WILLIAM BLAKE.

DEATH'S DOOR.

W. J. LINTON.

A TREATISE

ON

WOOD ENGRAVING

Historical and Practical

WITH UPWARDS OF THREE HUNDRED ILLUSTRATIONS
ENGRAVED ON WOOD

BY JOHN JACKSON.

THE HISTORICAL PORTION BY W. A. CHATTO.

————

Second Edition

WITH A NEW CHAPTER ON THE ARTISTS OF THE PRESENT DAY
BY HENRY G. BOHN
AND 145 ADDITIONAL WOOD ENGRAVINGS.

LONDON
HENRY G. BOHN, YORK STREET, COVENT GARDEN.
1861
REPUBLISHED BY GALE RESEARCH COMPANY, BOOK TOWER, DETROIT, 1969

Bibliographical Note

*For this edition a section of forty pages was added
to Chapter VIII and are numbered 561* through 600*.*

Library of Congress Catalog Card Number 69–16477

NOTICE TO THE SECOND EDITION.

THE former edition of this History of Wood Engraving having become extremely scarce and commercially valuable, the publisher was glad to obtain the copyright and wood-blocks from Mr. Mason Jackson, son of the late Mr. Jackson, original proprietor of the work, with the view of reprinting it.

It will be seen by the two distinct prefaces which accompanied the former edition, and are here reprinted, that there was some existing schism between the joint producers at the time of first publication. Mr. Jackson, the engraver, paymaster, and proprietor, conceived that he had a right to do what he liked with his own; while Mr. Chatto, his literary coadjutor, very naturally felt that he was entitled to some recognition on the title-page of what he had so successfully performed. On the book making its appearance without Mr. Chatto's name on the title-page, and with certain suppressions in his preface to which he had not given consent, a virulent controversy ensued, which was embodied in a pamphlet termed "a third preface," and afterwards carried on in the *Athenæum* of August and September, 1839. As this preface has nothing in it but the outpourings of a quarrel which can now interest no one, I do not republish any part of it; and looking back on the controversy after the lapse of twenty years, I cannot help feeling that Mr. Chatto had reasonable ground for complaining that his name was omitted, although I think Mr. Jackson had full right to determine what the book should be called, seeing that it was his own exclusive speculation. It is not for me to change a title now so firmly established, but I will do Mr. Chatto the civility to introduce his name on it, without concerning myself with the question of what he did or did not do, or what Mr. Jackson contributed beyond his practical remarks and anxious superintendence.

Although I have the pleasure of a personal acquaintance with Mr. Chatto, and communicated to him my intention of republishing the work, I declined letting him see it through the press; resolving to stand wholly responsible for any alterations or improvements I might choose to make. On the other hand, I have been quite as chary of letting even the shade of Mr. Jackson raise a new commotion—I say the shade, because, having his own copy full of manuscript remarks, it was at my option to use them; but I have adopted nothing from this source save a few palpable amendments. What additions have been made are entirely my own, and have arisen from a desire to increase the number of illustrations where I thought them previously deficient and had the means of supplying them. With the insertion of these additional illustrations, which it appears amount to seventy-five, it became necessary to describe them, and this has occasioned the introduction of perhaps a hundred or two lines, which are distributed in the form of notes or paragraphs throughout the volume. For the chief of these additions the critical examiner is referred to the following pages: 321, 322, 340, 352, 374, 428, 468, 477, 480, 493, 530, 531, 532, 539, 540, 541, 542, 543, 545, 546, 547, 548, 617, 639. The chapter on the artists of the present day is entirely new, and was not contemplated, as may be gathered from the remarks at pages 549 and 597, until the book was on the eve of publication. It contains upwards of seventy high class wood engravings, and gives a fair specimen of the talents of some of our most distinguished artists. Getting that supplementary matter together and into shape, was not so light and sudden a task as I meant it to be; but now it is done I feel that it was right to do it, and I can only hope that my unpretending labours will be deemed a step in the right direction. Should I retain my health, strength, and means, I purpose, at no very distant period, to follow up the present volume with one perhaps as large, giving a more complete series of Examples of the artists of the day, as well those of France and Germany as of England.

In conclusion, I think it due to Mr. Clay to acknowledge the attention and skill which, he has exercised in "bringing up" the numerous and somewhat difficult cuts to the agreeable face they now present. A good engraving without good printing is like a diamond without its polish.

HENRY G. BOHN.

January 4th, 1861.

MR. JACKSON'S PREFACE.

————✦————

I FEEL it my duty to submit to the public a few remarks, introductory to the Preface, which bears the signature of Mr. Chatto.

As my attention has been more readily directed to matters connected with my own profession than any other, it is not surprising that I should find almost a total absence of practical knowledge in all English authors who have written the early history of wood engraving. From the first occasion on which my attention was directed to the subject, to the present time, I have had frequent occasion to regret, that the early history and practice of the art were not to be found in any book in the English language. In the most expensive works of this description the process itself is not even correctly described, so that the reader— supposing him to be unacquainted with the subject—is obliged to follow the author in comparative darkness. It has not been without reason I have come to the conclusion, that, if the *practice*, as well as the *history* of wood engraving, were *better understood*, we should not have so many speculative opinions put forth by almost all writers on the subject, taking on trust what has been previously written, without giving themselves the trouble to examine and form an opinion of their own. Both with a view to amuse and improve myself as a wood engraver, I had long been in the habit of studying such productions of the old masters as came within my reach, and could not help noting the simple mistakes that many authors made in consequence of their knowing nothing of the practice. The farther I prosecuted the inquiry, the more interesting it became ; every additional piece of information strengthening my first opinion, that, "if the *practice*, as well as the *history* of wood engraving, were *better understood*," we should not have so many erroneous statements respecting both the history and capabilities of the art. At length, I determined upon engraving at my leisure hours a fac-simile of anything I thought worth preserving. For some time I continued to pursue this course, reading such English authors as have written on the origin and early history of wood engraving, and making memoranda, without proposing to myself any particular plan. It was not until I had proceeded thus far that I stopped to consider whether the information I had gleaned could not be applied to some specific purpose.

My plan, at this time, was to give a short introductory history to
precede the practice of the art, which I proposed should form the
principal feature in the Work. At this period, I was fortunate in
procuring the able assistance of Mr. W. A. Chatto, with whom I have
examined every work that called for the exercise of practical knowledge.
This naturally anticipated much that had been reserved for the practice,
and has, in some degree, extended the historical portion beyond what
I had originally contemplated; although, I trust, the reader will have
no occasion to regret such a deviation from the original plan, or that
it has not been *written* by myself. The number and variety of the
subjects it has been found necessary to introduce, rendered it a task of
some difficulty to preserve the characteristics of each individual master,
varying as they do in the style of execution. It only remains for me
to add, that, although I had the hardihood to venture upon such an
undertaking, it was not without a hope that the history of the art, with
an account of the practice, illustrated with numerous wood engravings,
would be looked upon with indulgence from one who only professed
to give a fac-simile of whatever appeared worthy of notice, with opinions
founded on a practical knowledge of the art.

JOHN JACKSON.

London, *December 15th*, 1838.

MR. CHATTO'S PREFACE.

THOUGH several English authors have, in modern times, written on
the origin and early history of wood engraving, yet no one has hitherto
given, in a distinct work, a connected account of its progress from the
earliest period to the present time; and no one, however confidently
he may have expressed his opinion on the subject, appears to have
thought it necessary to make himself acquainted with the practice of
the art. The antiquity and early history of wood engraving appear to
have been considered as themes which allowed of great scope for
speculation, and required no practical knowledge of the art. It is from
this cause that we find so many erroneous statements in almost every
modern dissertation on wood engraving. Had the writers ever thought
of appealing to a person practically acquainted with the art, whose
early productions they professed to give some account of, their conjectures might, in many instances, have been spared; and had they,

in matters requiring research, taken the pains to examine and judge for themselves, instead of adopting the opinions of others, they would have discovered that a considerable portion of what they thus took on trust, was not in accordance with facts.

As the antiquity and early history of wood engraving form a considerable portion of two expensive works which profess to give some account of the art, it has been thought that such a work as the present, combining the history with the practice of the art, and with numerous cuts illustrative of its progress, decline, and revival, might not be unfavourably received.

In the first chapter an attempt is made to trace the principle of wood engraving from the earliest authentic period; and to prove, by a continuous series of facts, that the art, when first applied to the impression of pictorial subjects on paper, about the beginning of the fifteenth century, was not so much an original invention, as the extension of a principle which had long been known and practically applied.

The second chapter contains an account of the progress of the art as exemplified in the earliest known single cuts, and in the block-books which preceded the invention of typography. In this chapter there is also an account of the Speculum Salvationis, which has been ascribed to Laurence Coster by Hadrian Junius, Scriverius, Meerman, and others, and which has frequently been described as an early block-book executed previous to 1440. A close examination of two Latin editions of the book has, however, convinced me, that in the earliest the text is entirely printed from movable types, and that in the other—supposed by Meerman to be the earliest, and to afford proofs of the progress of Coster's invention—those portions of the text which are printed from wood-blocks have been copied from the corresponding portions of the earlier edition with the text printed entirely from movable types. Fournier was the first who discovered that one of the Latin editions was printed partly from types, and partly from wood-blocks; and the credit of showing, from certain imperfections in the cuts, that this edition was subsequent to the other with the text printed entirely from types, is due to the late Mr. Ottley.

As typography, or printing from movable types, was unquestionably suggested by the earliest block-books with the text engraved on wood, the third chapter is devoted to an examination of the claims of Gutemberg and Coster to the honour of this invention. In the investigation of the evidence which has been produced in the behalf of each, the writer has endeavoured to divest his mind of all bias, and to decide according to facts, without reference to the opinions of either party. He has had no theory to support; and has neither a partiality for Mentz, nor a dislike to Harlem. It perhaps may not be unnecessary to mention here, that the cuts of arms from the History of the Virgin, given at pages 75, 76, and 77, were engraved before the writer had seen Koning's work on the Invention of Printing, Harlem, 1816, where they are also copied, and several of them assigned to Hannau, Burgundy, Brabant, Utrecht, and Leyden, and to certain Flemish noblemen, whose names are not mentioned. It is not improbable that, like the two rash Knights in the fable, we may have seen the shields on opposite sides;—the bearings may be common to states and families, both of Germany and the Netherlands.

The fourth chapter contains an account of wood engraving in connexion with the press, from the establishment of typography to the latter end of the fifteenth century. The fifth chapter comprehends the period in which Albert Durer flourished,—that is, from about 1498 to 1528. The sixth contains a notice of the principal wood-cuts designed by Holbein, with an account of the extension and improvement of the art in the sixteenth century, and of its subsequent decline. In the seventh chapter the history of the art is brought down from the commencement of the eighteenth century to the present time.

The eighth chapter contains an account of the practice of the art, with remarks on metallic relief engraving, and the best mode of printing wood-cuts. As no detailed account of the practice of wood engraving has hitherto been published in England, it is presumed that the information afforded by this part of the Work will not only be interesting to amateurs of the art, but useful to those who are professionally connected with it.

It is but justice to Mr. Jackson to add, that the Work was commenced by him at his sole risk ; that most of the subjects are of his selection ; and that nearly all of them were engraved, and that a great part of the Work was written, before he thought of applying to a publisher. The credit of commencing the Work, and of illustrating it so profusely, regardless of expense, is unquestionably due to him.

W. A. CHATTO.

LONDON, *December 5th*, 1838.

LIST OF ILLUSTRATIONS.

CHAPTER III.

THE INVENTION OF TYPOGRAPHY, 118—163.

CHAPTER IV.

WOOD ENGRAVING IN CONNEXION WITH THE PRESS, 164—229.

CHAPTER V.

CHAPTER VI.

CHAPTER VIII.

ARTISTS AND ENGRAVERS ON WOOD OF THE PRESENT DAY, 549—560.

CHAPTER IX.

THE PRACTICE OF WOOD ENGRAVING, 561—652.

ON

WOOD ENGRAVING.

CHAPTER I.

ANTIQUITY OF ENGRAVING.

ENGRAVING—THE WORD EXPLAINED—THE ART DEFINED—DISTINCTION BETWEEN ENGRAVING ON
COPPER AND ON WOOD—EARLY PRACTICE OF THE ART OF IMPRESSING CHARACTERS BY MEANS
OF STAMPS INSTANCED IN BABYLONIAN BRICKS; FRAGMENTS OF EGYPTIAN AND ETRUSCAN
EARTHENWARE; ROMAN LAMPS, TILES, AND AMPHORÆ—THE CAUTERIUM OR BRAND—PRIN-
CIPLE OF STENCILLING KNOWN TO THE ROMANS—ROYAL SIGNATURES THUS AFFIXED—PRACTICE
OF STAMPING MONOGRAMS ON DOCUMENTS IN THE MIDDLE AGES—NOTARIAL STAMPS—MER
CHANTS'-MARKS—COINS, SEALS, AND SEPULCHRAL BRASSES—EXAMINATION OF MR. OTTLEY'S
OPINIONS CONCERNING THE ORIGIN OF THE ART OF WOOD ENGRAVING IN EUROPE, AND ITS
EARLY PRACTICE BY TWO WONDERFUL CHILDREN, THE CUNIO.

 S few persons know, even amongst those who
profess to be admirers of the art of Wood En-
graving, by what means its effects, as seen in
books and single impressions, are produced,
and as a yet smaller number understand in
what manner it specifically differs in its procedure from the art of engraving on copper
or steel, it appears necessary, before entering
into any historic detail of its progress, to pre-
mise a few observations explanatory of the
word ENGRAVING in its general acceptation, and more particularly descriptive of that branch of the art which several persons call Xylography;
but which is as clearly expressed, and much more generally understood,
by the term WOOD ENGRAVING.

The primary meaning of the verb "to engrave" is defined by Dr.
Johnson, "to picture by incisions in any matter;" and he derives it from

the French "*engraver*." The great lexicographer is not, however, quite correct in his derivation ; for the French do not use the verb "engraver" in the sense of "to engrave," but to signify a ship or a boat being embedded in sand or mud so that she cannot float. The French synonym of the English verb "to engrave," is "graver ;" and its root is to be found in the Greek γράφω (*grapho*, I cut), which, with its compound ἐπιγράφω, according to Martorelli, as cited by Von Murr,* is always used by Homer to express cutting, incision, or wounding ; but never to express writing by the superficial tracing of characters with a reed or pen. From the circumstance of laws, in the early ages of Grecian history, being cut or engraved on wood, the word γράφω came to be used in the sense of, " I sanction, or I pass a law ;" and when, in the progress of society and the improvement of art, letters, instead of being cut on wood, were indented by means of a skewer-shaped instrument (stylus) on wax spread on tablets of wood or ivory, or written by means of a pen or reed on papyrus or on parchment, the word γράφω, which in its primitive meaning signified "to cut," became expressive of writing generally.

From γράφω is derived the Latin *scribo*,† " I write ;" and it is worthy of observation, that "*to scrive*,"—most probably from *scribo*,—signifies, in our own language, to cut numerals or other characters on timber with a tool called a *scrive :* the word thus passing, as it were, through a circle of various meanings and in different languages, and at last returning to its original signification.

Under the general term SCULPTURE—the root of which is to be found in the Latin verb *sculpo*, " I cut"—have been classed copper-plate engraving, wood engraving, gem engraving, and carving, as well as the art of the statuary or figure-cutter in marble, to which art the word *sculpture* is now more strictly applied, each of those arts requiring in its process the act of *cutting* of one kind or other. In the German language, which seldom borrows its terms of art from other languages, the various modes of cutting in sculpture, in copper-plate engraving, and in engraving on wood, are indicated in the name expressive of the operator or artist. The sculptor is named a *Bildhauer*, from *Bild*, a statue, and *hauen*, to hew, indicating the operation of cutting with a mallet and chisel ; the copper-plate engraver is called a *Kupfer-stecher*, from *Kupfer*, copper, and *stechen*, to dig or cut with the point ; and the wood engraver is a *Holzschneider*, from *Holz*, wood, and *schneiden*, to cut with the edge.

It is to be observed, that though both the copper-plate engraver and

* C. G. Von Murr, in his Journal zur Kunstgeschichte, 2 Theil, S. 253, referring to Martorelli, De Regia Theca Calamaria.

† If this etymology be correct, the English *Scrivener* and French *Greffier* may be related by descent as well as professionally ; both words being thus referable to the same origin, the Greek γράφω. The modern *Writer* in the Scottish courts of law performs the duties both of Scrivener and Greffier, with whose name his own is synonymous.

the wood engraver may be said to *cut* in a certain sense, as well as the sculptor and the carver, they have to execute their work *reversed*,—that is, contrary to the manner in which impressions from their plates or blocks are seen; and that in copying a painting or a drawing, it requires to be reversely transferred,—a disadvantage under which the sculptor and the carver do not labour, as they copy their models or subjects *direct.*

ENGRAVING, as the word is at the present time popularly used, and considered in its relation to the pictorial art, may be defined to be—" The art of representing objects on metallic substances, or on wood, expressed by lines and points produced by means of corrosion, incision, or excision, for the purpose of their being impressed on paper by means of ink or other colouring matter."

The impressions obtained from engraved *plates* of metal or from *blocks* of wood are commonly called engravings, and sometimes prints. Formerly the word *cuts** was applied indiscriminately to impressions, either from metal or wood; but at present it is more strictly confined to the pro-ductions of the wood engraver. Impressions from copper-plates only are properly called *plates;* though it is not unusual for persons who profess to review productions of art, to speak of a book containing, perhaps, a number of indifferent woodcuts, as " a work embellished with a profusion of the *most charming plates* on wood ;" thus affording to every one who is in the least acquainted with the art at once a specimen of their taste and their knowledge.

Independent of the difference of the material on which copper-plate engraving and wood engraving are executed, the grand distinction between the two arts is, that the engraver on copper corrodes by means of aqua-fortis, or cuts out with the burin or dry-point, the lines, stipplings, and hatchings from which his impression is to be produced ; while, on the contrary, the wood engraver effects his purpose by cutting away those parts which are to appear white or colourless, thus leaving the lines which produce the impression prominent.

In printing from a copper or steel plate, which is previously warmed by being placed above a charcoal fire, the ink or colouring matter is rubbed into the lines or incisions by means of a kind of ball formed of woollen cloth ; and when the lines are thus sufficiently charged with ink, the surface of the plate is first wiped with a piece of rag, and is then further cleaned and smoothed by the fleshy part of the palm of the hand, slightly touched with whitening, being once or twice passed rather quickly and lightly over it. The plate thus prepared is covered with the paper intended to receive the engraving, and is subjected to the action of

* Towards the close of the seventeenth century we find books " adorned with *sculptures* by a curious hand ;" about 1730 we find them " ornamented with *cuts ;*" at present they are " illustrated with *engravings.*"

the rolling or copper-plate printer's press ; and the impression is obtained by the paper being pressed *into* the inked incisions.

As the lines of an engraved block of wood are prominent or in relief, while those of a copper-plate are, as has been previously explained, *intagliate* or hollowed, the mode of taking an impression from the former is precisely the reverse of that which has just been described. The usual mode of taking impressions from an engraved block of wood is by means of the printing-press, either from the block separately, or wedged up in a *chase* with types. The block is inked by being beat with a roller on the surface, in the same manner as type ; and the paper being turned over upon it from the *tympan*, it is then run in under the *platen;* which being acted on by the lever, presses the paper *on to* the raised lines of the block, and thus produces the impression. Impressions from wood are thus obtained by the *on-pression* of the paper against the raised or prominent lines ; while impressions from copper-plates are obtained by the *in-pression* of the paper into hollowed ones. In consequence of this difference in the process, the inked lines impressed on paper from a copper-plate appear prominent when viewed direct; while the lines communicated from an engraved wood-block are indented in the front of the impression, and appear raised at the back.

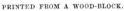

PRINTED FROM A WOOD-BLOCK.   PRINTED FROM A COPPER-PLATE.

The above impressions—the one from a wood-block, and the other from an etched copper-plate—will perhaps render what has been already said, explanatory of the difference between copper-plate printing from hollowed lines, and *surface printing* by means of the common press from prominent lines, still more intelligible. The subject is a representation of the copper-plate or rolling press.

Both the preceding impressions are produced in the same manner by means of the common printing-press. One is from wood ; the other, where the white lines are seen on a black ground, is from copper ;— the hollowed lines, which in copper-plate printing yield the impression, receiving no ink from the printer's balls or rollers; while the surface, which in copper-plate printing is wiped clean after the lines are filled with ink, is perfectly covered with it. It is, therefore, evident, that if this etching were printed in the same manner as other copper-plates, the impression would be a fac-simile of the one from wood. It has been judged necessary to be thus minute in explaining the difference between copper-plate and wood engraving, as the difference in the mode of obtaining impressions does not appear to have been previously pointed out with sufficient precision.

As it does not come within the scope of the present work to inquire into the origin of sculpture generally, I shall not here venture to give an opinion whether the art was invented by ADAM or his good angel RAZIEL, or whether it was introduced at a subsequent period by TUBAL-CAIN, NOAH, TRISMEGISTUS, ZOROASTER, or MOSES. Those who feel interested in such remote speculations will find the "authorities" in the second chapter of Evelyn's "Sculptura."

Without, therefore, inquiring when or by whom the art of engraving for the purpose of producing impressions was invented, I shall endeavour to show that such an art, however rude, was known at a very early period; and that it continued to be practised in Europe, though to a very limited extent, from an age anterior to the birth of Christ, to the year 1400. In the fifteenth century, its principles appear to have been more generally applied;—first, to the simple cutting of figures on wood for the purpose of being impressed on paper; next, to cutting figures and explanatory text on the same block, and then entire pages of text without figures, till the "ARS GRAPHICA ET IMPRESSORIA" attained its perfection in the discovery of PRINTING by means of movable fusile types.*

At a very early period stamps of wood, having hieroglyphic characters engraved on them, were used in Egypt for the purpose of producing impressions on bricks, and on other articles made of clay. This fact, which might have been inferred from the ancient bricks and fragments of earthenware containing characters evidently communicated by means of a stamp, has been established by the discovery of several of those wooden stamps, of undoubted antiquity, in the tombs at Thebes, Meroe, and other places. The following cuts represent the face and the back of one of the most perfect of those stamps, which was found in a tomb at Thebes, and has recently been brought to this country by Edward William Lane, Esq.†

The original stamp is made of the same kind of wood as the

* Astle on the Origin and Progress of Writing, p. 215, 2nd edit.

† Author of "An Account of the Manners and Customs of the Modern Egyptians, written in Egypt during the years 1833, '34, and '35."

mummy chests, and has an arched handle at the back, cut out of the same piece of wood as the face. It is of an oblong figure, with the ends rounded off; five inches long, two inches and a quarter broad, and half an inch thick. The hieroglyphic characters on its

 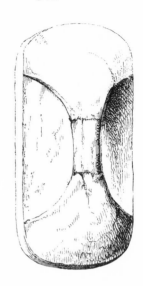

face are rudely cut in *intaglio*, so that their impression on clay would be in relief; and if printed in the same manner as the preceding copy, would present the same appearance,—that is, the characters which are cut into the wood, would appear white on a black ground. The phonetic power of the hieroglyphics on the face of the stamp may be represented respectively by the letters, A, M, N, F, T, P, T, H, M; and the vowels being supplied, as in reading Hebrew without points, we have the words, "Amonophtep, Thmei-mai,"—"Amonoph, beloved of truth." * The name is supposed to be that of Amonoph or Amenoph the First, the second king of the eighteenth dynasty, who, according to the best authorities, was contemporary with Moses, and reigned in Egypt previous to the departure of the Israelites. There are two ancient Egyptian bricks in the British Museum on which the impression of a similar stamp is quite distinct; and there are also several articles of burnt clay, of an elongated conical figure, and about nine inches long, which have their broader extremities impressed with hieroglyphics in a similar manner. There is also in the same collection a wooden

* On a mummy in the royal collection at Paris, the six first characters of this stamp occur. Champollion reads them, "Amenoftep," or "Amonaftep." He supposes the name to be that of Amonoph the First; and says that it signifies "approuvé par Ammon."— Précis du Système Hiéroglyphique. Planches et Explication, p. 20, No. 161.

stamp, of a larger size than that belonging to Mr. Lane, but not in so perfect a condition. Several ancient Etruscan terra-cottas and fragments of earthenware have been discovered, on which there are alphabetic characters, evidently impressed from a stamp, which was probably of wood. In the time of Pliny terra-cottas thus impressed were called Typi.

In the British Museum are several bricks which have been found on the site of ancient Babylon. They are larger than our bricks, and somewhat different in form, being about twelve inches square and three inches thick. They appear to have been made of a kind of muddy clay with which portions of chopped straw have been mixed to cause it to bind; and their general appearance and colour, which is like that of a common brick before it is burnt, plainly enough indicate that they have not been hardened by fire, but by exposure

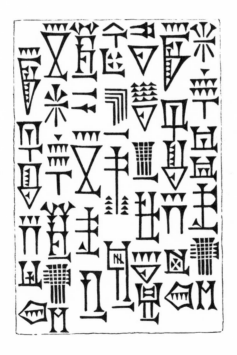

to the sun. About the middle of their broadest surface, they are impressed with certain characters which have evidently been indented when the brick was in a soft state. The characters are indented,— that is, they are such as would be produced by pressing a wood-block with raised lines upon a mass of soft clay; and were such a block printed on paper in the usual manner of wood-cuts, the impression would be similar to the preceding one, which has been copied, on a reduced scale, from one of the bricks above noticed. The characters have been variously described as cuneiform or wedge-shaped, arrow-headed, javelin-headed, or nail-headed; but their meaning has not hitherto been deciphered.

Amphoræ, lamps, tiles, and various domestic utensils, formed of clay, and of Roman workmanship, are found impressed with letters, which in some cases are supposed to denote the potter's name, and in others the contents of the vessel, or the name of the owner. On the tiles,—of which there are specimens in the British Museum,—the letters are commonly inscribed in a circle, and appear raised; thus showing that the stamp had been hollowed, or engraved in intaglio, in a manner similar to a wooden butter-print. In a book entitled "Ælia Lælia Crispis non nata resurgens," by C. C. Malvasia, 4to. Bologna, 1683, are several engravings on wood of such tiles, found in the neighbourhood of Rome, and communicated to the author by Fabretti, who, in the seventh chapter of his own work,* has given some account of the "figlinarum signa,"—the stamps of the ancient potters and tile-makers.

The stamp from which the following cut has been copied is preserved

in the British Museum. It is of brass, and the letters are in relief and reversed; so that if it were inked from a printer's ball and stamped on paper, an impression would be produced precisely the same as that which is here given.

It would be difficult now to ascertain why this stamp should be marked with the word LAR, which signifies a household god, or the image of the supposed tutelary genius of a house; but, without much stretch of imagination, we may easily conceive how appropriate such an inscription would be impressed on an amphora or large wine-vessel, sealed and set apart on the birth of an heir, and to be kept sacred—inviolate as the household gods—till the young Roman assumed the "toga virilis," or arrived at years of maturity. That vessels containing wine were kept for many years, we learn from Horace and Petronius; †

---

* Inscriptionum Explicatio, fol. Romæ, 1699.

† "O nata mecum consule Manlio !" says Horace, addressing an amphora of wine as old as himself; and Petronius mentions some choice Falernian which had attained the ripe age of a hundred : "Statim allatæ sunt amphoræ vitreæ diligenter gypsatæ, quarum in cervicibus pittacia erant affixa, cum hoc titulo : *Falernum Opimianum annorum centum.*" *Pittacia* were small labels—schedulæ breves—attached to the necks of wine-vessels, and on which were marked the name and age of the wine.

—————— Prome reconditum,
Lyde, strenua, Cæcubum,
Munitæque adhibe vim sapientiæ.
Inclinare meridiem
Sentis : ac veluti stet volucris dies,
Parcis deripere horreo
Cessantem Bibuli Consulis amphoram.

Carmin. lib. III. xxviii.

" Quickly produce, Lyde, the hoarded Cæcuban, and make an attack upon wisdom, ever on her guard. You perceive the noontide is on its decline ; and yet, as if the fleeting day stood still, you delay to bring out of the store-house the loitering cask, (that bears its date, from the Consul Bibulus."—*Smart's Translation.*

Mr. Ottley, in his " Inquiry into the Origin and Early History of Engraving," pages 57 and 58, makes a distinction between *impression* where the characters impressed are produced by "*a change of form*" —meaning where they are either indented in the substance impressed, or raised upon it in relief—and *impression* where the characters are produced by *colour ;* and requires evidence that the ancients ever used stamps " charged with ink or some other tint, for the purpose of stamping paper, parchment, or other substances, little or not at all capable of indentation."

It certainly would be very difficult, if not impossible, to produce a piece of paper, parchment, or cloth of the age of the Romans impressed with letters in ink or other colouring matter ; but the existence of such stamps as the preceding,—and there are others in the British Museum of the same kind, containing more letters and of a smaller size,—renders it very probable that they were used for the purpose of marking cloth, paper, and similar substances, with ink, as well as for being impressed in wax or clay.

Von Murr, in an article in his Journal, on the Art of Wood Engraving, gives a copy from a similar bronze stamp, in Praun's Museum, with the inscription " GALLIANI," which he considers as most distinctly proving that the Romans had nearly arrived at the arts of wood engraving and book printing. He adds : " Letters cut on wood they certainly had, and very likely grotesques and figures also, the hint of which their artists might readily obtain from the coloured stuffs which were frequently presented by Indian ambassadors to the emperors." *

At page 90 of Singer's " Researches into the History of Playing-Cards " are impressions copied from stamps similar to the preceding ;

* Journal zur Kunstgeschichte, 2 Theil, S. 81. By grotesque—" Laubwerk "—ornamental foliage is here meant ;—*grot*-esque, bower-work,—not caricatures.

which stamps the author considers as affording "examples of such a near approach to the art of printing as first practised, that it is truly extraordinary there is no remaining evidence of its having been exercised by them;—unless we suppose that they were acquainted with it, and did not choose to adopt it from reasons of state policy." It is just as extraordinary that the Greek who employed the expansive force of steam in the Æolipile to blow the fire did not invent Newcomen's engine;—unless, indeed, we suppose that the construction of such an engine was perfectly known at Syracuse, but that the government there did not choose to adopt it from motives of "state policy." It was not, however, a reason of "state policy" which caused the Roman cavalry to ride without stirrups, or the windows of the palace of Augustus to remain unglazed.

The following impressions are also copied from two other brass stamps, preserved in the collection of Roman antiquities in the British Museum.

As the letters in the originals are hollowed or cut into the metal, they would, if impressed on clay or soft wax, appear raised or in relief; and if inked and impressed on paper or on white cloth, they would present the same appearance that they do here—white on a black ground. Not being able to explain the letters on these stamps, further than that the first may be the dative case of a proper name Ovirillius, and indicate that property so marked belonged to such a person, I leave them, as Francis Moore, physician, leaves the hieroglyphic in his Almanack,—"to time and the curious to construe."

Lambinet, in his "Recherches sur l'Origine de l'Imprimerie," gives an account of two stone stamps of the form of small tablets, the letters of which were cut in *intaglio* and reverse, similar to the two of which impressions are above given. They were found in 1808, near the village of Nais, in the department of the Meuse; and as the letters, being in reverse, could not be made out, the owner of the tablets sent them to the Celtic Society of Paris, where M. Dulaure, to whose examination they were submitted, was of opinion that they were a kind of matrices or hollow stamps, intended to be applied to soft substances or such as were in a state of fusion. He thought they were stamps for vessels containing medical compositions; and if his reading of one of the inscriptions be correct, the practice of stamping the name of a quack and the nature of his remedy, in relief on the side of an ointment-pot or a bottle, is of high antiquity. The letters

Q. JUN. TAURI. ANODY.
NUM. AD OMN. LIPP.

M. Dulaure explains thus: *Quinti Junii Tauridi anodynum ad omnes lippas;** an inscription which is almost literally rendered by the title of a specific still known in the neighbourhood of Newcastle-on-Tyne, "*Dr. Dud's lotion, good for sore eyes.*"

Besides such stamps as have already been described, the ancients used brands, both figured and lettered, with which, when heated, they marked their horses, sheep, and cattle, as well as criminals, captives, and refractory or runaway slaves.

The Athenians, according to Suidas, marked their Samian captives with the figure of an owl; while Athenians captured by the Samians were marked with the figure of a galley, and by the Syracusans with the figure of a horse. The husbandman at his leisure time, as we are informed by Virgil, in the first book of the Georgics,

"Aut pecori signa, aut numeros impressit acervis;"

and from the third book we learn that the operation was performed by branding:

"Continuoque notas et nomina gentis *inurunt.*"†

---

* M. Dulaure's latinity is bad. "*Lippas*" certainly is not the word. His translation is, "Remède anodin de Quintus Junius Tauridus, pour *tous les maux* d'yeux." Other stone stamps, supposed to have been used by oculists to mark the vessels containing their medicaments, were discovered and explained long before M. Dulaure published his interpretation. See "WALCHII Antiquitates Medicæ Selectæ, Jenæ, 1772," Num. 1 and 2, referred to by Von Murr.

† HERMANNUS HUGO, De prima Origine Scribendi, cap. xix. De Notis Servilibus, et cap. xx. De Notis pecudum. A further account of the ancient *stigmata*, and of the manner in which slaves were marked, is to be found in PIGNORIUS, De Servis.

Such brands as those above noticed, commonly known by the name of *cauteria* or *stigmata*, were also used for similar purposes during the middle ages ; and the practice, which has not been very long obsolete, of burning homicides in the hand, and vagabonds and "sturdy beggars" on the breast, face, or shoulder, affords an example of the employment of the brand in the criminal jurisprudence of our own country. By the 1st Edward VI. cap. 3, it was enacted, that whosoever, man or woman, not being lame or impotent, nor so aged or diseased that he or she could not work, should be convicted of loitering or idle wandering by the highway-side, or in the streets, like a servant wanting a master, or a beggar, he or she was to be marked with a hot iron on the breast with the letter V [for Vagabond], and adjudged to the person bringing him or her before a justice to be his slave for two years ; and if such adjudged slave should run away, he or she, upon being taken and convicted, was to be marked on the forehead, or on the ball of the cheek, with the letter S [for Slave], and adjudged to be the said master's slave for ever. By the 1st of James I. cap. 7, it was also enacted, that such as were to be deemed "rogues, vagabonds, and sturdy beggars" by the 39th of Elizabeth, cap. 4, being convicted at the sessions and found to be incorrigible, were to be branded in the left shoulder with a hot iron, of the breadth of an English shilling, marked with a great Roman R [for Rogue] ; such branding upon the shoulder to be so thoroughly burned and set upon the skin and flesh, that the said letter R should be seen and remain for a perpetual mark upon such rogue during the remainder of his life.*

From a passage in Quintilian we learn that the Romans were acquainted with the method of *tracing* letters, by means of a piece of thin wood in which the characters were pierced or cut through, on a principle similar to that on which the present art of *stencilling* is founded. He is speaking of teaching boys to write, and the passage referred to may be thus translated : "When the boy shall have entered upon *joining-hand*, it will be useful for him to have a *copy-head* of wood in which the letters are well cut, that through its furrows, as it were, he may trace the characters with his *style*. He will not thus be liable to make slips as on the wax [alone], for he will be confined by the boundary of the letters, and neither will he be able to deviate from his text. By thus more rapidly and frequently following a definite outline, his hand will become *set*, without his requiring any assistance from the master to guide it."†

---

* History of the Poor Laws, 8vo. 1764, by Richard Burn, LL.D., who in his observations on such punishments says : "It is affecting to humanity to observe the various methods that have been invented for the *punishment* of vagrants ; none of all which wrought [the desired effect . . . . . . This part of our history looks like the history of the savages in America. Almost all severities have been exercised against vagrants, except scalping."

† "Quum puer jam ductus sequi cœperit, non inutile erit, litteras tabellæ quam optime insculpi, ut per illos, velut sulcos, ducatur stylus. Nam neque errabit, quemadmodum in

A thin stencil-plate of copper, having the following letters *cut out* of it,

DN CONSTAN

TIO AVG SEM

PER VICTORI

was received, together with some rare coins, from Italy by Tristan, author of "Commentaires Historiques, Paris, 1657," who gave a copy of it at page 68 of the third volume of that work. The letters thus formed, "ex nulla materia,"* might be traced on paper by means of a pen, or with a small brush, charged with body-colour, as stencillers *slap-dash* rooms through their pasteboard patterns, or dipped in ink in the same manner as many shopkeepers now, through similar thin copper-plates, mark the prices of their wares, or their own name and address on the paper in which such wares are wrapped.

In the sixth century it appears, from Procopius, that the Emperor Justin I. made use of a tablet of wood pierced or cut in a similar manner, through which he traced in red ink, the imperial colour, his signature, consisting of the first four letters of his name. It is also stated that Theodoric, King of the Ostrogoths, the contemporary of Justin, used after the same manner to sign the first four letters of his name through a plate of gold ;† and in Peringskiold's edition of the Life of Theodoric, the annexed is given as the monogram‡ of that monarch. The authenticity of this account has, however, been questioned, as Cochlæus, who died in 1552, cites no ancient authority for the fact.

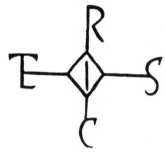

ceris, continebitur enim utrimque marginibus, neque extra præscriptum poterit egredi ; et celerius ac sæpius sequendo certa vestigia firmabit articulos, neque egebit adjutorio manum suam, manu superimposita, regentis." Quintiliani Instit. Orator., lib. i. cap. 1.

* Prosper Marchand, at page 9 of his "Histoire de l'Imprimerie," gives the following title of a book in 8vo. which was wholly, both text and figures, executed in this manner, *percé au jour*, in vellum : "Liber Passionis Domini Nostri Jesu Christi, cum figuris et characteribus *ex nulla materia* compositis." He states that in 1640 it was in the collection of Albert Henry, Prince de Ligne, and quotes a description of it from Anton. Sanderi Bibliotheca Belgica Manuscripta, parte ii. p. 1.

† "Rex Theodoricus inliteratus erat, et sic obruto sensu ut in decem annos regni sui quatuor literas subscriptionis edicti sui discere nullatenus potuisset. De qua re laminam auream jussit interrasilem fieri quatuor literas regis habentem, unde ut si subscribere voluisset, posita lamina super chartam, per eam pennam duceret et subscriptio ejus tantum videretur." —Vita Theodorici Regis Ostrogothorum et Italiæ, autore Joanne Cochlæo ; cum additamentis Joannis Peringskiold, 4to. Stockholmiæ, 1699, p. 199.

‡ A monogram, properly, consists of all, or the principal letters of a name, combined in such a manner that the whole appear but as one *character ;* a portion of one letter being understood to represent another, two being united to form a third, and so on.

It has been asserted by Mabillon, (Diplom. lib. ii. cap. 10,) that Charlemagne first introduced the practice of signing documents with a monogram, either traced with a pen by means of a thin tablet of gold, ivory, or wood, or impressed with an inked stamp, having the characters in relief, in a manner similar to that in which letters are stamped at the Post-office.* Ducange, however, states that this mode of signing documents is of greater antiquity, and he gives a copy of the monogram of the Pope Adrian I. who was elected to the see of Rome in 774, and died in 795. The annexed monogram of Charlemagne has been copied from Peringskiold, "Annotationes in Vitam Theodorici," p. 584; it is also given in Ducange's Glossary, and in the "Nouveau Traité de Diplomatique."

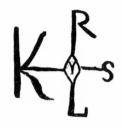

The monogram, either stencilled or stamped, consisted of a combination of the letters of the person's name, a fanciful character, or the figure of a cross,† accompanied with a peculiar kind of flourish, called by French writers on diplomatics *parafe* or *ruche*. This mode of signing appears to have been common in most nations of Europe during the ninth, tenth, and eleventh centuries ; and it was practised by nobles and the higher orders of the clergy, as well as by kings. It continued to be used by the kings of France to the time of Philip III. and by the Spanish monarchs to a much later period. It also appears to have been adopted by some of the Saxon kings of England ; and the authors of the "Nouveau Traité de Diplomatique" say that they had seen similar marks produced by a stamp of William the Conqueror, when Duke of Normandy. We have had a recent instance of the use of the *stampilla*, as it is called by diplomatists, in affixing the royal signature. During the illness of George IV. in 1830, a silver stamp, containing a fac-simile of the king's sign-manual, was executed by Wyon, which was stamped on documents requiring the royal signature, by commissioners, in his Majesty's presence. A similar stamp was used during the last illness of Henry VIII. for the purpose of affixing the royal signature. The king's warrant empowering commissioners to use the stamp may be seen in Rymer's Fœdera, vol. xv. p. 101, anno 1546. It is believed that the

---

* Mabillon's opinion is founded on the following passage in the Life of Charlemagne, by his secretary Eginhard : " *Ut scilicet imperitiam hanc [scribendi] honesto ritu suppleret, monogrammatis usum loco proprii signi invexit.*"

† " Triplex cruces exarandi modus : 1. penna sive calamo ; 2. lamina interrasili ; 3. stampilla sive typo anaglyptico. Laminæ interrasiles ex auro aliove metallo, vel ex ebore etiam confectæ sunt, atque ita perforatæ, ut hiatus, pro re nata, crucium cet. speciem præ se ferrent, per quos velut sulcos, calamus sive penna ducebatur. Stampillæ vero ita sculptæ sunt, ut figuræ superficiem eminerent, quæ deinde atramento tinctæ sunt, chartæque impressæ."—Gatterer, Elementa Artis Diplomaticæ, § 264, De Staurologia.

warrant which sent the poet Surrey to the scaffold was signed with this stamp, and not with Henry's own hand.

In Sempère's "History of the Cortes of Spain," several examples are given of the use of fanciful monograms in that country at an early period, and which were probably introduced by its Gothic invaders. That such marks were stamped is almost certain; for the first, which is that of Gundisalvo Tellez, affixed to a charter of the date of 840, is the same as the "sign" which was affixed by his widow, Flamula, when she granted certain property to the abbot and monks of Cardeña for the good of her deceased husband's soul. The second, which is of the date of 886, was used both by the abbot Ovecus, and Peter his nephew; and the third was used by all the four children of one Ordoño, as their "sign" to a charter of donation executed in 1018. The fourth mark is a Runic cypher, copied from an ancient Icelandic manuscript, and given by Peringskiold in his "Annotations on the Life of Theodoric:" it is not given here as being from a stencil or a stamp, but that it may be compared with the apparently Gothic monograms used in Spain.

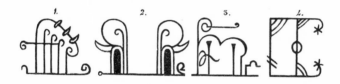

"In their inscriptions, and in the rubrics of their books," says a writer in the Edinburgh Review,* "the Spanish Goths, like the Romans of the Lower Empire, were fond of using combined capitals—of *monogram-matising*. This mode of writing is now common in Spain, on the sign-boards and on the shop-fronts, where it has retained its place in defiance of the canons of the council [of Leon]. The Goths, however, retained a truly *Gothic* custom in their writings. The Spanish Goth sometimes subscribed his name; or he drew a *monogram* like the Roman emperors, or the sign of the *cross* like the Saxon; but not unfrequently he affixed strange and fanciful marks to the deed or charter, bearing a close resemblance to the Runic or magical knots of which so many have been engraved by Peringskiold, and other northern antiquaries."

To the tenth or the eleventh century are also to be referred certain small silver coins—"something between counters and money," as is observed by Pinkerton—which are impressed, on one side only, with a kind of Runic monogram. They are formed of very thin pieces of

* No. lxi. p. 108, where the preceding Gothic marks, with the explanation of them, are given.

silver; and it has been supposed that the impression was produced from wooden dies. They are known to collectors as "*nummi bracteati*"— tinsel money; and Pinkerton, mistaking the Runic character for the Christian cross, says that "most of them are ecclesiastic." He is perhaps nearer the truth when he adds that they "belong to the tenth century, and are commonly found in Germany, and the northern kingdoms of Sweden and Denmark."* The four following copies from the original coins in the Brennerian collection are given by Peringskiold, in his "Annotations on the Life of Theodoric," previously referred to. The characters on the three first he reads as the letters EIR, OIR, and AIR, respectively, and considers them to be intended to represent the name of Eric the Victorious. The characters on the fourth he reads as EIM, and applies them to Emund Annosus, the nephew of Eric the Victorious, who succeeded to the Sueo-Gothic throne in 1051; about which time, through the influence of the monks, the ancient Runic characters were exchanged for Roman.

The notaries of succeeding times, who on their admission were required to use a distinctive sign or notarial mark in witnessing an instrument, continued occasionally to employ the stencil in affixing their

"sign;" although their use of the stamp for that purpose appears to have been more general. In some of those marks or stamps the name of the notary does not appear, and in others a small space is left in order that it might afterwards be inserted with a pen. The annexed monogram

NICOLAUS FERENTERIUS, 1236. was the official mark of an Italian notary, Nicolaus Ferenterius, who lived in 1236.†

The three following cuts represent impressions of German notarial stamps. The first is that of Jacobus Arnaldus, 1345; the second that of Johannes Meynersen, 1435; and the third that of Johannes Calvis, 1521.‡

* Essay on Medals, pp. 144, 145. Edit. 1784.

† It is given by Gatterer in his "Elementa Artis Diplomaticæ," p. 166; [4to. Gottingæ, 1765;] who refers to Muratori, Antiquit. Italiæ Medii Ævi, t. vi. p. 9.

‡ These stamps are copied from "D. E. Baringii Clavis Diplomatica," 4to. Hanoveræ, 1754. There is a work expressly treating of the use of the Diplomatic Stamp—J. C. C. Oelrichs de Stampilla Diplomatica, folio, Wismariæ, 1762, which I have not been able to obtain a sight of.

JACOBUS ARNALDUS, 1345.

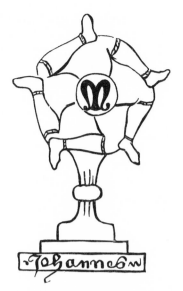

JOHANNES MEYNERSEN, 1435.

JOHANNES CALVIS, 1521.

Many of the merchants'-marks of our own country, which so frequently appear on stained glass windows, monumental brasses, and tombstones in the fourteenth, fifteenth, and sixteenth centuries, bear a considerable likeness to the ancient Runic monograms, from which it is not unlikely that they were originally derived. The English trader was accustomed to place his mark as his "sign" in his shop-front in the same manner as the Spaniard did his monogram: if he was a wool-stapler, he stamped it on his packs; or if a fish-curer, it was branded on the end of his casks. If he built himself a new house, his mark was frequently placed between his initials over the principal door-way, or over the fireplace of the hall; if he made a gift to a church or a chapel, his mark was emblazoned on the windows beside the knight's or the nobleman's shield of arms; and when he died, his mark was cut upon his tomb. Of the following merchants'-marks, the first is that of Adam de Walsokne, who died in 1349; the second that of Edmund Pepyr, who died in 1483; those two marks are from their tombs in St. Margaret's, Lynn; and the third is from a window in the same church.*

In Pierce Ploughman's Creed, written after the death of Wickliffe, which happened in 1384, and consequently more modern than many of Chaucer's poems, merchants'-marks are thus mentioned in the description of a window of a Dominican convent:

> " Wide windows y-wrought, y-written full thick,
> Shining with shapen shields, to shewen about,
> With *marks of merchants*, y-meddled between,
> Mo than twenty and two, twice y-numbered.†"

Having thus endeavoured to prove by a continuous chain of evidence that the principle of producing impressions from raised lines was known, and practised, at a very early period; and that it was applied for the purpose of impressing letters and other characters on paper, though perhaps confined to signatures only, long previous to 1423,—which is the earliest date that has been discovered on a wood-cut, in the modern sense of the word, impressed on paper, and accompanied with explanatory words cut on the same block;‡ and having shown that the principle of stencilling—the manner in which the above-named cut is

* The marks here given are copied from Mackarel's History of King's Lynn, 8vo. 1737. In the same book there are upwards of thirty more of a similar kind, from the middle of the fourteenth century to the latter end of the seventeenth. Perhaps no two counties in the kingdom afford so many examples of merchants'-marks and monumental brasses as Norfolk and Suffolk.

† " *Y-meddled* is mixed; the *marks* of merchants are put in opposition to the 'shapen shields,' because merchants had no coats of arms."—Specimens of the Early English Poets, by George Ellis, Esq. vol. i. p. 163. Edit. 1811.

‡ "Till lately this was the earliest dated evidence of block printing known; but there has just been discovered at Malines, and now deposited at Brussels, a woodcut of similar character, but assumed to be Dutch or Flemish, dated MCCCCXVIII.; and though there seems no reason to doubt the genuineness of the cut, it is currently asserted that the date bears evidence of having been tampered with."—Extract from Bohn's Lecture on Printing.

coloured *—was also known in the middle ages; it appears requisite, next to briefly notice the contemporary existence of the cognate arts of die-sinking, seal-cutting, and engraving on brass, and afterwards to examine the grounds of certain speculations on the introduction and early practice of wood-engraving and block-printing in Europe.

Concerning the first invention of stamping letters and figures upon coins, and the name of the inventor, it is fruitless to inquire, as the origin of the art is lost in the remoteness of antiquity. "Leaving these uncertainties," says Pinkerton, in his Essay on Medals, "we know from respectable authorities that the first money coined in Greece was that struck in the island of Ægina, by Phidon king of Argos. His reign is fixed by the Arundelian marbles to an era correspondent to the 885th year before Christ; but whether he derived this art from Lydia or any other source we are not told." About three hundred years before the birth of Christ, the art of coining, so far as relates to the beauty of the heads impressed, appears to have attained its perfection in Greece;—we may indeed say its perfection generally, for the specimens which were then produced in that country remain unsurpassed by modern art. Under the Roman emperors the art never seems to have attained so high a degree of perfection as it did in Greece; though several of the coins of Hadrian, probably executed by Greek artists, display great beauty of design and execution. The art of coining, with the rest of the ornamental arts, declined with the empire; and, on its final subversion in Italy, the coins of its rulers were scarcely superior to those which were subsequently minted in England, Germany, and France, during the darkest period of the middle ages.

The art of coining money, however rude in design and imperfect in its mode of stamping the impression, which was by repeated blows with a hammer, was practised from the twelfth to the sixteenth century in a greater number of places than at present; for many of the more powerful bishops and nobles assumed or extorted the right of coining money as well as the king; and in our own country the archbishops of Canterbury and York, and the bishop of Durham, exercised the right of coinage till the Reformation; and local mints for coining the king's money were occasionally fixed at Norwich, Chester, York, St. Edmundsbury, Newcastle-on-Tyne, and other places. Independent of those establishments for the coining of *money*, almost every abbey struck its own *jettons* or

* The woodcut referred to is that of St. Christopher, discovered by Heineken, pasted within the cover of a book in the Monastery of Buxheim, near Memmingen, in Suabia. It is of a folio size, and is coloured by means of stencils; a practice which appears to have been adopted at an early part of the fifteenth century by the German Formschneiders and Briefmalers, literally, figure-cutters and cardpainters, to colour their cuts and their cards. The St. Christopher is now in Earl Spencer's library. (See a reduced copy of it at p. 46).

counters; which were thin pieces of copper, commonly impressed with a pious legend, and used in *casting up accounts*, but which the general introduction of the numerals now in use, and an improved system of arithmetic, have rendered unnecessary. As such mints were at least as numerous in France and Germany as in our own country, Scheffer, the partner of Faust, when he conceived the idea of casting letters from matrices formed by punches, would have little difficulty in finding a workman to assist him in carrying his plans into execution. "The art of impressing legends on coins," says Astle in his Account of the Origin and Progress of writing, "is nothing more than the art of printing on medals." That the art of casting letters in relief, though not separately, and most likely from a mould of sand, was known to the Romans, is evident from the names of the emperors Domitian and Hadrian on some pigs of lead in the British Museum; and that it was practised during the middle and succeeding ages, we have ample testimony from the inscriptions on our ancient bells.*

In the century immediately preceding 1423, the date of the wood-cut of St. Christopher, the use of seals, for the purpose of authenticating documents by their impression on wax, was general throughout Europe; kings, nobles, bishops, abbots, and all who "came of *gentle* blood," with corporations, lay and clerical, all had seals. They were mostly of brass, for the art of engraving on precious stones does not appear to have been at that time revived, with the letters and device cut or cast in hollow— *en creux*—on the face of the seal, in order that the impression might appear raised. The workmanship of many of those seals, and more especially of some of the conventional ones, where figures of saints and a view of the abbey are introduced, displays no mean degree of skill. Looking on such specimens of the graver's art, and bearing in mind the character of many of the drawings which are to be seen in the missals and other manuscripts of the fourteenth century and of the early part of the fifteenth, we need no longer be surprised that the cuts of the earliest block-books should be so well executed.

The art of engraving on copper and other metals, though not with the intention of taking impressions on paper, is of great antiquity. In the late Mr. Salt's collection of Egyptian antiquities there was a small axe, probably a model, the head of which was formed of sheet-copper, and was tied, or rather bandaged, to the helve with slips of cloth. There were certain characters engraved upon the head in such a manner that if it were inked and submitted to the action of the rolling-press, impressions would be obtained as from a modern copper-plate. The axe, with other

---

* The small and thick brass coins, struck by Grecian cities under the Roman emperors, and known to collectors as "colonial Greek," appear to have been cast, and moulds for such a purpose have been discovered in our own country.

models of a carpenter's tools, also of copper, was found in a tomb in Egypt, where it must have been deposited at a very early period. That the ancient Greeks and Romans were accustomed to engrave on copper and other metals in a similar manner, is evident from engraved pateræ and other ornamental works executed by people of those nations. Though no ancient writer makes mention of the art of engraving being employed for the purpose of producing impressions on paper, yet it has been conjectured by De Pauw, from a passage in Pliny,* that such an art was invented by Varro for the purpose of multiplying the portraits of eminent men. "No Greek," says De Pauw, speaking of engraving, "has the least right to claim this invention, which belongs exclusively to Varro, as is expressed by Pliny in no equivocal terms, when he calls this method *inventum Varronis.* Engraved plates were employed which gave the profile and the principal traits of the figures, to which the appropriate colours and the shadows were afterwards added with the pencil. A woman, originally of Cyzica, but then settled in Italy, excelled all others in the talent of illumining such kind of prints, which were inserted by Varro in a large work of his entitled ' *Imagines* ' or ' *Hebdomades,*' which was enriched with seven hundred portraits of distinguished men, copied from their statues and busts. The necessity of exactly repeating each portrait or figure in every copy of the work suggested the idea of multiplying them without much cost, and thus gave birth to an art till then unknown."† The grounds, however, of this conjecture are extremely slight, and will not without additional support sustain the superstructure which De Pauw—an "ingenious" guesser, but a superficial inquirer—has so plausibly raised. A prop for this theory has been sought for by men of greater research than the original propounder, but hitherto without success.

About the year 1300 we have evidence of monumental brasses, with large figures engraved on them, being fixed on tombs in this country ; and it is not unlikely that they were known both here and on the

* " That a strong passion for portraits formerly existed, is attested both by Atticus, the friend of Cicero, who wrote a work on this subject, and by M. Varro, who conceived the very liberal idea of inserting by some means or other, in his numerous volumes, the portraits of seven hundred individuals ; as he could not bear the idea that all traces of their features should be lost, or that the lapse of centuries should get the better of mankind."—Pliny's Natural History, Book xxxv. chap. 2.—(Bohn's Ed. vol. vi. p. 226. M. Deville is of opinion that these portraits were made in relief upon plates of metal, perhaps bronze, and coloured with minium, a red tint much esteemed by the Romans).

† See De Pauw, Recherches Philosophiques sur les Grecs, t. ii. p. 100. The subject is discussed in Meusel's " Neue Miscellaneen von artistischen Inhalts," part xii. p. 380—387, in an article, "Sind wirklich die Römer die Erfinder der Kupferstecherkunst ?—Were the Romans truly the inventors of copper-plate engraving ?"—by A. Rode. Böttiger, one of the most learned and intelligent of all German writers on the fine arts, and Fea, the editor of Winkleman's History of Art, do not admit De Pauw's conjecture, but decide the question in the negative.

Continent at an earlier period. The best specimens known in this country are such as were in all probability executed previous to 1400. In the succeeding century the figures and ornamental work generally appear to be designed in a worse taste and more carelessly executed; and in the age of Queen Elizabeth the art, such as it was, appears to have reached the lowest point of degradation, the monumental brasses of that reign being generally the worst which are to be met with.

The figures on several of the more ancient brasses are well drawn, and the folds of the drapery in the dresses of the females are, as a painter would say, "well cast;" and the faces occasionally display a considerable degree of correct and elevated expression. Many of the figures are of the size of life, marked with a bold outline well ploughed into the brass, and having the features, armour, and drapery indicated by single lines of greater or less strength as might be required. Attempts at shading are also occasionally to be met with; the effect being produced by means of lines obliquely crossing each other in the manner of cross-hatchings. Whether impressions were ever taken or not from such early brasses by the artists who executed them, it is perhaps now impossible to ascertain; but that they might do so is beyond a doubt, for it is now a common practice, and two immense volumes of impressions taken from monumental brasses, for the late Craven Ord, Esq., are preserved in the print-room of the British Museum.

One of the finest monumental brasses known in this country is that of Robert Braunche and his two wives, in St. Margaret's Church, Lynn, where it appears to have been placed about the year 1364. Braunche, and his two wives, one on each side of him, are represented standing, of the size of life. Above the figures are representations of five small niches surmounted by canopies in the florid Gothic style. In the centre niche is the figure of the Deity holding apparently the infant Christ in his arms. In each of the niches adjoining the centre one is an angel swinging a censer; and in the exterior niches are angels playing on musical instruments. At the sides are figures of saints, and at the foot there is a representation of a feast, where persons are seen seated at table, others playing on musical instruments, while a figure kneeling presents a peacock. The length of this brass is eight feet eleven inches, and its breadth five feet two inches. It is supposed to have been executed in Flanders, with which country at that period the town of Lynn was closely connected in the way of trade.*

It has frequently been asserted that the art of wood engraving in Europe was derived from the Chinese; by whom, it is also said, that the

---

* An excellent representation of this celebrated monument is given in Cotman's " Engravings from the most remarkable Sepulchral Brasses in Norfolk," folio, 1819 (republished with considerable additions in 2 vols. folio, 1839).

art was practised in the reign of the renowned emperor Wu-Wang, who flourished 1120 years before the birth of Christ. As both these statements seem to rest on equal authorities, I attach to each an equal degree of credibility; that is, by believing neither. As Mr. Ottley has expressed an opinion in favour of the Chinese origin of the art,— though without adopting the tale of its being practised in the reign of Wu-Wang, which he shows has been taken by the wrong end,—I shall here take the liberty of examining the tenability of his arguments.

At page 8, in the first chapter of his work, Mr. Ottley cautiously says that the "art of printing from engraved blocks of wood appears to be of very high antiquity amongst the Chinese;" and at page 9, after citing Du Halde, as informing us that the art of printing was not discovered until about fifty years before the Christian era, he rather inconsistently observes: "So says Father Du Halde, whose authority I give without any comment, as the defence of Chinese chronology makes no part of the present undertaking." Unless Mr. Ottley is satisfied of the correctness of the chronology, he can by no means cite Du Halde's account as evidence of the very high antiquity of printing in China; which in every other part of his book he speaks of as a well-established fact, and yet refers to no other authority than Du Halde, who relies on the correctness of that Chinese chronology with the defence of which Mr. Ottley will have nothing to do.

It is also worthy of remark, that in the same chapter he corrects two writers, Papillon and Jansen, for erroneously applying a passage in Du Halde as proving that the art of printing was known in the reign of Wu-Wang,—he who flourished Ante Christum 1120; whereas the said passage was not alleged "by Du Halde to prove the antiquity of printing amongst the Chinese, but solely in reference to their ink." The passage, as translated by Mr. Ottley, is as follows: "As the stone Me" (a word signifying ink in the Chinese language), "which is used to blacken the *engraved* characters, can never become white; so a heart blackened by vices will always retain its blackness." The engraved characters were not inked, it appears, for the purpose of taking impressions, as Messrs. Papillon and Jansen have erroneously inferred. "It is possible," according to Mr. Ottley, "that the ink might be used by the Chinese at a very early period to blacken, and thereby render more easily legible, the characters of engraved inscriptions."* The *possibility* of this may be granted certainly; but at the same time we must admit that it is equally *possible* that the engraved characters were blackened with ink for the purpose of being printed, if they were of wood; or that, if

* At page 7, Mr. Ottley, borrowing from Du Halde, has erroneously stated that the delicate nature of their paper would not permit the use of a press. He must have forgot, for he cannot but have known, that impressions on the finest India paper had been frequently taken

cut in copper or other metal, they were filled with a black composition which would harden or *set* in the lines,—as an ingenious inquirer might infer from ink being represented by the *stone* ME; and thus it is *possible* that something very like "niello," or the filling of letters on brass doorplates with black wax, was known to the Chinese in the reign of Wu-Wang, who flourished in the year before our Lord, 1120. The one conjecture is as good as the other, and both good for nothing, until we have better assurance than is afforded by Du Halde, that engraved characters blackened with ink—for whatever purpose—were known by the Chinese in the reign of Wu-Wang.*

Although so little is positively known of the ancient history of "the great out-lying empire of China," as it is called by Sir William Jones, yet it has been most confidently referred to as affording authentic evidence of the high degree of the civilization and knowledge of the Chinese at a period when Europe was dark with the gloom of barbarism and ignorance. Their early history has been generally found, when opportunity has been afforded of impartially examining it, to be a mere tissue of absurd legends; compared to which, the history of the settlement of King Brute in Britain is authentic. With astronomy as a science they are scarcely acquainted; and their specimens of the fine arts display little more than representations of objects executed not unfrequently with minute accuracy, but without a knowledge of the most simple elements of correct design, and without the slightest pretensions to art, according to our standard.

One of the two Mahometan travellers who visited China in the ninth century, expressly states that the Chinese were unacquainted with the sciences; and as neither of them takes any notice of printing, the mariner's compass, or gunpowder, it seems but reasonable to conclude that the Chinese were unacquainted with those inventions at that period.†

Mr. Ottley, at pages 51 and 52 of his work, gives a brief account of

from wood-blocks by means of the common printing-press many years previous to 1816, the date of the publication of his book. I have never seen Chinese paper that would bear printing by hand, which would not also bear the action of the press, if printed without being wet in the same manner as common paper.

* It would appear that Chinese annalists themselves were not agreed as to the period when printing by the hand from wood-blocks was first practised in that country. "Nicholas Trigaltius, a member of our order," writes Herman Hugo, "who has recently returned from China, gives the following information respecting printing, which he professes to have carefully extracted from the annals of the Chinese themselves. '*Typography is of somewhat earlier date in China than in Europe, for it is certain that it was practised in that country about five centuries ago. Others assert that it was practised in China at a period prior to the Christian era.*'"—Hermannus Hugo, De Prima Origine Scribendi, p. 211. Antwerpiæ, 1617.

† The pretensions of the Chinese to excellence in science are ably exposed by the learned Abbé Renaudot in a disquisition "Sur les sciences des Chinois," appended to his translation, from the Arabic, entitled "Anciennes Relations des Indes et de la Chine, de deux Voyageurs Mahométans, qui y allèrent dans le neuvième siècle."—8vo. Paris, 1718.

the early commerce of Venice with the East, for the purpose of showing in what manner a knowledge of the art of printing in China might be obtained by the Venetians. He says: "They succeeded, likewise, in establishing a direct traffic with Persia, Tartary, China, and Japan; sending, for that purpose, several of their most respectable citizens, and largely providing them with every requisite." He cites an Italian author for this account, but he observes a prudent silence as to the period when the Venetians first established a *direct traffic* with China and Japan; though there is little doubt that Bettinelli, the authority referred to, alludes to the expedition of the two brothers Niccolo and Maffeo Polo, and of Marco Polo, the son of Niccolo, who in 1271 or 1272 left Venice on an expedition to the court of the Tartar emperor Kublai-Khan, which had been previously visited by the two brothers at some period between 1254 and 1269.* After having visited Tartary and China, the two brothers and Marco returned to Venice in 1295. Mr. Ottley, however, does not refer to the travels of the Polos for the purpose of showing that Marco, who at a subsequent period wrote an account of his travels, might introduce a knowledge of the Chinese art of printing into Europe: he cites them that his readers may suppose that a direct intercourse between Venice and China had been established long before; and that the art of engraving wood-blocks, and taking impressions from them, had been thus derived from the latter country, and had been practised in Venice long before the return of the travellers in 1295.

It is necessary here to observe that the invention of the mariner's compass, and of gunpowder and cannon, have been ascribed to the Chinese as well as the invention of wood engraving and block-printing; and it has been conjectured that *very probably* Marco Polo communicated to his countrymen, and through them to the rest of Europe, a knowledge of those arts. Marco Polo, however, does not in the account which he wrote of his travels once allude to gunpowder, cannon, or to the art of printing as being known in China;† nor does he once mention the compass as being used on board of the Chinese vessel in which he sailed from the coast of China to the Persian Gulf. "Nothing is more common,"

---

* See the Travels of Marco Polo. (In Bohn's Antiq. Library).

† It has been conjectured that the following passages in the travels of Marco Polo might suggest the idea of block-printing, and consequently wood engraving : " Gradatim reliquos belli duces in digniorem ponit statum, donatque illis aurea et argentea vasa, tabulas, privilegia atque immunitatem. Et hæc quidem privilegia tabulis vel bracteis per sculpturas imprimuntur." "Moneta magni Cham non fit de auro vel argento, aut alio metallo, sed corticem accipiunt medium ab arbore mori, et hunc consolidant, atque in particulas varias et rotundas, magnas et parvas, scindunt, atque regale imprimunt signum."—M. Pauli Veneti Itiner. lib. ii. capp. vii. & xxi. The mention of paper money impressed with the royal stamp also occurs in the Eastern History of Haython, an Armenian, whose work was written in 1307, in Latin, and has been printed several times, of which the last edition is by And. Müller, Colon. 1671, 4to.

says a writer in the Quarterly Review, "than to find it repeated from book to book, that gunpowder and the mariner's compass were first brought from China by Marco Polo, though there can be very little doubt that both were known in Europe some time before his return."—"That Marco Polo," says the same writer, "would have mentioned the mariner's compass, if it had been in use in China, we think highly probable; and his silence respecting gunpowder may be considered as at least a negative proof that this also was unknown to the Chinese in the time of Kublai-Khan."* In a manner widely different from this does Mr. Ottley reason, respecting the cause of Marco Polo not having mentioned printing as an art practised by the Chinese. He accounts for the traveller's silence as follows: "Marco Polo, it may be said, did not notice this art [of engraving on wood and block-printing] in the account which he left us of the marvels he had witnessed in China. The answer to this objection is obvious: it was no marvel; it had no novelty to recommend it; it was practised, as we have seen, at Ravenna, in 1285, and had perhaps been practised a century earlier in Venice. His mention of it, therefore, was not called for, and he preferred instructing his countrymen in matters with which they were not hitherto acquainted." This "obvious" answer, rather unfortunately, will equally apply to the question, "Why did not Marco Polo mention cannon as being used by the Chinese, who, as we are informed, had discovered such formidable engines of war long before the period of his visit?"

That the art of engraving wood-blocks and of taking impressions from them was introduced into Europe from China, I can see no sufficient reason to believe. Looking at the frequent practice in Europe, from the twelfth to the fifteenth century, of impressing inked stamps on paper, I can perceive nothing in the earliest specimens of wood engraving but the same principles applied on a larger scale. When I am once satisfied that a man had built a small boat, I feel no surprise on learning that his grandson had built a larger; and made in it a longer voyage than his ancestor ever ventured on, who merely used his slight skiff to ferry himself across a river.

In the first volume of Papillon's "Traité de la Gravure en Bois," there is an account of certain old wood engravings which he professes to have seen, and which, according to their engraved explanatory title, were executed by two notable young people, Alexander Alberic Cunio, *knight*, and Isabella Cunio, his twin sister, and finished by them when they were only sixteen years old, at the time when Honorius IV. was pope; that is, at some period between the years 1285 and 1287. This

* An article on Marsden's "Translation of the Travels of Marco Polo," in the Quarterly Review, No. xli. May, 1819, from p. 191 to 195, contains some curious particulars respecting the early use of the mariner's compass, and of gunpowder and cannon in Europe.

story has been adopted by Mr. Ottley, and by Zani, an Italian, who give it the benefit of their support. Mr. Singer, in his "Researches into the History of Playing Cards," grants the truth-like appearance of Papillon's tale; and the writer of the article "Wood-engraving" in the Encyclopedia Metropolitana considers it as authentic. It is, however, treated with contempt by Heineken, Huber, and Bartsch, whose knowledge of the origin and progress of engraving is at least equal to that of the four writers previously named.

The manner in which Papillon recovered his memoranda of the works of the Cunio is remarkable. In consequence of those curious notes being mislaid for upwards of thirty-five years, the sole record of the productions of those "ingenious and amiable twins" was very nearly lost to the world. The *three sheets of letter-paper* on which he had written an account of certain old volumes of wood engravings,—that containing the cuts executed by the Cunio being one of the number, —he had lost for upwards of thirty-five years. For long he had only a confused idea of those sheets, though he had often searched for them in vain, when he was writing his first essay on wood engraving, which was printed about 1737, but never published. At length he accidentally found them, on All-Saints' Day, 1758, rolled up in a bundle of specimens of paper-hangings which had been executed by his father. The finding of those three sheets afforded him the greater pleasure, as from them he discovered, by means of a pope's name, an epoch of engraving figures and letters on wood for the purpose of being printed, which was certainly much earlier than *any* at that period known in Europe, and at the same time a history relative to this subject equally curious and interesting. He says that he had so completely forgotten all this,—though he had so often recollected to search for his memoranda,—that he did not deign to take the least notice of it in his previously printed history of the art. The following is a faithful abstract of Papillon's account of his discovery of those early specimens of wood engraving. The title-page, as given by him in French from Monsieur De Greder's *vivâ voce* translation of the original,—which was " en mauvais Latin ou ancien Italien Gothique, avec beaucoup d'abréviations,"—is translated without abridgment, as are also his own descriptions of the cuts.

" When young, being engaged with my father in going almost every day to hang rooms with our papers, I was, some time in 1719 or 1720, at the village of Bagneux, near Mont Rouge, at a Monsieur De Greder's, a Swiss captain, who had a pretty house there. After I had papered a small room for him, he ordered me to cover the shelves of his library with paper in imitation of mosaic. One day after dinner he surprised me reading a book, which occasioned him to show me some very old ones which he had borrowed of one of his friends, a Swiss officer,* that

---

* A Monsieur Spirchtvel, as Papillon informs us. Tom. i. p 92.

he might examine them at his leisure. We talked about the figures which they contained, and of the antiquity of wood engraving; and what follows is a description of those ancient books as I wrote it before him, and as he was so kind as to explain and dictate to me."

" In a *cartouch*,* or frontispiece,—of fanciful and Gothic ornaments, though pleasing enough,—nine inches wide, and six inches high, having at the top the arms, doubtless, of Cunio, the following words are coarsely engraved on the same block, in bad Latin, or ancient Gothic Italian with many abbreviations.

" 'THE CHIVALROUS DEEDS, in figures, of the great and magnanimous Macedonian king, the courageous and valiant Alexander, dedicated, presented, and humbly offered to the most holy father, Pope Honorius IV. the glory and stay of the Church, and to our illustrious and generous father and mother, by us Alexander Alberic Cunio, knight, and Isabella Cunio, twin brother and sister; first reduced, imagined, and attempted to be executed in relief with a little knife, on blocks of wood, joined and smoothed by this learned and beloved sister, continued and finished together at Ravenna, after eight pictures of our designing, painted six times the size here represented; cut, explained in verse, and thus marked on paper to multiply the number, and to enable us to present them as a token of friendship and affection to our relations and friends. This was done and finished, the age of each being only sixteen years complete.' "

After having given the translation of the title-page, Papillon thus continues the narrative in his own person: " This *cartouch* [or ornamented title-page] is surrounded by a coarse line, the tenth of an inch broad, forming a square. A few slight lines, which are irregularly executed and without precision, form the shading of the ornaments. The impression, in the same manner as the rest of the cuts, has been taken in Indian blue, rather pale, and in distemper, apparently by the hand being passed frequently over the paper laid upon the block, as card-makers are accustomed to impress their addresses and the envelopes of their cards. The hollow parts of the block, not being sufficiently cut away in several places, and having received the ink, have smeared the paper, which is rather brown ; a circumstance which has caused the following words to be written in the margin underneath, that the fault might be remedied.

---

* *Cartouch.* " This word is used to denote those fantastic ornaments which were formerly introduced in decorating the wainscots of rooms ; and frequently served the purpose of frames, surrounding inscriptions, small paintings, or other devices. These *cartouches* were much in vogue in the sixteenth and seventeenth centuries for the frontispieces of books of prints ; and indeed *Callot* and *Della Bella* etched many entire sets of small subjects surrounded by similar ornaments. From the irregularity of their forms, the terms tablet shield, or panel, would be but ill expressive of their character."—Ottley's Inquiry, vol. i. p. 12.

They are in Gothic Italian, which M. de Greder had considerable difficulty in making out, and certainly written by the hand either of the Chevalier Cunio or his sister, on this first proof—evidently from a block—such as are here translated."

" ' *It is necessary to cut away the ground of the blocks more, that the paper may not touch it in taking impressions.*' "

" Following this frontispiece, and of the same size, are the subjects of the eight pictures, engraved on wood, surrounded by a similar line forming a square, and also with the shadows formed of slight lines. At the foot of each of those engravings, between the border-line and another, about a finger's breadth distant, are four Latin verses engraved on the block, poetically explaining the subject, the title of which is placed at the head. In all, the impression is similar to that of the frontispiece, and rather grey or cloudy, as if the paper had not been moistened. The figures, tolerably designed, though in a semi-gothic taste, are well enough characterized and draped ; and we may perceive from them that the arts of design were then beginning gradually to resume their vigour in Italy. At the feet of the principal figures their names are engraved, such as Alexander, Philip, *Darius*, Campaspe, and others."

" SUBJECT 1.—Alexander mounted on Bucephalus, which he has tamed. On a stone are these words : *Isabel. Cunio pinx. & scalp.*"

" SUBJECT 2.—Passage of the Granicus. Near the trunk of a tree these words are engraved : *Alex. Alb. Cunio Equ. pinx. Isabel Cunio scalp.*"

" SUBJECT 3.—Alexander cutting the Gordian knot. On the pedestal of a column are these words : *Alexan. Albe. Cunio Equ. pinx. & scalp.* This block is not so well engraved as the two preceding."

" SUBJECT 4.—Alexander in the tent of Darius. This subject is one of the best composed and engraved of the whole set. Upon the end of a piece of cloth are these words : *Isabel. Cunio pinxit & scalp.*"

" SUBJECT 5.—Alexander generously presents his mistress Campaspe to Apelles who was painting her. The figure of this beauty is very agreeable. The painter seems transported with joy at his good fortune. On the floor, on a kind of antique tablet, are these words : *Alex. Alb. Cunio Eques, pinx. & scalp.*"

" SUBJECT 6.—The famous battle of Arbela. Upon a small hillock are these words : *Alex. Alb. Equ. & Isabel. pictor. and scalp.* For composition, design, and engraving, this subject is also one of the best."

" SUBJECT 7.—Porus, vanquished, is brought before Alexander. This subject is so much the more beautiful and remarkable, as it is composed nearly in the same manner as that of the famous Le Brun ; it would seem that he had copied this print. Both Alexander and Porus have a grand

and magnanimous air. On a stone near a bush are engraved these words : *Isabel. Cunio pinx. & scalp.*"

"SUBJECT 8 AND LAST.—The glory and grand triumph of Alexander on entering Babylon. This piece, which is well enough composed, has been executed, as well as the sixth, by the brother and sister conjointly, as is testified by these characters engraved at the bottom of a wall: *Alex. Alb. Equ. et Isabel. Cunio, pictor. & scalp.* At the top of this impression, a piece about three inches long and one inch broad has been torn off."

However singular the above account of the works of those "amiable twins" may seem, no less surprising is the history of their birth, parentage, and education ; which, taken in conjunction with the early development of their talents as displayed in such an art, in the choice of such a subject, and at such a period, is scarcely to be surpassed in interest by any narrative which gives piquancy to the pages of the Wonderful Magazine.

Upon the blank leaf adjoining the last engraving were the following words, badly written in old Swiss characters, and scarcely legible in consequence of their having been written with pale ink. " Of course Papillon could not read Swiss," says Mr. Ottley, " M. de Greder, therefore, translated them for him into French."—" This precious volume was given to my grandfather Jan. Jacq. Turine, a native of Berne, by the illustrious Count Cunio, chief magistrate of Imola, who honoured him with his generous friendship. Above all my books I prize this the highest on account of the quarter from whence it came into our family, and on account of the knowledge, the valour, the beauty, and the noble and generous desire which those amiable twins Cunio had to gratify their relations and friends. Here ensues their singular and curious history as I have heard it many a time from my venerable father, and which I have caused to be more correctly written than I could do it myself."

Though Papillon's long-lost manuscript, containing the whole account of the works of the Cunio and notices of other old books of engravings, consisted of only three sheets of letter-paper, yet the history alone of the learned, beautiful, and amiable twins, which Turine the grandson caused to be written out as he had heard it from his father, occupies in Papillon's book four long octavo pages of thirty-eight lines each. To assume that his long-lost manuscript consisted of brief notes which he afterwards wrote out at length from memory, would at once destroy any validity that his account might be supposed to possess ; for he states that he had lost those papers for upwards of thirty five years, and had entirely forgotten their contents.

Without troubling myself to transcribe the whole of this choice morsel of French Romance concerning the history of the "amiable twins" Cunio,—the surprising beauty, talents, and accomplishments of the maiden,—the early death of herself and her lover,—the heroism of the youthful knight, Alexander Alberic Cunio, displayed when only fourteen years old,—I shall give a brief abstract of some of the passages which seem most important to the present inquiry.*

From this narrative,—which Papillon informs us was written in a much better hand, though also in Swiss characters, and with much blacker ink than Turine the grandson's own memorandum,—we obtain the following particulars : The Count de Cunio, father of the twins, was married to their mother, a noble maiden of Verona and a relation of Pope Honorius IV. without the knowledge of their parents, who, on discovering what had happened, caused the marriage to be annulled, and the priest by whom it was celebrated to be banished. The divorced wife, dreading the anger of her own father, sought an asylum with one of her aunts, under whose roof she was brought to bed of twins. Though the elder Cunio had compelled his son to espouse another wife, he yet allowed him to educate the twins, who were most affectionately received and cherished by their father's new wife. The children made astonishing progress in the sciences, more especially the girl Isabella, who at thirteen years of age was regarded as a prodigy ; for she understood, and wrote with correctness, the Latin language ; she composed excellent verses, understood geometry, was acquainted with music, could play on several instruments, and had begun to design and to paint with correctness, taste, and delicacy. Her brother Alberic, of a beauty as ravishing as his sister's, and one of the most charming youths in Italy, at the age of fourteen could manage the great horse, and understood the practice of arms and all other exercises befitting a young man of quality. He also understood Latin, and could paint well.

The troubles in Italy having caused the Count Cunio to take up arms, his son, young Alexander Alberic, accompanied him to the field to make his first campaign. Though not more than fourteen years old, he was entrusted with the command of a squadron of twenty-five horse, with which, as his first essay in war, he attacked and put to flight near two hundred of the enemy. His courage having carried him too far, he was surrounded by the fugitives, from whom, however, he fought himself clear without any further injury than a wound in his left arm. His father, who had hastened to his succour, found him returning with the enemy's banner, which he had wrapped about his wound. Delighted at the valour displayed by his son, the Count Cunio knighted him on the spot. The young man then asked permission to visit his mother, which

* Readers of French romances will find the tale of the Cunio at p. 89, tom i. of Papillon's "Traité de la Gravure en Bois," or at p. 17, vol. i. of Mr. Ottley's "History of Engraving."

was readily granted by the count, who was pleased to have this opportunity of testifying the love and esteem he still retained towards that
noble and afflicted lady, who continued to reside with her aunt ; of which
he certainly would have given her more convincing proofs, now that his
father was dead, by re-establishing their marriage and publicly espousing
her, if he had not been in duty bound to cherish the wife whom he
had been compelled to marry, and who had now borne him a large
family.

After Alexander Alberic had visited his mother, he returned home,
and shortly after began, together with his sister Isabella, to design and
work upon the pictures of the achievements of Alexander. He then
made a second campaign with his father, after which he continued to
employ himself on the pictures in conjunction with Isabella, who
attempted to reduce them and engrave them on wood. After the
engravings were finished, and copies had been printed and given to
Pope Honorius, and their relations and friends, Alexander Alberic
proceeded again to join the army, accompanied by Pandulphio, a young
nobleman, who was in love with the charming Isabella. This was his
last campaign, for he was killed in the presence of his friend, who was
dangerously wounded in defending him. He was slain when not more
than nineteen ; and his sister was so affected by his death that she
resolved never to marry, and died when she was scarcely twenty. The
death of this lovely and learned young lady was followed by that of her
lover, who had fondly hoped that she would make him happy. The
mother of those amiable twins was not long in following them to the
grave, being unable to survive the loss of her children. The Countess
de Cunio took seriously ill at the loss of Isabella, but fortunately
recovered ; and it was only the count's grandeur of soul that saved
him from falling sick also.

Some years after this, Count Cunio gave the copy of the achievements of Alexander, in its present binding, to the grandfather of the
person who caused this account to be written. The binding, according
to Papillon's description of it, was, for the period, little less remarkable
than the contents. " This ancient and Gothic binding," as Papillon's note
is translated by Mr. Ottley, "is made of thin tablets of wood, covered
with leather, and *ornamented with flowered compartments, which appear
simply stamped and marked with an iron a little warmed, without any
gilding.*" It is remarkable that this singular volume should afford not
only specimens of wood engraving, earlier by upwards of a hundred and
thirty years than any which are hitherto known, but that the binding, of
the same period as the engravings, should also be such as is rarely, if
ever, to be met with till upwards of one hundred and fifty years after
the wonderful twins were dead.

As this volume is no longer to be found, as no mention is made of such a work by any old writer, and as another copy has not been discovered in any of the libraries of Italy, nor the least trace of one ever having been there, the evidence of its ever having existed rests solely on the account given of it by Papillon. Before saying a word respecting the credit to be attached to this witness, or the props with which Zani and Ottley endeavour to support his testimony, I shall attempt to show that the account affords internal evidence of its own falsehood.

Before noticing the description of the subjects, I shall state a few objections to the account of the twins as written out by order of the youngest Turine, the grandson of Jan. Jacq. Turine, who received the volume from Count Cunio himself, the father of the twins, a few years after their death, which could not well happen later than 1291; as Pope Honorius, to whom their work was dedicated when they were sixteen years old, died in 1287, and Isabella Cunio, who survived her brother, died when she was not more than twenty. Supposing that Count Cunio gave the volume to his friend, J. J. Turine, a native of Berne, in 1300, and that the grandson of the latter caused the history of the twins to be written out eighty years afterwards,—and we cannot fairly assume that it was written later, if indeed so late,—we have thus 1380 as the date of the account written "in old Swiss characters, in a better hand, and with much blacker ink," than the owner's own memorandum of the manner in which the volume came into his family, and his reasons for prizing it so highly. The probable date of the pretended Swiss history of the Cunio, Papillon's advocates carefully keep out of sight; for what impartial person could believe that a Swiss of the fourteenth century could give utterance to the sentimental fustian which forms so considerable a portion of the account? Of the young knight Cunio he knows every movement; he is acquainted with his visit to his repudiated mother; he knows in which arm he was wounded; the number of men that he lost, when with only five-and-twenty he routed two hundred; the name of Isabella's lover; the illness and happy recovery of Count Cunio's wife, and can tell the cause why the count himself did not fall sick.

To any person who reflects on the doctrine of the church of Rome in the article of marriage, it certainly must appear strange that the parents of the Count Cunio and his first wife, the mother of the twins, should have had the power of dissolving the marriage and of banishing the priest by whom it was solemnized; and still more singular it is that the Count Cunio, whom we must suppose to have been a good Catholic, should speak, after his father's death, of re-establishing his marriage with his first wife and of publicly espousing her; and that he should make such a communication to her through the medium of her son, who,

as well as his sister, must have been declared illegitimate by the very
fact of their mother's divorce. It is also strange that this piece of
family history should come to the knowledge of the grandson of
Jan. Jacq. Turine. The Count Cunio's second marriage surely must
have been canonically legal, if the first were not; and if so, it would
not be a sense of duty alone to his second wife that would prevent him
divorcing her and re-marrying the first. On such subjects the church
was to be consulted; and to such playing fast-and-loose with the
sacrament of marriage the church said " NO."   Taking these circumstances into consideration, I can come to no other conclusion than that,
on this point, the writer of the history of the Cunio did not speak
truth; and that the paper containing such history, even if it could be
produced, is not genuine, as every other part of it which has the slightest
bearing on the point at issue, is equally, if not more, improbable.

With respect to the cuts pretended to be executed by the twins
themselves, I shall waive any objections which might be urged on the
ground of it being unlikely that they should be executed by a boy and
a girl so young. Supposing that the twins were as learned and accomplished as they are represented, still it would be a very surprising
circumstance that, in the thirteenth century, they should have executed
a series of wood engravings of the actions of Alexander the Great as an
appropriate present to the pope; and that the composition of one of
those subjects, No. 7, should so closely resemble one of Le Brun's—an
artist remarkable for the complication of his designs—that it would
seem he had copied this very print. Something like the reverse of this
is more probable; that the description of the pretended work of the
Cunio was suggested by the designs of Le Brun.* The execution of a
set of designs, in the thirteenth century, illustrating the actions of
Alexander in the manner described by Papillon, would be a rarity indeed
even if not engraved on wood; but that a series of wood engravings, and
not a saint in one of them, should be executed by a boy and a girl,
and presented to a *pope*, in 1286, is scarcely short of miraculous. The
twins must have been well read in Quintus Curtius. Though we are
informed that both were skilled in the Latin language, yet it plainly
appears on two occasions, when we might suppose that they would be
least liable to trip, that their Latinity is questionable. The sixth and
the eighth subjects, which were accomplished by their joint efforts, are

---

* Of Le Brun's five subjects illustrative of the actions of Alexander the Great, four of
them are precisely the same as four of those said to be executed by the Cunio: 1. Alexander
passing the Granicus ; 2. the battle of Arbela ; 3. the reception of Porus by Alexander ;
4. Alexander's triumphant entry into Babylon. There certainly has been some copying
here ; but it is more likely that Papillon or his informant had seen Le Brun's paintings,
than that Le Brun had seen the original wood engravings executed by the Cunio.

described as being marked : *Alex. Alb. Equ. et Isabel. Cunio pictor. et scalp.*

" Thus painters *did not* write their names at Co."

Why do not the advocates of those early specimens of wood engraving in Italy point out to their readers that these two children were the first who ever affixed the words *pinx. et scalp.* to a woodcut ? I challenge any believer in Papillon to point out a wood engraving on which the words *pinxit* and *scalpsit*, the first after the painter's name, and the second after the engraver's, appear previous to 1580. This apparent copying—and by a person ignorant of Latin too—of the formula of a later period, is of itself sufficient to excite a suspicion of forgery ; and, coupled with the improbable circumstances above related, it irresistibly compels me to conclude that the whole account is a mere fiction.

With respect to the credibility of Papillon, the sole evidence upon which the history of the wonderful twins rests, I shall have occasion to say very few words. That he was credulous, and excessively vain of what he considered his discoveries in the history of wood engraving, is admitted by those who profess to believe him. He appears also from an early age to have been subject to mental hallucination ; and in 1759, the year after he found his papers containing the account of the Cunio, he had a fit of decided insanity which rendered it necessary to convey him to a mad-house, where by copious bleeding he soon recovered his senses.[*] To those interested in the controversy I leave to decide how far the unsupported testimony of such a person, and in such a case, ought to be relied on. How easily he might be deceived on a subject relating to the early history of his art, it is not difficult to comprehend ; and eve nallowing him to be sincere in the belief of what he related, he was a person very likely to occasionally deceive both himself and others.[†]

Papillon's insanity had been previously adverted to by Heineken ; and this writer's remarks have produced the following correction from Mr. Ottley : " Heineken takes some pains to show that poor Papillon was not in his right mind ; and, amongst his other arguments, quotes a pas-

---

[*] From the age of sixteen, cruel and secret annoyances interrupted his studies ; shortly after his marriage, in 1723, his absent manner was a source of uneasiness to his wife ; and in 1759 he fairly lost his senses. See Papillon, Traité de la Gravure en Bois, 8vo. 1766, Preface, p. xi. ; & p. 335, tom. i. et Supplement, p. 39.

[†] It is worthy of remark that Papillon, when questioned by Heineken, who called on him in Paris after the publication of his work, respecting the account of the Cunio, did not produce his three sheets of original memoranda. He might thus have afforded a proof of his own good faith, by producing the manuscript written by him in 1720 from the dictation of Captain de Greder.

sage from his book, t. i. p. 335, in which he says, '*Par un accident et une fatalité commune à plusieurs graveurs, aussi bien qu'à moi, Le Fevre est devenu aliéné d'esprit:*' as if a little pleasantry of expression, such as the French writers, especially, have ever felt themselves at full liberty to indulge in, could really constitute fit grounds for a statute of lunacy."*

Had Mr. Ottley, instead of confidently correcting Heineken when the latter had stated nothing but the fact, turned to the cited page of Papillon's volume, he would there have found that Papillon was indulging in no "little pleasantry of expression," but was seriously relating a melancholy fact of two brother artists losing their senses about the same time as himself; and had he ever read the supplement, or third volume, of Papillon's work, he would have seen, at p. 39, the account which Papillon himself gives of his own insanity.

Having disposed of the story as told by Papillon, it remains now to notice "the learning and deep research" with which it has been supported by Zani, and some of the arguments which have been alleged in its favour by Mr. Ottley.

In the first place, Zani has discovered that a family of the name of Cunio, in which the name of Alberico more than once occurs, actually resided in the neighbourhood of Ravenna at the very period mentioned in the title-page to the cuts by the Cunio, and in the history written in old Swiss characters. Upon this, and other similar pieces of evidence, Mr. Ottley remarks as follows: "Now both these cities [Ravenna and Imola] are in the vicinity of Faenza, where the family, or a branch of it, is spoken of by writers of undoubted credit in the twelfth, the thirteenth, and the fourteenth centuries. These circumstances, therefore, far from furnishing any just motive of additional doubt, form together such a phalanx of corroborative evidence in support of the story, as, in my opinion, those who would impeach the truth of Papillon's statement can never break through." "*Argal*," Rowley's poems are genuine, because such a person as "Maistre William Canynge" lived at Bristol at the period when he is mentioned by the pseudo Rowley. Zani, however, unfortunately for his own argument, let us know that the names and residence of the family of the Cunio might be obtained from "Tonduzzi's History of Faenza," printed in 1675. Whether this book appeared in French, or not, previous to the publication of Papillon's works, I have not been able to learn; but a Swiss captain, who could read "old Gothic Italian," would certainly find little difficulty in picking a couple of names out of a modern Italian volume.

The reasoning faculties of Signor Zani appear to have been very imperfectly developed, for he cites the following as a case in point; and

* Inquiry into the Early History of Engraving, vol. i. p. 23.

Mr. Ottley, who gives it in his text, seems to concur in its applicability·
He is noticing the objections which have been made to Papillon's
account, on the ground of no previous author mentioning the existence
of such a work, and that no person subsequently had ever seen a copy.
Zani's argument, as given by Mr. Ottley,* is as follows : " He, however,
who should reason in this manner, might, upon the same grounds, deny
the loss of many manuscripts, and even of printed books, which, according to the testimony of credible authors, have become a prey to the
flames, or have perished during the anarchy of revolutions, or the dis-
tresses occasioned by wars. The learned part of my readers will not
require examples. Nevertheless, let him who wants such conviction
search throughout all the libraries of Europe for the work entitled ' Meditationes Reverendissimi patris Domini Johannis de Turre-cremata,' printed
at Rome by Ulrich Hahn, in 1467, and he will presently be informed by
the learned librarians, that of that edition there exists but one copy,
which is preserved in the library of Nuremberg. This book is, therefore,
unique.† Now let us suppose that, by some accident, this book should
perish ; could our descendants on that account deny that it ever had
existed ?" And this is a corroborative argument in support of the truth
of Papillon's tale! The comment, however, is worthy of the text. It is
to be observed that Ulrich Hahn's edition of Turre-cremata appeared ten
years after Faust and Scheffer's Psalter, of the date 1457, was printed ;
and that the existence of several hundred volumes printed before 1467
proves that the art of printing was then practised to a considerable
extent. That Ulrich Hahn was a printer at Rome in 1468 and subsequent years is proved by many copies of works which proceeded from
his press ; and the existence of the identical " unique " copy, referred
to by Zani, is vouched for by upwards of fifty learned men who have
seen it ; and, what is more, mentioned the place where it was preserved,
so that, if a person were sceptical, he might satisfy himself by the
evidence of his own senses. But who, except Papillon, has ever seen
the engravings of the Cunio, executed upwards of a hundred and thirty
years prior to the earliest authentic specimen of the art, and who has
ever mentioned the place where they were to be seen? Had any person
of equal credibility with Papillon described a volume printed at Rome
in 1285, the date of the pretended wood-cuts of the Cunio, the case
would then have been in point, and the decision of every person in the
slightest degree acquainted with the subject, and not rendered blind to
simple truth by the vivid brightness of his own speculations, would be

* History of Engraving, vol. i. p. 28.
† Three copies of this supposed unique book have long been known to bibliographers ;
one in the public library of Nuremberg, another in the Imperial library of Vienna, and
the third in Lord Spenser's library.

inevitably the same ; that is, the evidence in both cases would not be relied on.

"It is possible," say Zani, "that at this moment I may be blinded by partiality to my own nation ; but I would almost assert, that *to deny the testimony of the French writer, would be like denying the existence of light on a fine sun-shiny day.*" His mental optics must have been of a peculiar character, and it can be no longer doubtful that he

> "Had lights where better eyes are blind,
> As pigs are said to see the wind."

Mr. Ottley's own arguments in support of Papillon's story are scarcely of a higher character than those which he has adopted from Zani. At page 40, in answer to an objection founded on the silence of all authorities, not merely respecting the particular work of the Cunio, but of the frequent practice of such an art, and the fact of no contemporary specimens being known, he writes as follows : "We cannot safely argue from the silence of contemporaneous authorities, that the art of engraving on wood was not practised in Europe in those early times ; however, such silence may be an argument that it was not an art in high repute. Nor is our ignorance of such records a sufficient proof of their non-existence." The proof of such a negative would be certainly difficult ; but, according to this mode of argument, there is no modern invention which might not also be mentioned in "certain ancient undiscovered records." In the general business of life, that rule of evidence is a good one which declares "*de non-apparentibus et non-existentibus eadem est ratio ;*" and until it shall be a maxim in logic that "we ought readily to believe that to be true which we cannot prove to have been impossible," Mr. Ottley's solution of the difficulty does not seem likely to obtain general credence.

At page 41, speaking of the probability of wood-engraving, for the purpose of taking impressions, being practised at an earlier period than has been generally supposed, Mr. Ottley expresses himself as follows : "Nor is it any proof or strong argument against the antiquity of such a practice, that authentic specimens of wood-engraving of those early times are not now to be found. They were, it may be supposed, for the most part, detached pieces, whose merits, as works of art, were not such as to render their preservation at all probable. They were the toys of the day ; and, after having served the temporary purpose for which they were manufactured, were, no doubt, swept away to make room for others of newer fashion." He thus requires those who entertain an opinion contrary to his own to prove a negative ; while he assumes the point in dispute as most clearly established in his own favour.

If such wood engravings—"the toys of the day"—had been known in the thirteenth, or even the fourteenth century, is it not likely that some mention would be made of them in the writings of some one of the minstrels of the period to whom we are indebted for so many minute particulars illustrative of the state of society at the period referred to? Not the slightest allusion to anything of the kind has hitherto been noticed in their writings. Respecting such "toys" Boccaccio is silent, and our countryman Chaucer says not a word. Of wood-cuts not the least mention is made in Petrarch; and Richard de Bury, bishop of Durham, who lived in the reign of Edward III., in his curious Essay on the Love of Books, says not a syllable of wood-cuts, either as toys, or as illustrations of devotional or historical subjects. Upon this question, affirmed by Papillon, and maintained as true by Zani and Ottley, contemporary authorities are silent; and not one solitary fact bearing distinctly upon the point has been alleged in support of Papillon's narrative.

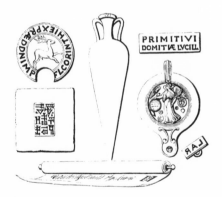

CHAPTER II.

PROGRESS OF WOOD ENGRAVING.

PLAYING-CARDS PRINTED FROM WOOD-BLOCKS—EARLY GERMAN WOOD-ENGRAVERS AT AUGS-
BURG, NUREMBERG, AND ULM—CARD-MAKERS AND WOOD-ENGRAVERS IN VENICE IN 1441—
FIGURES OF SAINTS ENGRAVED ON WOOD—THE ST. CHRISTOPHER, THE ANNUNCIATION, AND
THE ST. BRIDGET IN THE COLLECTION OF EARL SPENCER, WITH OTHER OLD WOOD-CUTS
DESCRIBED—BLOCK-BOOKS—THE APOCALYPSE, THE HISTORY OF THE VIRGIN, AND THE WORK
CALLED BIBLIA PAUPERUM—SPECULUM SALVATIONIS—FIGURED ALPHABET FORMERLY BELONG-
ING TO SIR GEORGE BEAUMONT—ARS MEMORANDI, AND OTHER SMALLER BLOCK-BOOKS.

 ROM the facts which have been produced in the preceding chapter, there cannot be a doubt that the principle on which wood engraving is founded,—that of taking impressions on paper or parchment, with ink, from prominent lines, —was known and practised in attesting documents in the thirteenth and fourteenth centuries. Towards the end of the fourteenth, or about the beginning of the fifteenth century, there is reason to believe that this principle was adopted by the German card-makers for the purpose of marking the outlines of the figures on their cards, which they afterwards coloured by means of a stencil.*

The period at which the game of cards was first known in Europe, as well as the people by whom they were invented, has been very learnedly, though not very satisfactorily discussed. Bullet has claimed the invention for the French, and Heineken for the Germans ; while other writers have maintained that the game was known in Italy earlier than in any other part of Europe, and that it was introduced from the East.

From a passage discovered by M. Van Praet, in an old manuscript copy of the romance of *Renard le Contrefait*, it appears that cards were known in France about 1340, although Bullet was of opinion that they

---

* A stencil is a piece of pasteboard, or a thin plate of metal, pierced with lines and figures, which are communicated to paper, parchment, or linen, by passing a brush charged with ink or colour over the stencil.

were invented in that country about 1376. At whatever period the game
was introduced, it appears to have been commonly known in France and
Spain towards the latter part of the fourteenth century. John I., King of
Castile, by an edict issued in 1387, prohibited the game of cards ; and in
1397, the Provost of Paris, by an ordonnance, forbid all working people
to play at tennis, bowls, dice, *cards*, or nine-pins, on working days. From
a passage in the Chronicle of Petit-Jehan de Saintré, written previous to
1380, it would appear that the game of cards at that period was in disrepute. Saintré had been one of the pages of Charles V. of France ; and on
his being appointed, on account of his good conduct, to the situation of
carver to the king, the squire who had charge of the pages, lectured some
of them on the impropriety of their behaviour ; such as playing at dice
and cards, keeping bad company, and haunting taverns and cabarets,
those not being the courses by which they might hope to arrive at the
honourable post of "ecuyer tranchant," to which their companion, Saintré,
had been raised.

In an account-book of Charles Poupart, treasurer to Charles VI. of
France, there is an entry, made about 1393, of "fifty-six sols of Paris,
given to Jacquemin Gringonneur, painter, for three packs of cards, gilt
and coloured, and of different sorts, for the diversion of his majesty."
From this passage the learned Jesuit Menestrier, who was not aware of
cards being mentioned by any earlier writer, concluded that they were
then invented by Gringonneur to amuse the king, who, in consequence of
a *coup de soleil*, had been attacked with delirium, which had subsided
into an almost continual depression of spirits. There, however, can be
no doubt that cards were known in France at least fifty years before ;
though, from their being so seldom noticed previous to 1380, it appears
likely that the game was but little played until after that period.
Whether the figures on the cards supplied for the king's amusement
were drawn and coloured by the hand, or whether the outlines were
impressed from wood-blocks, and coloured by means of a stencil, it is
impossible to ascertain ; though it has been conjectured that, from the
smallness of the sum paid for them, they were of the latter description.
That cards were cheap in 1397, however they might be manufactured,
may be presumed from the fact of their being then in the hands of the
working people.

To whatever nation the invention of cards is owing, it appears that
the Germans were the first who practised card-making as a trade. In
1418 the name of a "Kartenmacher"—card-maker—occurs in the
burgess-book of the city of Augsburg ; and in an old rate-book of the city
of Nuremburg, under the year 1433, we find " *Ell. Kartenmacherin;*"
that is, Ell.—probably for Elizabeth—the card-maker. In the same
book, under the year 1435, the name of " *Eliz. Kartenmacherin*," probably

the same person, is to be found; and in 1438 there occurs the name "Margret Kartenmalerin"—Margaret the card-painter. It thus appears that the earliest card-makers who are mentioned as living at Nuremberg were females; and it is worthy of note that the Germans seem to have called cards "*Karten*" before they gave them the name of "*Briefe.*" Heineken, however, considers that they were first known in Germany by the latter name; for, as he claimed the invention for his countrymen, he was unwilling to admit that the name should be borrowed either from Italy or France. He has not, however, produced anything like proof in support of his opinion, which is contradicted by the negative evidence of history.*

The name *Briefe*, which the Germans give to cards, also signifies letters [epistolæ]. The meaning of the word, however, is rather more general than the French term *lettres*, or the Latin *epistolæ* which he gives as its synonyms, for it is also applied in the sense in which we sometimes use the word "paper." For instance, "*ein Brief Stecknadeln, ein Brief Tabak*," are literally translated by the words "a *paper* of pins, a *paper* of tobacco;" in which sense the word "*Brief*" would, in Latin, be more correctly rendered by the term *charta* than *epistola*. As it is in a similar sense—cognate with "paper," as used in the two preceding examples—that "Briefe" is applied to cards, I am inclined to consider it as a translation of the Latin *chartæ*, the Italian *carte*, or the French *cartes*, and hence to conclude that the invention of cards does not belong to the people of Germany, who appear to have received cards, both "name and thing," from another nation, and after some time to have given them a name in their own language.

In the town-books of Nuremberg, the term *Formschneider*—figure-cutter,—the name appropriated to engravers on wood, first occurs in 1449;† and as it is found in subsequent years mentioned in the same page with "Kartenmaler," it seems reasonable to conclude that in 1449, and probably earlier, the business of the wood-engraver proper, and that of the card-maker, were distinct. The primary meaning of the word *form* or *forma* is almost precisely the same in most of the European languages.

---

* Cards—*Carten*—are mentioned in a book of bye-laws of Nuremberg, between 1380 and 1384. They are included in a list of games at which the burghers might indulge themselves, provided they ventured only small sums. "Awzgenommen rennen mit Pferder, Schiessen mit Armbrusten, *Carten*, Schofzagel, Pretspil, und Kugeln, umb einen pfenink zwen zu vier poten." That is: always excepting horse-racing, shooting with cross-bows, *cards*, shovel-board, tric-trac, and bowls, at which a man may bet from twopence to a groat."—C. G. Von Murr, Journal zur Kunstsgesch. 2 Theil, S. 99.

† In the town-books of Nuremberg a Hans *Formansneider* occurs so early as 1397, which De Murr says is not meant for "wood engraver," but is to be read thus: *Hans Forman, Schneider;* that is, "Ihon Forman, maister-fashionere," or, in modern phrase, "tailor." The word "*Karter*" also occurs in the same year, but it is meant for a carder, or wool-comber, and not for a card-maker.—C. G. Von Murr, Journal, 2 Theil, S. 99.

It has erroneously been explained, in its relation to wood engraving, as signifying a *mould*, whereas it simply means a shape or figure. The model of wood which the carpenter makes for the metal-founder is properly a *form*, and from it the latter prepares his mould in the sand. The word *form*, however, in course of time declined from its primary signification, and came to be used as expressive both of a model and a mould. The term *Fornschneider*, which was originally used to distinguish the professed engraver of figures from the mere engraver and colourer of cards, is still used in Germany to denote what we term a wood-engraver.

About the time that the term *Formschneider* first occurs we find *Briefmalers* mentioned, and at a later period *Briefdruckers*—card-printers ; and, though there evidently was a distinction between the two professions, yet we find that between 1470 and 1500 the *Briefmalers* not only engraved figures occasionally, but also printed books. The *Formschneiders* and the *Briefmalers*, however, continued to form but one guild or fellowship till long after the art of wood-engraving had made rapid strides towards perfection, under the superintendence of such masters as Durer, Burgmair, and Holbein, in the same manner as the barbers and surgeons in our own country continued to form but one company, though the " chirurgeon had long ceased to trim beards and cut hair, and the barber had given up bleeding and purging to devote himself more exclusively to the ornamental branch of his original profession." " *Kartenmacher* and *Kartenmaler*," says Von Murr, " or *Briefmaler*, as they were afterwards called [1473], were known in Germany eighty years previous to the invention of book-printing. The Kartenmacher was originally a Formschneider, though, after the practice of cutting figures of saints and of sacred subjects was introduced, a distinction began to be established between the two professions."

The German card-makers of Augsburg, Nuremberg, and Ulm, it is stated, sent large quantities of cards into Italy ; and it was probably against those foreign manufacturers that the fellowship of painters at Venice obtained an order in 1441 from the magistracy, declaring that no foreign manufactured cards, or printed coloured figures, should be brought into the city, under the penalty of forfeiting such articles, and of being fined xxx liv. xii soldi. This order was made in consequence of a petition presented by the Venetian painters, wherein they set forth that " the art and mystery of card-making and of printing figures, which were practised in Venice, had fallen into total decay through the great quantity of foreign playing-cards and coloured printed figures, which were brought into the city."* It is hence evident that the art both of the German

* " Conscioscia che l'arte e mestier delle carte & figure stampide, che se fano in Venesia è vegnudo a total deffaction, e questo sia per la gran quantità de carte a zugar, e fegure depente stampide, le qual vien fate de fuora de Venezia." The curious document in which

Kartenmacher and of the *Formschneider* was practised in Venice in 1441 ; and, as it is then mentioned as being in decay, it no doubt was practised there some time previously.

Heineken, in his "Neue Nachrichten," gives an extract from a MS. chronicle of the city of Ulm, completed in 1474, to the following effect : "Playing-cards were sent *barrelwise* [that is, in small casks] into Italy, Sicily, and also over sea, and exchanged for spices and other wares. From this we may judge of the number of card-makers who resided here." The preceding passage occurs in the index, under the head, "Business of card-making." Heineken also gives the passage in his "Idée Générale," p. 245 ; but from the French translation, which he there gives, it appears that he had misunderstood the word "*leglenweiss*"—barrelwise—which he renders "en ballots." In his "Neue Nachrichten," however, he inserts the explanation between parentheses, ("das ist, in kleinen Fässern")—i. e. in small casks ; which Mr. Singer renders "hogsheads," and Mr. Ottley, though he gives the original in a note, "large bales." The word "lägel," a barrel, is obsolete in Germany, but its diminutive, "leglin,"—as if "lägelen"—is still used in Scotland for the name of the ewe-milker's *kit*.

Some writers have been of opinion that the art of wood-engraving was derived from the practice of the ancient caligraphists and illuminators of manuscripts, who sometimes formed their large capital letters by means of a stencil or of a wooden stamp. That large capitals were formed in such a manner previous to the year 1400 there can be little doubt ; and it has been thought that stencils and stamps were used not only for the formation of capital letters, but also for the impression of a whole volume. Ihre, in a dissertation on the Gospels of Ulphilas,[*] which are supposed to be as old as the fifth century, has asserted that the silver letters of the text on a purple ground were impressed by means of heated iron stamps. This, however, is denied by the learned compilers of the "Nouveau Traité de Diplomatique," who had seen other volumes of a similar kind, the silver letters of which were evidently formed with a pen. A modern Italian author, D. Vincenzo Requeno, has published a tract[†] to prove that many supposed manuscripts from the tenth to the fourteenth century, instead of being written with a pen, were actually impressed by means of stamps. It is, however, extremely

the above passage occurs was discovered by Temanza, an Italian architect, in an old book of rules and orders belonging to the company of Venetian painters. His discovery, communicated in a letter to Count Algarotti, appeared in the Lettere Pittoriche, tom. v. p. 320, et sequent. and has since been quoted by every writer who has written upon the subject.

[*] This celebrated version, in the Mœso-Gothic language, is preserved in the library of Upsal in Sweden.

[†] Osservazioni sulla Chirotipografia, ossia Antica Arte di Stampare a mano. Opera di D. Vincenzo Requeno. Roma 1810, 8vo.

probable that he is mistaken ; for if his pretended discoveries were true, this art of stamping must have been very generally practised ; and if so, it surely would have been mentioned by some contemporary writers. Signor Requeno's examination, I am inclined to suspect, has not been sufficiently precise ; for he seems to have been too willing to find what he sought. In almost every collection that he examined, a pair of fine compasses being the test which he employed, he discovered voluminous works on vellum, hitherto supposed to be manuscript, but which according to his measurement were certainly executed by means of a stamp.

It has been conjectured that the art of wood-engraving was employed on sacred subjects, such as the figures of saints and holy persons, before it was applied to the multiplication of those "books of Satan," playing-cards. It however is not unlikely that it was first employed in the manufacture of cards ; and that the monks, availing themselves of the same principle, shortly afterwards employed the art of wood-engraving for the purpose of circulating the figures of saints ; thus endeavouring to supply a remedy for the evil, and extracting from the serpent a cure for his bite.

Wood-cuts of sacred subjects were known to the common people of Snabia, and the adjacent districts, by the name of *Helgen* or *Helglein*, a corruption of Heiligen, saints ;—a word which in course of time they used to signify prints—*estampes*—generally.* In France the same kind of cuts, probably stencil-coloured, were called "dominos,"—the affinity of which name with the German Helgen is obvious. The word "domino" was subsequently used as a name for coloured or marbled paper generally, and the makers of such paper, as well as the engravers and colourers of wood-cuts, were called "dominotiers." †

As might, *à priori*, be concluded, supposing the Germans to have been the first who applied wood-engraving to card-making, the earliest wood-cuts have been discovered, and in the greatest abundance, in that district where we first hear of the business of a card-maker and a wood-engraver. From a convent, situated within fifty miles of the city of Augsberg, where, in 1418, the first mention of a Kartenmacher occurs, has been obtained the earliest wood-cut known,—the St. Christopher, now in the possession of Earl Spencer, with the date 1423. That this was the first cut of the kind we have no reason to suppose ; but though others executed in a similar manner are known, to not one of them, upon anything like probable grounds, can a higher degree of antiquity be

---

* Fuseli, at p. 85 of Ottley's Inquiry ; and Breitkopf, Versuch d. Ursprungs der Spielkarten Zuerforschen, 2 Theil, S. 175.

† Fournier, Dissertation sur l'Origine et les Progrès de l'Art de Graver en Bois, p. 79 ; and Papillon, Traité de la Gravure en Bois, tom. i. p. 20, and Supplement, p. 80.

assigned.　From 1423, therefore, as from a known epoch, the practice of wood engraving, as applied to pictorial representations, may be dated.

The first person who published an account of this most interesting wood-cut was Heineken, who had inspected a greater number of old wood-cuts and block-books than any other person, and whose unwearied perseverance in searching after, and general accuracy in describing such

early specimens of the art of wood-engraving, are beyond all praise.　He found it pasted on the inside of the right-hand cover of a manuscript volume in the library of the convent of Buxheim, near Memmingen in Suabia.　The manuscript, entitled LAUS VIRGINIS,* and finished in 1417,

* " Liber iste, *Laus Virginis* intitulatus, continet Lectiones Matutinales accommodatas Officio B. V. Mariæ per singulos anni dies," &c.　At the beginning of the volume is the following memorandum : " Istum librum legavit domna Anna filia domni Stephani baronis

was left to the convent by Anna, canoness of Buchaw, who was living in 1427 ; but who probably died previous to 1435. The above reduced copy conveys a pretty good idea of the composition and style of engraving of the original cut, which is of a folio size, being eleven and a quarter inches high, and eight inches and one-eighth wide.*

The original affords a specimen of the combined talents of the Form-schneider or wood-engraver, and the Briefmaler or card-colourer. The engraved portions, such as are here represented, have been taken off in dark colouring matter similar to printers' ink, after which the impression appears to have been coloured by means of a stencil. As the back of the cut cannot be seen, in consequence of its being pasted on the cover of the volume, it cannot be ascertained with any degree of certainty whether the impression has been taken by means of a press, or *rubbed off* from the block by means of a burnisher or rubber, in a manner similar to that in which wood-engravers of the present day take their proofs.

This cut is much better designed than the generality of those which we find in books typographically executed from 1462, the date of the Bamberg Fables, to 1493, when the often-cited Nuremberg Chronicle was printed. Amongst the many coarse cuts which " illustrate " the latter, and which are announced in the book itself† as having been " got up " under the superintendence of Michael Wolgemuth, Albert Durer's master, and William Pleydenwurff, both " most skilful in the art of painting," I cannot find a single subject which either for spirit or feeling can be compared to the St. Christopher. In fact, the figure of the saint, and that of the youthful Christ whom he bears on his shoulders, are, with the exception of the extremities, designed in such a style, that they would scarcely discredit Albert Durer himself.

To the left of the engraving the artist has introduced, with a noble disregard of perspective,‡ what Bewick would have called a " bit of Nature." In the foreground a figure is seen driving an ass loaded with

---

de Gundelfingen, canonica in Büchow Aule bte. Marie v'ginis in Buchshaim ord'is Cartusien prope Memingen Augusten. dyoc."—Von Murr, Journal, 2 Theil, S. 104—105.

* A fac-simile, of the size of the original, is given in Von Murr's Journal, vol. ii. p. 104, and in Ottley's Inquiry, vol. i. p. 90, both engraved on wood. There is an imitation engraved on copper, in Jansen's Essai sur l'Origine de la Gravure, tom. i.

† The following announcement appears in the colophon of the Nuremberg Chronicle. " Ad intuitum autem et preces providorum civium Sebaldi Schreyer et Sebastiani Romer-maister hunc librum Anthonius Koberger Nurembergiæ impressit. Adhibitis tamen viris mathematicis pingendique arte peritissimis, Michaele Wolgemut et Wilhelmo Pleydenwurff, quorum solerti accuratissimaque animadversione tum civitatum tum illustrium virorum figuræ insertæ sunt. Consummatum autem duodecima mensis Julii. Anno Salutis ñre 1493."

‡ As great a neglect of the rules of perspective may be seen in several of the cuts in the famed edition of Theurdanck, Nuremberg, 1517, which are supposed to have been designed by Hans Burgmair, and engraved by Hans Schaufflein.

a sack towards a water-mill; while by a steep path a figure, perhaps
intended for the miller, is seen carrying a full sack from the back-door of
the mill towards a cottage. To the right is seen a hermit—known by
the bell over the entrance of his dwelling—holding a large lantern to
direct St. Christopher as he crosses the stream. The two verses at the
foot of the cut,

> Cristofori faciem die quacunque tueris,
> Illa nempe die morte mala non morieris,

may be translated as follows :

> Each day that thou the likeness of St. Christopher shalt see,
> That day no frightful form of death shall make an end of thee.

They allude to a popular superstition, common at that period in all
Catholic countries, which induced people to believe that the day on
which they should see a figure or image of St. Christopher, they should
not meet with a violent death, nor die without confession.* To this
popular superstition Erasmus alludes in his " Praise of Folly ;" and it is
not unlikely, that to his faith in this article of belief, the squire, in
Chaucer's " Canterbury Tales," wore

> " A Christofre on his brest, of silver shene."

The date " *Millesimo cccc° xx° tercio*"—1423—which is seen at the
right-hand corner, at the foot of the impression, most undoubtedly
designates the year in which the engraving was made.

The engraving, though coarse, is executed in a bold and free manner ;
and the folds of the drapery are marked in a style which would do credit
to a proficient. The whole subject, though expressed by means of few
lines, is not executed in the very simplest style of art. In the draperies
a diminution and a thickening of the lines, where necessary to the effect,
may be observed ; and the shades are indicated by means of parallel
lines both perpendicular, oblique, and curved, as may be seen in the
saint's robe and mantle. In many of the wood-cuts executed between
1462 and 1500, the figures are expressed, and the drapery indicated, by
simple lines of one undeviating degree of thickness, without the
slightest attempt at shading by means of parallel lines running in a
direction different to those marking the folds of the drapery or the outlines of the figure. If mere rudeness of design, and simplicity in the
mode of execution, were to be considered as the sole tests of antiquity
in wood-engravings, upwards of a hundred, positively known to have
been executed between 1470 and 1500, might be produced as affording
intrinsic evidence of their having been executed at a period antecedent
to the date of the St. Christopher.

* See Brand's Popular Antiquities, vol. i. pp. 359—364.—Bohn's edition.

In the Royal Library at Paris there is an impression of St. Christopher with the youthful Christ, which was supposed to be a duplicate of that in the possession of Earl Spencer. On comparing them, however, " it was quite evident," says Dr. Dibdin, "at the first glance, as M. Du Chesne admitted, that they were impressions taken from *different blocks*. The question therefore was, after a good deal of pertinacious argument on both sides—which of the two impressions was the more ancient? Undoubtedly it was that of Lord Spencer." At first Dr. Dibdin thought that the French impression was a copy of Earl Spencer's, and that it might be as old as the year 1460 ; but, from a note added in the second edition of his tour, he seems to have received a new light. He there says : "The reasons upon which this conclusion [that the French cut was a copy of a later date] was founded, are stated at length in the preceding edition of this work : since which, I very strongly incline to the supposition that the Paris impression is a *proof*—of one of the *cheats* of DE MURR." *

On the inside of the first cover or " board " of the Laus Virginis, the volume which contains the St. Christopher, there is also pasted a wood engraving of the Annunciation, of a similar size to the above-named cut, and impressed on the same kind of paper. As they are both worked off in the same kind of dark-coloured ink, and as they evidently have been coloured in the same manner, by means of a stencil, there can be little doubt of their being executed about the same time. From the left-hand corner of the Annunciation the figure of the Almighty has been torn out. The Holy Ghost, who appears descending from the Father upon the Virgin in the material form of a dove, could not well be torn out without greatly disfiguring the cut. An idea may be formed of the original from the following reduced copy.

Respecting these cuts, which in all probability were engraved by some one of the Formschneiders of Augsburg, Ulm, or Nuremberg,†

---

* Bibliographical and Picturesque Tour, by the Rev. T. F. Dibdin, D.D. p. 58, vol. ii. second edition, 1829. The De Murr to whom Dr. Dibdin alludes, is C. G. Von Murr, editor of the Journal of Arts and General Literature, published at Nuremberg in 1775 and subsequent years. Von Murr was the first who published, in the second volume of his journal, a *fac-simile*, engraved on wood by Sebast. Roland, of the Buxheim St. Christopher, from a tracing sent to him by P. Krismer, the librarian of the convent. Von Murr, in his Memorabilia of the City of Nuremberg, mentions that Breitkopf had seen a duplicate impression of the Buxheim St. Christopher in the possession of M. De Birkenstock at Vienna.

† There is every reason in the world to suppose that this wood-cut was executed either in Nuremberg or Augsburg. Buxheim is situated almost in the very heart of Suabia, the circle in which we find the earliest wood engravers established. Buxheim is about thirty English miles from Ulm, forty-four from Augsburg, and one hundred and fifteen from Nuremberg. Von Murr does not notice the pretensions of Ulm, which on his own grounds are stronger than those of his native city, Nuremberg.

P. Krismer, who was librarian of the convent of Buxheim, and who showed
the volume in which they are pasted to Heineken, writes to Von Murr to
the following effect : " It will not be superfluous if I here point out a
mark, by which, in my opinion, old wood engravings may with certainty
be distinguished from those of a later period.   It is this : In the oldest
wood-cuts only do we perceive that the engraver [Formschneider] has

frequently omitted certain parts, leaving them to be afterwards filled up
by the card-colourer [Briefmaler].   In the St. Christopher there is no
such deficiency, although there is in the other cut which is pasted on the
inside of the fore covering of the same volume, and which, I doubt not,
was executed at the same time as the former.   It represents the salu-
tation of the Virgin by the angel Gabriel, or, as it is also called, the
Annunciation ; and, from the omission of the colours, the upper part

of the body of the kneeling Virgin appears naked, except where it is covered with her mantle. Her inner dress had been left to be added by the pencil of the card-colourer. In another wood-cut of the same kind, representing St. Jerome doing penance before a small crucifix placed on a hill, we see with surprise that the saint, together with the instruments of penance, which are lying near him, and a whole forest beside, are suspended in the air without anything to support them, as the whole of the ground had been left to be inserted with the pencil. Nothing of this kind is to be seen in more recent wood-cuts, when the art had made greater progress. What the early wood-engravers could not readily effect with the graver, they performed with the pencil,—for the most part in a very coarse and careless manner,—as they were at the same time both wood-engravers and card-colourers."*

Besides the St. Christopher and the Annunciation, there is another old wood-cut in the collection of Earl Spencer which appears to belong to the same period, and which has in all probability been engraved by a German artist, as all who can read the German inscription above the figure would reasonably infer. Before making any remarks on this engraving, I shall first lay before the reader a reduced copy.

The figure writing is that of St. Bridget of Sweden, who was born in 1302 and died in 1373. From the representation of the Virgin with the infant Christ in her arms we may suppose that the artist intended to show the pious widow writing an account of her visions or revelations, in which she was often favoured with the blessed Virgin's appearance. The pilgrim's hat, staff, and scrip may allude to her pilgrimage to Jerusalem, which she was induced to make in consequence of a vision. The letters S. P. Q. R. in a shield, are no doubt intended to denote the place, Rome, where she saw the vision, and where she died. The lion, the arms of Sweden, and the crown at her feet, are most likely intended to denote that she was a princess of the blood royal of that kingdom. The words above the figure of the saint are a brief invocation in the German language, " *O Brigita bit Got für uns !*" "O Bridget, pray to God for us !" At the foot of the desk at which St. Bridget is writing are the letters M. I. CHRS., an abbreviation probably of Mater Jesu Christi, or if German, Mutter Iesus Christus.†

From the appearance of the back of this cut, as if it had been rubbed

---

* Von Murr, Journal, 2 Theil, S. 105, 106.

† St. Bridget was a favourite saint in Germany, where many religious establishments of the rule of St. Saviour, introduced by her, were founded. A folio volume, containing the life, revelations, and legends of St. Bridget, was published by A. Koberger, Nuremberg, 1502, with the following title : " Das puch der Himlischen offenbarung der Heiligen wittiben Birgitte von dem Kunigreich Schweden."

smooth with a burnisher or rubber, there can be little doubt of the
impression having been taken by means of friction. The colouring
matter of the engraving is much lighter than in the St. Christopher and
the Annunciation, and is like distemper or water-colour; while that of
the latter cuts appears, as has been already observed, more like printer's

ink. It is coarsely coloured, and apparently by the hand, unassisted
with the stencil. The face and hands are of a flesh colour. Her gown,
as well as the pilgrim's hat and scrip, are of a dark grey; her veil, which
she wears hoodwise, is partly black and partly white; and the wimple
which she wears round her neck is also white. The bench and desk, the
pilgrim's staff, the letters S. P. Q. R., the lion, the crown, and the nimbus

surrounding the head of St. Bridget and that of the Virgin, are yellow. The ground is green, and the whole cut is surrounded with a border of a shining mulberry or lake colour.

Mr. Ottley, having at the very outset of his Inquiry adopted Papillon's story of the Cunio, is compelled, for consistency's sake, in the subsequent portion of his work, when speaking of early wood engravings such as the above, to consider them, not as the earliest known specimens of the art, but merely as wood engravings such as were produced upwards of a hundred and thirty years after the amiable and accomplished Cunio, a mere boy and a girl, had in Italy produced a set of wood engravings, one of which was so well composed that Le Brun might be suspected of having borrowed from it the design of one of his most complicated pictures. In his desire, in support of his theory, to refer the oldest wood-cuts to Italy, Mr. Ottley asks: "What if these two prints [the St. Christopher and the Annunciation] should prove to be, not the productions of Germany, but rather of Venice, or of some district of the territory then under the dominion of that republic?"

His principal reasons for the preceding conjecture, are the ancient use of the word *stampide*—"printed"—in the Venetian decree against the introduction of foreign playing-cards in 1441 ; and the resemblance which the Annunciation bears to the style of the early Italian schools. Now, with respect to the first of these reasons, it is founded on the assumption that both those impressions have been obtained by means of a press of some kind or other,—a fact which remains yet to be proved ; for until the backs of both shall have been examined, and the mark of the burnisher or rubber found wanting, no person's mere opinion, however confidently declared, can be decisive of the question. It also remains to be proved that the word *stampide*, which occurs in the Venetian decree, was employed there to signify *"printed with a press."* For it is certain that the low Latin word *stampare*, with its cognates in the different languages of Europe, was used at that period to denote *impression* generally. But even supposing that "*stampide*" signifies "printed" in the modern acceptation of the word, and that the two impressions in question were obtained by means of a press; the argument in favour of their being Italian would gain nothing, unless we assume that the *foreign* printed cards and figures, which were forbid to be imported into Venice, were produced either within the territory of that state or in Italy ; for the word *stampide*—"*printed,*" is applied to them as well as those manufactured within the city. Now we know that the German card-makers used to send great quantities of cards to Venice about the period when the decree was made, while we have no evidence of any Italian cities manufacturing cards for exportation in 1441 ; it is therefore most likely that if the Venetians were acquainted with the use of the press in taking impressions from wood-blocks, the Germans were so too, and for these more probable reasons, admitting the cuts in question to have been printed by means of a press :—First, the fact of those wood-cuts being discovered in Germany in the very district where we first hear of wood-engravers ; and secondly, that if the Venetian wood-engravers were acquainted with the use of the press in taking impressions while the Germans were not, it is very unlikely that the latter would be able to undersell the Venetians in their own city. Until something like a probable reason shall be given for supposing the cuts in question to be productions "of Venice, or some other district of the territory then under the dominion of that republic," I shall continue to believe that they were executed in the district in which they were discovered, and which has supplied to the collections of amateurs so many old wood engravings of a similar kind. No wood engravings executed in Italy, are known of a date earlier than those contained in the " Meditationes Johannis de Turre-cremata," printed at Rome 1467,—and printed, be it observed, by a German, Ulrick Hahn. The circular wood engravings in the British Museum,* which Mr. Ottley says are indisputably Italian, and of the old dry taste of the fifteenth century, can scarcely be referred to an earlier period than 1500, and my own opinion is that they are not older than 1510. The manner in which they are engraved is that which we find prevalent in Italian wood-cuts executed between 1500 and 1520.

With respect to the resemblance which the Annunciation bears to the style of the early Italian school,—I beg to observe that it equally resembles many of the productions of contemporary "schools" of England and France, as displayed in many of the drawings contained in old illuminated manuscripts. It would be no difficult matter to point out in many old German engravings attitudes at least as graceful as the Virgin's ; and as to her drapery, which is said to be " wholly unlike the angular sharpness, the stiffness and the flutter of the ancient German school," I beg to observe that those peculiarities are not of so frequent occurrence in the works of German artists, whether sculptors, painters, or wood-engravers, who lived before 1450, as in the works of those who lived after that period. Angular sharpness and flutter in the draperies are not so characteristic of early German art generally, as of German art towards the end of the fifteenth, and in the early part of the sixteenth century.

---

* Those cuts consist of illustrations of the New Testament. There are ten of them, apparently a portion of a larger series, in the British Museum ; and they are marked in small letters, a. b. c. d. e. f. g. h. i. k. n. That which is marked g. also contains the words " Opus Jacobi." In this cut a specimen of cross-hatching may be observed, which was certainly very little practised—if at all—in Italy, before 1500.

Even the St. Bridget, which he considers to be of a date not later than the close of the fourteenth century,* Mr. Ottley, with a German inscription before his eyes, is inclined to give to an artist of the Low Countries ; and he kindly directs the attention of Coster's partisans to the shield of arms—probably intended for those of Sweden—at the right-hand corner of the cut. Meerman had discovered a seal, having in the centre a shield charged with a lion rampant—the bearing of the noble family of Brederode—a label of three points, and the mark of illegitimacy —a bend sinister, and surrounded by the inscription, "S[igillum] Lowrens Janssoen," which with him was sufficient evidence of its being the identical seal of Laurence, the Coster or churchwarden of Harlem.†

We thus perceive on what grounds the right of Germany to three of the oldest wood-cuts known is questioned ; and upon what traits of resemblance they are ascribed to Italy and the Low Countries. By adopting Mr. Ottley's mode of reasoning, it might be shown with equal probability that a very considerable number of early wood engravings— whether printed in books or separately—hitherto believed to be German, were really executed in Italy.

An old wood engraving of the martyrdom of St. Sebastian, of a quarto size, with a short prayer underneath, and the date 1437, apparently from the same block, was preserved in the monastery of St. Blaze, in the Black Forest on the confines of Suabia ;‡ and another, with the date 1443 inserted in manuscript, was pasted in a volume belonging to the library of the monastery of Buxheim. The latter is thus described by Von Murr : "Through the kindness of the celebrated librarian, Krismer, whom I have so often mentioned, I am enabled to give an account of an illuminated wood-cut, which at the latest must have been engraved in 1443. It is pasted on the inside of the cover of a volume which contains ' *Nicolai Dunkelspül* § Sermonum Partem Hyemalem.' It is of quarto

---

* Mr. Ottley's reason for considering this cut to be so old is, that " after that period [1400] an artist, who was capable of designing so good a figure, could scarcely have been so grossly ignorant of every effect of linear perspective, as was evidently the case with the author of the performance before us."—Inquiry, p. 87. Offences, however, scarcely less gross against the rules of linear perspective, are to be found in the wood-cuts in the Adventures of Sir Theurdank, 1517, many of which contain figures superior to that of St. Bridget. Errors in perspective are indeed frequent in the designs of many of the most eminent of Albert Durer's contemporaries, although in other respects the figures may be correctly drawn, and the general composition good.

† An engraving of this seal is given in the first volume of Meerman's Origines Typographicæ.

‡ Heineken, Neue Nachrichten von Künstlern und Kunstsachen. Dresden und Leipzig, 1786, S. 143.

§ In the Table des Matières to Jansen's Essai sur l'Origine de la Gravure, Paris, 1808, we find " Dünkelspül (Nicolas) graveur Allemand en 1443." After this specimen of accuracy, it

size, being seven and a half inches high, and five and a quarter wide, and
is inclosed within a border of a single line. It is much soiled, as we
perceive in the figures on cards which have been impressed by means of
a rubber. The style in which it is executed is like that of no other
wood-cut which I have ever seen. The cut itself represents three
different subjects, the upper part of it being divided into two compartments, each three inches square, and separated from each other by
means of a broad perpendicular line. In that to the right is seen St.
Dorothy sitting in a garden, with the youthful Christ presenting flowers
to her, of which she has her lap full. Before her stands a small hand-
basket,—also full of flowers,—such as the ladies of Franconia and Suabia
were accustomed to carry in former times. In the left compartment is
seen St. Alexius, lying at the foot of a flight of steps, upon which a man
is standing and emptying the contents of a pot upon the saint.* Between
these compartments there appears in manuscript the date ' *anno d'ni*
1443.' Both the ink and the characters correspond with those of the
volume. This date indicates the time when the writer had finished the
book and got it bound, as is more clearly proved by a memorandum at
the conclusion. In the year 1483, before it came into the possession
of the monastery of Buxheim, it belonged to Brother Jacobus Matzen-
berger, of the order of the Holy Ghost, and curate of the church of the
Virgin Mary in Memmingen. The whole of the lower part of the cut is
occupied with Christ bearing his cross, at the moment that he meets
with his mother, whom one of the executioners appears to be driving
away. Simon of Cyrene is seen assisting Christ to carry the cross. The
engraving is executed in a very coarse manner."†

In the Royal Library at Paris there is an ancient wood-cut of St.
Bernardin, who is represented on a terrace, the pavement of which
consists of alternate squares of yellow, red, and green. In his right
hand the saint holds something resembling the consecrated wafer or
host, in the midst of which is inscribed the name of Christ ; and
in his left a kind of oblong casket, on which are the words
" *Vide, lege, dulce nomen.*" Upon a scroll above the head of the
saint is engraved the sentence, " *Ihesus semper sit in ore meo,*"
and behind him, on a black label, is his name in yellow letters,
" *Sanct' Bernard'.*" The cut is surrounded by a border of foliage,
with the emblems of the four Evangelists at the four corners, and

---

is rather surprising that we do not find St. Alexius referred to also as "un graveur
Allemand."

* St. Alexius returning unknown to his father's house, as a poor pilgrim, was treated with
great indignity by the servants.

† Von Murr, Journal, 2 Theil, S. 113—115.

at the foot are the five following lines, with the date, impressed from prominent lines :—

O . splendor . pudicitie . zelator . paupertatis . a
mator . innocentie . cultor . virginitatis . lustra
cors . apientie . protector . veritatis . thro
num . fulgidum . eterne . majestatis . para
nobis . additum . divine . pietatis . amen . (1454)

This rare cut was communicated to Jansen by M. Vanpraet, the well-known bibliographer and keeper of the Royal Library.*

" Having visited in my last tour," says Heineken, after describing the St. Christopher, " a great many convents in Franconia, Suabia, Bavaria, and in the Austrian states, I everywhere discovered in their libraries many of those kinds of figures, engraved on wood, and pasted either at the beginning or the end of old volumes of the fifteenth century. I have indeed obtained several of them. These facts, taken altogether, have confirmed me in my opinion that the next step of the engraver in wood, after playing-cards, was to engrave figures of saints, which, being distributed and lost among the laity, were in part preserved by the monks, who pasted them in the earliest printed books with which they furnished their libraries."†

A great many wood-cuts of devotional subjects, of a period probably anterior to the invention of book-printing by Gutenberg, have been discovered in Germany. They are all executed in a rude style, and many of them are coloured. It is not unlikely that the most of these woodcuts were executed at the instance of the monks for distribution among the common people as helps to devotion ; and that each monastery, which might thus avail itself of the aid of wood engraving in the work of piety, would cause to be engraved the figure of its patron saint. The practice, in fact, of distributing such figures at monasteries and shrines to those who visit them, is not yet extinct on the Continent. In Belgium it is still continued, and, I believe, also in Germany, France, and Italy. The figures, however, are not generally impressions from wood-blocks, but are for the most part wholly executed by means of stencils. One of the latter class, representing the shrine of " Notre Dame de Hal,"—coloured in the most wretched taste with brick-dust red and shining green,—is

---

* Jansen, Essai sur l'Origine de la Gravure, tom. i. p. 237. Jansen's own authority on subjects connected with wood engraving is undeserving of attention. He is a mere compiler, who scarcely appears to have been able to distinguish a wood-cut from a copper-plate engraving.

† Idée Générale, p. 251. Hartman Schedel, the compiler of the Nuremberg Chronicle, was accustomed to paste both old wood-cuts and copper-plate engravings within the covers of his books, many of which were preserved in the Library of the Elector of Bavaria at Munich.— Idée Gén. p. 287 ; and Von Murr, Journal, 2 Theil, S. 115.

now lying before me. It was given to a gentleman who visited Halle, near Brussels, in 1829. It is nearly of the same size as many of the old devotional wood-cuts of Germany, being about four inches high, by two and three-quarters wide.*

The next step in the progress of wood engraving, subsequent to the production of single cuts, such as the St. Christopher, the Annunciation, and the St. Bridget, in each of which letters are sparingly introduced, was the application of the art to the production of those works which are known to bibliographers by the name of BLOCK-BOOKS: the most cele-brated of which are the Apocalypsis, seu Historia Sancti Johannis; the Historia Virginis ex Cantico Canticorum; and the Biblia Pauperum. The first is a history, pictorial and literal, of the life and revelations of St. John the Evangelist, derived in part from the traditions of the church, but chiefly from the book of Revelations. The second is a similar history of the Virgin, as it is supposed to be typified in the Songs of Solomon; and the third consists of subjects representing some of the most important passages in the Old and New Testament, with texts either explaining the subject, or enforcing the example of duty which it may afford. With the above, the Speculum Humanæ Salvationis is usually, though improperly, classed, as the whole of the text, in that which is most certainly the first edition, is printed from movable metal types. In the others the explanatory matter is engraved on wood, on the same block with the subject to which it refers.

All the above books have been claimed by Meerman and other Dutch writers for their countryman, Laurence Coster: and although no date, either impressed or manuscript, has been discovered in any one copy from which the period of its execution might be ascertained,† yet such appears to have been the clearness of the intuitive light which guided those authors, that they have assigned to each work the precise year in which it appeared. According to Seiz, the History of the Old and New Testament, otherwise called the Biblia Pauperum, appeared in 1432; the History of the Virgin in 1433; the Apocalypse in 1434; and the Speculum in 1439. For such assertions, however, he has not the slightest ground. That the three first might appear at some period between 1430 and 1450, is not unlikely;‡ but that the Speculum—*the text of which*

---

* Heineken thus speaks of those old devotional cuts: "On trouve dans la Bibliothèque de Wolfenbüttel de ces sortes d'estampes, qui représentent différens sujets de l'histoire sainte et de dévotion, avec du texte vis à vis de la figure, tout gravé en bois. Ces pièces sont de la même grandeur que nos cartes à jouer: elles portent 3 pouces de hauteur sur 2 pouces 6 lignes de largeur."—Idée Générale, p. 249.

† A copy of the Speculum belonging to the city of Harlem had at the commencement, "*Ex Officina Laurentii Joannis Costeri. Anno* 1440." But this inscription had been inserted by a modern hand —Idée Générale, p. 449.

‡ In the catalogue of Dr. Kloss's Library, No. 2024, is a "Historia et Apocalypsis Johannis

in the first edition was printed from metal types—should be printed before 1460, is in the highest degree improbable.

Upon extremely slight grounds it has been conjectured that the Biblia Pauperum, the Apocalypse, and the Ars Moriendi,—another block-book,— were engraved before the year 1430. The Rev. T. H. Horne, "a gentleman long and well known for his familiar acquaintance with books printed abroad," says Dr. Dibdin, "had a copy of each of the three books above mentioned, bound in one volume, upon the cover of which the following words were stamped: Hic liber relegatus fuit per Plebanum ecclesie"—with the date, according to the best of the Rev. Mr. Horne's recollection, 142(8). As he had broken up the volume, and had parted with the contents, he gave the above information on the strength of his memory alone. He was, however, confident that "the binding was the ancient legitimate one, and that the treatises had not been subsequently introduced into it, and that the date was 142 odd; but positively anterior to 1430." *

In such a case as this, however, mere recollection cannot be admitted as decisive of the fact, more especially when we know the many instances in which mistakes have been committed in reading the numerals in ancient dates. At page 88 of his Inquiry, Mr. Ottley, catching at every straw that may help to support his theory of wood engraving having been practised by the Cunio and others in the fourteenth century, refers to a print which a Monsieur Thierry professed to have seen at Lyons, inscribed "Schoting of Nuremberg," with the date 1384; and at p. 256 he alludes to it again in the following words: "The date 1384 on the woodcut preserved at Lyons, said to have been executed at Nuremberg, appears, I know not why, to have been suspected." It has been more than suspected; for, on examination, it has been found to be 1584. Paul Von Stettin published an account of a Biblia Pauperum, the date of which he supposed to be 1414; but which, when closely examined, was found to be 1474: and Baron Von Hupsch, of Cologne, published in 1787 an account of some wood-cuts which he supposed to have been executed in 1420; but which, in the opinion of Breitkopf, were part of the cuts of a Biblia Pauperum, in which it was probably intended to give the

Evangelistæ," imperfect, printed from wooden blocks. The following are the observations of the editor or compiler of the catalogue: "At the end of the volume is a short note, written by Pope Martin V., who occupied the papal chair from 1417 to 1431. This appears to accord with the edition described by Heineken at page 360, excepting in the double *a*, No. 3 and 4." If the note referred to were genuine, and actually written in the book, a certain date would be at once established. The information, however, comes in a questionable shape, as the English *rédacteur's* power of ascertaining who were the writers of ancient MS. notes appears little short of miraculous.

* Bibliotheca Spenceriana, vol. i. p. 4, cited in Ottley's Inquiry, vol. i. p. 99.

explanations in moveable types underneath the cuts, and probably of a later date than 1470.*

It is surprising that the Rev. Mr. Horne, who is no incurious observer of books, but an author who has written largely on Bibliography, should not have carefully copied so remarkable a date, or communicated it to a friend, when it might have been confirmed by a careful examination of the binding ; and still more surprising is it that such binding should have been destroyed. From the very fact of his not having paid more parti-cular attention to this most important date, and from his having permitted the evidence of it to be destroyed, the Rev. Mr. Horne seems to be an incompetent witness. Who would think of calling a person to prove from recollection the date of an old and important deed, who, when he had it in his possession, was so little aware of its value as to throw it away ? The three books in question, when covered by such a binding, would surely be much greater than when bound in any other manner. Such a volume must have been unique ; and, if the date on the binding were correct, it must have been admitted as decisive of a fact interesting to every bibliographer in Europe. It is not even mentioned in what kind of numerals the date was expressed, whether in Roman or Arabic. If the numerals had been Arabic, we might very reasonably suppose that the Rev. Mr. Horne had mistaken a seven for a two, and that, instead of " 142 odd," the correct date was " 147 odd." In Arabic numerals, such as were used about the middle of the fifteenth century, the seven may very easily be mistaken for a two.

The earliest ancient binding known, on which a date is impressed, is, I believe, that described by Laire.† It is that of a copy of "Sancti Hieronymi Epistolæ ;" and the words, in the same manner as that of the binding of which the Rev. Mr. Horne had so accurate a recollection, were " stamped at the extremity of the binding, towards the edge of the squares." It is only necessary to cite the words impressed on one of the boards, which were as follows :

" Illigatus est Anno Domini 1469
Per me Johannem
Richenbach Capellanum
In Gyslingen." ‡

The numerals of the date it is to be observed were Arabic. In the library of Dr. Kloss of Frankfort, sold in London by Sotheby and Son in 1835, were two volumes, "St. Augustini de Civitat. Dei, Libri xxii.

---

* Singer's Researches into the History of Playing-cards, p. 107.

† Index Librorum ab inventa Typographia ad annum 1500, No. 37.

‡ Mr. Bohn is in possession of a similarly bound volume, namely, " Astexani de Ast, Scrutinium Scripturarum," printed by Mentelin, without date, but about 1468, on the pig-skin covers of which is printed in bold black letter, *Per me Rich-en-bach illigatus in Gysslingen* 1470.

1469," and "St. Augustini Confessiones" of the same date ; both of which were bound by "Johannes Capellanus in Gyslingen," and who in the same manner had impressed his name on the covers with the date 1470. Both volumes had belonged to "Dominus Georgius Ruch de Gamundia."* That the volume formerly in the Rev. Mr. Horne's possession was bound by the curate of Geisslingen I by no means pretend to say, though I am firmly of opinion that it was bound subsequent to 1470, and that the character which he supposed to be a two was in reality a different figure. It is worthy of remark that it appears to have been bound by the "Plebanus" of some church, a word which is nearly synonymous with "Capellanus." †

As it does not come within the plan of the present volume to give a catalogue of all the subjects contained in the block-books to which it may be necessary to refer as illustrating the progress of wood engraving, I shall confine myself to a general notice of the manner in which the cuts are executed, with occasional observations on the designs, and such remarks as may be likely to explain any peculiarity of appearance, or to enable the reader to form a distinct idea of the subject referred to.

At whatever period the Apocalypse, the History of the Virgin, and the Biblia Pauperum may have been executed, the former has the appearance of being the earliest ; and in the absence of everything like proof upon the point, and as the style in which it is engraved is certainly more simple than that of the other two, it seems entitled to be first noticed in tracing the progress of the art.

Of the Apocalypse,—or "Historia Sancti Johannis Evangelistæ ejusque Visiones Apocalypticæ," as it is mostly termed by bibliographers, for the book itself has no title,—Heineken mentions no less than six editions, the earliest of which he considers to be that described by him at page 367 of his "Idée Générale d'une Collection complète d'Estampes." He, however, declares that the marks by which he has assigned to each edition its comparative antiquity are not infallible. It is indeed very evident that the marks which he assumed as characteristic of the relative order of the different editions were merely arbitrary, and could by no means be admitted as of the slightest consequence in enabling any

---

* "Catalogue of the Library of Dr. Kloss of Frankfort," Nos. 460 and 468. Geisslingen is about fifteen miles north-west of Ulm in Suabia, and Gemund about twelve miles northward of Geisslingen.

† Mr. Singer, at page 101 of his Researches into the History of Playing-cards, speaks of "one Plebanus of Augsburg," as if Plebanus were a proper name. It has nearly the same meaning as our own word "Curate." " PLEBANUS, Parœcus, Curio, Sacerdos, qui plebi præesț; Italis, Piovano ; Gallo-Belgis, Pleban. Balbus in Catholico : ' Plebanus, dominus plebis, Presbyter, qui plebem regit.'—Plebanum vero maxime vocant in ecclesiis cathedralibus seu collegiatis canonicum, cui plebis earum jurisdictioni subditæ cura committitur."—Du Cange, Glossarium, in verbo " Plebanus."

person to form a correct opinion on the subject. He notices two editions as the first and second, and immediately after he mentions a circumstance which might almost entitle the third to take precedence of them both; and that which he saw last he thinks the oldest of all. The designs of the second edition described by him, he says, are by another master than those of the first, although the artist has adhered to the same subjects and the same ideas. The third, according to his observations, differs from the first and second, both in the subjects and the descriptive text. The fourth edition is from the same blocks as the third; the only difference between them being, that the fourth is without the letters in alphabetical order which indicate the succession of the cuts. The fifth differed from the third or fourth only in the text and the directing letters, as the designs were the same; the only variations that could be observed being extremely trifling. After having described five editions of the book, he decides that a sixth, which he saw after the others, ought to be considered the earliest of all.* In all the copies which he had seen, the impressions had been taken by means of a rubber, in such a manner that each leaf contained only one engraving; the other side, which commonly bore the marks of the rubber, being without a cut. The impressions when collected into a volume faced each other, so that the first and last pages were blank.

The edition of the Apocalypse to which I shall now refer is that described by Heineken, at page 364, as the fifth; and the copy is that mentioned by him, at page 367, as then being in the collection of M. de Gaignat, and as wanting two cuts, Nos. 36 and 37. It is at present in the King's Library at the British Museum.

It is a thin folio in modern red morocco binding, and has, when perfect, consisted of fifty wood engravings, with their explanatory text also cut in wood, generally within an oblong border of a single line, within the *field* of the engraving, and not added underneath, as in the Speculum Salvationis, nor in detached compartments, both above and below, as in the Biblia Pauperum. The paper, which is somewhat of a cream colour, is stout, with rather a coarse surface, and such as we find the most ancient books printed on. As each leaf has been pasted down on another of modern paper, in order to preserve it, the marks of the rubber at the back of each impression, as described by Heineken, cannot be seen. The annexed outline is a reduced copy of a paper-mark, which may be perceived on some of the leaves. It is very like that numbered "vii." at p. 224, vol. i. of Mr. Ottley's Inquiry, and which he says occurs in the edition called the first Latin of the Speculum Salvationis. It is nearly the same as that which is to be seen in Earl Spencer's "Historia Virginis;" and Santander

* Idée Générale, pp. 334—370.

states that he has noticed a similar mark in books printed at Cologne by Ulric Zell, and Bart. de Unkel; at Louvain by John Veldener and Conrad Braen; and in books printed at Utrecht by Nic. Ketelaer and Gerard de Leempt.

The size of the largest cuts, as defined by the plain lines which form the border, is about ten and five-eighths inches high, by seven and six-eighths inches wide; of the smallest, ten and two-eighths inches high, by seven and three-eighths wide.* The order in which they are to be placed in binding is indicated by a letter of the alphabet, which serves the same purpose as our modern signatures,—engraved in a conspicuous part of the cut. For instance, the first two, which, as well as the others, might either face each other or be pasted back to back, are each marked with the letter a; the two next with the letter b, and so on through the alphabet. As the alphabet—which has the i the same as the j, the v the same as the u, and has not the w—became exhausted at the forty-sixth cut, the forty-seventh and forty-eighth are marked with a character which was used to represent the words "et cetera;" and the forty-ninth and fiftieth with the terminal abbreviation of the letters "us." In the copy described by Heineken, he observed that the directing letters m and n were wanting in the twenty-fourth and twenty-sixth cuts, and in the copy under consideration they are also omitted. The m, however, appears to have been engraved, though for some reason or other not to have been inked in taking an impression; for on a careful examination of this cut,—without being aware at the time of Heineken having noticed the omission,—I thought that I could very plainly discern the indention of the letter above one of the angels in the upper compartment of the print.

Of the forty-eight cuts† contained in the Museum copy, the greater number are divided by a horizontal line, nearly in the middle, and thus each consists of two compartments; of the remainder, each is occupied by a single subject, which fills the whole page. In some, the explanatory text consists only of two or three lines; and in others it occupies so

* In the copy of the Biblia Pauperum in the British Museum,

	Inches.		Inches.	
The largest cut is	$10\frac{4}{8}$	high, and	$7\frac{5}{8}$	wide.
The smallest —	$10\frac{1}{8}$	— —	$7\frac{5}{8}$	—

In the Historia Virginis, also in the British Museum,

The largest cut is	$10\frac{3}{8}$	high, and	$7\frac{2}{8}$	wide.
The smallest —	$9\frac{7}{8}$	— —	$6\frac{7}{8}$	—

† The two which are wanting are those numbered 36 and 37—that is, the second s, and the first t—in Heineken's collation. Although there is a memorandum at the commencement of the book that those cuts are wanting, yet the person who has put in the numbers, in manuscript, at the foot of each, has not noticed the omission, but has continued the numbers consecutively, marking that 36 which in a perfect copy is 38, and so on to the rest. A reference to Heineken from those manuscript numbers subsequent to the thirty-fifth cut would lead to error.

large a space, that if it were set up in moderately sized type, it would
be sufficient to fill a duodecimo page. The characters are different from
those in the History of the Virgin and the Biblia Pauperum, and are
smaller than those of the former, and generally larger and more distinctly cut than those of the latter; and although, as well as in the two
last-named books, the words are much abbreviated, yet they are more
easy to be made out than the text of either of the others. The impressions on the whole are better taken than those of the Biblia Pauperum,
though in lighter-coloured ink, something like a greyish sepia, and
apparently of a thinner body. It does not appear to have contained any
oil, and is more like distemper or water-colour than printer's ink. From
the manner in which the lines are indented in the paper, in several of
the cuts, it is evident that they must either have been subjected to a
considerable degree of pressure or have been very hard rubbed.

Although some of the figures bear a considerable degree of likeness
to others of the same kind in the Biblia Pauperum, I cannot think that
the designs for both books were made by the same person. The figures
in the different works which most resemble each other are those of saints
and angels, whose form and expression have been represented according
to a conventional standard, to which most of the artists of the period
conformed, in the same manner as in representing the Almighty and
Christ, whether they were painters, glass-stainers, carvers, or wood-
engravers. In many of the figures the drapery is broken into easy and
natural folds by means of single lines; and if this were admitted as a
ground for assigning the cut of the Annunciation to Italy, with much
greater reason might the Apocalypse be ascribed to the same country.

Without venturing to give an opinion whether the cuts were engraved
in Germany, Holland, or in the Low Countries, the drawing of many of
the figures appears to correspond with the idea that I have formed of the
style of Greek art, such as it was in the early part of the fifteenth
century. St. John was the favourite apostle of the Greeks, as St. Peter
was of the church of Rome; and as the Revelations were more especially
addressed to the churches of Greece, they were more generally read in
that country than in Western Europe. Artists mostly copy, in the heads
which they draw, the general expression of the country * to which they
belong, and where they have received their first impressions; and in the
Apocalypse the character of several of the heads appears to be decidedly
Grecian. The general representation, too, of several visions would seem
to have been suggested by a Greek who was familiar with that portion of
the New Testament which was so generally perused in his native land,
and whose annunciations and figurative prophecies were, in the early

---

* Witness Rembrandt, who never gets rid of the Dutch character, no matter how elevated
his subject may be.

part of the fifteenth century, commonly supposed by his countrymen to relate to the Turks, who at that time were triumphing over the cross. With them Mahomet was the Antichrist of the Revelations, and his followers the people bearing the mark of the beast, who were to persecute, and for a time to hold in bondage, the members of the church of Christ. As many Greeks, both artists and scholars, were driven from their country by the oppression of the Turks several years before the taking of Constantinople in 1453, I am induced to think that to a Greek we owe the designs of this edition of the Apocalypse. In the lower division of the twenty-third cut, m, representing the fight of Michael and his angels with the dragon, the following shields are borne by two of the heavenly host.

The crescent, as is well known, was one of the badges of Constantinople long previous to its capture by the Turks. The sort of cross in the other shield is very like that in the arms of the knights of St. Constantine, a military order which is said to have been founded at Constantinople by the Emperor Isaac Angelus Comnenus, in 1190. The above coincidences, though trifling, tend to support the opinion that the designs were made by a Greek artist. It is, however, possible, that the badges on the shields may have been suggested by the mere fancy of the designer, and that they may equally resemble the heraldic bearings of some order or of some individuals of Western Europe.

Though some of the designs are very indifferent, yet there are others which display considerable ability, and several of the single figures are decidedly superior to any that are contained in the other block-books. They are drawn with greater vigour and feeling; and though the designs of the Biblia Pauperum show a greater knowledge of the mechanism of art, yet the best of them, in point of expression and emphatic marking of character, are inferior to the best in the Apocalypse.

With respect to the engraving, the cuts are executed in the simplest manner, as there is not the least attempt at shading, by means of cross lines or hatchings, to be perceived in any one of the designs. The most difficult part of the engraver's task, supposing the drawings to have been made by another person, would be the cutting of the letters, which in several of the subjects must have occupied a considerable portion of

F

time, and have required no small degree of care. The following is a
reduced copy of the first cut.

In the upper portion of the subject, St. John is seen addressing four
persons, three men and a woman ; and the text at the top informs us of
the success of his ministry : " *Conversi ab idolis, per predicationem beati
Johannis, Drusiana et ceteri.*"—" By the preaching of St. John, Drusiana
and others are withdrawn from their idols." The letter a, a little above
the saint's outstretched hand, indicates that the cut is the first of the
series. In the lower compartment St. John is seen baptizing Drusiana,
who, as she stands naked in the font, is of very small size compared with
the saint. The situation in which Drusiana is placed might be alleged
in support of their peculiar tenets, either by the Baptists, who advocate
immersion as the proper mode of administering the rite, or by those who
consider sprinkling as sufficient ; but in each case with a difficulty which
it would not be easy to explain : for if Drusiana were to be baptized by
immersion, the font is too small to allow her to be dipped overhead ; and

if the rite were to be administered by mere sprinkling, why is she standing naked in the font? To the right of the cut are several figures, two of whom are provided with axes, who seem wishful to break open the door of the chapel in which St. John and his proselyte are seen. The inscription above their heads lets us know that they are—" *Cultores ydolorum explorantes facta ejus;*"—" Worshippers of idols watching the saint's proceedings."

The following cut is a copy of the eighteenth of the Apocalypse, which is illustrative of the xith and xiiith chapters of Revelations. The upper portion represents the execution of the two witnesses of the Lord, who are in the tablet named Enoch and Helyas, by the

command of the beast which ascendeth out of the bottomless pit, and which is Antichrist. He is seen issuing his commands for the execution of the witnesses; and the face of the executioner who has just used his sword, and who is looking towards him with an expression of brutal exultation, might have served Albert Durer for that of the mocker in his cut of Christ crowned with thorns.

The inscription to the right, is the 7th verse of the xith chapter, with the names of Enoch and Helyas inserted as those of the two witnesses : " *Cum finierunt Enoch et Helyas testimonium suum, bestia quæ ascendit de abisso faciet contra eos bellum, et vincet eos et occidet illos.*" In our translation the verse is rendered thus : "And when they shall have finished their testimony, the beast that ascendeth out of the bottomless pit shall make war against them, and shall overcome them and kill them."

The tablet to the left contains the following inscription : " *Et jacebunt corpora eorum in plateis, et non sinent poni in monumentis.*" It is formed of two passages, in the 8th and 9th verses of the xith chapter of Revelations, which are thus rendered in our version of the Bible : "And their dead bodies shall lie in the street, ... and they of the people ... shall not suffer their dead bodies to be put in graves."

In the lower compartment Antichrist is seen working his miracles, uprooting the two olive trees, typical of the two witnesses whom he had caused to be slain.* Two of his followers are seen kneeling as if worshipping him, while more to the left are the supporters of the true faith delivered into the hands of executioners. The design is illustrative of the xiiith chapter of Revelations. The following is the inscription above the figure of Antichrist :—" *Hic facit Antichristus miracula sua, et credentes in ipsum honorat, et incredentes variis interficit pœnis.*"—" Here Antichrist is performing his miracles, honouring those who believe in him, and putting the incredulous to death by various punishments." The leaves of the trees which Antichrist has miraculously uprooted are extremely like those of the tree of life engraved in one of the cuts of the Biblia Pauperum, and of which a copy will be found in a subsequent page.

In several of the cuts, the typical expressions which occur in the texts are explained. Thus, in cut eighth, we are informed that " *Stolæ albæ animarum gloriam designant.*"—" The white vestments denote the glory of departed souls." In the lower compartment of the same cut, the " *cœli recessio*"—" the opening of the heavens "—is explained to be the communication of the Bible to the Gentiles. In the lower compartment of the ninth cut, "much incense " is said to signify the precepts of the Gospel ; the "censers," the hearts of the Apostles ; and the "golden altar," the Church.

The next block-book which demands notice is that named " Historia seu Providentia Virginis Mariæ, ex Cantico Canticorum : " that is, " The History or Prefiguration of the Virgin Mary, from the Song of Songs." It is of small-folio size, and consists of sixteen leaves, printed on one side only by means of friction ; and the ink is of a dark brown, approaching nearly to black. Each impressed page contains two sub-

* Revelations, chap. xi. verses 3d and 4th.

jects, one above the other; the total number of subjects in the book is, consequently, thirty-two.

Of this book, according to the observations of Heineken, there are two editions; which, from variations noticed by him in the explanatory text, are evidently from different blocks; but, as the designs are precisely the same, it is certain that the one has been copied from the other.* That which he considers to be the first edition, has, in his opinion, been engraved in Germany; the other, he thinks, was a copy of the original, executed by some engraver in Holland. The principal ground on which he determines the priority of the editions is, that in the one the text is much more correctly given than in the other; and he thence concludes that the most correct would be the second. In this opinion I concur; not that his rule will universally hold good, but that in this case the conclusion which he has drawn seems the most probable. The designs, it is admitted, are precisely the same; and as the cuts of the one would in all probability be engraved from tracings or transfers of the other, it is not likely that we should find such a difference in the text of the two editions if that of the first were correct. A wood-engraver—on this point I speak from experience—would be much more likely to commit literal errors in copying manuscript, than to deviate in cutting a fac-simile from a correct impression. Had the text of the first edition been correct,—considering that the designs of the one edition are exact copies of those of the other,—it is probable that the text of both would have been more nearly alike. But as there are several errors in the text of the first edition, it is most likely that many of them would be discovered and corrected by the person at whose instance the designs were copied for the second. Diametrically opposite to this conclusion is that of Mr. Ottley, who argues as follows: †
" Heineken endeavours to draw another argument in favour of the originality of the edition possessed by Pertusati, Verdussen, and the Bodleian library, from the various errors, in that edition, in the Latin inscriptions on the scrolls; which, he says, are corrected in the other edition. But it is evident that this circumstance makes in favour of an opposite conclusion. The artist who originally invented the work must have been well acquainted with Latin, since it is, in fact, no other than an union of many of the most beautiful verses of the Book of Canticles, with a series of designs illustrative of the divine mysteries supposed to be revealed in that sacred poem; and, consequently, we have reason to consider that edition the original in which the inscriptions are given with the most correctness; and to ascribe the gross blunders in the other to the ignorance of some ordinary wood-engraver by whom the work was copied." Even granting the assumption that the

* Idée Générale, p. 376.   † Inquiry, vol. i. p. 140.

engraver of the edition, supposed by Mr. Ottley to be the first, was well acquainted with Latin, and that he who engraved the presumed second did not understand a word of that language, yet it by no means follows that the latter could not make a correct tracing of the engraved text lying before him. Because a draughtsman is unacquainted with a language, it would certainly be most erroneous to infer that he would be incapable of copying the characters correctly. Besides, though it does not benefit his argument a whit, it is surely assuming too much to assert that the artist who made the designs also selected the texts, and that he *must* have been well acquainted with Latin ; and that he who executed Mr. Ottley's presumed second edition was some ignorant ordinary wood-engraver. Did the artists who executed the fac-similes in Mr. Ottley's work, or in Dr. Dibdin's "Bibliotheca Spenceriana," understand the abbreviated Latin which in many instances they had to engrave ; and did they in consequence of their ignorance of that language copy incorrectly the original texts and sentences which were before them ?

In a copy which Heineken considers to be of the second edition, belonging to the city of Harlem, that writer observed the following inscription, from a wood block, impressed, as I understand him, at the top of the first cut. "𝕯𝖎𝖙 𝖎𝖘 𝖉𝖎𝖊 𝖇𝖔𝖊𝖗𝖘𝖎𝖓𝖎𝖈𝖍𝖊𝖎𝖙 𝖇𝖆 𝕸𝖆𝖗𝖎𝖊 𝖉𝖊𝖗 𝖒𝖔𝖉 . 𝖌𝖔𝖉𝖊𝖘 . 𝖊𝖓 𝖎𝖘 𝖌𝖊𝖍𝖊𝖙𝖊 𝖎𝖓 𝖑𝖆𝖙𝖍 . *Cāti.*" This inscription—which Heineken says is "en langue Flamande, ou plûtôt en Plât-Alemand"—may be expressed in English as follows : "This is the prefiguration of Mary the mother of God, and is in Latin named the Canticles." Heineken expresses no doubt of this inscription being genuine, though he makes use of it as an argument in support of his opinion, that the copy in which it occurs was one of later edition ; "for it is well known," he observes, "that the earliest editions of printed books are without titles, and more especially those of block-books." As this inscription, however, has been found in the Harlem copy only, I am inclined to agree with Mr. Ottley in considering it as a silly fraud devised by some of the compatriots of Coster for the purpose of establishing a fact which it is, in reality, much better calculated to overthrow." *

Heineken, who appears to have had more knowledge than taste on the subject of art, declares the History of the Virgin to be "the most Gothic of all the block-books ; that it is different from them both in the style of the designs and of the engraving ; and that the figures are very like the ancient sculptures in the churches of Germany." If by the term "Gothic" he means rude and tasteless, I differ with him entirely ; for, though there be great sameness in the subjects, yet the figures, generally, are more gracefully designed than those of any other block-

* Inquiry, p. 140.

book that I have seen. Compared with them, those of the Biblia
Pauperum and the Speculum might be termed "Gothic" indeed.

The above group,—from that which Heineken considers the first
edition,—in which the figures are of the size of the originals, is taken
from the seventh subject in Mr. Ottley's enumeration ;* that is, from the
upper portion of the fourth cut.

The text is the 14th verse of the 1st chapter of the Song of Solomon :
" *Botrus cipri dilectus meus inter vineas enngadi ;* " which in our Bible is
translated : "My beloved is unto me as a cluster of camphire in the vine-
yards of En-gedi." In every cut the female figures are almost precisely
the same, and the drapery and the expression scarcely vary. From the
easy and graceful attitudes of his female figures, as well as from the

* Inquiry, p. 144, vol. i.

manner in which they are clothed, the artist may be considered as the Stothard of his day.

The two preceding subjects are impressed on the second leaf, in the order in which they are here represented, forming Nos. 3 and 4 in Mr. Ottley's enumeration. They are reduced copies from the originals in the first edition, and afford a correct idea of a complete page.*

On the scroll to the left, in the upper subject, the words are intended for—" *Trahe me, post te curremus in odore unguentorum tuorum.*" They are to be found in the 4th and 3rd verses of the 1st chapter of the Song of Solomon. In our Bible the phrases are translated as follows : " Draw me, we will run after thee, . . . [in] the savour of thy good ointments."

---

* The copy from which the preceding specimens are given was formerly the property of the Rev. C. M. Cracherode, by whom it was left, with the rest of his valuable collection of books, to the British Museum.

In the scroll to the right, the inscription is from the 14th verse of the IInd chapter : " *Sonet vox tua in auribus meis, vox enim tua dulcis et facies tua decora:*" which is thus rendered in our Bible : " Let me hear thy voice, for sweet is thy voice, and thy countenance is comely."

On the scroll to the left, in the lower compartment, is the following inscription, from verse 10th, chapter IInd : " *En dilectus meus loquitur mihi, Surge, propera, amica mea:*" in our Bible translated thus : " My beloved spake, and said unto me, Rise up, my love, my fair one, and come away." The inscription on the scroll to the right is from 1st verse of chapter IVth : " *Quam pulchra es amica mea, quam pulchra es! Oculi tui columbarum, absque eo quod intrinsecus latet.*" The translation of this passage in our Bible does not correspond with that of the Vulgate in the last clause : " Behold thou art fair, my love ; behold thou art fair ; thou hast doves' eyes *within thy locks.*"

The style in which the cuts of the History of the Virgin are engraved indicates a more advanced state of art than those in the Apocalypse. The field of each cut is altogether better filled, and the subjects contain more of what an engraver would term " work ;" and shadowing, which is represented by courses of single lines, is also introduced. The back-grounds are better put in, and throughout the whole book may be observed several indications of a perception of natural beauty ; such as the occasional introduction of trees, flowers, and animals. A vine-stock, with its trellis, is happily and tastefully introduced at folio 4 and folio 10 ; and at folio 12 a goat and two sheep, drawn and engraved with considerable ability, are perceived in the background. Several other instances of a similar kind might be pointed out as proofs that the artist, whoever he might be, was no unworthy precursor of Albert Durer.

From a fancied delicacy in the engraving of the cuts of the History of the Virgin, Dr. Dibdin was led to conjecture that they were the " production of some metallic substance, and not struck off from wooden blocks." * This speculation is the result of a total ignorance of the practical part of wood engraving, and of the capabilities of the art ; and the very process which is suggested involves a greater difficulty than that which is sought to be removed. But, in fact, so far from the engravings being executed with a delicacy unattainable on wood, there is nothing in them—so far as the mere cutting of fancied delicate lines is concerned— which a mere apprentice of the present day, using very ordinary tools, would not execute as well, either on pear-tree, apple-tree, or beech, the kinds of wood on which the earliest engravings are supposed to have been made. Working on box, there is scarcely a line in all the series which a skilful wood-engraver could not split. In a similar manner Mr. John

---

* Bibliotheca Spenceriana, vol. i. p. 36. Mr. Ottley cites the passage at p. 139, vol. i. of his Inquiry, for the purpose of expressing his dissent from the theory.

Landseer conjectured from the frequent occurrence of cross-hatching in the wood engravings of the sixteenth century, that they, instead of being cut on wood, had in reality been executed on type-metal; although, as is known to every wood-engraver, the execution of such hatchings on type-metal would be more difficult than on wood. When, in refutation of his opinion, he was shown impressions from such presumed blocks or plates of type-metal, which from certain marks in the impressions had been evidently worm-eaten, he—in the genuine style of an "ingenious disputant" who could

"Confute the exciseman and puzzle the vicar,—

abandoned type-metal, and fortified his "*stubborn* opinion behind *vegetable putties* or pastes that are capable of being hardened—or any substance that is capable of being *worm-eaten.*" * Such "commenta opinionum"— the mere figments of conjecture—only deserve notice in consequence of their extravagance.

The History of the Virgin, in the same manner as every other ancient block-book, has been claimed for Coster by those who ascribe to him the invention both of wood engraving and printing with moveable types ; but if even the churchwarden of St. Bavon's in Harlem ever had handled a graver, or made a design, or if he was even the cause of wood-cuts being engraved by others,—every one of which assertions I very much doubt,— I should yet feel strongly inclined to believe that the work in question was the production of an artist residing either in Suabia or Alsace.

Scarcely any person who has had an opportunity of examining the works of Martin Schön, or Schöngauer,—one of the earliest German copper-plate engravers,—who is said to have died in 1486, can fail, on looking over the designs in the History of the Virgin, to notice the resemblance which many of his female figures bear to those in the above-named work. The similarity is too striking to have been accidental. I am inclined to believe that Martin Schön must have studied—and diligently too—the subjects contained in the History, or that he had received his professional education in a school which might possibly be founded by the artist who designed and engraved the wood-cuts in question, or under a master who had thoroughly adopted their style.

Martin Schön was a native of Colmar in Alsace, where he was born about 1453, but was a descendant of a family, probably of artists, which originally belonged to Augsburg. Heineken and Von Murr both bear testimony,† though indirectly, to the resemblance which his works bear to the designs in the History of the Virgin. The former states that the figures in the History are very like the ancient sculptures in the churches

* Landseer's Lectures on the Art of Engraving, pp. 201—205, 8vo. London, 1807.
† Heineken, Idée Générale, p. 374. Von Murr, Journal, 2 Theil, S. 43.

of Germany, and Von Murr asserts that such sculptures were probably Martin Schön's models.

In two or three of the designs in the History of the Virgin several shields of arms are introduced, either borne by figures, or suspended from a wall. As the heraldic emblems on such shields were not likely to be entirely suggested by the mere fancy of the artist, I think that most of them will be found to belong to Germany rather than to Holland; and the charge on one of them,—two fish back to back, which is rather remarkable, and by no means common, is one of the quarterings of the former Counts of Wirtemberg, the very district in which I am inclined to think the work was executed. I moreover fancy that in one of the cuts I can perceive an allusion to the Council of Basle, which in 1439 elected Amadeus of Savoy as Pope, under the title of Felix V, in opposition to Eugene IV. In order to afford those who are better acquainted with the subject an opportunity of judging for themselves, and of making further discoveries which may support my opinions if well-founded, or which may correct them if erroneous, I shall give copies of all the shields of arms which occur in the book. The following cut of four figures—a pope, two cardinals, and a bishop—occurs in the upper compartment of the nineteenth folio. The shield charged with a black eagle also occurs in the same compartment.

The preceding figures are seen looking over the battlements of a house in which the Virgin, typical of the Church, is seen in bed. On a scroll is inscribed the following sentence, from the Song of Solomon, chap. iii. v. 2: "*Surgam et circumibo civitatem ; per vicos et plateas queram quem diligit anima mea:*" which is thus translated in our Bible: "I will rise now, and go about the city in the streets, and in the broad ways I will seek him whom my soul loveth." In the same design, the Virgin, with her three attendants, are seen in a street, where two men on horseback appear taking away her mantle. One of the men bears upon his shield the figure of a black eagle, the same as that which appears underneath the wood-cut above given. Upon a scroll is this inscription, from Solomon's Song, chapter v. verse 7 : "*Percusserunt et vulneraverunt me, tulerunt pallium meum custodes murorum.*" In our Bible the entire verse is thus translated : "The watchmen that went about the city found me ; they smote me, they wounded me : the keepers of the walls took away my veil from me."

As the incidents in the life of the Virgin, described in the Canticles, were assumed by commentators to be typical of the history of the Church, I am inclined to think that the above cut may contain an allusion to the disputes between Pope Eugene IV. and the Council assembled at Basle in 1439. The passage in the first inscription, "I will seek him whom my soul loveth," might be very appropriately applied to a council which professed to represent the Church, and which had chosen for itself a new head. The second inscription would be equally descriptive of the treatment which, in the opinion of the same council, the Church had received from Eugene IV, whom they declared to be deposed, because "he was a disturber of the peace and union of the Church ; a schismatic and a heretic ; guilty of simony ; perjured and incorrigible." On the shield borne by the figure of a pope wearing a triple crown, is a fleur-de-lis ; but whether or no this flower formed part of the armorial distinctions of Amadeus Duke of Savoy, whom the council chose for their new pope, I have not been able to ascertain. The lion borne by the second figure, a cardinal, is too general a cognizance to be assigned to any particular state or city. The charge on the shield borne by the third figure, also a cardinal, I cannot make out. The cross-keys on the bishop's shield are the arms of the city of Ratisbon.

The following shields are borne by angels, who appear above the battlements of a wall in the lower compartment of folio 4, forming the eighth subject in Mr. Ottley's enumeration.

On these I have nothing to remark futher than that the double-headed eagle is the arms of the German empire. The other three I leave to be deciphered by others. The second, with an indented chief, and something like a rose in the field, will be found, I am inclined to think, to be the arms of some town or city in Wirtemberg or Alsace. I give the three inscriptions here, not that they are likely to throw any light on the subject, but because the third has not hitherto been deciphered. They are all from the ivth chapter of the Song of Solomon. The first is from verse 12 : "*Ortus conclusus est soror, mea sposa ; ortus conclusus, fons signatus :*" in our translation of the Bible : "A garden enclosed is my sister, my spouse ; a spring shut up, a fountain sealed." The second is from verse 15 : "*Fons ortorum, puteus aquarum vivencium quæ fluunt impetu de Lybano :*" in our Bible : "A fountain of gardens, a well of living waters, and streams from Lebanon." The third is from verse 16: "*Surge Aquilo ; veni Auster, perfla ortum et fluant aromata illius :*" in our Bible : "Awake, O north wind ; and come, thou south ; blow upon my garden, that the spices thereof may flow out."

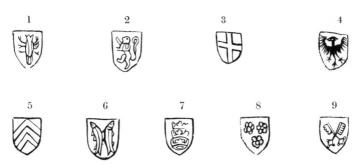

In the upper division of folio 15, which is the twenty-ninth subject in Mr. Ottley's enumeration, the above shields occur. They are suspended on the walls of a tower, which is represented by an inscription as "the armoury whereon hang a thousand bucklers, all shields of mighty men."*

On the first four I shall make no remark beyond calling the attention of those skilled in German heraldry to the remarkable charge in the first shield, which appears something like a cray-fish. The sixth, "two trouts hauriant and addorsed," is one of the quarterings of the house of Wirtemberg as lords of Mompelgard. The seventh is charged with three crowns, the arms of the city of Cologne. The charge of the eighth I take to be three cinquefoils, which are one of the puarterings of the family of Aremberg. The cross-keys in the ninth are the arms of the city of Ratisbon.

The four following shields occur in the lower division of folio 15. They are borne by men in armour standing by the side of a bed. On a scroll is the following inscription, from the 7th and 8th verses of the third chapter of Solomon's Song. "*En lectulum Salomonis sexaginta fortes ambiunt, omnes tenentes gladios :*" in our Bible : "Behold his bed, which is Solomon's ; three score valiant men are about it . . . . . they all hold swords."

The first three of the shields on the following page I shall leave to be

* Song of Solomon, chap. iv. verse 4.

assigned by others. The fourth, which is charged with a rose, was the arms of Hagenau, a town in Alsace.

As so little is known respecting the country where, and the precise time when, the principal block-books appeared,—of which the History of the Virgin is one,—I think every particular, however trifling, which may be likely to afford even a gleam of light, deserving of notice. It is for this reason that I have given the different shields contained in this and the preceding pages; not in the belief that I have made any importan discovery, or established any considerable facts; but with the desire of directing to this subject the attention of others, whose further inquiries and comparisons may perhaps establish such a perfect identity between the arms of a particular district, and those contained in the volume, as may determine the probable locality of the place where it was executed. The coincidences which I have noticed were not sought for. Happening to be turning over Sebastian Munster's Cosmography when a copy of the History of the Virgin was before me, I observed that the two fish in the arms of the Counts of Wirtemberg,* and those in the 15th folio of the History, were the same. The other instances of correspondence were also discovered without search, from having occasionally, in tracing the progress of wood engraving, to refer to Merian's Topographia.

Considering the thickness of the paper on which the block-books are printed,—if I may apply this term to them,—and the thin-bodied ink which has been used, I am at a loss to conceive how the early wood-engravers have contrived to take off their impressions so correctly; for in all the block-books which I have seen, where friction has evidently been the means employed to obtain the impression, I have only noticed two subjects in which the lines appeared double in consequence of the shifting of the paper. From the want of body in the ink, which appears in the Apocalypse to have been little more than water-colour, it is not likely the paper could be used in a damp state, otherwise the ink would run or spread; and, even if this difficulty did not exist, the paper in a damp state could not have borne the excessive rubbing which it appears to have received in order to obtain the impression.† Even with

---

* Those arms are to be seen in Sebastiana Munsteri Cosmographia, cap. De Regione Wirtenbergensi, p. 592. Folio, Basiliæ, apud Henrichum Petri, 1554.

† The backs of many of the old wood-cuts which have been taken by means of friction,

such printer's ink as is used in the present day,—which being tenacious, renders the paper in taking an impression by means of friction much less liable to slip or shift,—it would be difficult to obtain clear impressions on thick paper from blocks the size of those which form each page of the Apocalypse, or the History of the Virgin.

Mr. Ottley, however, states that no less than two pages of the History of the Virgin have been engraved on the same block. His observations on this subject are as follows: " Upon first viewing this work, I was of opinion that each of the designs contained in it was engraved upon a separate block of wood: but, upon a more careful examination, I have discovered that the contents of each two pages—that is, four subjects— were engraved on the same block. The number of wooden blocks, there- fore, from which the whole was printed, was only eight. This is proved in the first two pages of the copy before me;* where, near the bottom of the two upper subjects, the block appears to have been broken in two, in a horizontal direction,—after it was engraved,—and joined together again; although not with such exactness but that the traces of the operation clearly show themselves. The traces of a similar accident are still more apparent in the last block, containing the Nos. 29, 30, 31, 32. The whole work was, therefore, printed on eight sheets of paper from the same number of engraved blocks, the first four subjects being printed from the same block upon the same sheet,—and so on with the rest; and, indeed, in Lord Spencer's copy, each sheet, being mounted upon a guard, distinctly shows itself entire."†

The appearance of a corresponding fracture in two adjacent pages would certainly render it likely that both were engraved on the same block; though I should like to have an opportunity of satisfying myself by inspection whether such appearances are really occasioned by a fracture or not; for it is rather singular that such appearances should be observable on the *first* and the *last* blocks only. I always reluctantly speculate, except on something like sufficient grounds; but as I have not seen a copy of the edition to which Mr. Ottley refers, I beg to ask if the traces of supposed fracture in the last two pages do not correspond with those in the first two? and if so, would it not be equally reasonable to infer that eight subjects instead of four were engraved on the same block? A block containing only two pages would be about seventeen inches by ten, allowing for inner margins; and to obtain clear impressions from it by means of friction, on dry thick paper, and with mere water-

still appear bright in consequence of the rubbing which the paper has sustained in order to obtain the impression. They would not have this appearance if the paper had been used in a damp state.

* This must have been a copy of that which Heineken calls the second edition; no such appearances of a fracture or joining are to be seen in the first.

† Inquiry, p. 142.

colour ink, would be a task of such difficulty that I cannot conceive how it could be performed. No traces of points by which the paper might be kept steady on the block are perceptible ; and I unhesitatingly assert that no wood-engraver of the present day could by means of friction take clear impressions from such a block on equally thick paper, and using mere distemper instead of printer's ink. As the impressions in the History of the Virgin have unquestionably been taken by means of friction, it is evident to me that if the blocks were of the size that Mr. Ottley supposes, the old wood-engravers, who did not use a press, must have resorted to some contrivance to keep the paper steady, with which we are now unacquainted.

Heineken describes an edition of the Apocalypse consisting of forty-eight leaves, with cuts on one side only, which, when bound, form a volume of three "*gatherings*," or collections, each containing sixteen leaves. Each of these gatherings is formed by eight folio sheets folded in the middle, and placed one within the other, so that the cuts are worked off in the following manner : On the outer sheet of the gathering, forming the first and the sixteenth leaf, the first and the sixteenth cuts are impressed, so that when the sheet is folded they face each other, and the first and the last pages are left blank. In a similar manner the 2nd and 15th ; the 3d and 14th ; the 4th and 13th ; the 5th and 12th ; the 6th and 11th ; the 7th and 10th, and the 8th and 9th, are, each pair respectively, impressed on the same side of the same sheet. These sheets when folded for binding are then placed in such a manner that the first is opposite the second ; the third opposite the fourth, and so on throughout the whole sixteen. Being arranged in this manner, two cuts and two blank pages occur alternately. The reason for this mode of arrangement was, that the blank pages might be pasted together, and the cuts thus appear as if one were impressed on the back of another. A familiar illustration of this mode of folding, adopted by the early wood-engravers before they were accustomed to impress their cuts on both sides of a leaf, is afforded by forming a sheet of paper into a little book of sixteen leaves, and numbering the second and third pages 1 and 2, leaving two pages blank ; then numbering the fifth and sixth 3 and 4, and so to No. 16, which will stand opposite to No. 15, and have its back, forming the outer page of the gathering, unimpressed.

Of all the block-books, that which is now commonly called " BIBLIA PAUPERUM,"—the Bible of the Poor,—is most frequently referred to as a specimen of that kind of printing from wood-blocks which preceded typography, or printing by means of moveable characters or types. This title, however, has given rise to an error which certain learned biblio-graphers have without the least examination adopted, and have after-wards given to the public considerably enlarged, at least, if not corrected.* It has been gravely stated that this book, whose text is in abbreviated Latin, was printed for the use of the *poor* in an age when even the *rich* could scarcely read their own language. Manuscripts of the Bible were certainly at that period both scarce and costly, and not many individuals even of high rank were possessed of a copy ; but to conclude that the first editions of the so-called " Biblia Pauperum " were engraved and printed for the use of the poor, appears to be about as legitimate an inference as to conclude that, in the present day, the reprints of the Roxburghe club were published for the benefit of the poor who could not afford to purchase the original editions. That a merchant or a wealthy trader might occasionally become the purchaser of " Biblia Pauperum," I am willing to admit,—though I am of opinion that the book was never expressly intended for the laity ;—but that it should be printed for the use of the poor, I cannot bring myself to believe. If the poor of Germany in the fifteenth century had the means of purchasing such books, and were capable of reading them, I can only say that they must have had more money to spare than their descendants, and have been more learned than most of the rich people throughout Europe in the present day. If the accounts which we have of the state of knowledge about 1450 be correct, the monk or friar who could read and expound such a work must have been esteemed as a person of considerable literary attainments.

The name " Biblia Pauperum " was unknown to Schelhorn and Schœpflin, and was not adopted by Meerman. Schelhorn, who was the first that published a fac-simile of one of the pages engraved on wood, gives it no distinctive name ; but merely describes it as " a book which contained in text and figures certain histories and prophecies of the Old Testament, which, in the author's judgment, were figurative of Christ, and of the works performed by him for the salvation of man-kind."† Schœpflin calls it, " Vaticinia Veteris Testamenti de Christo ;"‡ —"Prophecies of the Old Testament concerning Christ;" but neither this title, nor the description of Schelhorn, is sufficiently comprehensive; for the book contains not only prophecies and typical figures from the Old Testament, but also passages and subjects selected from the New.

* " It is a manual or kind of Catechism of the Bible," says the Rev. T. H. Horne, " for the use of young persons and of the common people, whence it derives its name *Biblia Pauperum,—the Bible of the Poor,*—who were thus enabled to acquire, at a comparatively low price, an imperfect knowledge of some of the events recorded in the Scripture."—Introduction to the Critical Study of the Scriptures, vol. ii. p. 224—5. The young and the poor must have been comparatively learned at that period to be able to read cramped Latin, when many a priest could scarcely spell his breviary.

† J. G. Schelhorn, Amœnitates Literariæ, tom. iv. p. 297. 8vo. Francofurt. & Lips. 1730. Lichtenberger, Initia Typographica, p. 4, says erroneously, that Schelhorn's fac-simile was engraved on copper. It is on wood, as Schelhorn himself states at p. 296.

‡ J. D. Schœpflin, Vindiciæ Typographicæ, p. 7, 4to. Argentorati, 1760.

G

The title which Meerman gives to it is more accurately descriptive of the contents: "Figuræ typicæ Veteris atque antitypicæ Novi Testamenti, seu Historia Jesu Christi in figuris;" that is, "Typical figures of the Old Testament and antitypical of the New, or the History of Jesus Christ pictorially represented."*

Heineken appears to have been the first who gave to this book the name "Biblia Pauperum," as it was in his opinion the most appropriate ; "the figures being executed for the purpose of giving a knowledge of the Bible to those who could not afford to purchase a manuscript copy of the Scriptures."† This reason for the name is not, however, a good one ; for, according to his own statement, the only copy which he ever saw with the title or inscription "Biblia Pauperum," was a manuscript on vellum of the fourteenth century, in which the figures were drawn and coloured by hand.‡ Meerman, however, though without adopting the title, had previously noticed the same manuscript, which in his opinion was as old as the twelfth or thirteenth century. As the word "Pauperum" formed part of the title of the book long before presumed cheap copies were printed from wood-blocks for the use of the poor, it could not be peculiarly appropriate as the title of an illumined manuscript on vellum, which the poor could as little afford to purchase as they could a manuscript copy of the Bible. In whatever manner the term "poor" became connected with the book, it is clear that the name "Biblia Pauperum" was not given to it in consequence of its being printed at a cheap rate for circulation among poor people. It is not indeed likely that its ancient title ever was "Biblia Pauperum ;" while, on the contrary, there seems every reason to believe that Heineken had copied an abridged title and thus given currency to an error.

Heineken says that he observed the inscription, "Incipit Biblia Pauperum," in a manuscript in the library at Wolfenbuttel, written on vellum in a Gothic character, which appeared to be of the fourteenth century. The figures, which were badly designed, were coloured in distemper, and the explanatory text was in Latin rhyme. It is surprising that neither Heineken nor any other bibliographer should have suspected that a word was wanting in the above supposed title, more especially as the word wanting might have been so readily suggested by another work so much resembling the pretended "Biblia Pauperum" that the one has

---

* Ger. Meerman, Origines Typographicæ, P. 1, p. 241. 4to. Hagæ Comit. 1765.

† Idée Générale, p. 292, note.

‡ Camus, speaking of one of those manuscripts compared with the block-book, observes : "Ce dernier abrégé méritoit bien le nom de BIBLIA PAUPERUM, par comparison aux tableaux complets de la Bible que je viens d'indiquer. Des ouvrages tels que les tableaux complets ne pouvoient être que BIBLIA DIVITUM."—Notice d'un Livre imprimé à Bamberg en 1462, p. 12, note. 4to. Paris, 1800.

frequently been confounded with the other.* In the proemium of this other work, which is no other than the "Speculum Salvationis," the writer expressly states that he has compiled it "propter pauperes predicatores,"—for *poor* preachers.

Prebictu' p'hemiu' hujus libri de conte'tis compilabi,
Et p'pter paup'es p'dicatores hoc apponere curabi;
Qui si forte nequieru't totum librum sibi co'p'are,
Possu't ex ipso p'hemio, si sciu't p'dicare.

This preface of contents, stating what this book's about,
For the sake of all *poor preachers* I have fairly written out ;
If the purchase of the book entire should be above their reach,
This preface yet may serve them, if they know but how to preach.

That the other book might be called "Biblia Pauperum *Predicatorum*," in consequence of its general use by mendicant preachers, I can readily believe ; and no doubt the omission of the word "predicatorum" in the inscription copied by Heineken has given rise to the popular error, that the pretended "Biblia Pauperum" was a kind of cheap pictorial Bible, especially intended for the use of the poor. It is, in fact, a series of "skeleton sermons" ornamented with wood-cuts to warm the preacher's imagination, and stored with texts to assist his memory. In speaking of this book in future, I shall always refer to it as the "Biblia Pauperum Predicatorum,"—"the Poor Preachers' Bible ;" for the continuance of its former title only tends, in my opinion, to disseminate an error.

Nyerup, who in 1784 published an "Account of such books as were read in schools in Denmark prior to the Reformation,"† objected to the title "Biblia Pauperum," as he had seen portions of a manuscript copy in which the drawings were richly coloured. The title which he preferred was BIBLIA TYPICO-HARMONICA. In this objection, however, Camus does not concur: "It is not from the embellishments of a single copy," he observes, "that we ought to judge of the current price of a book ; and, besides, we must not forget to take into consideration the other motives which might suggest the title, 'Bible of the Poor,' for we have proofs that other abridgments of greater extent were called 'Poor men's books.' Such is the 'Biblia Pauperum' of St. Bonaventure, consisting of extracts for the use of *preachers*, and the 'Dictionarius Pauperum.' Of the last the title is explained in the book itself: 'Incipit summula omnibus *verbi divini seminatoribus* pernecessaria.'" It is surprising that Camus did

---

* "Entre ces abrégés [de la Bible] on remarque le SPECULUM HUMANÆ SALVATIONIS et le BIBLIA PAUPERUM. Ces deux ouvrages ont beaucoup d'affinité entre eux pour le volume, le choix des histoires, les moralités, la composition des tableaux. Ils existent en manuscrits dans plusieurs bibliothèques."—Camus, Notice d'un Livre, &c. p. 12.

† "Librorum qui ante Reformationem in scholis Daniæ legebantur, Notitia. Hafniæ, 1784 ;" referred to by Camus, Notice d'un Livre, &c. p. 10.

not perceive that the very titles which he cites militate against the opinion of the "Biblia" being intended for the use of poor *men.* St. Bonaventure's work, and the Dictionary, which he refers to as instances of "Poor men's books," both bear on the very face of them a refutation of his opinion, for in the works themselves it is distinctly stated that they were compiled, not "ad usum pauperum *hominum ;*" but "ad usum pauperum *predicatorum,* et *verbi divini seminatorum :*" not for the use of "poor *men,*" but for "poor *preachers* and *teachers of the divine word.*" Camus has unwittingly supplied a club to batter his own argument to pieces.

Of the "Biblia Pauperum Predicatorum," there are, according to Heineken, five different editions with the text in Latin. Four of them contain each forty leaves, printed on one side only from wood-blocks by means of friction, and which differ from each other in so trifling a degree, that it is not unlikely that three of them are from the same set of blocks. The other edition,—the fifth described by Heineken—contains fifty leaves, printed in a similar manner, but apparently with the figures designed by a different artist. Besides the above, there are two different editions, also from wood-blocks, with the text in German : one with the date 1470 ; and the other, 1471 or 1475, for the last numeral appears as like a 1 as a 5. There are also two editions, one Latin, and the other German, with the text printed from moveable types by Albert Pfister, at Bamberg, about 1462.

Without pretending to decide on the priority of the first five editions, —as I have not been able to perceive any sufficient marks from which the order in which they were published might be ascertained,—I shall here give a brief account of a copy of that edition which Heineken ranks as the third. It is in the King's Library at the British Museum, and was formerly in the collection of Monsieur Gaignat, at whose sale it was bought for George III.

It is a small folio of forty leaves, impressed on one side only, in order that the blank pages might be pasted together, so that two of the printed sides would thus form only one leaf. The order of the first twenty pages is indicated by the letters of the alphabet, from ɑ to ƀ, and of the second twenty by the same letters, having as a distinguishing mark a point both before and after them, thus : . ɑ . In that which Heineken considers the first edition, the letters ɴ, o, r, s, of the second alphabet, making pages 33, 34, 37, and 38, want those two distinguishing points, which, according to him, are to be found in each of the other three Latin editions of forty pages each. Mr. Ottley has, however, observed that Earl Spencer's copy wants the points,—on each side of the letters ɴ, o, r, s, of the second alphabet,—thus agreeing with that which Heineken calls the first edition, while in all other respects it answers the description which that writer gives of the presumed second. Mr. Ottley says, that Heineken errs in asserting that the want of those points on each side of the said letters is a distinction exclusively belonging to the first edition, since the edition called by him the second is likewise without them.* In fact, the variations noticed by Heineken are not only insufficient to enable a person to judge of the priority of the editions, but they are such as might with the greatest ease be introduced into a block after a certain number of copies had been taken off. Those which he considers as distinguishing marks might easily be broken away by the burnisher or rubber, and replaced by the insertion of other pieces, differing in a slight degree. From the trifling variations noticed by Heineken † in the first three editions, it is not unlikely that they were all taken from the same blocks. Each of the triangular ornaments in which he has observed a difference, might easily be re-inserted in the event of its being injured in taking an impression. The tiara of Moses, in page 35, letter . p . would be peculiarly liable to accident in taking an impression by friction, and I am disposed to think that a part of it has been broken off, and that in repairing it a trifling alteration has been made in the ornament on its top. Heineken, noticing the alteration, has considered it as a criterion of two different editions, while in all probability it only marks a trifling variety in copies taken from the same blocks.

On each page are four portraits,—two at the top, and two at the bottom,—intended for the prophets, and other holy men, whose writings are cited in the text. The middle part of the page between each pair of portraits consists of three compartments, each of which is occupied with a subject from the Old or the New Testament. In the 14th page, however, letter o, two of the compartments—that in the centre, and the adjoining one to the right—are both occupied by the same subject, Christ's entry into Jerusalem. The greatest portion of the explanatory text is at the top on each side of the uppermost portraits ; and on each side of those below there is a Leonine, or rhyming Latin, verse. A similar verse underneath those portraits forms the concluding line of each page. Texts of Scripture, and moral or explanatory sentences, having reference to the subjects in the three compartments, also appear on scrolls. The following cut, which is a reduced copy of the 14th page, letter k, will afford a better idea of the arrangement of the subjects, and of the explanatory texts, than any lengthened description.

The whole of this subject—both text and figures—appears intended to inculcate the necessity of restraining appetite. The inscription to the right, at the top, contains a reference to the 3rd chapter of Genesis, wherein there is to be found an account of the temptation and fall of

---

* Inquiry, vol. i. p. 129.   † Idée Générale, p. 307, 308.

Adam and Eve, who were induced by the Serpent to taste the forbidden fruit. This temptation of our first parents through the medium of the palate, was, as may be gathered from the same inscription, figurative of the temptation of Christ after his fasting forty days in the wilderness, when the Devil came to him and said, "If thou be the Son of God, command that these stones be made bread."

In the inscription to the left, reference is made to the 25th chapter of Genesis, as containing an account of Esau, who, in consequence of his unrestrained appetite, sold his birth-right for a mess of pottage.

In the compartments in the middle of the page, are three illustrations of the preceding text. In the centre is seen the pattern to imitate,— Christ resisting the temptation of the Devil; and on each side the examples to deter,—Adam and Eve with the forbidden fruit; and hungry Esau receiving the mess of pottage from Jacob.

Underneath the two half-length figures at the top, is inscribed "David 34," and "Ysaie xxix." * The numerals are probably intended to indicate the chapters in the Psalms, and in the Prophecies of Isaiah, where the inscriptions on the adjacent scrolls are to be found. On similar scrolls, towards the bottom of the page, are references to the 7th chapter of the 2nd book of Kings, and to the 16th chapter of Job. The two half-length figures are most likely intended for the writers of those sacred books. The likenesses of the prophets and holy persons, thus introduced at the top and bottom of each page, are, as Schelhorn has observed,† purely imaginary; for the same character is seldom seen twice with the same face. As most of the supposed figurative descriptions of Christ and his ministry are to be found in the Psalms, and in the Prophecies of Isaiah, the portraits of David and the last-named prophet are those which most frequently occur; and the designer seems to have been determined that neither the king nor the prophet should ever appear twice with the same likeness.

The rhyming verses are as follows. That to the right, underneath the subject of Adam and Eve :

Serpens vicit, Adam vetitam sibi sugerat escam.

The other, on the opposite side, underneath Jacob and Esau :

Lentis ob ardorem proprium male perdit honorem.

And the third, at the bottom of the page, underneath the two portraits :

Christum temptavit Sathanas ut eum superaret.

The following cuts are fac-similes, the size of the originals, of each of the compartments of the page referred to, and of which a reduced copy has been already given.

The first contains the representation of David and Isaiah, and the characters which follow the name of the former I consider to be intended for 34. They are the only instances in the volume of the use of Arabic, or rather Spanish numerals. The letter ƙ, at the foot, is the "signature," as a printer would term it, indicating the order of the page. On each side of it are portions of scrolls containing inscriptions, of which some of the letters are seen.

The next cut represents Satan tempting Christ by offering him stones to be converted into bread.

---

* The passages referred to are probably the 8th, 9th, and 10th verses of the xxxivth Psalm ; and the 8th verse of the xxixth chapter of Isaiah.

† "Has autem icones ex sola sculptoris imaginatione et arbitrio fluxisse vel inde liquet, quod idem scriptor sacer in diversis foliis diversa plerumque et alia facie delineatus sistatur, sicuti, v. g. Esaias ac David, sæpius obvii, Protei instar, varias induerunt in hoc opere formas."—Amœnitates Literariæ, tom. iv. p. 297.

In the distance are seen the high mountain, to the top of which Christ was taken up by the Devil, and the temple from whose pinnacle Christ was tempted to cast himself down.   The figure of Christ in this compartment is not devoid of sober dignity ; nor is Satan deficient in diabolical ugliness ; but, though clawed and horned proper, he wants the usual appendage of a tail.   The deficiency is, however, in some degree compensated by giving to his hip the likeness of a fiendish face.   In two or three other old wood engravings I have noticed a repulsive face indicated in a similar manner on the hip of the Devil.   A person well acquainted with the superstitions of the fourteenth and fifteenth centuries may perhaps be able to give a reason for this.   It may be intended to show that Satan, who is ever going about seeking whom he may devour, can see both before and behind.

The cut on the following page (90), which forms the compartment to the right, represents Adam and Eve, each with an apple: and the state in which Eve appears to be, is in accordance with an opinion maintained by several of the schoolmen of the twelfth and thirteenth centuries. The tree of knowledge is without fruit, and the serpent, with a human face, is seen twined round its stem.   The form of the tree and the shape of the leaves are almost precisely the same as those of the olive-trees in the Apocalypse, uprooted by Antichrist.   The character of the designs, however, in the two books is almost as different as the manner of the engraving.   In the Apocalypse there is no attempt at shading, while in the book under consideration it is introduced in every page, though merely by courses of single lines, as may be perceived in the drapery of Christ in the preceding cut, and in the trunk of the tree and in the serpent in the cut subjoined. In this cut the figure of Adam cannot be considered as a specimen of manly beauty; his face is that of a man who is past his prime, and his attitude is very like that of one of the splay-footed boors of Teniers. In point of personal beauty Eve appears

to be a partner worthy of her husband; and though from her action she seems conscious that she is naked, yet her expression and figure are extremely unlike the graceful timidity and beautiful proportions of the Medicean Venus. The face of the serpent displays neither malignity nor fiendish cunning; but, on the contrary, is marked with an expression not unlike that of a Bavarian broom-girl. This manner of representing the temptation of our first parents appears to have been conventional

among the early German Formschneiders; for I have seen several old
wood-cuts of this subject, in which the figures were almost precisely the
same.   Notwithstanding the bad drawing and the coarse engraving of
the following cut, many of the same subject, executed in Germany
between 1470 and 1510, are yet worse.

In the opposite cut, which forms the compartment to the left, Esau,
who is distinguished by his bow and quiver, is seen receiving a bowl of
pottage from his brother Jacob.   At the far side of the apartment is
seen a "kail-pot," suspended from a "crook," with something like a ham
and a gammon of bacon hanging against the wall.   This subject is
treated in a style which is thoroughly Dutch.   Isaac's family appear to

have been lodged in a tolerably comfortable house, with a stock of pro-
visions near the chimney nook; and his two sons are very like some of
the figures in the pictures of Teniers, more especially about the legs.

The following cut, a copy of that which is the lowest in the page,
represents the two prophets or inspired penmen, to whom reference is
made on the two scrolls whose ends may be perceived towards the lower
corners of each arch. The words underneath the figures are a portion of
the last rhyming verse quoted at page 87. It is from a difference in
the triangular ornament, above the pillar separating the two figures,
though not in this identical page, that Heineken chiefly decides on three
of the editions of this book; though nothing could be more easy than to

introduce another ornament of a similar kind, in the event of the original either being damaged in printing or intentionally effaced. In some of the earliest wood-blocks which remain undestroyed by the rough handling of time there are evident traces of several letters having been broken away, and of the injury being afterwards remedied by the introduction of a new piece of wood, on which the letters wanting were re-engraved.

The ink with which the cuts in the "Poor Preachers' Bible" have been printed, is evidently a kind of distemper of the colour of bistre, lighter than in the History of the Virgin, and darker than in the Apocalypse. In many of the cuts certain portions of the lines appear surcharged with ink,—sometimes giving to the whole page rather a blotched appearance,—while other portions seem scarcely to have received any.* This appearance is undoubtedly in consequence of the light-bodied ink having, from its want of tenacity, accumulated on the block where the line was thickest, or where two lines met, leaving the thinner portions adjacent with scarce any colouring at all. The block must, in my opinion, have been charged with such ink by means of something like a brush, and not by means of a ball. In some parts of the cuts—more especially where there is the greatest portion of text—

---

* Schelhorn has noticed a similar appearance in the old block-book entitled "Ars Memorandi:" "Videas hic nonnunquam literas atramento confluenti deformatas, ventremque illarum, alias album et vacuum, atramentaria macula repletum." Amœnitat. Liter. tom. i. p. 7.

small white spaces may be perceived, as if a graver had been run through the lines. On first noticing this appearance, I was inclined to think that it was owing to the spreading of the hairs of the brush in inking, whereby certain parts might have been left untouched. The same kind of break in the lines may be observed, however, in some of the impressions of the old wood-cuts published by Becker and Derschau,* and which are worked off by means of a press, and with common printer's ink. In these it is certainly owing to minute furrows in the grain of the wood; and I am now of opinion that the same cause has occasioned a similar appearance in the cuts of the "Biblia Pauperum Predicatorum." Mr. Ottley, speaking of the impressions in Earl Spencer's copy, makes the following remarks: "In many instances they have a sort of horizontally striped and confused appearance, which leads me to suppose that they were taken from engravings executed on some kind of wood of a coarse grain." † This correspondence between Earl Spencer's copy and that in the King's Library at the British Museum tends to confirm my opinion that there are not so many editions of the book as Heineken,—from certain accidental variations,—has been induced to suppose.

The manner in which the cuts are engraved, and the attempts at something like effect in the shading and composition, induce me to think that this book is not so old as either the Apocalpyse or the History of the Virgin. That it appeared before 1428, as has been inferred from the date which the Rev. Mr. Horne fancied that he had seen on the ancient binding, I cannot induce myself to believe. It is more likely to have been executed at some time between 1440 and 1460; and I am inclined to think that it is the production of a Dutch or Flemish, rather than a German artist.

A work, from which the engraved "Biblia Pauperum Predicatorum" is little more than an abstract, appears to have been known in France and Germany long before block-printing was introduced. Of such a work there were two manuscript copies in the National Library at Paris; the one complete, and the other—which, with a few exceptions, had been copied from the first—imperfect. The work consisted of a brief summary of the Bible, arranged in the following manner. One or two phrases in Latin and in French formed, as it were, the text; and each text was followed by a moral reflection, also in Latin and in French. Each

---

* This collection of wood engravings from old blocks was published in three parts, large folio, at Gotha in 1808, 1810, and 1816, under the following title: "Holzschnitte alter Deutscher Meister in den Original-Platten gesammelt von Hans Albrecht Von Derschau: Als ein Beytrag zur Kunstgeschichte herausgegeben, und mit einer Abhandlung über die Holzschneidekunst und deren Schicksale begleitet von Rudolph Zacharias Becker." The collector has frequently mistaken rudeness of design, and coarseness of execution, for proofs of antiquity.

† Inquiry, vol. i. p. 130.

article, which thus consisted of two parts, was illustrated by two draw-ings, one of which related to the historical fact, and the other to the moral deduced from it. The perfect copy consisted of four hundred and twenty-two pages, on each of which there were eight drawings, so that the number contained in the whole volume was upwards of five thousand. In some of the single drawings, which were about two and one-third inches wide, by three and one-third inches high, Camus counted not less than thirty heads.*

In a copy of the " Biblia Pauperum Predicatorum " from wood-blocks, Heineken observed written : " S. ANSGARIUS est autor hujus libri,"— St. Ansgarius is the author of this book. St. Ansgarius, who was a native of France, and a monk of the celebrated Abbey of Corbey, was sent into Lower Saxony, and other places in the north, for the purpose of reclaiming the people from paganism. He was appointed the first bishop of Hamburg in 831, and in 844 Bishop of Bremen, where he died in 864.† From a passage cited by Heineken from Ornhielm's Ecclesiastical History of Sweden and Gothland, it appears that Ansgarius was reputed to have compiled a similar book ; ‡ and Heineken observes that it might be from this passage that the " Biblia Pauperum Predicatorum " was ascribed to the Bishop of Hamburg.

In the cloisters of the cathedral at Bremen, Heineken saw two bas-reliefs sculptured on stone, of which the figures, of a moderate size, were precisely the same as those in two of the pages—the first and eighth—of the German " Biblia Pauperum Predicatorum." The inscriptions, which were in Latin, were the same as in block-book. He thinks it very probable that the other arches of the cloisters were formerly ornamented in the same manner with the remainder of the subjects, but that the sculptures had been destroyed in the disturbances which had occurred in Bremen. Though he by no means pretends that the cuts were engraved in the time of Ansgarius, he thinks it not impossible that the sculptures might be executed at that period according to the bishop's directions. This last passage is one of the most silly that occurs in Heineken's book.§ It is just about as likely that the cuts in the " Biblia Pauperum Predica-torum " were engraved in the time of Ansgarius, as that the bas-reliefs in the cloisters of the cathedral of Bremen should have been sculptured under his direction.

* Notice d'un Livre, &c. p. 11.   † Heineken, Idée Générale, p. 319.

‡ Ornhielm's book was printed in 4to. at Stockholm, 1689. The passage referred to is as follows : " Quos *per numeros et signa* conscripsisse eum [Ansgarium] libros Rembertus memo-rat indigitatos *pigmentorum* vocabulo, eos continuisse, palam est, quasdam aut e divinarum literarum, aut pie doctorum patrum scriptis, pericopas et sententias."

§ " Ces conjectures sont foibles ; elles ont été attaquées par Erasme Nyerup dans un écrit publié à Copenhague en 1784. . . . . Nyerup donne à penser que Heinecke a reconnu lui-même, dans la suite, la foiblesse de ses conjectures."—Camus, Notice d'un Livre, &c. p. 9.

The book usually called the "Speculum Humanæ Salvationis,"*—the Mirror of Human Salvation,—which is ascribed by Hadrian Junius to Lawrence Coster, has been more frequently the subject of discussion among bibliographers and writers who have treated of the origin of printing, than any other work. A great proportion, however, of what has been written on the subject consists of groundless speculation ; and the facts elicited, compared with the conjectures propounded, are as "two grains of wheat to a bushel of chaff." It would be a waste of time to recite at length the various opinions that have been entertained with respect to the date of this book, the manner in which the text was printed, and the printer's name. The statements and the theories put forth by Junius and Meerman in Coster's favour, so far as the execution of the Speculum is concerned, are decidedly contradicted by the book itself. Without, therefore, recapitulating arguments which are contradicted by established facts, I shall endeavour to give a correct account of the work, leaving those who choose to compare it, and reconcile it if they can, with the following assertions made by Coster's advocates : 1. that the Speculum was first printed by him in Dutch with wooden types ; 2. that while engraving a Latin edition on blocks of wood he discovered the art of printing with moveable letters ; 3. that the Latin edition, in which the text is partly from moveable types and partly from wood-blocks, was printed by Coster's heirs and successors, their moveable types having been stolen by John Gutemberg before the whole of the text was set up.

The Speculum which has been the subject of so much discussion is of a small folio size, and without date or printer's name. There are four editions of it known to bibliographers, all containing the same cuts ; two of those editions are in Latin, and two in Dutch. In the Latin editions the work consists of sixty-three leaves, five of which are occupied by an introduction or prologue, and on the other fifty-eight are printed the cuts and explanatory text. The Dutch editions, though containing the same number of cuts as the Latin, consist of only sixty-two leaves each, as the preface occupies only four. In all those editions the leaves are printed on one side only. Besides the four editions above noticed, which have been ascribed to Coster and have excited so much controversy, there are two or three others in which the cuts are more coarsely engraved, and probably executed, at a later period, in Germany. There is also a quarto edition of the Speculum, printed in 1483, at Culemburg, by John Veldener, and ornamented with the identical cuts of the folio editions ascribed to Coster and his heirs.

The four controverted editions of the Speculum may be considered as holding a middle place between block-books,—which are wholly executed,

---

* It is sometimes named "Speculum Figuratum ;" and Junius in his account of Coster's invention calls it " Speculum Nostræ Salutis."

both text and cuts, by the wood-engraver,—and books printed with moveable types : for in three of the editions the cuts are printed by means of friction with a rubber or burnisher, in the manner of the History of the Virgin, and other block-books, while the text, set in moveable type, has been worked off by means of a press ; and in a fourth edition, in which the cuts are taken in the same manner as in the former, twenty pages of the text are printed from wood-blocks by means of friction, while the remainder are printed in the same manner as the whole of the text in the three other editions ; that is, from moveable metal types, and by means of a press.

There are fifty-eight cuts in the Speculum, each of which is divided into two compartments by a slender column in the middle. In all the editions the cuts are placed as head-pieces at the top of each page, having underneath them, in two columns, the explanatory text. Under each compartment the title of the subject, in Latin, is engraved on the block.

The following reduced copy of the first cut will give an idea of their form, as every subject has pillars at the side, and is surmounted by an arch in the same style.

The style of engraving in those cuts is similar to those of the Poor Preachers' Bible. The former are, however, on the whole executed with greater delicacy, and contain more work. The shadows and folds of the drapery in the first forty-eight cuts are indicated by short parallel lines, which are mostly horizontal. In the forty-ninth and subsequent cuts, as has been noticed by Mr. Ottley, a change in the mode of indicating the shades and the folds in the draperies is perceptible ; for the short parallel lines, instead of being horizontal as in the former, are mostly slanting. Heineken observes, that to the forty-eighth cut inclusive, the chapters in the printed work are conformable with the old Latin manuscripts ; and as a perceptible change in the execution commences with the forty-ninth, it is not unlikely that the cuts were engraved by two different persons. The two following cuts are fac-similes of the compartments of the first, of which a reduced copy has been previously given.

casus lucifer

In the above cut, its title, " Casus Luciferi,"—the Fall of Lucifer,—is engraved at the bottom ; and the subject represented is Satan and the rebellious angels driven out of heaven, as typical of man's disobedience and fall. The following are the first two lines of the column of text underneath the cut in the Latin editions :

Inchoatur speculum humanae salbacionis
In quo patet casus hominis et modus repacionis.

Which may be translated into English thus :

In the Mirror of Salvation here is represented plain
The fall of man, and by what means he made his peace again.

The following is the right-hand compartment of the same cut. The

H

title of this subject, as in all the others, is engraved at the bottom ; the contracted words when written in full are, "Deus creavit hominem ad ymaginem et similitudinem suam,"—God created man after his own image and likeness.

ꝺꝭ ꙇꙇmꞇboꙇꙅ ꙇꙅ ꙇmꙇꙇꙅꙅ ꞇꙉꙇꙇꙇꙇꙇꙅ ꙇꙇꙇꙉ

The first two lines of the text in the column underneath this cut are,

Mulier autem in paradiso est formato
De costis viri dormienti est parata.

That is, in English rhyme of similar measure,

The woman was in Paradise for man an help meet made,
From Adam's rib created as he asleep was laid.

The cuts in all the editions are printed in light brown or sepia colour which has been mixed with water, and readily yields to moisture. The impressions have evidently been taken by means of friction, as the back of the paper immediately behind is smooth and shining from the action of the rubber or burnisher, while on the lower part of the page at the back of the text, which has been printed with moveable types, there is no such appearance. In the second Latin edition, in which the explanatory text to twenty of the cuts * has been printed from engraved wood-blocks by means of friction, the reverse of those twenty pages presents the same smooth appearance as the reverse of the cuts. In those twenty pages of text from engraved wood-blocks the ink is lighter-coloured than in the remainder of the book which is printed from moveable types, though much darker than that of the cuts. It is, therefore, evident that the two impressions,—the one from the block containing the cut, and the other from the block containing the text,—have been taken separately. In the pages printed from moveable types, the ink, which has evidently been compounded with oil, is full-bodied, and of a dark brown colour, approaching nearly to black. In the other three editions, one Latin and two Dutch, in which the text is entirely from moveable types, the ink is also full-bodied and nearly jet black, forming a strong contrast with the faint colour of the cuts.

The plan of the Speculum is almost the same as that of the Poor Preachers' Bible, and is equally as well entitled as the latter to be called " A History typical and anti-typical of the Old and New Testament." Several of the subjects in the two books are treated nearly in the same manner, though in no single instance, so far as my observation goes, is the design precisely the same in both. In several of the cuts of the Speculum, in the same manner as in the Poor Preachers' Bible, one compartment contains the supposed type or prefiguration, and the other its fulfilment; for instance: at No. 17 the appearance of the Lord to Moses in the burning bush is typical of the Annunciation; at No. 23 the brazen bath in the temple of Solomon is typical of baptism; at No. 31 the manna provided for the children of Israel in the Desert is typical of the Lord's Supper; at No. 45 the Crucifixion is represented in one compartment, and in the other is Tubal-Cain, the inventor of iron-work, and consequently of the nails with which Christ was fixed to the cross; and at No. 53 the descent of Christ to Hades, and the liberation of the patriarchs and fathers, is typified by the escape of the children of Israel from Egypt.

Though most of the subjects are from the Bible or the Apocrypha, yet there are two or three which the designer has borrowed from profane history: such as Semiramis contemplating the hanging gardens of Babylon; the Sibyl and Augustus; and Codrus king of Athens incurring death in order to secure victory to his people.

The Speculum Salvationis, as printed in the editions previously noticed, is only a portion of a larger work with the same title, and

* The cuts which have the text printed from wood-blocks are Nos. 1, 2, 4, 5, 6, 7, 8, 9, 10, 11, 13, 14, 16, 17, 21, 22, 26, 27, 46, and 55.—Heineken, Idée Générale, p. 444.

ornamented with similar designs, which had been known long before in manuscript. Heineken says, at page 478 of his Idée Générale, that the oldest copy he ever saw was in the Imperial Library at Vienna; and, at page 468, he observes that it appeared to belong to the twelfth century.

The manuscript work, when complete, consisted of forty-five chapters in rhyming Latin, to which was prefixed an introduction containing a list of them. Each of the first forty-two chapters contained four subjects, the first of which was the principal, and the other three illustrative of it. To each of these chapters were two drawings, every one of which, as in the printed copies of the work, consisted of two compartments. The last three chapters contained each eight subjects, and each subject was ornamented with a design.* The whole number of separate illustrations in the work was thus one hundred and ninety-two. The printed folio editions contain only fifty-eight cuts, or one hundred and sixteen separate illustrations.

Though the Speculum from the time of the publication of Junius's work † had been confidently claimed for Coster, yet no writer, either for or against him, appears to have particularly directed his attention to the manner in which the work was executed before Fournier, who in 1758, in a dissertation on the Origin and Progress of the Art of Wood-engraving,‡ first published some particulars respecting the work in question, which induced Meerman and Heineken to speculate on the priority of the different editions. Mr. Ottley, however, has proved, in a manner which carries with it the certainty of mathematical demonstration, that the conjectures of both the latter writers respecting the priority of the editions of the Speculum are absolutely erroneous. To elicit the truth does not, with respect to this work, seem to have been the object of those two writers. Both had espoused theories on its origin without much inquiry with respect to facts, and each presumed that edition to be the first which seemed most likely to support his own speculations.

Heineken, who assumed that the work was of German origin, insisted that the *first* edition was that in which the text is printed partly from moveable types and partly from letters engraved on wood-blocks, and that the Dutch editions were executed subsequently in the Low Countries. The Latin edition with the text entirely printed from moveable types he is pleased to denominate the second, and to assert, contrary to the evidence which the work itself affords, that the type resembles that of Faust and

---

* Heineken, Idée Générale, p. 474.

† The "Batavia" of Junius, in which the name of Lawrence Coster first appears as a printer, was published in 1588.

‡ Dissertation sur l'Origine et les Progrès de l'Art de Graver en Bois. Par M. Fournier le Jeune, 8vo. Paris, 1758.

Scheffer, and that the cuts in this *second* Latin edition, as he erroneously calls it, are coarser and not so sharp as those in the Latin edition which he supposes to be the first.

Fournier's discoveries with respect to the execution of the Speculum seem to have produced a complete change as to its origin in the opinions of Meerman; who, in 1757, the year before Fournier's dissertation was printed, had expressed his belief, in a letter to his friend Wagenaar, that what was alleged in favour of Coster being the inventor of printing was mere gratuitous assertion; that the text of the Speculum was probably printed after the cuts, and subsequent to 1470; that there was not a single document, nor an iota of evidence, to show that Coster ever used moveable types; and lastly, that the Latin was prior to the Dutch edition of the Speculum, as was apparent from the Latin names engraved at the foot of the cuts, which certainly would have been in Dutch had the cuts been originally destined for a Dutch edition.* In the teeth of his own previous opinions, having apparently gained a new light from Fournier's discoveries, Meerman, in his Origines Typographicæ, printed in 1765, endeavours to prove that the Dutch edition was the first, and that it was printed with moveable wooden types by Coster. The Latin edition in which the text is printed partly from moveable types and partly from wood-blocks he supposes to have been printed by Coster's heirs after his decease, thus endeavouring to give credibility to the story of Coster having died of grief on account of his types being stolen, and to encourage the supposition that his heirs in this edition supplied the loss by having engraved on blocks of wood those pages which were not already printed.

Fournier's discoveries relative to the manner in which the Speculum was executed were: 1st, that the cuts and the text had been printed at separate times, and that the former had been printed by means of friction; 2d, that a portion of the text in one of the Latin editions had been printed from engraved wood-blocks.† Fournier, who was a type-founder and wood-engraver, imagined that the moveable types with which the Speculum was printed were of wood. He also asserted that Faust and Scheffer's Psalter and an early edition of the Bible were printed with moveable wooden types. Such assertions are best

* A French translation of Meerman's letter, which was originally written in Dutch, is given by Santander in his Dictionnaire Bibliographique, tom. i. pp. 14—18, 8vo. Bruxelles, 1805.

† Dissertation, pp. 29—32. The many mistakes which Fournier commits in his Dissertation, excite a suspicion that he was either superficially acquainted with his subject, or extremely careless. He published two or three other small works on the subject of engraving and printing,—after the manner of " Supplements to an Appendix,"—the principal of which is entitled " De l'Origine et des Productions de l'Imprimerie primitive en taille de bois ; avec une refutation des préjugés plus ou moins accredités sur cet art ; pour servir de suite à la Dissertation sur l'Origine de l'Art de graver en bois. Paris, 1759."

answered by a simple negative, leaving the person who puts them forth to make out a probable case.

The fact having been established that in one of the editions of the Speculum a part of the text was printed from wood-blocks, while the whole of the text in the other three was printed from moveable types, Heineken, without diligently comparing the editions with each other in order to obtain further evidence, decides in favour of that edition being the first in which part of the text is printed from wood-blocks. His reasons for supposing this to be the first edition, though specious in appearance, are at variance with the facts which have since been incontrovertibly established by Mr. Ottley, whose scrutinizing examination of the different editions has clearly shown the futility of all former speculations respecting their priority. The argument of Heineken is to this effect: "It is improbable that a printer who had printed an edition wholly with moveable types should afterwards have recourse to an engraver to cut for him on blocks of wood a portion of the text for a second edition; and it is equally improbable that a wood-engraver who had discovered the art of printing with moveable types, and had used them to print the entire text of the first edition, should, to a certain extent, abandon his invention in a second by printing a portion of the text from engraved blocks of wood." The following is the order in which he arranges the different editions:

1. The Latin edition in which part of the text is printed from wood-blocks.
2. The Latin edition in which the text is entirely printed from moveable types.
3. The Dutch edition with the text printed wholly from moveable types, supposed by Meerman to be the *first edition* of all.*
4. The Dutch edition with the text printed wholly from moveable types, and which differs only from the preceding one in having the two pages of text under cuts No. 45 and 56 printed in a type different from the rest of the book.

The preceding arrangement—including Meerman's opinion respecting the priority of the Dutch edition—rests entirely on conjecture, and is almost diametrically contradicted in every instance by the evidence afforded by the books themselves; for through the comparisons and investigations of Mr. Ottley it is proved, to an absolute certainty, that the Latin edition supposed by Heineken to be the second is the *earliest of all;* that the edition No. 4, called the second Dutch, is the next in order to the actual first Latin; and that the two editions, No. 1 and No. 3, respectively proclaimed by Heineken and Meerman as the earliest,

---

* Heineken seems inclined to consider this as the second Dutch edition; and he only mentions it as the first Dutch edition because it is called so by Meerman.—Idée Gén. pp. 453, 454.

have been printed subsequently to the other two.* Which of the pretended *first* editions was in reality the *last,* has not been satisfactorily determined ; though there seems reason to believe that it was the Latin one which has part of the text printed from wood-blocks.

It is well known to every person acquainted with the practice of wood-engraving, that portions of single lines in such cuts as those of the Speculum are often broken out of the block in the process of printing. If two books, therefore, containing the same wood-cuts, but evidently printed at different times, though without a date, should be submitted to the examination of a person acquainted with the above fact and bearing it in mind, he would doubtless declare that the copy in which the cuts were most perfect was first printed, and that the other in which parts of the cuts appeared broken away was of a later date. If, on comparing other copies of the same editions he should find the same variations, the impression on his mind as to the priority of the editions would amount to absolute certainty. The identity of the cuts in all the four editions ot the Speculum being unquestionable, and as certain minute fractures in the lines of some of them, as if small portions of the block had been broken out in printing, had been previously noticed by Fournier and Heineken, Mr. Ottley conceived the idea of comparing the respective cuts in the different editions, with a view of ascertaining the order in which they were printed. He first compared two copies of the edition called the *first Latin* with a copy of that called the *second Dutch*, and finding, that, in several of the cuts of the former, parts of lines were wanting which in the latter were perfect, he concluded that the miscalled *second Dutch* edition was in fact of an earlier date than the pretended *first Latin* edition of Heineken. In further comparing the above editions with the supposed *second Latin* edition of Heineken and the supposed *first Dutch* edition of Meerman, he found that the cuts in the miscalled second Latin edition were the most perfect of all; and that the cuts in Heineken's first Latin and Meerman's first Dutch editions contained more broken lines than the edition named by those authors the *second Dutch*. The conclusion which he arrived at from those facts was irresistible, namely, that the earliest edition of all was that called by Heineken the second Latin ; and that the edition called the second Dutch was the next in order. As the cuts in the copies examined of the pretended *first* Latin and Dutch editions contained similar fractures, it could not be determined with certainty which was actually the *last*.

* Inquiry into the Origin and Early History of Engraving, pp. 205—217. Though differing from Mr. Ottley in the conclusions which he draws from the facts elicited by him respecting the priority of the editions of the Speculum, I bear a willing testimony to the value of his discoveries on this subject, which may rank among the most interesting that have resulted from bibliographical research.

As it is undoubted that the cuts of all the editions have been printed separately from the text, it has been objected that Mr. Ottley's examination has only ascertained the order in which the cuts have been printed, but by no means decided the priority of the editions of the entire book. All the cuts, it has been objected, might have been taken by the engraver before the text was printed in a single edition, and it might thus happen that the book first printed with text might contain the last, and consequently the most imperfect cuts. This exception, which is founded on a very improbable presumption, will be best answered by the following facts established on a comparison of the two Latin, and which, I believe, have not been previously noticed :—On closely comparing those pages which are printed with moveable types in the true second edition with the corresponding pages in that edition which is properly the first, it was evident from the different spelling of many of the words, and the different length of the lines, that they had been printed at different times : but on comparing, however, those pages which are printed in the second edition from engraved wood-blocks with the corresponding pages, from moveable type, in the first edition, I found the spelling and the length of the lines to be the same. The page printed from the wood-block was, in short, a fac-simile of the corresponding page printed from moveable types. So completely did they correspond, that I have no doubt that an impression of the page printed from moveable types had been " transferred," * as engravers say, to the block. In the last cut † of the first edition I noticed a scroll which was quite black, as if meant to contain an inscription which the artist had neglected to engrave ; and in the second edition I perceived that the black was cut away, thus leaving the part intended for the inscription white. Another proof, in addition to those adduced by Mr. Ottley of that Latin edition being truly the first in which the whole of the text is printed from moveable types.

Though there can no longer be a doubt in the mind of any impartial person of that Latin edition, in which part of the text is printed from engraved wood-blocks, and the rest from moveable types, being later than the other ; yet the establishment of this fact suggests a question, as to the cause of part of the text of this second Latin edition being printed from wood-blocks, which cannot perhaps be very satisfactorily answered.

* Wood-engravers of the present day are accustomed to transfer an old impression from a cut or a page of letter-press to a block in the following manner. They first moisten the back of the paper on which the cut or letter-press is printed with a mixture of concentrated potash and essence of lavender in equal quantities, which causes the ink to separate readily from the paper ; next, when the paper is nearly dry, the cut or page is placed above a prepared block, and by moderate pressure the ink comes off from the paper, and leaves an impression upon the wood.

† The subject is Daniel explaining to Belshazzar the writing on the wall.

All writers previous to Mr. Ottley, who had noticed that the text was printed partly from moveable types and partly from wood-blocks, decided, without hesitation, that this edition was the first; and each, accordingly as he espoused the cause of Gutemberg or Coster, proceeded to theorise on this assumed fact. As their arguments were founded in error, it cannot be a matter of surprise that their conclusions should be inconsistent with truth. The fact of this edition being subsequent to that in which the text is printed wholly from moveable types has been questioned on two grounds : 1st. The improbability that the person who had printed the text of a former edition entirely from moveable types should in a later edition have recourse to the more tedious operation of engraving part of the text on wood-blocks. 2d. Supposing that the owner of the cuts had determined in a later edition to engrave the text on blocks of wood, it is difficult to conceive what could be his reason for abandoning his plan, after twenty pages of the text were engraved, and printing the remainder with moveable types.

Before attempting to answer those objections, I think it necessary to observe that the existence of a positive fact can never be affected by any arguments which are grounded on the difficulty of accounting for it. Objections, however specious, can never alter the immutable character of truth, though they may affect opinions, and excite doubts in the minds of persons who have not an opportunity of examining and judging for themselves.

With respect to the first objection, it is to be remembered that in all the editions, the text, whether from wood-blocks or moveable types, has been printed separately from the cuts ; consequently the cuts of the first edition might be printed by a wood-engraver, and the text set up and printed by another person who possessed moveable types. The engraver of the cuts might not be possessed of any moveable types when the text of the first edition was printed ; and, as it is a well-known fact that wood-engravers continued to execute entire pages of text for upwards of thirty years after the establishment of printing with moveable types, it is not unlikely that he might attempt to engrave the text of a second edition and print the book solely for his own advantage. This supposition is to a certain extent corroborated by the fact of the twenty pages of engraved text in the second Latin edition being fac-similes of the twenty corresponding pages of text from moveable types in the first.

To the second objection every day's experience suggests a ready answer ; for scarcely anything is more common than for a person to attempt a work which he finds it difficult to complete, and, after making some progress in it, to require the aid of a kindred art, and abandon his original plan.

As the first edition of the Speculum was printed subsequent to the

discovery of the art of printing with moveable types, and as it was probably printed in the Low Countries, where the typographic art was first
introduced about 1472, I can discover no reason for believing that the
work was executed before that period.   Santander, who was so well
acquainted with the progress of typography in Belgium and Holland, is
of opinion that the Speculum is not of an earlier date than 1480.   In
1483 John Veldener printed at Culemburg a quarto edition of the Speculum, in which the cuts are the same as in the earlier folios.   In order to
adapt the cuts to this smaller edition Veldener had sawn each block in
two, through the centre pillar which forms a separation between the two
compartments in each of the original engravings.   Veldener's quarto
edition, which has the text printed on both sides of the paper from moveable types, contains twelve more cuts than the older editions, but designed
and executed in the same style.*   If Lawrence Coster had been the
inventor of printing with moveable types, and if any one folio edition of
the Speculum had been executed by him, we cannot suppose that Veldener, who was himself a wood-engraver, as well as a printer, would have
been ignorant of those facts.   He, however, printed two editions of the
Fasciculus Temporum,—one at Louvain in 1476, and the other at Utrecht
in 1480,—a work which contains a short notice of the art of printing
being discovered at Mentz, but not a syllable concerning its discovery at
Harlem by Lawrence Coster.   The researches of Coster's advocates have
clearly established one important fact, though an unfortunate one for
their argument; namely, that the Custos or Warden of St. Bavon's was
not known as a printer to one of his contemporaries.   The citizens of
Harlem, however, have still something to console themselves with :
though Coster may not be the inventor of printing, there can be little
doubt of Junius, or his editor, being the discoverer of Coster,—

              " Est quoddam prodire tenus, si non datur ultra."

   There is in the Print Room of the British Museum a small volume of
wood-cuts, which has not hitherto been described by any bibliographer,
nor by any writer who has treated on the origin and progress of wood
engraving.   It appears to have been unknown to Heineken, Breitkopf,
Von Murr, and Meerman ; and it is not mentioned, that I am aware of,
either by Dr. Dibdin or Mr. Douce, although it certainly was submitted
to the inspection of the latter.   It formerly belonged to the late Sir
George Beaumont, by whom it was bequeathed to the Museum ; but
where he obtained it I have not been able to learn.   It consists of an

---

* Heineken gives an account of those twelve additional cuts at page 463 of his Idée
Générale.   It appears that Veldener also published in the same year another edition of the
Speculum, also in quarto, containing the same cuts as the older folios, but without the twelve
above mentioned.

alphabet of large capital letters, formed of figures arranged in various attitudes ; and from the general character of the designs, the style of the engraving, and the kind of paper on which the impressions have been taken, it evidently belongs to the same period as the Poor Preachers' Bible. There is only one cut on each leaf, the back being left blank as in most of the block-books, and the impressions have been taken by means of friction. The paper at the back of each cut has a shining appearance when held towards the light, in consequence of the rubbing which it has received ; and in some it appears as if it had been blacked with charcoal, in the same manner that some parts of the cartoons were blacked which have been pricked through by the tapestry worker. The ink is merely a distemper or water-colour, which will partly wash out by the application of hot water, and its colour is a kind of sepia. Each leaf, which is about six inches high, by three and six-eighths wide, consists of a separate piece of paper, and is pasted, at the inner margin, on to a slip either of paper or parchment, through which the stitching of the cover passes. Whether the paper has been cut in this manner before or after that the impressions were taken, I am unable to determine.*

The greater part of the letter A is torn out, and in that which remains there are pin-marks, as if it had been traced by being pricked through. The letters S, T, and V are also wanting. The following is a brief description of the letters which remain. The letter B is composed of five figures, one with a pipe and tabor, another who supports him, a dwarf, an old man kneeling, and an old woman with a staff. C, a youthful figure rending open the jaws of a lion, with two grotesque heads like those of satyrs. D, a man on horseback, and a monk astride on a fiendish-looking monster. E, two grotesque heads, a figure holding the horn of one of them, and another figure stretching out a piece of cloth. F, a tall figure blowing a trumpet, and a youth beating a tabor, with an animal like a dog at their feet.† G, David with Goliah's head, and a figure stooping, who appears to kiss a flagellum. H, a figure opening the jaws of a dragon. I, a tall man embracing a woman. K, a female with a wreath, a youth kneeling, an old man on his knees, and a young man with his heels uppermost. [Engraved as a specimen at page 109.] L, a man with a long sword, as if about to pierce a figure reclining. [Engraved as

* The following is a reduced copy of the paper-mark, which appears to be a kind of anchor with a small cross springing from a ball or knob at the junction of the arms with the shank. It bears a considerable degree of resemblance to the mark given at page 62, from an edition of the Apocalypse. An anchor is to be found as a paper-mark in editions of the Apocalypse, and of the Poor Preachers' Bible. According to Santander, a similar paper-mark is to be found in books printed at Cologne, Louvain, and Utrecht, from about 1470 to 1480.

† The initial F, at the commencement of this chapter, is a reduced copy of the letter here described.

a specimen at page 110.]   M, two figures, each mounted on a kind of
monster; between them, an old man.   N, a man with a sword, another
mounted on the tail of a fish.   O, formed of four grotesque heads.   P,
two figures with clubs.   Q, formed of three grotesque heads, similar to
those in O.   R, a tall, upright figure, another with something like a club
in his hand; a third, with his heels up, blowing a horn.   X, composed of
four figures, one of which has two bells, and another has one; on the
shoulder of the upper figure to the right a squirrel may be perceived.
Y, a figure with something like a hairy skin on his shoulder; another
thrusting a sword through the head of an animal.   Z, three figures; an
old man about to draw a dagger, a youth lying down, and another who
appears as if flying.   [Engraved as a specimen at page 111.]   The last
cut is the ornamental flower, of which a copy is given at page 113.

In the same case with those interesting, and probably unique specimens of early wood engraving, there is a letter relating to them, dated
27th May, 1819, from Mr. Samuel Lysons to Sir George Beaumont, from
which the following is an extract: "I return herewith your curious
volume of ancient cuts.   I showed it yesterday to Mr. Douce, who agrees
with me that it is a great curiosity.   He thinks that the blocks were
executed at Harlem, and are some of the earliest productions of that
place.   He has in his possession most of the letters executed in copper,
but very inferior to the original cuts.   Before you return from the Continent I shall probably be able to ascertain something further respecting
them."   What might be Mr. Douce's reasons for supposing that those
cuts were executed at Harlem I cannot tell; though I am inclined to
think that he had no better foundation for his opinion than his faith
in Junius, Meerman, and other advocates of Lawrence Coster, who unhesitatingly ascribe every early block-book to the spurious "Officina
Laurentiana."

In the manuscript catalogue in the Print Room of the British Museum
the volume is thus described by Mr. Ottley: "Alphabet of initial letters
composed of grotesque figures, wood engravings of the middle of the
fifteenth century, apparently the work of a Dutch or Flemish artist; the
impressions taken off by friction in the manner of the early block-books.
. . . I perceive the word 'London' in small characters written upon the
blade of a sword in one of the cuts, [the letter L,] and I suspect they
were engraved in England."

As to whether these cuts were engraved in England or no I shall not
venture to give an opinion.   I am, however, satisfied that they were
neither designed nor engraved by the artists who designed and engraved
the cuts in the Apocalypse, the History of the Virgin, and the Poor
Preachers' Bible.   With respect to drawing, expression, and engraving,
the cuts of the Alphabet are decidedly superior to those of every block-

book, and generally to all wood engravings executed previous to 1500, with the exception of such as are by Albert Durer, and those contained in the Hypnerotomachia, an Italian rhapsody, with wood-cuts supposed to have been designed by Raffaele or Andrea Mantegna, and printed by Aldus at Venice, 1499. Although the cuts of the Alphabet may not have been engraved in England, it is, however, certain that the volume had been at rather an early period in the possession of an Englishman.

The cover consists of a double fold of thick parchment, on the inside of which, between the folds, there is written in large old English characters what I take to be the name "Edwardus Lowes." On the blank side of the last leaf there is a sketch of a letter commencing "Right reverent and wershipfull masters and frynds; In the moste loweliste maner that I canne or may, I here recomende me, duely glade to her of yor good prosperitye and welth." The writing, as I have been informed, is of the period of Henry VIII; and on the slips of paper and parchment to which the inner margins of the leaves are pasted are portions of English manuscripts, which are probably of the same date. There can, however, be little doubt that the leaves have been mounted, and the volume covered, about a hundred years subsequent to the engraving of the cuts.

I agree with Mr. Ottley in thinking that those cuts were engraved about the middle of the fifteenth century, but I can perceive nothing in them to induce me to suppose they were the work of a Dutch artist; and I am as little inclined to ascribe them to a German. The style of the drawing is not unlike what we see in illuminated French manuscripts of the middle of the fifteenth century; and as the only two engraved words which occur in the volume are French, I am rather inclined to suppose that the artist who made the drawings was a native of France.

The costume of the female to whom the words are addressed appears to be French; and the action of the lover kneeling seems almost characteristic of that nation. No Dutchman certainly ever addressed his mistress with such an air. He holds what appears to be a ring as gracefully as a modern Frenchman holds a snuff-box, and upon the scroll before him are engraved a heart, and the words which he may be supposed to utter, "*Mon Ame.*" At page 109, is a fac-simile of the cut referred to, the letter K, of the size of the original, and printed in the same kind of colour.

Upon the sword-blade in the original cut of the following letter, L, there is written in small characters, as Mr. Ottley has observed,

the word "*London;*" and in the white space on the right, or upper side, of the figure lying down, there appears written in the same hand the name "*Bethemsted.*" In this name the letter B is not unlike a W; and I have heard it conjectured that the name might be that of

John Wethamstede, abbot of St. Alban's, who was a great lover of books, and who died in 1440. This conjecture, however, will not hold good, for the letter is certainly intended for a B ; and in the cut of the letter B there is written " *R. Beths.*," which is in all probability intended for an abbreviation of the name, "*Bethemsted*," which occurs in another part of the book. The ink with which these names are written is

nearly of the same colour as that of the cuts. The characters appear to be of an earlier date than those on the reverse of the last leaf.

The cut at page 111, is that of the letter Z, which stands the wrong way in consequence of its not having been drawn reversed upon the block. The subject might at first sight be supposed to represent the angel staying Abraham when about to sacrifice Isaac; but on examining the cut more closely it will be perceived that the figure which might be mistaken for an angel is without wings, and appears to be in the act of supplicating the old man, who with his left hand holds him by the hair.

The opposite cut, which is the last in the book, is an ornamental flower designed with great freedom and spirit, and surpassing everything of the kind executed on wood in the fifteenth century. I speak not of the style of engraving, which, though effective, is coarse ; but of the taste displayed in the drawing. The colour of the cuts on pages 109, 110, 111, from the late Sir George Beaumont's book, will give the reader, who has not had an opportunity of examining the originals, some idea of the colour in which the cuts of the Apocalypse, the History of the Virgin, the Poor Preachers' Bible, and the Speculum, are printed ; which in all of them is a kind of sepia, in some inclining more to a yellow, and in others more to a brown.

In the volume under consideration we may clearly perceive that the art of wood engraving had made considerable progress at the time the cuts were executed. Although there are no attempts at cross-hatching, which was introduced about 1486, yet the shadows are generally well indicated, either by thickening the line, or by courses of short parallel lines, marking the folds of the drapery, or giving the appearance of rotundity to the figures. The expression of the heads displays considerable talent, and the wood-engraver who at the present time could design and execute such a series of figures, would be entitled to no small degree of commendation. Comparing those cuts with such as are to be seen in books typographically executed between 1461 * and 1490, it is surprising that the art of wood engraving should have so materially declined when employed by printers for the illustration of their books. The best of the cuts printed with letter-press in the period referred to are decidedly inferior to the best of the early block-books.

As it would occupy too much space, and would be beyond the scope of the present treatise to enter into a detail of the contents of all the block-books noticed by Heineken, I shall give a brief description of that named " Ars Memorandi," and conclude the chapter with a list of such others as are chiefly referred to by bibliographers.

The " ARS MEMORANDI " is considered by Schelhorn † and by Dr. Dibdin as one of the earliest block-books, and in their opinion I concur. Heineken, however,—who states that the style is almost the same as in the figures of the Apocalypse,—thinks that it is of later date than the Poor Preachers' Bible and the History of the

---

* The first book with moveable types and wood-cuts both printed by means of the press is the Fables printed at Bamberg, by Albert Pfister, " Am Sant Valentinus tag," 1461.

† " Nostrum vero libellum, cujus gratia hæc præfati sumus, intrepide, si non primum artis inventæ fœtum, certe inter primos fuisse asseveramus."—Amœnitates Literariæ, tom. 1. p. 4.

Virgin. It is of a quarto size, and consists of fifteen cuts, with the same number of separate pages of text also cut on wood, and printed on one side of each leaf only by means of friction.* At the foot of each page of text is a letter of the alphabet, commencing with a, indicating the order in which they are to follow each other. In every cut an animal is represented,—an eagle, an angel, an ox, or a lion,— emblematic of the Evangelist whose Gospel is to be impressed on the memory. Each of the animals is represented standing upright, and marked with various signs expressive of the contents of the different chapters. To the Gospel of St. John, with which the book commences, three cuts with as many pages of text are allotted. St. Matthew has five cuts, and five pages of text. St. Mark three cuts and three pages of text ; and St. Luke four cuts and four pages of text.†

"It is worthy of observation," says J. C. Von Aretin, in his Essay on the earliest Results of the Invention of Printing, "that this book, which the most intelligent bibliographers consider to be one of the earliest of its kind, should be devoted to the improvement of the memory, which, though divested of much of its former importance by the invention of writing, was to be rendered of still less consequence by the introduction of printing." ‡

The first cut is intended to express figuratively the first six chapters of St. John's Gospel. The upright eagle is the emblem of the saint, and the numerals are the references to the chapters. The contents of the first chapter are represented by the dove perched on the eagle's head, and the two faces,—one of an old, the other of a young man,—probably intended for those of Moses and Christ.§ The lute on the breast of the eagle, with something like three bells‖ suspended from it, indicate the contents of the second chapter, and are supposed by Schelhorn to refer to the marriage of Cana. The numeral 3, in Schelhorn's opinion, relates to "nonnihil apertum et prosectum circa ventrem," which he thinks may be intended as a reference to the words of Nicodemus : " Nunquid homo senex potest in ventrem matris suæ

---

* Heineken had seen two editions of this book, and he gives fac-similes of their titles, which are evidently from different blocks. The title at full length is as follows : *Ars memorandi notabilis per figuras Evangelistarum hic ex post descriptam quam diligens lector diligenter legat et practiset per signa localia ut in practica experitur.*—" En horridum et incomtum dicendi genus, Priscianumque misere vapulantem ! " exclaims Schelhorn.

† Heineken, Idée Générale, p. 394.

‡ Über die frühesten universal historischen Folgen der Erfindung der Buchdruckerkunst, von J. Christ. Freyherrn Von Aretin, S. 18. 4to. Munich, 1808.

§ "For the law was given by Moses, but grace and truth came by Jesus Christ."— St. John's Gospel, chap. i. v. 17.

‖ " Forte tamen ea, quæ tintinnabulis haud videntur dissimilia, nummulariorum loculos et pecuniæ receptacula referunt."—Schelhorn, Amœnit. Liter. tom. i. p. 10.

iterum introire et renasci ?" Between the feet of the eagle is a water-bucket surmounted by a sort of coronet or crown, intended to represent the principal events narrated in the 4th chapter, which are Christ's talking with the woman of Samaria at the well, and his healing the son of a nobleman at Capernaum. The 5th chapter is indicated by a fish above the eagle's right wing, which is intended to bring to mind the pool of Bethesda. The principal event related in the 6th chapter, Christ feeding the multitude, is indicated by the two fishes and five small loaves above the eagle's left wing. The cross within a circle, above the fishes, is emblematic of the consecrated wafer in the Lord's supper, as celebrated by the church of Rome.*

The above reduced copy of the cut will afford some idea of the manner in which the memory is to be assisted in recollecting the first six chapters of St. John. Those who wish to know more respecting this curious book are referred to Schelhorn's Amœnitates Literariæ, tom. i.

* The following are the contents of the first page, descriptive of the cut : " Evangelium Johannis habet viginti unum capittula. Primum. In principio erat verbum de eternitate verbi et de trinitate. Secundum capittulum. Nupcie facte sunt in Chana Galilee et qualiter Christus subvertit mensas nummulariorum. Tertium capittulum. Erat autem homo ex Phariseis Nycodemus nomine. Quartum capittulum. Qualiter Ihesus peciit a muliere Samaritana bibere circum puteum Jacob et de regulo. Quintum capittulum. De probatica piscina ubi dixit Ihesus infirmo Tolle grabatum tuum & vade. Sextum capit-tulum. De refectione ex quinque panibus & duobus piscibus Et de ewkaristia."—Schelhorn, Amœnit. Lit. tom. i. p. 9.

pp. 1—17 ; Heineken, Idée Générale, pp. 394, 395 ; and to Dr. Dibdin's Bibliotheca Spenceriana, vol. i. p. 4, where a copy is given of the first cut relating to the Gospel of St. Matthew.

Block-books containing both text and figures were executed long after the introduction of typography, or printing by means of moveable types ; but the cuts in such works are decidedly inferior to those executed at an earlier period. The book entitled "Die Kunst Cyromantia,"* which consists chiefly of text, is printed from wood-blocks on both sides of each leaf by means of a press. At the conclusion of the title is the date 1448 ; but this is generally considered to refer to the period when the book was written, and not the time when it was engraved. On the last page is the name : "jorg schapff zu augspurg," If this George Schapff was a wood-engraver of Augsburg, the style of the cuts in the book sufficiently declares that he must have been one of the very lowest class. More wretched cuts were never chiselled out by a printer's apprentice as a head-piece to a half-penny ballad.

Of the block-book entitled "Ars Moriendi," Heineken enumerates no less than seven editions, of which one is printed on both sides of the leaves, and by means of a press. Besides these he mentions another edition, impressed on one side of the paper only, in which appear the following name and date : "Hans eporer, 1473, hat diss puch pruff= mo er."†

Of the book named in German "Der Entkrist"—Antichrist—printed from wood-blocks, Heineken mentions two editions. In that which he considers the first, containing thirty-nine cuts, each leaf is printed on one side only by means of friction ; in the other, which contains thirty-eight cuts, is the "brief-maler's" or wood-engraver's name : "Der jung hanss priffmaler hat das puch zu nurenberg, 1472."

At Nuremberg, in the collection of a physician of the name of Treu, Heineken noticed a small volume in quarto, consisting of thirty-two wood-cuts of Bible subjects, underneath each of which were fifteen verses in German, engraved on the same block. Each leaf was printed on one side only, and the impressions, which were in pale ink, had been taken by means of friction.

The early wood-engravers, besides books of cuts, executed others

---

* This work on Palmistry was composed in German by a Doctor Hartlieb, as is expressed at the beginning : "Das nachgeschriben buch von der hand hätt zu teutsch gemacht Doctor Hartlieb." Specimens of the first and the last pages, and of one of the cuts, are given in Heineken's Idée Générale, plates 27 and 28.

† I am of opinion that this is the same person who executed the cuts for a German dition of the Poor Preachers' Bible in 1475. His name does not appear ; but on a shield of arms there is a spur, which may be intended as a rebus of the name ; in the same manner as Albert Durer's surname appears in his coat of arms, a pair of doors,—*Durer*, or, as his father's name was sometimes spelled, *Thurer*.

consisting of text only, of which several portions are preserved in public libraries in Germany,* France, and Holland; and although it is certain that block-books continued to be engraved and printed several years after the invention of typography, there can be little doubt that editions of the grammatical primer called the "Donatus," from the name of its supposed compiler, were printed from wood-blocks previous to the earliest essays of Gutemberg to print with moveable types. It is indeed asserted that Gutemberg himself engraved, or caused to be engraved on wood, a "Donatus" before his grand invention was perfected.

In the Royal Library at Paris are preserved the two old blocks of a "Donatus" which are mentioned by Heineken at page 257 of his Idée Générale. They are both of a quarto form; but as the one contains twenty lines and the other only sixteen, and as there is a perceptible difference in the size of the letters, it is probable that they were engraved for different editions.† Those blocks were purchased in Germany by a Monsieur Faucault, and after passing through the hands of three other book-collectors they came into the possession of the Duke de la Vallière, at whose sale they were sold for two hundred and thirty livres. In De Bure's catalogue of the La Vallière library, impressions are given from the original blocks. The letters in both those blocks, though differing in size, are of the same proportions and form; and Heineken and Fischer consider that they bear a great resemblance to the characters of Faust and Scheffer's Psalter, printed with moveable types in 1457, although the latter are considerably larger.

The art of wood engraving, having advanced from a single figure with merely a name cut underneath it, to the impression of entire pages of text, was now to undergo a change. Moveable letters formed of metal, and wedged together within an iron frame, were to supersede the engraved page; and impressions, instead of being taken by the slow and tedious process of friction, were now to be obtained by the speedy and powerful action of the press. If the art of wood engraving suffered a temporary decline for a few years after the general introduction of typography, it was only to revive again under the protecting influence of the PRESS; by means of which its productions were to be multiplied a hundred fold, and, instead of being confined to a few towns, were to be disseminated throughout every part of Europe.

* Aretin says that in the Royal Library at Munich there are about forty books and about a hundred single leaves printed from engraved wood-blocks.—Über die Folgen, &c. S. 6.

† Meerman had an old block of a Donatus, which was obtained from the collection of a M. Hubert of Basle, and which appeared to belong to the same edition as that containing sixteen lines in the Royal Library at Paris.—Heineken, Idée Générale, p. 258.

CHAPTER III.

INVENTION OF TYPOGRAPHY.

THE DISCOVERY OF DESROCHES.—THE STAMPING OF LODEWYC VAN VAELBEKE.—EARLY
"PRENTERS" OF ANTWERP AND BRUGES NOT TYPOGRAPHERS.—COLOGNE CHRONICLE.
—DONATUSES PRINTED IN HOLLAND.—GUTEMBERG'S BIRTH AND FAMILY—PROGRESS OF
HIS INVENTION—HIS LAW-SUIT WITH THE DRYTZEHNS AT STRASBURG—HIS RETURN TO
MENTZ, AND PARTNERSHIP WITH FAUST — PARTNERSHIP DISSOLVED. — POSSIBILITY OF
PRINTING WITH WOODEN TYPES EXAMINED.—SUPPOSED EARLY PRODUCTIONS OF GUTEM-
BERG AND FAUST'S PRESS.—PROOFS OF GUTEMBERG HAVING A PRESS OF HIS OWN.—THE
VOCABULARY PRINTED AT ELFELD.—GUTEMBERG'S DEATH AND EPITAPHS.—INVENTION OF
PRINTING CLAIMED FOR LAWRENCE COSTER.—THE ACCOUNT GIVEN BY JUNIUS—CONTRA-
DICTED, ALTERED, AND AMENDED AT WILL BY MEERMAN, KONING, AND OTHERS.—WORKS
PRETENDED TO BE PRINTED WITH COSTER'S TYPES.—THE HORARIUM DISCOVERED BY
ENSCHEDIUS.

 EFORE proceeding to trace the progress of wood
engraving in connexion with typography, it
appears necessary to give some account of the
invention of the latter art. In the following
brief narrative of Gutemberg's life, I shall adhere to positive facts; and until evidence
equally good shall be produced in support of
another's claim to the invention, I shall consider him as the father of typography. I shall
also give Hadrian Junius's account of the invention of wood engraving, block-printing, and
typography by Lawrence Coster, with a few
remarks on its credibility. Some of the conjectures and assertions of
Meerman, Koning, and other advocates of Coster, will be briefly noticed,
and their inconsistency pointed out. To attempt to refute at length the
gratuitous assumptions of Coster's advocates, and to enter into a detail
of all their groundless arguments, would be like proving a medal to be
a forgery by a long dissertation, when the modern fabricator has plainly
put his name in the legend. The best proof of the fallacy of Coster's
claims to the honour of having discovered the art of printing with
moveable types is to be found in the arguments of those by whom
they have been supported.

Meerman, with all his research, has not been able to produce a single fact to prove that Lawrence Coster, or Lawrence Janszoon as he calls him, ever printed a single book; and it is by no means certain that his hero is the identical Lawrence Coster mentioned by Junius. In order to suit his own theory he has questioned the accuracy of the statements of Junius, and has thus weakened the very foundation of Coster's claims. The title of the custos of St. Bavon's to the honour of being the inventor of typography must rest upon the authenticity of the account given by Junius; and how far this corresponds with established facts in the history of wood engraving and typography I leave others to decide for themselves.

Among the many fancied discoveries of the real inventor of the art of printing, that of Monsieur Desroches, a member of the Imperial Academy of Sciences and Belles Lettres at Brussels, seems to require an especial notice. In a paper printed in the transactions of that society,* he endeavoured to prove, that the art of printing books was practised in Flanders about the beginning of the fourteenth century; and one of the principal grounds of his opinion was contained in an old chronicle of Brabant, written, as is supposed, by one Nicholas le Clerk, [Clericus,] secretary to the city of Antwerp. The chronicler, after having described several remarkable events which happened during the government of John II. Duke of Brabant, who died in 1312, adds the following lines :

> In dieser tyt sterf menschelyc
> Die goede vedelare Lodewyc ;
> Die de beste was die voor dien
> In de werelt ye was ghesien
> Van makene ende metter hant ;
> Van Vaelbeke in Brabant
> Alsoe was hy ghenant.
> Hy was d'erste die vant
> Van Stampien die manieren
> Diemen noch hoert antieren.

This curious record, which Monsieur Desroches considered as so plain a proof of "die goede vedelare Lodewyc" being the inventor of printing, may be translated in English as follows :

> This year the way of all flesh went
> Ludwig, the fidler most excellent ;
> For handy-work a man of name ;
> From Vaelbeke in Brabant he came.

* Nouvelles Recherches sur l'origine de l'Imprimerie, dans lesquelles on fait voir que la première idée est due aux Brabançons. Par M. Desroches. Lu à la séance du 8 Janvier, 1777.—Mémoires de l'Académie Impériale des Sciences et Belles Lettres, tom. i. pp. 523—547. Edit. 1780.

He was the first who did find out
The art of beating time, no doubt,
(Displaying thus his meikle skill,
And fidlers all practise it still.*

The laughable mistake of Monsieur Desroches in supposing that
fidler Ludwig's invention, of beating time by stamping with the foot,
related to the discovery of printing by means of the press, was pointed
out in 1779 by Monsieur Ghesquiere in a letter printed in the Esprit
des Journaux.† In this letter Monsieur Ghesquiere shows that the
Flemish word "Stampien," used by the chronicler in his account of
the invention of the "good fidler Ludwig," had not a meaning similar
to that of the word "stampus" explained by Ducange, but that it
properly signified "met de voet kleppen,"—to stamp or beat with
the feet.

In support of his opinion of the antiquity of printing, Monsieur
Desroches refers to a manuscript in his possession, consisting of lives
of the saints and a chronicle written in the fourteenth century. At the
end of this manuscript was a catalogue of the books belonging to the
monastery of Wiblingen, the writing of which was much abbreviated,
and which appeared to him to be of the following century. Among
other entries in the catalogue was this: "(It.) dōicali īpv̄o lĭƀ° ſtm̄p^{to}
ī bappiro nō scrpo." On supplying the letters wanting Monsieur
Desroches says that we shall have the following words: "Item. Domi-
nicalia in parvo libro stampato in bappiro [papyro,] non scripto;"
that is, "Item. Dominicals [a form of prayer or portion of church
service] in a small book printed [or stamped] on paper, not written."
In the abbreviated word ſtm̄p^{to}, he says that the letter m could not
very well be distinguished; but the doubt which might thus arise he
considers to be completely resolved by the words "non scripto," and by
the following memorandum which occurs, in the same hand-writing, at
the foot of the page: "Anno Dñi 1340 viguit q̄ fēt stāpā Dñatos,"—

---

* The following is the French translation of Monsieur Desroches : " En ces temps mourut
de la mort commune à tous les hommes, Louis *cet excellent faiseur d'instrumens de musique*,
le meilleur artist qu'on eut vû jusques-là dans l'univers, en fait d'ouvrages mechaniques.
Il étoit de Vaelbeke en Brabant, et il en porta le nom. Il fut le premier qui inventa la
manière d'imprimer, qui est presentement en usage." The reason of Monsieur Desroches
for his periphrasis of the simple word "vedelare"—fidler—is as follows : " J'ai rendu
Vedelare par 'faiseur d'instrumens de musique.' Le mot radical est *vedel*, violin : par
consequent, *Vedelare* doit signifier celui qui en joue, ou qui en fait. Je me suis determiné
pour le dernier à cause des vers suivans, où il n'est point question de jouer mais de faire.
Si l'on préfère le premier, je ne m'y opposerai pas ; rien empêche que ce habile homme n'ait
été musicien."—Mem. de l'Acad. de Brux. tom. i. p. 536.

† Lettre de M. J. G[hesquiere] à M. l'Abbé Turberville Needham, directeur de l'Aca-
demie Impériale et Royale de Bruxelles.—Printed in l'Esprit des Journaux for June 1779,
pp. 232—260.

"In 1340 he flourished who caused Donatuses to be printed." If the catalogue were really of the period supposed by Monsieur Desroches, the preceding extracts would certainly prove that the art of printing or stamping books, though not from moveable types, was practised in the fourteenth century; but, as the date has not been ascertained, its contents cannot be admitted as evidence on the point in dispute. Monsieur Ghesquiere is inclined to think that the catalogue was not written before 1470; and, as the compiler was evidently an ignorant person, he thinks that in the note, "Anno Domini 1340 viguit qui fecit stampare Donatos," he might have written 1340 instead of 1440.

Although it has been asserted that the wood-cut of St. Christopher with the date 1423, and the wood-cut of the Annunciation—probably of the same period—were printed by means of a press, yet I consider it exceedingly doubtful if the press were employed to take impressions from wood-blocks before Gutemberg used it in his earliest recorded attempts to print with moveable types. I believe that in every one of the early block-books, where opportunity has been afforded of examining the back of each cut, unquestionable evidence has been discovered of their having been *printed*, if I may here use the term, by means of friction. Although there is no mention of a *press* which might be used to take impressions before the process between Gutemberg and the heirs of one of his partners, in 1439, yet "Prenters" were certainly known in Antwerp before his invention of printing with moveable types was brought to perfection. Desroches in his Essay on the Invention of Printing gives an extract from an order of the magistracy of Antwerp, in the year 1442, in favour of the fellowship or guild of St. Luke, called also the Company of Painters, which consisted of Painters, Statuaries, Stone-cutters, Glass-makers, Illuminators, and "*Prenters.*" This fellow-ship was doubtless similar to that of Venice, in whose favour a decree was made by the magistracy of that city in 1441, and of which some account has been given, at page 43, in the preceding chapter. There is evidence of a similar fellowship existing at Bruges in 1454; and John Mentelin, who afterwards established himself at Strasburg as a typo-grapher or printer proper, was admitted a member of the Painters' Company of that city as a "Chrysographus" or illuminator in 1447.*

Whether the "Prenters" of Antwerp in 1442 were acquainted with the use of the press, or not, is uncertain; but there can be little doubt of their not being *Printers*, as the word is now generally understood; that is, persons who printed books with moveable types. They were most likely block-printers, and such as engraved and printed cards and

---

* Lichtenberger, Initia Typographica, § De Prenteris ante inventam Typographiam, p. 140.—Lambinet, Recherches sur l'Origine de l'Imprimerie, p. 115.

images of saints ; and it would seem that typographers were not admitted
members of the society ; for of all the early typographers of Antwerp
the name of one only, Mathias Van der Goes, appears in the books of
the fellowship of St. Luke ; and he perhaps may have been admitted as
a wood-engraver, on account of the cuts in an herbal printed with his
types, without date, but probably between 1485 and 1490.

Ghesquiere, who successfully refuted the opinion of Desroches that
typography was known at Antwerp in 1442, was himself induced to
suppose that it was practised at Bruges in 1445, and that printed books
were then neither very scarce nor very dear in that city.* In an old
manuscript journal or memorandum book of Jean-le-Robèrt, abbot of
St. Aubert in the diocese of Cambray, he observed an entry stating that
the said abbot had purchased at Bruges, in January 1446, a " Doctrinale
gette en mole " for the use of his nephew. The words "gette en mole "
he conceives to mean, "printed in type ; " and he thinks that the
Doctrinale mentioned was the work which was subsequently printed
at Geneva, in 1478, under the title of Le Doctrinal de Sapience, and
at Westminster by Caxton, in 1489, under the title of The Doctrinal of
Sapyence. The Abbé Mercier de St. Leger, who wrote a reply to the
observations of Ghesquiere, with greater probability supposes that the
book was printed from engraved wood-blocks, and that it was the
" Doctrinale Alexandri Galli," a short grammatical treatise in monkish
rhyme, which at that period was almost as popular as the " Donatus,"
and of which odd leaves, printed on both sides, are still to be seen in
libraries which are rich in early specimens of printing.

Although there is every reason to believe that the early Printers
of Antwerp and Bruges were not acquainted with the use of moveable
types, yet the mention of such persons at so early a period, and the
notice of the makers " of cards and printed figures" at Venice in 1441,
sufficiently declare that, though wood engraving might be first established
as a profession in Suabia, it was known, and practised to a considerable
extent, in other countries previous to 1450.

The Cologne Chronicle, which was printed in 1499, has been most
unfairly quoted by the advocates of Coster in support of their assertions ;
and the passage which appeared most to favour their argument they have
ascribed to Ulric Zell, the first person who established a press at Cologne.
A shrewd German,† however, has most clearly shown, from the same
chronicle, that the actual testimony of Ulric Zell is directly in opposition

---

* Reflexions sur deux pièces relatives à l'Hist. de l'Imprimerie. Nivelles, 1780.—
Lambinet, Recherches, p. 394.

† Friedrich Lehne, Einige Bemerkungen über das Unternehmen der gelehrten Gesellschaft
zu Harlem, ihrer Stadt die Ehre der Erfindung der Buchdruckerkunst zu ertrotzen, S. 24—26.
Zweite Ausgabe, Mainz. 1825.

to the claims advanced by the advocates of Coster. The passage on which they rely is to the following effect : " Item : although the art [of printing] as it is now commonly practised, was discovered at Mentz, yet the first conception of it was discovered in Holland from the Donatuses, which before that time were printed there." This we are given to understand by Meerman and Koning is the statement of Ulric Zell. A little further on, however, the Chronicler, who in the above passage appears to have been speaking in his own person from popular report, thus proceeds : " But the first inventor of printing was a citizen of Mentz, though born at Strasburg,* named John Gutemberg : Item : from Mentz the above-named art first came to Cologne, afterwards to Strasburg, and then to Venice. This account of the commencement and progress of the said art was communicated to me by word of mouth by that worthy person Master Ulric Zell of Hanau, at the present time [1499] a printer in Cologne, through whom the said art was brought to Cologne." At this point the advocates of Coster stop, as the very next sentence deprives them of any advantage which they might hope to gain from the " impartial testimony of the Cologne Chronicle," the compiler of which proceeds as follows : " Item : there are certain *fanciful people* who say that books were printed before ; but *this is not true ;* foe in no country are books to be found printed before that time." †

That " Donatuses " and other small elementary books for the use of schools were printed from wood-blocks previous to the invention of typography there can be little doubt ; and it is by no means unlikely that they might be first printed in Holland or in Flanders. At any rate an opinion seems to have been prevalent at an early period that the idea of printing with moveable types was first derived from a " Donatus,"‡ printed from wood-blocks. In the petition of Conrad Sweinheim and Arnold Pannartz, two Germans, who first established

* This is a mistake into which the compiler of the chronicle printed at Rome, 1474, by Philippus de Lignamine, has also fallen. Gutemberg was not a native of Strasburg, but of Mentz.

† Mallinkrot appears to have been the first who gave a translation of the entire passage in the Cologne Chronicle which relates to the invention of printing. His version of the last sentence is as follows : " Reperiuntur Scioli aliquot qui dicant, dudum ante hæc tempora typorum ope libros excusos esse, qui tamen et se et alios decipiunt ; nullibi enim terrarum libri eo tempore impressi reperiuntur."—De Ortu et Progressu Artis Typographicæ, p. 38. Colon. Agrippinæ, 1640.

‡ Angelus Rocca mentions having seen a " Donatus " on parchment, at the commencement of which was written in the hand of Mariangelus Accursius, who flourished about 1530 : " Impressus est autem hic *Donatus* et *Confessionalia* primùm omnium anno MCCCCL. Admonitus certè fuit ex *Donato* Hollandiæ, prius impresso in tabula incisa."—Bibliotheca Vaticana commentario illustrata, 1591, cited by Prosper Marchand in his Hist. de l'Imprimerie, 2nde Partie, p. 35. It is likely that Accursius derived his information about a Donatus being printed in Holland from the Cologne Chronicle.

a press at Rome, addressed to Pope Sixtus IV. in 1472, stating the expense which they had incurred in printing books, and praying for assistance, they mention amongst other works printed by them, " DONATI pro puerulis, unde IMPRIMENDI INITIUM sumpsimus ; " that is : " Dona- tuses for boys, whence we have taken the beginning of printing." If this passage is to be understood as referring to the origin of typography, and not to the first proofs of their own press, it is the earliest and the best evidence on the point which has been adduced ; for it is very likely that both these printers had acquired a knowledge of their art at Mentz in the very office where it was first brought to perfection.

About the year 1400, Henne, or John Gænsfleisch de Sulgeloch, called also John Gutemberg zum Jungen, appears to have been born at Mentz. He had two brothers ; Conrad who died in 1424, and Friele who was living in 1459. He had also two sisters, Bertha and Hebele, who were both nuns of St. Clare at Mentz. Gutemberg had an uncle by his father's side, named Friele, who had three sons, named John, Friele, and Pederman, who were all living in 1459.

Gutemberg was descended of an honourable family, and he himself is said to have been by birth a knight.* It would appear that the family had been possessed of considerable property. They had one house in Mentz called zum Gænsfleisch, and another called zum Gudenberg, or Gutenberg, which Wimpheling translates, " Domum boni montis." The local name of Sulgeloch, or Sorgenloch, was derived from the name of a village where the family of Gænsfleisch had resided previous to their removing to Mentz. It seems probable that the house zum Jungen at Mentz came into the Gutembergs' possession by inheritance. It was in this house, according to the account of Trithemius, that the printing business was carried on during his partnership with Faust.†

When Gutemberg called himself der Junge, or junior, it was doubt- less to distinguish himself from Gænsfleisch der Elter, or senior, a name which frequently occurs in the documents printed by Koehler. Meerman has fixed upon the latter name for the purpose of giving to Gutemberg a brother of the same christian name, and of making him the thief who stole Coster's types. He also avails himself of an error committed by Wimpheling and others, who had supposed John Gutemberg and John Gænsfleisch to be two different persons. In two deeds of sale, however, of the date 1441 and 1442, entered in the Salic book of the church of

---

* Schwartz observes that in the instrument drawn up by the notary Ulric Helmasperger, Gutemberg is styled "*Juncker*," an honourable addition which was at that period ex- pressive of nobility.—Primaria quædam Documenta de Origine Typographiæ, p. 20, 4to. Altorfii, 1740.

† " Morabatur autem prædictus Joannes Gutenberg Moguntiæ in domo *zum Jungen*, quæ domus usque in præsentem diem [1513] illius novæ Artis nomine noscitur insignita."— Trithemii Chronicum Spanhemiense, ad annum 1450.

St. Thomas at Strasburg, he is thus expressly named : "*Joannes dictus Gensfleisch alias nuncupatus Gutenberg de Moguncia, Argentinæ commorans;*" that is, "John Gænsfleisch, otherwise named Gutemberg, of Mentz, residing at Strasburg." * Anthony à Wood, in his History of the University of Oxford, calls him Tossanus ; and Chevillier, in his Origine de l'Imprimerie de Paris, Toussaints. Seiz† is within an ace of making him a knight of the Golden Fleece. That he was a man of property is proved by various documents ; and those writers who have described him as a person of mean origin, or as so poor as to be obliged to labour as a common workman, are certainly wrong.

From a letter written by Gutemberg in 1424 to his sister Bertha it appears that he was then residing at Strasburg ; and it is also certain that in 1430 he was not living at Mentz ; for in an act of accommodation between the nobility and burghers of that city, passed in that year with the authority of the archbishop Conrad III., Gutemberg is mentioned among the nobles "*die ytzund nit inlendig sint*"—"who are not at present in the country." In 1434 there is positive evidence of his residing at Strasburg ; for in that year he caused the town-clerk of Mentz to be arrested for a sum of three hundred florins due to him from the latter city, and he agreed to his release at the instance of the magistrates of Strasburg within whose jurisdiction the arrest took place.‡ In 1436 he entered into partnership with Andrew Drytzehn and others ; and there is every reason to believe that at this period he was engaged in making experiments on the practicability of printing with moveable types, and that the chief object of his engaging with those persons was to obtain funds to enable him to perfect his invention.

From 1436 to 1444 the name of Gutemberg appears among the " *Constaflers*" or civic nobility of Strasburg. In 1437 he was summoned before the ecclesiastical judge of that city at the suit of Anne of Iron-Door,§ for breach of promise of marriage. It would seem that he afterwards fulfilled his promise, for in a tax-book of the city of Strasburg, Anne Gutemberg is mentioned, after Gutemberg had returned to Mentz, as paying the toll levied on wine.

Andrew Drytzehn, one of Gutemberg's partners, having died in 1438, his brothers George and Nicholas instituted a process against Gutemberg to compel him either to refund the money advanced by their brother, or to admit them to take his place in the partnership. From the depositions

---

* In the release which he grants to the town-clerk of Mentz, in 1434, he describes himself as, " Johann Gensefleisch der Junge, genant Gutemberg."

† In " Het derde Jubeljaer der uitgevondene Boekdrukkonst door Laurens Jansz Koster," p. 71. Harlem, 1740.—Oberlin, Essai d'Annales.

‡ The release is given in Schœpflin's Vindiciæ Typographicæ, Documentum I.

§ " *Ennelin zu der Iserin Thure.*" She was then living at Strasburg, and was of an honourable family, originally of Alsace.—Schœpflin. Vind. Typ. p. 17.

of the witnesses in this cause, which, together with the decision of the judges, are given at length by Schœpflin, there can be little doubt that one of the inventions which Gutemberg agreed to communicate to his partners was an improvement in the art of printing, such as it was at that period.

The following particulars concerning the partnership of Gutemberg with Andrew Drytzehn and others are derived from the recital of the case contained in the decision of the judges. Some years before his death, Andrew Drytzehn expressed a desire to learn one of Gutemberg's arts, for he appears to have been fond of trying new experiments, and the latter acceding to his request taught him a method of polishing stones, by which he gained considerable profit. Some time afterwards, Gutemberg, in company with a person named John Riff, began to exercise a certain art whose productions were in demand at the fair of Aix-la-Chapelle. Andrew Drytzehn, hearing of this, begged that the new art might be explained to him, promising at the same time to give whatever premium should be required. Anthony Heilman also made a similar request for his brother Andrew Heilman.* To both these applications Gutemberg assented, agreeing to teach them the art; it being stipulated that the two new partners were to receive a fourth part of the profits between them; that Riff was to have another fourth; and that the remaining half should be received by the inventor. It was also agreed that Gutemberg should receive from each of the new partners the sum of eighty florins of gold payable by a certain day, as a premium for communicating to them his art. The great fair of Aix-la-Chapelle being deferred to another year, Gutemberg's two new partners requested that he would communicate to them without reserve all his wonderful and rare inventions; to which he assented on condition that to the former sum of one hundred and sixty florins they should jointly advance two hundred and fifty more, of which one hundred were to be paid immediately, and the then remaining seventy-five florins due by each were to be paid at three instalments. Of the hundred florins stipulated to be paid in ready money, Andrew Heilman paid fifty, according to his engagement, while Andrew Drytzehn only paid forty, leaving ten due. The term of the partnership for carrying on the "wonderful art" was fixed at five years; and it was also agreed that if any of the partners should die within that period, his interest in the utensils and stock should become vested in the surviving partners, who at the completion of the term were to pay to the heirs of the deceased the sum of one

---

* When Andrew Heilman was proposed as a partner, Gutemberg observed that his friends would perhaps treat the business into which he was about to embark as mere jugglery [göckel werck], and object to his having anything to do with it.—Schœpflin, Vind. Typ. Document. p. 10.

hundred florins. Andrew Drytzehn having died within the period, and when there remained a sum of eighty-five florins unpaid by him, Gutemberg met the claim of his brothers by referring to the articles of partnership, and insisted that from the sum of one hundred florins which the surviving partners were bound to pay, the eighty-five remaining unpaid by the deceased should be deducted. The balance of fifteen florins thus remaining due from the partnership he expressed his willingness to pay, although according to the terms of the agreement it was not payable until the five years were expired, and would thus not be strictly due for some years to come. The claim of George Drytzehn to be admitted a partner, as the heir of his brother, he opposed, on the ground of his being unacquainted with the obligations of the partnership; and he also denied that Andrew Drytzehn had ever become security for the payment of any sum for lead or other things purchased on account of the business, except to Fridelin von Seckingen, and that this sum (which was owing for lead) Gutemberg himself paid. The judges having heard the allegations of both parties, and having examined the agreement between Gutemberg and Andrew Drytzehn, decided that the eighty-five florins which remained unpaid by the latter should be deducted from the hundred which were to be repaid in the event of any one of the partners dying; and that Gutemberg should pay the balance of fifteen florins to George and Nicholas Drytzehn, and that when this sum should be paid they should have no further claim on the partnership.*

From the depositions of some of the witnesses in this process, there can scarcely be a doubt that the "wonderful art" which Gutemberg was attempting to perfect was typography or printing with moveable types. Fournier† thinks that Gutemberg's attempts at printing, as may be gathered from the evidence in this cause, were confined to printing from wood-blocks; but such expressions of the witnesses as appear to relate to printing do not favour this opinion. As Gutemberg lived near the monastery of St. Arbogast, which was without the walls of the city, it appears that the attempts to perfect his invention were carried on in the house of his partner Andrew Drytzehn. Upon the death of the latter, Gutemberg appears to have been particularly anxious that "four *pieces*" which were in a "press" should be "distributed,"—making use of the very word which is yet used in Germany to express the distribution or separation of a form of types—so that no person should know what they were.

Hans Schultheis, a dealer in wood, and Ann his wife, depose to the following effect: After the death of Andrew Drytzehn, Gutemberg's

---

* This decision is dated " On the Eve of St. Lucia and St. Otilia, [12th December,] 1439."

† Traité de l'origine et des productions de l'Imprimerie primitive en taille de bois, Paris, 1758 ; et Remarques sur un Ouvrage, &c. pour servir de suite au Traité, Paris, 1762.

servant, Lawrence Beildeck, came to their house, and thus addressed their relation Nicholas Drytzehn : "Your deceased brother Andrew had four "pieces" placed under a press, and John Gutemberg requests that you will take them out and lay them separately [or apart from each other] upon the press so that no one may see what it is."

Conrad Saspach states that one day Andrew Heilman, a partner of Gutemberg's, came to him in the Merchants' Walk and said to him, "Conrad, as Andrew Drytzehn is dead, and *as you made the press* and know all about it, go and take the *pieces* † out of the press and separate [zerlege] them so that no person may know what they are." This witness intended to do as he was requested, but on making inquiry the day after St. Stephen's Day ‡ he found that the work was removed.

Lawrence Beildeck, Gutemberg's servant, deposes that after Andrew Drytzehn's death he was sent by his master to Nicholas Drytzehn to tell him not to show the press which he had in his house to any person. Beildeck also adds that he was desired by Gutemberg to go to the presses, and to open [or undo] the press which was fastened with two screws, so that the "pieces" [which were in it] should fall asunder. The said "pieces" he was then to place in or upon the press, so that no person might see or understand them.

Anthony Heilman, the brother of one of Gutemberg's partners, states that he knew of Gutemberg having sent his servant shortly before Christmas both to Andrew Heilman and Andrew Drytzehn to bring away all the "forms" [formen] that they might be separated in his presence, as he found several things in them of which he disapproved.§ The same witness also states that he was well aware of many people being wishful

---

* " Andres Dritzehn uwer bruder selige hat iiij stücke undenan inn einer *pressen* ligen, da hat uch Hanns Gutemberg gebetten das ir die darusz nement ünd uff die presse legent von einander so kan man nit gesehen was das ist."—Schœpflin, Vind. Typ. Document. p. 6.

† " Nym die stücke usz der *pressen* und *zerlege* sü von einander so weis nyemand was es ist :" literally : " Take the pieces out of the press and distribute [or separate] them, so that no man may know what it is."—Schœpflin, Vind. Typ. Document. p. 6. " The word *zerlegen*," says Lichtenberger, Initia Typograph. p. 11, " is used at the present day by printers to denote the distribution of the types which the compositor has set up." The original word " stücke" —pieces—is always translated " paginæ "—pages—by Schelhorn. Dr. Dibdin calls them " *forms* kept together by *two screws* or press-*spindles*."—Life of Caxton, in his edition of Ames's and Herbert's Typ. Antiq. p. lxxxvii. note.

‡ St. Stephen's Day is on 26th December. Andrew Drytzehn, being very ill, confessed himself to Peter Eckhart on Christmas-day, 1438, and it would seem that he died on the 27th.

§ " Dirre gezuge hat ouch geseit das er wol wisse das Gutenberg unlange vor Wihnahten sinen kneht sante zu den beden Andresen, alle *formen* zu holen, und würdent zur lossen das er ess sehe, un jn joch ettliche formen ruwete."—Schœpflin, Vind. Typ. Document. p. 12. The separate letters, which are now called "types," were frequently called " formæ " by the early printers and writers of the fifteenth century. They are thus named by Joh. and Vindelin de Spire in 1469 ; by Franciscus Philelphus in 1470 ; by Ludovicus Carbo in 1471 ; and by Phil. de Lignamine in 1474.—Lichtenberger, Init. Typ. p. 11.

to see the press, and that Gutemberg had desired that they should send some person to prevent its being seen.

Hans Dünne, a goldsmith, deposed that about three years before, he had done work for Gutemberg on account of printing alone to the amount of a hundred florins.[*]

As Gutemberg evidently had kept his art as secret as possible, it is not surprising that the notice of it by the preceding witnesses should not be more explicit. Though it may be a matter of doubt whether his invention was merely an improvement on block-printing, or an attempt to print with moveable types, yet, bearing in mind that express mention is made of a *press* and of *printing*, and taking into consideration his subsequent partnership with Faust, it is morally certain that Gutemberg's attention had been occupied with some new discovery relative to printing at least three years previous to December 1439.

If Gutemberg's attempts when in partnership with Andrew Drytzehn and others did not extend beyond block-printing, and if the four "pieces" which were in the press are assumed to have been four engraved blocks, it is evident that the mere unscrewing them from the "*chase*" or frame in which they might be enclosed, would not in the least prevent persons from knowing what they were; and it is difficult to conceive how the undoing of the two screws would cause "the pieces" to fall asunder. If, however, we suppose the four "pieces" to have been so many pages of moveable types screwed together in a frame, it is easy to conceive the effect of undoing the two screws which held it together. On this hypothesis, Gutemberg's instructions to his servant, and Anthony Heilman's request to Conrad Saspach, the maker of the press, that he would take out the "pieces" and distribute them, are at once intelligible. If Gutemberg's attempts were confined to block-printing, he could certainly have no claim to the discovery of a new art, unless indeed we are to suppose that his invention consisted in the introduction of the press for the purpose of taking impressions; but it is apparent that his anxiety was not so much to prevent people seeing the press as to keep them ignorant of the purpose for which it was employed, and to conceal what was in it.

The evidence of Hans Dünne the goldsmith, though very brief, is in favour of the opinion that Gutemberg's essays in printing were made with moveable types of metal; and it also is corroborated by the fact of *lead* being one of the articles purchased on account of the partnership. It is certain that goldsmiths were accustomed to engrave letters and figures upon silver and other metals long before the art of copper-plate printing was introduced; and Fournier not attending to the distinction

---

[*] " Hanns Dünne der goltsmyt hat gesait, das er vor dryen jaren oder daby Gutemberg by den hundert guldin verdienet habe, alleine das zu dem *trucken* gehöret."—Schœpflin, Vind. Typ. Document. p. 13.

between simple engraving on metal and engraving on a plate for the purpose of taking impressions on paper, has made a futile objection to the argument of Bär,* who very naturally supposes that the hundred florins which Hans Dünne received from Gutemberg for work done on account of printing alone, might be on account of his having cut the types, the formation of which by means of punches and matrices was a subsequent improvement of Peter Scheffer.   It is indeed difficult to conceive in what manner a goldsmith could earn a hundred florins for work done on account of printing, except in his capacity as an engraver ; and as I can see no reason to suppose that Hans Dünne was an engraver on wood, I am inclined to think that he was employed by Gutemberg to cut the letters on separate pieces of metal.

There is no evidence to show that Gutemberg succeeded in printing any books at Strasburg with moveable types : and the most likely conclusion seems to be that he did not.   As the process between him and the Drytzehns must have given a certain degree of publicity to his invention, it might be expected that some notice would have been taken of its first-fruits had he succeeded in making it available in Strasburg. On the contrary, all the early writers in the least entitled to credit, who have spoken of the invention of printing with moveable types, agree in ascribing the honour to Mentz, after Gutemberg had returned to that city and entered into partnership with Faust.   Two writers, however, whose learning and research are entitled to the highest respect, are of a different opinion.   "It has been doubted," says Professor Oberlin, "that Gutemberg ever printed books at Strasburg.   It is, nevertheless, probable that he did ; for he had a press there in 1439, and continued to reside in that city for five years afterwards.   He might print several of those small tracts without date, in which the inequality of the letters and rudeness of the workmanship indicate the infancy of the art.   Schœpflin thinks that he can identify some of them ; and the passages cited by him clearly show that printing had been carried on there." †   It is, however, to be remarked that the passages cited by Schœpflin, and referred to by Oberlin,

---

* The words of Bär, who was almoner of the Swedish chapel at Paris in 1761, are these : "Tout le monde sait que dans ce temps les orfèvres exerçoient aussi l'art de la gravûre ; et nous concluons de-là que Guttemberg a commencé par des caractères de bois, que de-là il a passé aux caractères de plomb."   On this passage Fournier makes the following observations : "Tout le monde sait au contraire que dans ce temps il n'y avoit pas un seul graveur dans le genre dont vous parlez, et cela par une raison bien simple : c'est que cet art de la gravûre n'a été inventé que vingt-trois ans après ce que vous citez, c'est-à-dire en 1460, par *Masso Piniguera*."—Remarques, &c. p. 20.   Bär mentioned no particular kind of engraving ; and the name of the Italian goldsmith who is supposed to have been the first who discovered the art of taking impressions from a plate on paper, was Finiguerra, not Piniguera, as Fournier, with his usual inaccuracy, spells it.

† Essai d'Annales de la Vie de Jean Gutenberg, par Jer. J. Oberlin.   8vo.   Strasbourg, An ix. [1802.]

by no means show that the art of printing had been practised at Strasburg by Gutemberg; nor do they clearly prove that it had been continuously carried on there by his partners or others to the time of Mentelin, who probably established himself there as a printer in 1466.

It has been stated that Gutemberg's first essays in typography were made with wooden types; and Daniel Specklin, an architect of Strasburg, who died in 1589, professed to have seen some of them. According to his account there was a hole pierced in each letter, and they were arranged in lines by a string being passed through them. The lines thus formed like a string of beads were afterwards collected into pages, and submitted to the press. Particles and syllables of frequent occurrence were not formed of separate letters, but were cut on single pieces of wood. We are left to conjecture the size of those letters; but if they were sufficiently large to allow of a hole being bored through them, and to afterwards sustain the action of the press, they could not well be less than the missal types with which Faust and Scheffer's Psalter is printed. It is however likely that Specklin had been mistaken; and that he had supposed some old initial letters, large enough to admit of a hole being bored through them without injury, to have been such as were generally used in the infancy of the art.

In 1441 and 1442, Gutemberg, who appears to have been always in want of money, executed deeds of sale to the dean and chapter of the collegiate church of St. Thomas at Strasburg, whereby he assigned to them certain rents and profits in Mentz which he inherited from his uncle John Leheymer, who had been a judge in that city. In 1443 and 1444 Gutemberg's name still appears in the rate or tax book of Strasburg; but after the latter year it is no longer to be found. About 1445, it is probable that he returned to Mentz, his native city, having apparently been unsuccessful in his speculations at Strasburg. From this period to 1450 it is likely that he continued to employ himself in attempts to perfect his invention of typography. In 1450 he entered into partnership with John Faust, a goldsmith and native of Mentz, and it is from this year that Trithemius dates the invention. In his Annales Hirsaugienses, under the year 1450, he gives the following account of the first establishment and early progress of the art. "About this time [1450], in the city of Mentz upon the Rhine, in Germany, and not in Italy as some have falsely stated, this wonderful and hitherto unheard of art of printing was conceived and invented by John Gutemberg, a citizen of Mentz. He had expended nearly all his substance on the invention; and being greatly pressed for want of means, was about to abandon it in despair, when, through the advice and with the money furnished by John Faust, also a citizen of Mentz, he completed his undertaking. At first they printed the vocabulary called the *Catholicon*, from letters cut on blocks of wood.

K 2

These letters however could not be used to print anything else, as they were not separately moveable, but were cut on the blocks as above stated. To this invention succeeded others more subtle, and they afterwards invented a method of casting the shapes, named by them *matrices*, of all the letters of the Roman alphabet, from which they again cast letters of copper or tin, sufficient to bear any pressure to which they might be subjected, and which they had formerly cut by hand. As I have heard, nearly thirty years ago, from Peter Scheffer, of Gernsheim, citizen of Mentz, who was son-in-law of the first inventor, great difficulties attended the first establishment of this art; for when they had commenced printing a Bible they found that upwards of four thousand florins had been expended before they had finished the third *quaternion* [or quire of four sheets]. Peter Scheffer, an ingenious and prudent man, at first the servant, and afterwards, as has been already said, the son-in-law of John Faust, the first inventor, discovered the more ready mode of casting the types, and perfected the art as it is at present exercised. These three for some time kept their method of printing a secret, till at length it was divulged by some workmen whose assistance they could not do without. It first passed to Strasburg, and gradually to other nations." *

As Trithemius finished the work which contains the preceding account in 1514, Marchand concludes that he must have received his information from Scheffer about 1484, which would be within thirty-five years of Gutemberg's entering into a partnership with Faust. Although Trithemius had his information from so excellent an authority, yet the account which he has thus left is far from satisfactory. Schœpflin, amongst other objections to its accuracy, remarks that Trithemius is wrong in stating that the invention of moveable types was subsequent to Gutemberg's connexion with Faust, seeing that the former had previously employed them at Strasburg; and he also observes that in the learned abbot's account there is no distinct mention made of moveable letters cut by hand, but that we are led to infer that the improvement of casting types from matrices immediately followed the printing of the Catholicon from wood-blocks. The words of Trithemius on this point are as follows: "Post hæc, inventis successerunt subtiliora, inveneruntque modum fundendi formas omnium Latini alphabeti litterarum, quas ipsi *matrices* nominabant, ex quibus rursum æneos sive stanneos characteres fundebant ad omnem pressuram sufficientes quos prius manibus sculpebant." From this passage it might be objected in opposition to the opinion of Schœpflin: † 1. That the "subtiliora,"—more subtle contrivances, mentioned *before* the invention of casting moveable letters, may relate to the cutting

---

* Trithemii Annales Hirsaugienses, tom. ii. ad annum 1450. The original passage is printed in Prosper Marchand's Histoire de l'Imprimerie, 2nde Partie, p. 7.

† Vindiciæ Typographicæ, pp. 77, 78.

of such letters by hand. 2. That the word "quos" is to be referred to the antecedent "æneos sive stanneos characteres,"—letters of copper or tin, —and not to the "characteres in tabulis ligneis scripti,"—letters engraved on wood-blocks,—which are mentioned in a preceding sentence. The inconsistency of Trithemius in ascribing the origin of the art to Gutemberg, and twice immediately afterwards calling Scheffer the son-in-law of "the first inventor," Faust, is noticed by Schœpflin, and has been pointed out by several other writers.

In 1455 the partnership between Gutemberg and Faust was dissolved at the instance of the latter, who preferred a suit against his partner for the recovery, with interest, of certain sums of money which he had advanced. There is no mention of the time when the partnership commenced in the sentence or award of the judge ; but Schwartz infers, from the sum claimed on account of interest, that it must have been in August 1449. It is probable that his conclusion is very near the truth ; for most of the early writers who have mentioned the invention of printing at Mentz by Gutemberg and Faust, agree in assigning the year 1450 as that in which they began to practise the new art. It is conjectured by Santander that Faust, who seems to have been a selfish character,* sought an opportunity of quarrelling with Gutemberg as soon as Scheffer had communicated to him his great improvement of forming the letters by means of punches and matrices.

The document containing the decision of the judges was drawn up by Ulric Helmasperger, a notary, on 6th November, 1455, in the presence of Peter Gernsheim [Scheffer], James Faust, the brother of John, Henry Keffer, and others.† From the statement of Faust, as recited in this instrument, it appears that he had first advanced to Gutemberg eight hundred florins at the annual interest of six per cent., and afterwards eight hundred florins more. Gutemberg having neglected to pay the interest, there was owing by him a sum of two hundred and fifty florins on account of the first eight hundred ; and a further sum of one hundred and forty on account of the second. In consequence of Gutemberg's

---

* In the first work which issued from Faust and Scheffer's press, with a date and the printer's names,—the Psalter of 1457,—and in several others, Scheffer appears on an equal footing with Faust. In the colophon of an edition of Cicero de Officiis, 1465, Faust has inserted the following degrading words : " Presens opus Joh. Fust Moguntinus civis . . . . arte quadam perpulcra Petri manu *pueri mei* feliciter effeci." His partner, to whose ingenuity he is chiefly indebted for his fame, is here represented in the character of a menial. Peter Scheffer, of Gernsheim, clerk, who perfected the art of printing, is now degraded to " Peter, my *boy*," by whose hand—not by his ingenuity—John Faust exercises a certain beautiful art.

† Henry Keffer was employed in Gutemberg and Faust's printing-office. He afterwards went to Nuremberg, where his name appears as a printer, in 1473, in conjunction with John Sensenschmid.—Primaria quædam Documenta de origine Typographiæ, edente C. G. Schwartzio. 8vo. Altorfii, 1740.

neglecting to pay the interest, Faust states that he had incurred a further expense of thirty-six florins from having to borrow money both of Christians and Jews. For the capital advanced by him, and arrears of interest, he claimed on the whole two thousand and twenty florins.*

In answer to these allegations Gutemberg replied : that the first eight hundred florins which he received of Faust were advanced in order to purchase utensils for printing, which were assigned to Faust as a security for his money. It was agreed between them that Faust should contribute three hundred florins annually for workmen's wages and house-rent, and for the purchase of parchment, paper, ink, and other things.† It was also stipulated that in the event of any disagreement arising between them, the printing materials assigned to Faust as a security should become the property of Gutemberg on his repaying the sum of eight hundred florins. This sum, however, which was advanced for the completion of the work, Gutemberg did not think himself bound to expend on book-work alone ; and although it was expressed in their agreement that he should pay six florins in the hundred for an annual interest, yet Faust assured him that he would not accept of it, as the eight hundred florins were not paid down at once, as by their agreement they ought to have been. For the second sum of eight hundred florins he was ready to render Faust an account. For interest or usury he considered that he was not liable. ‡

The judges, having heard the statements of both parties, decided that Gutemberg should repay Faust so much of the capital as had not been expended in the business ; and that on Faust's producing witnesses, or swearing that he had borrowed upon interest the sums advanced, Gutemberg should pay him interest also, according to their agreement. Faust having made oath that he had borrowed 1550 florins, which he paid over to Gutemberg, to be employed by him for their common benefit, and that he had paid yearly interest, and was still liable on account of the same, the notary, Ulric Helmasperger, signed his attestation of the award on

---

* " Er [Johan Fust] denselben solt fürter under Christen und Iudden hab müssen ussne-men, und davor sess und dreyssig Gulden ungevärlich zu guter Rechnung zu Gesuch geben, das sich also zusamen mit dem Hauptgeld ungevärlich trifft an zvvytusend und zvvanzig Gulden." Schwartz in an observation upon this passage conceives the sum of 2,020 florins to be thus made up : capital advanced, in two sums of 800 each, 1,600 florins : interest 390 ; on account of compound interest, incurred by Faust, 36 ; making in all 2,026. He thinks that 2,020 florins only were claimed as a round sum ; and that the second sum of 800 florins was advanced in October 1452.—Primaria quædam Documenta, pp. 9—14.

† " .... und das JOHANNES [FUST] ym ierlichen 300 Gulden vor Kosten geben, und auch Gesinde Lone, Huss Zinss, Vermet, Papier, Tinte, &c. verlegen solte." Primaria quædam Doc. p. 10.

‡ " .... von den ubrigen 800 Gulden vvegen begert er ym ein rechnung zu thun, so gestett er auch ym keins Soldes noch Wuchers, und hofft ym im rechten darum nit pflichtigk sin." Primaria quædam Doc. p. 11.

6th November, 1455.* It would appear that Gutemberg not being able to repay the money was obliged to relinquish the printing materials to Faust.

Salmuth, who alludes to the above document in his annotations upon Pancirollus, has most singularly perverted its meaning, by representing Gutemberg as the person who advanced the money, and Faust as the ingenious inventor who was sued by his rich partner. "From this it evidently appears," says he, after making Gutemberg and Faust exchange characters, "that Gutemberg was not the first who invented and practised typography; but that some years after its invention he was admitted a partner by John Faust, to whom he advanced money." If for "Gutemberg" we read "Faust," and *vice versâ*, the account is correct.

Whether Faust, who might be an engraver as well as a goldsmith, assisted Gutemberg or not by engraving the types, does not appear. It is stated that Gutemberg's earliest productions at Mentz were an alphabet cut on wood, and a Donatus executed in the same manner. Trithemius mentions a "*Catholicon*" engraved on blocks of wood as one of the first books printed by Gutemberg and Faust, and this Heineken thinks was the same as the Donatus.† Whatever may have been the book which Trithemius describes as a "Catholicon," it certainly was not the "*Catholicon Joannis Januensis*," a large folio which appeared in 1460 without the name or residence of the printer, but which is supposed to have been printed by Gutemberg after the dissolution of his partnership with Faust.

It has been stated that previous to the introduction of metal types Gutemberg and Faust used moveable types of wood; and Schœpflin speaks confidently of such being used at Strasburg by Mentelin long after Scheffer had introduced the improved method of forming metal types by means of punches and matrices. On this subject, however, Schœpflin's opinion is of very little weight, for on whatever relates to the practice of typography or wood engraving he was very slightly informed. He fancies that all the books printed at Strasburg previous to the appearance of *Vincentii Bellovacensis Speculum Historiale* in 1473, were printed with moveable types of wood. It is, however, doubtful if ever a single book was printed in this manner.

* Mercier, who is frequently referred to as an authority on subjects connected with Bibliography, has, in his supplement to Prosper Marchand's Histoire de l'Imprimerie, confounded this document with that containing an account of the process between the Drytzehns and Gutemberg at Strasburg in 1439; and Heineken, at p. 255 of his Idée Générale, has committed the same mistake.

† " Je crois, que ces tables [deux planches de bois autrefois chez le Duc de la Valliere] sont du livre que le Chroniqueur de Cologne appelle un *Donat* et que *Trithem* nomme un *Catholicon*, (livre universel,) ce qu'on a confondu ensuite avec le grand ouvrage intitulé *Catholicon Januensis*."—Idée Générale, p. 258.

Willett in his Essay on Printing, published in the eleventh volume of the Archæologia, not only says that no entire book was ever printed with wooden types, but adds, "I venture to pronounce it impossible." He has pronounced rashly. Although it certainly would be a work of considerable labour to cut a set of moveable letters of the size of what is called Donatus type, and sufficient to print such a book, yet it is by no means impossible. That such books as "*Eyn Manung der Cristenheit widder die durken,*" of which a fac-simile is given by Aretin, and the first and second Donatuses, of which specimens are given by Fischer, might be printed from wooden types I am perfectly satisfied, though I am decidedly of opinion that they were not. Marchand has doubted the possibility of printing with wooden types, which he observes would be apt to warp when wet for the purpose of cleaning; but it is to be observed that they would not require to be cleaned before they were used.

Fournier, who was a letter-founder, and who occasionally practised wood engraving, speaks positively of the Psalter first printed by Faust and Scheffer in 1457, and again in 1459, being printed with wooden types; and he expresses his conviction of the practicability of cutting and printing with such types, provided that they were not of a smaller size than Great Primer Roman. Meerman shows the possibility of using such types; and Camus caused two lines of the Bible, supposed to have been printed by Gutemberg, to be cut in separate letters on wood, and which sustained the action of the press.* Lambinet says, it is certain that Gutemberg cut moveable letters of wood, but he gives no authority for the assertion; and I am of opinion that no unexceptionable testimony on this point can be produced. The statements of Serarius and Paulus Pater,† who profess to have seen such ancient wooden types at Mentz, are entitled to as little credit as Daniel Specklin, who asserted that he had seen such at Strasburg. They may have seen large initial letters of wood with holes bored through, but scarcely any lower-case letters which were ever used in printing any book.

That experiments might be made by Gutemberg with wooden types I can believe, though I have not been able to find any sufficient authority for the fact. Of the possibility of cutting moveable types of a certain size in wood, and of printing a book with them, I am convinced from experiment; and could convince others, were it worth the expense, by

---

* Oberlin, Essai d'Annales de la Vie de Gutenberg.

† " . . . . ligneos typos, ex buxi frutice, perforatos in medio, ut zona colligari una jungique commode possint, ex Fausti officina reliquos, Moguntiæ aliquando me conspexisse memini." —Paulus Pater, in Dissertatione de Typis Literarum, &c. p. 10. 4to. Lipsiæ, 1710. Heineken, at p. 254 of his Idée Gén., declares himself to be convinced that Gutemberg had cut separate letters on wood, but he thinks that no person would be able to cut a quantity sufficient to print whole sheets, and, still less, large volumes as many pretend.

printing a fac-simile, from wooden types, of any page of any book which is of an earlier date than 1462. But, though convinced of the possibility of printing small works in letters of a certain size, with wooden types, I have never seen any early specimens of typography which contained positive and indisputable indications of having been printed in that manner. It was, until of late, confidently asserted by persons who pretended to have a competent knowledge of the subject, that the text of the celebrated Adventures of Theurdank, printed in 1517, had been engraved on wood-blocks, and their statement was generally believed. There cannot, however, now be a doubt in the mind of any person who examines the book, and who has the slightest knowledge of wood engraving and printing, of the text being printed with metal types.

During the partnership of Gutemberg and Faust it is likely that they printed some works, though there is scarcely one which can be assigned to them with any degree of certainty. One of the supposed earliest productions of typography is a letter of indulgence conceded on the 12th of August, 1451, by Pope Nicholas V, to Paulin Zappe, counsellor and ambassador of John, King of Cyprus. It was to be in force for three years from the 1st of May, 1452, and it granted indulgence to all persons who within that period should contribute towards the defence of Cyprus against the Turks. Four copies of this indulgence are known, printed on vellum in the manner of a patent or brief. The characters are of a larger size than those of the "Durandi Rationale," 1459, or of the Latin Bible printed by Faust and Scheffer in 1462. The following date appears at the conclusion of one of the copies: "Datum *Erffurdie* sub anno Domini m cccc liiij, die vero *quinta decima* mensis *novembris.*" The words which are here printed in Italic, are in the original written with a pen. A copy of the same indulgence discovered by Professor Gebhardi is more complete. It has at the end, a "*Forma plenissimæ absolutionis et remissionis in vita et in mortis articulo,*"—a form of plenary absolution and remission in life and at the point of death. At the conclusion is the following date, the words in Italics being inserted with a pen: "Datum in *Luneborch* anno Domini m cccc l *quinto,* die vero *vicesima sexta* mensis *Januarii.*" Heineken, who saw this copy in the possession of Breitkopf, has observed that in the original date, m cccc liiij, the last four characters had been effaced and the word *quinto* written with a pen; but yet in such a manner that the numerals iiij might still be perceived. In two copies of this indulgence in the possession of Earl Spencer, described by Dr. Dibdin in the Bibliotheca Spenceriana, vol. i. p. 44, the final units (iiij) have not had the word "quinto" overwritten, but have been formed with a pen into the numeral V. In the catalogue of Dr. Kloss's library, No. 1287, it is stated that a fragment of a "Donatus" there described, consisting of two leaves of parchment, is printed with the same type as the Mazarine Bible; and it is added, on the authority of George Appleyard, Esq., Earl Spencer's librarian, that the " Littera Indulgentiæ" of Pope Nicholas V, in his lordship's possession, contains two lines printed with the same type.   Breitkopf had some doubts respecting this instrument; but a writer in the Jena Literary Gazette is certainly wrong in supposing that it had been ante-dated ten years.   It was only to be in force for three years; and Pope Nicholas V, by whom it was granted, died on the 24th March, 1455.*   Two words, UNIVERSIS and PAULINUS, which are printed in capitals in the first two lines, are said to be of the same type as those of a Bible of which Schelhorn has given a specimen in his " Dissertation on an early Edition of the Bible," Ulm, 1760.

The next earliest specimen of typography with a date is the tract entitled "*Eyn Manung der Cristenheit widder die durken*,"—An Appeal to Christendom against the Turks,—which has been alluded to at page 136. A lithographic fac-simile of the whole of this tract, which consists of nine printed pages of a quarto size, is given by Aretin at the end of his " Essay on the earliest historical results of the invention of Printing," published at Munich in 1808.   This " Appeal" is in German rhyme, and it consists of exhortations, arranged under every month in the manner of a calendar, addressed to the pope, the emperor, to kings, princes, bishops, and free states, encouraging them to take up arms and resist the Turks. The exhortation for January is addressed to Pope Nicholas V, who died, as has been observed, in March 1455.   Towards the conclusion of the prologue is the date "*Als man zelet noch din' geburt offenbar m.cccc.lv. iar sieben wochen und iiii do by von nativitatis bis esto michi.*"   At the conclusion of the exhortation for December are the following words. " Eyn gut selig nuwe Jar:" A happy new year! From these circumstances Aretin is of opinion that the tract was printed towards the end of 1454. M. Bernhart, however, one of the superintendents of the Royal Library at Munich, of which Aretin was the principal director, has questioned the accuracy of this date; and from certain allusions in the exhortation for December, has endeavoured to show that the correct date ought to be 1472.†

Fischer in looking over some old papers discovered a calendar of a folio size, and printed on one side only, for 1457.   The letters, according to his description, resemble those of a Donatus, of which he has given a specimen in the third part of his Typographic Rarities, and he supposes that both the Donatus and the Calendar were printed by Gutemberg. ‡

* Oberlin, Essai d'Annales de la Vie de Gutenberg.
† Dr. Dibdin, Bibliog. Tour, vol. iii. p. 135, second edition.
‡ Gotthelf Fischer, Notice du premier livre imprimé avec date. 4to. Mayence, An xi. Typographisch. Seltenheit. 6te. Lieferung, S. 25. 8vo. Nürnberg, 1804.   When Fischer

It is, however, certain that the Donatus which he ascribed to Gutemberg was printed by Peter Scheffer, and in all probability after Faust's death ; and from the similarity of the type it is likely that the Calendar was printed at the same office. Fischer, having observed that the large ornamental capitals of this Donatus were the same as those in the Psalter printed by Faust and Scheffer in 1457, was led most erroneously to conclude that the large ornamental letters of the Psalter, which were most likely of wood, had been cut by Gutemberg. The discovery of a Donatus with Peter Scheffer's imprint has completely destroyed his conjectures, and invalidated the arguments advanced by him in favour of the Mazarine Bible being printed by Gutemberg alone.

As Trithemius and the compiler of the Cologne Chronicle have mentioned a Bible as one of the first books printed by Gutemberg and Faust, it has been a fertile subject of discussion among bibliographers to ascertain the identical edition to which the honour was to be awarded. It seems, however, to be now generally admitted that the edition called the Mazarine * is the best entitled to that distinction. In 1789 Maugerard produced a copy of this edition to the Academy of Metz, containing memoranda which seem clearly to prove that it was printed at least as early as August 1456. As the partnership between Gutemberg and Faust was only dissolved in November 1455, it is almost impossible that such could have been printed by either of them separately in the space of eight months ; and as there seems no reason to believe that any other typographical establishment existed at that period, it is most likely that this was the identical edition alluded to by Trithemius as having cost 4,000 florins before the partners, Gutemberg and Faust, had finished the third quaternion, or quire of four sheets.

The copy produced by Maugerard is printed on paper, and is now in the Royal Library at Paris. It is bound in two volumes ; and every complete page consists of two columns, each containing forty-two lines. At the conclusion of the first volume the person by whom it was rubricated † and bound has written the following memorandum : *" Et sic est finis prime partis biblie. Scr. Veteris testamenti. Illuminata seu rubricata et illuminata p' henricum Albeh alius Cremer anno dn'i m.cccc.lvi festo Bartholomei apli—Deo gratias—alleluja."* At the end of the second

---

published his account of the Calendar, Aretin had not discovered the tract entitled " *Eyn Manung der Cristenheit widder die durken.*"

* It is called the Mazarine Bible in consequence of the first known copy being discovered in the library formed by Cardinal Mazarine. Dr. Dibdin, in his Bibliographical Tour, vol. ii. p. 191, mentions having seen not fewer than ten or twelve copies of this edition, which he says must not be designated as " of the very first degree of rarity." An edition of the Bible, supposed to have been printed at Bamberg by Albert Pfister about 1461, is much more scarce.

† In most of the early printed books the capitals were left to be inserted in red ink by the pen or pencil of the " rubricator."

volume the same person has written the date in words at length : " *Iste liber illuminatus, ligatus & completus est p' henricum Cremer vicariū ecclesie collegatʒ Sancti Stephani maguntini sub anno D'ni millesimo quadringentesimo quinquagesimo sexto festo assumptionis gloriose virginis Marie. Deo gracias alleluja.*" * Fischer † says that this last memorandum assigns "einen spatern tag"—a later day—to the end of the rubricator's work. In this he is mistaken ; for the feast of the Assumption of the Virgin, when the *second* volume was finished, is on the 15th of August : while the feast of St. Bartholomew, the day on which he finished the *first*, falls on August 24th. Lambinet, ‡ who doubts the genuineness of those inscriptions, makes the circumstance of the second volume being finished nine days before the first, a ground of objection. This seeming inconsistency however can by no means be admitted as a proof of the inscriptions being spurious. It is indeed more likely that the rubricator might actually finish the second volume before the first, than that a modern forger, intent to deceive, should not have been aware of the objection.

The genuineness of the inscriptions is, however, confirmed by other evidence which no mere conjecture can invalidate. On the last leaf of this Bible there is a memorandum written by Berthold de Steyna, vicar of the parochial church of " Ville-Ostein," § to the sacrist of which the Bible belonged. The sum of this memorandum is that on St. George's day [23d April] 1457 there was chaunted, for the first time by the said Berthold, the mass of the holy sacrament. In the Carthusian monastery without the walls of Mentz, Schwartz ‖ says that he saw a copy of this edition, the last leaves of which were torn out ; but that in an old catalogue he perceived an entry stating that this Bible was presented to the monastery by Gutemberg and Faust. If the memorandum in the catalogue could be relied on as genuine, it would appear that this Bible had been completed before the dissolution of Gutemberg and Faust's partnership in November 1455.

Although not a single work has been discovered with Gutemberg's imprint, yet there cannot be a doubt of his having established a press of his own, and printed books at Mentz after the partnership between him and Faust had been dissolved. In the chronicle printed by Philip de Lignamine at Rome in 1474, it is expressly stated, under the year 1458,

---

* There are fac-simile tracings of those memorandums, on separate slips of paper, in the copy of the Mazarine Bible in the King's Library at the British Museum ; and fac-simile engravings of them are given in the M'Carthy Catalogue.

† Typograph. Seltenheit. S. 20, 3te. Lieferung.

‡ Recherches sur l'Origine de l'Imprimerie, p. 135.

§ Oberlin says that " Ville-Ostein" lies near Erfurth, and is in the diocese of Mentz.

‖ Index librorum sub incunabula typograph. impressorum. 1739 ; cited by Fischer, Typograph. Seltenheit. S. 21, 3te. Lieferung.

that there were then two printers at Mentz skilful in printing on parchment with metal types. The name of one was *Cutemberg,* and the other Faust; and it was known that each of them could print three hundred sheets in a day.* On St. Margaret's day, 20th July, 1459, Gutemberg, in conjunction with his brother Friele and his cousins John, Friele, and Pederman, executed a deed in favour of the convent of St. Clara at Mentz, in which his sister Hebele was a nun. In this document, which is preserved among the archives of the university of Mentz, there occurs a passage, "which makes it as clear," says Fischer, who gives the deed entire, " as the finest May-day noon, that Gutemberg had not only printed books at that time, but that he intended to print more." The passage alluded to is to the following effect: " And with respect to the books which I, the above-named John, have given the library of the said convent, they shall remain for ever in the said library; and I, the above-named John, will furthermore give to the library of the said convent all such books required for pious uses and the service of God,—whether for reading or singing, or for use according to the rules of the order,—as I, the above-named John, have printed or shall hereafter print." †

That Gutemberg had a press of his own is further confirmed by a bond or deed of obligation executed by Dr. Conrad Homery on the Friday after St. Matthias' day, 1468, wherein he acknowledges having received " certain forms, letters, utensils, materials, and other things belonging to printing," left by John Gutemberg deceased ; and he binds himself to the archbishop Adolphus not to use them beyond the territory of Mentz, and in the event of his selling them to give a preference to a person belonging to that city.

The words translated " certain forms, letters, utensils, materials, and other things belonging to printing," in the preceding paragraph, are in the original enumerated as : " *etliche formen, buchstaben, instrument, gezuge und anders zu truckwerck gehoerende.*" As there is a distinction made between " formen " and " buchstaben,"—literally, " forms " and " letters," —Schwartz is inclined to think that by " formen " engraved wood-blocks might be meant, and he adduces in favour of his opinion the word " formen-schneider," the old German name for a wood-engraver. One or more pages of type when wedged into a rectangular iron frame called a " chase," and ready for the press, is termed a " form " both by English and German printers; but Schwartz thinks that such were not the " forms "

* Philippi de Lignamine Chronica Summorum Pontificum Imperatorumque, anno 1474, Romæ impressa. A second edition of this chronicle was printed at Rome in 1476 by "Schurener de Bopardia." In both editions Gutemberg is called " Jacobus,"—James, and is said to be a native of Strasburg. Under the same year John Mentelin is mentioned as a printer at Strasburg.

† Fischer, Typograph. Seltenheit. S. 44, 1ste. Lieferung. In this instrument Gutemberg describes himself as " Henne Genssfleisch von Sulgeloch, genennt Gudinberg."

mentioned in the document. As there appears to be a distinction also between "*instrument*" and "*gezuge*,"—translated utensils and materials, —he supposes that the latter word may be used to signify the metal of which the types were formed. He observes that German printers call their old worn-out types "*der Zeug*"—literally, "stuff," and that the mixed metal of which types are composed is also known as "der Zeug, oder Metall." * It is to be remembered that the earliest printers were also their own letter-founders.

The work called the Catholicon, compiled by Johannes de Balbis, Januensis, a Dominican, which appeared in 1460 without the printer's name, has been ascribed to Gutemberg's press by some of the most eminent German bibliographers. It is a Latin dictionary and introduction to grammar, and consists of three hundred and seventy-three leaves of large folio size. Fischer and others are of opinion that a Vocabulary, printed at Elfeld,—in Latin, Altavilla,—near Mentz, on 6th November, 1467, was executed with the same types. At the end of this work, which is a quarto of one hundred and sixty-five leaves, it is stated to have been begun by Henry Bechtermuntze, and finished by his brother Nicholas, and Wigand Spyess de Orthenberg.† A second edition of the same work, printed by Nicholas Bechtermuntze, appeared in 1469. The following extract from a letter written by Fischer to Professor Zapf in 1803, contains an account of his researches respecting the Catholicon and Vocabulary : "The frankness with which you retracted your former opinions respecting the printer of the Catholicon of 1460, and agreed with me in assigning it to Gutemberg, demands the respect of every unbiassed inquirer. I beg now merely to mention to you a discovery that I have made which no longer leaves it difficult to conceive how the Catholicon types should have come into the hands of Bechtermuntze. From a monument which stands before the high altar of the church of Elfeld it is evident that the family of Sorgenloch, of which that of Gutemberg or Gænsfleisch was a branch, was connected with the family of Bechtermuntze by marriage. The types used by Bechtermuntze were not only similar to those formerly belonging to Gutemberg, but were the very same, as I always maintained, appealing to the principles of the type-founder's art. They had come into the possession of Bechtermuntze by inheritance, on the death of Gutemberg, and hence Dr. Homery's reclamation." ‡

---

* Primaria quædam Document. pp. 26—34.

† " .... per henricum bechtermuncze pie memorie in altavilla est inchoatum. et demū sub anno dñi M.CCCCLXII. ipō die Leonardi confessoris qui fuit quarta die mensis novembris p. nycolaum bechtermūcze fratrem dicti Henrici et Wygandū Spyess de orthenberg ē consummatū." There is a copy of this edition in the Royal Library at Paris.

‡ Typographisch. Seltenheit. S. 101, 5te. Lieferung.

Zapf, to whom Fischer's letter is addressed, had previously communicated to Oberlin his opinion that the types of the Catholicon were the same as those of an *Augustinus de Vita Christiana*, 4to, without date or printer's name, but having at the end the arms of Faust and Scheffer. In his account, printed at Nuremberg, 1803, of an early edition of " Joannis de Turre-cremata explanatio in Psalterium," he acknowledged that he was mistaken; thus agreeing with Schwartz, Meerman, Panzer, and Fischer, that no book known to be printed by Faust and Scheffer is printed with the same types as the Catholicon and the Vocabulary.

Although there can be little doubt of the Catholicon and the Elfeld Vocabulary being printed with the same types, and of the former being printed by Gutemberg, yet it is far from certain that Bechtermuntze inherited Gutemberg's printing materials, even though he might be a relation. It is as likely that Gutemberg might sell to the brothers a portion of his materials and still retain enough for himself. If they came into their possession by inheritance, which is not likely, Gutemberg must have died some months previous to 4th November, 1467, the day on which Nicholas Bechtermuntze and Wygand Spyess finished the printing of the Vocabulary. If the materials had been purchased by Bechtermuntze in Gutemberg's lifetime, which seems to be the most reasonable supposition, Conrad Homery could have no claim upon them on account of money advanced to Gutemberg, and consequently the types and printing materials which after his death came into Homery's possession, could not be those employed by the brothers Bechtermuntze in their establishment at Elfeld.*

By letters patent, dated at Elfeld on St. Anthony's day, 1465, Adolphus, archbishop and elector of Mentz, appointed Gutemberg one of his courtiers, with the same allowance of clothing as the rest of the nobles attending his court, with other privileges and exemptions. From this period Fischer thinks that Gutemberg no longer occupied himself with business as a printer, and that he transferred his printing materials to Henry Bechtermuntze. " If Wimpheling's account be true," says Fischer, " that Gutemberg became blind in his old age, we need no longer be surprised that during his lifetime his types and utensils should come into

---

* The two following works, without date or printer's name, are printed with the same types as the Catholicon, and it is doubtful whether they were printed by Gutemberg, or by other persons with his types.

1. Matthei de Cracovia tractatus, seu dialogus racionis et consciencie de sumpcione pabuli salutiferi corporis domini nostri ihesu christi. 4to. foliis 22.

2. Thome de Aquino summa de articulis fidei et ecclesie sacramentis. 4to. foliis 13.

A declaration of Thierry von Isenburg, archbishop of Mayence, offering to resign in favour of his opponent, Adolphus of Nassau, printed in German and Latin in 1462, is ascribed to Gutemberg : it is of quarto size and consists of four leaves.—Oberlin, Annales de la Vie de Gutenberg.

the possession of Bechtermuntze." The exact period of Gutemberg's decease has not been ascertained, but in the bond or deed of obligation executed by Doctor Conrad Homery the Friday after St. Matthias's day,* 1468, he is mentioned as being then dead. He was interred at Mentz in the church of the Recollets, and the following epitaph was composed by his relation, Adam Gelthaus : †

" D. O. M. S.

" Joanni Genszfleisch, artis impressoriæ repertori, de omni natione et lingua optime merito, in nominis sui memoriam immortalem Adam Gelthaus posuit. Ossa ejus in ecclesia D. Francisci Moguntina feliciter cubant."

From the last sentence it is probable that this epitaph was not placed in the church wherein Gutemberg was interred. The following inscription was composed by Ivo Wittich, professor of law and member of the imperial chamber at Mentz :

" Jo. Guttenbergensi, Moguntino, qui primus omnium literas ære imprimendas invenit, hac arte de orbe toto bene merenti Ivo Witigisis hoc saxum pro monimento posuit M.D.VII."

This inscription, according to Serarius, who professes to have seen it, and who died in 1609, was placed in front of the school of law at Mentz. This house had formerly belonged to Gutemberg, and was supposed to be the same in which he first commenced printing at Mentz in conjunction with Faust. ‡

From the documentary evidence cited in the preceding account of the life of Gutemberg, it will be perceived that the art of printing with moveable types was not perfected as soon as conceived, but that it was a work of time. It is highly probable that Gutemberg was occupied with his invention in 1436 ; and from the obscure manner in which his " admirable discovery " is alluded to in the process between him and the Drytzehns in 1439, it does not seem likely that he had then proceeded beyond making experiments. In 1449 or 1450, when the sum of 800 florins was advanced by Faust, it appears not unreasonable to suppose that he had so far improved his invention, as to render it practically available without reference to Scheffer's great improvement in casting the types from matrices formed by punches, which was most likely discovered between 1452 and 1455. § About fourteen years must have

---

* St. Matthias's day is on 24th February.

† In the instrument dated 1434, wherein Gutemberg agrees to release the town-clerk of Mentz, whom he had arrested, mention is made of a relation of his, Ort Gelthus, living at Oppenheim. Schœpflin, mistaking the word, has printed in his Documenta, p. 4, " Artgeld huss," which he translates " Artgeld domo," the house of Artgeld.

‡ Serarii Historia Mogunt. lib. 1. cap. xxxvii. p. 159. Heineken, Nachrichten von Kunstlern und Kunst-Sachen, 2te. Theil, S. 299.

§ In the colophon to " Trithemii Breviarium historiarum de origine Regum et Gentis

elapsed before Gutemberg was enabled to bring his invention into practice. The difficulties which must have attended the first establishment of typography could only have been surmounted by great ingenuity and mechanical knowledge combined with unwearied perseverance. After the mind had conceived the idea of using moveable types, those types, whatever might be the material employed, were yet to be formed, and when completed they were to be arranged in pages, divided by proper spaces, and bound together in some manner which the ingenuity of the inventor was to devise. Nor was his invention complete until he had contrived a PRESS, by means of which numerous impressions from his types might be perfectly and rapidly obtained.

Mr. Ottley, at page 285 of the first volume of his Researches, informs us that " almost all great discoveries have been made by accident ;" and at page 196 of the same volume, when speaking of printing as the invention of Lawrence Coster, he mentions it as an " art which had been at first taken up as the amusement of a leisure hour, became improved, and was practised by him as a profitable trade." Let any unbiassed person enter a printing-office ; let him look at the single letters, let him observe them formed into pages, and the pages wedged up in forms ; let him see a sheet printed from one of those forms by means of the press ; and when he has seen and considered all this, let him ask himself if ever, since the world began, the amusement of an old man practised in his hours of leisure was attended with such a result? " Very few great discoveries," says Lord Brougham, " have been made by chance and by ignorant persons, much fewer than is generally supposed.—They are generally made by persons of competent knowledge, and who are in search of them." *

Having now given some account of the grounds on which Gutemberg's claims to the invention of typography are founded, it appears necessary to give a brief summary, from the earliest authorities, of the pretensions of Lawrence Coster not only to the same honour, but to something more ; for if the earliest account which we have of him be true, he was not only the inventor of typography, but of block-printing also.

The first mention of Holland in connexion with the invention of typography occurs in the Cologne Chronicle, printed by John Kœlhoff in 1499, wherein it is said that the first idea of the art was suggested by the Donatuses printed in Holland ; it being however expressly stated in

Francorum," printed at Mentz in 1515 by John Scheffer, son of Peter Scheffer and Christina, the daughter of Faust, it is stated that the art of printing was perfected in 1452, through the labour and ingenious contrivances of Peter Scheffer of Gernsheim, and that Faust gave him his daughter Christina in marriage as a reward.

* On the Pleasures and Advantages of Science, p. 160. Edit. 1831.

the same work that the art of printing as then practised was invented at Mentz. In a memorandum, which has been referred to at page 123, written by Mariangelus Accursius, who flourished about 1530, the invention of printing with metal types is erroneously ascribed to Faust; and it is further added, that he derived the idea from a Donatus printed in Holland from a wood-block. That a Donatus might be printed there from a wood-block previous to the invention of typography is neither impossible nor improbable; although I esteem the testimony of Accursius of very little value. He was born and resided in Italy, and it is not unlikely, as has been previously observed, that he might derive his information from the Cologne Chronicle.

John Van Zuyren, who died in 1594, is said to have written a book to prove that typography was invented at Harlem; but it never was printed, and the knowledge that we have of it is from certain fragments of it preserved by Scriverius, a writer whose own uncorroborated testimony on this subject is not entitled to the slightest credit. The substance of Zuyren's account is almost the same as that of Junius, except that he does not mention the inventor's name. The art according to him was invented at Harlem, but that while yet in a rude and imperfect state it was carried by a stranger to Mentz, and there brought to perfection.

Theodore Coornhert, in the dedication of his Dutch translation of Tully's Offices to the magistrates of Harlem, printed in 1561, says that he had frequently heard from respectable people that the art of printing was invented at Harlem, and that the house where the inventor lived was pointed out to him. He proceeds to relate that by the dishonesty of a workman the art was carried to Mentz and there perfected. Though he says that he was informed by certain respectable old men both of the inventor's name and family, yet, for some reason or other, he is careful not to mention them. When he was informing the magistrates of Harlem of their city being the nurse of so famous a discovery, it is rather strange that he should not mention the parent's name. From the conclusion of his dedication we may guess why he should be led to mention Harlem as the place where typography was invented. It appears that he and certain friends of his, being inflamed with a patriotic spirit, designed to establish a new printing-office at Harlem, "in honour of their native city, for the profit of others, and for their own accommodation, and yet without detriment to any person." His claiming the invention of printing for Harlem was a good advertisement for the speculation.

The next writer who mentions Harlem as the place where printing was invented is Guicciardini, who in his Description of the Low Countries, first printed at Antwerp in 1567, gives the report, without vouching for its truth, as follows: "In this place, it appears, not only from the general opinion of the inhabitants and other Hollanders, but from the testimony of several writers and from other memoirs, that the art of printing and impressing letters on paper such as is now practised, was invented. The inventor dying before the art was perfected or had come into repute, his servant, as they say, went to live at Mentz, where making this new art known, he was joyfully received; and applying himself diligently to so important a business, he brought it to perfection and into general repute. Hence the report has spread abroad and gained credit that the art of printing was first practised at Mentz. What truth there may be in this relation, I am not able, nor do I wish, to decide; contenting myself with mentioning the subject in a few words, that I might not prejudice [by my silence the claims of] this district." *

It is evident that the above account is given from mere report. What other writers had previously noticed the claims of Harlem, except Coornhert and Zuyren, remain yet to be discovered. They appear to have been unknown to Guicciardini's contemporary, Junius, who was the first to give a name to the Harlem inventor; a "local habitation" had already been provided for him by Coornhert.

The sole authority for one Lawrence Coster having invented woodengraving, block-printing, and typography, is Hadrian Junius, who was born at Horn in North Holland, in 1511. He took up his abode at Harlem in 1560. During his residence in that city he commenced his Batavia,—the work in which the account of Coster first appeared,—which, from the preface, would seem to have been finished in January, 1575. He died the 16th June in the same year, and his book was not published until 1588, twelve years after his decease.† In this work, which is a topographical and historical account of Holland, or more properly of the country included within the limits of ancient Batavia, we find the first account of Lawrence Coster as the inventor of typography. Almost every succeeding advocate of Coster's pretensions has taken the liberty of

* Ludovico Guicciardini, Descrittione di tutti i Paesi Bassi : folio, Anversa, 1581. The original passage is given by Meerman. The original words *altre memorie*—translated in the above extract "other memoirs"—are rendered by Mr. Ottley "other records." This may pass ; but it scarcely can be believed that Guicciardini consulted or personally knew of the existence of any such records. Mr. Ottley also, to match his "records," refers to the relations of Coornhert, Zuyren, Guicciardini, and Junius as "documents."

† Junius was a physician, and unquestionably a learned man. He is the author of a nomenclator in Latin, Greek, Dutch, and French. An edition, with the English synonyms, by John Higins and Abraham Fleming, was printed at London in 1585. The following passage concerning Junius occurs in Southey's Biographical Sketch of the Earl of Surrey in the "Select Works of the British Poets from Chaucer to Jonson :" " Surrey is next found distinguishing himself at the siege of Landrecy. At that siege Bonner, who was afterwards so eminently infamous, invited Hadrian Junius to England. When that distinguished scholar arrived, Bonner wanted either the means, or more probably the heart, to assist him ; but Surrey took him into his family in the capacity of physician, and gave him a pension of fifty angels."

altering, amplifying, or contradicting the account of Junius according as it might suit his own line of argument; but not one of them has been able to produce a single solitary fact in confirmation of it. Scriverius, Seiz, Meerman, and Koning are fertile in their conjectures about the thief that stole Coster's types, but they are miserably barren in their proofs of his having had types to be stolen. " If the variety of opinions," observes Naude, speaking of Coster's invention, " may be taken as an indication of the falsehood of any theory, it is impossible that this should be true." Since Naude's time the number of Coster's advocates has been increased by Seiz, Meerman, and Koning ; * who, if they have not been able to produce any evidence of the existence of Lawrence Coster as a printer, have at least been fertile in conjectures respecting the thief. They have not strengthened but weakened the Costerian triumphal arch raised by Junius, for they have all more or less knocked a piece of it away ; and even where they have pretended to make repairs, it has merely been " one nail driving another out."

Junius's account of Coster is supposed to have been written about 1568 ; and in order to do justice to the claims of Harlem I shall here give a faithful translation of the " document,"—according to Mr. Ottley, —upon which they are founded. After alluding, in a preliminary rhetorical flourish, to Truth being the daughter of Time, and to her being concealed in a well, Junius thus proceeds to draw her out.

" If he is the best witness, as Plutarch says, who, bound by no favour and led by no partiality, freely and fearlessly speaks what he thinks, my testimony may deservedly claim attention. I have no connexion through kindred with the deceased, his heirs, or his posterity, and I expect on this account neither favour nor reward. What I have done is performed through a regard to the memory of the dead. I shall therefore relate what I have heard from old and respectable persons who have held offices in the city, and who seriously affirmed that they had heard what they told from their elders, whose authority ought justly to entitle them to credit."

"About a hundred and twenty-eight years ago,+ Lawrence John, called the churchwarden or keeper,‡ from the profitable and honourable office which his family held by hereditary right, dwelt in a large house, which is yet standing entire, opposite the Royal Palace. This is

---

* Koning's Dissertation on the Invention of Printing, which was crowned by the Society of Sciences of Harlem, was first printed at Harlem in the Dutch language in 1816. It was afterwards abridged and translated into French with the approbation, and under the revision, of the author. In 1817 he published a first supplement ; and a second appeared in 1820.

+ Reckoning from 1568, the period referred to would be 1440.

‡ " Ædituus Custosve." The word " Koster" in modern Dutch is synonymous with the English " Sexton."

the person who now on the most sacred ground of right puts forth his claims to the honour of having invented typography, an honour so nefariously obtained and possessed by others. Walking in a neighbouring wood, as citizens are accustomed to do after dinner and on holidays, he began to cut letters of beech-bark, with which for amusement, the letters being inverted as on a seal, he impressed short sentences on paper for the children of his son-in-law. Having succeeded so well in this, he began to think of more important undertakings, for he was a shrewd and ingenious man ; and, in conjunction with his son-in-law Thomas Peter, he discovered a more glutinous and tenacious kind of ink, as he found from experience that the ink in common use occasioned blots. This Thomas Peter left four sons, all of whom were magistrates ; and I mention this that all may know that the art derived its origin from a respectable and not from a mean family. He then printed whole figured pages with the text added. Of this kind I have seen specimens executed in the infancy of the art, being printed only on one side. This was a book composed in our native language by an anonymous author, and entitled *Speculum Nostræ Salutis*. In this we may observe that in the first productions of the art—for no invention is immediately perfected—the blank pages were pasted together, so that they might not appear as a defect. He afterwards exchanged his beech types for leaden ones, and subsequently he formed his types of tin, as being less flexible and of greater durability. Of the remains of these types certain old wine-vessels were cast, which are still preserved in the house formerly the residence of Lawrence, which, as I have said, looks into the market-place, and which was afterwards inhabited by his great-grandson Gerard Thomas, a citizen of repute, who died an old man a few years ago.

" The new invention being well received, and a new and unheard-of commodity finding on all sides purchasers, to the great profit of the inventor, he became more devoted to the art, his business was increased, and new workmen—the first cause of his misfortune—were employed. Among them was one called John ; but whether, as is suspected, he bore the ominous surname of Faust,—*infaustus** and unfaithful to his master —or whether it were some other John, I shall not labour to prove, as I do not wish to disturb the dead already enduring the pangs of conscience for what they had done when living.† This person, who was admitted under an oath to assist in printing, as soon as he thought he had attained

---

* " Sive is (ut fert suspicio) Faustus fuerit ominoso cognomine, hero suo infidus et infaustus." The author here indulges in an ominous pun. The Latinised name *"Faustus,"* signifies lucky ; the word *"infaustus,"* unlucky. The German name Füst may be literally translated " Fist." A clenched hand is the crest of the family of Faust.

† This is an admirable instance of candour. A charge is insinuated, and presumed to be a fact, and yet the writer kindly forbears to bring forward proof, that he may not disturb the dead. History has long since given the lie to the insinuation of the thief having been Faust.

the art of joining the letters, a knowledge of the fusile types, and other matters connected with the business, embracing the convenient opportunity of Christmas Eve, when all persons are accustomed to attend to their devotions, stole all the types and conveyed away all the utensils which his master had contrived by his own skill; and then leaving home with the thief, first went to Amsterdam, then to Cologne, and lastly to Mentz, as his altar of refuge, where being safely settled, beyond bowshot as they say, he might commence business, and thence derive a rich profit from the things which he had stolen. Within the space of a year from Christmas, 1442, it is certain that there appeared printed with the types which Lawrence had used at Harlem '*Alexandri Galli Doctrinale*,' a grammar then in frequent use, with '*Petri Hispani Tractatus.*'

"The above is nearly what I have heard from old men worthy of credit who had received the tradition as a shining torch transferred from hand to hand, and I have heard the same related and affirmed by others. I remember being told by Nicholas Galius, the instructor of my youth, —a man of iron memory, and venerable from his long white hair,—that when a boy he had often heard one Cornelius, a bookbinder, not less than eighty years old (who had been an assistant in the same office), relate with such excited feelings the whole transaction,—the occasion of the invention, its progress, and perfection, as he had heard of them from his master,—that as often as he came to the story of the robbery he would burst into tears; and then the old man's anger would be so roused on account of the honour that had been lost through the theft, that he appeared as if he could have hanged the thief had he been alive; and then again he would vow perdition on his sacrilegious head, and curse the nights that he had slept in the same bed with him, for the old man had been his bedfellow for some months. This does not differ from the words of Quirinus Talesius, who admitted to me that he had formerly received nearly the same account from the mouth of the same bookseller."*

As Junius died upwards of twelve years before his book was published, it is doubtful whether the above account was actually written by him or not. It may have been an interpolation of an editor or a bookseller anxious for the honour of Harlem, and who might thus expect to gain currency for the story by giving it to the world under the sanction of Junius's name. There was also another advantage attending this mode of publication; for as the reputed writer was dead, he could not be called on to answer the many objections which remain yet unexplained.

The manner in which Coster, according to the preceding account, first discovered the principle of obtaining impressions from separate

---

* Hadriani Junii Batavia, p. 253, et sequent. Edit. Ludg. Batavor. 1588.

letters formed of the bark of the beech-tree requires no remark.* There are, however, other parts of this narrative which more especially force themselves on the attention as being at variance with reason as well as fact.

Coster, we are informed, lived in a large house, and, at the time of his engaging the workman who robbed him, he had brought the art to such perfection that he derived from it a great profit; and in consequence of the demand for the new commodity, which was eagerly sought after by purchasers, he was obliged to increase his establishment and engage assistants. It is therefore evident that the existence of such an art must have been well known, although its details might be kept secret. Coster, we are also informed, was of a respectable family; his grand-children were men of authority in the city, and a great-grandson of his died only a few years before Junius wrote, and yet not one of his friends or descendants made any complaint of the loss which Coster had sustained both in property and fame. Their apathy, however, was compensated by the ardour of old Cornelius, who used to shed involuntary tears whenever the theft was mentioned; and used to heap bitter curses on the head of the thief as often as he thought of the glory of which Coster and Harlem had been so villanously deprived. It is certainly very singular that a person of respectability and authority should be robbed of his materials and deprived of the honour of the invention, and yet neither himself nor any one of his kindred publicly denounce the thief; more especially as the place where he had established himself was known, and where in conjunction with others he had the frontless audacity·to claim the honour of the invention.

Of Lawrence Coster, his invention, and his loss, the world knew nothing until he had been nearly a hundred and fifty years in his grave. The presumed writer of the account which had to do justice to his memory had been also twelve years dead when his book was published. His information, which he received when he was a boy, was derived from an old man who when a boy had heard it from another old man who lived with Coster at the time of the robbery, and who had heard the account of the invention from his master. Such is the list of the Harlem witnesses. If Junius had produced any evidence on the autho-

---

* Scriverius—whose book was printed in 1628—thinking that there might be some objection raised to the letters of beech-bark, thus, according to his own fancy, amends the account of Cornelius as given by Junius : " Coster walking in the wood picked up a small bough of a beech, or rather of an oak-tree blown off by the wind ; and after amusing himself with cutting some letters on it, wrapped it up in paper, and afterwards laid himself down to sleep. When he awoke, he perceived that the paper, by a shower of rain or some accident having got moist, had received an impression from these letters ; which induced him to pursue the accidental discovery." This is more imaginative than the account of Cornelius, but scarcely more probable.

rity of Coster's great-grandson that any of his predecessors—his father or his grandfather—had carried on the business of a printer at Harlem, this might in part have corroborated the narrative of Cornelius; but, though subsequent advocates of the claims of Harlem have asserted that Coster's grand-children continued the printing business, no book or document has been discovered to establish the fact.

The account of Cornelius involves a contradiction which cannot be easily explained away. If the thief stole the whole or greater part of Coster's printing materials,—types and press and all, as the narrative seems to imply,—it is difficult to conceive how he could do so without being discovered, even though the time chosen were Christmas Eve; for on an occasion when all or most people were engaged at their devotions, the fact of two persons being employed would in itself be a suspicious circumstance: a tenant with a small stock of furniture who wished to make a "moonlight flitting" would most likely be stopped if he attempted to remove his goods on a Sunday night. As the dishonest workman had an assistant, who is rather unaccountably called "*the* thief*," it is evident from this circumstance, as well as from the express words of the narrative,[*] that the quantity of materials stolen must have been considerable. If, on the contrary, the thief only carried away a portion of the types and matrices, with a few other instruments,—"all that could be moved without manifest danger of immediate detection," to use the words of Mr. Ottley,—what was there to prevent Coster from continuing the business of printing? Did he give up the lucrative trade which he had established, and disappoint his numerous customers, because a dishonest workman had stolen a few of his types? But even if every letter and matrice had been stolen,—though how likely this is to be true I shall leave every one conversant with typography to decide, —was the loss irreparable, and could this "shrewd and ingenious man" not reconstruct the types and other printing materials which he had originally contrived?

If the business of Coster was continued uninterruptedly, and after his death carried on by his grand-children, we might naturally expect that some of the works which they printed could be produced, and that some record of their having practised such an art at Harlem would be in existence. The records of Harlem are however silent on the subject; no mention is made by any contemporary author, nor in any contemporary document, of Coster or his descendants as printers in that city; and no book printed by them has been discovered except by persons who decide upon the subject as if they were endowed with the faculty of intuitive discrimination. If Coster's business had been

---

[*] " Choragium omne typorum involat, instrumentorum herilium ei artificio comparatorum suppelectilem convasat, deinde *cum fure* domo se proripit."—H. Junii Batavia, p. 255.

suspended in consequence of the robbery, his customers, from all parts, who eagerly purchased the "new commodity," must have been aware of the circumstance ; and to suppose that it should not have been mentioned by some old writer, and that the claims of Coster should have lain dormant for a century and a half, exceeds my powers of belief. Where pretended truth can only be perceived by closing the eyes of reason I am content to remain ignorant ; nor do I wish to trust myself to the unsafe bridge of conjecture—a rotten plank without a hand-rail,—

" O'er which lame faith leads understanding blind."

If all Coster's types had been stolen and he had not supplied himself with new ones, it would be difficult to account for the wine vessels which were cast from the old types ; and if he or his heirs continued to print subsequent to the robbery, all that his advocates had to complain of was the theft. For since it must have been well known that he had discovered and practised the art, at least ten years previous to its known establishment at Mentz, and seventeen years before a book appeared with the name of the printers claiming the honour of the invention, the greatest injury which he received must have been from his fellow citizens ; who perversely and wilfully would not recollect his previous discovery and do justice to his claims. Even supposing that a thief had stolen the whole of Coster's printing-materials, types, chases, and presses, it by no means follows that he deprived of their memory not only all the citizens of Harlem, but all Coster's customers who came from other places* to purchase the "new commodity" which his press supplied. Such however must have been the consequences of the robbery, if the narrative of Cornelius were true ; for except himself no person seems to have remembered Coster's invention, or that either he or his immediate descendants had ever printed a single book.

Notwithstanding the internal evidence of the improbability of Cornelius's account of Coster and his invention, its claims to credibility are still further weakened by those persons who have shown themselves most wishful to establish its truth. Lawrence Janszoon, whom Meerman and others suppose to have been the person described by Cornelius as the inventor of printing, appears to have been custos of the church of St. Bavon at Harlem in the years 1423, 1426, 1432 and 1433. His death is placed by Meerman in 1440 ; and as, according to the narrative of Cornelius, the types and other printing materials were stolen on Christmas eve 1441, the inventor of typography must have been in his grave at the time the robbery was committed. Cornelius must have known of his master's death, and yet in his account of the robbery he

---

* "..... quum nova merx, nunquam antea visa, emptores undique exciret cum huber rimo questu."—Junii Batavia.

makes no mention of Coster being dead at the time, nor of the business being carried on by his descendants after his decease. It was at one time supposed that Coster died of grief on the loss of his types, and on account of the thief claiming the honour of the invention. But this it seems is a mistake; he was dead according to Meerman at the time of the robbery, and the business was carried on by his grandchildren.

Koning has discovered that Cornelius the bookbinder died in 1522, aged at least ninety years. Allowing him to have been ninety-two, this assistant in Coster's printing establishment, and who learnt the account of the invention and improvement of the art from Coster himself, must have been just ten years old when his master died; and yet upon the improbable and uncorroborated testimony of this person are the claims of Coster founded.

Lehne, in his "Chronology of the Harlem fiction,"* thus remarks on the authorities, Galius, and Talesius, referred to by Junius as evidences of its truth. As Cornelius was upwards of eighty when he related the story to Nicholas Galius, who was then a boy, this must have happened about 1510. The boy Galius we will suppose to have been at that time about fifteen years old: Junius was born in 1511, and we will suppose that he was under the care of Nicholas Galius, the instructor of his youth, until he was fifteen; that is, until 1526. In this year Galius, the man venerable from his grey hairs, would be only thirty-six years old, an age at which grey hairs are premature. Grey hairs are only venerable in old age, and it is not usual to praise a young man's faculty of recollection in the style in which Junius lauds the "iron memory" of his teacher. Talesius, as Koning states, was born in 1505, and consequently six years older than Junius; and on the death of Cornelius, in 1522, he would be seventeen, and Junius eleven years old. Junius might in his eleventh year have heard the whole account from Cornelius himself in the same manner as the latter when only ten must have heard it from Coster; and it is remarkable that Galius who was so well acquainted with Cornelius did not afford his pupil the opportunity. We thus perceive that in the whole of this affair children and old men play the principal parts, and both ages are proverbially addicted to narratives which savour of the marvellous.

Meerman, writing to his correspondent Wagenaar in 1757, expresses his utter disbelief in the story of Coster being the inventor of typography, which, he observes, was daily losing credit : whatever historical evidence Seiz had brought forward in favour of Coster was gratuitously

* In " Einige Bemerkungen über das Unternehmen der gelehrten Gesellschaft zu Harlem," &c. S. 31.

assumed; in short, the whole story of the invention was a fiction.* After the publication of Schœpflin's Vindiciæ Typographicæ in 1760, giving proofs of Gutemberg having been engaged in 1438 with some invention relating to *printing*, and in which a *press* was employed, Meerman appears to have received a new light; for in 1765 he published his own work in support of the very story which he had previously declared to be undeserving of credit. The mere change, however, of a writer's opinions cannot alter the immutable character of truth; and the guesses and assumptions with which he may endeavour to gloss a fiction can never give to it the solidity of fact. What he has said of the work of Seiz in support of Coster's claims may with equal truth be applied to his own arguments in the same cause: "Whatever historical evidence he has brought forward in favour of Coster has been gratuitously assumed." Meerman's work, like the story which it was written to support, "is daily losing credit." It is a dangerous book for an advocate of Coster to quote; for he has scarcely advanced an argument in favour of Coster, and in proof of his stolen types being the foundation of typography at Mentz, but what is contradicted by a positive fact.

In order to make the documentary evidence produced by Schœpflin in favour of Gutemberg in some degree correspond with the story of Cornelius, Junius's authority, he has assumed that Gutemberg had an elder brother also called John; and that he was known as Gænsfleisch the elder, while his younger brother was called by way of distinction Gutemberg. In support of this assumption he refers to Wimpheling,†

'* Santander has published a French translation of this letter in his Dictionnaire Bibliographique, tom. i. pp. 14—18.

† Wimpheling, who was born at Sletstadt in 1451, thus addresses the inventor of printing,—whose name, Gænsfleisch, he Latinises "Ansicarus,"—in an epigram printed at the end of "Memoriæ Marsilii ab Inghen," 4to. 1499.

> "Felix *Ansicare*, per te Germania felix
> Omnibus in terris præmia laudis habet.
> Urbe Moguntina, divino fulte Joannes
> Ingenio, primus imprimis ære notas.
> Multum Relligio, multum tibi Græca sophia,
> Et multum debet lingua Latina."

In his "Epitome Rerum Germanicarum," 1502, he says that the art of printing was discovered at Strasburg in 1440 by a native of that city, who afterwards removing to Mentz there perfected the art. In his "Episcoporum Argentinensium Catalogus," 1508, he says that printing was invented by a native of Strasburg, and that when the inventor had joined some other persons engaged on the same invention at Mentz, the art was there perfected by one John Gænsfleisch, who was blind through age, in the house called Gutemberg, in which, in 1508, the College of Justice held its sittings. Wimpheling does not seem to have known that Gænsfleisch was also called Gutemberg, and that his first attempts at printing were made in Strasburg.

who in one place has called the inventor Gænsfleisch, and in another
Gutemberg; and he also supposes that the two epitaphs which have
been given at page 144, relate to two different persons. The first,
inscribed by Adam Gelthaus to the memory of John *Gænsfleisch*, he
concludes to have been intended for the elder brother. The second,
inscribed by Ivo Wittich to the memory of John *Gutemberg*, he
supposes to relate to the younger brother, and to have been erected from
a feeling of envy. The fact of Gutemberg being also named Gænsfleisch
in several contemporary documents, is not allowed to stand in the way
of Meerman's hypothesis of the two "brother Johns," which has been
supposed to be corroborated by the fact of a John Gænsfleisch the Elder
being actually the contemporary of John Gænsfleisch called also
Gutemberg.

Having thus provided Gutemberg with an elder brother also named
John, Meerman proceeds to find him employment; for at the period of
his writing much light had been thrown on the early history of printing,
and no person in the least acquainted with the subject could believe
that Faust was the thief who stole Coster's types, as had been insinuated
by Junius and affirmed by Boxhorn and Scriverius. Gænsfleisch the
Elder is accordingly sent by Meerman to Harlem, and there engaged as
a workman in Lawrence Coster's printing office. It is needless to ask
if there be any proof of this: Meerman having introduced a new
character into the Harlem farce may claim the right of employing him
as he pleases. As there is evidence of Gutemberg, or Gænsfleisch the
Younger, being engaged at Strasburg about 1436 in some experiments
connected with printing, and mention being made in the same documents
of the fair of Aix-la-Chapelle, Meerman sends him there in 1435.
From Aix-la-Chapelle, as the distance is not very great, Meerman
makes him pay a visit to his elder brother, then working as a printer
in Coster's office at Harlem. He thus has an opportunity of seeing
Coster's printing establishment, and of gaining some information respecting the art, and hence his attempts at printing at Strasburg in 1436. In
1441 he supposes that John Gænsfleisch the Elder stole his master's
types, and printed with them, at Mentz, in 1442, "Alexandri Galli
Doctrinale," and "Petri Hispani Tractatus," as related by Junius. As
this trumpery story rests solely on the conjecture of the writer, it might
be briefly dismissed for reconsideration when the proofs should be
produced; but as Heineken * has afforded the means of showing its
utter falsity, it may perhaps be worth while to notice some of the facts
produced by him respecting the family and proceedings of Gutemberg.

John Gænsfleisch the Elder, whom Meerman makes Gutemberg's
elder brother, was descended from a branch of the numerous family of

* Nachrichten von Kunstlern und Kunst-Sachen, 1te. Theil, S. 286—293.

Gænsfleisch, which was also known by the local names of zum Jungen, Gutenberg or Gutemberg, and Sorgenloch. This person, whom Meerman engages as a workman with Coster, was a man of property ; and at the time that we are given to understand he was residing at Harlem, we have evidence of his being married and having children born to him at Mentz. This objection, however, could easily be answered by the ingenuity of a Dutch commentator, who, as he has made the husband a thief, would find no difficulty in providing him with a suitable wife. He would also be very likely to bring forward the presumed misconduct of the wife in support of his hypothesis of the husband being a thief. John Gænsfleisch the Elder was married to Ketgin, daughter of Nicholas Jostenhofer of Schenkenberg, on the Thursday after St. Agnes's day, 1437. In 1439 his wife bore him a son named Michael ; and in 1442 another son, who died in infancy. In 1441 we have evidence of his residing at Mentz ; for in that year his relation Rudiger zum Landeck appeared before a judge to give Gænsfleisch an acknowledgment of his having properly discharged his duties as trustee, and of his having delivered up to the said Rudiger the property left to him by his father and mother.

That John Gænsfleisch the Elder printed "Alexandri Galli Doctrinale," and "Petri Hispani Tractatus," at Mentz in 1442 with the types which he had stolen from Coster, is as improbable as every other part of the story. There is, in fact, not the slightest reason to believe that the works in question were printed at Mentz in 1442, or that any book was printed there with types until nearly eight years after that period. In opposition, however, to a host of historical evidence we have the assertion of Cornelius, who told the tale to Galius, who told it to Junius, who told it to the world.

Meerman's web of sophistry and fiction having been brushed away by Heineken, a modern advocate of Coster's undertook to spin another, which has also been swept down by a German critic. Jacobus Koning,* town-clerk of Amsterdam, having learnt from a document printed by Fischer, that Gutemberg had a brother named Friele, sends him to Harlem to work with Coster, and makes him the thief who stole the types ; thus copying Meerman's plot, and merely substituting Gutemberg's known brother for John Gænsfleisch the Elder. On this attempt of Koning's to make the old sieve hold water by plastering it with his own mud, Lehne † makes the following remarks :—

"He gives up the name of John,—although it might be supposed that old Cornelius would have known the name of his bedfellow better

---

* In a Memoir on the Invention of Printing, which was crowned by the Academy of Sciences at Harlem in 1816.

† Einige Bemerkungen, &c. S. 18, 19.

than Koning,—and without hesitation charges Gutemberg's brother with the theft. In order to flatter the vain-glory of the Harlemers, poor Friele, after he had been nearly four hundred years in his grave, is publicly accused of robbery on no other ground than that Mynheer Koning had occasion for a thief. It is, however, rather unfortunate for the credit of the story that this Friele should have been the founder of one of the first families in Mentz, of the order of knighthood, and possessed of great property both in the city and the neighbourhood. Is it likely that this person should have been engaged as a workman in the employment of the Harlem churchwarden, and that he should have robbed him of his types in order to convey them to his brother, who then lived at Strasburg, and who had been engaged in his own invention at least three years before, as is proved by the process between him and the Drytzehns published by Schœpflin? From this specimen of insulting and unjust accusation on a subject of literary inquiry, we may congratulate the city of Amsterdam that Mynheer Koning is but a law-writer and not a judge, should he be not more just as a man than as an author."

In a book of old accounts belonging to the city of Harlem, and extending from April 1439 to April 1440, Koning having discovered at least nine entries of expenses incurred on account of messengers despatched to the Justice-Court of Amsterdam, he concludes that there must have been some conference between the judges of Harlem and Amsterdam on the subject of Coster's robbery. There is not a word mentioned in the entries on what account the messengers were despatched, but he decides that it must have been on some business connected with this robbery, for the first messenger was despatched on the last day of the Christmas holidays ; and the thief, according to the account of Junius, made choice of Christmas-eve as the most likely opportunity for effecting his purpose. To this most logical conclusion there happens to be an objection, which however Mynheer Koning readily disposes of. The first messenger was despatched on the last day of the Christmas holidays 1439, and the accounts terminate in April 1440 ; but according to the narrative of Cornelius the robbery was committed on Christmas-eve 1441. This trifling discrepancy is however easily accounted for by the fact of the Dutch at that period reckoning the commencement of the year from Easter, and by supposing,—as the date is printed in numerals, —that Junius might have written 1442, instead of 1441, as the time when the two books appeared at Mentz printed with the stolen types, and within a year after the robbery. Notwithstanding this *satisfactory* explanation there still remains a trifling error to be rectified, and it will doubtless give the clear-headed advocate of Coster very little trouble. Admitting that the accounts are for the year commencing at Easter 1440 and ending at Easter 1441, it is rather difficult to comprehend how they should contain any notice of an event which happened at the Christmas following. The Harlem scribe possibly might have the gift of seeing into futurity as clearly as Mynheer Koning has the gift of seeing into the past. The arguments derived from paper-marks which Koning has advanced in favour of Coster are not worthy of serious notice.

He has found, as Meerman did before him, that one Lawrence Janszoon was living in Harlem between 1420 and 1436, and that his name occurs within that period as custos or warden of St. Bavon's church. As he is never called "Coster," a name acquired by the family, according to Junius, in consequence of the office which they enjoyed by hereditary right, the identity of Lawrence Janszoon and Lawrence Coster is by no means clearly established; and even if it were, the sole evidence of his having been a printer rests on the testimony of Cornelius, who was scarcely ten years old when Lawrence Janszoon died. The correctness of Cornelius's narrative is questioned both by Meerman and Koning whenever his statements do not accord with their theory, and yet they require others to believe the most incredible of his assertions. They themselves throw doubts on the evidence of their own witness, and yet require their opponents to receive as true his deposition on the most important point in dispute—that Coster invented typography previous to 1441,—a point on which he is positively contradicted by more than twenty authors who wrote previous to 1500; and negatively by the silence of Coster's contemporaries. Supposing that the account of Cornelius had been published in 1488 instead of 1588, it would be of very little weight unless corroborated by the testimony of others who must have been as well aware of Coster's invention as himself; for the silence of contemporary writers on the subject of an important invention or memorable event, will always be of greater negative authority than the unsupported assertion of an individual who when an old man professes to relate what he had heard and seen when a boy. If therefore the uncorroborated testimony of Cornelius would be so little worth, even if published in 1488, of what value can it be printed in 1588, in the name of a person who was then dead, and who could not be called on to explain the discrepancies of his part of the narrative? Whatever might be the original value of Cornelius's testimony, it is deteriorated by the channel through which it descends to us. He told it to a boy, who, when an old man, told it to another boy, who when nearly sixty years old inserts it in a book which he is writing, but which is not printed until twelve years after his death.

It is singular how Mr. Ottley, who contends for the truth of Papillon's story of the Cunio, and who maintains that the art of engraving figures and text upon wood was well known and practised previous to 1285, should believe the account given by Cornelius of the origin of Coster's invention. If he does not believe this part of the account, with what consistency can he require other people to give credit to the rest? With respect to the origin and progress of the invention, Cornelius was as likely to be correctly informed as he was with regard to the theft and the establishment of printing at Mentz; if therefore Coster's advocates themselves establish the incorrectness of his testimony in the first part of the story, they destroy the general credibility of his evidence.

With respect to the fragments of "Alexandri Galli Doctrinale" and "Catonis Disticha" which have been discovered, printed with the same, or similar types as the Speculum Salvationis, no good argument can be founded on them in support of Coster's claims, although the facts which they establish are decisive of the fallacy of Meerman's assumptions. In order to suit his own theory, he was pleased to assert that the first edition of the Speculum was the only one of that book printed by Coster, and that it was printed with wooden types. Mr. Ottley has, however, shown that the edition which Meerman and others supposed to be the first was in reality the second; and that the presumed second was unquestionably the first, and that the text was throughout printed with metal types by means of a press. It is thus the fate of all Coster's advocates that the last should always produce some fact directly contradicting his predecessors' speculations, but not one confirmatory of the truth of the story on which all their arguments are based. Meerman questions the accuracy of Cornelius as reported by Junius; Meerman's arguments are rejected by Koning; and Mr. Ottley, who espouses the same cause, has from his diligent collation of two different editions of the Speculum afforded a convincing proof that on a most material point all his predecessors are wrong. His inquiries have established beyond a doubt, that the text of the first edition of the Speculum was printed wholly with metal types; and that in the second the text was printed partly from metal types by means of a press, and partly from wood-blocks by means of friction. The assertion that Coster printed the first edition with wooden types, and that his grandsons and successors printed the second edition with types of metal, is thus most clearly refuted. As no printer's name has been discovered in any of the fragments referred to, it is uncertain where or when they were printed. It however seems more likely that they were printed in Holland or the Low Countries than in Germany. The presumption of their antiquity in consequence of their rarity is not a good ground of argument. Of an edition of a "Donatus," printed by Sweinheim and Pannartz, between 1465 and 1470, and consisting of three hundred copies, not one is known to exist. From sundry fragments of a "Donatus," embellished with the same ornamented small capitals as are used in Faust and Scheffer's Psalter, Fischer was pleased to conjecture that the book had been printed by Gutemberg and Faust previous to 1455. A copy, however, has been discovered bearing the imprint of Scheffer, and printed, in all probability, subsequent to 1467, as it is in this year that Scheffer's name first appears alone. The "Historia Alexandri Magni," pretendedly printed with wooden types, and ascribed by Meerman to Coster, was printed by Ketelar and Leempt, who first established a printing-office at Utrecht in 1473.

John Enschedius, a letter-founder and printer of Harlem, and a strenuous assertor of Coster's pretensions, discovered a very curious specimen of typography which he and others have supposed to be the identical "short sentences" mentioned by Junius as having been printed by Coster for the instruction of his grand-children. This unique specimen of typography consists of eight small pages, each being about one inch and six-eighths high, by one and five-eighths wide, printed on parchment and on both sides. The contents are an alphabet; the Lord's Prayer; the Creed; the Ave Mary; and two short prayers, all in Latin. Meerman has given a fac-simile of all the eight pages in the second volume of his "Origines Typographicæ;"* and if this be correct, I am strongly inclined to suspect that this singular "Horarium" is a modern forgery. The letters are rudely formed, and the shape of some of the pages is irregular; but the whole appears to me rather as an imitation of rudeness and a studied irregularity, than as the first essay of an inventor. There are very few contractions in the words; and though the letters are rudely formed, and there are no points, yet I have seen no early specimen of typography which is so easy to read. It is apparent that the printer, whoever he might be, did not forget that the little manual was intended for children. The letters I am positive could not be thus printed with types formed of beech-bark; and I am further of opinion that they were not, and could not be, printed with moveable types of wood. I am also certain that, whatever might be the material of which the types were formed, those letters could only be printed on

---

* Enschedius published a fac-simile himself, with the following title: "Afbeelding van 't A. B. C. 't Pater Noster, Ave Maria, 't Credo, en Ave Salus Mundi, door Laurens Janszoon, te Haarlem, ten behoeven van zyne dochters Kinderen, met beweegbaare Letteren gedrukt, en teffens aangeweesen de groote der Stukjes pergament, zekerlyk 't oudste overblyfsel der eerste Boekdrukkery, 't welk als zulk een eersteling der Konst bewaard word en berust in de Boekery van *Joannes Enschedé*, Lettergieter en Boekdrukker te Haarlem, 1768.—*A. J. Polak sculps. ex originali.*"

M

parchment on both sides by means of a press. The most strenuous of Coster's advocates have not ventured to assert that he was acquainted with the use of metal types in 1423, the pretended date of his first printing short sentences for the use of his grand-children, nor have any of them suggested that he used a press for the purpose of obtaining impressions from his letters of beech-bark; how then can it be pretended with any degree of consistency that this "Horarium" agrees exactly with the description of Cornelius? It is said that Enschedius discovered this singular specimen of typography pasted in the cover of an old book. It is certainly such a one as he was most wishful to find, and which he in his capacity of type-founder and printer would find little difficulty in producing. I am firmly convinced that it is neither printed with wooden types nor a specimen of early typography; on the contrary, I suspect it to be a Dutch typographic essay on popular credulity.

Of all the works which have been claimed for Coster, his advocates have not succeeded in making out his title to a single one; and the best evidence of the fallacy of his claims is to be found in the writings of those persons by whom they have been most confidently asserted. Having no theory of my own to support, and having no predilection in favour of Gutemberg, I was long inclined to think that there might be some rational foundation for the claims which have been so confidently advanced in favour of Harlem. An examination, however, of the presumed proofs and arguments adduced by Coster's advocates has convinced me that the claims put forward on his behalf, as the inventor of typography, are untenable. They have certainly discovered that a person of the name of Lawrence Janszoon was living at Harlem between the years 1420 and 1440, but they have not been able to show anything in proof of this person ever having printed any book either from wood-blocks or with moveable types. There is indeed reason to believe that at the period referred to there were three persons of the name of Lawrence Janszoon,—or Fitz-John, as the surname may be rendered;—but to which of them the pretended invention is to be ascribed is a matter of doubt. At one time we find the inventor described as an illegitimate scion of the noble family of Brederode, which was descended from the ancient sovereigns of Holland; at another he is said to have been called Coster in consequence of the office of custos or warden of St. Bavon's church being hereditary in his family; and in a third account we find Lawrence Janszoon figuring as a promoter of sedition and one of the leaders of a body of rioters. The advocates for the claims of Harlem have brought forward every Lawrence that they could find at that period whose father's name was John; as if the more they could produce the more conclusive would be the *proof* of one of them at least being the inventor of printing. As the books which are ascribed to Coster furnish positive evidence of the incorrectness of the story of Cornelius and of the comments of Meerman ; and as records, which are now matters of history, prove that neither Gutemberg nor Faust stole any types from Coster or his descendants, the next supporter of the claims of Harlem will have to begin *de novo ;* and lest the palm should be awarded to the wrong Lawrence Janszoon, he ought first to ascertain which of them is really the hero of the old book-binder's tale.

CHAPTER IV.

WOOD ENGRAVING IN CONNEXION WITH THE PRESS.

FAUST AND SCHEFFER'S PSALTER OF 1457—PRINTING AT BAMBERG IN 1461—BOOKS CON-
TAINING WOOD-CUTS PRINTED THERE BY ALBERT PFISTER—OPPOSITION OF THE WOOD
ENGRAVERS OF AUGSBURG TO THE EARLIEST PRINTERS ESTABLISHED IN THAT CITY—
TRAVELLING PRINTERS—WOOD-CUTS IN " MEDITATIONES JOHANNIS DE TURRE-CREMATA,"
ROME, 1467 ; AND IN " VALTURIUS DE RE MILITARI," VERONA, 1472 — WOOD-CUTS
FREQUENT IN BOOKS PRINTED AT AUGSBURG BETWEEN 1474 AND 1480—WOOD-CUTS IN
BOOKS PRINTED BY CAXTON — MAPS ENGRAVED ON WOOD, 1482 — PROGRESS OF MAP
ENGRAVING—CROSS-HATCHING — FLOWERED BORDERS—HORTUS SANITATIS—NUREMBERG
CHRONICLE—WOOD ENGRAVING IN ITALY—POLIPHILI HYPNEROTOMACHIA—DECLINE OF
BLOCK-PRINTING—OLD WOOD-CUTS IN DERSCHAU'S COLLECTION.

ONSIDERING Gutemberg as the inventor of printing with moveable types ; that his first attempts were made at Strasburg about 1436 ; and that with Faust's money and Scheffer's ingenuity the art was perfected at Mentz about 1452, I shall now proceed to trace the progress of wood engraving in its connexion with the press.

In the first book which appeared with a date and the printers' names—the Psalter printed by Faust and Scheffer, at Mentz, in 1457—the large initial letters, engraved on wood and printed in red and blue ink, are the most beautiful specimens of this kind of ornament which the united efforts of the wood-engraver and the pressman have produced. They have been imitated in modern times, but not excelled. As they are the first letters, in point of time, printed with two colours, so are they likely to continue the first in point of excellence.

Only seven copies of the Psalter of 1457 are known, and they are all printed on vellum. Although they have all the same colophon, containing the printers' names and the date, yet no two copies exactly correspond. A similar want of agreement is said to have been observed in different copies of the Mazarine Bible, but which are, notwithstanding, of one and the same edition. As such works would in the infancy of the art be a long time in printing—more especially the Psalter, as, in consequence of the large capitals being printed in two colours, each side of many of the sheets would have to be printed thrice—it can be a matter of no surprise that alterations and amendments should be made in the text while the work was going through the press. In the Mazarine Bible, the entire Book of Psalms, which contains a considerable number of red letters, would have to pass four times through the press, including what printers call the "reiteration."*

The largest of the ornamented capitals in the Psalter of 1457 is the letter B, which stands at the commencement of the first psalm, "Beatus vir." The letters which are next in size are an A, a C, a D, an E, and a P; and there are also others of a smaller size, similarly ornamented, and printed in two colours in the same manner as the larger ones. Although only two colours are used to each letter, yet when the same letter is repeated a variety is introduced by alternating the colours: for instance, the shape of the letter is in one page printed red, with the ornamental portions blue; and in another the shape of the letter is blue, and the ornamental portions red. It has been erroneously stated by Papillon that the large letters at the beginning of each psalm are printed in three colours, red, blue, and purple; and Lambinet has copied the mistake. A second edition of this Psalter appeared in 1459; a third in 1490; and a fourth in 1502, all in folio, like the first, and with the same ornamented capitals. Heineken observes that in the edition of 1490 the large letters are printed in red and green instead of red and blue.

In consequence of those large letters being printed in two colours, two blocks would necessarily be required for each; one for that portion of the letter which is red, and another for that which is blue. In the body, or shape, of the largest letter, the B at the beginning of the first psalm, the mass of colour is relieved by certain figures being cut out in the block, which appear white in the impression. On the stem of the letter a dog like a greyhound is seen chasing a bird; and flowers and ears of corn are represented on the curved portions. These figures being white, or the colour of the vellum, give additional brightness to the full-bodied red by which they are surrounded, and materially add to the beauty and effect of the whole letter.

In consequence of two blocks being required for each letter, the

---

* By the common press only one side of a sheet can be printed at once. The reiteration is the second printing of the same sheet on the blank side. Thus in the Psalter of 1457 every sheet containing letters of two colours on each side would have to pass six times through the press. It was probably in consequence of printing so much in red and black that the early printers used to employ so many presses. Melchior de Stamham, abbot of St. Ulric and St. Afra at Augsburg, and who established a printing-office within that monastery, about 1472, bought five presses of John Schüssler; a considerable number for what may be considered an amateur establishment. He also had two others made by Sixtus Saurloch.—Zapf, Annales Typographicæ Augustanæ, p. xxiv.

means were afforded of printing any of them twice in the same sheet or the same page with alternate colours; for while the body of the first was printed in red from one block, the ornamental portion of the second might be printed red at the same time from the other block. In the second printing, with the blue colour, it would only be necessary to transpose the blocks, and thus the two letters would be completed, identical in shape and ornament, and differing only from the correspond-ing portions being in the one letter printed red and in the other blue. In the edition of 1459 the same ornamented letter is to be found repeated on the same page; but of this I have only noticed one instance; though there are several examples of the same letter being printed twice in the same sheet.

Although the engraving of the most highly ornamented and largest of those letters cannot be considered as an extraordinary instance of skill, even at that period, for many wood-cuts of an earlier date afford proof of greater excellence, yet the artist by whom the blocks were engraved must have had considerable practice. The whole of the ornamental part, which would be the most difficult to execute, is clearly and evenly cut, and in some places with great neatness and delicacy. " This letter," says Heineken, " is an authentic testimony that the artists employed on such a work were persons trained up and exercised in their profession. The art of wood engraving was no longer in its cradle."

The name of the artist by whom those letters were engraved is unknown. In Sebastian Munster's Cosmography, book iii. chapter 159, John Meydenbach is mentioned as being one of Gutemberg's assistants; and an anonymous writer in Serarius states the same fact. Heineken in noticing these two passages writes to the following effect. " This Meydenbach is doubtless the same person who proceeded with Gutem-berg from Strasburg to Mentz in 1444.* It is probable that he was a wood engraver or an illuminator, but this is not certain; and it is still more uncertain that this person engraved the cuts in a book entitled *Apocalipsis cum figuris*, printed at Strasburg in 1502, because these are copied from the cuts in the Apocalypse engraved and printed by Albert Durer at Nuremberg. Whether this copyist was the *Jacobus Meydenbach* who printed books at Mentz in 1491,† or he was some other engraver, I have not been able to determine."‡

---

* Heineken in his Nachrichten, T. I. S. 108, also states that Meydenbach came from Strasburg with Gutemberg. Oberlin however observes, " Je ne sais où de Heinecke a trouvè que ce Meydenbach est venu en 1444 avec Gutenberg à Mayence." Heineken says, " In der Nachricht von Strassburg findet man dass ein gewisser Meydenbach 1444 nach Maynz gezogen," and refers to Fournier, p. 40. Dissert. sur l'Orig. de l'Imprimerie primitive.

† An edition of the Hortus Sanitatis with wood-cuts was printed at Mentz, by *Jacobus Meydenbach*, in 1491.

‡ Idée Générale, p. 286.

Although so little is positively known respecting John Meydenbach, Gutemberg's assistant, yet Von Murr thinks that there is reason to suppose that he was the artist who engraved the large initial letters for the Psalter of 1457. Fischer, who declares that there is no sufficient grounds for this conjecture, confidently assumes, from false premises, that those letters were engraved by Gutemberg, "a person experienced in such work," adds he, "as we are taught by his residence at Strasburg." From the account that we have of his residence and pursuits at Strasburg, however, we are taught no such thing. We only learn from it he was engaged in some invention which related to printing. We learn that Conrad Saspach made him a press, and it is conjectured that the goldsmith Hanns Dunne was employed to engrave his letters; but there is not a word of his being an experienced wood engraver, nor is there a well authenticated passage in any account of his life from which it might be concluded that he ever engraved a single letter. Fischer's reasons for supposing that Gutemberg engraved the large letters in Faust and Scheffer's Psalter are, however, contradicted by facts. Having seen a few leaves of a Donatus ornamented with the same initial letters as the Psalter, he directly concluded that the former was printed by Gutemberg and Faust prior to the dissolution of their partnership; and not satisfied with this leap he takes another, and arrives at the conclusion that they were engraved by Gutemberg, as "*his* modesty only could allow such works to appear without his name."

Although we have no information respecting the artist by whom those letters were engraved, yet it is not unlikely that they were suggested, if not actually drawn by Scheffer, who, from his profession of a scribe or writer* previous to his connexion with Faust, may be supposed to have been well acquainted with the various kinds of flowered and ornamented capitals with which manuscripts of that and preceding centuries were embellished. It is not unusual to find manuscripts of the early part of the fifteenth century embellished with capitals of two colours, red and blue, in the same taste as in the Psalter; and there is now lying before me a capital P, drawn on vellum in red and blue ink, in a manuscript apparently of the date of 1430, which is so like the same letter in the Psalter that the one might be supposed to have suggested the other.

It was an object with Faust and Scheffer to recommend their Psalter

---

* Scheffer previous to his connexion with Faust was a "clericus,"—not a *clerk* as distinguished from a layman, but a writer or scribe. A specimen of his "set-hand," written t Paris in 1449, is given by Schœpflin in his Vindiciæ Typographicæ. Several of the earliest printers were writers or illuminators; among whom may be mentioned John Mentelin of Strasburg, John Baemler of Augsburg, Ulric Zell of Cologne, and Colard Mansion of Bruges.

—probably the first work printed by them after Gutemberg had been obliged to withdraw from the partnership—by the beauty of its capitals and the sufficiency and distinctness of its "rubrications ;"* and it is evident that they did not fail in the attempt. The Psalter of 1457 is, with respect to ornamental printing, their greatest work ; for in no subsequent production of their press does the typographic art appear to have reached a higher degree of excellence. It may with truth be said that the art of printing—be the inventor who he may—was perfected by Faust and Scheffer ; for the earliest known production of their press remains to the present day unsurpassed as a specimen of skill in ornamental printing.

A fac-simile of the large B at the commencement of the Psalter, printed in colours the same as the original, is given in the first volume of Dibdin's Bibliotheca Spenceriana, and in Savage's Hints on Decorative Printing ; but in neither of those works has the excellence of the original letter been attained. In the Bibliotheca Spenceriana, although the volume has been printed little more than twenty years, the red colour in which the body of the letter is printed has assumed a coppery hue, while in the original, executed nearly four hundred years ago, the freshness and purity of the colours remain unimpaired. In Savage's work, though the letter and its ornaments are faithfully copied† and tolerably well printed, yet the colours are not equal to those of the original. In the modern copy the blue is too faint ; and the red, which in the original is like well impasted paint, has not sufficient body, but appears like a wash, through which in many places the white paper may be seen. The whole letter compared with the original seems like a water-colour copy compared with a painting in oil.

Although it has been generally supposed that the art of printing was first carried from Mentz in 1462 when Faust and Scheffer's sworn workmen were dispersed ‡ on the capture of that city by the archbishop

* This is intimated in the colophon, which, with the contracted words written at length, is as follows : " Presens Spalmorum codex venustate capitalium decoratus Rubricationibusque sufficienter distinctus . Adinventione artificiosa imprimendi ac caracterizandi absque calami ulla exaracione sic effigiatus . Et ad eusebiam dei industrie est consummatus . Per Johannem Fust, Civem maguntinum . Et Petrum Schoffer de Gernzheim, Anno domini Millesimo . cccc lvii . In vigilia Assumpcionis." In the second edition the mis-spelling, " Spalmorum " for " Psalmorum," is corrected.

† It is to be observed that in Savage's copy the perpendicular flourishes are given horizontally, above and below the letter, in order to save room. In a copy of the edition of 1459, in the King's Library, part of the lower flourish has not been inked, as it would have interfered with the letter Q at the commencement of the second psalm " *Quare fremuerunt gentes.*" Traces of the flourish where not coloured may be observed impressed in the vellum.

‡ The following passage occurs in the colophon of two works printed by John Scheffer at Mentz in 1515 and 1516 ; the one being the " Trithemii Breviarium Historiæ Francorum," and the other " Breviarium Ecclesiæ Mindensis :" " Retinuerunt autem hi duo jam præ-nominati, *Johannes Fust et Petrus Scheffer,* hanc artem in secreto, (omnibus ministris et

Adolphus of Nassau, yet there can be no doubt that it was practised at Bamberg before that period ; for a book of fables printed at the latter place by Albert Pfister is expressly dated on St. Valentine's day, 1461 ; and a history of Joseph, Daniel, Judith, and Esther was also printed by Pfister at Bamberg in 1462, "𝔑𝔦𝔱 𝔩𝔞𝔫𝔤 𝔫𝔞𝔠𝔥 𝔰𝔞𝔫𝔡 𝔴𝔞𝔩𝔭𝔲𝔯𝔤𝔢𝔫 𝔱𝔞𝔤,"— not long after St. Walburg's day.* It is therefore certain that the art was practised beyond Mentz previous to the capture of that city, which was not taken until the eve of St. Simon and St. Jude ; that is, on the 28th of October in 1462. As it is very probable that Pfister would have to superintend the formation of his own types and the construction of his own presses,—for none of his types are of the same fount as those used by Gutemberg or by Faust and Scheffer,—we may presume that he would be occupied for some considerable time in preparing his materials and utensils before he could begin to print. As his first known work with a date, containing a hundred and one wood-cuts, was finished on the 14th of February 1461, it is not unlikely that he might have begun to make preparations three or four years before. Upon these grounds it seems but reasonable to conclude with Aretin, that the art was carried from Mentz by some of Gutemberg and Faust's workmen on the dissolution of their partnership in 1455 ; and that the date of the capture of Mentz—when for a time all the male inhabitants capable of bearing arms were compelled to leave the city by the captors —marks the period of its more general diffusion. The occasion of the disaster to which Mentz was exposed for nearly three years was a contest for the succession to the archbishopric. Theodoric von Erpach having died in May 1459, a majority of the chapter chose Thierry von Isenburg to succeed him, while another party supported the pretensions of Adolphus of Nassau. An appeal having been made to Rome, the election of Thierry was annulled, and Adolphus was declared by the Pope to be the lawful archbishop of Mentz. Thierry, being in possession and supported by the citizens, refused to resign, until his rival, assisted by the forces of his adherents and relations, succeeded in obtaining possession of the city.†

familiaribus eorum, ne illam quoquo modo manifestarent, jure jurando adstrictis :) quæ tandem anno Domini M.CCCC.LXII. per eosdem familiares in diversas terrarum provincias divulgata, haud parvum sumpsit incrementum."

* St. Walburg's day is on the 25th of February ; though her feast is also held both on the 1st of May and on the 12th of October. The eve of her feast on the 1st of May is more particularly celebrated ; and it is then that the witches and warlocks of Germany hold their annual meeting on the Brocken. St. Walburg, though born of royal parents in Saxony, was yet educated in England, at the convent of Wimborn in Dorsetshire, of which she became afterwards abbess, and where she died in 779.

† A mournful account of the expulsion of the inhabitants and the plundering of the city is given by Trithemius at page 30 of his " Res Gestæ Frederici Palatini," published with notes by Marquard Freher, at Heidelberg, 4to. 1603.

Until the discovery of Pfister's book containing the four histories, most bibliographers supposed that the date 1461, in the fables, related to the composition of the work or the completion of the manuscript, and not to the printing of the book. Saubert, who was the first to notice it, in 1643, describes it as being printed, both text and figures, from wood-blocks; and Meerman has adopted the same erroneous opinion. Heineken was the first to describe it truly, as having the text printed with moveable types, though he expresses himself doubtfully as to the date, 1461, being that of the impression.

As the discovery of Pfister's tracts has thrown considerable light on the progress of typography and wood engraving, I shall give an account of the most important of them, as connected with those subjects; with a brief notice of a few circumstances relative to the early connexion of wood engraving with the press, and to the dispersion of the printers on the capture of Mentz in 1462.

The discovery of the history of Joseph, Daniel, Judith, and Esther, with the date 1462, printed at Bamberg by Pfister, has established the fact that the dates refer to the years in which the books were printed, and not to the period when the works were composed or transcribed. An account of the history above named, written by M. J. Steiner, pastor of the church of St. Ulric at Augsburg, was first printed in Meusel's Historical and Literary Magazine in 1792; and a more ample description of this and other tracts printed by Pfister was published by Camus in 1800,* when the volume containing them, which was the identical one that had been previously seen by Steiner, was deposited in the National Library at Paris.

The book of fables † printed by Pfister at Bamberg in 1461 is a small folio consisting of twenty-eight leaves, and containing eighty-five fables in rhyme in the old German language. As those fables, which are ascribed to one "Boner, dictus der Edelstein," are known to have been written previous to 1330, the words at the end of the volume,—"Zu Bamberg dies Büchlein geendet ist,"—At Bamberg this book is finished, —most certainly relate to the time when it was printed, and not when it was written. It is therefore the earliest book printed with moveable types which is illustrated with wood-cuts containing figures. Not having an opportunity of seeing this extremely rare book,—of which only one perfect copy is known,—I am unable to speak from personal examination of the style in which its hundred and one cuts are engraved. Heineken,

---

* Under the title of "Notice d'un Livre imprimé à Bamberg en ciɔcccclxii. lue à l'Institut National, par Camus." 4to. Paris, An vii. [1800.]

† The copy of those fables belonging to the Wolfenbuttel Library, and which is the only one known, was taken away by the French and placed in the National Library at Paris, but was restored on the surrender of Paris in 1815.

however, has given a fac-simile of the first, and he says that the others are of a similar kind. The following is a reduced copy of the fac-simile given by Heineken, and which forms the head-piece to the first fable.

On the manner in which it is engraved I shall make no remark, until I shall have produced some specimens of the cuts contained in a " Biblia Pauperum Predicatorum," also printed by Pfister, and having the text in the German language.

The volume described by Camus contains three different works; and although Pfister's name, with the date 1462, appears in only one of them, the " Four Histories," yet, as the type is the same in all, there can be no doubt of the other two being printed by the same person and about the same period. The following particulars respecting its contents are derived from the " Notice " of Camus. It is a small folio consisting altogether of a hundred and one leaves of paper of good quality, moderately thick and white, and in which the water-mark is an ox's head. The text is printed in a large type, called missal-type ; and though the characters are larger, and there is a trifling variation in three or four of the capitals, yet they evidently appear to have been copied from those of the Mazarine Bible.

The first work is that which Heineken calls " une Allégorie sur la Mort ;"* but this title does not give a just idea of its contents. It is in fact a collection of accusations preferred against Death, with his answers to them. The object is to show that such complaints are unavailing, and that, instead of making them, people ought rather to employ themselves in endeavouring to live well. In this tract, which

* Idée Générale, p. 276. Dr. Dibdin in his Bibliographical Tour says that this work "is entitled by Camus the ALLEGORY OF DEATH." This is a mistake ; for Camus, who objects to this title,—which was given to it by Heineken,—always refers to the book under the title of " Les Plaintes contre la Mort."

consists of twenty-four leaves, there are five wood-cuts, each occupying
an entire page. The first represents Death seated on a throne. Before
him there is a man with a child, who appears to accuse Death of having
deprived him of his wife, who is seen on a tomb wrapped in a winding-
sheet.—In the second cut, Death is also seen seated on a throne, with
the same person apparently complaining against him, while a number
of persons appear approaching sad and slow, to lay down the ensigns
of their dignity at his feet.—In the third cut there are two figures of
Death ; one on foot mows down youths and maidens with a scythe,
while another, mounted, is seen chasing a number of figures on horseback, at whom he at the same time discharges his arrows.—The fourth
cut consists of two parts, the one above the other. In the upper part,
Death appears seated on a throne, with a person before him in the act
of complaining, as in the first and second cuts. In the lower part, to
the left of the cut, is seen a convent, at the gate of which there are two
persons in religious habits ; to the right a garden is represented, in which
are perceived a tree laden with fruit, a woman crowning an infant, and
another woman conversing with a young man. In the space between
the convent and the garden certain signs are engraved, which Camus
thinks are intended to represent various branches of learning and
science,—none of which can afford protection against death,—as they
are treated of in the chapter which precedes the cut. In the fifth cut,
Death and the Complainant are seen before Christ, who is seated on a
throne with an angel on each side of him, under a canopy ornamented
with stars. Although neither Heineken nor Camus give specimens of
those cuts, nor speak of the style in which they are executed, it may be
presumed that they are not superior either in design or engraving to those
contained in the other tracts.

The text of the work is divided into thirty-four chapters, each of
which, except the first, is preceded by a summary ; and their numbers
are printed in Roman characters. The initial letter of each chapter is
red, and appears to have been formed by means of a stencil. The first
chapter, which has neither title nor numeral, commences with the
Complainant's recital of his injuries ; in the second, Death defends
himself ; in the third the Complainant resumes, in the fourth Death
replies ; and in this manner the work proceeds, the Complainant and
Death speaking alternately through thirty-two chapters. In the thirty-
third, God decides between the parties ; and after a few common-place
reflections and observations on the readiness of people to complain on all
ccasions, sentence is pronounced in these words : " The Complainant is
condemned, and Death has gained the cause. Of right, the Life of every
man is due to Death ; to Earth his Body, and to Us his Soul." In the
thirty-fourth chapter, the Complainant, perceiving that he has lost his

suit, proceeds to pray to God on behalf of his deceased wife. In the summary prefixed to the chapter the reader is informed that he is now about to peruse a model of a prayer ; and that the name of the Complainant is expressed by the large red letters which are to be found in the chapter. Accordingly, in the course of the chapter, six red letters, besides the initial at the beginning, occur at the commencement of so many different sentences. They are formed by means of a stencil, while the letters at the commencement of other similar sentences are printed black. Those red letters, including the initial at the beginning of the chapter, occur in the following order, IHESANW. Whether the name is expressed by them as they stand, or whether they are to be combined in some other manner, Camus will not venture to decide.* From the prayer it appears that the name of the Complainant's deceased wife was Margaret. In this singular composition, which in the summary is declared to be a model, the author, not forgetting the court language of his native country, calls the Almighty " the Elector who determines the choice of all Electors," " Hoffmeister" of the court of Heaven, and " Herzog" of the Heavenly host. The text is in the German language, such as was spoken and written in the fifteenth century.

The German words " *Hoffmeister* " and " *Herzog* " appear extremely ridiculous in Camus's French translation,—" le Maître-d'hôtel de la cour céleste," and " le Grand-duc de l'armée céleste." But this is clothing ancient and dignified German in modern French frippery. The word " Hoffmeister "—literally, "court-master or governor"—is used in modern German in nearly the same sense as the English word " steward ; " and the governor or tutor of a young prince or nobleman is called by the same name. The word " Herzog"—the " Grand-duc " of Camus—in its original signification means the leader of a host or army. It is a German title of honour which defines its original meaning, and is in modern language synonymous with the English title "Duke." The ancient German " Herzog" was a leader of hosts ; the modern French " Grand-duc" is a clean-shaved gentleman in a court-dress, redolent of eau-de-Cologne, and bedizened with stars and strings. The two words are characteristic of the two languages.

The second work in the volume is the Histories of Joseph, Daniel, Judith, and Esther. It has no general frontispiece nor title ; but each separate history commences with the words : " Here begins the history

---

* " Outre la lettre initiale, on remarque, dans le cours du chapitre, six lettres rouges non imprimées, mais peintes à la plaque, qui commencent six phrases diverses. Les lettres initiales des autres phrases du même chapitre sont imprimées en noir. Les lettres rouges sont IHESANW. Doit-on les assembler dans l'ordre où elles sont placées, ou bien doivent-elles recevoir un autre arrangement ? Je ne prends pas sur moi de le décider."—Camus, Notice, p. 6.

of . . . ." in German. Each history forms a separate gathering, and the
whole four are contained in sixty leaves, of which two, about the middle,
are blank, although there is no appearance of any deficiency in the
history. The text is accompanied with wood-cuts which are much less
than those in the "Complaints against Death," each occupying only the
space of eleven lines in a page, which when full contains twenty-eight.
The number of the cuts is sixty-one; but there are only fifty-five
different subjects, four of them having been printed twice, and one
thrice. Camus gives a specimen of one of the cuts, which represents
the Jews of Bethuliah rejoicing and offering sacrifice on the return of
Judith after she had cut off the head of Holofernes. It is certainly a
very indifferent performance, both with respect to design and engraving;
and from Camus's remarks on the artist's ignorance and want of taste it
would appear that the others are no better. In one of them Haman is
decorated with the collar of an order from which a cross is suspended;
and in another Jacob is seen travelling to Egypt in a carriage* drawn by
two horses, which are harnessed according to the manner of the fifteenth
century, and driven by a postilion seated on a saddle, and with his feet
in stirrups. All the cuts in the "Four Histories" are coarsely coloured.

It is this work which Camus, in his title-page, professes to give an
account of, although in his tract he describes the other two contained
in the same volume with no less minuteness. He especially announced
a notice of this work as "a book printed at Bamberg in 1462," in consequence of its being the most important in the volume; for it contains
not only the date and place, but also the printer's name. In the book of
Fables, printed with the same types at Bamberg in 1461, Pfister's name
does not appear.

The text of the "Four Histories" ends at the fourth line on the recto
of the sixtieth leaf; and after a blank space equal to that of a line,
thirteen lines succeed, forming the colophon, and containing the place,
date, and printer's name. Although those lines run continuously on,
occupying the full width of the page as in prose, yet they consist of
couplets in German rhyme. The end of each verse is marked with a
point, and the first word of the succeeding one begins with a capital.

---

* Camus calls it a "voiture," but I question if such a carriage was known in 1462; and
am inclined to think that he has converted a kind of light waggon into a modern "voiture."
A light sort of waggon, called by Stow a "Wherlicote," was used in England by the mother
of Richard the Second in the manner of a modern coach. I have noticed in an old wood-cut
a light travelling waggon, drawn by what is called a "unicorn team" of three horses; that
is, one as a "leader," and two "wheelers," with the driver riding on the "near side" wheeler.
This cut is in the Bagford collection in the British Museum, and is one of a series of ninety
subjects from the Old and New Testament which have been cut out of a book. A manuscript note in German states that they are by Michael Wolgemuth, and printed in 1491. In
no wood-cut executed previous to 1500 have I seen a vehicle like a modern French voiture.

Camus has given a fac-simile of those lines, that he might at once present his readers with a specimen of the type and a copy of this colophon, so interesting to bibliographers as establishing the important fact in the history of printing, namely, that the art was practised beyond Mentz prior to 1462. The following copy, though not a fac-simile, is printed line for line from Camus.

> Ein ittlich mensch von herzen gert . Das er wer weiss
> und wol gelert . An meister un' schrift das nit mag
> sein . So kun' wir all auch nit latein . Darauff han
> ich ein teil gedacht . Und vier historii zu samen pra=
> cht . Joseph daniel un' auch judith . Und hester auch
> mit gutem sith . die vier het got in seiner hut . Als er
> noch ye de' guten thut . Dar durch wir pessern unser
> lebe' . De' puchlein ist sein ende gebe' . Lzu bambergk
> in der selbe' stat . Das albrecht pfister gedrucket hat
> Do ma' zalt tausent un' vierhu'dert iar . Im zwei und
> sechzigste' das ist war . Nit lang nach sand walpur=
> gen tag . Die uns wol gnad erberben mag . Frid un'
> das ewig lebe' . Das wolle uns got alle' gebe' . Ame'.

The following is a translation of the above, in English couplets of similar rhythm and measure as the original:

> With heart's desire each man doth seek
> That he were wise and learned eke :
> But books and teacher he doth need,
> And all men cannot Latin read.
> As on this subject oft I thought,
> These hist'ries four I therefore wrote ;
> Of Joseph, Daniel, Judith too,
> And Esther eke, with purpose true :
> These four did God with bliss requite,
> As he doth all who act upright.
> That men may learn their lives to mend
> This book at Bamberg here I end.
> In the same city, as I've hinted,
> It was by Albert Pfister printed,
> In th' year of grace, I tell you true,
> A thousand four hundred and sixty-two ;
> Soon after good St. Walburg's day,
> Who well may aid us on our way,
> And help us to eternal bliss :
> God, of his mercy, grant us this. Amen.

The third work contained in the volume described by Camus is an edition of the "Poor Preachers' Bible," with the text in German, and printed on both sides. The number of the leaves is eighteen, of which only seventeen are printed ; and as there is a "history" on each page, the total number in the work is thirty-four, each of which is illustrated with five cuts. The subjects of those cuts and their arrangement on the page is not precisely the same as in the earlier Latin editions ; and as in the latter there are forty "histories," six are wanting in the Bamberg edition, namely : 1. Christ in the garden ; 2. The soldiers alarmed at the sepulchre ; 3. The Last Judgment ; 4. Hell ; 5. The eternal Father receiving the righteous into his bosom ; and 6. The crowning of the Saints. As the cuts illustrative of these subjects are the last in the Latin editions, it is possible that the Bamberg copy described by Camus might be defective ; he, however, observes that there is no appearance of any leaves being wanting.* In each page of the Bamberg edition the text is in two columns below the cuts, which are arranged in the following manner in the upper part of the page :

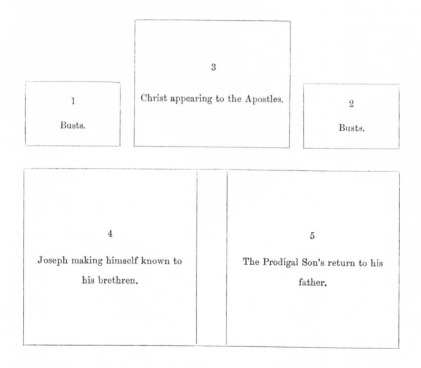

	3	
1	Christ appearing to the Apostles.	2
Busts.		Busts.

4	5
Joseph making himself known to his brethren.	The Prodigal Son's return to his father.

The following cuts are fac-similes of those given by Camus ; and the numbers underneath each relate to their position in the preceding

* The copy of the Bamberg edition in the Wolfenbuttel Library, seen and described by Heineken, Idée Générale, pp. 327—329, contained only twenty-six "histories," or general subjects.

example of their arrangement. In No. 1 the heads are intended for David and the author of the Book of Wisdom ; in No. 2, for Isaiah and Ezekiel.

No. 1.

No. 2.

The subject represented in the following cut, No. 3, forming the centre piece at the top in the arrangement of the original page, is Christ appearing to his disciples after his resurrection. The figure on the right of Christ is intended for St. Peter, and that on his left for St. John. I believe that in no wood-cut, ancient or modern, is Christ represented with so uncomely an aspect and so clumsy a figure.

No. 3.

The subject of No. 4 is Joseph making himself known to his brethren ; from Genesis, chapter XLV.

N

No. 4.

In No. 5 the subject represented is the Prodigal Son received by his father ; from St. Luke, chapter xv.   Camus says that the cuts given by him were engraved on wood by Duplaa with the greatest exactitude from tracings of the originals by Dubrena.

No. 5.

Supposing that all the cuts in the four works, printed by Pfister and described in the preceding pages, were designed in a similar taste and executed in a similar manner to those of which specimens are given, the persons by whom they were engraved—for it is not likely that they were all engraved by one man—must have had very little knowledge of the art. Looking merely at the manner in which they are engraved, without reference to the wretched drawing of the figures and want of "feeling" displayed in the general treatment of the subjects, a moderately apt lad, at the present day, generally will cut as well by the time that he has had a month or two's practice. If those cuts were to be considered as fair specimens of wood engraving in Germany in 1462, it would be evident that the art was then declining; for none of the specimens that I have seen of the cuts printed by Pfister can bear a comparison with those contained in the early block-books, such as the Apocalypse, the History of the Virgin, or the early editions of the Poor Preachers' Bible. To the cuts contained in the latter works they are decidedly inferior, both with respect to design and engraving. Even the earliest wood-cuts which are known,—for instance, the St. Christopher, the St. Bridget, and the Annunciation, in Earl Spencer's collection,—are executed in a superior manner.

It would, however, be unfair to conclude that the cuts which appear in Pfister's works were the best that were executed at that period. On the contrary, it is probable that they are the productions of persons who in their own age would be esteemed only as inferior artists. As the progress of typography was regarded with jealousy by the early wood engravers and block printers, who were apprehensive that it would ruin their trade, and as previous to the establishment of printing they were already formed into companies or fellowships, which were extremely sensitive on the subject of their exclusive rights, it is not unlikely that the earliest type-printers who adorned their books with wood-cuts would be obliged to have them executed by a person who was not professionally a wood engraver. It is only upon this supposition that we can account for the fact of the wood-cuts in the earliest books printed with type being so very inferior to those in the earliest block-books. This supposition is corroborated by the account which we have of the proceedings of the wood engravers of Augsburg shortly after type-printing was first established in that city. In 1471 they opposed Gunther Zainer's* admission to the privileges of a burgess, and endeavoured to prevent him printing wood engravings in his books.

* Gunther Zainer was a native of Reutlingen, in Wirtemberg, and was the first printer in Germany who used Roman characters,—in an edition of "Isidori Episcopi Hispalensis Etymologia," printed by him in 1472. He first began to print at Augsburg in 1468. In 1472 he printed a German translation of the book entitled "Belial," with wood-cuts. A Latin edition of this book was printed by Schussler in the same year. Von Murr says that Schussler printed another edition of "Belial" in 1477 ; but this would seem to be a mistake, for Veith asserts in his "Diatribe de Origine et Incrementis Artis Typographicæ in urbe Augusta Vindelica," prefixed to Zapf's "Annales," that Schussler only printed in the years 1470, 1471, and 1472.

Melchior Stamham, however, abbot of St. Ulric and Afra, a warm promoter of typography, interested himself on behalf of Zainer, and obtained an order from the magistracy that he and John Schussler— another printer whom the wood engravers had also objected to—should be allowed to follow without interruption their art of printing. They were, however, forbid to print initial letters from wood-blocks or to insert wood-cuts in their books, as this would be an infringement on the privileges of the fellowship of wood engravers. Subsequently the wood engravers came to an understanding with Zainer, and agreed that he should print as many initial letters and wood-cuts as he pleased, provided that they engraved them.* Whether Schussler came to the same agreement or not is uncertain, as there is no book known to be printed by him of a later date than 1472. It is probable that he is the person,—named John *Schüssler* in the memorandum printed by Zapf,—of whom Melchior de Stamham in that year bought five presses for the printing-office which he established in his convent of St. Ulric and St. Afra. To John Bämler, who at the same time carried on the business of a printer at Augsburg, no objection appears to have been made. As he was originally a "calligraphus" or ornamental writer, it is probable that he was a member of the wood engravers' guild, and thus entitled to engrave and print his own works without interruption.

As it is probable that the wood-cuts which appear in books printed within the first thirty years from the establishment of typography at Mentz were intended to be coloured, this may in some degree account for the coarseness with which they are engraved ; but as the wood-cuts in the earlier block-books were also intended to be coloured in a similar manner, the inferiority of the former can only be accounted for by supposing that the best wood engravers declined to assist in promoting what they would consider to be a rival art, and that the earlier printers would generally be obliged to have their cuts engraved by persons connected with their own establishments, and who had not by a regular course of apprenticeship acquired a knowledge of the art. About seventy or eighty years ago, and until a more recent period, many country printers in England used themselves to engrave such rude wood-cuts as they might occasionally want. A most extensive assortment of such wood-cuts belonged to the printing-office of the late Mr. George Angus of Newcastle-upon-Tyne, who used them as headpieces and general illustrations to ballads and chap-books. A considerable number of them were cut with a penknife, on pear-tree wood, by an apprentice named Randell, who died about forty years ago.

---

* Von Murr, Journal, 2 Theil, S. 144.—Zapf, Buchdruckergeschichte von Augsburg, 1 Band.

Persons who are fond of a "rough harvest" of such modern-antiques are referred to the "Historical Delights," the "History of Ripon," and other works published by Thomas Gent at York about 1733.

Notwithstanding the rudeness with which the cuts are engraved in the four works printed by Pfister, yet from their number a considerable portion of time must have been occupied in their execution. In the "Four Histories" there are sixty-one cuts, which have been printed from fifty-five blocks. In the "Fables" there are one hundred and one cuts; in the "Complaints against Death," five; and in the "Poor Preachers' Bible," one hundred and seventy, reckoning each subject separately. Supposing each cut in the *three* last works was printed from a separate block, the total number of blocks required for the *four* would be three hundred and thirty-one.* Supposing that each cut on an average contained as much work as that which is numbered 4 in the preceding specimens—Joseph making himself known to his brethren—and supposing that the artist drew the subjects himself, the execution of those three hundred and thirty-one cuts would occupy one person for about two years and a half, allowing him to work three hundred days in each year. It is true that a modern wood engraver might finish more than three of such cuts in a week, yet I question if any one of the profession would complete the whole number, with his own hands, in less time than I have specified.

From the similarity between Pfister's types and those with which a Bible without place or date is printed, several bibliographers have ascribed the latter work to his press. This Bible, which in the Royal Library at Paris is bound in three volumes folio, is the rarest of all editions of the Scriptures printed in Latin. Schelhorn, who wrote a dissertation on this edition, endeavoured to show that it was the first of the Bibles printed at Mentz, and that it was partly printed by Gutemberg and Faust previous to their separation, and finished by Faust and Scheffer in 1456.† Lichtenberger, without expressly assenting to Schelhorn's opinion, is inclined to think that it was printed at Mentz, and by Gutemberg. The reasons which he assigns, however, are not such as are likely to gain assent without a previous willingness to believe. He admits that Pfister's types are similar to those of the Bible, though he says that the former are somewhat ruder.

* Lichtenberger, in his Initia Typographica, referring to Sprenger's History of Printing at Bamberg, says that, besides those four, five other tracts are printed with Pfister's types, of which three contain wood-cuts. One of those three, however, a "Poor Preachers' Bible," with the text in Latin, has the same cuts as the "Poor Preachers' Bible" with the text in German. Only one of those other five works contains the place and date.

† De Antiquissima Latinorum Bibliorum editione .... Jo. Georgii Schelhorn Diatribe. Ulmæ, 4to. 1760.

Camus considers that the tracts unquestionably printed by Pfister throw considerable light on the question as to whom this Bible is to be ascribed. There are two specimens of this Bible, the one given by Masch in his Bibliotheca Sacra, and the other by Schelhorn, in a dissertation prefixed to Quirini's account of the principal works printed at Rome. Camus, on comparing these specimens with the text of Pfister's tracts, immediately perceived the most perfect resemblance between the characters; and on applying a tracing of the last thirteen lines of the "Four Histories" to the corresponding letters in Schelhorn's specimen, he found that the characters exactly corresponded. This perfect identity induced him to believe that the Bible described by Schelhorn was printed with Pfister's types. A correspondent in Meusel's Magazine, No. VII. 1794, had previously advanced the same opinion; and he moreover thought that the Bible had been printed previous to the Fables dated 1461, because the characters of the Bible are cleaner, and appear as if they had been impressed from newer types than those of the Fables.* In support of this opinion an extract is given, in the same magazine, from a curious manuscript of the date of 1459, and preserved in the library of Cracow. This manuscript is a kind of dictionary of arts and sciences, composed by Paul of Prague, doctor of medicine and philosophy, who, in his definition of the word "Libripagus," gives a curious piece of information to the following effect. The barbarous Latin of the original passage, to which I shall have occasion to refer, will be found in the subjoined note.† "He is an artist who dexterously cuts figures, letters, and whatever he pleases on plates of copper, of iron, of solid blocks of wood, and other materials, that he may print upon paper, on a wall, or on a clean board. He cuts whatever he pleases; and he proceeds in this manner with respect to pictures. In my time somebody of Bamberg cut the entire Bible upon plates; in four weeks he impressed the whole Bible, thus sculptured, upon thin parchment."

Although I am of opinion that the weight of evidence is in favour of Pfister being the printer of the Bible in question, yet I cannot think that the arguments which have been adduced in his favour derive any additional support from this passage. The writer, like many other dictionary makers, both in ancient and modern times, has found it a more difficult matter to give a clear account of a *thing* than to find the

* Dr. Dibdin says that a copy of this Bible, which formerly belonged to the Earl of Oxford, and is now in the Royal Library at Paris, contains "an undoubted coeval MS. date, in red ink, of 1461."—Bibliog. Tour, vol. ii. p. 108. Second edition.

† "Libripagus est artifex sculpens subtiliter in laminibus æreis, ferreis, ac ligneis solidi ligni, atque aliis, imagines, scripturam et omne quodlibet, ut prius imprimat papyro aut parieti aut asseri mundo. Scindit omne quod cupit, et est homo faciens talia cum picturis; et tempore mei Bambergæ quidam sculpsit integram bibliam super lamellas, et in quatuor septimanis totam bibliam in pergameno subtili præsignavit sculpturam."

synonym of a *word*. But, notwithstanding his confused account, I think that I can perceive in it the "disjecta membra" of an ancient Form-schneider and a Briefmaler, but no indication of a typographer.

In a jargon worthy of the "Epistolæ obscurorum virorum" he describes an artist, or rather an artizan, "sculpens subtiliter in laminibus* [laminis] æreis, ferreis, ac ligneis solidi ligni, atque aliis, imagines, scripturam et omne quodlibet." In this passage the business of the "Form-schneider" may be clearly enough distinguished : he cuts figures and animals in plates of copper and iron ;—but not in the manner of a modern copper-plate engraver ; but in the manner in which a stenciller pierces his patterns. That this is the true meaning of the writer is evident from the context, wherein he informs us of the artist's object in cutting such letters and figures, namely, "ut prius imprimat papyro aut parieti aut asseri mundo,"—that he may print upon paper, on a wall, or on a clean board. This is evidently descriptive of the practice of stencilling, and proves, if the manuscript be authentic, that the old "Briefmalers" were accustomed to "slapdash" walls as well as to engrave and colour cards. In the distinction which is made of the "laminibus ligneis *ligni solidi,*" it is probable that, the writer meant to specify the difference between cutting *out* letters and figures on thin plates of metal, and cutting *upon* blocks of solid wood. When he speaks of a Bible being cut, at Bamberg, "super lamellas," he most likely means a "Poor Preachers' Bible," engraved on blocks of wood. An impression of a hundred or more copies of such a work might easily enough be taken in a month when the blocks were all ready engraved ; but we cannot suppose that the Bible ascribed to Pfister could be worked off in so short a time. This Bible consists of eight hundred and seventy leaves ; and to print an edition of three hundred copies at the rate of three hundred sheets a day would require four hundred and fifty days. About three hundred copies of each work appears to have been the usual number which Sweinheim and Pannartz and Ulric Hahn printed, on the establishment of the art in Italy ; and Philip de Lignamine in his chronicle mentions, under the year 1458, that Gutemberg and Faust, at Mentz, and Mentelin at Strasburg, printed three hundred sheets in a day.†

Of Pfister nothing more is positively known than what the tracts printed by him afford ; namely, that he dwelt at Bamberg, and exercised the business of a printer there in 1461 and 1462. He might indeed print there both before and after those years, but of this we have no direct

---

* In 1793, a learned doctor of divinity of Cambridge is said in a like manner to have broken Priscian's head with "*paginibus.*" An epigram on this "blunder*bus*" is to be found in the "Gradus ad Cantabrigiam."

† Lichtenberger, Initia Typographica, p. 51.

evidence. From 1462 to 1481 no book is known to have been printed at Bamberg. In the latter year, a press was established there by John Sensenschmidt of Egra, who had previously, that is from 1470, printed several works at Nuremberg.

Panzer, alluding to Pfister as the printer only of the Fables and of the tracts contained in the volume described by Camus, says that he can scarcely believe that he had a fixed residence at Bamberg ; and that those tracts most likely proceeded from the press of a travelling printer.[*] Several of the early printers, who commenced on their own account, on the dispersion of Faust and Scheffer's workmen in 1462, were accustomed to travel with their small stock of materials from one place to another ; sometimes finding employment in a monastery, and sometimes taking up their temporary abode in a small town ; removing to another as soon as public curiosity was satisfied, and the demand for the productions of their press began to decline. As they seldom put their names, or that of the place, to the works which they printed, it is extremely difficult to decide on the locality or the date of many old books printed in Germany. It is very likely that they were their own letter-founders, and that they themselves engraved such wood-cuts as they might require. As their object was to gain money, it is not unlikely that they might occasionally sell a portion of their types to each other ;[†] or to a novice who wished to begin the business, or to a learned abbot who might be desirous of establishing an amateur press within the precinct of his monastery, where copies of the Facetiæ of Poggius might be multiplied as well as the works of St. Augustine. Although it has been asserted the monks regarded with jealousy the progress of printing, as if it were likely to make knowledge too cheap, and to interfere with a part of their business as transcribers of books, such does not appear to have been the fact. In every country in Europe we find them to have been the first to encourage and promote the new art ; and the annals of typography most clearly show that the greater part of the books printed within the first thirty years from the time of Gutemberg and Faust's partnership were chiefly for the use of the monks and the secular clergy.

From 1462 to 1467 there appears to have been no book printed containing wood-cuts. In the latter year Ulric Hahn, a German, printed at Rome a book entitled "Meditationes Johannis de Turrecremata,"[‡] which

---

* "Opuscula quæ typis mandavit typographus hic, hactenus ignotus, ad litteraturam Teutonicam pertinent. Imprimis Pfisterum hunc Bambergæ fixam habuisse sedem vix crediderim. Videntur potius hi libri Teutonici monumenta transeuntis typographi."—Annal. Typogr. tom. i. p. 142, cited by Camus.

† Breitkopf, Ueber Bibliographie, S. 25. 4to. Leipzig, 1793.

‡ The following is the title at length as it is printed, in red letters, underneath the first cut : "Meditationes Reverēdissimi patris dñi Johannis de turre cremata sacrosce Romane

contains wood-cuts engraved in simple outline in a coarse manner. The work is in folio, and consists of thirty-four leaves of stout paper, on which the water-mark is a hunter's horn. The number of cuts is also thirty-four ; and the following—the creation of animals—is a reduced copy of the first.

The remainder of the cuts are executed in a similar style ; and though designed with more spirit than those contained in Pfister's tracts, yet it can scarcely be said that they are better engraved. The following is an enumeration of the subjects. 1. The Creation, as above represented. 2. The Almighty speaking to Adam. 3. Eve taking the apple. (From No. 3 the rest of the cuts are illustrative of the New Testament or of Ecclesiastical History.) 4. The Annunciation. 5. The Nativity. 6. Circumcision of Christ. 7. Adoration of the Magi. 8. Simeon's Benediction. 9. The Flight into Egypt. 10. Christ disputing with the Doctors in the Temple. 11. Christ baptized. 12. The Temptation in the Wilderness. 13. The keys given to Peter. 14. The Transfiguration. 15. Christ washing the Apostles' feet. 16. The Last Supper. 17. Christ betrayed by Judas. 18. Christ led before the High Priest. 19. The Crucifixion. 20. Mater Dolorosa. 21. The Descent into Hell. 22. The Resurrection. 23. Christ appearing to his Disciples. 24. The Ascension. 25. The feast of Pentecost. 26. The Host borne by a bishop. 27. The mystery of the Trinity ; Abraham sees three and adores one. 28. St. Dominic extended like the " *Stam-Herr*" or first ancestor in a pedigree, and sending forth

eccl'ie cardinalis posite & depicte de ipsius mādato ī eccl'ie ambitu Marie de Minerva. Rome." The book is described in Von Murr's Memorabilia Bibliothecar. Publicar. Norimbergensium and in Dibdin's Ædes Althorpianæ, vol. ii. p. 273, with specimens of the cuts.

numerous branches as Popes, Cardinals, and Saints. 29. Christ appearing
to St. Sixtus.   30. The Assumption of the Virgin.   31. Christ seated
amidst a choir of Angels.   32. Christ seated at the Virgin's right hand
in the assembly of Saints.   33. The Office of Mass for the Dead.   34.
The Last Judgment.

Zani says that those cuts were engraved by an Italian artist, but
beyond his assertion there is no authority for the fact. It is most likely
that they were cut by one of Hahn's workmen, who could occasionally
"turn his hand" to wood-engraving and type-founding, as well as compose and work at press ; and it is most probable that Hahn's workmen
when he first established a press in Rome were Germans, and not
Italians.

The second book printed in Italy with wood-cuts is the "Editio
Princeps" of the treatise of R. Valturius de Re Militari, which appeared
at Verona from the press of "Johannes de Verona," son of Nicholas
the surgeon, and master of the art of printing.* This work is dedicated
by the author to Sigismund Malatesta, lord of Rimini, who is styled in
pompous phrase, "Splendidissimum Arminensium Regem ac Imperatorem
semper invictum." The work, however, must have been written several
years before it was printed, for Baluze transcribed from a MS. dated
1463 a letter written in the name of Malatesta, and sent by the author
with a copy of his work to the Sultan Mahomet II. The bearer of this
letter was the painter Matteo Pasti, a friend of the author, who visited
Constantinople at the Sultan's request in order that he might paint his
portrait. It is said that the cuts in this work were designed by Pasti ;
and it is very probable that he might make the drawings in Malatesta's
own copy, from which it is likely that the book was printed. As
Valturius has mentioned Pasti as being eminently skilful in the arts of
Painting, Sculpture, and *Engraving*,† Maffei has conjectured,—and Mr.
Ottley adds, "with some appearance of probability,"—that the cuts in
question were executed by his hand. If such were the fact, it only
could be regretted that an artist so eminent should have mis-spent his
time in a manner so unworthy of his reputation ; for, allowing that a considerable degree of talent is displayed in many of the designs, there is
nothing in the engraving, as they are mere outlines, but what might be cut
by a novice. There is not, however, the slightest reasonable ground to
suppose that those engravings were cut by Matteo Pasti, for I believe that
he died before printing was introduced into Italy ; and it surely would be

---

* The following is a copy of the colophon : " Johannes ex verona oriundus : Nicolai
cyrurgie medici filius : Artis impressorie magister : hunc de re militari librum elegantissimum :
litteris et figuratis signis sua in patria primus impressit. An. MCCCCLXXII."

† " Valturius speaks of Pasti in one of his letters as being eminently skilful in the arts of
Painting, Sculpture, and Engraving."—Ottley, Inquiry, p. 257.

presuming beyond the verge of probability to assert that they might be engraved in anticipation of the art being introduced, and of the book being printed at some time or other, when the blocks would be all ready engraved, in a simple style of art indeed, but with a master's hand. A master-sculptor's hand, however, is not very easily distinguished in the mere rough-dressing of a block of sandstone, which any country mason's apprentice might do as well. It is very questionable if Matteo Pasti was an engraver in the present sense of the word ; the engraving meant by Valturius was probably that of gold and silver vessels and ornaments ; but not the engraving of plates of copper or other metal for the purpose of being printed.

Several of those cuts occupy an entire folio page, though the greater number are of smaller size. They chiefly represent warlike engines, which display considerable mechanical skill on the part of the contriver ; modes of attack and defence both by land and water, with various contrivances for passing a river which is not fordable, by means of rafts, inflated bladders, and floating bridges. In some of them inventions may be noticed which are generally ascribed to a later period : such as a boat with paddle-wheels, which are put in motion by a kind of crank ; a gun with a stock, fired from the shoulder ; and a bomb-shell. It has frequently been asserted that hand-guns were first introduced about the beginning of the sixteenth century, yet the figure of one in the work of Valturius makes it evident that they were known some time before. It is also likely that the drawing was made and the description written at least ten years before the book was printed. It has also been generally asserted that bomb-shells were first used by Charles VIII. of France when besieging Naples in 1495. Valturius, however, in treating of cannon, ascribes the invention to Malatesta.* Gibbon, in chapter lxviii. of his History of the Decline and Fall of the Roman Empire, notices this cut of a bomb-shell. His reference is to the second edition of the work, in Italian, printed also at Verona by Bonin de Bononis in 1483, with the same cuts as the first edition in Latin.† The two following cuts are fac-similes of the bomb-shell and the hand-gun, as represented in the edition of 1472. The figure armed with the gun,—a portion of a

---

* " Inventum est quoque alterum machinæ hujusce tuum Sigismonde Panpulfe [Malatesta] : qua pilæ æneæ tormentarii pulveris plenæ cum fungi aridi fomite urientis emittuntur."—We hence learn that the first bomb-shells were made of copper, and that the fuzee was a piece of a dried fungus. As the first edition has neither numerals nor signatures, I cannot refer to the page in which the above passage is to be found. It is, however, opposite to the cut in which the bomb-shell appears, and that is about the middle of the volume.

† " Robert Valturio published at Verona, in 1483, his twelve books de Re Militari, in which he first mentions the use of bombs. By his patron Sigismond Malatesti, Prince of Rimini, it had been addressed with a Latin epistle to Mahomet II."—Decline and Fall of the Roman Empire, chap. lxviii., note.

large cut,—is firing from a kind of floating battery; and in the original two figures armed with similar weapons are stationed immediately above him.

The following fac-simile of a cut representing a man shooting with a cross-bow is the best in the book. The drawing of the figure is good, and the attitude graceful and natural. The figure, indeed, is not only the best in the work of Valturius, but is one of the best, so far as respects the drawing, that is to be met with in any book printed in the fifteenth century.

The practice of introducing wood-cuts into printed books seems to have been first generally adopted at Augsburg, where Gunther Zainer, in 1471, printed a German translation of the " Legenda Sanctorum " with figures of the saints coarsely engraved on wood. This, I believe, is the first book, after Pfister's tracts, printed in Germany with wood-cuts and containing a date. In 1472 he printed a second volume of the same work, and an edition of the book entitled " Belial,"* both containing wood-cuts. Several other works printed by him between 1471 and 1475 are illustrated in a similar manner. Zainer's example was followed at Augsburg by his contemporaries John Bämler and John Schussler;

* Von Murr says that the person who engraved the cuts for this book also engraved the cuts in a German edition of the Speculum without date, but printed at Augsburg, and dedicated to John [von Giltingen] abbot of the monastery of St. Ulric and St. Afra, who was chosen to that office in 1482. Heineken supposed that the person to whom the book was dedicated was John von Hohenstein, but he resigned the office of abbot in 1459 ; and the book was certainly not printed at that period.—See Heineken, Idée Gén. p. 466 ; and Von Murr, Journal, 2 Theil, S. 145.

and by them, and Anthony Sorg, who first began to print there about 1475, more books with wood-cuts were printed in that city previous to 1480 than at any other place within the same period. In 1477 the first German Bible with wood-cuts was printed by Sorg, who printed another edition with the same cuts and initial letters in 1480. In 1483 he printed an account of the Council of Constance held in 1431, with upwards of a thousand wood-cuts of figures and of the arms of the principal persons both lay and spiritual who attended the council.

Upon this work Gebhard, in his Genealogical History of the Heritable States of the German Empire, makes the following observations :—" The first printed collection of arms is that of 1483 in the History of the Council of Constance written by Ulrich Reichenthal. To this council we are indebted accidentally for the collection. From the thirteenth century it was customary to hang up the shields of noble and honour-able persons deceased in churches ; and subsequently the practice was introduced of painting them upon the walls, or of placing them in the windows in stained glass. A similar custom prevailed at the Council of Constance ; for every person of consideration who attended

had his arms painted on the wall in front of his chamber; and thus
Reichenthal, who caused those arms to be copied and engraved on wood,
was enabled to give in his history the first general collection of coat-
armour which had appeared; as eminent persons from all the Catholic
states of Europe attended this council."*

The practice of introducing wood-cuts became in a few years general
throughout Germany. In 1473, John Zainer of Reutlingen, who is said
to have been the brother of Gunther, printed an edition of Boccacio's
work "De mulieribus claris," with wood-cuts, at Ulm. In 1474 the
first edition of Werner Rolewinck de Laer's chronicle, entitled "Fasciculus
Temporum," was printed with wood-cuts by Arnold Ther-Hoernen at
Cologne; and in 1476 an edition of the same work, also with wood-cuts,
was printed at Louvain by John Veldener, who previously had been a
printer at Cologne. In another edition of the same work printed by
Veldener at Utrecht in 1480, the first page is surrounded with a border
of foliage and flowers cut on wood; and another page, about the middle
of the volume, is ornamented in a similar manner. These are the
earliest instances of ornamental borders from wood-blocks which I have
observed. About the beginning of the sixteenth century title-pages
surrounded with ornamental borders are frequent. From the name of
those borders, *Rahmen*, the German wood engravers of that period are
sometimes called *Rahmenschneiders*. Prosper Marchand, in his "Dictionnaire Historique," tom. ii. p. 156, has stated that Erhard Ratdolt, a native
of Augsburg, who began to print at Venice about 1475, was the first
printer who introduced flowered initial letters, and vignettes—meaning
by the latter term wood-cuts; but his information is scarcely correct.
Wood-cuts—without reference to Pfister's tracts, which were not known
when Marchand wrote—were introduced at Augsburg six years before
Ratdolt and his partners† printed at Venice in 1476 the "Calendarium
Joannis Regiomontani," the work to which Marchand alludes. It may
be true that he introduced a new kind of initial letters ornamented
with flowers in this work, but much more beautiful initial letters had
appeared long before in the Psalter, in the "Durandi Rationale," and
the "Donatus" printed by Faust and Scheffer. The first person who
mentions Ratdolt as the inventor of "florentes litteræ," so named from
the flowers with which they are intermixed, is Maittaire, in his Annales
Typographici, tom. i. part i. p. 53.

* L. A. Gebhard, Genèalogische Geschichte, 1 Theil, Vorrede, S. 11. Cited by Veith in
his "Diatribe," prefixed to Zapf's "Annales Typographiæ Augustanæ."

† The following colophon to an edition of Appian informs us that his partners were
Bernard the painter and Peter Loslein, who also acted as corrector of the press : " Impressum
est hoc opus Venetiis per Bernardū pictorem & Erhardum ratdolt de Augusta una cum Petro
Loslein de Langenzen correctore ac socio. Laus Deo. MCCCCLXXVII."

In 1483 Veldener,* as has been previously observed at page 106, printed at Culemburg an edition in small quarto of the Speculum Salvationis, with the same blocks as had been used in the earlier folio editions, which are so confidently ascribed to Lawrence Coster. In Veldener's edition each of the large blocks, consisting of two compartments, is sawn in two in order to adapt them to a smaller page. A German translation of the Speculum, with wood-cuts, was printed at Basle, in folio, in 1476 ; and Jansen says that the first book printed in France with wood-cuts was an edition of the Speculum, at Lyons, in 1478 ; and that the second was a translation of the book named " Belial," printed at the same place in 1482.

The first printed book in the English language that contains wood-cuts is the second edition of Caxton's " Game and Playe of the Chesse," a small folio, without date or place, but generally supposed to have been printed about 1476.† The first edition of the same work, without cuts, was printed in 1474. On the blank leaves at the end of a copy of the first edition in the King's Library, at the British Museum, there is written in a contemporary hand a list of the bannerets and knights‡ made at the battle of " Stooke by syde newerke apon trent the xvi day of june the ii^de yer of harry the vii." that is, in 1487. In this battle Martin Swart was killed. He commanded the Flemings, who were sent by the Duchess of Burgundy to assist Lambert Simnel. It was at the request of the duchess, who was Edward the Fourth's sister, that Caxton translated the " Recuyell of the Historyes of Troye," the first book printed in the English language, and which appeared at Cologne in 1471 or 1472.

In Dr. Dibdin's edition of Ames's Typographical Antiquities there is a " Description of the Pieces and Pawns" in the second edition of Caxton's Chess ; which description is said to be illustrated with fac-

---

* Veldener at the conclusion of a book printed by him in 1476, containing " *Epistolares quasdam formulas*," thus informs the reader of his name and qualifications : " Accipito huic artifici nomen esse magistro Johanni Veldener, cui quidem certa manu insculpendi, celandi, intorculandi, caracterandi adsit industria ; adde et figurandi et effigiendi." That is, his name was John Veldener ; he could engrave, could work both at press and case, and moreover he knew something of sculpture, and could paint a little.

† Heineken, Idée Gén. p. 207, erroneously states that the first book with wood-cuts printed in England was the Golden Legend, by Caxton, in 1483. It is probable that the second edition of the Game of Chess preceded it by seven years, and it certainly was printed after the Mirror of the World.

‡ The following are some of the names as they are written : " S gilbert talbott . S john cheiny . S williā stoner . Theis iij wer made byfore the bataile, and after the bataile were made the same day : S^r. john of Arundell . Thomas Cooksey . John forteskew . Edmond benyngfeld . james blount . ric . of Croffte . Geofrey Stanley . ric . delaber. John mortymer. williā troutbeke." The above appear to have been created *Bannerets*, for after them follows a list of " *Knyghtes* made at the same bataile." It is likely that the owner of the volume was at the battle, and that the names were written immediately after.

simile wood-cuts. There are indeed fac-similes of some of the figures given, but not of the wood-cuts generally ; for in almost every cut given by Dr. Dibdin the back-ground of the original is omitted. In the description of the first fac-simile there is also an error: it is said to be " the *first* cut in the work," while in fact it is the *second*. The following I believe to be a correct list of these first fruits of English wood-engraving.

1. An executioner with an axe cutting to pieces, on a block, the limbs of a man. On the head, which is lying on the ground, there is a crown. Birds are seen seizing and flying away with portions of the limbs. There are buildings in the distance, and three figures, one of whom is a king with a crown and sceptre, appear looking on. 2. A figure sitting at a table, with a chess-board before him, and holding one of the chess-men in his hand. This is the cut which Dr. Dibdin says is the first in the book. 3. A king and another person playing at chess. 4. The king at chess, seated on a throne. 5. The king and queen. 6. The " alphyns," now called " bishops" in the game of chess, " in the maner of judges sittyng." 7. The knight. 8. The " rook," or castle, a figure on horseback wearing a hood and holding a staff in his hand. From No. 9 to No. 15 inclusive, the pawns are thus represented. 9. Labourers and workmen, the principal figure representing the first pawn, with a spade in his right hand and a cart-whip in his left. 10. The second pawn, a smith with his buttriss in the string of his apron, and a hammer in his right hand. 11. The third pawn, represented as a *clerk,* that is a writer or transcriber, in the same sense as Peter Scheffer and Ulric Zell are styled *clerici,* with his case of writing materials at his girdle, a pair of shears in one hand, and a large knife in the other. The knife, which has a large curved blade, appears more fit for a butcher's chopper than to make or mend pens. 12. The fourth pawn, a man with a pair of scales, and having a purse at his girdle, representing " marchauntes or chaungers." 13. The fifth pawn, a figure seated on a chair, having in his right hand a book, and in his left a sort of casket or box of ointments, representing a physician, spicer, or apothecary. 14. The sixth pawn, an innkeeper, receiving a guest. 15. The seventh pawn, a figure with a yard measure in his right hand, a bunch of keys in his left, and an open purse at his girdle, representing " customers and tolle gaderers." 16. The eighth pawn, a figure with a sort of badge on his breast near to his right shoulder, after the manner of a nobleman's retainer, and holding a pair of dice in his left hand, representing dice-players, messengers, and " currours," that is " couriers." In old authors the numerous idle retainers of the nobilityare frequently represented as gamblers, swashbucklers, and tavern-haunters.

Although there are twenty-four impressions in the volume, yet there are only sixteen subjects, as described above ; the remaining eight being repetitions of the cuts numbered 4, 5, 6, 7, 8 and 10, with two impressions of the cut No. 2, besides that towards the commencement.

The above cut is a reduced copy of the knight, No. 7 ; and his character is thus described : " The knyght ought to be maad al armed upon an hors in suche wise that he have an helme on his heed and a spere in his right hond, and coverid with his shelde, a swerde and a mace on his left syde . clad with an halberke and plates tofore his breste . legge harnoys on his legges . spores on his heelis, on hys handes hys gauntelettes . hys hors wel broken and taught and apte to bataylle and coveryd with hys armes. When the Knyghtes been maad they ben bayned or bathed . That is the signe that they sholde lede a newe lyf and newe maners . also they wake alle the nyght in prayers and orisons unto god that he wil geve hem grace that they may gete that thyng that they may not gete by nature. The kyng or prynce gyrdeth a boute them a swerde in signe that they shold abyde and kepen hym of whom they taken their dispences and dignyte."

The following cut of the sixth or bishop's pawn, No. 14, " whiche is lykened to taverners and vytayllers," is thus described in Caxton's own words : " The sixte pawn whiche stondeth before the alphyn on the lyfte syde is made in this forme . ffor hit is a man that hath the right hond stretched out for to calle men, and holdeth in his left honde a loof of breed and a cuppe of wyn . and on his gurdel hangyng a bondel of keyes, and this resemblith the taverners hostelers and sellars of vytayl . and

O

these ought properly to be sette to fore the alphyn as to fore a juge, for there sourdeth oft tymes amonge hem contencion noyse and stryf, which behoveth to be determyned and trayted by the alphyn which is juge of the kynge."

The next book containing wood-cuts printed by Caxton is the " Mirrour of the World, or thymage of the same," as he entitles it at the head of the table of contents. It is a thin folio consisting of one hundred leaves ; and, in the Prologue, Caxton informs the reader that it " conteyneth in all lxvii chapitres and xxvii figures, without which it may not lightly be understāde." He also says that he translated it from the French at the " request, desire, coste, and dispense of the honourable and worshipful man Hugh Bryce, alderman cytezeyn of London," who intended to present the same to William, Lord Hastings, chamberlain to Edward IV, and lieutenant of the same for the town of Calais and the marches there. On the last page he again mentions Hugh Bryce and Lord Hastings, and says of his translation : " Whiche book I begun first to trāslate the second day of Janyuer the yere of our lord M.cccc.lxxx. And fynysshed the viii day of Marche the same yere, and the xxi yere of the reign of the most crysten kynge, Kynge Edward the fourthe."*

* Edward IV. began to reign 4th March 1461 ; the twenty-first year of his reign would consequently commence on 4th March 1481 ; Caxton's dates therefore do not agree, unless we suppose that he reckoned the commencement of the year from 21st March. If so, his date viii March 1480, and the xxi year of the reign of Edward IV. would agree ; and the year of Christ, according to our present mode of reckoning, would be 1481. Dr. Dibdin assigns to the Mirror the date 1481.—Typ. Ant. i. p. 100.

The "xxvii figures" mentioned by Caxton, without which the work might not be easily understood, are chiefly diagrams explanatory of the principles of astronomy and dialling; but besides those twenty-seven cuts the book contains eleven more, which may be considered as illustrative rather than explanatory. The following is a list of those eleven cuts in the order in which they occur. They are less than the cuts in the "Game of Chess;" the most of them not exceeding three inches and a half by three.*

1. A school-master or "doctor," gowned, and seated on a high-backed chair, teaching four youths who are on their knees. 2. A person seated on a low-backed chair, holding in his hand a kind of globe; astronomical instruments on a table before him. 3. Christ, or the Godhead, holding in his hand a ball and cross. 4. The creation of Eve, who appears coming out of Adam's side.—The next cuts are figurative of the "seven arts liberal." 5. Grammar. A teacher with a large birch-rod seated on a chair, his four pupils before him on their knees. 6. Logic. Figure bare-headed seated on a chair, and having before him a book on a kind of reading-stand, which he appears expounding to his pupils who are kneeling. 7. Rhetoric. An upright figure in a gown, to whom another, kneeling, presents a paper, from which a seal is seen depending. 8. Arithmetic. A figure seated, and having before him a tablet inscribed with numerical characters. 9. Geometry. A figure standing, with a pair of compasses in his hand, with which he seems to be drawing diagrams on a table. 10. Music. A female figure with a sheet of music in her hand, singing, and a man playing on the English flute. 11. Astronomy. Figure with a kind of quadrant in his hand, who seems to be taking an observation.—An idea may be formed of the manner in which those cuts are engraved from the fac-simile on the next page of No. 10, "Music."

There are wood-cuts in the Golden Legend, 1483; the Fables of Esop, 1484; Chaucer's Canterbury Tales, and other books printed by Caxton; but it is unnecessary either to enumerate them or to give specimens, as they are all executed in the same rude manner as the cuts in the Book of Chess and the Mirror of the World. In the Book of Hunting and Hawking printed at St. Albans, 1486, there are rude wood-cuts; as also in a second and enlarged edition of the same book printed by Wynkyn de Worde, Caxton's successor, at Westminster in 1496. The most considerable wood-cut printed in England previous to 1500 is, so far as regards the design, a representation of the Crucifixion at the end of the Golden Legend printed by Wynkyn de Worde in

* Fac-similes of six of those cuts are given in Dr. Dibdin's edition of Ames's Typographical Antiquities, vol. i. p. 110—112.

1493.* In this cut, neither of the thieves on each side of Christ appears to be nailed to the cross. The arms of the thief on the right of Christ hang behind, and are bound to the transverse piece of the cross, which passes underneath his shoulders. His feet are neither bound nor nailed to the cross. The feet of the thief to the left of Christ are tied to the upright piece of the cross, to which his hands are also bound, his shoulders resting upon the top, and his face turned upward towards the sky. To the left is seen the Virgin,—who has fallen down,—supported by St. John. In the back-ground to the right, the artist, like several others of that period, has represented Christ bearing his cross.

Dr. Dibdin, at page 8 of the "Disquisition on the Early State of Engraving and Ornamental Printing in Great Britain," prefixed to Ames's and Herbert's Typographical Antiquities, makes the following observations on this cut : "The 'Crucifixion' at the end of the 'Golden Legend' of 1493, which Wynkyn de Worde has so frequently subjoined to his religious pieces, is, unquestionably, the effort of some ingenious foreign artist. It is not very improbable that Rubens had a recollection of one of the thieves, twisted, from convulsive agony, round the top of the cross, when he executed his celebrated picture of the same subject."†

* A large flowered letter, a T, cut on wood, occurs on the same page as the Crucifixion.

† In a note upon this passage Dr. Dibdin gives the following extract from Sir Joshua Reynolds. " To give animation to this subject, Rubens has chosen the point of time when an executioner is piercing the side of Christ, while another with a bar of iron is breaking the

In De Worde's cut, however, it is to be remarked that the contorted attitude of both the thieves results rather from the manner in which they are bound to the cross, than from the convulsions of agony.

At page 7 of the same Disquisition it is said that the figures in the Game of Chess, the Mirror of the World, and other works printed by Caxton "are, in all probability, not the genuine productions of this country ; and may be traced to books of an earlier date printed abroad, from which they were often borrowed without acknowledgment or the least regard to the work in which they again appeared. Caxton, however, has judiciously taken one of the prints from the ' Biblia Pauperum ' to introduce in his ' Life of Christ.' The cuts for his second edition of ' Chaucer's Canterbury Tales' may perhaps safely be considered as the genuine invention and execution of a British artist."

Although I am well aware that the printers of the fifteenth century were accustomed to copy without acknowledgment the cuts which appeared in each other's books, and though I think it likely that Caxton might occasionally resort to the same practice, yet I am decidedly of opinion that the cuts in the " Game of Chess" and the " Mirror of the World" were designed and engraved in this country. Caxton's Game of Chess is certainly the first book of the kind which appeared with wood-cuts in any country ; and I am further of opinion that in no book printed previous to 1481 will the presumed originals of the eleven principal cuts in the Mirror of the World be found. Before we are required to believe that the cuts in those two books were copied from similar designs by some foreign artist, we ought to be informed in what work such originals are to be found. If there be any merit in a first design, however rude, it is but just to assign it to him who first employs the unknown artist and makes his productions known. Caxton's claims to the merit of " illustrating" the Game of Chess and the Mirror of the World with wood-cuts from original designs, I conceive to be indisputable.

Dr. Dibdin, in a long note at pages 33, 34, and 35 of the Typographical Antiquities, gives a confused account of the earliest editions of books on chess. He mentions as the first, a Latin edition—supposed by Santander to be the work of Jacobus de Cessolis—in folio, printed about the year 1473, by Ketelaer and Leempt. In this edition, however, there are no cuts, and the date is only conjectural. He says that two editions of the work of Jacobus de Cessolis on the Morality of Chess, in German and Italian, with wood-cuts, were printed, without date, in the fifteenth century, and he adds : " Whether Caxton borrowed the

limbs of one of the malefactors, who in his convulsive agony, which his body admirably expresses, has torn one of his feet from the tree to which it was nailed. The expression in the action of the figure is wonderful."

cuts in his second edition from those in the 8vo. German edition without date, or from this latter Italian one, I am not able to ascertain, having seen neither." He seems satisfied that Caxton had *borrowed* the cuts in his book of chess, though he is at a loss to discover the party who might have them to *lend*. Had he even seen the two editions which he mentions, he could not have known whether Caxton had borrowed his cuts from them or not until he had ascertained that they were printed previously to the English edition. There is a German edition of Jacobus de Cessolis, in folio, with wood-cuts supposed to be printed in 1477, at Augsburg, by Gunther Zainer, but both date and printer's name are conjectural. The first German edition of this work with wood-cuts, and having a positive date, I believe to be that printed at Strasburg by Henry Knoblochzer in 1483. Until a work on chess shall be produced of an earlier date than that ascribed to Caxton's, and containing similar wood-cuts, I shall continue to believe that the wood-cuts in the second English edition of the "Game and Playe of the Chesse" were both designed and executed by an English artist; and I protest against bibliographers going a-begging with wood-cuts found in old English books, and ascribing them to foreign artists, before they have taken the slightest pains to ascertain whether such cuts were executed in England or not.

The wood-cuts in the Game of Chess and the Mirror of the World are equally as good as the wood-cuts which are to be found in books printed abroad about the same period. They are even decidedly better than those in Anthony Sorg's German Bible, Augsburg, 1480, or those in Veldener's edition of the Fasciculus Temporum, printed at Utrecht in the same year.

It has been supposed that most of the wood-cuts which appear in books printed by Caxton and De Worde were executed abroad; on the presumption that there were at that period no professed wood engravers in England. Although I am inclined to believe that within the fifteenth century there were no persons in this country who practised wood engraving as a distinct profession, yet it by no means follows from such an admission that Caxton's and De Worde's cuts must have been engraved by foreign artists. The manner in which they are executed is so coarse that they might be cut by any person who could handle a graver. Looking at them merely as specimens of wood engraving, they are not generally superior to the practice-blocks cut by a modern wood-engraver's apprentice within the first month of his noviciate. I conceive that there would be no greater difficulty in finding a person capable of engraving them than there would be in finding the pieces of wood on which they were to be executed. Persons who have noticed the embellishments in manuscripts, the carving, the monuments, and the stained glass in churches, executed in England about the time of Caxton, will scarcely suppose that there were no artists in this country capable of making the designs for those cuts. There is in fact reason to believe that in England in the fifteenth and sixteenth centuries the walls of apartments, more especially in taverns and hostelries, frequently contained paintings, most probably in distemper, of subjects both from sacred and general history. That paintings of sacred subjects were not unusual in churches at those periods is well known.

In most of the cuts which are to be found in books printed by Caxton, the effect is produced by the simplest means. The outline of the figures is coarse and hard, and the shades and folds of the draperies are indicated by short parallel lines. Cross-hatchings occur in none of them, though in one or two I have noticed a few angular dots picked out of the black part of a cut in order that it might not appear like a mere blot. The foliage of the trees is generally represented in a manner similar to those in the background of the cut of the knight, of which a copy is given at page 193. The oak leaves in a wood-cut[*] at the commencement of the preface to the Golden Legend, 1483, are an exception to the general style of Caxton's foliage; and represent what they are intended for with tolerable accuracy. Having thus noticed some of the earliest books with wood-engravings printed in England, I shall now resume my account of the progress of the art on the Continent.

In an edition of Ptolemy's Cosmography, printed at Ulm in 1482 by Leonard Holl, we have the first instance of maps engraved on wood. The work is in folio, and the number of the maps is twenty-seven. In a general map of the world the engraver has thus inserted his name at the top: "Insculptum est per Johannē Schnitzer de Armssheim."[†] At the corners of this map the winds are represented by heads with puffed-out cheeks, very indifferently engraved. The work also contains ornamental initial letters engraved on wood. In a large one, the letter at the beginning of the volume, the translator is represented offering his book to Pope Paul II. who occupied the see of Rome from 1464 to 1471.

Each map occupies two folio pages, and is printed on the verso of one page and the recto of the next, in such a manner that when the book is open the adjacent pages seem as if printed from one block. What may be considered as the skeleton of each map,—such as

---

[*] A copy of this cut is given at p. 186, vol. i. of Dr. Dibdin's edition of the Typographical Antiquities.

[†] Arnsheim, which is probably the place intended, is about twenty miles to the southwest of Mentz.

indications of rivers and mountains,—is coarsely cut ; but as the names of the places are also engraved on wood, the execution of those thirty-seven maps must have been a work of considerable labour. In 1486 another edition with the same cuts was printed at Ulm by John Regen at the cost of Justus de Albano of Venice.

The idea of Leonard Holl's Ptolemy was most likely suggested by an edition of the same work printed at Rome in 1478 by Arnold Bukinck, the successor of Conrad Sweinheim. In this edition the maps are printed from plates of copper ; and from the perfect similarity of the letters, as may be observed in the names of places, there can be no doubt of their having been stamped upon the plate by means of a punch in a manner similar to that in which a bookbinder impresses the titles at the back of a volume. It is absolutely impossible that such perfect uniformity in the form of the letters could have been obtained, had they been separately engraved on the plate by hand. Each single letter is as perfectly like another of the same character,— the capital M for instance,—as types cast by a letter-founder from the same mould. The names of the places are all in capitals, but different sizes are used for the names of countries and cities. The capitals at the margins referring to the degrees of latitude are of very beautiful shape, and as delicate as the capitals in modern hair-type.

At the back of some of the maps in the copy in the King's Library at the British Museum, the paper appears as if it had received, when in a damp state, an impression from linen cloth. As this appearance of threads crossing each other does not proceed from the texture of the paper, but is evidently the result of pressure, I am inclined to think that it has been occasioned by a piece of linen being placed between the paper and the roller when the impressions were taken.

In the dedication of the work to the Pope it is stated that this edition was prepared by Domitius Calderinus of Verona, who promised to collate the Latin version with an ancient Greek manuscript ; and that Conrad Sweinheim, who was one of the first who introduced the art of printing at Rome, undertook, with the assistance of "certain mathematical men," whom he taught, to "impress" the maps upon plates of copper. Sweinheim, after having spent three years in preparing these plates, died before they were finished ; and Arnold Bukinck, a learned German printer, completed the work, "that the emendations of Calderinus,—who also died before the book was printed,—and the results of Sweinheim's most ingenious mechanical contrivances might not be lost to the learned world."[*]

* " Magister vero Conradus Suueynheyn, Germanus, a quo formandorum Romæ librorum ars primum profecta est, occasione hinc sumpta posteritati consulens animum ad hanc

An edition of Ptolemy in folio, with the maps engraved on copper, was printed at Bologna by Dominico de Lapis with the erroneous date M.CCCC.LXII. This date is certainly wrong, for no work from the press of this printer is known of an earlier date than 1477 ; and the editor of this edition, Philip Beroaldus the elder, was only born in 1450, if not in 1453. Supposing him to have been born in the former year, he would only be twelve years old in 1462. Raidel, who in 1737 published a dissertation on this edition, thinks that two numerals—xx—had accidentally been omitted, and that the date ought to be 1482. Breitkopf thinks that one x might be accidentally omitted in a date and pass uncorrected, but not two. He rather thinks that the compositor had placed an I instead of an L, and that the correct date ought to stand thus : M CCCC L XLI—1491. I am however of opinion that no instance of the Roman numerals, L XLI, being thus combined to express 91, can be produced. It seems most probable that the date 1482 assigned by Raidel is correct ; although his opinion respecting the numerals—xx—being accidentally omitted may be wrong. It is extremely difficult to account for the erroneous dates of many books printed previous to 1500. Several of those dates may have been accidentally wrong set by the compositor, and overlooked by the corrector ; but others are so obvious that it is likely they were designedly introduced. The bibliographer who should undertake to enquire what the printers' reasons might be for falsifying the dates of their books, would be as likely to arrive at the truth, as he would be in an enquiry into the reason of their sometimes adding their name, and sometimes omitting it. The execution of the maps in the edition of De Lapis is much inferior to that of the maps begun by Sweinheim, and finished by Bukinck in 1478.

Bukinck's edition of Ptolemy, 1478, is the second book which contains impressions from copper-plates. Heineken, at page 233, refers to the " Missale Herbipolense," folio, 1481, as the first book printed in Germany containing a specimen of copper-plate engraving. Dr. Dibdin, however, in the 3rd volume of his Tour, page 306, mentions the same work as having the date of 1479 in the prefatory admonition, and says that the plate of a shield of arms—the only one in the volume—is noticed by Bartsch in his " Peintre-Graveur," vol. x. p. 57. The printer

doctrinam capessendam applicuit. Subinde mathematicis adhibitis viris quemadmodum tabulis eneis imprimerentur edocuit, triennioque in hac cura consumpto diem obiit. In cujus vigilarum laborumque partem non inferiori ingenio ac studio Arnoldus Buckinck e Germania vir apprime eruditus ad imperfectum opus succedens, ne Domitii Conradique obitu eorum vigiliæ emendationesque sine testimonio perirent neve virorum eruditorum censuram fugerent immensæ subtilitatis machinimenta, examussim ad unum perfecit."—Dedication to the Pope, of Ptolemy's Cosmography, Rome, 1478.

of the edition of 1481 appears from Heineken to have been George Reyser. In the "Modus Orandi secundum chorum Herbipolensem," folio, printed by George Reyser, "Herbipoli," [at Wurtzburg,] 1485, there is on folio II. a copper-plate engraving of the arms of Rudolph de Scherenberg, bishop of that see. This plate is also described by Bartsch in his "Peintre-Graveur," vol. x. p. 156. The first book which appeared with copper-plate engravings is intitled "Il Monte Sancto di Dio," written by Antonio Bettini, and printed at Florence in 1477 by Nicolo di Lorenzo della Magna. As this book is of extreme rarity, I shall here give an account of the plates from Mercier, who first called the attention of bibliographers to it as being of an earlier date than the folio edition of Dante, with copper-plate engravings, printed also by Nicolo Lorenzo in 1481. This edition of Dante was generally supposed to be the first book containing copper-plate engravings until Bettini's work was described by Mercier.

The work called "Il Monte Sancto di Dio" is in quarto, and according to Mercier there ought to be a quire or gathering of four leaves at the commencement, containing a summary of the work, which is divided into three parts, with a table of the chapters. On the reverse of the last of those four leaves is the first plate, which occupies the whole page, and "measures nine inches and seven-eighths in height, by seven inches in width."* This plate represents the Holy Mountain, on the top of which Christ is seen standing in the midst of adoring angels. A ladder is placed against this mountain, to which it is fastened with iron chains, and on each step is engraved the name of a virtue, for instance, Prudence, Temperance, Fortitude, and others. A figure clothed in a long robe, and who appears to be a monk, is seen mounting the ladder. His eyes are directed towards a large crucifix placed half way up the hill to the right of the ladder, and from his mouth there proceeds a label inscribed with these words: "*Tirami doppo ti*,"—"Draw me up after thee." Another figure is seen standing at the foot of the mountain, looking towards the top, and uttering these words: "*Levavi oculos meos in montes*," &c. The second plate occurs at signature I v† after the 115th chapter. It also represents Christ in his glory, surrounded by angels. It is only four inches and five lines high, by six inches wide, French measure. The third plate, which is the same size as the second, occurs at signature Pvij, and represents a view of Hell according to the description of Dante. Those plates, which for the period are well enough designed and executed, especially the second, were most likely engraved

---

* This is Mr. Ottley's measurement, taken within the black line which bounds the subject. The width as given by Mercier does not accord with the above. He says that the plate " a neuf pouces et demi de haut sur six de large."

† Mr. Ottley says, " on the reverse of signature N viij."

on copper; and they seem to be by the same hand as those in the edition of Dante of 1481, from the press of Nicolo di Lorenzo, who also printed the work of Bettini.* A copy of "Il Monte Sancto di Dio" is in Earl Spencer's Library; and a description and specimens of the cuts are given by Dr. Dibdin in the Bibliotheca Spenceriana, vol. iv. p. 30; and by Mr. Ottley in the Inquiry into the Origin and Early History of Engraving, vol. i. pp. 375—377.

In the execution of the maps, the copper-plate engraver possesses a decided advantage over the engraver on wood, owing to the greater facility and clearness with which letters can be cut *in* copper than *on* wood. In the engraving of letters on copper, the artist cuts the form of the letter *into* the plate, the character being thus in *intaglio;* while in engraving on a block, the wood surrounding has to be cut away, and the letter left in *relief.* On copper, using only the graver,—for etching was not known in the fifteenth century,—as many letters might be cut in one day as could be cut on wood in three. Notwithstanding the disadvantage under which the ancient wood engravers laboured in the execution of maps, they for many years contended with the copper-plate printers for a share of this branch of business; and the printers, at whose presses maps engraved on wood only could be printed, were well inclined to support the wood engravers. In a folio edition of Ptolemy, printed at Venice in 1511, by Jacobus Pentius de Leucho, the outlines of the maps, with the indications of the mountains and rivers, are cut on wood, and the names of the places are printed in type, of different sizes, and with red and black ink. For instance, in the map of Britain, which is more correct than any which had previously appeared, the word "ALBION" is printed in large capitals, and the word "GADINI" in small capitals, and both with red ink. The words "Curia" and "Bremenium" are printed in small Roman characters, and with black ink. The names of the rivers are also in small Roman, and in black ink. Such of those maps as contain many names, are almost full of type. The double borders surrounding them, within which the degrees of latitude are marked, appear to have been formed of separate pieces of metal, in the manner of wide double rules. At the head of several of the maps there are figures of animals emblematic of the country. In the first map of Africa there are two parrots; in the second an animal like a jackal, and a non-descript; in the third, containing Egypt, a crocodile, and a monstrous kind of fish like a dragon; and in the

---

* "Lettres de M. l'Abbé de St. L***, [St. Léger, autrefois le pere Le Mercier, ancien Bibliothecaire de St. Genevieve] à M. le Baron de H*** sur différentes Editions rares du XVᵉ. Siécle," p. 4—5. 8vo. Paris, 1783. A short biographic sketch of the Abbé Mercier St. Léger, one of the most eminent French Bibliographers of the last century, will be found in Dr. Dibdin's Tour, vol. ii. p. 180.

fourth, two parrots. In the last, the "curious observer" will note a specimen of decorative printing from two blocks of wood ; for the beak, wing, and tail of one of the parrots is printed in red.

In the last map,—of Loraine,—in an edition of Ptolemy, in folio, printed at Strasburg in 1513, by John Schott, the attempt to print in colours, in the manner of chiaro-scuro wood engravings, is carried yet further. The hills and woods are printed green ; the indications of towns and cities, and the names of the most considerable places, are red ; while the names of the smaller places are black. For this map, executed in three colours, green, red, and black, there would be required two wood engravings and two forms of type, each of which would have to be separately printed. The arms which form a border to the map are printed in their proper heraldic colours.* The only other specimen of armorial bearings printed in colours from wood-blocks, that I am aware of, is Earl Spencer's arms in the first part of Savage's Hints on Decorative Printing, which was published in 1818, upwards of three hundred years after the first essay.

At a later period a new method was adopted by which the wood engraver was spared the trouble of cutting the letters, while the printer was enabled to obtain a perfect copy of each map by a single impression. The mode in which this was effected was as follows. The indications of mountains, rivers, cities, and villages were engraved on the wood as before, and blank spaces were left for the names. Those spaces were afterwards cut out by means of a chisel or drill, piercing quite through the block : and the names of the places being inserted in type, the whole constituted only one " form," from which an impression both of the cut and the letters could be obtained by its being passed once through the press. Sebastian Munster's Cosmography, folio, printed at Basle in 1554, by Henry Petri, affords several examples of maps executed in this manner. This may be considered as one of the last efforts of the old wood engravers and printers to secure to themselves a share of the business of map-engraving. Their endeavours, however, were unavailing ; for within twenty years of that date, this branch of art was almost exclusively in the hands of the copper-plate engravers. From the date of the maps of Ortelius, Antwerp, 1570, engraved on copper by Ægidius Diest, maps engraved on wood are rarely to be seen. The practice of engraving the outlines and rivers on wood, and then piercing the block and inserting the names of the places in type has, however, lately been revived ; and where publishers are obliged either to print maps with the type or to

---

* I regret that I have not had an opportunity of personally examining this map. There is a copy of Schott's edition in the British Museum ; but all the maps, except one of the sphere, are taken out. The above account of the map of Loraine is from Breitkopf's interesting essay " Ueber den Druck der Geographischen Charten," S. 7. 4to. Leipzig, 1777.

give none at all, this mode may answer very well, more especially when the object is to give the relative position of a few of the principal places, rather than a crowded list of names. Most of the larger maps in the Penny Cyclopædia are executed in this manner. The holes in the blocks are pierced with the greatest rapidity by gouges of different sizes acting vertically, and put in motion by machinery contrived by Mr. Edward Cowper, to whose great mechanical skill the art of steam-printing chiefly owes its perfection.

Having thus noticed consecutively the progress of map engraving, it may not here be out of place to give a brief account of Breitkopf's experiment to print a map with separate pieces of metal in the manner of type.* Previous to 1776 some attempts had been made by a person named Preusch, of Carlsruhe, to print maps by a process which he named typometric, and who published an account of his plan, printed at the press of Haass the Younger, of Basil. In 1776 Breitkopf sent a communication to Busching's Journal, containing some remarks on the invention of Preusch, and stating that he had conceived a similar plan upwards of twenty years previously, and that he had actually set up a specimen and printed off a few copies, which he had given to his friends. The veracity of this account having been questioned by an illiberal critic, Breitkopf, in 1777, prefixed to his Essay on the Printing of Maps a specimen composed of moveable pieces of metal in the manner of types. He expressly declares that he considered his experiment a failure ; and that he only produced his specimen—a quarto map of the country round Leipsic—in testimony of the truth of what he had previously asserted, and to show that two persons might, independently of each other, conceive an idea of the same invention, although they might differ considerably in their mode of carrying it into effect.

He was first led to think on the practicability of printing maps with moveable pieces of metal by considering that when the letters are omitted there remain but hills, rivers, and the indications of places ; and for these he was convinced that representations consisting of moveable pieces of metal might be contrived. Having, however, made the experiment, he felt satisfied that the appearance of such a map was unpleasing to the eye, and that the invention was not likely to be practically useful. Had it not been for the publication of Preusch, he says that he never would have thought of mentioning his invention, except as a mechanical experiment ; and to show that the execution of maps in such a manner was within the compass of the printer's art.

In the specimen which he gives, rivers are represented by minute parallel lines, which are shorter or longer as the river contracts or

* The following particulars respecting Breitkopf's invention are derived from his essay " Ueber den Druck der Geographischen Charten," previously referred to.

expands ; and the junction of the separate pieces may be distinctly perceived. For hills and trees there are distinct characters representing those objects. Towns and large villages are distinguished by a small church, and small villages by a small circle. Roads are indicated by dotted parallel lines. For the title of the map large capitals are used. The name of the city of LEIPSIC is in small capitals. The names of towns and villages are in *Italic ;* and of woods, rivers, and hills, in Roman type. The general appearance of the map is unpleasing to the eye. Breitkopf has displayed his ingenuity by producing such a typographic curiosity, and his good sense in abandoning his invention when he found that he could not render it useful.

Mr. Ottley, at page 755 of the second volume of his Inquiry, makes the following remarks on the subject of cross-hatching in wood engravings :—" It appears anciently to have been the practice of those masters who furnished designs for the wood engravers to work from, carefully to avoid all cross-hatchings, which, it is probable, were considered beyond the power of the Xylographist to represent. Wolgemuth perceived that, though difficult, this was not impossible ; and in the cuts of the Nuremberg Chronicle, the execution of which, (besides furnishing the designs,) he doubtless superintended, a successful attempt was first made to imitate the bold hatchings of a pen-drawing, crossing each other, as occasion prompted the designer, in various directions : to him belongs the praise of having been the first who duly appreciated the powers of this art."

Although it is true that cross-hatchings are not to be found in the earliest wood engravings, yet Mr. Ottley is wrong in assigning this material improvement in the art to Michael Wolgemuth ; for cross-hatching is introduced in the beautiful cut forming the frontispiece to the Latin edition of Breydenbach's Travels, folio, first printed at Mentz, by Erhard Reuwich, in 1486,* seven years before the Nuremberg Chronicle appeared. The cut in the following page is a reduced but accurate copy of Breydenbach's frontispiece, which is not only the finest wood engraving which had appeared up to that date, 1486, but is in point of design and execution as superior to the best cuts in the Nuremberg Chronicle, as the designs of Albert Durer are to the cuts in the oldest editions of the " Poor Preachers' Bible."

In this cut, cross-hatching may be observed in the drapery of the female figure, in the upper part of the two shields on each side of her, in the border at the top of the cut, and in other places. Whether the female figure be intended as a personification of the city of Mentz, as is

---

* An edition of this work in German, with the same cuts, was printed by Reuwich in 1488. Within ten years, at least six different editions of this work were printed in Germany. It was also translated into Low Dutch, and printed in Holland.

sometimes seen in old books of the sixteenth century, or for St. Catherine, whose shrine on Mount Sinai was visited by Breydenbach in his travels, I shall not pretend to determine. The arms on her right are Breydenbach's own ; on her left are the arms of John, Count of Solms and Lord of Mintzenberg, and at the bottom of the cut those of Philip de Bicken, knight, who were Breydenbach's companions to the holy sepulchre at Jerusalem and the shrine of St. Catherine on Mount Sinai.

St. Catherine, it may be observed, was esteemed the patroness of learned men, and her figure was frequently placed in libraries in Catholic countries, in the same manner as the bust of Minerva in the libraries of ancient Greece and Rome. The name of the artist by whom the frontispiece to Breydenbach's travels was executed is unknown ; but I have no hesitation in declaring him to be one of the best wood engravers of the period. As this is the earliest wood-cut in which I have noticed cross-hatching, I shall venture to ascribe the merit of the invention to the unknown artist, whoever he may have been ; and shall consider the date 1486 as marking the period when a new style of wood engraving was introduced. Wolgemuth, as associated with wood engraving, has too long been decked out with borrowed plumes ; and persons who knew little or nothing either of the history or practice of the art, and who are misled by writers on whose authority they rely, believe that Michael Wolgemuth was not only one of the best wood engravers of his day, but that he was the first who introduced a material improvement into the practice of the art. This error becomes more firmly rooted when such persons come to be informed that he was the master of Albert Durer, who is generally, but erroneously, supposed to have been the best wood engraver of his day. Albert Durer studied under Michael Wolgemuth as a painter, and not as a wood engraver ; and I consider it as extremely questionable if either of them ever engraved a single block. There are many evidences in Germany of Wolgemuth having been a tolerably good painter for the age and country in which he lived ; but there is not one of his having engraved on wood. In the Nuremberg Chronicle he is represented as having, in conjunction with William Pleydenwurf, superintended the execution of the wood-cuts contained in that book. Those cuts, which are frequently referred to as excellent specimens of old wood engraving, are in fact the most tasteless and worthless things that are to be found in any book, ancient or modern. It is a book, however, that is easy to be obtained; and it serves as a land-mark to superficial enquirers who are perpetually referring to it as containing wood-cuts designed, if not engraved, by Albert Durer's master,—and such, they conclude, must necessarily possess a very high degree of excellence.

Breydenbach was a canon of the cathedral church of Mentz, and he dedicates the account of his pilgrimage to the Holy Land and visit to Mount Sinai to Berthold, archbishop of that see. The frontispiece, although most deserving of attention as a specimen of wood engraving, is not the only cut in the book which is worthy of notice. Views are given, engraved on wood, of the most remarkable places which he visited ;—and those of Venice, Corfu, Modon, and the country round Jerusalem, which are of great length, are inserted in the book as "folding plates." Each of the above views is too large to have been engraved on one block. For that of Venice, which is about five feet long, and ten inches high, several blocks must have been required, from each of which impressions would have to be taken singly, and afterwards pasted together, as is at present done in such views as are too wide to be contained on one sheet. Those views, with respect to the manner in which they are executed, are superior to everything of the same kind which had previously appeared. The work also contains smaller cuts printed with the type, which are not generally remarkable for their execution, although some of them are drawn and engraved in a free and spirited manner. The following cut is a reduced copy of that which is prefixed to a chapter intitled "De Surianis qui Ierosolimis et locis illis manentes etiam se asserunt esse Christianos :"—

In a cut of animals there is a figure of a giraffe,* named by Breydenbach "seraffa," of a unicorn, a salamander, a camel, and an animal something like an oran-outang, except that it has a tail. Of the last the traveller observes, "non constat de nomine." Some account of this book, with fac-similes of the cuts, will be found in Dibdin's Bibliotheca Spenceriana, vol. iii. pp. 216—228. In the copy there described, belonging to Earl Spencer, the beautiful frontispiece was wanting.

Although a flowered border surrounding a whole page may be observed as occurring twice in Veldener's edition of the Fasciculus Temporum, printed at Utrecht in 1480, yet I am inclined to think that the practice of surrounding every page with an ornamental flowered border cut in wood, was first introduced by the Parisian printers at a period somewhat later. In 1488, an edition of the "Horæ in Laudem beatissimæ virginis Mariæ," in octavo, was printed at Paris by Anthony Verard, the text of which is surrounded with ornamental borders. The practice thus introduced was subsequently adopted by the printers of

* This is probably the first figure of the giraffe that was communicated to the "reading public" of Europe. Its existence was afterwards denied by several naturalists ; and it is only within a comparatively recent period that the existence of such an animal was clearly established.

Germany and Holland, more especially in the decoration of devotional works, such as Horæ, Breviaries, and Psalters. Verard appears to have chiefly printed works of devotion and love, for a greater number of Horæ and Romances proceeded from his press than that of any other printer of his age. Most of them contain wood-cuts, some of which, in books printed by him about the beginning of the sixteenth century, are designed with considerable taste and well engraved; while others, those for instance in " La Fleur des Battailes," 4to, 1505, are not superior to those in Caxton's Chess: it is, however, not unlikely that the cuts in " La Fleur des Battailes" of this date had been used for an earlier edition.*

The "Hortus Sanitatis," folio, printed at Mentz in 1491 by Jacobus Meydenbach, is frequently referred to by bibliographers; not so much on account of the many wood-cuts which it contains, but as being supposed in some degree to confirm a statement in Sebastian Munster's Cosmography, and in Serrarius, De Rebus Moguntinis, where a *John* Meydenbach is mentioned as being a partner with Gutemberg and Faust. Von Murr, as has been previously noticed, supposed that this person was a wood engraver; and Prosper Marchand,† though without any authority, calls *Jacobus* Meydenbach his son or his relation.

This work, which is a kind of Natural History, explaining the uses and virtues of herbs, fowls, fish, quadrupeds, minerals, drugs, and spices, contains a number of wood-cuts, many of which are curious, as containing representations of natural objects, but none of which are remarkable for their execution as wood engravings. On the opposite page is a fac-simile of the cut which forms the head-piece to the chapter " De Ovis." The figure, which possesses considerable merit, represents an old woman going to market with her basket of eggs.

This is a fair specimen of the manner in which the cuts in the Hortus Sanitatis are designed and executed. Among the most curious and best designed are: the interior of an apothecary's shop, on the reverse of the first leaf; a monkey seated on the top of a fountain, in the chapter on water; a butcher cutting up meat; a man selling cheese at a stall; a woman milking a cow; and figures of the male and female mandrake. At chapter 119, " De Pediculo," a woman is represented brushing the head of a boy with a peculiar kind of brush, which answers the purpose of a small-toothed comb; and she appears

---

* A good specimen of early French wood engraving may be seen in the large cut forming a kind of frontispiece to the " Roman du Roy Artus," folio, printed at Rouen in 1488 by Jehan de Bourgeois. This cut, which occupies the whole page, represents King Arthur and his knights dining off the round table. A smaller one occurs at the beginning of the second part, and both are surrounded by ornamental borders.

† Hist. de l'Imprimerie, p. 49.

to bestow her labour on no infertile field, for each of her "sweepings," which are seen lying on the floor, would scarcely slip through the teeth of a garden rake. Meydenbach's edition has been supposed to be the first; and Linnæus, in the Bibliotheca Botanica, has ascribed the work to one John Cuba, a physician of Mentz; but other writers have doubted if this person were really the author. The first edition of this work, under the title of "Herbarus," with a hundred and fifty wood-cuts, was printed at Mentz by Peter Scheffer in 1484; and in 1485 he printed an enlarged edition in German, containing three hundred and eighty cuts, under the title of "Ortus Sanitatis oder Garten der Gesundheit." Of the work printed by Scheffer, Breydenbach is said

to have been one of the compilers. Several editions of the Hortus Sanitatis were subsequently printed, not only in Germany, but in France Holland, and Switzerland.

Having previously expressed my opinion respecting the wood-cuts in the Nuremberg Chronicle, there will be less occasion to give a detailed account of the book and the rubbish it contains here : in speaking thus it may perhaps be necessary to say that this character is meant to apply to the wood-cuts and not to the literary portion of the work, which Thomas Hearne, of black-letter memory, pronounces to be extremely "pleasant, useful, and curious." With the wood-cuts the Rev. Dr. Dibdin appears to have been equally charmed.

The work called the "Nuremberg Chronicle" is a folio, compiled by
Hartman Schedel, a physician of Nuremberg, and printed in that city
by Anthony Koburger in 1493.   In the colophon it is stated that the
views of cities, and figures of eminent characters, were executed under
the superintendence of Michael Wolgemuth and William Pleydenwurff,
"mathematical men"* and skilled in the art of painting.   The total
number of impressions contained in the work exceeds two thousand, but
several of the cuts are repeated eight or ten times.   The following
fac-simile will afford an idea of the style in which the portraits of
illustrious men contained in this often-cited chronicle are executed.

The above head, which the owner appears to be scratching with so
much earnestness, first occurs as that of Paris the lover of Helen; and
it is afterwards repeated as that of Thales, Anastasius, Odofredus, and
the poet Dante.   In a like manner the economical printer has a stock-
head for kings and emperors; another for popes; a third for bishops;
a fourth for saints, and so on.   Several cuts representing what might be
supposed to be particular events are in the same manner pressed into
the general service of the chronicler.

The peculiarity of the cuts in the Nuremberg Chronicle is that they
generally contain more of what engravers term "colour" than any which

---

* The expression "adhibitis tamen viris mathematicis" in the Nuremberg Chronicle, is
evidently borrowed from that,—"subinde mathematicis adhibitis viris,"—in the dedication of
Bukinck's Ptolemy, 1478, to the Pope.   "Mathematical men," in the present sense of the
term, might be required to construct the maps in the edition of Ptolemy, but scarcely to
design or engrave the vulgar figures and worthless views in the Nuremberg Chronicle.

had previously appeared. Before proceeding, however, to make any further observations on these cuts, I shall endeavour to explain what engravers mean by the term "colour," as applied to an impression taken with black ink from a copper-plate or a wood-block.

Though there is no "colour," strictly speaking, in an engraving consisting merely of black and white lines, yet the term is often conventionally applied to an engraving which is supposed, from the varied character of its lines and the contrast of light and shade, to convey the idea of varied local colour as seen in a painting or a water-colour drawing. For instance, an engraving is said to contain much "colour" which appears clearly to indicate not only a variety of colour, but also its different degrees of intensity in the several objects, and which at the same time presents an effective combination of light and shade. An engraver cannot certainly express the difference between green and yellow, or red and orange, yet in engraving a figure, say that of a cavalier by Vandyke, with brown leather boots, buff-coloured woollen hose, doublet of red silk, and blue velvet cloak, a master of his art will not only express a difference in the texture, but will also convey an idea of the different parts of the dress being of different colours. The Rent Day, engraved by Raimbach from a painting by Wilkie, and Chelsea Pensioners hearing the Gazette of the Battle of Waterloo read, engraved by Burnet from a picture by the same artist, may be instanced as copper-plate engravings which contain much "colour."

Mr. Landseer, at pages 175, 176, of his Lectures on Engraving, makes the following remarks on the term "colour," as conventionally applied by engravers in speaking of impressions from plates or from wood-blocks :—" It is not uncommon among print-publishers, nor even amongst engravers themselves, to hear the word COLOUR mistakenly employed to signify *shade ;* so that if they think an engraving too dark, they say it has too much *colour,* too little colour if too light— and so forth. The same ignorance which has hitherto reigned over the pursuits of this Art, has here imposed its authority, and with the same unfortunate success : I cannot however yield to it the same submission, since it is not only a palpable misuse of a word, but would lead to endless confusion when I come to explain to you my ideas of the means the Art of engraving possesses of rendering local colour in the abstract. Wherefore, whenever I may use the term *colour,* I mean it in no other than its ordinary acceptation."

" By MIDDLE TINT, I understand and mean, 'the medium between strong light and strong shade.'—These are Mr. Gilpin's words ; and he adds, with a propriety that confers value on the definition—' the phrase is *not at all* expressive of colour.' "

Whether we owe the term "colour," as applied to engravings, to the

ignorance of printsellers or not, I shall not inquire ; I only know that
a number of terms equally objectionable, if their primitive meaning
be considered, are used in speaking of the arts of painting and engraving
by persons who are certainly not ignorant. We have the words *high*
and *deep*, which strictly relate to objects of lineal altitude or profundity,
applied to denote intensity of colour ; and the very word *intensity*, when
thus applied, is only relative ; the speaker being unable to find a word
directly expressive of his meaning, explains himself by referring to
some object or thing previously known, as, in this instance, by reference
to the *tension* of a string or cord. The word *tone*, which is so frequently
used in speaking of pictures, is derived from the sister art of music.
I presume that none of these terms were introduced into the nomenclature of painting and engraving by ignorant persons, but that they were
adopted from a necessity originating from the very constitution of the
human mind. It is well known to every person who has paid any
attention to the construction of languages, that almost every abstract
term is referable to, and derived from, the name of some material
object. The very word to "think," implying the exercise of our mental
faculties, is probably an offset from the substantive "thing."

It is also to be observed, that Mr. Landseer speaks as if the term
colour was used by ignorant printsellers, and of course ignorant engravers,
to signify *shade* only. It is, however, used by them to signify that there
is a considerable proportion of dark lines and hatchings in an engraving,
although such lines and hatchings are not expressive of shade, but
merely indicative of deep colours. Dark brown, red, and purple, for
instance, even when receiving direct rays of light, would naturally
contain much conventional " colour " in an engraving ; and so would a
bay horse, a coal barge, or the trunk of an old oak tree, when receiving
the light in a similar manner ; all would be represented as comparatively
dark, when contrasted with lighter coloured objects,—for instance, with
a blue sky, grass, or light green foliage,—although not in shade. An
engraving that appears too light, compared with the painting from which
it is copied, is said to want " colour," and the copper-plate engraver
remedies the defect by thickening the dark lines, or by adding cross
lines and hatchings. As a copper-plate engraver can always obtain more
" colour," he generally keeps his work light in the first stage of a plate ;
on the contrary, a wood engraver keeps his first proof dark, as he cannot
afterwards introduce more " colour," or give to an object a greater depth
of shade. A wood engraver can make his lines thinner if they be too
thick, and thus cause his subject to appear lighter ; but if he has made
them too fine at first, and more colour be wanted, it is not in his power
to remedy the defect.

What Mr. Landseer's ideas may be of the "means [which] the art of engraving possesses of rendering local colour in the abstract," I cannot very well comprehend. I am aware of the lines used conventionally by engravers to indicate heraldic colours in coat-armour; but I can see no natural relation between perpendicular lines in an engraving and the red colour of a soldier's coat. I believe that no person could tell the colour of the draperies in Leonardo da Vinci's Last Supper from an inspection of Raphael Morghen's engraving of it. When Mr. Landseer says that he will use the term "colour" in its "ordinary acceptation," he ought to have explained what the ordinary acceptation of the word meant when applied to impressions from copper-plates which consist of nothing but lines and interstices of black and white.

In the second paragraph Mr. Landseer displays great inconsistency in praising Mr. Gilpin for his definition of the word "tint," which, when applied to engravings, is as objectionable as the term "colour." It appears that Mr. Gilpin may employ a conventional term with "singular propriety," while printsellers and engravers who should use the same liberty would be charged with ignorance. Is there such a thing as a *tint* in nature which is of no colour? Mr. Gilpin's lauded definition involves a contradiction even when the word is applied to engravings, in which every "tint" is indicative of positive colour. That "medium between strong light and strong shade," and which is yet of no colour, remains to be discovered. Mr. Gilpin has supplied us with the " word," but it appears that no definite idea is necessary to be attached to it. Having thus endeavoured to give a little brightness to the " colour" of "ignorant printsellers and engravers," I shall resume my observations on the cuts in the Nuremberg Chronicle, to the " colour" of which the preceding digression is to be ascribed.

The preceding cut, representing the Creation of Eve, is copied from one of the best in the Nuremberg Chronicle, both with respect to design and engraving. In this, compared with most other cuts previously executed, much more colour will be perceived, which results from the closeness of the single lines, as in the dark parts of the rock immediately behind the figure of Eve ; from the introduction of dark lines crossing each other,—called "cross-hatching,"—as may be seen in the drapery of the Divinity ; and from the contrast of the shade thus produced with the lighter parts of the cut.

The subjoined cut, of the same subject, copied from the Poor Preachers' Bible,* will, by comparison with the preceding, illustrate

more clearly than any verbal explanation the difference with respect to colour between the wood-cuts in the old block-books and in most others printed between 1462 and 1493, and those contained in the Nuremberg

* In the original, this cut, with one of Christ's side pierced by a soldier, and another of Moses striking the rock, are intended to illustrate the mystery of the Sacrament of the Lord's Supper.

Chronicle. In this cut there is no indication of colour ; the shades in the drapery which are expressed by hard parallel lines are all of equal strength, or rather weakness ; and the hair of Adam's head and the foliage of the tree are expressed nearly in the same manner.

This manner of representing the creation of Eve appears to have been general amongst the wood engravers of the fifteenth century, for the same subject frequently occurs in old cuts executed previous to 1500. It is frequently represented in the same manner in illuminated missals ; and in Flaxman's Lectures on Sculpture a lithographic print is given, copied from an ancient piece of sculpture in Wells Cathedral, where Eve is seen thus proceeding from the side of Adam. In a picture by Raffaele the creation of Eve is also represented in the same manner.

In the wood-cuts which occur in Italian books printed previous to 1500 the engravers have seldom attempted anything beyond a simple outline with occasionally an indication of shade, or of colour, by means of short parallel lines. The following is a fac-simile of a cut in Bonsignore's Italian prose translation of Ovid's Metamorphoses, folio, printed at Venice by the brothers De Lignano in 1497. It may serve at once as a specimen of the other cuts contained in the work and of the general style of engraving on wood in Italy for about ten years preceding that period.

The subject illustrated is the difficult labour of Alcmena through the malign influence of Lucina, as related by Ovid in the IXth book of the Metamorphoses, from verse 295 to 314. This would appear to have been rather a favourite subject with designers, for it is again selected for illustration in Ludovico Dolce's Transformationi, a kind of paraphrase of the Metamorphoses, 4to, printed at Venice by Gabriel Giolito in 1557 ; and it is also represented in the illustrations to the Metamorphoses designed by Virgil Solis, and printed at Frankfort, in oblong 4to, by George Corvinus and Sigismund Feyrabent, in 1569.*

Of all the wood-cuts executed in Italy within the fifteenth century there are none that can bear a comparison for elegance of design with those contained in an Italian work entitled "Hypnerotomachia Poliphili," a folio without printer's name or place, but certainly printed at Venice by Aldus in 1499. This "Contest between Imagination and Love, by a general Lover,"—for such seems to be the import of the title,—is an obscure medley of fable, history, antiquities, mathematics, and various other matters, highly seasoned with erotic sketches† suggested by the prurient imagination of a monk,—for such the author was,—who, like many others of his fraternity, in all ages, appears to have had "a *law* not to marry, and a *custom* not to live chaste." The language in which this chaos of absurdities is composed is almost as varied as the subjects. The ground-work is Italian, on which the author engrafts at will whole phrases of Latin, with a number of words borrowed from the Greek, Hebrew, Arabic, and Chaldee. "Certain persons," says Tiraboschi, "who admire a work the more the less they understand it, have fancied that they could perceive in the Hypnerotomachia a complete summary of human knowledge." ‡

The name of the author was Francis Colonna, who was born at Venice, and at an early age became a monk of the order of St. Dominic. In 1467 he professed Grammar and Classical Literature in the convent of his order at Trevisa ; and he afterwards became Professor of Theology at Padua, where he commenced Doctor in 1473, a degree which, according to the rule of his order, he could not assume until he was forty. At the time of his death, which happened in 1527, he could not thus be less than ninety-four years old. The true name of this amorous dreaming monk, and the fictitious one of the woman with whom he was in love, are thus expressed by combining, in the order in which they follow each other, the initial letters of the several chapters : "POLIAM FRATER FRANCISCUS COLUMNA PERAMAVIT."§ If any reliance can be placed on

---

* Mr. Ottley in speaking of an edition of the Metamorphoses printed at Venice in 1509, with wood-cuts, mentions one of them as representing the "Birth of Hercules," which is probably treated in a manner similar to those above noticed. Mr. Ottley also states that he had discovered the artist to be Benedetto Montagna, who also engraved on copper.—Inquiry, vol. ii. p. 576.

† Bibliographers and booksellers in their catalogues specify with delight such copies as contain "la figura rappresentante il Sacrifizio à Priapo bene conservata," for in some copies this choice subject is wanting, and in others partially defaced.

‡ Some account of the Hypnerotomachia and its author is to be found in Prosper Marchand's Dictionnaire Historique.

§ In the life of Colonna in the Biographie Universelle, the last word is said to be "*adamavit*," which is a mistake. The word formed by the initial letters of the nine last chapters is "*peramavit*," as above.

the text and the cuts as narrating and representing real incidents, we may gather that the stream of love had not run smooth with father Francis any more than with simple laymen.   With respect to the true name of the mistress of father Francis, biographers are not agreed. One says that her name was Lucretia Maura; and another that her name was Ippolita, and that she belonged to the noble family of Poli, of Trevisa, and that she was a nun in that city.   From the name Ippolita some authors thus derive the fictitious name Polia: Ippolita; Polita; Polia.

A second edition, also from the Aldine press, appeared in 1545 ; and in the following year a French translation was printed at Paris under the following title : " Le Tableau des riches inventions couvertes du voile des feintes amourouses qui sont representées dans le Songe de Poliphile, devoilées des ombres du Songe, et subtilment exposées."   Of this translation several editions were published ; and in 1804 J. G. Legrand, an architect of some repute in Paris, printed a kind of paraphrase of the work, in two volumes 12mo, which, however, was not published until after his death in 1807.   In 1811 Bodoni reprinted the original work at Parma in an elegant quarto volume.

In the original work the wood-cuts with respect to design may rank among the best that have appeared in Italy.   The whole number in the volume is one hundred and ninety-two ; of which eighty-six relate to mythology and ancient history ; fifty-four represent processions and emblematic figures : there are thirty-six architectural and ornamental subjects ; and sixteen vases and statues.   Several writers have asserted that those cuts were designed by Raffaele,[*] while others with equal confidence, though on no better grounds, have ascribed them to Andrea Mantegna.   Except from the resemblance which they are supposed to bear to the acknowledged works of those artists, I am not aware that there is any reason to suppose that they were designed by either of them. As Raffaele, who was born in 1483, was only sixteen when the Hypnerotomachia was printed, it is not likely that all, or even any of hose cuts were designed by him; as it is highly probable that all the drawings would be finished at least twelve months before, and many of them contain internal evidence of their not being the productions of a youth of fifteen.   That Andrea Mantegna might design them is possible ; but this certainly cannot be a sufficient reason for positively asserting that he actually did.   Mr. Ottley, at page 576, vol. ii, of his Inquiry, asserts that they were designed by Benedetto Montagna, an

---

[*] Heineken, in his catalogue of Raffaele's works, mentions the cuts in the Hypneroto-machia, but he says that it is questionable whether he designed them all or only the eighty-six mythological and historical subjects.—Nachrichten von Künstlern und Kunst-Sachen, 2er Theil, S. 360. 8vo. Leipzig, 1769.

artist who flourished about the year 1500, and who is chiefly known as an engraver on copper.   The grounds on which Mr. Ottley forms his opinion are not very clear, but if I understand him correctly they are as follows :

In the collection of the late Mr. Douce there were sixteen wood engravings which had been cut out of a folio edition of Ovid's Metamorphoses, printed at Venice in 1509.   All those engravings, except two, were marked with the letters ía, which according to Mr. Ottley are the initials of the engraver, Ioanne Andrea di Vavassori.   Between some of the cuts from the Ovid, and certain engravings executed by Montagna, it seems that Mr. Ottley discovered a resemblance ; and as he thought that he perceived a perfect similarity between the sixteen cuts from the Ovid and those contained in the Hypnerotomachia, he considers that Benedetto Montagna is thus proved to have been the designer of the cuts in the latter work.

Not having seen the cuts in the edition of the Metamorphoses of 1509, I cannot speak, from my own examination, of the resemblance between them and those in the Hypnerotomachia; it, however, seems that Mr. Douce had noticed the similarity as well as Mr. Ottley : but even admitting that there is a perfect identity of style in the cuts of the above two works, yet it by no means follows that, because a few of the cuts in the Ovid resemble some copper-plate engravings executed by Benedetto Montagna, he must have designed the cuts in the Hypnerotomachia.   As the cuts in the Ovid may, as Mr. Ottley himself remarks, have been used in an earlier edition than that of 1509, it is not unlikely that they might appear before Montagna's copper-plates ; and that the latter might copy the designs of a greater artist than himself, and thus by his very plagiarism acquire, according to Mr. Ottley's train of reasoning, the merit which may be justly due to another.   If Benedetto Montagna be really the designer of the cuts in the Hypnerotomachia, he has certainly excelled himself, for they certainly display talent of a much higher order than is to be perceived in his copper-plate engravings.   Besides the striking difference with respect to drawing between the wood-cuts in Poliphilo * and the engravings of Benedetto Montagna, two of the cuts in the former work have a mark which never appears in any of that artist's known productions, which generally have either his name at length or the letters B. M.   In the third cut of Poliphilo, the designer's or engraver's mark, a small b, may be perceived at the foot, to the right; and the same mark is repeated in a cut at signature C.

---

* The author thus names his hero in his Italian title : " *Poliphilo* incomincia la sua hypnerotomachia ad descrivere et l'hora et il tempo quando gli appar ve in somno, &c."

A London bookseller in his catalogue published in 1834, probably speaking on Mr. Ottley's hint that the cuts in the Ovid of 1509 might have appeared in an earlier edition, thus describes Bonsignore's Ovid, a work in which the wood-cuts are of a very inferior description, and of which a specimen is given in a preceding page : "Ovidii Metamorphoseos Vulgare, con le Allegorie, [Venezia, 1497,] with numerous beautiful wood-cuts, apparently by the artist who executed the Poliphilo, printed by Aldus in 1499." The wood-cuts in the Ovid of 1497 are as inferior to those in Poliphilo as the commonest cuts in children's school-books are inferior to the beautiful wood-cuts in Rogers's Pleasures of Memory, printed in 1812, which were designed by Stothard and engraved by Clennell. It is but fair to add, that the cuts used in the Ovid of 1497, printed by the brothers De Lignano, cannot be the same as those in the Ovid of 1509 referred to by Mr. Ottley ; for though the subjects may be nearly the same, the cuts in the latter edition are larger than those in the former, and have besides an engraver's mark which is not to be seen in any of the cuts in the edition of 1497.

The five following cuts are fac-similes traced line for line from the originals in Poliphilo. In the first, Mercury is seen interfering to save Cupid from the anger of Venus, who has been punishing him and

plucking the feathers from his wings. The cause of her anger is explained by the figure of Mars behind the net in which he and Venus had been inclosed by Vulcan. Love had been the cause of his mother's misfortune.

In the following cut Cupid is represented as brought by Mercury
before Jove, who in the text, "in Athica lingua," addresses the God of
Love, as "ΣΤΜΟΙΓΛΤΚΤΣ ΚΑΙ ΠΙΚΡΟΣ"—"at once sweet and
bitter." In the inscription in the cut, "ΑΛΛΑ" is substituted for
"ΚΑΙ."

In the next cut Cupid appears piercing the sky with a dart, and
thus causing a shower of gold to fall. The figures represent persons of
all conditions whom he has wounded, looking on with amazement.

The three preceding cuts, in the original work, appear as compartments from left to right on one block. They are here given separate for the convenience of printing, as the page is not wide enough to allow of their being placed as in the original folio.

The subjoined cut is intended to represent Autumn, according to a description of the figure in the text, where the author is speaking of an altar to be erected to the four seasons. On one of the sides he proposes that the following figure should be represented "with a iolly countenance, crowned with vine leaves, holding in one hand a

bunch of grapes, and in the other a cornucopia, with an inscription: ' MUSTULENTO AUTUMNO S.' "* The face of jolly Autumn is indeed like that of one who loved new wine, and his body seems like an ample skin to keep the liquor in;—Sir John Falstaff playing Bacchus ere he had grown old and inordinately fat.

* The epithets applied to the different seasons as represented on this votive altar are singularly beautiful and appropriate: " Florido Veri ; Flavæ Messi ; Mustulento Autumno ; Hyemi Æoliæ, Sacrum."

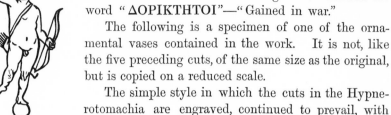

The following figure of Cupid is copied from the top of a fanciful military standard described by the author; and on a kind of banner beneath the figure is inscribed the word " ΔΟΡΙΚΤΗΤΟΙ "—" Gained in war."

The following is a specimen of one of the ornamental vases contained in the work. It is not, like the five preceding cuts, of the same size as the original, but is copied on a reduced scale.

The simple style in which the cuts in the Hypnerotomachia are engraved, continued to prevail, with certain modifications, in Italy for many years after the method of cross-hatching became general in Germany; and from 1500 to about 1530 the characteristic of most Italian wood-cuts is the simple manner in which they are executed compared with the more laboured productions of the German wood engravers. While the German proceeds with considerable labour to obtain " colour," or shade, by means of cross-hatching, the Italian in the early part of the sixteenth century endeavours to attain his object by easier means, such as leaving his lines thicker in certain parts, and in others, indicating shade by means of short slanting parallel lines. In the execution of flowered or ornamented initial letters a decided difference may frequently be noticed between the work of an Italian and a German artist. The German mostly, with considerable trouble, cuts  his flourishes, figures, and flowers in relief, according to the general practice of wood engravers; the Italian, on the contrary, often cuts them, with much greater ease, in *intaglio;* and thus the form of the letter, and its ornaments, appear, when printed, white upon a black ground.* The letter C at the commencement of the present chapter is an example of the German style, with the ornamental parts in *relief;* the letter M at the commencement of chapter v. is a specimen of the manner frequently adopted by old Italian wood engravers, the form of the letter and the ornamental foliage being cut in *intaglio.* At a subsequent period a more elaborate manner of engraving began to prevail in Italy, and cross-hatching was almost as generally employed to obtain depth of colour and shade as in Germany. The wood-cuts which appear in works printed at Venice between 1550 and 1570 are generally as good as most German wood-cuts of the same period; and

* The letter M at the commencement of the next chapter affords an example of this style of engraving.

many of them, more especially those in books printed by the Giolitos, are executed with a clearness and delicacy which have seldom been surpassed.

Before concluding the present chapter, which is more especially devoted to the consideration of wood engraving in the first period of its connexion with typography, it may not be improper to take a brief glance at the state of the art as practised by the Briefmalers and Formschneiders of Germany, who were the first to introduce the practice of block-printing, and who continued to exercise this branch of their art for many years after typography had been generally established throughout Europe. That the ancient wood engravers continued to practise the art of block-printing till towards the close of the fifteenth century, there can be little doubt. There is an edition of the Poor Preachers' Bible, with the date 1470, printed from wood-blocks, without place or engraver's name, but having at the end, as a mark, two shields, on one of which is a squirrel, and on the other something like two pilgrim's staves crossed. Another edition of the same work, though not from the same blocks, appeared in 1471. In this the engraver's mark is two shields, on one of which is a spur, probably a rebus for the name of "Sporer;" in the same manner that a pair of folding-doors represented the name "Thurer," or "Durer." An engraver of the name of Hans Sporer printed an edition of the Ars Moriendi from wood-blocks in 1473; and in the preceding year Young Hans, Brief-maler, of Nuremberg, printed an edition of the Antichrist in the same manner.*

It is probable that most of the single sheets and short tracts, printed from wood-blocks, preserved in the libraries of Germany, were printed between 1440 and 1480. Books consisting of two or more sheets printed from wood-blocks are of rare occurrence with a date subsequent to 1480. Although about that period the wood engravers appear to have resigned the printing of books entirely to typographers, yet for several years afterwards they continued to print broadsides from blocks of wood; and until about 1500 they continued to compete with the press for the printing of "Wand-Kalendars," or sheet Almanacks to be hung up against a wall. Several copies of such Almanacks, engraved between 1470 and 1500, are preserved in libraries on the Continent that are rich in specimens of early block-printing. But even this branch of their business the wood engravers were at length obliged to abandon; and at the end of the fifteenth century the practice of printing pages of text from engraved wood-blocks may be considered as almost extinct in Germany. It probably began with a single sheet, and with a

---

* Von Murr says that "Young Hans" was unquestionably the son of "Hans Form-schneider," whose name appears in the town-books of Nuremberg from 1449 to 1490. He also thinks that he might be the same person as Hans Sporer.—Journal, 2 Theil, S. 140, 141.

single sheet it ended; and its origin, perfection, decline, and extinction are comprised within a century. 1430 may mark its origin; 1450 its perfection; 1460 the commencement of its decline; and 1500 its fall.

In an assemblage of wood engravings printed at Gotha between 1808 and 1816,* from old blocks collected by the Baron Von Derschau, there are several to which the editor, Zacharias Becker, assigns an earlier date than the year 1500. It is not unlikely that two or three of those in his oldest class, A, may have been executed previous to that period; but there are others in which bad drawing and rude engraving have been mistaken for indubitable proofs of antiquity. There are also two or three in the same class which I strongly suspect to be modern forgeries. It would appear from a circumstance mentioned in Dr. Dibdin's Bibliographical Tour,† and referred to at page 236 of the present work, that the Baron was a person from whose collection copper-plate engravings of questionable date had proceeded as well as wood-blocks. The following is a reduced copy of one of those suspicious blocks, but which the editor considers to be of an earlier date than the St. Christopher in the collection of Earl Spencer. I am however of opinion that it is of comparatively modern manufacture.

The inscription, intended for old German, at the bottom of the cut, is literally as follows: "*Hiet uch, vor den Katczen dy vorn lecken unde*

---

* The title of this work is: " Holzschnitte alter Deutscher Meister in den Original-Platten gesammelt von Hans Albrecht Von Derschau. Als ein Beytrag zur Kunstgeschichte herausgegeben, und mit einer Abhandlung über die Holzschneidekunst begleitet, von Rudolph Zacharias Becker." It is in large folio, with the text in German and French. The first part was published at Gotha in 1808; the second in 1810; and the third in 1816.

† Vol. iii. p. 445, edit. 1829.

hinden kraiczen"—that is: "Beware of the cats that lick before and scratch behind." It is rather singular that the editor—who describes the subject as a cat which appears to teach her kitten "le Jeu de Souris"—should not have informed his readers that more was meant by this inscription than met the eye, and that it was in fact part of a German proverb descriptive of a class of females who are particularly dangerous to simple young men.* Among the cuts supposed to have been engraved previous to the year 1500, another is given which I suspect also of being a forgery, and by the same person that engraved the cat. The cut alluded to represents a woman sitting beside a young man, whose purse she is seen picking while she appears to fondle him. A hawk is seen behind the woman, and an ape behind the man. At one side is a lily, above which are the words "**Ich wart.**" At the top of the cut is an inscription,—which seems, like that in the cut of the cat, to be in affectedly old German,—describing the young man as a prey for hawks and a fool, and the woman as a flatterer, who will fawn upon him until she has emptied his pouch. The subjects of those two cuts, though not apparently, are, in reality, connected. In the first we are presented with the warning, and in the latter with the example. Von Murr—whom Dr. Dibdin suspects to have forged the French St. Christopher—describes in his Journal impressions from those blocks as old wood-cuts in the collection of Dr. Silberrad;† and it is certainly very singular that the identical blocks from which Dr. Silberrad's scarce old wood engravings were taken should afterwards happen to be discovered and come into the possession of the Baron Von Derschau.

In the same work there is a rude wood-cut of St. Catharine and three other saints; and at the back of the block there is also engraved the figure of a soldier. At the bottom of the cut of St. Catharine, the name of the engraver, "**Jorg Glockendon,**" appears in old German characters. As "Glockendon" or "Glockenton" was the name of a family of artists who appear to have been settled at Nuremberg early in the fifteenth century, Becker concludes that the cut in question was engraved prior to 1482, and that this "Jorg Glockendon" was "the first wood engraver known by name, and not John Schnitzer of Arnsheim,—who engraved the maps in Leonard Holl's Ptolemy, printed in the above year,—as Heineken and others pretend." That the cut was engraved previous to 1482 rests merely on Becker's conjecture; and a person who would assert that it was engraved ten or fifteen years later, would perhaps be nearer the truth. John Schnitzer, however, is not the first wood engraver known by name. The name of Hans Sporer appears in the Ars Moriendi of 1473; and it is not probable that Hartlieb's

* "**Huren sind böse katzen die bornen lecken und hinten kratzen.**"
† Journal zur Kunstgeschichte, 2er Theil, S. 125, 126.

Chiromantia, in which we find the name " **Jorg Schapff zu Augspurg**,"
was engraved subsequent to 1480. It would appear that Becker did
not consider " Hans Briefmaler," who occurs as a wood engraver between
1470 and 1480, as a person " known by name," though it is probable
that he had no other surname than that which was derived from his
profession.

Although Derschau's collection contains a number of old cuts which
are well worth preserving, more especially among those executed in the
sixteenth century ; yet it also contains a large portion of worthless cuts,
which are neither interesting from their subjects nor their antiquity,
and which throw no light on the progress of the art. There are also
not a few modern antiques which are only illustrative of the credulity
of the collector, who mistakes rudeness of execution for a certain test
of antiquity. According to this test the following cut ought to be
ascribed to the age of Caxton, and published with a long commentary
as an undoubted specimen of early English wood engraving. It is

however nothing more than an impression from a block engraved with
a pen-knife by a printer's apprentice between 1770 and 1780. It was
one of the numerous cuts of a similar kind belonging to the late Mr.
George Angus of Newcastle-upon-Tyne, who used them as head-pieces
to chap-books and broadside histories and ballads.

Besides the smaller block-books, almanacks, and broadsides of text,
executed by wood engravers between 1460 and 1500, they also executed
a number of single cuts, some accompanied with a few sentences of

text also cut in wood, and others containing only figures. Many of
the sacred subjects were probably executed for convents in honour of
a favourite saint; while others were engraved by them on their own
account for sale among the poorer classes of the people, who had neither
the means to purchase, nor the ability to read, a large "picture-book"
which contained a considerable portion of explanatory text. In almost
every one of the works executed by the Briefmalers and Formschneiders
subsequent to the invention of typography, there is scarcely a single cut
to be found that possesses the least merit either in design or execution.
They appear generally to have been mere workmen, who could draw and
engrave figures on wood in a rude style, but who had not the slightest
pretensions to a knowledge of art.

Having now brought the history of wood engraving to the end of
the fifteenth century, I shall here conclude the present chapter, without
expressly noticing such works of Albert Durer as were certainly
engraved on wood previous to the year 1500. The designs of this
great promoter of wood engraving mark an epoch in the progress of
the art; and will, with others of the same school, more appropriately
form the subject of the next chapter.

CHAPTER V.

WOOD ENGRAVING IN THE TIME OF ALBERT DURER.

CHIARO-SCURO ENGRAVING ON WOOD—A COPPER-PLATE BY MAIR MISTAKEN FOR THE FIRST
CHIARO-SCURO—DOTTED BACKGROUNDS IN OLD WOOD-CUTS—ALBERT DURER PROBABLY NOT A
WOOD-ENGRAVER—HIS BIRTH—A PUPIL OF MICHAEL WOLGEMUTH—HIS TRAVELS—CUTS OF
THE APOCALYPSE DESIGNED BY HIM—HIS VISIT TO VENICE IN 1506—THE HISTORY OF THE
VIRGIN AND CHRIST'S PASSION ENGRAVED ON WOOD FROM HIS DESIGNS—HIS TRIUMPHAL CAR
AND TRIUMPHAL ARCH OF THE EMPEROR MAXIMILIAN—HIS INVENTION OF ETCHING—HIS
CARVING—VISIT TO THE NETHERLANDS—HIS DEATH—WOOD-CUTS DESIGNED BY L. CRANACH, H.
BURGMAIR, AND H. SCHÆFFLEIN—THE ADVENTURES OF SIR THEURDANK—THE WISE KING—
THE TRIUMPHS OF MAXIMILIAN—UGO DA CARPI—LUCAS VAN LEYDEN—WILLIAM DE FIGUER-
SNIDER—URSGRAFF—CUTS DESIGNED BY UNKNOWN ARTISTS BETWEEN 1500 AND 1528.

 OST authors who have written on the
history of engraving have incidentally
noticed the art of chiaro-scuro engraving on wood, which began to be
practised early in the sixteenth century.*
The honour of the invention has been
claimed for Italy by Vasari and other
Italian writers, who seem to think that
no improvement in the arts of design
and engraving can originate on this
side of the Alps. According to their
account, chiaro-scuro engraving on wood
was first introduced by Ugo da Carpi, who executed several pieces in
that manner from the designs of Raffaele. But, though confident in
their assertions, they are weak in their proofs ; for they can produce
no chiaro-scuros by Ugo da Carpi, or by any other Italian engraver, of
an earlier date than 1518. The engravings of Italian artists in this style

* Chiaro-scuros are executed by means of two or more blocks, in imitation of a drawing
in sepia, India ink, or any other colour of two or more shades. The older chiaro-scuros are
seldom executed with more than three blocks ; on the first of which the general outline of
the subject and the stronger shades were engraved and printed in the usual manner ; from
the second the lighter shades were communicated ; and from the third a general tint was
printed over the impressions of the other two.

are not numerous, previous to 1530, and we can scarcely suppose that the earliest of them was executed before 1515. That the art was known and practised in Germany several years before this period there can be no doubt; for a chiaro-scuro wood engraving, a Repose in Egypt, by Lucas Cranach, is dated 1509; two others by Hans Baldung Grün are dated 1509 and 1510; and a portrait, in the same style, by Hans Burgmair, is dated 1512.

Some German writers, not satisfied with these proofs of the art being practised in Germany before it was known in Italy, refer to an engraving, dated 1499, by a German artist of the name of Mair, as one of the earliest executed in this manner. This engraving, which is from a copper-plate, cannot fairly be produced as evidence on the point in dispute; for though it bears the appearance of a chiaro-scuro engraving, yet it is not so in reality; for on a narrow inspection we may perceive that the light touches have neither been preserved, nor afterwards communicated by means of a block or a plate, but have been added with a fine pencil after the impression was taken. It is, in fact, nothing more than a copper-plate printed on dark-coloured paper, and afterwards heightened with a kind of white and yellow body-colour. It is very likely, however, that the subject was engraved and printed on a dark ground with the express intention of the lights being subsequently added by means of a pencil. The artist had questionless wished to produce an imitation of a chiaro-scuro drawing; but he certainly did not effect his purpose in the same manner as L. Cranach, H. Burgmair, or Ugo da Carpi, whose chiaro-scuro engravings had the lights preserved, and required no subsequent touching with the pencil to give to them that character.

The subject of this engraving is the Nativity, and there is an impression of it in the Print Room of the British Museum.* In the foreground, about the middle of the print, is the Virgin seated with the infant Jesus in her lap. At her feet is a cradle of wicker-work, and to the left is an angel kneeling in adoration. On the same side, but further distant, is Joseph leaning over a half door, holding a candle in one hand and shading it with the other. In the background is the stable, in which an ox and an ass are seen; and the directing star appears shining in the

---

* This print is one of the valuable collection left to the Museum by the Rev. C. M. Cracherode, and the following remark in that gentleman's writing is inserted on the opposite page of the folio in which it is preserved: "The Presepe is a plain proof that printing in chiaro-scuro was known before the time of Ugo da Carpi, who is erroneously reputed the inventor of this art at the beginning of the sixteenth century." The print in question is certainly not a proof of the art of engraving in chiaro-scuro; and Mr. Ottley has added the following correction in pencil: "But the white here is put on with a pencil, and not left in printing, as it would have been if the tint had been added by a wooden block after the copper-plate had been printed."

sky. The print is eight inches high, and five inches and three-eighths wide; at the top is the date 1499, and at the bottom the engraver's name, MAIR. It is printed in black ink on paper which previous to receiving the impression had been tinted or stained a brownish-green colour. The lights have neither been preserved in the plate nor communicated by means of a second impression, but have been laid on by the hand with a fine pencil. The rays of the star, and the circles of light surrounding the head of the Virgin, and also that of the infant, are of a pale yellow, and the colour from its chalky appearance seems very like the touches of a crayon. The lights in the draperies and in the architectural parts of the subject have been laid on with a fine pencil guided by a steady hand. That the engraver intended his work to be finished in this manner there can be little doubt; and the impression referred to affords a proof of it; for Joseph's candle, though he shades it with his left hand, in reality gives no light. The engraver had evidently intended that the light should be added in positive body colour; but the person—perhaps the engraver himself—whose business it was to add the finishing touches to the impression, has neglected to light Joseph's candle.*

Towards the latter end of the fifteenth century,† a practice was introduced by the German wood engravers of dotting the dark parts of their subjects with white, more especially in cuts where the figures were intended to appear light upon a dark ground; and about the beginning of the sixteenth, this mode of "killing the black," as it is technically termed, was very generally prevalent among the French wood engravers, who, as well as the Germans and Dutch, continued to practise it till about 1520, when it was almost wholly superseded by cross-hatching; a mode of producing shade which had been much practised by the German engravers who worked from the drawings of Durer, Cranach, and Burgmair, and which about that time seems to have been generally adopted in all countries where the art had made any progress. The two following cuts, which are from an edition of "Heures à l'Usaige de Chartres," printed at Paris by Simon Vostre, about 1502, are examples of this mode of diminishing the effects of a ground which would otherwise be entirely black. Books printed in France between 1500 and 1520 afford the most numerous instances of dark backgrounds dotted with white. In many cuts executed about the latter period the dots are of larger size and more numerous in proportion to the black, and they evidently have been

---

* Bartsch describes this print in his Peintre-Graveur, tom. vi. p. 364, No. 4; but he takes no notice of Joseph holding a candle, nor of its wanting a light.

† Some single cuts executed in this manner are supposed to be at least as old as the year 1450. The earliest that I have noticed in a book occur in a Life of Christ printed at Cologne about 1485.

produced by means of a lozenge-pointed tool, in imitation of cross-hatching.

The greatest promoter of the art of wood engraving, towards the close of the fifteenth and in the early part of the sixteenth century, was

unquestionably Albert Durer; not however, as is generally supposed, from having himself engraved the numerous wood-cuts which bear his mark, but from his having thought so well of the art as to have most of his greatest works engraved on wood from drawings made on the block by himself. Until within the last thirty years, most writers who have written on the subject of art, have spoken of Albert Durer as a wood engraver; and before proceeding to give any account of his life, or specimens of some of the principal wood engravings which bear his mark, it appears necessary to examine the grounds of this opinion.

There are about two hundred subjects engraved on wood which are marked with the initials of Albert Durer's name; and the greater part of them, though evidently designed by the hand of a master, are engraved in a manner which certainly denotes no very great excellence. Of the remainder, which are better engraved, it would be difficult to point out one which displays execution so decidedly superior as to enable any person to say positively that it must have been cut by Albert Durer himself. The earliest engravings on wood with Durer's mark are sixteen cuts illustrative of the Apocalypse, first published in 1498; and between that period and 1528, the year of his death, it is likely that nearly all the others were executed. The cuts of the Apocalypse generally are much superior to all wood engravings that had previously appeared, both in design and execution; but if they be carefully examined by any person conversant with the practice of the art, it will be perceived that their superiority is not owing to any delicacy in the lines which would render them difficult to engrave, but from the ability of the person by whom they were drawn, and from his knowledge of the capabilities of the art. Looking at the state of wood engraving at the period when those cuts were published, I cannot think that the artist who made the drawings would experience any difficulty in finding persons capable of engraving them. In most of the wood-cuts supposed to have been engraved by Albert Durer we find cross-hatching freely introduced; the readiest mode of producing effect to an artist drawing on wood with a pen or a black-lead pencil, but which to the wood engraver is attended with considerable labour. Had Albert Durer engraved his own designs, I am inclined to think that he would not have introduced cross-hatching so frequently, but would have endeavoured to attain his object by means which were easier of execution. What is termed "cross-hatching" in wood engraving is nothing more than black lines crossing each other, for the most part diagonally; and in *drawing* on wood it is easier to produce a shade by this means, than by thickening the lines; but in *engraving* on wood it is precisely the reverse; for it is easier to leave a thick line than to cut out the interstices of lines crossing each other. Nothing is more common than for persons who know little of the history of wood engraving, and still less of the practice, to refer to the frequent cross-hatching in the cuts supposed to have been engraved by Albert Durer as a proof of their excellence: as if the talent of the artist were chiefly displayed in such parts of the cuts as are in reality least worthy of him, and which a mere workman might execute as well. In opposition to this vulgar error I venture to assert, that there is not a wood engraver in London of the least repute who cannot produce *apprentices* to cut fac-similes of any cross-hatching that is to be found, not only in the wood engravings supposed to have been excuted by Albert Durer, but in those of any other master. The execution of cross-hatching requires time, but very little talent; and a moderately clever lad, with a steady hand and a lozenge-pointed tool, will cut in a year a *square yard* of such cross-hatching as is generally found in the largest of the cuts supposed to have been engraved by Albert Durer. In the works of Bewick, scarcely more than one trifling instance of cross-hatching is to be found; and in the productions of all other modern wood engravers who have made their own drawings, we find cross-hatching sparingly introduced; while in almost every one of the cuts designed by Durer, Cranach, Burgmair, and others who are known to have been painters of eminence in their day, it is of frequent occurrence. Had these masters engraved their own designs on wood, as has been very generally supposed, they probably would have introduced much less cross-hatching into their subjects; but as there is every reason to believe that they only made the drawing on the wood, the engravings which are ascribed to them abound in lines which are readily made with a pen or a pencil, but which require considerable time to cut with a graver.

At the period that Durer published his illustrations of the Apocalypse, few wood-cuts of much merit either in design or execution had appeared in printed books; and the wood engravers of that age seem generally to have been mere workmen, who only understood the mechanical branch of their art, but who were utterly devoid of all knowledge of composition or correct drawing; and there is also reason to believe that wood-cuts at that period, and even for some time after, were not unfrequently engraved by women.* As the names of those persons were probably not known beyond the town in which they resided, it cannot be a matter of surprise that neither their marks nor initials should be found on the cuts which they engraved from the drawings of such artists as Albert Durer.

It perhaps may be objected, that as Albert Durer's copper-plate engravings contain only his mark, in the same manner as the wood engravings, it might with equal reason be questioned if they were really executed by himself. Notwithstanding the identity of the marks, there is, however, a wide difference between the two cases. In the age of Albert Durer most of the artists who engraved on copper were also painters; and most of the copper-plate engravings which bear his mark are such as none but an artist of great talent could execute. It would require the abilities of a first-rate copper-plate engraver of the present day to produce a fac-simile of his best copper-plates; while a wood engraver of but moderate skill would be able to cut a fac-simile of one of his best wood engravings after the subject was drawn for him on the block. The best of Albert Durer's copper-plates could only have been engraved by a master; while the best of his wood-cuts might be engraved by a working Formschneider who had acquired a practical knowledge of his art by engraving, under the superintendence of Michael Wolgemuth and William Pleydenwurff, the wood-cuts for the Nuremberg Chronicle.

Von Murr, who was of opinion that Albert Durer engraved his own designs on wood, gives a letter of Durer's in the ninth volume of his Journal which he thinks is decisive of the fact. The letter, which relates to a wood engraving of a shield of arms, was written in 1511, and is to the following effect: " Dear Michael Beheim, I return you

---

* In a folio ot Albert Durer's drawings in the Print Room at the British Museum there is a portrait of " *Fronica, Formschneiderin*," with the date 1525. In 1433 we find a woman at Nuremberg described as a card-maker : " *Ell. Kartenmacherin.*" It is scarcely necessary to remind the reader that the earliest German wood engravers were card-makers.—See chapter II. p. 41.

the arms, and beg that you will let it remain as it is. No one will make it better, as I have done it according to art and with great care, as those who see it and understand the matter will tell you. If the labels were thrown back above the helmet, the volet would be covered."* This letter, however, is by no means decisive, for it is impossible to determine whether the "arms" which the artist returned were a finished engraving or merely a drawing on wood.† From one or two expressions it seems most likely to have been a drawing only ; for in a finished cut alterations cannot very well be introduced ; and it seems most probable that Michael Beheim's objections would be made to the drawing of the arms before they were engraved, and not to the finished cut. But even supposing it to have been the engraved block which Durer returned, this is by no means a proof of his having engraved it himself, for he might have engravers employed in his house in order that the designs which he drew on the blocks might be executed under his own superintendence. The Baron Derschau indeed told Dr. Dibdin that he was once in possession of the *journal* or day-book of Albert Durer, from which " it appeared that he was in the habit of drawing upon the blocks, and that his men performed the remaining operation of cutting away the wood."‡ This information, had it been communicated by a person whose veracity might be depended on, would be decisive of the question ; but the book unfortunately " perished in the flames of a house in the neighbourhood of one of the battles fought between Bonaparte and the Prussians ;" and from a little anecdote recorded by Dr. Dibdin the Baron appears to have been a person whose word was not to be implicitly relied on.§

Neudörffer, who in 1546 collected some particulars relative to the

---

* The following is Bartsch's French version of this letter, which is given in the original German in Von Murr's Journal, 9er Theil, S. 53. " Cher Michel Beheim. Je vous envoie les armoiries, en vous priant de les laisser comme elles sont. Personne d'ailleurs ne les corrigeroit en mieux, car je les ai faites exprès et avec art ; c'est pourquoi ceux qui s'y connoissent et qui les verront vous en rendront bonne raison. Si l'on haussoit les lambrequins du heaume, ils couvriroient le volet."—Bartsch, Peintre-Graveur, tom. vii. p. 27.

† In Durer's Journal of his visit to the Netherlands in 1520 there is the following passage : " Item hab dem von Rogendorff sein Wappen auf Holz gerissen, dafür hat er mir geschenckt vii. Eln Sammet."—" Also I have drawn for Von Rogendorff his arms on wood, for which he has presented me with seven yards of velvet."—Von Murr, Journal zur Kunstgeschichte, 7er Theil, S. 76.

‡ Bibliographical Tour, vol. iii. p. 442, second edition.

§ The Baron was the collector of the wood-cuts published with Becker's explanations, referred to at page 226, chapter IV. The anecdote alluded to will be found in Dr. Dibdin's Bibliographical Tour, vol. iii pp. 445, 446. The Baron sold a rare specimen of copperplate engraving with the date M. CCCC. XXX. to the Doctor, and it seems that he also sold *another* impression from the same plate to Mr. John Payne. There is no doubt of their being gross forgeries ; and it is not unlikely that the plate was in the Baron's possession.

history of the artists of Nuremberg, says that Jerome Resch, or Rösch, engraved most of the cuts designed by Albert Durer. He also says that Resch was one of the most skilful wood engravers of his day, and that he particularly excelled in engraving letters on wood. This artist also used to engrave dies for coining money, and had a printing establishment of his own. He dwelt in the Broad Way at Nuremberg, with a back entrance in Petticoat Lane ; * and when he was employed in engraving the Triumphal Car drawn by Albert Durer for the Emperor Maximilian, the Emperor used to call almost every day to see the progress of the work ; and as he entered at Petticoat Lane, it became a by-word with the common people : "The Emperor still often drives to Petticoat Lane."†

Although it is by no means unlikely that Albert Durer might engrave two or three wood-cuts of his own designing, yet, after a careful examination of most of those that bear his mark, I cannot find one which is so decidedly superior to the rest as to induce an opinion of its being engraved by himself ; and I cannot for a moment believe that an artist of his great talents, and who painted so many pictures, engraved so many copper-plates, and made so many designs, could find time to engrave even a small part of the many wood-cuts which have been supposed to be executed by him, and which a common wood engraver might execute as well. " If Durer himself had engraved on wood," says Bartsch in the seventh volume of his Peintre-Graveur, " it is most likely that among the many particular accounts which we have of his different pursuits, and of the various kind of works which he has left, the fact of his having applied himself to wood engraving would certainly have been transmitted in a manner no less explicit ; but, far from finding the least trace of it, everything that relates to this subject proves that he had never employed himself in this kind of work. He is always described as a painter, a designer, or an editor of works engraved on wood, but never as a wood engraver."‡ I also further agree with Bartsch, who thinks that the wood-cuts which contain the marks of Lucas Cranach, Hans Burgmair, and others who are known to

---

* "Dieser Hieronymus hat allhier im breiten Gassen gewohnt, dessen Wohnung hinten ins Frauengässlein ging."

† Neudörffer, quoted in Von Murr's Journal, 2ter Theil, S. 158, 159.

‡ At the end of the first edition of the cuts illustrative of the Apocalypse, 1498, we find the words : *Gedrukt durch Albrecht Durer, Maler*,"—Printed by Albert Durer, painter ; and the same in Latin in the second edition, printed about 1510. The passion of Christ and the History of the Virgin are respectively said to have been " *effigiata* " and " *per figuras digesta*"—" drawn" and "pictorially represented" by Albert Durer ; and the cuts of the Triumphal Car of the Emperor Maximilian are described as being " *erfunden und geordnet*"—" invented and arranged" by him.—Bartsch, Peintre-Graveur, tom. vii. p. 28.

have been painters of considerable reputation in their day, were not
engraved by those artists, but only designed or drawn by them on
the block.

Albert Durer was born at Nuremberg, on 20th May 1471.   His
father, whose name was also Albert, was a goldsmith, and a native of
Cola in Hungary.   His mother was a daughter of Jerome Haller, who
was also a goldsmith, and the master under whom the elder Durer had
acquired a knowledge of his art.   Albert continued with his father till
his sixteenth year, and had, as he himself says, learned to execute
beautiful works in the goldsmith's art, when he felt a great desire to
become a painter.   His father on hearing of his wish to change his
profession was much displeased, as he considered that the time he had
already spent in endeavouring to acquire a knowledge of the art of
a goldsmith was entirely lost.   He, however, assented to his son's
earnest request, and placed him, on St. Andrew's day, 1486, as a pupil
under Michael Wolgemuth for the term of three years, to learn the
art of painting.   On the expiration of his "lehr-jahre," or apprenticeship, in 1490, he left his master, and, according to the custom of
German artists of that period, proceeded to travel for the purpose of
gaining a further knowledge of his profession.   In what manner or
in what places he was chiefly employed during his "wander-jahre"*
is not very well known; but it is probable that his travels did not
extend beyond Germany.   In the course of his peregrinations he visited
Colmar, in 1492, where he was kindly received by Caspar, Paul, and
Louis, the brothers of Martin Schongauer; but he did not see, either
then or at any other period, that celebrated engraver himself.† He
returned to Nuremberg in the spring of 1494; and shortly afterwards
married Agnes, the daughter of John Frey, a mechanist of considerable
reputation of that city.   This match, which is said to have been made
for him by his parents, proved to be an unhappy one; for, though his
wife possessed considerable personal charms, she was a woman of a most
wretched temper; and her incessant urging him to continued exertion

---

* The time that a German artist spends in travel from the expiration of his apprenticeship to the period of his settling as a master is called his wander-jahre,"—his travelling
years. It is customary with many trades in Germany for the young men to travel for
a certain time on the termination of their apprenticeship before they are admitted to the
full privileges of the company or fellowship.

† It has been stated, though erroneously, that Albert Durer was a pupil of Martin
Schongauer, or Schön, as the surname was spelled by some writers, one of the most eminent
painters and copper-plate engravers of his day. It has been generally supposed that he died
in 1486; but, if an old memorandum at the back of his portrait in the collection of Count
de Fries can be depended on, his death did not take place till the 2d of February 1499. An
account of this memorandum will be found in Ottley's Inquiry into the Origin and Early
History of Engraving, vol. ii. p. 640.

in order that she might obtain money, is said to have embittered the life of the artist and eventually to have hastened his death.*

It has not been ascertained from whom Albert Durer learnt the art of engraving on copper ; for there seems but little reason to believe that his master Michael Wolgemuth ever practised that branch of art, though several copper-plates, marked with a W, have been ascribed to him by some authors.† As most of the early copper-plate engravers were also goldsmiths, it is probable that Durer might acquire some knowledge of the former art during the time that he continued with his father ; and, as he was endowed with a versatile genius, it is not unlikely that he owed his future improvement entirely to himself. The earliest date that is to be found on his copper-plates is 1494. The subject in which this date occurs represents a group of four naked women with a globe suspended above them, in the manner of a lamp, on which are inscribed the letters O. G. H. which have been supposed to signify the words " O Gott helf ! "—Help, O Lord !—as if the spectator on beholding the naked beauties were exceedingly liable to fall into temptation.‡

The earliest wood engravings that contain Albert Durer's mark are sixteen subjects, of folio size, illustrative of the Apocalypse, which were printed at Nuremberg, 1498. On the first leaf is the title in German : " Die heimliche Offenbarung Johannes "—" The Revelation of John ; "— and on the back of the last cut but one is the imprint : " Gedrücket zu Nurnbergk durch Albrecht Durer, maler, nach Christi geburt M. CCCC. und darnach im xcviij. iar "—" Printed at Nuremberg by Albert Durer, painter, in the year after the birth of Christ 1498." The date of those cuts marks an important epoch in the history of wood engraving. From this time the boundaries of the art became enlarged ; and wood engravers, instead of being almost wholly occupied in executing designs of the very lowest character, drawn without feeling, taste, or knowledge, were now to be engaged in engraving subjects of general interest, drawn, expressly for the purpose of being thus executed, by some of the most celebrated artists of the age. Though several cuts of the Apocalypse are faulty in drawing and extravagant in design, they are on the whole

---

* On a passage, in which Durer alludes to his wife, in one of his letters from Venice, 1506, to his friend Bilibald Pirkheimer, Von Murr makes the following remark : " This Xantippe must even at that time have vexed him much ; and he was obliged to drag on his life with her for twenty-two years longer, till she fairly plagued him to death."—Journal, 10er Theil, S. 32.

† Bartsch is decidedly of opinion that Michael Wolgemuth was not an engraver ; and he ascribes all the plates marked with a W, which others have supposed to be Wolgemuth's, to Wenceslaus of Olmutz, an artist of whom nothing is positively known.

‡ This subject has also been engraved by Israel Von Mecken, and by an artist supposed to be Wenceslaus of Olmutz. It is probable that those artists have copied Durer's engraving. On the globe in Israel Von Mecken's plate the letters are O. G. B.

much superior to any series of wood engravings that preceded them;
and their execution, though coarse, is free and bold. They are not equal,
in point of well-contrasted light and shade, to some of Durer's later
designs on wood ; but considering them as his first essays in drawing on
wood, they are not unworthy of his reputation. They appear as if they
had been drawn on the block with a pen and ink ; and though cross-
hatching is to be found in all of them, this mode of indicating a shade,
or obtaining "colour," is much less frequently employed than in some of
his later productions. The following is a reduced copy of one of the cuts,

No. 11, which is illustrative of the twelfth chapter of Revelations, verses
1—4 : " And there appeared a great wonder in heaven ; a woman clothed
with the sun, and the moon under her feet, and upon her head a crown
of twelve stars.————And there appeared another wonder in heaven ;
and behold a great red dragon, having seven heads and ten horns, and
seven crowns upon his heads. And his tail drew the third part of

the stars of heaven, and did cast them to the earth; and the dragon stood before the woman."

In 1502 a pirated edition of those cuts was published at Strasburg by Jerome Greff, who describes himself as a painter of Frankfort. In 1511 Durer published a second edition of the originals; and on the back of the last cut but one is a caution addressed to the plagiary, informing him of the Emperor's order, prohibiting any one to copy the cuts or to sell the spurious impressions within the limits of the German empire, under the penalty of the confiscation of goods, and at the peril of further punishment.*

Though no other wood engravings with Durer's mark are found with a date till 1504, yet it is highly probable that several subjects of his designing were engraved between 1498, the date of the Apocalypse, and the above year; and it is also likely that he engraved several copper-plates within this period; although, with the exception of that of the four naked women, there are only four known which contain a date earlier than 1505. About the commencement of 1506 Durer visited Venice, where he remained till October in the same year. Eight letters which he addressed to Bilibald Pirkheimer from Venice, are printed in the tenth volume of Von Murr's Journal. In the first letter, which is dated on the day of the Three Kings of Cologne, 1506, he informs his friend that he was employed to paint a picture for the German church at Venice, for which he was to receive a hundred and ten Rhenish guilders,† and that he expects to have it ready to place above the altar a month after Easter. He expresses a hope that he will be enabled to repay out of this money what he had borrowed of Pirkheimer. From this letter it seems evident that Durer's circumstances were not then in a very flourishing state, and that he had to depend on his exertions for the means of living. The comparatively trifling sums which he mentions as having sent to his mother and his wife sufficiently declare that he had not left a considerable sum at home. He also says, that should his wife want more money, her father must assist her, and that he will honourably repay him on his return.

* This caution is in the original expressed in the following indignant terms : " Heus, tu insidiator, ac alieni laboris et ingenii surreptor, ne manus temerarias his nostris operibus inicias cave. Scias enim a gloriosissimo Romanorum imperatore Maximiliano nobis concessum esse ne quis supposititiis formis has imagines imprimere seu impressas per imperii limites vendere audeat : q' per contemptum seu avariciæ crimen secus feceris, post bonorum confiscationem tibi maximum periculum subeundum esse certissime scias."

† Von Murr says that the subject of this picture was the martyrdom of St. Bartholomew, the saint to whom the church was dedicated ; and that the painting afterwards came into the possession of the Emperor Rudolf II. and was placed in his gallery at Prague. It seems that Durer had taken some pictures with him to Venice ; for in his fifth letter he says that he has sold two for twenty-four ducats, and exchanged three others for three rings, valued also at twenty-four ducats.

In the second letter, after telling Pirkheimer that he has no other friend but him on earth, he expresses a wish that he were in Venice to enjoy the pleasant company that he has met with there. The following passage, which occurs in this letter, is, perhaps, the most interesting in the collection : " I have many good friends among the Italians, who warn me not to eat or drink with their painters, of whom several are my enemies, and copy my picture in the church and others of mine, wherever they can find them ; and yet they blame them, and say they are not according to ancient art, and therefore not good. Giovanni Bellini* however has praised me highly to several gentlemen, and wishes to have something of my doing. He called on me himself, and requested that I would paint a picture for him, for which he said he would pay me well. People a·e all surprised that I should be so much thought of by a person of his reputation. He is very old, but is still the best painter of them all. The things which pleased me eleven years ago, please me no longer. If I had not seen it myself I could not have believed it. You must also know that there are many better painters within this city than Master Jacob is without, although Anthony Kolb swears that there is not on earth a better painter than Jacob.† The others laugh, and say if he were good for anything he would live in Venice."

The greater part of the other six letters are chiefly occupied with accounts of his success in executing sundry little commissions with which he had been entrusted by his friends, such as the purchase of a finger-ring and two pieces of tapestry ; to enquire after such Greek books as had been recently published ; and to get him some crane feathers. The sixth and seventh letters are written in a vein of humour which at the present time would be called gross. Von Murr illustrates one passage by a quotation from Swift which is not remarkable for its delicacy ; and he also says that Durer's eighth letter is written in the humorous style of that writer. Those letters show that chastity was not one of Bilibald Pirkheimer's virtues ; and that the learned counsellor of the imperial city of Nuremberg was devoted "tam Veneri quam Mercurio."‡

In the fourth letter Durer says that the painters were much opposed

---

* In the Venetian dialect of that period Giovanni Bellini was called Zan Belin ; and Durer spells the name " Sambellinus." He was the master of Titian, and died in 1514, at the age of ninety.—Von Murr, Journal, 10er Theil, S. 8.

† Von Murr says that he cannot discover what Jacob is here meant. It would not be Jacob Walsch, as he died in 1500. The person alluded to was certainly not an Italian.

‡ Bilibald Pirkheimer was a learned man, and a person of great authority in the city of Nuremberg. He was also a member of the Imperial Council, and was frequently employed in negociations with neighbouring states. He published several works ; and among others a humorous essay entitled " Laus Podagræ "—The Praise of the Gout. His memory is still held in great respect in Germany as the friend of Albert Durer and Ulrich Hutten, two of the most extraordinary men that Germany has produced. He died in 1530, aged 60.

to him ; that they had thrice compelled him to go before the magistracy ; and that they had obliged him to give four florins to their society. In the seventh letter, he writes as follows about the picture which he had painted for the German church : " I have through it received great praise, but little profit. I might well have gained two hundred ducats in the same time, and all the while I laboured most diligently in order that I might get home again. I have given all the painters a rubbing down who said that I could engrave* well, but that in painting I knew not how to manage my colours. Everybody here says they never saw colours more beautiful." In his last letter,which is dated, " at Venice, I know not what day of the month, but about the fourteenth day after Michaelmas, 1506," he says that he will be ready to leave that city in about ten days; that he intends to proceed to Bologna, and after staying there about eight or ten days for the sake of learning some secrets in perspective, to return home by way of Venice. He visited Bologna as he intended ; and was treated with great respect by the painters of that city. After a brief stay at Bologna, he returned to Nuremberg ; and there is no evidence of his ever having visited Italy again.

In 1511, the second of Durer's large works engraved on wood appeared at Nuremberg. It is generally entitled the History of the Virgin, and consists of nine-teen large cuts, each about eleven inches and three quarters high, by eight inches and a quarter wide, with a vignette of smaller size which ornaments the title-page.† Impressions are to be found without any accompanying text, but the greater number have explanatory verses printed from type at the back. The cut here represented is a reduced copy of the vignette on the title-page. The Virgin

---

* The kind of engraving meant was copper-plate engraving. Durer's words are : " Ich hab awch dy Moler all gesthrilt dy do sagten, Im *Stechen* wer ich gut, aber im molen west ich nit mit farben um zu gen." The word " *Stechen* " applies to engraving on copper ; " Schneiden" to engraving on wood.—Von Murr, Journal, 10er Theil, S. 28.

† The title at length is as follows : " Epitome in Divæ Parthenices Marie Historiam ab Alberto Durero Norico per figuras digestam, cum versibus annexis Chelidonii." Chelidonius, who was a Benedictine monk of Nuremberg, also furnished the descriptive text to the series of twelve cuts illustrative of Christ's Passion, of which specimens will be found between page 246 and page 250.

is seen seated on a crescent, giving suck to the infant Christ; and her
figure and that of the child are drawn with great feeling.   Of all Durer's
Madonnas, whether engraved on wood or copper, this, perhaps, is one of
the best.   Her attitude is easy and natural, and happily expressive of the
character in which she is represented—that of a nursing mother.   The
light and shade are well contrasted ; and the folds of her ample drapery,
which Durer was fond of introducing whenever he could, are arranged in
a manner which materially contributes to the effect of the engraving.

The following cuts are reduced copies of two of the larger subjects of
the same work.   That which is here given represents the birth of the

Virgin ; and were it not for the angel who is seen swinging a censer at
the top of the room, it might be taken for the accouchement of a German
burgomaster's wife in the year 1510.   The interior is apparently that of
a house in Nuremberg of Durer's own time, and the figures introduced

are doubtless faithful copies, both in costume and character, of such females as were generally to be found in the house of a German tradesman on such an occasion. From the number of cups and flagons that are seen, we may be certain that the gossips did not want liquor ; and that in Durer's age the female friends and attendants on a groaning woman were accustomed to enjoy themselves on the birth of a child over a cheerful cup. In the fore-ground an elderly female is perceived taking a draught, without measure, from a flagon ; while another, more in the distance and farther to the right, appears to be drinking, from a cup, health to the infant which a woman like a nurse holds in her arms. An elderly female, sitting by the side of the bed, has dropped into a doze ; but whether from the effects of the liquor or long watching it would not be easy to divine. On the opposite side of the bed a female figure presents a caudle, with a spoon in it, to St. Anne, the mother of the Virgin, while another is seen filling a goblet of wine. At the bottom of the cut is Durer's mark on a tablet. The original cut is not remarkable for the excellence of its engraving, but it affords a striking example of the little attention which Durer, in common with most other German painters of that period, paid to propriety of costume in the treatment of such subjects. The piece is Hebrew, of the age of Herod the Great ; but the scenery, dresses, and decorations are German, of the time of Maximilian I.

The second specimen of the large cuts of Durer's Life of the Virgin, given on the next page, represents the Sojourn of the Holy Family in Egypt. In the fore-ground St. Joseph is seen working at his business as a carpenter ; while a number of little figures, like so many Cupids, are busily employed in collecting the chips which he makes and in putting them into a basket. Two little winged figures, of the same family as the chip-collectors, are seen running hand-in-hand, a little more in the distance to the left, and one of them holds in his hand a plaything like those which are called "windmills" in England, and are cried about as "toys for girls and boys," and sold for a halfpenny each, or exchanged for old pewter spoons, doctors' bottles, or broken flint-glass. To the right the Virgin, a matronly-looking figure, is seen sitting spinning, and at the same time rocking with her foot the cradle in which the infant Christ is asleep. Near the Virgin are St. Elizabeth and her young son, the future Baptist. At the head of the cradle is an angel bending as if in the act of adoration ; while another, immediately behind St. Elizabeth, holds a pot .containing flowers. In the sky there is a representation of the Deity, with the Holy Ghost in the shape of a dove. The artist has not thought it necessary to mark the locality of the scene by the introduction of pyramids and temples in the back-ground, for the architectural parts of his subject, as well

as the human figures, have evidently been supplied by his own country
Durer's mark is at the bottom of the cut on the right.

Christ's Passion, consisting of a series of eleven large wood-cuts
and a vignette, designed by Albert Durer, appeared about the same
time as his History of the Virgin.* The descriptive matter was
compiled by Chelidonius; and, in the same manner as in the History of
the Virgin, a certain number of impressions were printed without any
explanatory text.† The large subjects are about fifteen inches and a

* The cuts of these two works appear to have been in the hands of the engraver at the
same time. Of those in the History of the Virgin one is dated 1509 ; and two bear the date
1510 ; and in the Passion of Christ four are dated 1510.

† The Latin title of the work is as follows : " Passio Domini nostri Jesu, ex Hieronymo
Paduano, Dominico Mancino, Sedulio, et Baptista Mantuana, per fratrem Chelidonium
collecta, cum figuris Alberti Dureri Norici Pictoris."

half high, by eleven inches and an eighth wide. The following cut is a reduced copy of the vignette on the title-page.

The subject is Christ mocked; but the artist has at the same time wished to express in the figure of Christ the variety of his sufferings: the Saviour prays as if in his agony on the mount; near him lies the instrument of his flagellation; his hands and feet bear the marks of the nails, and he appears seated on the covering of his sepulchre. The soldier is kneeling and offering a reed as a sceptre to Christ, whom he hails in derision as King of the Jews.

The three following cuts are reduced copies of the same number in the Passion of Christ. In the cut of the Last Supper, in the next page, cross-hatching is freely introduced, though without contributing much to the improvement of the engraving; and the same effect in the wall to the right, in the groins of the roof, and in the floor under the table, might be produced by much simpler means. No artist, I am persuaded, would introduce such work in a design if he had to engrave it himself. The same "colour" might be produced by single lines which could be executed in a third of the time required to cut out the interstices of the cross-hatchings. Durer's mark is at the bottom of the cut, and the date 1510 is perceived above it, on the frame of the table.

The cut on page 249, from the Passion, Christ bearing his Cross, is highly characteristic of Durer's style; and the original is one of the best of all the wood engravings which bear his mark. The characters introduced are such as he was fondest of drawing; and most of the heads and figures may be recognised in several other engravings either executed by himself on copper or by others on wood from his designs.

The figure which is seen holding a kind of halbert in his right hand is a favourite with Durer, and is introduced, with trifling variations, in at

least half a dozen of his subjects ; and the horseman with a kind of
turban on his head and a lance in his left hand occurs no less frequently.
St. Veronica, who is seen holding the " sudarium," or holy handkerchief,
in the fore-ground to the left, is a type of his female figures ; the head of
the executioner, who is seen urging Christ forward, is nearly the same as
that of the mocker in the preceding vignette ; and Simon the Cyrenian,

who assists to bear the cross, appears to be the twin-brother of St. Joseph
in the Sojourn in Egypt. The figure of Christ, bowed down with the
weight of the cross, is well drawn, and his face is strongly expressive of
sorrow.   Behind Simon the Cyrenian are the Virgin and St. John ; and
under the gateway a man with a haggard visage is perceived carrying a
ladder with his head between the steps. The artist's mark is at the
bottom of the cut.

The subject of the cut on page 250, from Christ's Passion, represents the descent into hell and the liberation of the ancestors.   The massive gates of the abode of sin and death have been burst open, and the banner of the cross waves triumphant.   Among those who have already been liberated from the pit of darkness are Eve, who has her back turned towards the spectator, and Adam, who in his right hand holds an apple,

the symbol of his fall, and with his left supports a cross, the emblem of his redemption.   In the front is Christ aiding others of the ancestors to ascend from the pit, to the great dismay of the demons whose realm is invaded.   A horrid monster, with a head like that of a boar surmounted with a horn, aims a blow at the Redeemer with a kind of rude lance; while another, a hideous compound of things that swim, and walk, and fly, sounds a note of alarm to arouse his kindred fiends.   On a stone, above the entrance to the pit, is the date 1510; and Durer's mark is perceived on another stone immediately before the figure of Christ· This cut, with the exception of the frequent cross-hatching, is designed more in the style and spirit of the artist's illustrations of the Apocalypse than in the manner of the rest of the series to which it belongs.

The preceding specimens of wood-cuts from Durer's three great works, the Apocalypse, the History of the Virgin, and Christ's Passion, afford not only an idea of the style of his drawing on wood, but also of the progress made by the art of wood engraving from the time of his first availing himself of its capabilities. In Durer's designs on wood we perceive not only more correct drawing and a greater knowledge of composition, but also a much more effective combination of light and shade, than are to be found in any wood-cuts executed before the date of his earliest work, the Apocalypse, which appeared in 1498. One of the peculiar advantages of wood engraving is the effect with which strong shades can be represented ; and of this Durer has generally availed himself with the greatest skill. On comparing his works engraved on wood with all those previously executed in the same manner, we shall find that his figures are not only much better drawn and more skilfully grouped, but that instead of sticking, in hard outline, against the background, they stand out with the natural appearance of rotundity. The rules of perspective are more attentively observed ; the back-grounds better filled ; and a number of subordinate objects introduced—such as trees, herbage, flowers, animals, and children—which at once give a pleasing variety to the subject and impart to it the stamp of truth. Though the figures in many of his designs may not indeed be correct in point of costume,—for though he diligently studied Nature, it was only in her German dress,—yet their character and expression are generally appropriate and natural. Though incapable of imparting to sacred subjects the elevated character which is given to them by Raffaele, his representations are perhaps no less like the originals than those of the great Italian master. It is indeed highly probable that Albert Durer's German representatives of saints and apostles are more like the originals than the more dignified ideal portraits of Raffaele. The latter, from his knowledge of the antique, has frequently given to his Jews a character and a costume borrowed from Grecian art of the age of Phidias ; while Albert Durer has given to them the features and invested them in the costume of Germans of his own age.

Shortly after the appearance of the large cuts illustrative of Christ's Passion, Durer published a series of thirty-seven of a smaller size, also engraved on wood, which Mr. Ottley calls " The Fall of Man and his Redemption through Christ," but which Durer himself refers to under the title of "The Little Passion."* All the cuts of the Little Passion, as well as seventeen of those of the Life of the Virgin and several other pieces of Durer's, were imitated on copper by Marc Antonio Raimondi, the celebrated Italian engraver, who is said to have sold his copies as the originals. Vasari, in his Life of Marc Antonio, says that when Durer was informed of this imitation of his works, he was highly incensed and

* The Latin title of this work is " Passio Christi," and the explanatory verses are from the pen of Chelidonius. Durer, in the Journal of his Visit to the Netherlands, twice mentions it as " die Kleine Passion," and each time with a distinction which proves that he did not mean the Passion engraved by him on copper and probably published in 1512. " Item Sebaldt Fischer hat mir zu Antorff [Antwerp] abkaufft 16 *kleiner Passion*, pro 4 fl. Mehr 32 grosser Bücher pro 8 fl. Mehr 6 gestochne Passion pro 3 fl."—" Darnach die drey Bücher unser Frauen Leben, Apocalypsin, und den grossen Passion, darnach *den klein Passion*, und den Passion in Kupffer."—Albrecht Dürers Reisejournal, in Von Murr, 7er Theil, S. 60 and 67. The size of the cuts of the Little Passion is five inches high by three and seven-eighths wide. Four impressions from the original blocks are given in Ottley's Inquiry, vol. ii. between page 730 and page 731

set out directly for Venice, and that on his arrival there he complained of Marc Antonio's proceedings to the government ; but could obtain no further redress than that in future Marc Antonio should not put Durer's mark to his engravings.

Though it is by no means unlikely that Durer might apply to the Venetian government to prevent the sale of spurious copies of his works within the bounds of their jurisdiction, yet Vasari's account of his personally visiting that city for the purpose of making a complaint against Marc Antonio, and of the government having forbid the latter to affix Durer's mark to his engravings in future, is certainly incorrect. The History of the Virgin, the earliest of the two works which were almost entirely copied by Marc Antonio, was not published before 1510, and there is not the slightest evidence of Durer having re-visited Venice after his return to Nuremberg about the latter end of 1506. Bartsch thinks that Vasari's account of Durer's complaining to the Venetian government against Marc Antonio is wholly unfounded ; not only from the fact of Durer not having visited Venice subsequent to 1506, but from the improbability of his applying to a foreign state to prohibit a stranger from copying his works. Mr. Ottley, however,—after observing that Marc Antonio had affixed Durer's mark to his copies of the seventeen cuts of the Life of the Virgin and of some other single subjects, but had omitted it in his copies of the cuts of the Little Passion,—thus expresses his opinion with respect to the correctness of this part of Vasari's account : " That Durer, who enjoyed the especial protection of the Emperor Maximilian, might be enabled through the imperial ambassador at Venice to lay his complaints before the government, and to obtain the prohibition before stated, may I think readily be imagined ; and it cannot be denied, that the circumstance of Marc Antonio's having omitted to affix the mark of Albert to the copies which he afterwards made of the series of the ' Life of Christ' is strongly corroborative of the general truth of the story."* As two of the cuts in the Little Passion, which Mr. Ottley here calls the " Life of Christ," are dated 1510, and as, according to Mr. Ottley, Marc Antonio arrived at Rome in the course of that year, it is difficult to conceive how the government of Venice could have the power to prohibit a native of Bologna, living in a state beyond their jurisdiction, from affixing Albert Durer's mark to such engravings as he might please to copy from the works of that master.

* Inquiry into the Origin and Early History of Engraving, vol. ii. p. 782. The objections to the general truth of Vasari's story appear to be much stronger than the presumptions in its favour. 1. The improbability of Albert Durer having visited Venice subsequent to 1506 ; 2. The fact of Marc Antonio's copies of the cuts of the Little Passion *not* containing Albert Durer's mark ; and 3. The probability of Mark Antonio residing beyond the jurisdiction of the Venetian government at the time of his engraving them.

Among the more remarkable single subjects engraved on wood from Durer's designs, the following are most frequently referred to : God the Father bearing up into heaven the dead body of Christ, with the date 1511 ; a Rhinoceros, with the date 1515 ; a portrait of Ulrich Varnbuler, with the date 1522 ; a large head of Christ crowned with thorns, without date ; and the Siege of a fortified town, with the date 1527. In the first of the above-named cuts, God the Father wears a kind of tiara like that of the Pope, and above the principal figure the Holy Ghost is seen hovering in the form of a dove. On each side of the Deity and the dead Christ are angels holding the cross, the pillar to which Christ was bound when he was scourged, the crown of thorns, the sponge dipped in vinegar, and other emblems of the Passion. At the foot are heads with puffed-out cheeks intended to represent the winds. This cut is engraved in a clearer and more delicate style than most of the other subjects designed by Durer on wood. There are impressions of the Rhinoceros, and the portrait of Varnbuler, printed in chiaro-scuro from three blocks ; and there are also other wood-cuts designed by Durer executed in the same manner. The large head of Christ, which is engraved in a coarse though spirited and effective manner, is placed by Bartsch among the doubtful pieces ascribed to Durer ; but Mr. Ottley says, "I am unwilling to deny to Durer the credit of this admirable and boldly executed production."* The cut representing the siege of a fortified town is twenty-eight inches and three-eighths wide, by eight inches and seven eighths high. It has been engraved on two blocks, and afterwards pasted together. A number of small figures are introduced, and a great extent of country is shown in this cut, which is, however, deficient in effect ; and the little figures, though drawn with great spirit, want relief, which causes many of them to appear as if they were riding or walking in the air. The most solid-like part of the subject is the sky; there is no ground for most of the figures to stand on ; and those which are in the distance are of the same size as those which are apparently a mile or two nearer the spectator. There is nothing remarkable in the execution, and the design adds nothing to Durer's reputation.

The great patron of wood engraving in the earlier part of the sixteenth century was the Emperor Maximilian I, who,—besides originating the three works, known by the titles of Sir Theurdank, the

---

* There is a copy of this head, also engraved on wood, of the size of the original, but without Durer's, or any other mark. Underneath an impression of the copy, in the Print Room of the British Museum, there is written in a hand which appears to be at least as old as the year 1550, " Dieser hat ʍP ehaim gerissen"—" H. S. Behaim drew this." Hans Sebald Behaim, a painter and designer on wood, was born at Nuremberg in 1500, and was the pupil of his uncle, also named Behaim, a painter and engraver of that city. The younger Behaim abandoned the arts to become a tavern-keeper at Frankfort, where he died in 1550.

Wise King, and the Triumphs of Maximilian, which he caused to be illustrated with numerous wood engravings, chiefly from the designs of Hans Burgmair and Hans Schaufflein,—employed Albert Durer to make the designs for two other series of wood engravings, a Triumphal Car and a Triumphal Arch.

The Triumphal *Car*, engraved by Jerome Resch from Durer's drawings on wood, is frequently confounded with the larger work called the Triumphs of Maximilian, most of the designs of which were made by Hans Burgmair. It is indeed generally asserted that all the designs for the latter work were made by Hans Burgmair; but I think I shall be able to show, in a subsequent notice of that work, that some of the cuts contained in the edition published at Vienna and London in 1796 were, in all probability, designed by Albert Durer. The Triumphal Car consists of eight separate pieces, which, when joined together, form a continuous subject seven feet four inches long; the height of the highest cut—that containing the car—is eighteen inches from the base line to the upper part of the canopy above the Emperor's head. The Emperor is seen seated in a highly ornamented car, attended by female figures, representing Justice, Truth, Clemency, and other virtues, who hold towards him triumphal wreaths. One of the two wheels which are seen is inscribed " Magnificentia," and the other " Dignitas ; " the driver of the car is Reason,—" Ratio,"—and one of the reins is marked " Nobilitas," and the other " Potentia." The car is drawn by six pair of horses splendidly harnessed, and each horse is attended by a female figure. The names of the females at the head of the first pair from the car are " Providentia" and " Moderatio ; " of the second, " Alacritas " and " Opportunitas ; " of the third, " Velocitas" and " Firmitudo ; " of the fourth, " Acrimonia " and " Virilitas ;" of the fifth, " Audacia " and " Magnanimitas ;" and the attendants on the leaders are " Experientia " and " Solertia." Above each pair of horses there is a portion of explanatory matter printed in letter-press ; and in that above the leading pair is a mandate from the Emperor Maximilian, dated Inspruck, 1518, addressed to Bilibald Pirkheimer, who appears to have suggested the subject; and in the same place is the name of the inventor and designer, Albert Durer.* The first edition of those cuts appeared at Nuremberg in 1522 ; and in some copies the text is in German, and in others in Latin. A second edition, with the text in Latin only, was printed at the same place in the following year. A third edition, from the same blocks, was

---

* In the edition with Latin inscriptions, 1523, are the words, " Excogitatus et depictus est currus iste Nurembergæ, impressus vero per Albertum Durer. Anno MDXXIII. The Latin words "excogitatus et depictus" are expressed by "gefunden und geordnet" in the German inscriptions in the edition of 1522. A sketch by Durer, for the Triumphal Car, is preserved in the Print Room in the British Museum.

printed at Venice in 1588 ; and a fourth at Amsterdam in 1609. The execution of this subject is not particularly good, but the action of the horses is generally well represented, and the drawing of some of the female figures attending them is extremely spirited. ·Guido seems to have availed himself of some of the figures in Durer's Triumphal Car in his celebrated fresco of the Car of Apollo, preceded by Aurora, and accompanied by the Hours.

It is said that the same subject painted by Durer himself is still to be seen on the walls of the Town-hall of Nuremberg ; but how far this is correct I am unable to positively say ; for I know of no account of the painting written by a person who appears to have been acquainted with the subject engraved on wood. Dr. Dibdin, who visited the Town-hall of Nuremberg in 1818, speaks of what he saw there in a most vague and unsatisfactory manner, as if he did not know the Triumphal Car designed by Durer from the larger work entitled the Triumphs of Maximilian. The notice of the learned bibliographer, who professes to be a great admirer of the works of Albert Durer, is as follows : " The great boast of the collection [in the Town-hall of Nuremberg] are the Triumphs of Maximilian executed by *Albert Durer,*—which, however, have by no means escaped injury."* It is from such careless observations as the preceding that erroneous opinions respecting the Triumphal Car and the Triumphs of Maximilian are continued and propagated, and that most persons confound the two works ; which is indeed not surprising, seeing that Dr. Dibdin himself, who is considered to be an authority on such matters, has afforded proof that he does not know one from the other. In the same volume that contains the notice of the "Triumphs of Maximilian" in the Town-hall of Nuremberg, Dr. Dibdin says that he saw the "ORIGINAL PAINTINGS" from which the large wood blocks were taken for the well-known work entitled the " *Triumphs of the Emperor Maximilian,*" in large folio, in the Imperial Library at Vienna.† Such observations are very much in the style of the countryman's, who had seen *two* genuine skulls of Oliver Cromwell,—one at Oxford, and another in the British Museum. Though I have not been able to ascertain satisfactorily the subject of Durer's painting in the Town-hall of Nuremberg, I am inclined to think that it is the Triumphal *Car* of Maximilian. In a memorandum in the hand-writing of Nollekins, preserved with his copies of Durer's Triumphal Car and Triumphal Arch of Maximilian, in the Print Room of the British Museum, it is said, though erroneously, that the former is painted in the Town-hall of *Augsburg* with the figures as large as life.

The Triumphal *Arch* of the Emperor Maximilian, engraved on wood from Durer's designs, consists of ninety-two separate pieces, which, when

---

* Bibliographical Tour, vol. iii. p. 438. Edit. 1829. † Ibid. p. 330.

joined together, form one large composition about ten feet and a half high by nine and a half wide, exclusive of the margins and five folio sheets of explanatory matter by the projector of the design, John Stabius, who styles himself the historiographer and poet of the Emperor, and who says, at the commencement of his description, that this arch was drawn " after the manner of those erected in honour of the Roman emperors at Rome, some of which are destroyed and others still to be seen." In the arch of Maximilian are three gates or entrances; that in the centre is named the Gate of Honour and Power; that to the left the Gate of Fame; and that to the right the Gate of Nobility.* Above the middle entrance is what Stabius calls the "grand tower," surmounted with the imperial crown, and containing an inscription in German to the memory of Maximilian. Above and on each side of the gates or entrances, which are of very small dimensions, are portraits of the Roman emperors from the time of Julius Cæsar to that of Maximilian himself; there are also portraits of his ancestors, and of kings and princes with whom he was allied either by friendship or marriage; shields of arms illustrative of his descent or of the extent of his sovereignty; with representations of his most memorable actions, among which his adventures in the Tyrolean Alps, when hunting the chamois, are not forgotten. Underneath each subject illustrative of his own history are explanatory verses, in the German language, engraved on wood; and the names of the kings and emperors, as well as the inscriptions explanatory of other parts of the subject, are also executed in the same manner. The whole subject is, in fact, a kind of pictorial epitome of the history of the German empire; representing the succession of the Roman emperors, and the more remarkable events of Maximilian's own reign; with illustrations of his descent, possessions, and alliances.

At the time of Maximilian's death, which happened in 1519, this great work was not finished; and it is said that Durer himself did not live to see it completed, as one small block remained to be engraved at the period of his death, in 1528. At whatever time the work might be finished, it certainly was commenced at least four years before the Emperor's death, for the date 1515 occurs in two places at the foot of the subject. Though Durer's mark is not to be found on any one of the cuts, there can be little doubt of his having furnished the designs for the whole. In the ninth volume of Von Murr's Journal it is stated that Durer received a hundred guilders a year from the Emperor,—probably on account of this large work; and in the same volume there is a letter

---

* The two last names are, in the first edition, pasted over others which appear to have been "The Gate of Honour" and "The Gate of Relationship, Friendship, and Alliance." The last name alludes to the emperor's possessions as acquired by descent or marriage, and to his power as strengthened by his friendly alliances with neighbouring states.

of Durer's addressed to a friend, requesting him to apply to the emperor on account of arrears due to him. In this letter he says that he has made many drawings besides the " *Tryumps*"* for the emperor; and as he also thrice mentions Stabius, the inventor of the Triumphal Arch, there can be little doubt but that this was the work to which he alludes.

As a work of art the best single subjects of the Triumphal Arch will not bear a comparison with the best cuts in Durer's Apocalypse, the History of the Virgin, or Christ's Passion; and there are several in which no trace of his effective style of drawing on wood is to be found. Most of the subjects illustrative of the emperor's battles and adventures are in particular meagre in point of drawing, and deficient in effect. The whole composition indeed appears like the result of continued application without much display of talent. The powers of Durer had been evidently constrained to work out the conceptions of the historiographer and poet, Stabius; and as the subjects were not the suggestions of the artist's own feelings, it cannot be a matter of surprise that we should find in them so few traces of his genius. The engraving of the cuts is clear, but not generally effective; and the execution of the whole, both figures and letters, would occupy a single wood engraver not less than four years; even allowing him to engrave more rapidly on pear-tree than a modern wood engraver does on box; and supposing him to be a master of his profession.

From his varied talents and the excellence which he displayed in every branch of art that he attempted, Albert Durer is entitled to rank with the most extraordinary men of his age. As a painter he may be considered as the father of the German school; while for his fidelity in copying nature and the beauty of his colours he may bear a comparison with most of the Italian artists of his own age. As an engraver on copper he greatly excelled all who preceded him; and it is highly questionable if any artist since his time, except Rembrandt, has painted so many good pictures and engraved so many good copper-plates. But besides excelling as an engraver on copper after the manner in which the art had been previously practised, giving to his subjects a breadth of light and a depth of shade which is not to be found in the productions of the earlier masters, he further improved the art by the invention of

---

* " Item wist auch das Ich K. Mt. ausserhalb des Tryumps sonst viel mancherley Fisyrung gemacht hab."—" You must also know that I have made many other drawings for the emperor besides those of the Triumph." The date of this letter is not given, but Durer informs his friend that he had been already three years employed for the emperor, and that if he had not exerted himself the beautiful " work" would not have been so soon completed. If this is to be understood of the Triumphal Arch, it would seem that the designs at least were all finished before the emperor's death.—Von Murr, Journal, 9er Theil, S. 4.

S

etching,* which enables the artist to work with greater freedom and to
give a variety and an effect to his subjects, more especially landscapes,
which are utterly unattainable by means of the graver alone.

There are two subjects by Albert Durer, dated 1512, which Bartsch
thinks were etched upon plates of iron, but which Mr. Ottley considers
to have been executed upon plates of a softer metal than copper, with the
dry-point. There are, however, two undoubted etchings by Durer with
the date 1515 ; two others executed in the same manner are dated 1516 ;
and a fifth, a landscape with a large cannon in the fore-ground to the left,
is dated 1518. There is another undoubted etching by Durer, representing naked figures in a bath ; but it contains neither his mark nor a date.
The three pieces which Mr. Ottley thinks were not etched, but executed
on some soft kind of metal with the dry-point, are : 1. The figure of
Christ, seen in front, standing, clothed with a mantle, having his hands
tied together, and on his head a crown of thorns ; date 1512. 2. St.
Jerome seated amongst rocks, praying to a crucifix, with a book open
before him, and a lion below to the left ; date 1512. 3. The Virgin, seated
with the infant Christ in her lap, and seen in front, with St. Joseph
behind her on the left, and on the right three other figures ; without
mark or date.—One of the more common of Durer's undoubted etchings
is that of a man mounted on a unicorn, and carrying off a naked woman,
with the date 1516.

Albert Durer not only excelled as a painter, an engraver on copper,
and a designer on wood, but he also executed several pieces of sculpture
with surprising delicacy and natural expression of character. An admirable specimen of his skill in this department of art is preserved in
the British Museum, to which institution it was bequeathed by the late

---

* In the process of etching the plate is first covered with a resinous composition—called
etching ground—on which the lines intended to be *etched*, or bit into the plate, are drawn
through to the surface of the metal by means of a small pointed tool called an etching needle,
or an etching point. When the drawing of the subject upon the etching ground is finished,
the plate is surrounded with a slightly raised border, or " wall," as it is technically termed,
formed of rosin, bee's-wax, and lard ; and, a corrosive liquid being poured upon the plate, the
lines are " bit" into the copper or steel. When the engraver thinks that the lines are
corroded to a sufficient depth, he pours off the liquid, cleans the plate by means of turpentine,
and proceeds to finish his work with the graver and dry-point. According to the practice of
modern engravers, where several *tints* are required, as is most frequently the case, the process
of " biting-in" is repeated ; the corrosive liquid being again poured on the plate to corrode
deeper the stronger lines, while the more delicate are " stopped out,"—that is, covered with
a kind of varnish that soon hardens, to preserve them from further corrosion. Most of our
best engravers now use a diamond point in etching. *Nitrous* acid is used for " biting-in" on
copper in the proportion of one part acid to four parts water, and the mixture is considered
to be better after it has been once or twice used. Before using the acid it is advisable to take
the stopper out of the bottle for twenty-four hours in order to allow a portion of the strength
to evaporate. During the process of biting-in a large copper-plate the fumes which arise are
so powerful as frequently to cause an unpleasant stricture in the throat, and sometimes to

R. Payne Knight, Esq., by whom it was purchased at Brussels for five hundred guineas upwards of forty years ago. This most exquisite piece of sculpture is of small dimensions, being only seven and three quarter inches high, by five and a half wide. It is executed in hone-stone, of a cream colour, and is all of one piece, with the exception of a dog and one or two books in front. The subject is the naming of John the Baptist.* In front, to the right, is an old man with a tablet inscribed with Hebrew characters; another old man is seen immediately behind him, further to the right; and a younger man,—said to be intended by the artist for a portrait of himself,—appears entering the door of the apartment. An old woman with the child in her arms is seated near the figure with the tablet; St. Elizabeth is perceived lying in bed, on the more distant side of which a female attendant is standing, and on the other, nearer to the spectator, an elderly man is seen kneeling. It is supposed that the latter figure is intended for Zacharias, and that the artist had represented him in the act of making signs to Elizabeth with his hands. The figures in the fore-ground are executed in high relief, and the character and expression of the heads have perhaps never been surpassed in any work of sculpture executed on the same scale. Durer's mark is perceived on a tablet at the foot of the bed, with the date 1510. This curious specimen of Durer's talents as a sculptor is carefully preserved in a frame with a glass before it, and is in most perfect condition, with the exception of the hands of Zacharias and of Elizabeth, some of the fingers of which are broken off.

Shortly after Whitsuntide, 1520, Durer set out from Nuremberg, accompanied by his wife and her servant Susanna, on a visit to the Netherlands; and as he took with him several copies of his principal works, engravings on copper as well as on wood, and painted and drew a

bring on a spitting of blood when they have been incautiously inhaled by the engraver. At such times it is usual for the engraver to have near him some powerful essence, generally hartshorn, in order to counteract the effects of the noxious vapour. For biting-in on steel *nitric* acid is used in the proportion of thirty drops to half a pint of distilled water; and the mixture is never used for more than one plate.—When a *copper*-plate is sufficiently bit-in, it is only necessary to wash it with a little water previous to removing the etching ground with turpentine; but, besides this, with a *steel* plate it is further necessary to set it on one of its edges against a wall or other support, and to blow it with a pair of small bellows till every particle of moisture in the lines is perfectly evaporated. The plate is then rubbed with oil, otherwise the lines would rust from the action of the atmosphere and the plate be consequently spoiled. Previous to a steel plate being laid aside for any length of time it ought to be warmed, and the engraved surface rubbed carefully over with virgin wax so that it may be completely covered, and every line filled. A piece of thick paper the size of the plate, laid over the wax while it is yet adhesive, will prove an additional safeguard. For this information respecting the process of biting-in, the writer is indebted to an eminent engraver, Mr. J. T. Wilmore.

* The account of the naming of John the Baptist will be found in St. Luke's Gospel, chap. i. verse 59—64.

number of portraits during his residence there, the journey appears to have been taken as much with a view to business as pleasure. He kept a journal from the time of his leaving Nuremberg till the period of his reaching Cologne on his return, and from this curious record of the artist's travels the following particulars of his visit to the Netherlands have been obtained.*

Durer proceeded foom Nuremberg direct to Bamberg, where he presented to the bishop a painting of the Virgin, with a copy of the Apocalypse and the Life of the Virgin engraved on wood. The bishop invited Durer to his table, and gave him a letter exempting his goods from toll, with three others which were, most likely, letters of recommendation to persons of influence in the Netherlands.† From Bamberg, Durer proceeded by way of Eltman, Sweinfurth, and Frankfort to Mentz, and from the latter city down the Rhine to Cologne. In this part of his journey he seems to have met with little which he deemed worthy of remark : at Sweinfurth Dr. Rebart made him a present of some wine ; at Mentz, Peter Goldsmith's landlady presented him with two flasks of the same liquor ; and when Veit Varnbuler invited him to dinner there, the tavern-keeper would not receive any payment, but insisted on being Durer's host himself. At Lohnstein, on the Rhine, between Boppart and Coblentz, the toll-collector, who was well acquainted with Durer's wife, presented him with a can of wine, and expressed himself extremely glad to see him.

From Cologne, Durer proceeded direct to Antwerp, where he took up his abode in the house of "Jobst Planckfelt ;" and on the evening of his arrival‡ he was invited to a splendid supper by Bernard Stecher, an

---

* Durer's Journal of his Travels is given by Von Murr, 7er Theil, S. 55—98. The title which the Editor has prefixed to it is, " Reisejournal Albrecht Dürer's von seiner Niederländischen Reise, 1520 und 1521. E. Bibliotheca Ebneriana." In the same volume, Von Murr gives some specimens of Durer's poetry. The first couplet which he made in 1509 is as follows :

"Du aller Engel Spiegel und Erlöser der Welt,
Deine grosse Marter sey für mein Sünd ein Widergelt."

Thou mirror of all Angels and Redeemer of mankind,
Through thy martyrdom, for all my sins may I a ransom find.

This couplet being ridiculed by Bilibald Pirkheimer, who said that rhyming verses ought not to consist of more than eight syllables, Durer wrote several others in a shorter measure, but with no better success ; for he says at the conclusion, that they did not please the learned counsellor. With Durer's rhymes there is an epistle in verse from his friend Lazarus Sprengel, written to dissuade him from attempting to become a poet. Durer's verses want " the right butter-woman's trot to market," and are sadly deficient in rhythm when compared with the more regular clink of his friend's.

† Subsequently, Durer mentions having delivered to the Margrave John, at Brussels, a letter of recommendation [Fürderbrief] from the Bishop of Bamberg.

‡ As Durer was at Cologne about the 26th July, it is probable that he would arrive at Antwerp about the last day of that month.

agent of the Fuggers, the celebrated family of merchants of Nuremberg, and the most wealthy in Germany. On St. Oswald's day, Sunday, 5th August, the Painters' Company of Antwerp invited Durer, with his wife and her maid,* to a grand entertainment in their hall, which was ornamented in a splendid manner, and all the vessels on the table were of silver. The wives of the painters were also present ; and when Durer was conducted to his seat at the table "all the company stood up on each side, as if some great lord had been making his entrance." Several honourable persons, who had also been invited, bowed to him ; and all expressed their respect and their wishes to afford him pleasure. While he was at table the messenger of the magistrates of Antwerp made his appearance, and presented him in their name with four flaggons of wine, saying, that the magistrates thus testified their respect and their good-will towards him. Durer, as in duty bound, returned thanks, and tendered to the magisterial body his humble service. After this little affair was despatched, entered Peter the city carpenter *in propria persona,* and presented Durer with two more flaggons of wine, and complimented him with the offer of his services. After the party had enjoyed themselves cheerfully till late in the night, they attended Durer to his lodgings with torches in a most honourable manner, expressing their good-will towards him, and their readiness to assist him in whatever manner he might choose.—Shortly after this grand Fellowship-feast, Durer was entertained by Quintin Matsys,—frequently called the Blacksmith of Antwerp,—whose celebrated picture of the Misers is now in the Royal Collection at Windsor.

On the Sunday after the Assumption,† Durer witnessed a grand procession in honour of the Virgin, and the account which he has given of it presents so curious a picture of the old religious pageantries that it appears worthy of being translated without abridgement. "On the Sunday after the Assumption of our Lady," says the artist, "I saw the grand procession from our Lady's church at Antwerp, where all the inhabitants of the city assembled, gentry as well as trades-people, each, according to his rank, gayly dressed. Every class and fellowship was distinguished by its proper badge ; and large and valuable crosses were borne before several of the crafts. There were also silver trumpets of the old Frankish fashion ; with German drums and fifes playing loudly. I also saw in the street, marching after each other in rank, at a certain

---

* The maid, Susanna, seems to have been rather a "humble friend" than a menial servant; for she is mentioned in another part of the Journal as being entertained with Durer's wife at the house of "Tomasin Florianus," whom Durer describes as "*Romanus,* von Luca bürtig."

† The Assumption of the Virgin is celebrated in the Roman Catholic Church on the 15th August.

distance, the Goldsmiths, the Painters, the Masons, the Embroiderers, the
Statuaries, the Cabinet-makers, the Carpenters, the Sailors, the Fisher-
men, the Butchers, the Curriers, the Weavers, the Bakers, the Tailors, the
Shoemakers, and all kinds of craftsmen with labourers engaged in
producing the necessaries of life. In the same manner came the Shopkeepers and Merchants with their assistants. After these came the
Shooters, with firelocks, bows, and cross-bows, some on horseback and
some on foot; and after them came the City Guard. These were followed
by persons of the higher classes and the magistrates, all dressed in their
proper habits; and after them came a gallant troop arrayed in a noble
and splendid manner. In this procession were a number of females of a
religious order who subsist by means of their labour, all clothed in white
from head to foot, and forming a very pleasing sight. After them came
a number of gallant persons and the canons of our Lady's church, with
all the clergy and scholars, followed by a grand display of characters.
Twenty men carried the Virgin and Christ, most richly adorned, to the
honour of God. In this part of the procession were a number of
delightful things, represented in a splendid manner. There were several
waggons in which were representations of ships and fortifications. Then
came a troop of characters from the Prophets in regular order, followed
by others from the New Testament, such as the Annunciation, the Wise
Men of the East, riding on great camels and other wonderful animals,
and the Flight into Egypt, all very skilfully appointed. Then came a
great dragon, and St. Margaret, with the image of the Virgin at her
girdle, exceedingly beautiful; and last St. George and his squire. In
this troop rode a number of boys and girls very handsomely arrayed in
various costumes, representing so many saints. This procession, from
beginning to end, was upwards of two hours in passing our house; and
there were so many things to be seen, that I could never describe them
all even in a book."*

Though Durer chiefly resided at Antwerp during his stay in the
Netherlands, he did not entirely confine himself to that city, but
occasionally visited other places. On the 2nd of September 1520, he
left Antwerp for Brussels, proceeding by way of Malines and Vilvorde.
When at Brussels, he saw a number of valuable curiosities which had
been sent to the Emperor from Mexico, among which he enumerates
a golden sun, a fathom broad, and a silver moon of the same size, with
weapons, armour, and dresses, and various other admirable things of
great beauty and cost. He says that their value was estimated at a
hundred thousand guilders; and that he never saw any thing that pleased
him so much in his life. Durer was evidently fond of seeing sights; he
speaks with delight of the fountains, the labyrinths, and the parks in the

* Albrecht Dürer's Reisejournal, in Von Murr, 7er Theil, S. 63—65.

neighbourhood of the Royal Palace, which he says were like Paradise ; and among the wonders which he saw at Brussels, he notices a large fish-bone which was almost a fathom in circumference and weighed fifteen " centner ; " * a great bed that would hold fifty men ; and a stone which fell from the sky in a thunder-storm in presence of the Count of Nassau. He also mentions having seen at Antwerp the bones of a giant who had been eighteen feet high. Durer and his wife seem to have had a taste for zoology : Herr Lazarus Von Ravenspurg complimented him with a monkey ; and " Signor Roderigo," a Portuguese, presented his ill-tempered spouse with a green parrot.

When at Brussels, Durer painted the portrait of the celebrated Eras-mus, from whom, previous to leaving Antwerp, he had received as a present a Spanish mantle and three portraits. He remained about a week at Brussels, during which time he drew or painted seven portraits ; and in his Journal he makes the following memorandum: "Item, six persons whose likenesses I have taken at Brussels, have not given me anything." Among those portraits was that of Bernard Van Orley, an eminent Flemish painter who had studied under Raffaele, and who at that time held the office of painter to the Archduchess Margaret, regent of the Netherlands, and aunt of the Emperor Charles V. When at Brussels, Durer bought for a stiver † two copies of the " Eulenspiegel," a celebrated engraving by Lucas Van Leyden, now of very great rarity.

After remaining at Antwerp till the latter end of September, Durer proceeded to Aix-la-Chapelle, where, on the 23rd of October, he wit-nessed the coronation of the Emperor Charles V. He afterwards proceeded to Cologne, where, on the Sunday after All Saints' day, he saw a grand banquet and dance given by the emperor, from whom, on the Monday after Martinmas day, he received the appointment of court-painter to his Imperial Majesty. When at Cologne, Durer bought a copy of the " Condemnation of that good man, Martin Luther, for a white-penny." This Condemnation was probably a copy of the bull of excommunication issued against Luther by Pope Leo X. on 20th June

---

* This " gross Fischpein " was probably part of the back-bone of a whale.

† The stiver was the twenty-fourth part of a guilder or florin of gold, which was equal to about nine shillings English money of the present time ; the stiver would therefore be equal to about four pence half-penny. About the same time, Durer sold a copy of his Christ's Passion, probably the large one, for twelve stivers, and an impression of his copper-plate of Adam and Eve for four stivers. Shortly after his first arrival at Antwerp, he sold sixteen copies of the Little Passion for four guilders or florins ; and thirty-two copies of his larger works,—probably the Apocalypse, the History of the Virgin, and the Great Passion, –for eight florins, being at the rate of sixteen stivers for each copy. He also sold six copies of the Passion engraved on copper at the same price. He gave to his host a painting of the Virgin on canvass to sell for two Rhenish florins. The sum that he received for each portrait in pencil [the German is mit Kohlen, which is literally charcoal], when the parties did pay, appears to have been a florin.

1520. In a day or two after receiving his appointment, Durer left Cologne and proceeded down the Rhine, and visited Nimeguen. He then went to Bois-le-duc, where he was entertained by Arnold de Beer, a painter of considerable reputation in his day, and treated with great respect by the goldsmiths of the place. On the Thursday after the Presentation of the Virgin,*—21st November,—Durer again arrived at Antwerp. "In the seven weeks and upwards that I was absent," he writes in his Journal, "my wife and her maid spent seven gold crowns. The first had her pocket cut off in St. Mary's church on St. Mary's day; there were two guilders in it."

On the 3rd of December, Durer left Antwerp on a short journey through Zealand, proceeding by way of Bergen-op-Zoom. In the Abbey at Middleburg he saw the great picture of the Descent from the Cross by Mabeuse; of which he remarks that "it is better painted than drawn." When he was about to land at Armuyden, a small town on the island of Walcheren, the rope broke, and a violent wind arising, the boat which he was in was driven out to sea. Some persons, however, at length came to their assistance, and brought all the passengers safely ashore. On the Friday after St. Lucia's day he again returned to Antwerp, after having been absent about twelve days.

On Shrove Tuesday, 1521, the company of goldsmiths invited Durer and his wife to a dinner, at which he was treated with great honour; and as this was an early meal, he was enabled at night to attend a grand banquet to which he was invited by one of the chief magistrates of Antwerp. On the Monday after his entertainment by the goldsmiths he was invited to another grand banquet which lasted two hours, and where he won, at some kind of game, two guilders of Bernard of Castile. Both at this and at the magistrates' banquet there was masquerading. At another entertainment given by Master Peter the Secretary, Durer and Erasmus were present. He was not idle at this period of festivity, but drew several portraits in pencil. He also made a drawing for "Tomasin," and a painting of St. Jerome for Roderigo of Portugal, who appears to have been one of the most liberal of all Durer's Antwerp friends. Besides the little green parrot which he gave his wife, he also presented Durer with one for himself; he also gave him a small cask of comfits, with various other sweetmeats, and specimens of the sugar-cane. He also made him a present of cocoa-nuts and of several other things; and shortly before the painting was finished, Signor Roderigo

---

* In Von Murr the words are "Am Donnnerstage nach Marien Himmelfahrt,"—On the Thursday after the *Assumption* of the Virgin. But this is evidently incorrect, the feast of the Assumption being kept on 15th August. The "Marien Opferung"— the Presentation of the Virgin—which is commemorated on 21st November, is evidently meant.

gave him two large pieces of Portuguese gold coin, each of which was worth ten ducats.

On the Saturday after Easter, Durer visited Bruges, where he saw in St. James's church some beautiful paintings by Hubert Van Eyck and Hugo Vander Goes ; and in the Painters' chapel, and in other churches, he saw several by John Van Eyck ; he also mentions having seen, in St. Mary's church, an image of the Virgin in alabaster by Michael Angelo. The guild of painters invited him to a grand banquet in their hall. Two of the magistrates, Jacob and Peter Mostaert, presented him with twelve flaggons of wine ; and on the conclusion of the entertainment, all the company, amounting to sixty persons, accompanied him with torches to his lodgings. He next visited Ghent, where the company of painters also treated him with great respect. He there saw, in St. John's church, the celebrated picture of the Elders worshipping the Lamb, from the Revelations, painted by John Van Eyck for Philip the Good, Duke of Burgundy. Durer thus expresses his opinion of it : " This is a well conceived and capital picture ; the figures of Eve, the Virgin, and God the Father, are, in particular, extremely good." After being about a week absent, he again returned to Antwerp, where he was shortly after seized with an intermitting fever, which was accompanied with a violent head-ache and great sense of weariness. This illness, however, does not seem to have lasted very long ; his fever commenced in the third week after Easter, and on Rogation Sunday he attended the marriage feast of " Meister Joachim,"—probably Joachim Patenier, a landscape painter whom Durer mentions in an earlier part of his Journal.

Durer was a man of strong religious feelings ; and when Luther began to preach in opposition to the church of Rome, he warmly espoused his cause. The following passages from his Journal sufficiently demonstrate the interest which he felt in the success of the great champion of the Reformation. Luther on his return from Worms, where he had attended the Diet under a safe-conduct granted by the Emperor Charles V, was waylaid, on 4th May 1521, by a party of armed men, who caused him to descend from the light waggon in which he was travelling, and to follow them into an adjacent wood. His brother James, who was in the waggon with him, made his escape on the first appearance of the horsemen. Luther having been secured, the driver and others who were in the waggon were allowed to pursue their journey without further hindrance. This secret apprehension of Luther was, in reality, contrived by his friend and supporter, Frederick, Elector of Saxony,* in order to withdraw him

---

* Luther's safe-conduct from Worms to Wittenberg was limited to twenty-one days, at the expiration of which he was declared to be under the ban of the empire, or, in other words, an outlaw, to whom no prince or free city of Germany was to afford a refuge. Luther, previous

for a time from the apprehended violence of his enemies, whose hatred towards him had been more than ever inflamed by the bold and undisguised statement of his opinions at Worms. Luther's friends, being totally ignorant of the elector's design, generally supposed that the safe-conduct had been disregarded by those whose duty it was to respect it, and that he had been betrayed and delivered into the hands of his enemies. Durer, on hearing of Luther's apprehension, writes in his Journal as follows.

"On the Friday after Whitsuntide, 1521, I heard a report at Antwerp, that Martin Luther had heen treacherously seized; for the herald of the Emperor Charles, who attended him with a safe-conduct, and to whose protection he was committed, on arriving at a lonely place near Eisenach, said he durst proceed no further, and rode away. Immediately ten horsemen made their appearance, and carried off the godly man thus betrayed into their hands. He was indeed a man enlightened by the Holy Ghost, and a follower of the true Christian faith. Whether he be yet living, or whether his enemies have put him to death, I know not; yet certainly what he has suffered has been for the sake of truth, and because he has reprehended the abuses of unchristian papacy, which strives to fetter Christian liberty with the incumbrance of human ordinances, that we may be robbed of the price of our blood and sweat, and shamefully plundered by idlers, while the sick and needy perish through hunger. Above all, it is especially distressing to me to think that God may yet allow us to remain under the blind doctrine which those men called 'the fathers' have imagined and set forth, whereby the precious word is either in many places falsely expounded or not at all observed." *

After indulging in sundry pious invocations and reflections to the extent of two or three pages, Durer thus proceeds to lament the supposed death of Luther, and to invoke Erasmus to put his hand to the work from which he believed that Luther had been removed. "And is Luther dead? Who henceforth will so clearly explain to us the Gospel? Alas! what might he not have written for us in ten or twenty years? Aid me,

to leaving Worms, was informed of the elector's intention of secretly apprehending him on the road and conveying him to a place of safety. After getting into the wood, Luther was mounted on horseback, and conveyed to Wartburg, a castle belonging to the elector, where he continued to live disguised as a knight—Junker Jörge—till March 1522. Luther was accustomed to call the castle of Wartburg his Patmos.

* Durer, though an advocate of Luther, does not seem to have withdrawn himself from the communion of the Church of Rome. In his Journal, in 1521, he enters a sum of ten stivers given to his confessor, and, subsequently, eight stivers given to a monk who visited his wife when she was sick. The passage in which the last item occurs is curious, and seems to prove that female practitioners were then accustomed both to dispense and administer medical preparations at Antwerp. "Meine Frau ward krank,—der Apothekerinn für Klystiren gegeben 14 Stüber; dem Mönch, der sie besuchte, 8 Stüber."—Von Murr, Journal, 7er Theil, S. 93.

all pious Christians, to bewail this man of heavenly mind, and to pray that God may send us another as divinely enlightened. Where, O Erasmus, wilt thou remain? Behold, now, how the tyranny of might and the power of darkness prevail. Hear, thou champion of Christ! Ride forward, defend the truth, and deserve the martyr's crown, for thou art already an old man.* I have heard from thy own mouth that thou hast allotted to thyself two years yet of labour in which thou mightst still be able to produce something good ; employ these well for the benefit of the Gospel and the true Christian faith : let then thy voice be heard, and so shall not the see of Rome, the gates of Hell, as Christ saith, prevail against thee. And though, like thy master, thou shouldst bear the scorn of the liars, and even die a short time earlier than thou otherwise mightst, yet wilt thou therefore pass earlier from death unto eternal life and be glorified through Christ. If thou drinkest of the cup of which he drank, so wilt thou reign with him and pronounce judgment on those who have acted unrighteously."†

About this time a large wood-cut, of which the following is a reduced copy, was published ; and though the satire which it contains will apply equally to any monk who may be supposed to be an instrument of the devil, it was probably directed against Luther in particular, as a teacher of false doctrine through the inspiration of the father of lies. In the cut the arch-enemy, as a bag-piper, is seen blowing into the ear of a monk, whose head forms the " bag," and by skilful fingering causing the nose, elongated in the form of a " chanter," to discourse sweet music. The preaching friars of former times were no less celebrated for their nasal melody than the "saints" in the days of Cromwell. A serious

---

* This inducement for Erasmus to stand forth as a candidate for the honour of martyrdom is, in the original, as simple in expression as it is novel in conception : " Du bist doch sonst ein altes Menniken." Literally : For thou art already an old *mannikin*. Erasmus, however, was not a spirit to be charmed to enter such a circle by such an invocation. As he said of himself, " his gift did not lie that way," and he had as little taste for martyrdom as he had for fish.—In one or two other passages in Durer's Journal there is an allusion to the diminutive stature of Erasmus.

† Von Murr, Journal, 7er Theil, S. 88—93. In volume X, p. 41, Von Murr gives from Peucer, the son-in-law of Melancthon, the following anecdote : " Melancthon, when at Nuremberg, on church and university affairs, was much in the society of Pirkheimer ; and Albert Durer, the painter, an intelligent man, whose least merit, as Melancthon used to say, was his art, was frequently one of the party. Between Pirkheimer and Durer there were frequent disputes respecting the recent [religious] contest, in which Durer, as he was a man of strong mind, vigorously opposed Pirkheimer, and refuted his arguments as if he had come prepared for the discussion. Pirkheimer growing warm, for he was very irritable and much plagued with the gout, would sometimes exclaim " Not so :—these things cannot be *painted*." —" And the arguments which you allege," Durer would reply, " can neither be correctly expressed nor comprehended."—Whatever might have been the particular points in dispute between the two friends, Pirkheimer, as well as Durer, was a supporter of the doctrines of Luther.

portrait of Luther, probably engraved or drawn on wood by Hans
Baldung Grün, a pupil of Durer, was also published in 1521. It is
printed in a quarto tract, entitled, "Acta et Res gestæ D. Martini Lutheri
in Comitiis Principum Vuormaciæ, Anno MDXXI," and also in a tract,
written by Luther himself in answer to Jerome Emser, without date, but
probably printed at Wittenberg about 1523. In this portrait, which
bears considerable resemblance to the head forming the bag of Satan's

pipe, Luther appears as if meditating on a passage that he has just read
in a volume which he holds open ; his head is surrounded with rays of
glory ; and the Holy Ghost, in the form of a dove, appears as if about to
settle on his shaven crown.   In an impression now before me, some one,
apparently a contemporary, who thought that Luther's inspiration was
derived from another source, has with pen and ink transformed the dove
into one of those unclean things between bat and serpent, which are

supposed to be appropriate to the regions of darkness, and which are generally to be seen in paintings and engravings of the temptation of St. Anthony.

A week after Corpus Christi day* Durer left Antwerp for Malines, where the Archduchess Margaret, the aunt of the emperor Charles V, was then residing. He took up his lodgings with Henry de Bles, a painter of considerable reputation, called Civetta by the Italians, from the owl which he painted as a mark in most of his pictures ; and the painters and statuaries, as at Antwerp and other places, invited him to an entertainment and treated him with great respect. He waited on the archduchess and showed her his portrait of the emperor, and would have presented it to her, but she would by no means accept of it ;— probably because she could not well receive such a gift without making the artist a suitable return, for it appears, from a subsequent passage in Durer's Journal, that she had no particular objection to receive other works of art when they cost her nothing.

In the course of a few days Durer returned to Antwerp, where he shortly afterwards saw Lucas Van Leyden, the celebrated painter and engraver, whose plates at that time were by many considered nearly equal to his own. Durer's brief notice of his talented contemporary is as follows : " Received an invitation from Master Lucas, who engraves on copper. He is a little man, and a native of Leyden in Holland." Subsequently he mentions having drawn Lucas's portrait in crayons ; and having exchanged some of his own works to the value of eight florins for a complete set of Lucas's engravings. Durer in this part of his Journal, after enumerating the portraits he had taken and the exchanges he had made since his return from Malines to Antwerp, thus speaks of the manner in which he was rewarded : " In all my transactions in the Netherlands—for my paintings, drawings, and in disposing of my works—both with high and low I have had the disadvantage. The Lady Margaret, especially, for all that I have given her and done for her, has not made me the least recompense."

Durer now began to make preparations for his return home. He engaged a waggoner to take him and his wife to Cologne ; he exchanged a portrait of the emperor for some white English cloth ; and, on 1st July, he borrowed of Alexander Imhoff a hundred gold guilders to be repaid at Nuremberg ; another proof that Durer, though treated with great distinction in the Low Countries, had not derived much pecuniary advantage during the period of his residence there. On the 2nd July, when he was about to leave Antwerp, the King of Denmark, Christian II, who had recently arrived in Flanders, sent for him to take his

* Corpus Christi day is a moveable festival, and is celebrated on the first Thursday after Trinity Sunday.

portrait.   He first drew his majesty with black chalk—mit der Kohlen —and afterwards went with him to Brussels, where he appears to have painted his portrait in oil colours, and for which he received thirty florins.   At Brussels, on the Sunday before St. Margaret's Day,* the King of Denmark gave a grand banquet to the Emperor and the Arch-duchess Margaret, to which Durer had the honour of being invited, and failed not to attend.   On the following Friday he left Brussels to return to Nuremberg, proceeding by way of Aix-la-Chapelle to Cologne.

Out of a variety of other matters which Durer has mentioned in his Journal, the following—which could not be conveniently given in chro-nological order in the preceding abstract—may not, perhaps, be wholly uninteresting.   He painted a portrait of one Nicholas, an astronomer, who was in the service of the King of England, and who was of great service to Durer on several occasions.†   He gave one florin and eight stivers for wood, but whether for drawing on, or for fuel, is uncertain.   He only mentions having made two drawings on wood during his residence in the Low Countries, and both were of the arms of Von Rogendorff, noticed at page 236.   In one of those instances, he distinctly says that he made the drawing, "*das man's schneiden mag*"—that it may be engraved.   The word "*man's*" clearly shows that it was to be engraved by another person.—He mentions that since Raffaele's death his works are dispersed—"*verzogen,*"—and that one of that master's pupils, by name "Thomas Polonier," had called on him and made him a present of an antique ring.   In a subsequent passage he calls this person "Thomas Polonius," and says that he had given him a set of his works to be sent to Rome and exchanged for "*Raphaelische Sache*"—things by Raffaele.

It has been said, though without sufficient authority, that Durer, weary of a home where he was made miserable by his bad-tempered, avaricious wife, left Nuremberg, and visited the Low Countries alone for the purpose of avoiding her constant annoyance.   There is, however, no evidence of Durer's visiting the Low Countries previous to 1520, when he was accompanied by his wife ; nor is there any authentic record of his ever again visiting Flanders subsequent to the latter end of August 1521, when he left Brussels to return to Nuremberg.   In 1522, Durer published the first edition of the Triumphal Car of the Emperor Maximilian, the designs for which had probably been made five or six years before.   One of the best portraits drawn by Durer on wood also bears the date 1522.   It is that of his friend Ulrich Varnbuler,‡—mentioned at page 253,—and is of large size, being about

---

* St. Margaret's day is the 20th July.

† Durer says that this astronomer was a German, and a native of Munich.

‡ Ulrich Varnbuler was subsequently the chancellor of the Emperor Ferdinand I.   Durer mentions him in a letter addressed to "Hernn Frey in Zurich," and dated from Nuremberg

seventeen inches high by twelve and three-fourths wide. The head is full of character, and the engraving is admirably executed. From 1522 to 1528, the year of Durer's death, he seems to have almost entirely given up the practice of drawing on wood, as there are only three cuts with his mark which contain a date between those years; they are his own arms dated 1523; his own portrait dated 1527; and the siege of a fortified city previously noticed at page 253, also dated 1527. The following is a reduced copy of the cut of Durer's arms.

The pair of *doors* on the shield—in German *Durer* or *Thurer*—is a rebus of the artist's name; after the manner of the Lucys of our own country, who bore three *luces*,* or pikes—fish, not weapons—argent, in their coat of arms.

on the Sunday *after St. Andrew's day*, 1523. With this letter Durer sent to his correspondent a humorous sketch, in pen and ink, of apes dancing, which in 1776 was still preserved in the Public Library of Basle. The date of this letter proves the incorrectness of Mr. Ottley's statement, in page 723 of his Inquiry, where he says that Durer did not return to Nuremberg from the Low Countries "until *the middle of the year* 1524." Mr. Ottley is not more correct when he says, at page 735, that the portrait of Varnbuler is the "size of nature."

* It is supposed that Shakspeare, in alluding to the "dozen white luces" in Master Shallow's coat of arms,—Merry Wives of Windsor, Act I,—intended to ridicule Sir Thomas Lucy of Charlecotte, Wiltshire, before whom he is said to have been brought in his youth on a charge of deer-stealing.

The last of Durer's engravings on copper is a portrait of Melancthon, dated 1526, the year in which the meek and learned reformer visited Nuremberg. The following is a reduced copy of his own portrait, perhaps the last drawing that he made on wood. It is probably a good likeness of the artist; at any rate it bears a great resemblance to the portrait said to be intended for Durer's own in his carving of the naming of St. John, of which some account is given at page 259. The size of the original is eleven inches and three-eighths high by ten inches wide. According to Bartsch, the earliest impressions have not the arms

and mark, and are inscribed above the border at the top : " *Albrecht Durer's Conterfeyt* "—Albert Durer's portrait. It would seem that the block had been preserved for many years subsequent to the date, for I have now before me an impression, on comparatively modern paper, from which it is evident that at the time of its being taken, the block had been much corroded by worms.

It is probable that between 1522 and 1528 the treatises of which Durer is the author were chiefly composed. Their Titles are An Essay on the Fortification of Towns and Villages ; Instructions for Measuring with the Rule and Compass; and On the Proportions of the Human Body.* They were all published at Nuremberg with illustrative wood-cuts; the first in 1527, and the other two in 1528. It is to the latter work that Hogarth alludes, in his Analysis of Beauty, when he speaks of Albert Durer, Lamozzo, and others, having "puzzled mankind with a heap of minute unnecessary divisions" in their rules for correctly drawing the human figure.

After a life of unremitted application,—as is sufficiently proved by the number of his works as a painter, an engraver, and a designer on wood,—Albert Durer died at Nuremberg on 6th April 1528, in the fifty-seventh year of his age. His wife's wretched temper had un-questionably rendered the latter years of his life very unhappy, and in her eagerness to obtain money she appears to have urged her husband to what seems more like the heartless toil of a slave than an artist's exercise of his profession. It is said that her sitting-room was under her husband's studio, and that she was accustomed to give an admonitory knock against the ceiling whenever she suspected that he was "not getting forward with his work." The following extracts from a letter, written by Bilibald Pirkheimer shortly after Durer's death, will show that common fame has not greatly belied this heartless, selfish woman, in ascribing, in a great measure, her husband's death to the daily vexation which she caused him, and to her urging him to continual application in order that a greater sum might be secured to her on his decease. The passages relating to Durer in Pirkheimer's letter are to the following effect.†

" I have indeed lost in Albert one of the best friends I had on earth ; and nothing pains me more than the thought of his death having been so melancholy, which, next to the will of Providence, I can ascribe to no one but his wife, for she fretted him so much and tasked him so hard that he departed sooner than he otherwise would. He was dried up like a bundle of straw ; durst never enjoy himself nor enter into company. This bad woman, moreover, was anxious about that for which she had no occasion to take heed,—she urged him to labour day and night solely that he might earn money, even at the cost of his life, and leave it to her ; she was content to live despised, as she does still, provided Albert might leave her six thousand guilders. But she cannot

---

* Etliche Underricht zu Befestigung der Stett, Schloss, und Flecken ; Underweysung der Messung mit der Zirckel und Richtscheyt ; Bucher von Menschlicher Proportion. All in folio. Those treatises were subsequently translated into Latin and several times reprinted. The treatise on the Proportions of the Human Body was also translated into French and printed at Paris in 1557. A collection of Durer's writings was published by J. Jansen, 1604.

† This letter is addressed to " Johann Tscherte," an architect residing at Vienna, the mutual friend of Pirkheimer and Durer.—Von Murr, Journal, 10er Theil, S. 36.

enjoy them : the sum of the matter is, she alone has been the cause of his death. I have often expostulated with her about her fretful, jealous conduct, and warned her what the consequences would be, but have only met with reproach. To the friends and sincere well-wishers of Albert she was sure to be the enemy ; while such conduct was to him a cause of exceeding grief, and contributed to bring him to the grave. I have not seen her since his death ; she will have nothing to say to me, although I have on many occasions rendered her great service. Whoever contradicts her, or gives not way to her in all things, is sure to incur her enmity ; I am, therefore, better pleased that she should keep herself away. She and her sister are not indeed women of loose character ; but, on the contrary, are, as I believe, of honest reputation and religious ; one would, however, rather have one of the other kind who otherwise conducts herself in a pleasant manner, than a fretful, jealous, scolding wife—however devout she may be—with whom a man can have no peace either day or night. We must, however, leave the matter to the will of God, who will be gracious and merciful to Albert, for his life was that of a pious and righteous man. As he died like a good Christian, we may have little doubt of his salvation. God grant us grace, and that in his own good time we may happily follow Albert."

The popular error,—as I believe it to be,—that Albert Durer was an engraver on wood, has not tended, in England, where his works as a painter are but little known, to increase his reputation. Many persons on looking over the wood engravings which bear his mark have thought but meanly of their execution ; and have concluded that his abilities as an artist were much over-rated, on the supposition that his fame chiefly rested on the presumed fact of his being the engraver of those works. Certain writers, too, speaking of him as a painter and an engraver on copper, have formed rather an unfavourable estimate of his talents, by comparing his pictures with those of his great Italian contemporaries,— Leonardo da Vinci, Michael Angelo, and Raffaele,—and by judging of his engravings with reference to the productions of modern art, in which the freedom and effect of etching are combined with the precision and clearness of lines produced by the burin. This, however, is judging the artist by an unfair standard. Though he has not attained, nor indeed attempted, that sublimity which seems to have been principally the aim of the three great Italian masters above mentioned, he has produced much that is beautiful, natural, and interesting ; and which, though it may not stand so high in the scale of art as the grand compositions of his three great contemporaries, is no less necessary to its completion. The field which he cultivated, though not yielding productions so noble or splendid as theirs, was of greater extent and afforded greater variety. If they have left us more sublime conceptions of past and future events,

Durer has transmitted to us more faithful pictures of the characters, manners, and customs of his own times. Let those who are inclined to depreciate his engravings on copper, as dry and meagre when compared with the productions of modern engravers, consider the state in which he found the art; and let them also recollect that he was not a mere translator of another person's ideas, but that he engraved his own designs. Setting aside his merits as a painter, I am of opinion that no artist of the present day has produced, from his own designs, three such engravings as Durer's Adam and Eve, St. Jerome seated in his chamber writing, and the subject entitled Melancolia.* Let it also not be forgotten that to Albert Durer we owe the discovery of etching; a branch of the art which gives to modern engravers, more especially in landscape, so great an advantage over the original inventor. Looking impartially at the various works of Durer, and considering the period and the country in which he lived, few, I think, will venture to deny that he was one of the greatest artists of his age. The best proof indeed of the solidity of his fame is afforded by the esteem in which his works have been held for three centuries by nearly all persons who have had opportunities of seeing them, except such as have, upon narrow principles, formed an exclusive theory with respect to excellence in art. With such authorities nothing can be beautiful or interesting that is not *grand;* every country parish church should be built in the style of a Grecian temple; our woods should grow nothing but oaks; a country gentleman's dovecot should be a fac-simile of the lantern of Demosthenes; the sign of the Angel at a country inn should be painted by a Guido; and a picture representing the meeting of the British Association for the Advancement of Science should be in the style of Raffaele's School of Athens.

Lucas Cranach, a painter of great repute in his day, like his contemporary Durer has also been supposed to be the engraver of the woodcuts which bear his mark, but which, in all probability, were only drawn by him on the block and executed by professional wood engravers. The family name of this artist was Sunder, and he is also sometimes called Muller or Maler—Painter—from his profession. He acquired the name Cranach, or Von Cranach, from Cranach, a town in the territory of Bamberg, where he was born in 1470. He enjoyed the patronage of the electoral princes of Saxony, and one of the most frequent of his marks is a shield of the arms of that family. Another of his marks is a shield with two swords crossed; a third is a kind of dragon; and a fourth is

---

* Those three engravings are respectively numbered 1, 60, and 67 in Bartsch's list of Durer's works in his Peintre-Graveur, tom. vii. The Adam and Eve is nine inches and three-fourths high by seven inches and a half wide,—date 1504; St. Jerome, nine inches and five-eighths high by seven inches and three-eighths wide,—date 1514; Melancolia, nine inches and three-eighths high by seven inches and one fourth wide,—date 1514.

the initial letters of his name, L. C. Sometimes two or three of those marks are to be found in one cut. There are four engravings on copper with the mark *L ϛ* which are generally ascribed to this artist. That they are from his designs is very likely, but whether they were engraved by himself or not is uncertain. One of them bears the date 1492, and it is probable that they were all executed about the same period. Two of those pieces were in the possession of Mr. Ottley, who says, " Perhaps the two last characters of the mark may be intended for *Cr.*" It seems, however, more likely that the last character is intended for the letter which it most resembles—a Z, and that it denotes the German word *zeichnet*—that is " *drew ;*" in the same manner as later artists occasionally subjoined the letter P or F to their names for *Pinxit* or *Fecit*, respectively as they might have painted the picture or engraved the plate.

One of the earliest chiaro-scuros, as has before been observed, printed from three blocks, is from a design of Lucas Cranach. It is dated 1509, nine years before the earliest chiaro-scuro with a date executed by Ugo da Carpi, to whom Vasari and others have erroneously ascribed the invention of this mode of imitating a drawing by impressions from two or more wood-blocks. The subject, like that of the following specimen, is a Repose in Egypt, but is treated in a different manner,—the Virgin being represented giving suck to the infant Christ.

The wood engravings that contain Cranach's mark are not so numerous as those which contain the mark of Albert Durer, and they are also generally inferior to the latter both in effect and design. The following reduced copy of a cut which contains three of Cranach's four marks will afford some idea of the style of his designs on wood. As a specimen of his ability in this branch of art it is perhaps superior to the greater part of his designs executed in the same manner. The subject is described by Bartsch as a Repose in Egypt. The action of the youthful angels who are dancing round the Virgin and the infant Christ is certainly truly juvenile if not graceful. The two children seen up the tree robbing an eagle's nest are perhaps emblematic of the promised peace of Christ's kingdom and of the destruction of the power of Satan : " No lion shall be there nor any ravenous beast shall go up thereon, it shall not be found there ; but the redeemed shall walk there."[*]   In the right-hand corner at the top is the shield of the arms of Saxony ; and to the left, also at the top, is another of Cranach's marks—a shield with two swords crossed ; in the right-hand corner at the bottom is a third mark,— the figure of a kind of dragon with a ring in its mouth. The size of the original cut is thirteen inches and one-fourth high by nine inches and one-fourth wide.

* Isaiah, chapter xxxv. verse 9.

Cranach was much esteemed in his own country as a painter, and several of his pictures are still regarded with admiration. He was in great favour with John Frederick, Elector of Saxony,* and at one period of his life was one of the magistrates of Wittenberg. He died at Weimar, on 16th October 1553, aged eighty-three.

Another eminent painter who has been classed with Durer and Cranach as a wood engraver is Hans Burgmair, who was born at Augsburg about 1473. The mark of this artist is to be found on a

* One of the largest wood-cuts designed by Cranach is a subject representing the baptism of some saint; and having on one side a portrait of Frederick, Elector of Saxony, and on the other a portrait of Luther. The block has consisted of three pieces, and from the impressions it seems as if the parts containing the portraits of the elector and Luther had been added after the central part had been finished. The piece altogether is comparatively worthless in design, and is very indifferently engraved.

great number of wood engravings, but beyond this fact there is not the least reason to suppose that he ever engraved a single block. To those who have described Burgmair as a wood engraver from this circumstance only, a most satisfactory answer is afforded by the fact that several of the original blocks of the Triumphs of Maximilian, which contain Burgmair's mark, have at the back the names of the different engravers by whom they were executed. As we have here positive evidence of cuts with Burgmair's mark being engraved by other persons, we cannot certainly conclude that any cut, from the mere fact of its containing his mark, was actually engraved by himself. Next to Albert Durer he was one of the best designers on wood of his age; and as one of the early masters of the German school of painting he is generally considered as entitled to rank next to the great painter of Nuremberg. It has indeed been supposed that Burgmair was a pupil of Durer; but for this opinion there seems to be no sufficient ground. It is certain that he made many of the designs for the wood-cuts published under the title of The Triumphs of Maximilian; and it is also probable that he drew nearly all the cuts in the book entitled Der Weiss Kunig—The Wise King, another work illustrative of the learning, wisdom, and adventures of tl.e Emperor Maximilian.* Before proceeding, however, to give any account of those works, it seems advisable to give two specimens from a different series of wood-cuts of his designing, and to briefly notice two or three of the more remarkable single cuts that bear his mark.

The cut on the opposite page is a reduced copy from a series designed by Burgmair. The subject is Samson and Delilah, and is treated according to the old German fashion, without the least regard to propriety of costume. Samson is represented like a grisly old German baron of Burgmair's own time, with limbs certainly not indicating extraordinary strength; and Delilah seems very deliberately engaged in cutting off his hair. The wine flagon and fowl, to the left, would seem to indicate the danger of yielding to sensual indulgence. The original cut is surrounded by an ornamental border, and is four inches and five-eighths high by three inches and five-eighths wide. Burgmair's mark H. B. is at the bottom of the cut, to the right.

The cut on page 280 is also a reduced copy from one of the same series, and is a proof that those who call the whole by the general title of "Bible Prints" are not exactly correct in their nomenclature. The somewhat humorous-looking personage, whom a lady is using as her pad, is thus described in an inscription underneath the cut : "Aristotle,

---

* Burgmair also made the designs for a series of saints, male and female, of the family of the emperor, which are also engraved on wood. The original blocks, with the names of the engravers written at the back, are still preserved, and are at present in the Imperial Library at Vienna.

a Greek, the son of Nicomachus. A disciple of Plato, and the master of Alexander the Great." Though Aristotle is said to have been extremely fond of his wife Pythaïs, and to have paid her divine honours after her death, there is no record, I believe, of her having amused herself with riding on her husband's back. The subject is probably intended to illustrate the power of the fair sex over even the wisest of mortals, and to show that philosophers themselves when under such influence occasionally forget their character as teachers of men, and exhibit them-

selves in situations which scarcely an ass might envy. The original is surrounded by a border, and is four inches and five-eighths high by three inches and five-eighths wide.

There are several chiaro-scuros from wood-blocks with Burgmair's mark. One of the earliest is a portrait of "Joannes Paungartner," from two blocks, with the date 1512; another of St. George on horseback, from two blocks, engraved by Jost or Josse de Negher, without date; a third representing a young woman flying from Death, who is seen killing

a young man,—from three blocks, without date ; and a fourth of the
Emperor Maximilian on horseback, from two blocks, with the date
1518.

The best cuts of Burgmair's designing, though drawn with great
spirit and freedom, are decidedly inferior to the best of the wood-cuts
designed by Albert Durer.   Errors in perspective are frequent in the cuts
which bear his mark ; his figures are not so varied nor their characters
so well indicated as Durer's ; and in their arrangement, or grouping, he

is also inferior to Durer, as well as in the art of giving effect to his
subjects by the skilful distribution of light and shade.   The cuts in the
Wise King, nearly all of which are said to have been designed by him,
are, for the most part, very inferior productions both with respect to
engraving and design.   His merits as a designer on wood are perhaps
shown to greater advantage in the Triumphs of Maximilian than in any
other of his works executed in this manner. —Some writers have asserted
that Burgmair died in 1517, but this is certainly incorrect ; for there is a

portrait of him, with that of his wife on the same pannel, painted by himself in 1529, when he was fifty-six years old. Underneath this painting was a couplet to the following effect :

> Our likeness such as here you view ;—
> The glass itself was not more true.*

Burgmair, like Cranach, lived till he was upwards of eighty ; but it would seem that he had given up drawing on wood for many years previous to his death, for I am not aware of there being any wood-cuts designed by him with a date subsequent to 1530. He died in 1559, aged eighty-six.

Hans Schäufflein is another of those old German painters who are generally supposed to have been also engravers on wood. Bartsch, however, thinks that, like Durer, Cranach, and Burgmair, he only made the designs for the wood-cuts which are ascribed to him, and that they were engraved by other persons. Schäufflein was born at Nuremberg in 1483 ; and it is said that he was a pupil of Albert Durer. Subsequently he removed to Nordlingen, a town in Suabia, about sixty miles to the south-westward of Nuremberg, where he died in 1550.

The wood-cuts in connexion with which Schäufflein's name is most frequently mentioned are the illustrations of the work usually called the Adventures of Sir Theurdank,† an allegorical poem, in folio, which is

---

* " Solche Gestalt unser baider was,
  Im Spigel aber nix dan das !"

A small engraving in a slight manner appears to have been made of the portraits of Burgmair and his wife by George Christopher Kilian, an artist of Augsburg, about 1774.— Von Murr, Journal, 4er Theil, S. 22.

† The original title of the work is : " Die gevarlichkeiten und eins teils der Geschichten des loblichen streytparen und hochberümbten Helds und Ritters Tewrdanckhs." That is : The adventurous deeds and part of the history of the famous, valiant, and highly-renowned hero Sir Theurdank. The name, Theurdank, in the language of the period, would seem to imply a person whose thoughts were only employed on noble and elevated subjects. Goethe, who in his youth was fond of looking over old books illustrated with wood-cuts, alludes to Sir Theurdank in his admirable play of Götz von Berlichingen : " Geht ! Geht !" says Adelheid to Weislingen, " Erzählt das Mädchen die den Teurdanck lesen, und sich so einen Mann wünschen."—" Go ! Go ! Tell that to a girl who reads Sir Theurdank, and wishes that she may have such a husband." In Sir Walter Scott's faulty translation of this play—under the name of *William* Scott, 1799,—the passage is rendered as follows : " Go ! Go ! Talk of that to some forsaken damsel whose Corydon has proved forsworn." In another passage where Goethe makes Adelheid allude to the popular " Märchen," or tale, of Number-Nip, the point is completely lost in the translation : " Entbinden nicht unsre Gesetze solchen Schwüren ?—Macht das Kindern weiss die den Rübezahl glauben." Literally, " Do not our laws release you from such oaths ?—Tell that to children who believe Number-Nip." In Sir Walter Scott's translation the passage is thus most incorrectly rendered : " Such agreement is no more binding than an unjust extorted oath. Every child knows what faith is to be kept with robbers." The name *Rübezahl* is literally translated by *Number-Neep ;* Rübe is the German name for a turnip,—Scoticè, a neep. The story is as well known in Germany as that of Jack the Giant-Killer in England.

said to have been the joint composition of the Emperor Maximilian and his private secretary Melchior Pfintzing, provost of the church of St. Sebald at Nuremberg. Though Köhler, a German author, in an Essay on Sir Theurdank,—De inclyto libro poetico Theurdank,—has highly praised the poetical beauties of the work, they are certainly not such as are likely to interest an English reader. "The versified allegory of Sir Theurdank," says Küttner,* "is deficient in true Epic beauty; it has also nothing, as a poem, of the romantic descriptions of the thirteenth century,—nothing of the delicate gallantry of the age of chivalry and the troubadours. The machinery which sets all in action are certain personifications of Envy, restless Curiosity, and Daring; these induce the hero to undertake many perilous adventures, from which he always escapes through Understanding and Virtue. Such is the groundwork of the fable which Pfintzing constructs in order to extol, under allegorical representations, the perils, adventures, and heroic deeds of the emperor. Everything is described so figuratively as to amount to a riddle; and the story proceeds with little connexion and without animation. There are no striking descriptive passages, no Homeric similes, and no episodes to allow the reader occasionally to rest; in fact, nothing admirable, spirit-stirring, or great. The poem is indeed rather moral than epic; Lucan's Pharsalia partakes more of the epic character than Pfintzing's Theurdank. Pfintzing, however, surpasses the Cyclic poets alluded to by Horace."†

The first edition of Sir Theurdank was printed by Hans Schönsperger the elder, at Nuremberg in 1517; and in 1519 two editions appeared at Augsburg from the press of the same printer. As Schönsperger's established printing-office was at the latter city and not at Nuremberg, Panzer has supposed that the imprint of Nuremberg in the first edition might have been introduced as a compliment to the nominal author, Melchior Pfintzing, who then resided in that city. Two or three other editions of Sir Theurdank, with the same cuts, appeared between 1519 and 1602; but Küttner, in his Characters of German poets and prose-writers, says that in all those editions alterations have been made in the text.

The character in which Sir Theurdank is printed is of great beauty

---

* Charaktere Teutscher Dichter und Prosaisten, S. 71. Berlin, 1781.

†   Nec sic incipies, ut scriptor cyclicus olim :
                " Fortunam Priami cantabo, et nobile bellum :"
                Q uid dignum tanto feret hic promissor hiatu ?
                Parturiunt montes ; nascetur ridiculus mus.
                         Ars Poetica, v. 136 –139.
In a Greek epigram the Cyclic poets are thus noticed :

        Τοὺς κυκλίους τούτους τοὺς αὐτὰρ ἔπειτα λέγοντας
        Μισῶ λωποδύτας ἀλλοτρίων ἐπέων.

and much ornamented with flourishes. Several writers, and among others Fournier, who was a type-founder and wood-engraver, have erroneously described the text as having been engraved on blocks of wood. This very superficial and incorrect writer also states that the cuts contained in the volume are " chefs-d'œuvres de la gravure en bois."* His opinion with respect to the cuts is about as correct as his judgment respecting the type; the most of them are in fact very ordinary productions, and are neither remarkable for execution nor design. He also informs his readers that he has discovered on some of those cuts an H and an S, accompanied with a little shovel, and that they are the monogram of *Hans Sebalde,* or Hans Schäufflein. By *Hans Sebalde* he perhaps means Hans Sebald Behaim, an artist born at Nuremberg in 1500, and who never used the letters H and S, accompanied with a little shovel, as a monogram. Fournier did not know that this mark is used exclusively by Hans Schäufflein; and that the little shovel, or baker's peel,—called in old German, Schäufflein, or Scheuffleine,—is a rebus of his surname. The careful examination of writers more deserving of credit has completely proved that the text of the three earliest editions—those only in which it was asserted to be from engraved wood-blocks—is printed from moveable types of metal. Breitkopf† has observed, that in the edition of 1517 the letter i, in the word *shickhet,* in the second line following the eighty-fourth cut, is inverted; and Panzer and Brunner have noticed several variations in the orthography of the second and third editions when compared with the first.

There are a hundred and eighteen wood-cuts in the Adventures of Sir Theurdank, which are all supposed to have been designed, if not engraved, by Hans Schäufflein, though his mark, ◌⟋ ⻌ , occurs on not more than five or six. From the general similarity of style I have, however, no doubt that the designs were all made by the same person, and I think it more likely that Schäufflein was the designer than the engraver. The cut on page 284 is a reduced copy of that numbered 14 in the first edition. The original is six inches and one-fourth high by five inches and a half wide. In this cut, Sir Theurdank is seen, in the dress of a hunter, encountering a huge bear; while to the right is perceived one of his tempters, *Fürwittig*—restless Curiosity,—and to the left, on

---

* Dissertation sur l'Origine et les Progres de l'Art de Graver en Bois, p. 74. Paris, 1758.

† The kind of character in which the text of Sir Theurdank is printed is called " Fractur " by German printers. "The first work," says Breitkopf, "which afforded an example of a perfectly-shaped *Fractur* for printing, was unquestionably the Theurdank, printed at Nuremberg, 1517."—Ueber Bibliographie und Bibliophile, S. 8. 1793.—Neudörffer, a contemporary, who lived at Nuremberg at the time when Sir Theurdank was first published, says that the specimens for the types were written by Vincent Rockner, the emperor's court-secretary.— Von Murr, Journal, 2er Theil, S. 159 ; and Lichtenberger, Initia Typographica, p. 194.

horseback, Theurdank's squire, Ernhold. The title of the chapter, or
fytte, to which this cut is prefixed is to the following effect: "How
Fürwittig led Sir Theurdank into a perilous encounter with a she-bear."
The subject of the thirteenth chapter is his perilous encounter with
a stag, and in the fifteenth we are entertained with the narration of one
of his adventures when hunting the chamois.

The opposite cut is a reduced copy of No. 111 in the Adventures
of Sir Theurdank. The title of the chapter to which this cut is prefixed
is : "How Unfalo [one of Theurdank's tempters] was hung." A monk
at the foot of the gallows appears to pray for the culprit just turned off ;
while Ernold seems to be explaining to a group of spectators to the left
the reason of the execution. The cut illustrative of the 110th chapter
represents the beheading of "Fürwittig ;" and in the 112th, "Neydelhart,"
the basest of Theurdank's enemies, is seen receiving the reward of his
perfidy by being thrown into a moat. The two original cuts which have
been selected as specimens of the wood engravings in the Adventures of
Sir Theurdank, though not the best, are perhaps, in point of design and
execution, rather superior to two-thirds of those contained in the work.

The copies, though less in size, afford a tolerably correct idea of the style of the originals, which no one who is acquainted with the best wood-cuts engraved after the designs of Durer and Burgmair will assert to be " chefs-d'œuvres " of the art of wood engraving.

There are a number of wood-cuts which contain Hans Schäufflein's mark, though somewhat different from that which occurs in the Adventures of Sir Theurdank ; the S being linked with one of the upright lines of the H, instead of being placed between them. When the letters are combined in this manner, there are frequently two little shovels crossed, " in saltire," as a herald would say, instead of a single one as in Sir Theurdank. The following mark, ⑤══, occurs on a series of wood-cuts illustrative of Christ's Passion, printed at Frankfort by C. Egenolf, 1542 ; on the cuts in a German almanack, Mentz, 1545, and 1547 ; and on several single subjects executed about that period. This mark, it is said, distinguishes the designs of Hans Schaufflein the younger. Bartsch, however, observes, that "what Strutt has said about there being two persons of this name, an elder and a younger, seems to be a mere conjecture."

The book entitled Der Weiss Kunig—the Wise King—is another of
the works projected by the Emperor Maximilian in order to inform the
world of sundry matters concerning his father Frederick III, his own
education, warlike and perilous deeds, government, wooing, and wedding.
This work is in prose ; and though Marx Treitzsaurwein, the emperor's
secretary, is put forth as the author, there is little doubt of its having
been chiefly composed by Maximilian himself. About 1512 it appears
that the materials for this work were prepared by the emperor, and that
about 1514 they were entrusted to his secretary, Treitzsaurwein, to be
put in order. It would appear that before the work was ready for the
press Maximilian had died ; and Charles V. was too much occupied
with other matters to pay much attention to the publication of an
enigmatical work, whose chief object was to celebrate the accomplishments, knowledge, and adventures of his grandfather. The obscurity
of many passages in the emperor's manuscript seems to have, in a great
measure, retarded the completion of the work. There is now in the
Imperial Library at Vienna a manuscript volume of queries respecting
the doubtful passages in the Weiss Kunig ; and as each had ultimately
to be referred to the emperor, it would seem that, from the pressure of
more important business and his increased age, he had wanted leisure
and spirits to give the necessary explanations. In the sixteenth century,
Richard Strein, an eminent philologer, began a sort of commentary or
exposition of the more difficult passages in the Wise King ; and
subsequently his remarks came into the hands of George Christopher
von Schallenberg, who, in 1631, had the good fortune to obtain at
Vienna impressions of most of the cuts which were intended by the
emperor to illustrate the work, together with several of the original
drawings. Treitzsaurwein's manuscript, which for many years had been
preserved at Ambras in the Tyrol, having been transferred to the
Imperial Library at Vienna, and the original blocks having been
discovered in the Jesuits' College at Gratz in Stiria, the text and cuts
were printed together, for the first time, in a folio volume, at Vienna in
1775.*
It is probable that the greater part, if not all the cuts, were finished
previous to the emperor's death ; and impressions of them, very likely
taken shortly after the blocks were finished, were known to collectors
long before the publication of the book. The late Mr. Ottley had
seventy-seven of the series, apparently taken as proofs by means of a

---

* The title of the volume is " Der Weiss Kunig. Eine Erzelhung von den Thaten
Kaiser Maximilian des Ersten. Von Marx Treitzsaurwein auf dessen Angeben zusammen
getragen, nebst von Hannsen Burgmair dazu verfertigten Holzschnitten. Herausgeben
aus dem Manuscripte der Kaiserl. Königl. Hofbibliothek. Wien, auf Kosten Joseph
Kurzböckens, 1775."

press. The paper on which these cuts are impressed appears to have consisted of fragments, on one side of which there had previously been printed certain state papers of the Emperor Maximilian, dated 1514. They were sold at the sale of the late Mr. Ottley's engravings in 1838, and are now in the Print Room of the British Museum. In the volume printed at Vienna in 1775, there are two hundred and thirty-seven* large cuts, of which number ninety-two contain Burgmair's mark, H. B ; one contains Schaufflein's mark ; another the mark of Hans Springinklee ; and a third, a modern cut, is marked "F. F. S. V. 1775." Besides the large cuts, all of which are old except the last noticed, there are a few worthless tail-pieces of modern execution, one of which, a nondescript bird, has been copied by Bewick, and is to be found at page 144 of the first edition of his Quadrupeds, 1790.

The cuts in the Weiss Kunig, with respect to the style in which they are designed, bear considerable resemblance to those in Sir Theurdank ; and from their execution it is evident that they have been cut by different engravers ; some of them being executed in a very superior manner, and others affording proofs of their either being cut by a novice or a very indifferent workman. It has been said that all those which contain the mark of Hans Burgmair show a decided superiority in point of engraving ; but this assertion is not correct, for several of them may be classed with the worst executed in the volume. The unequal manner in which the cuts with Burgmair's mark are executed is with me an additional reason for believing that he only furnished the designs for professional wood engravers to execute, and never engraved on wood himself.

It seems unnecessary to give any specimens of the cuts in the Weiss Kunig, as an idea of their style may be formed from those given at pages 284 and 285 from Sir Theurdank ; and as other specimens of Burgmair's talents as a designer on wood will be given subsequently from the Triumphs of Maximilian. The following abstract of the titles of a few of the chapters may perhaps afford some idea of the work, while they prove that the education of the emperor embraced a wide circle, forming almost a perfect Cyclopædia. The first fifteen chapters give an account of the marriage of the Old Wise King, Frederick III, the father of Maximilian, with Elenora, daughter of Alphonso V, King of Portugal ; his journey to Rome and his coronation

---

* In the Imperial Library at Vienna there is a series of old impressions of cuts intended for " Der Weiss Kunig," consisting of two hundred and fifty pieces ; it would therefore appear, supposing this set to be perfect, that there are fourteen of the original blocks lost. Why a single modern cut has been admitted into the book, and thirteen of the old impressions not re-engraved, it perhaps would be difficult to give a satisfactory reason.

there by the pope; with the birth, and christening of Maximilian, the Young Wise King. About thirty-five chapters, from XV. to L, are chiefly occupied with an account of Maximilian's education. After learning to write, he is instructed in the liberal arts; and after some time devoted to "Politik," or King-craft, he proceeds to the study of the *black-art*, a branch of knowledge which the emperor subsequently held to be vain and ungodly. He then commences the study of history, devotes some attention to medicine and law, and learns the Italian and Bohemian languages. He then learns to paint; studies the principles of architecture, and tries his hand at carpentry. He next takes lessons in music; and about the same time acquires a practical knowledge of the art of cookery:—the Wise King, we are informed, was a person of nice taste in kitchen affairs, and had a proper relish for savoury and well-cooked viands. To the accomplishment of dancing he adds a knowledge of numismatics; and, after making himself acquainted with the mode of working mines, he learns to shoot with the hand-gun and the cross-bow. The chase, falconry, angling, and fowling next occupy his attention; and about the same time he learns to fence, to tilt, and to manage the great horse. His course of education appears to have been wound up with practical lessons in the art of making armour, in gunnery, and in fortification. From the fiftieth chapter to the conclusion, the book is chiefly filled with accounts of the wars and adventures of Maximilian, which are for the most part allegorically detailed, and require the reader to be well versed in the true history of the emperor to be able to unriddle them. Küttner says that, notwithstanding its allegories and enigmatical allusions, the Weiss Kunig is a work which displays much mind in the conception and execution, and considerable force and elegance of language; and that it chiefly wants a more orderly arrangement of the events. "Throughout the whole," he adds, "there are evidences of a searching genius, improved by science and a knowledge of the affairs of the world."*

The series of wood-cuts called the Triumphs of Maximilian are, both with respect to design and engraving, the best of all the works thus executed by command of the emperor to convey to posterity a pictorial representation of the splendour of his court, his victories, and the extent of his possessions. This work appears to have been commenced about the same time as the Weiss Kunig; and from the subject, a triumphal procession, it was probably intended to be the last of the series of wood-cuts by which he was desirous of disseminating an opinion of his power and his fame. Of those works he only lived to see one published,—the Adventures of Sir Theurdank; the Wise King, the Triumphal Car, the Triumphal Arch, and the

* Charaktere Teutscher Dichter und Prosaisten, S. 70.

Triumphal Procession, appear to have been all unfinished at the time of his decease in 1519. The total number of cuts contained in the latter work, published under the title of the Triumphs of Maximilian, in 1796, is one hundred and thirty-five; but had the series been finished according to the original drawings, now preserved in the Imperial Library at Vienna, the whole number of the cuts would have been about two hundred and eighteen. Of the hundred and thirty-five published there are about sixteen designed in a style so different from the rest, that it is doubtful if they belong to the same series; and this suspicion receives further confirmation from the fact that the subjects of those sixteen doubtful cuts are not to be found among the original designs. It would therefore seem, that, unless some of the blocks have been lost or destroyed, little more than one-half of the cuts intended for the Triumphal Procession were finished when the emperor's death put a stop to the further progress of the work. It is almost certain, that none of the cuts were engraved after the emperor's death; for the date, commencing with 1516, is written at the back of several of the original blocks, and on no one is it later than 1519.

The plan of the Triumphal Procession,—consisting of a description of the characters to be introduced, the order in which they are to follow each other, their arms, dress, and appointments,—appears to have been dictated by the emperor to his secretary Treitzsaurwein, the nominal author of the Weiss Kunig, in 1512. In this manuscript the subjects for the rhyming inscriptions intended for the different banners and tablets are also noted in prose. Another manuscript, in the handwriting of Treitzsaurwein, and interlined by the emperor himself, contains the inscriptions for the banners and tablets in verse; and a third manuscript, written after the drawings were finished, contains a description of the subjects,—though not so much in detail as the first, and in some particulars slightly differing,—with all the inscriptions in verse except eight. From those manuscripts, which are preserved in the Imperial Library at Vienna, the descriptions in the edition of 1796 have been transcribed. Most of the descriptions and verses were previously given by Von Murr, in 1775, in the ninth volume of his Journal. The edition of the Triumphal Procession published in 1796 also contains a French translation of the descriptions, with numbers referring to those printed at the right-hand corner of the cuts. The numbers, however, of the description and the cut in very many instances do not agree; and it would almost seem, from the manner in which the text is printed, that the publishers did not wish to facilitate a comparison between the description and the cut which they have numbered as corresponding with it. The gross negligence of the publishers, or their editor, in this respect materially detracts from the interest of the work. To compare

U

the descriptions with the cuts is not only a work of some trouble, but it is also labour thrown away. Von Murr's volume, from its convenient size, is of much greater use in comparing the cuts with the description than the text printed in the edition of 1796 ; and though it contains no numbers for reference,—as no complete collection of the cuts had then been printed,—it contains no misdirections : and it is better to have no guide-posts than such as only lead the traveller wrong.

The original drawings for the Triumphal Procession,—or as the work is usually called, the Triumphs of Maximilian,—are preserved in the Imperial Library at Vienna. They are painted in water colours, on a hundred and nine sheets of vellum, each thirty-four inches long by twenty inches high, and containing two of the engraved subjects. Dr. Dibdin, who saw the drawings in 1818, says that they are rather gaudily executed, and that he prefers the engravings to the original paintings.* Whether those paintings are the work of Hans Burgmair, or not, appears to be uncertain. From the following extract from the preface to the Triumphs of Maximilian, published in 1796, it is evident that the writer did not think that the original drawings were executed by that artist. "The engravings of this Triumph, far from being servile copies of the paintings in miniature, differ from them entirely, so far as regards the manner in which they are designed. Most all the groups have a different form, and almost every figure a different attitude ; *consequently Hans Burgmair appears in his work in the character of author [original designer], and so much the more, as he has in many points surpassed his model.* But whatever may be the difference between the engravings and the drawings on vellum, the subjects still so far correspond that they may be recognised without the least difficulty. It is, however, necessary to except eighteen of the engravings, in which this corre- spondence would be sought for in vain. Those engravings are, the twelve from No. 89 to 100, and the six from 130 to 135." As the cuts appear to have been intentionally wrong numbered, it is not easy to determine from this reference which are actually the first twelve alluded to, for in most of the copies which I have seen, the numerals 91, 92, and 93 occur twice,—though the subjects of the cuts are different. In the copy now before me, I have to observe that there are *sixteen*† cuts designed in a style so different from those which contain Burgmair's mark, that I am convinced they have not been drawn by that artist.

* Bibliographical Tour, vol. iii. p. 330.

† The subjects of those sixteen cuts are chiefly the statues of the emperor's ancestors, with representations of himself, and of his family alliances. Several of the carriages are propelled by mechanical contrivances, which for laborious ingenuity may vie with the machine for uncorking bottles in one of the subjects of Hogarth's Marriage à la Mode. In the copy before me those engravings are numbered 89, 90, 91, 91, 92, 92, 93, 93, 94, 95, 96, 97, 99, 101, 102, 103.

Without enquiring whether the subjects are to be found in the paintings or not, I am satisfied that a considerable number of the engravings, besides those sixteen, were not drawn on the wood by Hans Burgmair. Both Breitkopf and Von Murr* have asserted that the drawings for the Triumphs of Maximilian were made by Albert Durer, but they do not say whether they mean the drawings on vellum, or the drawings on the blocks. This assertion is, however, made without any authority; and, whether they meant the drawings on vellum or the drawings on the block, it is unquestionably incorrect. The drawings on vellum are not by Durer, and of the whole hundred and thirty-five cuts there are not more than five or six that can be supposed with any degree of probability to have been of his designing.

Forty of the blocks from which the Triumphs of Maximilian are printed were obtained from Ambras in the Tyrol, where they had probably been preserved since the time of the emperor's death; and the other ninety-five were discovered in the Jesuits' College at Gratz in Stiria. The whole were brought to Vienna and deposited in the Imperial Library in 1779. A few proofs had probably been taken when the blocks were engraved; there are ninety of those old impressions in the Imperial Library; Monsieur Mariette had ninety-seven; and Sandrart had seen a hundred. The latter, in speaking of those impressions, expresses a suspicion of the original blocks having been destroyed in a fire at Augsburg; their subsequent discovery, however, at Ambras and Gratz, shows that his suspicion was not well founded. On the discovery of those blocks it was supposed that the remainder of the series, as described in the manuscript, might also be still in existence; but after a diligent search no more have been found. It is indeed highly probable that the further progress of the work had been interrupted by Maximilian's death, and that if any more of the series were finished, the number must have been few. About 1775, a few impressions were taken from the blocks preserved at Ambras, and also from those at Gratz; but no collection of the whole accompanied with text was ever printed until 1796, when an edition in large folio was printed at Vienna by permission of the Austrian government, and with the name of J. Edwards, then a bookseller in Pall-Mall, on the title-page, as the London publisher. It is much to be regretted that greater pains were not taken to afford the reader every information that could be obtained with respect to the

* Breitkopf, Ueber Bibliographie und Bibliophile, S. 4. Leipzig, 1793. Von Murr, Journal, 9er Theil, S. 1. At page 255 I have said: "Though I have not been able to ascertain satisfactorily the subject of Durer's painting in the Town-hall of Nuremberg, I am inclined to think that it is the Triumphal *Car* of Maximilian." Since the sheet containing the above passage was printed off I have ascertained that the subject *is* the Triumphal Car; and that it is described in Von Murr's Nürnbergischen Merkwürdigkeiten, S. 395.

cuts ; and it says very little for the English publisher's patriotism that
the translation of the original German descriptions should be in French ;
—but perhaps there might be a reason for this, for, where no precise
meaning is to be conveyed, French is certainly much better than English.
From the fact of several of the subjects not being contained in the
original drawings, and from the great difference in the style of many of
the cuts, it is by no means certain that they were all intended for the
same work.   There can, however, be little doubt of their all having been
designed for a triumphal procession intended to celebrate the fame of
Maximilian.

The original blocks, now preserved in the Imperial Library at
Vienna, are all of pear-tree, and several of them are partially worm-
eaten.   At the back of those blocks are written or engraved seventeen
names and initials, which are supposed, with great probability, to be
those of the engravers by whom they were executed.   At the back of
No. 18, which represents five musicians in a car, there is written, " Der
kert an die Elland,—hat *Wilhelm geschnitten :*" that is, "This follows
the Elks.—Engraved by William."   In the preceding cut, No. 17, are the
two elks which draw the car, and on one of the traces is Hans Burgmair's
mark.   At the back of No. 20 is written, "*Jobst putavit,* 14 *Aprilis*
1517.   *Die gehert an die bifel, und die bifel hatt Jos geschnitten.*"*
This inscription Mr. Ottley, at page 756, volume ii. of his Inquiry,
expounds as follows : "Josse putavit (perhaps for *punctavit*), the 14th of
April, 1517.   This block joins to that which represents the Buffaloes."
This translation is substantially correct ; but it is exceedingly doubtful if
putavit was written in mistake for *punctavit*.   The proposed substitution
indeed seems very like explaining an *ignotum per ignotius*.   The verb
punctare is never, that I am aware of, used by any writer, either classical
or modern, to express the idea of engraving on wood.   A German,
however, who was but imperfectly acquainted with Latin, would not be
unlikely to translate the German verb *schneiden*, which signifies *to cut*
generally, by the Latin *putare*, which is specially applied to the lopping
or pruning of trees.   I have heard it conjectured that *putavit* might
have been used in the sense of *imaginavit*, as if Jobst were the designer ;
but there can be little doubt of its being here intended to express
the cutting of the wood-engraver ; for Burgmair's mark is to be found
both on this cut and on the preceding one of the two buffaloes, No. 19 ;
and it cannot for a moment be supposed that he was a mere workman employed to execute the designs of another person.   Were such

---

* *Jobst* and *Jos*, in this inscription, are probably intended for the name of the same person.
For the name Jobst, Jost, Josse, or Jos—for it is thus variously spelled—we have no equi-
valent in English.   It is not unusual in Germany as a baptismal name—it can scarcely be
called *Christian*—and is Latinized, I believe, under the more lengthy form of *Jodocus*.

a supposition granted, it would follow that the wood-engraver of that period—at least so far as regards the work in question—was considered as a much superior person to him who drew the designs ; that the *workman*, in fact, was to be commemorated, but the *artist* forgotten ; a conclusion which is diametrically opposed to fact, for so little were the mere wood-engravers of that period esteemed, that we only incidentally become acquainted with their names ; and from their not putting their marks or initials to the cuts which they engraved has arisen the popular error that Durer, Cranach, Burgmair, and others, who are known to have been painters of great repute in their day, were wood-engravers and executed themselves the wood-cuts which bear their marks.

The following are the names and initial letters at the back of the blocks. 1. Jerome André, called also Jerome Resch, or Rösch, the engraver of the Triumphal Arch designed by Albert Durer. 2. Jan de Bonn. 3. Cornelius. 4. Hans Frank. 5. Saint German. 6. Wilhelm. 7. Corneille Liefrink. 8. Wilhelm Liefrink. 9. Alexis Lindt. 10. Josse de Negker. On several of the blocks Negker is styled, "engraver on wood, at Augsburg." 11. Vincent Pfarkecher. 12. Jaques Rupp. 13. Hans Schaufflein. 14. Jan Taberith. 15. F. P. 16. H. F. 17. W. R. It is not unlikely that "Cornelius," No. 3, may be the same as Corneille Liefrink, No. 7 ; and that "Wilhelm," No. 6, and Wilhelm Liefrink, No. 8, may also be the same person. At the back of the block which corresponds with the description numbered 120, Hans Schaufflein's name is found coupled with that of Cornelius Liefrink ; and at the back of the cut which corresponds with the description numbered 121 Schaufflein's name occurs alone.* The occurrence of Schaufflein's name at the back of the cuts would certainly seem to indicate that he was one of the engravers ; but his name also appearing at the back of that described under No. 120, in conjunction with the name of Cornelius Liefrink, who was certainly a wood-engraver,† makes me

---

* The printed numbers on those two cuts are 105 and 106, though the descriptions are numbered 120 and 121 in the text. The subjects are, No. 105, two ranks, of five men each, on foot, carrying long lances ; and No. 106, two ranks, of five men each, on foot, carrying large two-handed swords on their shoulders.—Perhaps it may not be out of place to correct here the following passage which occurs at page 285 of this volume : " Bartsch, however, observes, that ' what Strutt has said about there being two persons of this name [Hans Schaufflein], an elder and a younger, seems to be a mere conjecture.' " Since the sheet containing this passage was printed off, I have learnt from a paper, in Meusel's Neue Miscellaneen, 5tes. Stück, S. 210, that Hans Schäufflein had a son of the same name who was also a painter, and that the elder Schäufflein died at Nordlingen, in 1539. At page 281, his death, on the authority of Bartsch, is erroneously placed in 1550.

† The name of Cornelius Liefrink occurs at the back of some of the wood-cuts representing the saints of the family of Maximilian, designed by Burgmair, mentioned at page 278, note.

inclined to suppose that he might only have made the drawing on the block and not have engraved the cut ; and this supposition seems to be partly confirmed by the fact that the cuts which are numbered 104, 105, and 106, corresponding with the descriptions Nos. 119, 120, and 121, have not Hans Burgmair's mark, and are much more like the undoubted designs of Hans Schaufflein than those of that artist. That the cuts published under the title of the Triumphs of Maximilian were not all drawn on the block by the same person will, I think, appear probable to any one who even cursorily examines them ; and whoever carefully compares them can scarcely have a doubt on the subject.

From No. 15.　With Burgmair's mark.

Almost every one of the cuts that contains Burgmair's mark, in the Triumphal Procession, is designed with great spirit, and has evidently been drawn by an artist who had a thorough command of his pencil. His horses are generally strong and heavy, and the men on their backs of a stout and muscular form. The action of the horses seems natural ; and the indications of the joints and the drawing of the hoofs—which are mostly low and broad—evidently show that the artist had paid some attention to the structure of the animal. There are, however, a considerable number of cuts where both men and horses appear remarkable for their leanness ; and in which the hoofs of the horses are most incorrectly drawn, and the action of the animals represented in a manner which is by no means natural. Though it is not unlikely that Hans Burgmair was capable of drawing both a stout, heavy horse, and a long-backed, thin-quartered, lean one, I cannot persuade myself that he would, in almost every instance, draw the hoofs and legs of the one correctly, and those of the other with great inaccuracy. The cut on the opposite page and the five next following, of single figures, copied on a reduced scale from the Triumphs, will exemplify the preceding observations. The numbers are those printed on the cuts, and they all, except one, appear to correspond with the French descriptions in the text. The preceding cut is from that marked No. 15. The mark of Hans Burgmair is on the ornamental breast-plate, as an English saddler would call it, that passes across the horse's chest. This figure, in the original cut, carries a tablet suspended from a staff, of which the

From No. 65.   Apparently not drawn by Burgmair.

lower part only is perceived in the copy, as it has not been thought necessary to give the tablet and a large scroll which were intended to contain inscriptions.* The description of the subject is to the following effect : " After the chase, comes a figure on horseback, bearing a tablet, on which shall be written the five charges of the court,—

* In all the blocks, the tablets and scrolls, and the upper part of banners intended to receive verses and inscriptions, were left unengraved. In order that the appearance of the cuts might not be injured, the black ground, intended for the letters, was cut away in most of the tablets and scrolls, in the edition of 1796.

that is, of the butler, the cook, the barber, the tailor, and the shoemaker; and Eberbach shall be the under-marshal of the household, and carry the tablet."

The cut on page 295 is a reduced copy of a figure, the last, in No. 65, which is without Burgmair's mark. In the original the horseman bears a banner, having on it the arms of the state or city which he represents; and at the top of the banner a black space whereon a name or motto ought to have been engraved. The original cut contains three figures; and, if the description can be relied on, the banners which they bear are those of Fribourg, Bregentz, and Saulgau. The

From No. 33. With Burgmair's mark.

other two horsemen and their steeds in No. 65 are still more unlike those in the cuts which contain Burgmair's mark.

The above cut is a reduced copy of a figure on horseback in No. 33. Burgmair's mark, an H and a B, may be perceived on the trappings of the horse. This figure, in the original, bears a large tablet, and he is followed by five men on foot carrying flails, the *swingels** of which are of leather. The description of the cut,—which

---

* That part of the flail which comes in contact with the corn is, in the North of England, termed a *swingel*.

forms the first of seven representing the dresses and arms of combatants on foot,—is as follows: "Then shall come a person mounted and properly habited like a master of arms, and he shall carry the tablet containing the rhyme. Item, Hans Hollywars shall be the master of arms, and his rhyme shall be this effect: that he has professed the noble practice of arms at the court, according to the method devised by the emperor."*

The following is a reduced copy of a figure in the cut erroneously numbered 83, but which corresponds with the description that refers

From No. 83.　Apparently not drawn by Burgmair.

to 84. This figure is the last of the three, who, in the original, are represented bearing banners containing the arms of Malines, Salins and Antwerp.

* The substance of almost every rhyme and inscription is, that the person who bears the rhyme-tablet or scroll has derived great improvement in his art or profession from the instructions or suggestions of the emperor. Huntsmen, falconers, trumpeters, organists, fencing-masters, ballet-masters, tourniers, and jousters, all acknowledge their obligations in this respect to Maximilian. For the wit and humour of the jesters and the natural fools, the emperor, with great forbearance, takes to himself no credit; and Anthony von Dornstett, the leader of the drummers and fifers, is one of the few whose art he has not improved.

The following figure, who is given with his rhyme-tablet in full, is copied from the cut numbered 27. This jovial-looking personage, as we

From No. 27.   With Burgmair's mark.

learn from the description, is the Will Somers of Maximilian's court, and he figures as the leader of the professed jesters and the natural fools, who appear in all ages to have been the subjects of "pleasant mirth." The instructions to the painter are as follows: "Then shall come one on horseback habited like a jester, and carrying a rhyme-tablet for the jesters and natural fools; and he shall be Conrad von der Rosen." The

No. 74.   Apparently not drawn by Burgmair.

fool's cap with the bell at the peak, denoting his profession, is perceived hanging on his left shoulder; and on the breast-plate, crossing the chest of the horse, is Burgmair's mark.

The figure on page 299 of a horseman, bearing the banner of Burgundy, is from the cut numbered **74**. The drawing both of rider and horse is extremely unlike the style of Burgmair as displayed in those cuts which contain his mark. Burgmair's men are generally stout, and their attitudes free; and they all appear to sit well on horseback. The present lean, lanky figure, who rides a horse that seems admirably suited to him, cannot have been designed by Burgmair, unless he was accustomed to design in two styles which were the very opposites of each other; the one distinguished by the freedom and the boldness of the drawing, the stoutness of the men, and the bulky form of the horses introduced; and the other remarkable for laboured and stiff drawing, gaunt and meagre men, and leggy, starved-like cattle. The whole of the cuts from No. 57 to No. 88, inclusive,—representing, except three,* men on horseback bearing the banners of the kingdoms and states either possessed or claimed by the emperor,—are designed in the latter style. Not only are the men and horses represented according to a different standard, but even the very ground is indicated in a different manner; it seems to abound in fragments of stones almost like a Macadamized road after a shower of rain. There is indeed no lack of stones on Burgmair's ground, but they appear more like rounded pebbles, and are not scattered about with so liberal a hand as in the cuts alluded to. In not one of those cuts which are so unlike Burgmair's is the mark of that artist to be found; and their general appearance is so unlike that of the cuts undoubtedly designed by him, that any person in the least acquainted with works of art will, even on a cursory examination, perceive the strongly marked difference.

The following cut is a reduced copy of that numbered 57; and which is the first of those representing horsemen bearing the banners of the several kingdoms, states, and cities subject to the house of Austria or to which Maximilian laid claim. It is one of the most gorgeous of the series; but, from the manner in which the horses and their riders are represented, I feel convinced that it has not been drawn by Burgmair. The subject is thus described in the emperor's directions prefixed to the volume: " One on horseback bearing the banner of the arms of Austria; another on horseback bearing the old Austrian arms; another also on horseback bearing the arms of Stiria." On the parts which are left black in the banners it had been intended to insert inscriptions. The instructions to the painter for this part of the procession are to the following effect: " One on horseback bearing on a lance a rhyme-tablet. Then the arms of the hereditary dominions of the house of Austria on banners, with their shields, helms, and crests, borne by horsemen; and the

---

* Those three are the numbers 77, 78, 79, representing musicians on horseback. The same person who drew the standard-bearers has evidently drawn those three cuts also.

banners of those countries in which the emperor has carried on war shall be borne by riders in armour; and the painter shall vary the armour according to the old manner. The banners of those countries in which

No. 57. Apparently not drawn by Burgmair.

the emperor has not carried on war shall be borne by horsemen without armour, but all splendidly clothed, each according to the costume of the country he represents. Every one shall wear a laurel wreath."

The cut on the next page is copied from that numbered 107, but which accords with the description of No. 122. The subject is described by the emperor as follows: "Then shall come riding a man of Calicut, naked, except his loins covered with a girdle, bearing a rhyme-tablet, on which shall be inscribed these words, ' These people are the subjects of the famous crowns and houses heretofore named.' " In this cut the mark of Burgmair is perceived on the harness on the breast of the elephant. There are two other cuts of Indians belonging to the same part of the procession, each of which also contains Burgmair's mark.

The cuts which were to follow the Indians and close the procession were the baggage-waggons and camp-followers of the army. Of those there are five cuts in the work published in 1796, and it is evident that some are wanting, for the two which may be considered as the first and last of those five, respectively require a preceding and a following cut to render them complete ; and there are also one or two cuts wanting to complete the intermediate subjects. Those cuts are referred to in the French description under Nos. 125 to 129, but they are numbered 129, 128, 110, 111, 125. The last three, as parts of a large subject, follow each other as the numbers are here placed ; and though the right side of No. 110 accords with the left of No. 128, inasmuch as they each contain the half of a tree which appears complete when they are joined together, yet there are no horses in No. 128 to

No. 107. With Burgmair's mark.

draw the waggon which is seen in No. 110. The order of Nos. 110, 111, and 125, is easily ascertained ; a horse at the left of No. 110 wants a tail which is to be found in No. 111 ; and the outline of a mountain in the left of No. 111 is continued in the right of No. 125. From the back-grounds, trees, and figures in those cuts I am very much inclined to think that they have been engraved from designs by Albert Durer, if he did not actually draw them on the block himself. There is no mark to be found on any of them ; and they are extremely unlike any cuts which are undoubtedly of Burgmair's designing, and they are decidedly superior to any that are usually ascribed to Hans Schaufflein. The following, which is a reduced copy of that numbered 110, will perhaps afford some idea of those cuts, and enable persons who are acquainted with Durer's works to judge for themselves with respect to the probability of their having been engraved from his designs. One or two of the other four contain still more striking resemblances of Durer's style.

Besides the twelve cuts which, in the French preface to the Triumphal Procession of Maximilian, are said not to correspond with

No. 110.　Probably drawn by Albert Durer.

the original drawings, there are also six others which the editor says are not to be found in the original designs, and which he considers to have been additions made to the work while it was in the course of engraving. Those six cuts are described in an appendix, where their numbers are said to be from 130 to 135. In No. 130 the principal figures are a king and queen, on horseback, supposed to be intended for Philip the Fair, son of the Emperor Maximilian, and his wife Joanna of Castile. This cut is very indifferently executed, and has evidently been designed by the artist who made the drawings for the questionable cuts containing the complicated locomotive carriages, mentioned at page 290. No. 131, a princess on horseback, accompanied by two female attendants also on horseback, and guards on foot, has evidently been designed by the same artist as No. 130. These two, I am inclined to think, belong to some other work. Nos. 132, 133, and 134, are from the designs of Hans Burgmair, whose mark is to be found on each; and there can be little doubt of their having been intended for Maximilian's Triumphal Procession. They form one continuous subject, which represents twelve men, habited in various costume, leading the same number of horses splendidly caparisoned. A figure on horseback bearing a rhyme-tablet leads this part of the procession; and above the horses are large scrolls probably intended to contain their names, with those of the countries to which they belong. The cut on the opposite page is a reduced copy of the last, numbered 135, which is thus described in the appendix: "The fore part of a triumphal car, drawn by four horses yoked abreast, and managed by a winged female figure who holds in her left hand a wreath of laurel." There is no mark on the original cut; but from the manner in which the horses are drawn it seems like one of Burgmair's designing.

That the cuts of the Triumphal Procession of Maximilian were engraved by different persons is certain from the names at their backs; and I think the difference that is to be perceived in the style of drawing renders it in the highest degree probable that the subjects were designed, or at least drawn on the wood, by different artists. I am inclined to think that Burgmair drew very few besides those that contain his mark; the cuts of the banner-bearers I am persuaded are not of his drawing; a third artist, of inferior talent, seems to have made the drawings of the fanciful cars containing the emperor and his family; and the five cuts of the baggage-waggons and camp followers, appear, as I have already said, extremely like the designs of Albert Durer. The best engraved cuts are to be found among those which contain Burgmair's mark. Some of the banner-bearers are also very ably executed, though not in so free or bold a manner; which I conceive to be owing to the more laboured style in which the subject has been drawn on the block. The mechanical subjects, with their accompanying figures, are the worst engraved as well as the worst drawn of the whole. The five cuts which I suppose to have been designed by Albert Durer are engraved with great spirit, but not so well as the best of those which contain the mark of Burgmair.

Though there are still in existence upwards of a hundred of the original blocks designed by Albert Durer, and upwards of three hundred designed by the most eminent of his contemporaries, yet a person who professes to be an instructor of the public on subjects of art made the following statement before the Select Committee of the House of

Commons on Arts and their Connexion with Manufactures, appointed in 1835. He is asked, "Do you consider that the progress of the arts in this country is impeded by the want of protection for new inventions of importance?" and he proceeds to enlighten the committee as follows. "Very much impeded. Inventions connected with the arts of design, of new instruments, or new processes, for example, are, from the ease with which they can be pirated, more difficult of protection than any other inventions whatever. Such protection as the existing laws afford is quite inadequate. I cannot better illustrate my meaning, than by mentioning the case of *engraving in metallic relief*, an art which is supposed to have existed three or four centuries ago ; and the re-discovery of which has long been a desideratum among artists. Albert Durer, who was both a painter and engraver, *certainly possessed this art*

No. 135. Apparently designed by Burgmair.

that is to say, the art of transferring his designs, after they had been sketched on paper, *immediately into metallic relief*, so that they might be printed along with letter-press. At present, the only sort of engravings you can print along with letter-press are wood engravings, or stereotype casts from wood engravings ; and then those engravings are but copies, and often very rude copies, of their originals ; while, in the case of Albert Durer, it is QUITE CLEAR *that it was his own identical designs that were transferred into the metallic relief.* Wood engravings, too, are limited in point of size, *because they can only be executed on box-wood*, the width of which is very small ; in fact, we have no wood engravings on a single block of a larger size than octavo : when the engraving is larger, two or three blocks are joined together ; but this is attended with so much difficulty and inconvenience, that it is seldom done. From the

X

specimens of *metallic relief engraving*, left us by Albert Durer, there is
every reason to infer that he was under no such limitation ; that he could
produce plates of any size."* This statement abounds in errors, and
may justify a suspicion that the person who made it had never seen the
cuts designed by Albert Durer which he pretends were executed in
"metallic relief." At the commencement he says that the art of engraving
in metallic relief is *supposed* to have existed three or four centuries ago ;
and immediately afterwards he asserts that Albert Durer "certainly
possessed this art;" as if by his mere word he could convert a
groundless fiction into a positive fact. When he made this confident
assertion he seems not to have been aware that many of the original
pear-tree blocks of the cuts pretendedly executed in metallic relief are
still in existence ; and when, speaking of the difficulty of getting blocks
of a larger size than an octavo, he says, "From the specimens of metallic
relief engraving, left us by Albert Durer, there is every reason to infer
that he was under no such limitation,—that he could produce plates of
any size," he affords a positive proof that he knows nothing of the
subject on which he has spoken so confidently. Had he ever examined
the large cuts engraved from Durer's designs, he would have seen, in
several, undeniable marks of the junction of the blocks, proving directly
the reverse of what he asserts on this point. What he says with respect
to the modern practice of the art is as incorrect as his assertions about
Albert Durer's engraving in metallic relief. Though it is true that there
are few modern engravings on box-wood of a larger size than octavo,
it is not true that the forming of a large block of two or more pieces is
attended with much difficulty, and is seldom done. The making of such
blocks is now a regular trade ; they are formed without the least
difficulty, and hundreds of cuts on such blocks are engraved in London
every year.† When he says that wood engravings "can only be made
on box-wood," he gives another proof of his ignorance of the subject.
Most of the earlier wood engravings were executed on blocks of pear-
tree or crab ; and even at the present time box-wood is seldom used for
the large cuts on posting-bills. In short, every statement that this
person has made on the subject of wood and pretended metallic relief
engraving is incorrect; and it is rather surprising that none of the

---

* Minutes of Evidence before the Select Committee on Arts and Manufactures, p. 130.
Ordered to be printed, 16th August 1836.

† Among the principal modern wood-cuts engraved on blocks consisting of several pieces
the following may be mentioned : The Chillingham Bull, by Thomas Bewick, 1789 ; A view
of St. Nicholas' Church, Newcastle-on-Tyne, by Charlton Nesbit, from a drawing by R.
Johnson, 1798 ; The Diploma of the Highland Society, by Luke Clennell, from a design by
B. West, P.R.A. 1808 ; The Death of Dentatus, by William Harvey, from a painting by
B. R. Haydon, 1821 ; and The Old Horse waiting for Death, left unfinished, by T. Bewick,
and published in 1832.

members of the committee should have exposed his ignorance. When such persons put themselves forward as the instructors of mechanics on the subject of art, it cannot be a matter of surprise that in the arts as applied to manufactures we should be inferior to our continental neighbours.

The art of imitating drawings—called chiaro-scuro—by means of impressions from two or more blocks, was cultivated with great success in Italy by Ugo da Carpi about 1518. The invention of this art, as has been previously remarked, is ascribed to him by some writers, but without any sufficient grounds ; for not even the slightest evidence has been produced by them to show that he, or any other Italian artist, had executed a single cut in this manner previous to 1509, the date of a chiaro-scuro wood engraving from a design by Lucas Cranach. Though it is highly probable that Ugo da Carpi was not the inventor of this art, it is certain that he greatly improved it. The chiaro-scuros executed by him are not only superior to those of the German artists, who most likely preceded him in this department of wood engraving, but to the present time they remain unsurpassed. In the present day Mr. George Baxter has attempted to extend the boundaries of this art by calling in the aid of aquatint for his outlines and first ground, and by copying the positive colours of an oil or water-colour painting. Most of Ugo da Carpi's chiaro-scuros are from Raffaele's designs, and it is said that the great painter himself drew some of the subjects on the blocks. Independent of the excellence of the designs, the characteristics of Da Carpi's chiaro-scuros are their effect and the simplicity of their execution ; for all of them, except one or two, appear to have been produced from not more than three blocks. The following may be mentioned as the principal of Da Carpi's works in this style. A Sibyl reading with a boy holding a torch, from two blocks, said by Vasari to be the artist's first attempt in this style; Jacob's Dream ; David cutting off the head of Goliah ; the Death of Ananias ; Giving the Keys to Peter ; the miraculous Draught of Fishes ; the Descent from the Cross ; the Resurrection ; and Æneas carrying away his father Anchises on his shoulders from the fire of Troy ; * all the preceding from the designs of Raffaele. Among the subjects designed by other masters are St. Peter preaching, after Polidoro ; and Diogenes showing the plucked cock in ridicule of Plato's definition of man, "a two-legged animal without feathers," after Par-

* At the foot of this cut, to the right, after the name of the designer,—" RAPHAEL URBINAS,"—is the following privilege, granted by Pope Leo X. and the Doge of Venice, prohibiting all persons from pirating the work. " QUISQUIS HAS TABELLAS INVITO AUTORE IMPRIMET EX DIVI LEONIS X. ET ILL PRINCIPIS VENETIARUM DECRETIS EXCOMINICATIONIS SENTENTIAM ET ALIAS PENAS INCURRET." Below this inscription is the engraver's name with the date : " Romæ apud Ugum de Carpi impressum. MDXVIII."

megiano. The latter, which is remarkably bold and spirited, is from four blocks; and Vasari says that it is the best of all Da Carpi's chiaroscuros. Many of Da Carpi's productions in this style were copied by Andrea Andreani of Milan, about 1580. That of Æneas carrying his father on his shoulders was copied by Edward Kirkall, an English engraver in 1722. Kirkall's copy is not entirely from wood-blocks, like the original; the outlines and the greater part of the shadows are from a copper-plate engraved in mezzotint, in a manner similar to that which has more recently been adopted by Mr. Baxter in his picture-printing.

Lucas Dammetz, generally called Lucas van Leyden, from the place of his birth, was an excellent engraver on copper, and in this branch of art more nearly approached Durer than any other of his German or Flemish contemporaries. He is said to have been born at Leyden in 1496; and, if this date be correct, he at a very early age gave decided proofs of his talents as an engraver on copper. One of his earliest prints, the monk Sergius killed by Mahomet, is dated 1508, when he was only fourteen years of age; and at the age of twelve he is said to have painted, in distemper, a picture of St. Hubert which excited the admiration of all the artists of the time. Of his numerous copper-plate engravings there are no less than twenty-one which, though they contain no date, are supposed to have been executed previously to 1508. As several of those plates are of very considerable merit, it would appear that Lucas while yet a boy excelled, as a copper-plate engraver, most of his German and Dutch contemporaries. From 1508 to 1533, the year of his death, he appears to have engraved not less than two hundred copper-plates; and, as if these were not sufficient to occupy his time, he in the same period painted several pictures, some of which were of large size. He is also said to have excelled as a painter on glass; and like Durer, Cranach, and Burgmair, he is ranked among the wood engravers of that period.

The wood-cuts which contain the mark of Lucas van Leyden, or which are usually ascribed to him, are not numerous; and, even admitting them to have been engraved by himself, the fact would contribute but little to his fame, for I have not seen one which might not have been executed by a professional "formschneider" of very moderate abilities. The total of the wood-cuts supposed to have been engraved by him does not exceed twenty. The following is a reduced copy of a wood-cut ascribed to Lucas van Leyden, in the Print Room of the British Museum, but which is not in Bartsch's Catalogue, nor in the list of Lucas van Leyden's engravings in Meusel's Neue Miscellaneen. Though I very much question if the original cut were engraved by Lucas himself, I have no doubt of its being from his design. It represents the death of Sisera; and, with a noble contempt of the unity of time, Jael is seen giving Sisera a drink of milk, driving the nail into his head, and

then showing the body,—with herself in the act of driving the nail,—
to Barak and his followers : the absurdity of this threefold action has
perhaps never been surpassed in any cut ancient or modern. Sir Boyle
Roach said that it was impossible for any *person*, except a *bird* or a *fish*,
to be in two places at once ; but here we have a pictorial representation
of a female being in no less than three; and in one of the localities
actually pointing out to certain persons how she was then employed in
another.

Heineken, in his account of engravers of the Flemish school, has
either committed an egregious mistake, or expressed himself with
intentional ambiguity with respect to a wood-cut printed at Antwerp,
and which he saw in the collections of the Abbé de Marolles. His
notice of this cut is as follows : " I found in the collections of the
Abbé de Marolles, in the cabinet of the King of France, a detached

piece, which, in my opinion, is the most ancient of the wood engravings executed in the Low Countries which bear the name of the artist. This cut is marked, *Gheprint t'Antwerpen by my Phillery de figursnider*— Printed at Antwerp, by me Phillery, the engraver of figures. It serves as a proof that the engravers of moulds were, at Antwerp, in that ancient time, also printers."*

In this vague and ambiguous account, the writer gives us no idea of the period to which he refers in the words "cet ancien tems." If he means the time between the pretended invention of Coster, and the period when typography was probably first practised in the Low Countries,—that is, from about 1430 to 1472,—he is wrong, and his statement would afford ground for a presumption that he had either examined the cut very carelessly, or that he was so superficially acquainted with the progressive improvement of the art of wood engraving as to mistake a cut abounding in cross-hatching, and certainly executed subsequent to 1524, for one that had been executed about seventy years previously, when cross-hatching was never attempted, and when the costume was as different from that of the figures represented in the cut as the costume of Vandyke's portraits is dissimilar to Hogarth's. The words "*graveurs de moules,*" I have translated literally "engravers of moulds," for I cannot conceive what else Heineken can mean; but this expression is scarcely warranted by the word "*figuersnider*" on the cut, which is almost the same as the German "formschneider;" and whatever might be the original meaning of the word, it was certainly used to express merely a wood engraver. Compilers of Histories of Art, and Dictionaries of Painters and Engravers, who usually follow their leader, even in his slips, as regularly as a flock of sheep follow the bell-wether through a gap, have disseminated Heineken's mistake, and the antiquity of "*Phillery's*" wood-engraving is about as firmly established as Lawrence Coster's invention of typography. One of those "straightforward" people has indeed gone rather beyond his authority; for in a "Dictionary of the Fine Arts," published in 1826, we are expressly informed that "*Phillery, who lived near the end of the fourteenth century, was the first engraver on wood who practised in the Netherlands.*"† It is thus that

---

* " J'ai trouvé dans les Receueils de l'Abbé de Marolles, au Cabinet du Roi de France, une piece détachée, qui, suivant mon sentiment, est la plus ancienne de celles, qui sont gravées en bois dans les Païs-Bas, et qui portent le nom de l'artiste. Cette estampe est marquée : *Gheprint t'Antwerpen by my Phillery de figursnider—Imprimé à Anvers, chez moi Phillery, le graveur de figures.* Elle sert de preuve, que les graveurs de moules étoient aussi, dans cet ancien tems, imprimeurs à Anvers."—Idée Générale d'une Collection complette d'Estampes, p. 197.

† In a work of a similar kind, and of equal authority, published in 1834, we are informed that Ugo da Carpi was a historical painter, and that he died in 1500. He was only born in 1486.

error on the subject of art, and indeed on every other subject, is propagated : a writer of reputation makes an incorrect or an ambiguous statement ; other writers adopt it without examination, and not unfrequently one of that class whose confidence in deciding on a question is in the inverse ratio of their knowledge of the subject, proceeds beyond his original authority, and declares that to be certain which previously had only been doubtfully or obscurely expressed. In Heineken's notice of this cut there is an implied qualification under which he might screen himself from a charge of incorrectness with respect to the time of its execution, though not from a charge of ambiguity. He says that, in his opinion, it is "the most ancient of the wood engravings executed in the Low Countries *which bear the name of the artist ;*" and with this limitation his opinion may be correct, although the cut were only engraved in 1525 or 1526 ; for I am not aware of any wood engraving of an earlier date, executed in the Low Countries, that contains the *name* of the artist, though there are several which contain the artist's mark. It also may be argued that the words "*cet ancien tems*" might be about as correctly applied to designate the year 1525 as 1470 : if, however, he meant the first of those dates, he has expressed himself in an equivocal manner, for he is generally understood to refer the cut to a considerably earlier period. It has been indeed conjectured that Heineken, in speaking of this cut, might intentionally express himself obscurely, in order that he might not give offence to his friend Monsieur Mariette, who is said to have considered it to be one of the earliest specimens of wood engravings executed in the Low Countries. This is, however, without any sufficient reason, merely shifting the charge of ignorance, with respect to the difference of style in wood engravings of different periods, from Heineken to Monsieur Mariette. As there is no evidence to show that the latter ever expressed any such opinion as that ascribed to him respecting the antiquity of the cut in question, Heineken alone is answerable for the account contained in his book. Impressions of the cut by "*Phillery*" are not of very great rarity ; there are two in the Print Room at the British Museum, and from one of them the reduced copy in the following page has been carefully made.

Any person, however, slightly acquainted with the progress of wood engraving could scarcely fail to pronounce that the original of this cut must have been executed subsequent to 1500, and in all probability subsequent to the cuts of the Triumphal Procession of Maximilian, to the general style of which, so far as relates to the manner of engraving, it bears considerable resemblance. The costume of the figures, too, also proves that it does not belong to the fifteenth century ;

and on carefully examining the inscription, a person accustomed to
the old German or Dutch characters would be more likely to read
"*Willem*" than "*Phillery*" as the name of the artist. To one of the
impressions in the British Museum a former owner, after extracting
Heineken's account, has appended the following remark : "This is the

print above described. There seems to be an inconsiderable mistake
in the name, which I take to be D'villery." It is to be observed that
in the original, as in the preceding copy, the inscription is engraved
on wood, and not set up in type ; and that consequently the first
character of the doubtful name is rather indistinct. It is however

most probably a *W;* and the last is certainly an *m*, with a flourish at its tail. The intermediate letters *ille* are plain enough, and if the first be supposed to be a *W*, and the last an *m*, we have the name *Willem*,—a very probable prenomen for a Dutch wood engraver of the sixteenth century. The inscription when carefully examined is literally as follows : " *Gheprint Tantwerpen Bij mij Willem de Figuersnider.*" Heineken's mistake of *Phillery* for *Willem*, or William, and thus giving a heretofore unheard-of name to the list of artists, is not unlike that of Scopoli the naturalist, who, in one of his works, has commemorated " Horace Head" as a London bookseller.*

Though the cut which bears the name of the supposed "Phillery" contains internal evidence of its not having been engraved in the fifteenth century, there is yet further reason to believe that it is merely a copy of part of a cut of the same size by a Swiss artist of the name of Urse Graff, which is dated 1524. There is an impression of Urse Graff's cut† in the Print Room of the British Museum ; in the fore-ground are the figures which have obviously been copied by *Willem de Figuersnider*, alias *Phillery*, and immediately behind the middle figure, who holds in his right hand a large Swiss espadon, is a leafless tree with a figure of Death clinging to the upper part of the trunk, and pointing to a hour-glass which he holds in his left hand. A bird, probably intended for a raven, is perched above the hour-glass ; and on the trunk of the tree, near to the figure of Death, is Urse Graff's mark with the date as is here given. The back-ground presents a view of a lake, with buildings and mountains on the left. The general character of Urse Graff's subject is Swiss, both in the scenery and figures ; and the perfect identity of the latter with those in the cut "printed at Antwerp by William the figure-cutter" proves, beyond the possibility of a doubt, that one of those two artists has copied the work of the other. Urse Graff's subject, however, is complete, and corresponds both in the land-scape and in the costume of the figures with the country of the artist ; while the cut of William of Antwerp represents merely an unrelieved group of figures in the costume of Switzerland. Urse Graff was an artist of reputation in his time ; of " Willem," who was probably only an engraver of the designs of others, nothing more is known beyond what is afforded by the single cut in question. From these circumstances,

---

* The sign of Mr. Benjamin White, formerly a bookseller in Fleet Street, was Horace's Head. In Scopoli's Deliciæ, Flora, et Fauna Insubriæ, plate 24 is thus inscribed : " Auspiciis Benjamini White et Horatii Head, Bibliopol. Londinensium." The learned naturalist had mistaken Mr. White's sign for his partner in the business.

† This cut of Urse Graff is described in Bartsch's Peintre-Graveur, tom. vii. p. 465, No. 16.

though it cannot be positively decided which of those cuts is the original, it is almost morally certain that the Flemish figure-cutter has copied the work of the Swiss artist.—Urse Graff resided at Basle, of which city he was probably a native. In one of his engravings with the date 1523, he describes himself as a goldsmith and die-sinker. Wood-cuts containing his mark are not very common, and the most of them appear to have been executed between 1515 and 1528. A series of wood-cuts of the Passion of Christ, designed in a very inferior manner, and printed at Strasburg in 1509, are sometimes ascribed to him on account of their being marked with the letters V. G., which some writers have supposed to be the mark of an artist named Von Gamperlin. Professor Christ, in his Dictionary of Monograms, says that he can find nothing to determine him in favour of the name Gamperlin ; and that he is rather inclined to think that those letters are intended for the name Von Goar, which he believes that he has deciphered on an engraving containing this mark. The mark of Urse Graff, a V and a G interlaced, occurs in the ornamented border of the title-page of several books printed at Basle, and amongst others on the title of a quarto edition of Ulrich Hutten's Nemo, printed there by Frobenius in 1519. At the end of this edition there is a beautifully-designed cut of the printer's device, which is probably the work of the same artist.*

A painter, named Nicholas Emanuel Deutsch, a contemporary of Urse Graff, and who resided at Bern, is said, by Sandrart, to have been of a noble English family, and the same writer adds that he left his own country on account of his religion. The latter statement, however, is not likely to be correct, for there are wood-cuts, with this artist's mark, dated "Bern, 1518 ;" which was before the persecution in England on account of the doctrines of Luther had commenced. In J. R. Füssli's Dictionary of Artists it is stated that he was of a French family, of the name of Cholard, but that he was born at Bern in 1484, and died there in 1530. He was a poet as well as a painter, and held one of the highest offices in the magistracy of Bern.

Within the first thirty years of the sixteenth century the practice of illustrating books with wood-cuts seems to have been more general than at any other period, scarcely excepting the present ; for though within the last eight or ten years an immense number of wood-cuts have been executed in England and France, yet wood engravings at the time referred to were introduced into a greater variety of books, and the art was more generally practised throughout Europe. In

---

* The device of Frobenius at the end of an edition of the same work, printed by him in 1518, is much inferior to that in the edition of 1519. In both, the ornamental border of the title-page is the same.

modern German and Dutch works wood engravings are sparingly introduced; and in works printed in Switzerland and Italy they are still more rarely to be found. In the former period the art seems to have been very generally practised throughout Europe, though to a greater extent, and with greater skill, in Germany than in any other country. The wood-cuts which are to be found in Italian books printed between 1500 and 1530 are mostly meagre in design and very indifferently engraved; and for many years after the German wood engravers had begun to give variety of colour and richness of effect to their cuts by means of cross-hatchings, their Italian contemporaries continued to adhere to the old method of engraving their figures, chiefly in outline, with the shadows and the folds of the draperies indicated by parallel lines. These observations relate only to the ordinary wood engravings of the period, printed in the same page with type, or printed separately in the usual manner of surface printing at one impression. The admirable chiaro-scuros of Ugo da Carpi, printed from two or more blocks, are for effect and general excellence the most admirable specimens of this branch of the art that ever have been executed; they are as superior to the chiaro-scuros of German artists as the usual wood engravings of the latter excel those executed in Italy during the same period.

In point of drawing, some of the best wood-cuts executed in Italy in the time of Albert Durer are to be found in a folio work entitled Triompho di Fortuna, written by Sigismond Fanti, and printed at Venice in 1527.* The subject of this work, which was licensed by Pope Clement VII, is the art of fortune-telling, or of answering all kinds of questions relative to future events. The volume contains a considerable number of wood-cuts ; some designed and executed in the very humblest style of wood engraving, and others, which appear to have been drawn on the block with pen-and-ink, designed with great

---

* The title of this book is, in red letters, " Triompho di Fortuna, di Sigismondo Fanti, Ferrarese." The title-page is also ornamented with a wood-cut, representing the Pope, with Virtue on one side, and Vice on the other, seated above the globe, which is supported by Atlas, and provided with an axis, having a handle at each side, like a winch. At one of the handles is a devil, and at the other an angel ; to the left is a naked figure holding a die, and near to him is an astronomer taking an observation. At the foot of the cut is the mark I. M. or T. M., for I cannot positively decide whether the first letter be intended for an I or a T. The following is the colophon: " Impresso in la inclita citta di Venegia per Agostin da Portese. Nel anno dil virgineo parto MD.XXVII. Nel mese di Genaro, ad instãtia di Jacomo Giunta Mercatãte Florentino. Con il Privilegio di Clemente Papa VII, et del Senato Veneto a requisitione di l'Autore." In the Catalogue of the British Museum this book is erroneously entered as printed at Rome, 1526. The compiler had mistaken the date of the Pope's licence for the time when the book was printed. This trifling mistake is noticed here, as from similar oversights bibliographers have sometimes described books as having been twice or thrice printed, when, in fact, there had been only one edition.

spirit. The smallest and most inferior cuts serve as illustrations to the questions, and an idea may be formed of them from the three here

given, which occur under the question: " Qual fede o legge sia di queste tre la buona, o la Christiana, l'Hebrea, o quello di Mahumeto ? " * In English : " Which of these three religions is the best, the Christian, the Jewish, or the Mahometan ? " Several larger cuts are executed in a dry hard style, and evidently drawn by a person very inferior to the artist who designed the cuts executed in the manner of pen-and-ink drawings. The following is a fac-simile of one of the latter. It is entitled " Fortuna de Africo," in a series of twelve, intended for representations of the winds.

The following cut, which appears in folio 38, is intitled " Michael Fiorentino,"—Michael Angelo ; and it certainly conveys no bad idea

* The following questions, selected from a number of others, will perhaps afford some idea of this " Opera utilissima et jocosa," as it is called by the author. " Se glie bene a pigliar bella, o bruta donna ; se'l servo sara fidele al suo signore ; se quest' anno sara carestia o abundantia ; quanti mariti havera la donna ; se glie bene a far viaggio et a che tempo ; se'l parto della donna sara maschio o femina ; se'l sogno fatto sara vero ; se'l fin del huomo sara buonò." The three small illustrations of the last query are of evil omen ; in one, is seen a gallows ; in another, a man praying ; and in the third, the quarters of a human body hung up in terrorem.

of the energetic manner in which that great artist is said to have used his mallet and chisel when engaged on works of sculpture. This cut, however, is made to represent several other sculptors besides the great Florentine ; it is repeated seven times in the subsequent pages, and on each occasion we find underneath it a different name. The late T. Stothard, R.A. was of opinion that wood engraving was best adapted to express pen-and-ink drawing, and that the wood engraver generally failed when he attempted more. His illustrations of Rogers's poems, engraved on wood by Clennell and Thompson, are executed in a similar style to that of the following specimen, though with greater delicacy.

Certain wood-cuts with the mark A. G., executed towards the conclusion of the fifteenth century, have been ascribed to an artist named Albert Glockenton. Bartsch, however, says that the name of the artist is unknown ; and he seems to consider that Sandrart had merely conjectured that those letters might represent the name Albert Glockenton. For no better reason the letters I. V. on a tablet, with two pilgrim's-staffs crossed between them, which are to be found on several old chiaro-scuro wood engravings, have been supposed to represent the name, John Ulric Pilgrim. This name appears to be a pure invention of some ingenious expounder of monograms, for there is not the slightest evidence, that I am aware of, to show that any artist of this name ever lived. The chiaro-scuros with this mark were probably executed in the time of Durer, but none of them contains a date to establish the fact. Heineken considers them to have been the productions of a German artist; and he refers to them in proof of the art of chiaro-scuro having been practised in Germany long before the time of Ugo da Carpi. It is, however, highly questionable if they are of an earlier date than 1518; and it is by no means certain that the artist was a German. By some persons he has been supposed to have been the inventor of chiaro-scuro engraving, on no better grounds, it would seem, than that his pieces are without a date.

Next to the Germans, in the time of Albert Durer, the Dutch and Flemings seem to have excelled in the art of wood engraving; but the cuts executed in Holland and Flanders are generally much inferior to those designed and engraved by German artists. In a considerable number of Dutch wood engravings, of the period under review, I have observed an attempt to combine something like the effect of cross-hatching and of the dotted manner mentioned at page 232 as having been frequently practised by French wood engravers in the early part of the sixteenth century. In a series of cuts from a Dutch prayer-book, apparently printed between 1520 and 1530, this style of engraving is frequently introduced. Where a German artist would have introduced lines crossing each other with great regularity, the Dutch wood engraver has endeavoured to attain his object by irregularly picking out portions of the wood with the point of his graver; the effect, however, is not good. In the border surrounding those cuts, a Dance of Death is represented, consisting of several more characters than are to be found in the celebrated work ascribed to Holbein, but far inferior in point of design and execution.

An artist, named John Walter van Assen, is usually mentioned as one of the best Dutch wood engravers or designers of this period. Nothing further is known of him than that he lived at Amsterdam about 1517. The mark supposed to be Van Assen's is often ascribed by expounders of monograms to another artist whom they call Werner or Waer van Assanen.

A considerable number of French works, printed in the time of Albert Durer, contain wood engravings, but few of them possess much merit when compared with the more highly finished and correctly drawn productions of the German school of the same period. The ornamental borders, however, of many missals and prayer-books, which then issued in great numbers from the Parisian press, frequently display great beauty. The taste for surrounding each page with an ornamental border engraved on wood was very generally prevalent in Germany, France, and Flanders at that period, more especially in devotional works; and in the former country, and in Switzerland, scarcely a tract was printed—and the Lutheran controversy gave rise to many hundreds—without an ornamental border surrounding the title. In Germany such wood engravers as were chiefly employed in executing cuts of this kind were called *Rahmen-schneiders*—border-cutters,—as has been previously observed at page 190. In England during the same period wood engraving made but little progress ; and there seems to have been a lack of good designers and competent engravers in this country. The best cuts printed in England in the time of Durer are contained in a manual of prayers, of a small duodecimo size. On a tablet in the border of one of the cuts—the Flight into Egypt *—I perceive the date 1523. The total number of cuts in the volume is about a hundred ; and under each of the largest are four verses in English. Several of the smaller cuts, representing figures of saints, and preceding the prayers for their respective days, have evidently been designed by an artist of considerable talent. As most of the wood-cuts which constitute the ornaments or the illustrations of books printed at this period are without any name or mark, it is impossible to ascertain the names of the persons by whom they were designed or engraved.

The manner of wood engraving in *intaglio* so that the figures appear white on a black ground, so frequently adopted by early Italian wood engravers, was sometimes practised in Germany ; and in one of the earliest works containing portraits of the Roman emperors,† copied from ancient medals, printed in the latter country, the cuts are executed in this style. The subject of the work is the lives of the Roman emperors, written by Joannes Huttichius, and the portraits with which it is illustrated are copied from medals in a collection which had been formed by the Emperor Maximilian, the great promoter of wood engraving in Germany. The first edition, in Latin, was printed by Wolff Köpffel, at Strasburg, in 1525 ; and a second edition, in German, was published at the same place in the succeeding year. The cut on the next page, of the head of Nero, will afford an idea of the style in which the portraits are

* The following lines descriptive of this cut are printed underneath it :

𝕳𝖔𝖜 𝕸𝖆𝖗𝖞 𝖆𝖓𝖉 𝕵𝖔𝖘𝖊𝖕𝖍 𝖜𝖎𝖙𝖍 𝖎𝖊𝖘𝖚 𝖜𝖊𝖗𝖊 𝖋𝖆𝖞𝖓𝖊.
𝕴𝖓 𝖙𝖔 𝕰𝖌𝖞𝖕𝖙𝖊 𝖋𝖔𝖗 𝖘𝖔𝖈𝖔𝖚𝖗 𝖙𝖔 𝖋𝖑𝖊.
𝖂𝖍𝖆𝖓 𝖙𝖍𝖊 𝕴𝖓𝖓𝖔𝖈𝖊𝖓𝖙𝖊𝖘 𝖋𝖔𝖗 𝖍𝖎𝖘 𝖘𝖆𝖐𝖊 𝖜𝖊𝖗 𝖘𝖑𝖆𝖞𝖓𝖊.
𝕭𝖞 𝖈𝖔𝖒𝖎𝖘𝖘𝖞𝖔𝖓 𝖔𝖋 𝕳𝖊𝖗𝖔𝖉𝖊𝖘 𝖗𝖚𝖊𝖑𝖙𝖎𝖊.

† In a folio work entitled "Epitome Thesauri Antiquitatum, hoc est IMPP. Rom. Orientalium et Occidentalium Iconum, ex Antiquis Numismatibus quam fidelissime delinea tarum. Ex Musæo Jacobi de Strada Mantuani Antiquarii," Lyons, 1553, it is stated that the first work containing portraits of the Roman emperors engraved from their coins was that entitled "Illustrium Imagines," written by Cardinal Sadolet, and printed at Rome by Jacobus Mazochius.—In Strada's work the portraits are executed in the same manner as in that of Huttichius. The wood-cut containing the printer's device, on the title-page of Strada's work, is admirably engraved.

executed, and of the fidelity with which the artist has in general represented the likeness impressed on the original medals.

Besides Durer, Burgmair, Cranach, and Schaufflein, there are several other German painters of the same period who are also said to have engraved on wood, and among the most celebrated of this secondary class the following may be mentioned : Hans Sebald Behaim, previously noticed at page 253 ; Albert Altdorffer ; Hans Springinklee ; and Hans Baldung Grün. The marks of all those artists are to be found on wood-cuts executed in the time of Durer ; but I am extremely doubtful if

those cuts were actually engraved by themselves. If they were, I can only say that, though they might be good painters and designers, they were very indifferent wood engravers ; and that their time in executing the subjects ascribed to them must have been very badly employed. The common working *formschneider* who could not execute them as well, must have been a very ordinary wood-*cutter*, not to say wood-*engraver*,— by the latter term meaning one who excels in his profession, and not a mere cutter of lines, without skill or taste, on box or pear-tree.

Albert Altdorffer was born at Ratisbon in 1480, and afterwards became a magistrate of his native city. The engravings on wood and copper containing his mark are mostly of a small size, and he is generally known as one of the *little masters* of the German school of engraving.* Hans Springinklee was a painter of some eminence, and according to Doppelmayer, as referred to by Bartsch, was a pupil of Durer's. His mark is to be found on several wood-cuts ; and it occurs in one of the illustrations in the Wise King. Hans Baldung Grün was born at Gemund in Suabia, and studied at Nuremberg under Albert Durer. He excelled as a painter ; and the wood-cuts which contain his

---

* Heineken ranks the following in the class of *little masters* : Henry Aldgrever, Albert Altdorffer, Bartholomew Behaim, Hans Sebald Behaim, Hans Binck, Henry Goerting, George Penez, and Virgil Solis. Most of them were engravers on copper.

mark are mostly designed with great spirit. The earliest wood engraving that contains his mark is a frontispiece to a volume of sermons with the date 1508; and the latest is a group of horses, engraved in a hard, stiff manner, with the name "BALDUNG" and the date 1534.* He chiefly resided at Strasburg, where he died in 1545. He is mentioned by Durer, in his Journal, by the name of "Grün Hannsen."

We may here conveniently introduce fac-similes on a reduced scale of two rather interesting wood engravings given by Dr. Dibdin in his

Bibliomania, and copied from an early folio volume, entitled *Revelationes cœlestes sanctœ Brigittœ de Suecia*, printed at Nuremberg by Anthony Köberger, M CCC XXI. *mensis Septembris*, which some read 1500, on the 21st of September, others 1521, in the month of September. The first of these cuts is curious as representing the simplicity of an ancient reading room, with its three-legged joint stool, such as is so prettily described by Cowper, Task, I. v. 19; the other cut describes a punish-

---

* The following curious testimony respecting a lock of Albert Durer's hair, which had formerly been in the possession of Hans Baldung Grün, is translated from an article in Meusel's Neue Miscellaneen, 1799. The lock of hair and the document were then in the possession of Herr H. S. Hüsgen of Frankfort on the Mayn: " Herein is the hair which was cut from the head of that ingenious and celebrated painter Albert Durer, after his death at Nuremberg, 8th April 1528, as a token of remembrance. It afterwards came into the possession of that skilful painter Hans Baldung, burger of this city, Strasburg; and after his death, in 1545, my late brother-in-law, Nicholas Krämer, painter, of this city, having

ment which is said to have been revealed to St. Bridget against those ladies who have "ornamenta indecentia capitibus et pedibus, et reliquis membris, ad provocandam luxuriam, et irritandum Deum, in strictis

vestibus, ostensione mamillarum, unctionibus, &c." The artist is unknown, but seems to be among the best of the Nuremberg school.

It cannot be reasonably doubted that Durer and several other German painters of his time were accustomed to engrave their own designs on copper; for in many instances we have the express testimony of their contemporaries, and not unfrequently their own, to the fact. Copper-plate engraving for about sixty years from the time of its invention was generally practised by persons who were also painters, and who usually engraved their own designs. Wood engraving, on the contrary, from an early period was practised as a distinct profession by persons who are never heard of as painters. That some of the early German painters—of a period when " artists were more of workmen, and workmen more of artists "* than in the present day—*might* engrave some of the wood-cuts which bear their marks, is certainly not impossible ; but it is highly improbable that all the wood-cuts which are ascribed to them should have been executed by themselves. If any wood-cuts were actually engraved by Durer, Cranach, Burgmair, and other painters of reputation, I conceive that such cuts are not to be distinguished by their superior execution from those engraved by the professional *formschneider* and *brief-maler* of the day. The best copper-plates engraved by Albert Durer can scarcely be surpassed by the best copper-plate engraver of the present day,—that is, supposing him to execute his work by the same means ; while the best of the wood-cuts which he is supposed to have engraved himself might be readily executed by a score of modern

bought sundry of his works and other things, among them found this lock of hair, in an old letter, wherein was written an account of what it contained. On the death of my brother-in-law, in 1550, it was presented to me by my sister Dorothy, and I now enclose it in this letter for a memorial. 1559. SEBOLD BÜHELER." To this testimony are subjoined two or three others of subsequent date, showing in whose possession the valued relic had been before it came into the hands of Herr Hüsgen.

* Evidence of Dr. G. F. Waagen of Berlin before the Select Committee of the House of Commons on Arts and their Connexion with Manufactures, 1835.

wood engravers if the subject were drawn for them on the block.   In the age of Durer the best wood-cuts are of comparatively large size, and are distinguished more from the boldness and freedom of their design than from any peculiar excellence of engraving: they display, in fact, rather the talent of the *artist* than the skill of the *workman*.   Though wood engraving had very greatly improved from about the end of the fifteenth century to the time of Durer's decease, yet it certainly did not attain its perfection within that period.   In later years, indeed, the workman has displayed greater excellence; but at no time does the art appear to have been more flourishing or more highly esteemed than in the reign of its great patron, the Emperor Maximilian.

CHAPTER VI.

FURTHER PROGRESS AND DECLINE OF WOOD ENGRAVING.

THE DANCE OF DEATH—PAINTED IN SEVERAL OLD CHURCHES—TWO PAINTINGS OF THIS SUBJECT
AT BASLE—OLD EDITIONS OF LA DANSE MACABRE, WITH WOOD-CUTS—LES SIMULACHRES ET
HISTORIÉES FACES DE LA MORT, USUALLY CALLED THE DANCE OF DEATH, PRINTED AT LYONS,
1538—VARIOUS EDITIONS AND COPIES OF THIS WORK—ICONES HISTORIARUM VETERIS TES-
TAMENTI, OR BIBLE CUTS, DESIGNED BY HANS HOLBEIN—SIMILARITY BETWEEN THESE CUTS
AND THOSE OF THE LYONS DANCE OF DEATH—CUTS OF BOTH WORKS, PROBABLY DESIGNED BY
THE SAME PERSON—PORTRAIT OF SIR T. WYATT—CUTS IN CRANMER'S CATECHISM—AND IN
OTHER OLD ENGLISH WORKS—WOOD-ENGRAVING IN ITALY—CHIARO-SCURO—MARCOLINI'S
SORTI—S. MUNSTER'S COSMOGRAPHY—MAPS—VIRGIL SOLIS—BERNARD SOLOMON—JOST AMMON
—ANDREA ANDREANI—HENRY GOLTZIUS—ENGLISH WOOD-CUTS—CUTS BY CHRISTOPHER
JEGHER FROM THE DESIGNS OF RUBENS—GENERAL DECLINE OF THE ART IN THE SEVEN-
TEENTH CENTURY.

HE best of the wood-cuts of the time
of Albert Durer, more especially those
executed by German engravers, are for
the most part of rather large size ; the
best of those, however, which appeared
within forty years of his decease are
generally small. The art of wood engraving, both as regards design and
execution, appears to have attained its
highest perfection within about ten
years of the time of Durer's decease ;
for the cuts which, in my opinion,
display the greatest excellence of the art as practised in former times,
were published in 1538. The cuts to which I allude are those of the
celebrated Dance of Death, which were first published in that year at
Lyons. So admirably are those cuts executed,—with so much feeling
and with so perfect a knowledge of the capabilities of the art,—that I
do not think any wood engraver of the present time is capable of
surpassing them. The manner in which they are engraved is comparatively simple : there is no laboured and unnecessary cross-hatching
where the same effect might be obtained by simpler means ; no display

of fine work merely to show the artist's talent in cutting delicate lines. Every line is expressive ; and the end is always obtained by the simplest means. In this the talent and feeling of the engraver are chiefly displayed. He wastes not his time in mere mechanical execution—which in the present day is often mistaken for excellence ;—he endeavours to give to each character its appropriate expression ; and in this he appears to have succeeded better, considering the small size of the cuts, than any other wood engraver, either of times past or present.

Though two or three of the cuts which will subsequently be given may be of rather earlier date than those of the Dance of Death, it seems preferable to give first some account of this celebrated work ; and to introduce the cuts alluded to, though not in strict chronological order,—which is the less necessary as they do not illustrate the progress of the art,—with others executed in a similar style.

Long before the publication of the work now so generally known as "The Dance of Death," a series of paintings representing, in a similar manner, Death seizing on persons of all ranks and ages, had appeared on the walls of several churches. A Dance of Death was painted in the cloisters of the Church of the Innocents at Paris, in the cloisters of St. Paul's, London, and in the portico of St. Mary's, Lubec. The painting in St. Paul's is said to have been executed at the cost of one Jenkin Carpenter, who lived in the reign of Henry VI, and who was one of the executors of that famous "lord-mayor of London," Richard Whittington ; and Dugdale, in his History of St. Paul's Cathedral, says that it was in imitation of that in the cloisters of the Church of the Innocents at Paris.* This subject seems to have been usually known in former times by the name of "The Dance of Machabre," from a French or German poet—for this point is not settled by the learned—of the name of Macaber or Macabre, who is said to have written a poem on this subject.† The

---

* Besides those above mentioned, there is said to have been a "Death's Dance" at the following places : in Hungerford's Chapel, Salisbury Cathedral ; Hexham Church ; at Fescamp in Normandy, carved in stone ; at Dresden ; Leipsic ; Annaberg ; and Berne in Switzerland. The last, painted on the walls of the cloisters of the Dominican friars, was the work of Nicholas Emanuel Deutsch, previously mentioned at page 314. So early as 1560 this painting was destroyed in consequence of the cloisters being pulled down to widen a street. There are two copies of it in water-colours preserved at Berne. From one of them a series of lithographic engravings has been made. An ample list of old paintings of this subject will be found in Mr. Douce's Dance of Death, chapters iii. and iv, published by Pickering, 1833, and republished, with additions, by H. G. Bohn, 1858.

† Mr. Douce says, " Macaber was not a German or any other poet, but a nonentity." He supposes that the name *Macaber* is only a slight and obvious corruption of *Macarius*, a Saint who lived as a hermit in Egypt, and of whom there is a story of his showing to three kings or noblemen an emblem of mortality in the shape of three skeletons. " The word *Macabre*," observes Mr. Douce, " is found only in French authorities ; and the Saint's name, which in the modern orthography is *Macaire*, would in many ancient manuscripts be written *Macabre* instead of *Macaure*, the letter *b* being substituted for that of *u* from the caprice, ignorance,

Dance of Death, however, which as a painting has attained greater celebrity and given rise to much more discussion than any other, is that which was painted on the wall of a kind of court-house attached to the Church of the Dominicans at Basle. This painting has frequently been ascribed to Holbein ; but it certainly was executed before he was born ; and there is not the slightest reason to believe that he ever touched it in any of the repairs which it underwent in subsequent years.

The following particulars respecting this painting are such as seem best authenticated.

It is said to owe its origin to a plague which ravaged the city of Basle in 1439, during the time of the great council, which commenced in 1431, and did not terminate till 1448. A number of persons of almost all ranks, whom the council had brought to this city, having fallen victims to the plague, it is said that the painting was executed in remembrance of the event, and as a memento of the uncertainty of life. Though it may be true that the great mortality at Basle in 1439 might have been the occasion of such a picture in the church-court—*Kirchhofe*, as it is called by Hegner in his Life of Holbein—of the Dominicans in that city, it is almost certain that the subject must have been suggested by one of much earlier date painted on the walls of an old building which had formerly been the cloisters of a nunnery which stood in that part of Basle which is called the Little City. This convent was founded in 1275 ; and the painting appears to have been executed in 1312, according to the following date, which was to be seen above one of the figures, that of the Count, who was also one of the characters in the painting in the church-court of the Dominicans : " 𝕯𝖚𝖘𝖘𝖊𝖓𝖙 𝖏𝖆𝖗 𝖙𝖗𝖊𝖎𝖍𝖚𝖓𝖙𝖊𝖗𝖙 𝖚𝖓𝖉 𝖃𝖎𝖎 :" in English : One thousand three hundred and twelve. Several of the figures in this old painting were almost the same as in that of the church-court of the Dominicans, though executed in a coarser manner ; and, like the latter, were accompanied with explanatory inscriptions in verse. This curious old work appears to have remained unnoticed till 1766, when one Emanuel Büchel, of Basle, by trade a baker, but an admirer of art, and an industrious draughtsman, had his attention directed to it. He made a careful copy in colours of all that then remained of it, and his drawings are now in the public library of Basle.

or carelessness of transcribers." Mr. Douce's conjecture would have been more feasible had he produced a single instance from any ancient manuscript of the name having been written *Macabre* instead of *Macaure* or *Macarius*. By a similar process of reasoning, it would not be difficult to prove that a hundred old writers and poets non-entities. In the earliest French editions, the work is intitled " La Danse Macabre ;" and in a Parisian edition, " Per Magistrum Guidonem Mercatorem pro Godefrido de Marnef," folio, 1490, the title is as follows : " Chorea ab eximio Macabro versibus Alemanicis edita, et à Petro Desrey emendata." This seems to prove that Peter Desrey knew something of a person named Macaber who had written a description of the Dance in German.

" This oldest Dance of Death," says Hegner, writing in 1827, " is almost entirely effaced, and becomes daily more so, as well on account of age as from the cloisters of the old nunnery having been for many years used as a warehouse for salt."*

It is supposed that the Dance of Death in the church-court of the Dominicans at Basle was originally painted in *fresco* or distemper. The number of characters, each accompanied by a figure of Death, was originally forty ;† but in 1568, a painter, named Hans Hugo Klauber, who was employed by the magistrates to repair the old painting, introduced a figure of the reformer Oecolampadius as if preaching to the characters composing the Dance, with portraits of himself, his wife, and their little son, at the end. It is probable that he painted over the old figures in oil-colour, and introduced sundry alterations, suggested by other paintings and engravings of the same subject. It appears likely that, at the same time, many of the old inscriptions were changed for others more in accordance with the doctrines of the Reformation, which then prevailed at Basle. The verses above the figure of the Pope were certainly not such as would have been tolerated at the period when the subject is supposed to have been first painted.‡ In 1616 the painting was again repaired ; but, though a Latin inscription was then added containing the names of the magistrates who had thus taken care to preserve it, there is no mention made of any artist by whom the subject

---

* Hans Holbein der Jüngere. Von Ulrich Hegner, S. 309. Berlin, 1827.

† All the persons introduced were of the size of life. Death, in only one instance, was represented as a perfect skeleton, and that was in the subject of the Doctor, whom he was supposed to address as follows :

"Herr Doctor b'schaw die Anatomey
An mir, ob sie recht g'macht sey."

That is :
" Doctor, take of me a sight,—
Say if the skeleton be right."

It has been said that the Pope, the Emperor, and the King, were intended respectively for portraits of Pope Felix V, the Emperor Sigismund, and Albert II, his successor, as King of the Romans. This, however, is merely a conjecture, and not a very probable one. Sigismund died before the commencement of the plague which is said to have been the occasion of the painting.

‡ Those verses, as they appeared in later times, are as follows :

"Heilig war ich auff Erd genant
Ohn Gott der höchst führt ich mein stand.
Der Ablass that mir gar wol lohnen
Doch will der tod mein nicht verschonen."

Their meaning may be thus expressed in English :

" His Holiness, on earth my name ;
From God my power never came ;
Although by pardons wealth I got,
Death, alas, will pardon not !"

had been originally painted or subsequently retouched. Had there been any record of Holbein having been at any time employed on the work, such a circumstance would most likely have been noticed; as his memory was then held in the highest estimation, and Basle prided herself on having had so eminent an artist enrolled among the number of her citizens. In 1658 the painting was again renewed: and there seems reason to believe that further alterations were then introduced both in the costume and the colouring. It was retouched in 1703; but from that time, as the paint began to peel off from the decaying walls, all attempts for its further preservation appear to have been considered hopeless. It would indeed seem to have become in a great measure disregarded by the magistrates, for a rope-maker used to exercise his trade under the roof that protected it from the weather. As the old wall stood much in the way of new buildings, it is not unlikely that they might be rather wishful to have it removed. In 1805 the magistrates pronounced sentence against the Dance of Death, and the wall on which it was painted was by their orders pulled down, though not without considerable opposition on the part of many of the citizens, more especially those of the suburb of St. John, within which the old church-court of the Dominicans stood. Several pieces of the painting were collected, and are still preserved at Basle as memorials of the old "Todten-tanz," which was formerly an object of curiosity with all strangers who visited the city, and which has been so frequently the subject of discussion in the history of art.

Mr. Douce has given a list of many books containing the figures of a Dance of Death printed before the celebrated Simulachres et Historiées Faces de la Mort of Lyons, 1538; and among the principal the following may be here enumerated.—A German edition, intitled "Der Dodtendanz mit figuren. Clage und Antwort schon von allen staten der Welt." This work, which is small folio, is mentioned in Braun's Notitia librorum in Bibliotheca ad SS. Udalricum et Afram Augustæ, vol. ii. p. 62. It is without date, but Braun supposes that it may have been printed between 1480 and 1500. It consists of twenty-two leaves, with wood-cuts of the Pope, Cardinal, Bishop, Abbot, &c. &c. accompanied by figures of Death. The descriptions are in German verse, and printed in double columns.—The earliest printed book on this subject with a date is intitled "La Danse Macabre imprimée par ung nommé Guy Marchand," &c. Paris, 1485, small folio. In 1486 Guy Marchand,—or Guyot Marchant, as he is also called,—printed another edition, "La Danse Macabre nouvelle," with several additional cuts; and in the same year he printed "La Danse Macabre des Femmes," a small folio of fifteen leaves. This is the first edition of the Macaber Dance of females. Thirty-two subjects are described, but there are only cuts of two, the

Queen and the Duchess. In 1490 an edition appeared with the following title: "Chorea ab eximio Macabro versibus Alemanicis edita, et à Petro Desrey emendata. Parisiis, per magistrum Guidonem Mercatorem [Guy Marchand] pro Godefrido de Marnef." In the same year Marchand printed another edition of "La nouvelle Danse Macabre des Hommes;" and in the year following there appeared from his press a second edition of "La Danse Macabre des Femmes," with cuts of all the characters and other additions. A Dance of Death, according to Von der Hagen, in his Deutsche Poesie, p. 459, was printed at Leipsic in 1496; and in 1499 a "Grande Danse Macabre des Hommes et Femmes" was printed in folio at Lyons. The latter is supposed to be the earliest that contains cuts of both men and women. About 1500, Ant. Verard printed an edition, in folio, of the Danse Macabre at Paris; and in various years between 1500 and 1530 a work with the same title and similar cuts was printed at Paris, Troyes, Rouen, Lyons, and Geneva. Besides those works, characters from the Dance of Death were frequently introduced as incidental illustrations in books of devotion, more especially in those usually denominated Horæ or Hours of the Virgin, and printed in France.*

The celebrated "Dance of Death," the cuts of which have been so generally ascribed to Hans Holbein as the engraver as well as designer, was first published at Lyons, in 1538. It is of small quarto size, and the title is as follows: "Les Simulachres & Historiées faces de la Mort, autant elegammēt pourtraictes, que artificiellement imaginées. A Lyon, Soubz l'escu de Cologne. M.D.XXXVIII." On the title-page is an emblematic wood-cut, very indifferently executed, representing three heads joined together, with a wreath above them; the middle one a full face, and those on each side in profile. Instead of shoulders, the heads, or busts, are provided with a pair of wings of peacock's feathers; they

---

* Several characters are to be found in those Dances of Death which do not occur in the Simulachres et Historiées Faces de la Mort of Lyons, 1538. In the preface to the Emblems of Mortality,—with wood-cuts by John Bewick, 1789,—written by John Sidney Hawkins, Esq., the following list is given of the cuts in an edition of "La grande Danse de Macabre des Hommes et Femmes," 4to. printed at Troyes for John Garnier, but without a date. "The Pope, Emperor, Cardinal, King, Legate, Duke, Patriarch, Constable, Archbishop, Knight, Bishop, Squire, Abbot, Bailiff, Astrologer, Burgess, Canon, Merchant, Schoolmaster, Man of Arms, Chartreux, Serjeant, Monk, Usurer, Physician, Lover, Advocate, Minstrel, Curate, Labourer, Proctor, Gaoler, Pilgrim, Shepherd, Cordelier, Child, Clerk, Hermit, Adventurer, Fool. The women are the Queen, Duchess, Regent's Wife, Knight's Wife, Abbess, Squire's Wife, Shepherdess, Cripple, Burgess's Wife, Widow, Merchant's Wife, Bailiff's Wife, Young Wife, Dainty Dame, Female Philosopher, New-married Wife, Woman with Child, Old Maid, Female Cordelier, Chambermaid, Intelligence-Woman, Hostess, Nurse, Prioress, Damsel, Country Girl, Old Chambermaid, Huckstress, Strumpet, Nurse for Lying-in-Woman, Young Girl, Religious, Sorceress, Bigot, Fool." Nearly the same characters occur in borders of the old Dutch Prayer Book mentioned at page 318, though in the latter they are yet more numerous; among the men there is a fowler—*vogelaer*—and among the women, the beauty—*scone*—and the old woman—*alde vrou*—which do not occur in the preceding list.

rest on a kind of pedestal, on which is also an open book inscribed with the maxim, "ΓΝΩΘΙ ΣΕΑΥΤΟΝ." A large serpent is seen confined by the middle in a hole which must be supposed to pass through the pedestal; and to it (the pedestal) are chained two globes,—one surmounted by a small cross, like the emblem of imperial authority, and the other having two wings. This emblematic cut, which is certainly not "l'escu de Coloigne," is accompanied with the motto "*Usus me Genuit.*"* At the conclusion of the book is the imprint, within an ornamental wood-cut border: "EXCVDEBANT LVGDVNI MELCHIOR ET GASPAR TRECHSEL FRATRES. 1538." The title is succeeded by a preface, of six pages, which is followed by seven pages more, descriptive of "diverses tables de Mort, non painctes, mais extraictes de l'escripture saincte, colorées par Docteurs Ecclesiastiques, et umbragées par Philosophes." After those verbal sketches of Death come the cuts, one on each page; and they are succeeded by a series of descriptions of death and reflections on mortality, the general title to which, commencing at signature H, is, "Figures de la Mort moralement descriptes, & depeinctes selon l'authorité de l'scripture, & des sainctz Peres."

By far the most important passage in the book, at least so far as relates to the designer or engraver of the cuts, occurs in the preface, which is written much in the style of a pedantic father-confessor to a nunnery who felt a pleasure in ornamenting his Christian discourses and exhortations with the flowers of Pagan eloquence. The preface is addressed, "A moult reverende Abbesse du religieux convent S. Pierre de Lyon, Madame Jehanne de Touszele, Salut dun vray Zele,"† and the passage above mentioned is to the following effect. "But to return to our figured representations of Death, we have greatly to regret the death of him who has imagined such elegant figures as are herein contained, as much excelling all those heretofore printed,‡ as the pictures of Apelles or of Zeuxis surpass those of modern times; for, his funereal histories,

---

* It has been thought necessary to be thus particular in describing the title-page of this rare edition, as it is incorrectly described by Mr. Douce. In the copy in the British Museum the title-page is wanting.

† This "vray Zele" having said in the first page of the preface that the name and surname of the revered abbess had the same sound as his own, with the exception of the letter T, the editor of the Emblems conjectures "that his name was JEAN, or, as it was anciently written, JEHAN de OUSZELL, or OZELL as it is now usually spelt."

‡ In the original, "avancantes autât les patronées jusques ici." The word *patronées*, I conceive to refer to cuts printed from wood-blocks. The editor of the Emblems, 1688, who is followed by Mr. Ottley, translated the passage, "exceeding all the *examples* hitherto." Works executed by means of a stencil were in old French said to be *patronées*, and the word also appears to have been applied to impressions printed from wood-blocks. The verb *patroner* is thus explained in Noel and Chapsal's Nouveau Dictionnaire de la Langue Française, Paris, 1828: "Terme de cartier: enduire de couleur, au moyen du patron évidé, les endroits où cette couleur doit paraître."

with their gravely versified descriptions, excite such admiration in beholders, that the figures of Death appear to them most life-like, while those of the living are the very pictures of mortality. It therefore seems to me that Death, fearing that this excellent painter would paint him in a manner so lively, that he should be no longer feared as Death, and apprehensive that the artist would thus become immortal, determined to shorten his days, and thus prevent him finishing other subjects which he had already drawn. Among these is one of a waggoner, knocked down and crushed under his broken waggon, the wheels and horses of which appear so frightfully shattered and maimed that it is as fearful to see their overthrow as it is amusing to behold the liquorishness of a figure of Death, who is perceived roguishly sucking the wine out of a broken cask, by means of a reed. To such imperfect subjects, as to the inimitable heavenly bow named Iris,* no one has ventured to put the last hand, on account of the bold drawing, perspectives, and shadows contained in this inimitable chef-d'œuvre, there so gracefully delineated, that from it we may derive a pleasing sadness and a melancholy pleasure, as in a thing mournfully delightful." The cut of the waggoner, described by the French euphuist, was, however, afterwards finished, and, with others, inserted in a subsequent edition of the work. It is figured in the present volume at page 344.

The number of cuts in the first edition, now under examination, is forty-one ; above each is a text of Scripture, in Latin ; and below are four verses in French—the "descriptions severement rithmées," mentioned in the preface—containing some moral or reflection germane to the subject. A few sets of impressions of all those cuts, except one, appear to have been taken before the work appeared at Lyons. They have been printed by means of a press,—not taken by friction in the manner in which wood engravers usually take their proofs,—and at the top of each cut is the name in the German language, but in Italic type. " Why those German names," says Hegner, " in a work which, so far as we know, was first published at Lyons ? They appear to confirm the opinion of the cuts having been actually engraved at Basle ; and the descriptions correspond with the dialect of that city." The late Mr. Ottley had impressions of forty of those original cuts, and six of those which were inserted in a later edition. In his Inquiry into the Origin and Early History of Engraving, Mr. Ottley, speaking of the Dance of Death, says : " It is certain that the cuts had been previously printed at Basle ; and, indeed, some writers assert that the work was published in that city, with texts of Scripture, in the German language, above the cuts, and verses, in the

* Mr. Douce supposes that the rainbow here alluded to was that which appears in the cut of the Last Judgment, the last but one in the first edition. The writer evidently means the natural rainbow which is mostly seen imperfect.

same language, underneath, as early as 1530; although, hitherto, I have been unable to meet with or hear of any person who had seen a copy of such an edition." In a note upon this passage, Jansen, the compiler of an Essay on the Origin of Engraving, and the anonymous author of a work entitled Notices sur les Graveurs, Besançon, 1807, are cited as mentioning such an edition. To give every one his due, however, and to show the original authority for the existence of such an edition, I beg here to give an extract from Papillon, who never felt any difficulty in supposing a date, and whose conjectures such writers as Jansen have felt as little hesitation in converting into certainties. The substance of Papillon's observations on this point is as follows: "But to return to Holbein's Dance of Death, which is unquestionably a master-piece of wood engraving. There are several editions; the first of which, *so far as may be judged*, ought to be about 1530, as has been already said,* and was printed at Basle or Zurich, with a title to each cut, and, *I believe*, verses underneath, all in the German language." What Papillon puts forth as a matter of conjecture and opinion, Von Murr, Jansen, and the author of the Notices sur les Graveurs, promulgate as facts, and Mr. Ottley refers to the two latter writers as if he were well inclined to give credit to their assertions.

From the following passage it would appear that Mr. Ottley had also been willing to believe that those impressions might have been accompanied with explanatory verses and texts of Scripture. "I have only to add, upon the subject of this celebrated work, that I am myself the fortunate possessor of forty pieces, (the complete series of the first edition, excepting one,) which are printed with the greatest clearness and brilliancy of effect, on one side of the paper only; each cut having over it its title, printed in the German language with moveable type. It is possible that they may originally have had verses underneath, and texts of Scripture above, in addition to the titles just mentioned: but as the margins are clipped on the sides and at bottom, it is now impossible to ascertain the fact." †

Had the forty impressions in question been accompanied with verses and texts of Scripture, they certainly might be considered as having

---

* Traité de la Gravure en Bois, tom. i. p. 168. Papillon in a preceding page had observed: "These cuts must have been engraved about 1530, for we find the four first among the little figures of the Old Testament printed in 1539, from which it is easy to perceive that many thousand impressions had already been taken from the blocks."—Those four cuts in the first edition of the Dance of Death, have not the slightest appearance of having been from blocks that had already furnished many thousand impressions. In the copy now before me, I cannot perceive a break or an imperfection in the most delicate lines. The first edition of the " Historiarum Veteris Testamenti Icones," to which Papillon alludes, first appeared in the same year as the Simulachres, 1538, and from the office of the same publishers, the brothers Melchior and Gaspar Trechsel.

† Inquiry into the Origin and Early History of Engraving, vol. ii. p. 762.

belonged to an earlier edition of the work than that of 1538, and for the existence of which Mr. Ottley has referred to the testimony of Jansen and the editor of the Notices sur les Graveurs, printed at Besançon. There is, however, a set of those cuts preserved in the public library at Basle, which seems clearly to prove that they had only been taken as specimens without any further accompaniment than the titles. They are printed on four folio leaves, on only one side of the paper, and there are ten cuts on each page ; the title, in the German language, and in Italic type, like Mr. Ottley's, is printed above each ; and the same cut —that of the astrologer—is also wanting. From these circumstances there can scarcely be a doubt that the set formerly belonging to Mr. Ottley* had been printed in the same manner, and that each impression had subsequently been cut out, perhaps for the purpose of mounting them singly. The following are the titles given to those cuts, and to each is subjoined a literal translation. They are numbered as they follow each other in LES SIMULACHRES ET HISTORIEES FACES DE LA MORT, 1538, which perhaps may not be incorrectly expressed by the English title, " Pictorial and Historical Portraits of Death."

1. *Die schöpfung aller ding*— The creation of all things.
2. *Adam Eua im Paradyfs*— Adam and Eve in Paradise.
3. *Vertribung Ade Eue*—The driving out of Adam and Eve.
4. *Adam baugt die erden*—Adam cultivates the earth.
5. *Gebeyn aller menschen*— Skeletons of all men.
6. *Der Papst*—The Pope.
7. *Der Keyser*—The Emperor.
8. *Der Künig*—The King.
9. *Der Cardinal*—The Cardinal.
10. *Die Keyserinn.*—The Empress.
11. *Die Küniginn*—The Queen.
12. *Der Bischoff*—The Bishop.
13. *Der Hertzog*—The Duke.
14. *Der Apt*—The Abbot.
15. *Die Aptissinn*—The Abbess.
16. *Der Edelman*—The Nobleman.
17. *Der Thümherr*—The Canon.
18. *Der Richter*—The Judge.
19. *Der Fürspräch*—The Advocate.
20. *Der Rahtsherr*—The Magistrate.
21. *Der Predicant*—The Preaching Friar.
22. *Der Pfarrherr*—The Parish-priest.
23. *Der Münch*—The Monk.
24. *Die Nunne*—The Nun.
25. *Dass Altweyb*—The Old Woman.

* Those cuts, with that of the astrologer and five others, supplied from a later edition, were bought, at the sale of Mr. Ottley's prints, in 1837, for the British Museum, for £37 10s. In the catalogue, which, I understand, was chiefly drawn up from his own memoranda, they are thus described, under the head " HANS HOLBEIN," No. 458: " THE CELEBRATED DANCE OF DEATH, first impressions, printed (probably at Basle, about 1530,) upon one side only, with German titles at the top in type ; supposed to be UNIQUE." That they were printed in 1530 is highly *improbable*, and they certainly are NOT *unique*.

26. *Der Artzet*—The Doctor.
27. (Wanting in the specimens.) The Astrologer.
28. *Der Rychman*—The Rich Man.
29. *Der Kauffman*—The Merchant.
30. *Der Schiffman*—The Sailor.
31. *Der Ritter*—The Knight.
32. *Der Graff*—The Count.
33. *Der Alt man*—The Old Man.

34. *Die Greffinn*—The Countess.
35. *Die Edelfraw*—The Lady.
36. *Die Hertzoginn*—The Duchess.
37. *Der Krämer*—The Pedlar.
38. *Der Ackerman*—The Farmer.
39. *Das Jung Kint*—The Young Child.
40. *Das Jüngst Gericht*—The Last Judgment.
41. *Die Wapen des Thots*—Death's coat-of-arms.

In 1542 a second edition of the Dance of Death, with the same cuts as the first, was published at Lyons, " Soubz l'escu de Coloigne," by John and Francis Frellon, who appear to have succeeded to the business of the brothers Trechsel,—if, indeed, the latter were not merely the printers of the first edition. In a third edition, with the title Imagines Mortis, 1545, the verses underneath each cut are in Latin.* A cut of a lame beggar, which has no relation to the Dance of Death, is introduced as a tail-piece to one of the discourses on death—Cypriani Sermo de Mortalitate—at the end of the volume ; but it is neither designed nor executed in the same style as the others.

In a fourth edition, with the title " Imagines Mortis,"† 1547, eleven additional cuts are introduced ; namely : 1. Death fighting with a soldier in Swiss costume ; 2. Gamblers, with a figure of Death, and another of the Devil ; 3. Drunkards, with a figure of Death ; 4. The Fool, with a figure of Death playing on the bagpipes ; 5. The Robber seized by Death ; 6. The Blind Man and Death ; 7. The Waggoner and Death ; 8. Children, one of whom is borne on the shoulders of the others as a conqueror triumphing ; 9. A child with a shield and dart ; 10. Three children ; one riding on an arrow, another on a bow, as on a hobby-horse, the third carrying a hare over his shoulder, suspended·from a hunting pole ; 11. Children as Bacchanalians. The last four subjects have no relation to a Dance of Death, but have evidently been introduced merely to increase the number of the cuts ; they are, however, beautifully designed and well engraved. This edition contains twelve more cuts, reckoning the tail-piece of the Lame Beggar, than the first. Another edition, forming the fifth, was also published in 1547 under the title of " Les Images de la

---

* The French verses were translated into Latin by George Æmylius, "an eminent German divine of Mansfelt," says Mr. Douce, " and the author of many pious works."

† Some copies have the title " Icones Mortis ;" and though they correspond in every other respect with those of the same year, intitled Imagines Mortis, Mr. Douce seems to consider that this trifling variation is a sufficient ground for describing them as different editions.

Mort," with French verses, as in the edition of 1538. The number of cuts is the same as in the edition of 1547 with Latin verses, and the title " Imagines Mortis," or " Icones Mortis."

In 1549, a sixth edition, with the same number of cuts as the last, was published, under the title of " Simolachri, Historie, e Figure de la Morte," with the letter-press in Italian, with the exception of the texts of Scripture, which were in Latin, as in the others. In the preface, John Frellon—whose name appears alone in the edition of 1547, and in those of subsequent years—complains of a piracy of the book, which was printed at Venice in 1545, with fac-similes of the cuts of the first edition. " Frellon, by way of revenge," says Mr. Douce, " and to save the trouble of making a new translation of the articles that compose the volume, made use of that of his Italian competitor."* A seventh edition, with the title " Icones Mortis," and containing fifty-three cuts, appeared, without any printer's name, in 1554.

In an eighth edition, 1562, with the title " Les Images de la Mort, auxquelles sont adjoustees dix-sept figures," five additional cuts are introduced, thus making seventeen more than are contained in the first. The total number of cuts in the edition of 1562 is fifty-eight ; and that of the Lame Beggar, which first appeared as a tail-piece in the edition of 1545, has now a place among the others in the body of the book. The subjects of the five new cuts are : 1. The Husband, with a figure of Death ; 2. The Wife,—Death leading a young woman by the hand, preceded by a young man playing on a kind of guitar ; 3. Children as part of a triumph, one of them as a warrior on horseback ; 4. Three children ; one with a trophy of armour, another carrying a vase and a shield, the third seated naked on the ground ; 5. Children with musical instruments. The subjects of children are designed and executed in the same style as those first introduced in the edition of 1547. The last of those five new cuts does not appear in regular order with the other fifty-seven ; but is given as a tail-piece at the end of a preface to a devotional tract—La Medicine de l'Ame—in the latter part of the book. Mr. Douce mentions another edition with the date 1574. He, however, observes in a note : " This edition is given on the authority of Peignot,† page 62, but has not been seen by the author of this work. In the year 1547 there were three editions, and it is not improbable that, by the transposition of the two last figures, one of these might have been intended." As one of Mr. Douce's *three* editions of 1547 differs only

---

* Dance of Death, p. 107, edit. 1833 (Bohn's edition, p. 95). It is stated in the Italian piracy that it was printed " *Con gratia e privilegio de l'Illustriss. Senato Vinitiano, per anni dieci. Appresso Vincenzo Vaugris, al Segno d'Erasmo.* MDXLV."

† Author of the work intitled, " Recherches sur les Danses des Morts." Dijon et Paris, 1826.

from another of the same date by having "*Icones*" instead of "*Imagines*" in the title-page, he might as consistently have claimed a fourth for the same year on the ground of a *probable* transposition of 74 for 47. All the authentic editions of the "Dance of Death," previously noticed, were published at Lyons. The first, as has been already observed, was in small quarto; the others are described by Mr. Douce as being in duodecimo. In a Dutch Dance of Death, intitled "De Doodt vermaskert met swerelts ydelheit," duodecimo, Antwerp, 1654, fourteen of the cuts, according to Mr. Douce, were from the original blocks which had been used in the Lyons editions.

It seems probable that the earliest copies of the cuts in "Les Simulachres et Historiées Faces de la Mort," or Dance of Death, as the work is more frequently called, appeared in a small folio, intitled "Todtentantz," printed at Augsburg in 1544, by "*Jobst Denecker, Form-schneyder.*" As I have never seen a copy of this edition, I take the liberty of extracting the following notice of it from Mr. Douce: "This edition is not only valuable from its extreme rarity, but for the very accurate and spirited manner in which the fine original cuts are copied. It contains all the subjects that were then published, but not arranged as those had been. It has the addition of one singular print, intitled, 'Der Eebrecher,' *i. e.* the Adulterer, representing a man discovering the adulterer in bed with his wife, and plunging his sword through both of them, Death guiding his hands. On the opposite page to each engraving there is a dialogue between Death and the party, and at bottom a Latin hexameter. The subject of the Pleader has the unknown mark ⅏ ; and on that of the Duchess in bed, there is the date 1542."* Mr. Douce is of opinion that the "*Jobst Denecker, Formschneyder,*" who appears as the printer, was the same person as Jobst or Jost de Negker, the wood engraver whose name is at the back of one of the cuts of the Triumphal Procession of Maximilian.—The next copy of the work is that intitled "Simolachri, Historie, e Figure de la Morte," Venice, 1545, the piracy complained of by Frellon in his Italian edition of 1549. It contains forty-one cuts, as in the first Lyons edition of 1538. There is no variation in the figures ; but the expression of the faces is frequently lost, and the general execution of the whole is greatly inferior to that of the originals. Another edition, in Latin, was published in 1546; and Mr. Douce says that there are impressions of the cuts on single sheets, at the bottom of one of which is the date 1568.—In 1555, an edition with the title "Imagines Mortis," with fifty-three cuts, similar to those in the Lyons edition of 1547, was published at Cologne by the heirs of Arnold Birkman, Cologne, 1555 ; and there are four other editions of the same work, respectively dated 1557, 1566, 1567, and 1572. Alterations are

* Dance of Death, p. 118. Edit. 1833.

made in some of those cuts ; in five of them the mark $\mathcal{A}$ is introduced ; and in the cut of the Duchess the mark 'ʃ , seen on the bed-frame in the original, is omitted. All the alterations are for the worse ; some of the figures seem like caricatures of the originals ; and the cuts generally are, in point of execution, very inferior to those in the Lyons editions. The name of the artist to whom the mark $\mathcal{A}$ belongs is unknown. In the preface to the Emblems of Mortality, page xx, the writer says it is "that of SILVIUS ANTONIANUS, an artist of considerable merit." This, however, is merely one of the blunders of Papillon, who, according to Mr. Douce, has converted the owner of this mark into a cardinal. Papillon, it would seem, had observed it on the cuts of an edition of Faerno's Fables—printed at Antwerp, 1567, and dedicated to Cardinal Borromeo by Silvio Antoniano, professor of Belles Lettres at Rome, afterwards a cardinal himself—and without hesitation he concluded that the editor was the engraver.* The last of the editions published in the sixteenth century with wood-cuts copied from the Lyons work, appeared at Wittemberg in 1590.

Various editions of the Dance of Death, with copper-plate engravings generally copied from the work published at Lyons, are enumerated by Mr. Douce, but only one of them seems to require notice here. Between 1647 and 1651 Hollar etched thirty subjects from the Dance of Death, introducing occasionally a few alterations. From a careful examination of those etchings, I am inclined to think that most of them were copied not from the cuts in any of the Lyons editions, but from those in the edition published by the heirs of Birkman at Cologne. The original copper-plates of Hollar's thirty etchings having come into the possession of Mr. James Edwards, formerly a bookseller in Pall-Mall, he published an edition in duodecimo, without date, but about 1794,† with preliminary observations on the Dance of Death, written by the late Mr. F. Douce. Those preliminary observations are the germ of Mr. Douce's beautiful and more complete volume, published by W. Pickering in 1833 (and re-published with additions by Mr. Bohn in 1858). As Petrarch's amatory sonnets and poems have been called " a labour of Love," with equal

---

* Mr. Douce gives another amusing instance of Papillon's sagacity in assigning marks and names to their proper owners. " He (Papillon) had seen an edition of the Emblems of Sambucus with cuts, bearing the mark $\mathcal{A}$, in which there is a fine portrait of the author with his favourite dog, and under the latter the word BOMBO, which Papillon gravely states to be the name of the engraver ; and finding the same word on another of the emblems, which has also the dog, he concludes that all the cuts which have not the $\mathcal{A}$ were engraved by the same BOMBO."—Dance of Death, p. 114, 1833. Those blunders of Papillon are to be found in his Traité Historique et Pratique de la Gravure en Bois, tom. i. pp. 238 et 525.

† Mr. Douce himself says, " about 1794." A copy in the British Museum, formerly belonging to the late Reverend C. M. Cracherode, has, however, that gentleman's usual mark, and the date 1793.

propriety may Mr. Douce's last work be intitled "a labour of Death." Scarcely a cut or an engraving that contains even a death's head and cross-bones appears to have escaped his notice. Incorporated is a *Catalogue raisonné* which contains an enumeration of all the tomb-stones in England and Wales that are ornamented with those standard "Emblems of Mortality,"—skull, thigh-bones in saltire, and hour-glass. In his last "Opus Magnum Mortis," the notices of the several Dances of Death in various parts of Europe are very much enlarged, but he has not been able to adduce any further arguments or evidences beyond what appeared in his first essay, to show that the cuts in the original edition of the Dance of Death, published at Lyons, were not designed by Holbein. Throughout the work there are undeniable proofs of the diligence of the collector; but no evidences of a mind that could make them available to a useful end. He is at once sceptical and credulous; he denies that any poet of the name of Macaber ever lived; and yet he believes, on the sole authority of one T. Nieuhoff Picard, whose existence is as doubtful as Macaber's, that Holbein painted a Dance of Death as large as life, in fresco, in the old palace at Whitehall.

Having now given a list of all the authentic editions of the Dance of Death and of the principal copies of it, I shall next, before saying any-thing about the supposed designer or engraver, lay before the reader a few specimens of the original cuts. Mr. Douce observes, of the forty-nine cuts given in his Dance of Death, 1833, that "they may be very justly regarded as scarcely distinguishable from their fine originals." Now, without any intention of depreciating these clever copies, I must pro-nounce them inferior to the originals, especially in the heads and hands. In this respect the wood-cuts of the first Lyons edition of the Dance of Death are unrivalled by any other productions of the art of wood engraving, either in past or present times. In the present day, when mere delicacy of cutting in the modern French taste is often mistaken for good engraving, there are doubtless many admirers of the art who fancy that there would be no difficulty in finding a wood engraver who might be fully competent to accurately copy the•originals in the first edition of the Dance of Death. The experiment, however, would pro-bably convince the undertaker of such a task, whoever he might be, that he had in this instance over-rated his abilities. Let the heads in the Lyons cuts, and those of any copies of them, old or recent, be examined with a magnifying glass, and the excellence of the former will appear still more decidedly than when viewed with the naked eye.

The following cut is a copy of the same size as the original, which is the second of the Dance of Death, of the edition of 1538. The subject is Adam and Eve eating of the forbidden fruit; and in the series of early impressions, formerly Mr. Ottley's, but now in the Print Room of the British Museum, it is intitled *"Adam Eva im Paradyss"*—Adam and Eve in Paradise. The serpent, as in many other old engravings, as well as in paintings, is represented with a human face. In order to convey an idea of the original page, this cut is accompanied with its explanatory text and verses printed in similar type.

Quia audifti vocem vxoris tuæ, & comedifti
de ligno ex quo preceperam tibi ne come=
deres &c.

G E N E S I S   I I I

A D A M fut par E V E deceu
Et contre D I E V mangea la pomm
Dont tous deux ont la Mort receu,
Et depuis fut mortel tout homme.
C

In the two first cuts, which represent the Creation of Eve, and Adam taking the forbidden fruit, the figure of Death is not seen. In the third, Adam and Eve driven out of Paradise, Death, playing on a kind of lyre, is seen preceding them; and in the fourth, Adam cultivating the earth, Death is perceived assisting him in his labour. In the fifth, intitled *Gebeyn aller menschen*—Skeletons of all men—in the early impressions of the cuts, formerly belonging to Mr. Ottley, but now in the British Museum, all the figures are skeletons; one of them is seen beating a pair of kettle drums, while others are sounding trumpets, as if rejoicing in the power which had been given to Death in consequence of the fall of man. The texts above this cut are, "Væ væ væ habitantibus in terra. APOCALYPSIS VIII ;" and "Cuncta in quibus spiraculum vitæ est, mortua sunt. GENESIS VII." In the sixth cut there are two figures of Death,— one grinning at the pope as he bestows the crown on a kneeling emperor, and the other, wearing a cardinal's hat, as a witness of the ceremony. In the thirty-sixth cut, the Duchess, there are two figures of Death introduced, and there are also two in the thirty-seventh, the Pedlar ; but in all the others of this edition, from the seventh to the thirty-ninth, inclusive, there is only a single figure of Death, and in every instance his action and expression are highly comic, most distinctly evincing that man's destruction is his sport. In the fortieth cut there is no figure of Death ; the Deity seated on a rainbow, with his feet resting on the globe, is seen pronouncing final judgment on the human race. The forty-first, and last cut of the original edition, represents Death's coat-of-arms—*Die wapen des Thots.* On an escutcheon, which is rent in several

places, is a death's-head, with something like a large worm proceeding from the mouth ; above the escutcheon, a barred helmet, seen in front like that of a sovereign prince, is probably intended to represent the power of Death ; the crest is a pair of fleshless arms holding something like a large stone immediately above an hour-glass ; on the dexter side of the escutcheon stands a gentleman, who seems to be calling the attention of the spectator to this memento of Death, and on the opposite side is a lady ; in the distance are Alpine mountains, the top of the highest partly shaded by a cloud. The appropriate text is, "Memorare novis-

sima, et in æternum non peccabis. Eccle. vii ; " and the following are
the verses underneath :

> " Si tu veulx vivre sans peché
> Voy ceste imaige a tous propos,
> Et point ne seras empesché
> Quand tu t'en iras en repos."

The total number of cuts of the first edition in which Death is seen
attending on men and women of all ranks and conditions, mocking them,
seizing them, slaying them, or merrily leading them to their end, is
thirty-seven.

> Spiritus meus attenuabitur, dies mihi bre=
> viabuntur, & folum mihi fupereft fepul=
> chrum.

> IOB   XVII

> Mes efperitz font attendriz,
> Et ma uie f'en ua tout beau.
> Las mes longz iours font amoindriz
> Plus ne me refte qu'un tombeau.

The above cut is a copy of the thirty-third, the Old Man—*Der Alt
man*—whom Death leads in confiding imbecility to the grave, while he

pretends to support him and to amuse him with the music of a dulcimer. The text and verses are given as they stand in the original.

The following cut is a copy of the thirty-sixth, the Duchess—*Die Hertzoginn.* In this cut, as has been previously observed, there are two figures of Death ; one rouses her from the bed—where she appears to have been indulging in an afternoon nap—by pulling off the coverlet,

De lectulo fuper quem afcendi=
fti non defcendes, fed morte
morieris.

I I I   R E G.   I

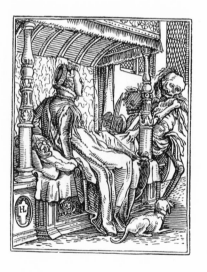

Du lict fus lequel as monté
Ne defcendras a ton plaifir.
Car Mort t'aura tantoft dompté,
Et en brief te uiendra faifir.

while the other treats her to a tune on the violin. On the frame of the bed, or couch, to the left, near the bottom of the cut, is seen the mark H, which has not a little increased the difficulty of arriving at any clear and unquestionable conclusion with respect to the designer or engraver of those cuts. The text and the verses are given literally, as in the two preceding specimens.

The following cut, the Child—*Das Iung Kint*—is a copy of the thirty-ninth, and the last but two in the original edition. Death having been represented in the preceding cuts as beguiling men and women in court and council-chamber, in bed-room and hall, in street and field, by sea and by land, is here represented as visiting the dilapidated cottage of the poor, and, while the mother is engaged in cooking, seizing her youngest child.

Homo natus de muliere, brevi vivens tempore
repletur multis miferiis, qui quafi flos egre=
ditur, & conteritur, & fugit velut umbra.

I O B   X I I I I

Tout homme de la femme yffant
Remply de mifere, & d'encombre,
Ainfi que fleur toft finiffant,
Sort & puis fuyt comme faict l'umbre.

The cut of the Waggon overturned, from which the following is copied, first appeared with ten others in the edition of 1547. From an inspection of this cut, which most probably is that mentioned as being left unfinished, in the prefatory address to Madame Jehanne de Touszele in the first edition, 1538, it will be perceived that the description which is there given of it is not correct, and hence arises a doubt if the writer had actually seen it. He describes the driver as knocked down, and lying bruised under his broken waggon, and he says that the figure of Death is perceived roguishly sucking the wine out of a broken cask by means of a reed.* In the cut itself, however, the waggoner is seen standing, wringing his hands as if in despair on account of the accident, and a figure of Death,—for there are two in this cut,—instead of sucking the wine, appears to be

Il cheut en son chariot.

I.   R O I S   IX.

Au passage de MORT perverse
Raison, Chartier tout esperdu,
Du corps le char, & chevaux verse,
Le vin (sang de vie) esperdu.

engaged in undoing the rope or chain by which the cask is secured to the waggon. A second figure of Death is perceived carrying off one of the waggon-wheels. In this cut the subject is not so well

---

* Mr. Douce, when correcting the mistake of the writer of the address, commits an error himself. He says that "Death is in the act of untwisting the *fastening to one of the hoops*." Now, it is very evident that he is undoing the rope or chain that steadies the cask and confines it to the waggon. He has hold of the stake or piece of wood, which serves as a *twitch* to tighten the rope or chain, in the manner in which large timber is secured to the waggon in the present day.

treated as in most of those in the edition of 1538 ; and it is also
not so well engraved.—The text and verses annexed are from the
edition of 1562.

Of the eleven additional cuts inserted in the edition of 1547, there
are four of children, which, as has already been observed in page 334,
have not the slightest connexion with the Dance of Death. The following
is a copy of one of them. The editor seems to have found no difficulty

Il sera percé de sagettes.

E X O D.   X I X.

L'eage du sens, du sang l'ardeur
Est legier dard, & foible escu
Contre MORT, qui un tel dardeur
De son propre dard rend vaincu.

in providing the subject with a text; and it serves as a peg to hang
a quatrain on as well as the others which contain personifications
of Death.

In the edition of 1562 five more cuts are inserted ; but two of them
only—the Bridegroom and the Bride—have relation to the Dance of
Death ; the other three are of a similar character to the four cuts of
children first inserted in the edition of 1547. All the seven cuts of

children have been evidently designed by the same person. They are well engraved, but not in so masterly a style as the forty-one cuts of the original edition. The following is a copy of one of the three which were inserted in the edition of 1562.

Having now given what, perhaps, may be considered a sufficiently ample account of the Lyons Dance of Death, it next appears necessary to make some enquiries respecting the designer of the cuts. Until the publication of Mr. Douce's observations, prefixed to the edition of

Il partira les despoilles avec les puissans.

I S A I E   L I I I.

Pour les victoires triumphées
Sur les plus forts des humains cœurs,
Les despoilles dresse en trophées
La MORT vaincresse des vainqueurs.

Hollar's etchings from those cuts, by Edwards, about 1794, scarcely any writer who mentions them seems to entertain a doubt of their having been designed by Holbein; and Papillon, in his usual manner, claims him as a wood engraver, and unhesitatingly declares that not only the cuts of the Lyons Dance of Death, but all the other cuts which are generally supposed to have been of his designing, were engraved by himself. Mr. Douce's arguments are almost entirely negative,—for he produces no satisfactory evidence to show that those cuts were certainly designed by some other artist,—and they are chiefly founded on the passage in the first Lyons edition, where the writer speaks of the death of the person "qui nous en a icy imaginé si elegantes figures."

The sum of Mr. Douce's objections to Holbein being the designer of the cuts in question is as follows. "The singularity of this curious and interesting dedication is deserving of the utmost attention. It seems very strongly, if not decisively, to point out the edition to which it is prefixed, as the first ; and what is of still more importance, to deprive Holbein of any claim to the invention of the work. It most certainly uses such terms of art as can scarcely be mistaken as conveying any other sense than that of originality of design. There cannot be words of plainer import than those which describe the painter, as he is expressly called, *delineating* the subjects and leaving several of them unfinished : and whoever the artist might have been, it clearly appears that he was not living in 1538. Now, it is well known that Holbein's death did not take place before the year 1554, during the plague which ravaged London at that time. If then the expressions used in this dedication signify anything, it may surely be asked what becomes of any claim on the part of Holbein to the designs of the work in question, or does it not *at least* remain in a situation of doubt and difficulty ? " * With respect to the true import of the passage referred to, my opinion is almost directly the reverse of that expressed by Mr. Douce.

What the writer of the address to Madame Jehanne de Touszele, in the Lyons edition of 1538, says respecting the unfinished cuts, taken all together, seems to relate more properly to the engraver than the designer ; more especially when we find that a cut—that of the Waggoner,—expressly noticed by him as being then unfinished, was given with others of a similar character in a subsequent edition.

From the incorrect manner in which the cut of the Waggoner is described, I am very much inclined to think that the writer had neither seen the original nor the other subjects already traced—the "*plusieurs aultres figures jà par luy trassées*"—of whose "bold drawing, perspectives, and shadows," he speaks in such terms of admiration. If the writer knew little of the process of wood engraving, he would be very likely to commit the mistake of supposing that the engraver was also the designer of the cuts. Though I consider it by no means unlikely that the engraver might have been dead before the publication of the first edition, yet I am very much inclined to believe that the passage in which the cuts are mentioned is purposely involved in obscurity : the writer, while he speaks of the deceased artist in terms of the highest commendation, at the same time carefully conceals his name. If the account in the preface be admitted as correct, it would

* Dance of Death, p. 88. Edit. 1833. (Bohn's edit. 1858, p. 77.)

appear that the cuts were both designed and engraved by the same
person, and that those already drawn on the block * remained unfinished
in consequence of his decease; for if he were *not* the engraver, what
prevented the execution of the other subjects already traced, and of
which the bold drawing, perspective, and shadows, all so gracefully
delineated, are distinctly mentioned ? The engraver, whoever he might
be, was certainly not only the best of his age, but continues unsurpassed
to the present day, and I am satisfied that such precision of line as is
seen in the heads could only be acquired by great practice. The designs
are so excellent in drawing and composition, and so admirably are the
different characters represented,—with such spirit, humour, and appropriate expression,—that to have produced them would confer additional
honour on even the greatest painters of that or any other period. Are we
then to suppose that those excellencies of design and of engraving were
combined in an obscure individual whose name is not to be found in
the roll of fame, who lived comparatively unknown, and whose death
is only incidentally noticed in an ambiguous preface written by a nameless pedant, and professedly addressed to an abbess whose very existence
is questionable ? † Such a supposition I conceive to be in the highest
degree improbable ; and, on the contrary, I am perfectly satisfied that
the cuts in question were *not* designed and engraved by the same
person. Furthermore, admitting the address to Madame Jehanne de
Touszele to be written in good faith, I am firmly of opinion that the
person whose death is there mentioned, was the engraver, and not the
designer of the cuts of the first edition.

The mark **H**, in the cut of the Duchess, is certainly not Holbein's ;
and Mr. Douce says, "that it was intended to express the name of the
designer, cannot be supported by evidence of any kind." That it is not
the mark of the designer, I agree with Mr. Douce, but my conclusion is
drawn from premises directly the reverse of his ; for had I not found
evidence elsewhere to convince me that this mark can only be that
of the engraver, I should most certainly have concluded that it was
intended for the mark of the designer. In direct opposition to what
Mr. Douce here says, up to the time of the publication of the Lyons

---

* The words "*jà par luy trassées*" will apply more properly to drawings already made on
the block, but unengraved, than to unfinished drawings on paper. It is indeed almost certain that the writer meant the former, for their " *audacieux traictz, perspectives, et umbrages*"
are mentioned ; they were moreover "*gracieusement deliniées.*" These expressions will apply
correctly to a finished, though unengraved design on the block, but scarcely to an unfinished
drawing on paper.

† I am very much inclined to think that Madame Jehanne de Touszele is a fictitious
character. I have had no opportunities of learning if such a person were really abbess of
the Convent of St. Peter at Lyons in 1538, and must therefore leave this point to be decided
by some other enquirer.

Dance of Death, the mark on wood-cuts is most frequently that of the designer, and whenever that of the engraver appears, it is as an exception to the general custom. It is, in fact, upon the evidence of the mark alone that the greater part of the wood-cut designs of Durer, Cranach, Burgmair, Behaim, Baldung, Grün, and other old masters, are respectively ascribed to them. The cuts of the Triumphal Procession of Maximilian with Hans Burgmair's mark in front, and the names of the engravers written at the back of the blocks, may serve as an illustration of the general practice, which is directly the reverse of Mr. Douce's opinion. If the weight of probability be not on the opposite side, the mark in question ought certainly, according to the usual practice of the period, to be considered as that of the designer.

In a subsequent page of the same chapter, Mr. Douce most inconsistently says, " There is an unfortunate ambiguity connected with the marks that are found on ancient engravings on wood, and it has been a *very great error* on the part of all the writers who treat on such engravings, in referring the marks that accompany them to the block-cutters, or as the Germans properly denominate them the *formschneiders*, whilst, perhaps, the greatest part of them really belong to the designers." He commits in the early part of the chapter the very error which he ascribes to others. According to his own principles, as expressed in the last extract, he was bound to allow the mark H_L to be that of the designer until he could show on probable grounds that it was not. But though Mr. Douce might deny that Holbein were the designer of those cuts, it seems that he durst not venture to follow up the line of his argument, and declare that Hans Lutzelburger *was* the designer, which he certainly might have done with at least as much reason as has led him to decide that Holbein *was not*. But he prudently abstained from venturing on such an affirmation, the improbability of which, notwithstanding the mark, might have led his readers to inquire, how it happened that so talented an artist should have remained so long undiscovered, and that even his contemporaries should not have known him as the designer of those subjects.

Though I am satisfied that the mark H_L is that of the *engraver* of the cuts in the first edition of the Lyons Dance of Death, I by no means pretend to account for its appearing alone—thus forming an exception to the general rule—without the mark of the designer, and without any mention of his name either in the title or preface to the book. We have no knowledge of the connexion in the way of business between the working wood engravers and the designers of that period ; but there seems reason to believe that the former sometimes got drawings made at their own expense and risk, and, when engraved, either published them on their own account, or disposed of them to booksellers and printers. It is also to be observed that about the time of the publication of the first Lyons edition of the Dance of Death, or a few years before, wood engravers began to occasionally introduce their name or mark into the cut, in addition to that of the designer. A cut, in a German translation of Cicero de Officiis, Frankfort, 1538, contains two marks; one of them being that of Hans Sebald Behaim, and the other, the letters H. W., which I take to be that of the engraver. At a later period this practice became more frequent, and a considerable number of wood-cuts executed between 1540 and 1580 contain two marks; one of the designer, and the other of the engraver : in wood-cuts designed by Virgil Solis in particular, double marks are of frequent occurrence. As it seems evident that the publishers of the Lyons Dance of Death were desirous of concealing the name of the designer, and as it appears likely that they had purchased the cuts ready engraved from a Swiss or a German,— for the designs are certainly not French,—it surely cannot be surprising that he should wish to affix his mark to those most admirable specimens of art. Moreover, if those cuts were not executed under the personal superintendence of the designer, but when he was chiefly resident in a distant country, the engraver would thus have the uncontrolled liberty of inserting his own mark ; and more especially, if those cuts were a private speculation of his own, and not executed for a publisher who had employed an artist to make the designs. Another reason, perhaps equally as good as any of the foregoing, might be suggested; as those cuts are decidedly the best executed of any of that period, the designer —even if he had opportunities of seeing the proofs—might have permitted the mark of the engraver to appear on one of them, in approbation of his talent.

This mark, H‾L, was first assigned to a wood engraver named Hans Lutzelburger, by M. Christian von Mechel, a celebrated engraver of Basle, who in 1780 published forty-five copper-plate engravings of a Dance of Death from drawings said to be by Holbein, and which almost in every respect agree with the corresponding cuts in the Lyons work, though of greater size.* M. Mechel's conjecture respecting the

* Mechel's work is in folio, with four subjects on each full page, and is entitled " Oeuvre de Jean Holbein, ou Receuil de Gravures d'après ses plus beaux ouvrages, &c. Première Partie. La Triomphe de Mort." It is dedicated to George III, and the presentation copy is in the King's Library at the British Museum. The first part contains, besides forty-five subjects of the Dance of Death, the design for the sheath of a dagger from a drawing ascribed to Holbein, which has been re-engraved in the work of Mr. Douce. It is extremely doubtful if the drawings of the Dance, from which Mechel's engravings are copied, be really by Holbein. They were purchased by M. Fleischmann of Strasburg, at Crozat's sale at Paris in 1741. It was stated in the catalogue that they had formed part of the Arundelian collection, and that they had afterwards come into the possession of Jan Bockhorst, commonly called Lang Jan, a contemporary of Vandyke. This piece of information, however, can only be received as an auctioneer's puff. M. Mechel himself, according to Mr. Douce, had not

engraver of those cuts appears to have been first published in the sixteenth volume of Von Murr's Journal ; but though I am inclined to think that he is correct, it has not been satisfactorily shown that Hans Lutzelburger ever used the mark **H**. He, however, lived at that period, and it is almost certain that he executed an alphabet of small initial letters representing a Dance of Death, which appear to have been first used at Basle by the printers Bebelius and Cratander about 1530. We give (on the following page) the entire series. He is also supposed to have engraved two other alphabets of ornamental initial letters, one representing a dance of peasants, " intermixed," says Mr. Douce, " with other subjects, some of which are not of the most delicate nature ; " the other representing groups of children in various playful attitudes. All those three alphabets are generally described by German and Swiss writers on art as having been designed by Holbein ; and few impartial persons I conceive can have much doubt on the subject, if almost perfect identity between most of the figures and those in his known productions be allowed to have any weight.

There is a set of proofs of the alphabet of the Dance of Death, printed on one sheet, preserved in the Public Library at Basle, and underneath is printed in moveable letters the name H𝔞𝔫𝔫𝔰 𝔏ü𝔱𝔷𝔢𝔩𝔟𝔲𝔯𝔤𝔢𝔯 𝔣𝔬𝔯𝔪𝔩𝔠𝔥𝔫𝔦𝔡𝔢𝔯, 𝔤𝔢𝔫𝔞𝔫𝔫𝔱 𝔍𝔯𝔞𝔫𝔠𝔨,—that is, " Hanns Lutzelburger, wood engraver, named Franck." The first H is an ornamented Roman capital; the other letters of the name are in the German character. The size of the cuts in this alphabet of the Dance of Death is one inch by seven-eighths. The reason for supposing that Hans Lutzelburger was the engraver of the cuts in the first edition of the Lyons Dance of Death are : 1. The similarity of style between the latter and those of the Basle alphabet of the same subject ; and 2. The correspondence of the mark in the cut of the Duchess with the initial letters of the name H[ans] L[utzelburger], and the fact of his being a wood engraver of that period. Mr. Douce, in the seventh chapter of his work, professes to

been able to trace those drawings previously to their falling into the hands of Monsieur Crozat. They were purchased of M Fleischmann by Prince Gallitzin, a Russian nobleman, by whom they were lent to M. Mechel. They are now in the Imperial Library at Petersburg. According to Mr. Coxe, who saw them when in M. Mechel's possession, they were drawn with a pen, and slightly shaded with Indian ink. Hegner, in his Life of Holbein, speaks slightingly of Mechel's engravings, which he says were executed by one of his workmen from copies of the pretended original drawings made by an artist named Rudolph Schellenburg of Winterthur. Those copper-plates certainly appear feeble when compared with the wood-cut in the Lyons work, and Hegner's criticism on the figure of Eve seems just, though Mr. Douce does not approve of it. Hegner says, " Let any one compare the figure of Eve under the tree in Mechel's second plate with the second wood-cut ; in the former she is sitting in as elegant an attitude as if she belonged to a French family by Boucher."—Boucher, a French painter, who died in 1770, was famous in his time for the pretty women introduced into his landscapes.

examine the "claim of Hans Lutzelburger as to the design or execution of the Lyons engravings of the Dance of Death," but his investigations seem very unsatisfactory; and his chapter is one of those "in which," as Fielding says, "nothing is concluded." He gives no opinion as to whether Lutzelburger was the designer of the Lyons cuts or not, though this is one of the professed topics of his investigation; and even his opinion, for the time being, as to the engraver, only appears in the heading of the following chapter, where it is thus announced : "*List of several editions of the Lyons work on the Dance of Death, with the mark of Lutzenburger.*"* His mind, however, does not appear to have been finally made up on this point; for in a subsequent page, 215, speaking of the mark **H** in the cut of the Duchess, which he had previously mentioned as that of Hans Lutzelburger, he says, "*but to whomsoever this mark may turn out to belong,* certain it is that Holbein never made use of it." His only unalterable decision appears to be that Holbein did not design the cuts of the Lyons Dance of Death, and in support of it he puts forth sundry arguments which are at once absurd and inconsistent; rejects unquestionable evidence which makes for the contrary opinion; and admits the most improbable that seems to favour his own.

Mr. Douce, in his seventh chapter, also gives a list of cuts, which he says were executed by Hans Lutzelburger; but out of the seven single cuts and three alphabets which he enumerates, I am inclined to think that Lutzelburger's name is only to be found attached to one single cut and to one alphabet,—the latter being that of the initial letters representing a Dance of Death. The single cut to which I allude—and which, I believe, is the only one of the kind that has his name underneath it,— represents a combat in a wood between some naked men and a body of peasants. Within the cut, to the left, is the mark, probably of the designer, on a reversed tablet, thus ; and underneath is the following inscription, from a separate block : HANNS . LEUCZELLBURGER . FURMSCHNIDER × 1.5.2.2. An impression of this cut is preserved in the Public Library at Basle ; and an alphabet of Roman capitals, engraved on wood, is printed on the same folio, below Lutzelburger's name. In not one of the other single cuts does this engraver's name occur, nor in fact any mark that can be fairly ascribed to him. The seventh cut, described by Mr. Douce,—a copy of Albert Durer's Decollation of John the Baptist,—is ascribed to Lutzelburger on the authority of Zani. According to this writer,—for I have not seen the cut myself any more than Mr. Douce,—it has "the mark H. L. reversed," which perhaps may prove to be L. H. "In the index of names," says Mr. Douce, "he (Zani) finds his name thus written, HANS

---

* Mr. Douce in every instance spells the name thus. In the proofs of the alphabet of the Dance of Death it is *Lützelburger*, and below the cut with the date 1522, *Leuczellburger*.

A A

LUTZELBURGER FORMSCHNIDER GENANT (chiamato) FRANCK, and calls him the true prince of engravers on wood." In what index Zani found the reversed mark thus expounded does not appear; I, however, am decidedly of opinion that there is no wood-cut in existence with the mark H. L. which can be ascribed with anything like certainty to Lutzelburger ; and his name is only to be found at length *under* the cut of the Fight above mentioned, and printed in moveable characters on the sheet containing the proofs of the alphabet of the Dance of Death.* The title of "true prince of engravers on wood," given by Zani to Lutzelburger, can only be admitted on the supposition of his being the engraver of the cuts in the first edition of the Lyons Dance of Death ; but it yet remains to be proved that he ever used the mark H.L or the separate letters H. L. on any previous or subsequent cut. Though, from his name appearing on the page containing the alphabet of the Dance of Death, and from the correspondence of his initials with the mark in the cut of the Duchess in the Lyons Dance of Death, I am inclined to think that he was the engraver of the cuts in the latter work, yet I have thought it necessary to enter thus fully into the grounds of his pretensions to the execution of those, and other wood engravings, in order that the reader may judge for himself.

Hegner, in his Life of Holbein, treats the claims that have been advanced on behalf of Lutzelburger too lightly. He not only denies that he was the engraver of the cuts in the first edition of the Lyons work, but also that he executed the cuts of the alphabet of the Dance of Death, although his name with the addition of "wood engraver"—*form-schnider*—be printed on the sheet of proofs. If we cannot admit the inscription in question as evidence of Lutzelburger being the engraver of this alphabet, we may with equal reason question if any wood engraver actually executed the cut or cuts under which his name only appears printed in type, or which may be ascribed to him in the title of a book. Mr. Douce, speaking of the three alphabets,—of peasants, boys, and a Dance of Death,—all of which he supposes to have been engraved by Lutzelburger, says that the proofs "may have been deposited by him in his *native* city," meaning Basle. Hegner, however, says that there is no trace of him to be found either in registers of baptism or burger-lists of Basle. He further adds, though I by no means concur with him in this opinion, "It is indeed likely that, as a travelling dealer in works of art— who, according to the custom of that period, took up their temporary residence sometimes in one place, sometimes in another,—he had obtained possession of those blocks, [of the alphabet of Death's Dance, and the Fight, with his name,] and that he sold impressions from them in

---

* There are proofs of this alphabet in the Royal Collection at Dresden, as well as in the Public Library at Basle.

the way of trade."* Mr. Douce says that it may admit of a doubt
whether the alphabets ascribed to Lutzelburger were cut on metal or
on wood. It may admit of a doubt, certainly, with one who knows very
little of the practice of wood engraving, but none with a person who is
accustomed to see cuts executed in a much more delicate style by wood
engravers of very moderate abilities. To engrave them on wood, would
be comparatively easy, so far as relates to the mere delicacy of the lines ;
but it would be a task of great difficulty to engrave them in relief in
any metal which should be much harder than that of which types are
composed. To suppose that they might have been executed in type-
metal, on account of the delicacy of the lines, would involve a contradiction ; for not only can finer lines be cut on box-wood than on type-metal,
but also with much greater facility.

It perhaps may not be unnecessary to give here two instances of the
many vague and absurd conjectures which have been propounded
respecting the designer or the engraver of the cuts in the Lyons editions
of the Dance of Death. In a copy of this work of the edition 1545
now in the British Museum, but formerly belonging to the Reverend C.
M. Cracherode, a portrait of a painter or engraver named Hans Ladenspelder is inserted opposite to the cut of the Duchess, as if in support of
the conjecture that *he* might be the designer of those cuts, merely from
the circumstance of the initial letters of his name corresponding with
the mark **HL**. The portrait is a small oval engraved on copper, with
an ornamental border, round which is the following inscription : "Imago
Joannis Ladenspelder, Essendiensis, Anno ætatis suæ xxviii. 1540." †
The mark **L** is perceived on this portrait, and underneath is written the
following MS. note, referring to the mark in the cut of the Duchess :
"**HL** the mark of the designer of these designs of Death's Dance, not
H. Holbein. By several persons that have seen Holbein's Death Dance
at Basil, it is not like these, nor in the same manner." This note, so far
as relates to the implied conjecture about Ladenspelder, may be allowed
to pass without remark for what it is worth ; but it seems necessary to
remind the reader that the painting of the Dance of Death at Basle, here
evidently alluded to, *was not* the work of Holbein, and to observe that
this note is not in the handwriting of Mr. Cracherode, but that it has
apparently been written by a former owner of the volume.

In a copy of the first edition, now lying before me, a former owner
has written on the fly-leaf the following verses from page 158 of the
Nugæ—Lyons, 1540,—of Nicholas Borbonius, a French poet :

* Hans Holbein der Jüngere, S. 332.

† Hans Ladenspelder was a native of Essen, a frontier town in the duchy of Berg. The
following mark is to be found on his engravings $\frac{s}{\sqrt{\cdot}}$, which Bartsch thinks may be
intended for the single letters I. L. V. E. S.,—representing the words *Joannes Ladenspelder
Von Essen Sculpsit.*

> " Videre qui vult Parrhasium cum Zeuxide,
>   Accersat a Britannia
>   Hansum Ulbium, et Georgium Reperdium
>   Lugduno ab urbe Galliæ."

The meaning of these verses may be thus expressed in English :

> Whoever wishes to behold,
> Painters like to those of old,
> To England straightway let him se d,
> And summon Holbein to attend ;
> Reperdius,* too, from Lyons bring,
> A city of the Gallic King.

To the extract from Borbonius,—or Bourbon, as he is more frequently called, without the Latin termination,—the writer has added a note : " *An Reperdius harum Iconum sculptor fuerit ?* " That is : " Query, if Reperdius were the engraver of these cuts ? "—meaning the cuts contained in the Lyons Dance of Death. Mr. Douce also cites the preceding verses from Nicholas Bourbon ; and upon so slight and unstable a foundation he, *more solito*, raises a ponderous superstructure. He, in fact, says, that " it is *extremely probable* that he might have begun the work in question [the designs for the Dance of Death], and have died before he could complete it, and that the Lyons publishers might have afterwards employed Holbein to finish what was left undone, as well as to make designs for additional subjects which appeared in the subsequent editions. Thus would Holbein be so connected with the work as to obtain in future such notice as would constitute him by general report the real inventor of it."

Perhaps in the whole of the discussion on this subject a more tortuous piece of argument is not to be found. It strikingly exemplifies Mr Douce's eagerness to avail himself of the most trifling circumstance which seemed to favour his own views ; and his manner of twisting and twining it is sufficient to excite a suspicion even in the mind of the most careless inquirer, that the chain of argument which consists of a series of such links must be little better than a rope of sand. Mr. Douce must have had singular notions of probability, when, upon the mere mention of the name of Reperdius, by Bourbon, as a painter then residing at Lyons, he asserts that it is *extremely probable* that he, Reperdius, might have begun the work : it is evident that he does not employ the term in its usual and proper sense. If for " *extremely probable* " the words " *barely possible* " be substituted, the passage will be unobjectionable ; and will then fairly represent the value of the conjecture of Reperdius having designed any of the cuts in question. If it be *extremely probable*

---

* Of this George Reperdius, or his works, nothing, I believe, is known beyond the brief mention of his name in conjunction with that of Holbein in the verses of Bourbon.

that the cuts of the first edition of the Lyons Dance of Death were designed by Reperdius, from the mere occurrence of his name in Bourbon, the evidence in favour of their being designed by Holbein ought with equal reason to be considered as *plusquam-perfect ;* for the voices of his contemporaries are expressly in his favour, the cuts themselves bear a strong general resemblance to those which are known to be of his designing, and some of the figures and details in the cuts of the Dance of Death correspond so nearly with others in the Bible-cuts designed by Holbein, and also printed at Lyons by the brothers Trechsel, and in the same year, that there cannot be a doubt in the mind of any impartial inquirer who shall compare them, that either both series must have been designed by the same person, or that Holbein had servilely copied the works of an unknown artist greater than himself. Upon one of the horns of this dilemma, Mr. Douce, and all who assert that the cuts of the Lyons Dance of Death *were not designed by Holbein,* must inevitably be fixed.

One of the earliest evidences in favour of Holbein being the designer of the cuts in the Lyons Dance of Death is Nicholas Bourbon, the author of the epigram previously cited. In an edition of his Nugæ, published at Basle in 1540, are the following verses :*

De morte picta à Hanso pictore nobili.

Dum mortis Hansus pictor imaginem exprimit,
Tanta arte mortem retulit ut mors vivere
Videatur ipsa : et ipse se immortalibus
Parem Diis fecerit operis hujus gloria.

Now,—after premising that the term *picta* was applied to designs engraved on wood, as well as to paintings in oil or water-colours,†—it may be asked to what work of Holbein's do these lines refer? The painting in the church-court at Basle was not executed by Holbein ; neither was it ascribed to him by his contemporaries ; for the popular error which assigns it to him appears to have originated with certain travellers who visited Basle upwards of a hundred years after Holbein's decease. It indeed may be answered that Bourbon might allude to the *alphabet* of the Dance of Death which has been ascribed to Holbein. A mere supposition of this kind, however, would be untenable in this instance ; for there is no direct evidence to show that Holbein was the designer of this alphabet, and the principal reason for supposing it to

---

* Neither these verses, nor those previously cited, occur in the first edition of the Nugæ, Paris, 1533.

† At that period a wood-cut, as well as a painting, was termed *pictura.*—On the title-page of an edition of the New Testament, with wood-cuts, Zurich, 1554, by Froschover, we find the following : " Novi Testamenti Editio postrema per Des. Erasmum Roterodamum. Omnia *picturis* illustrata."

have been designed by him rests upon the previous assumption of his being the designer of the cuts of the Lyons Dance of Death. Deny him the honour of this work, and assert that the last quoted verses of Bourbon must relate to some other, and the difficulty of showing by anything like credible evidence, that he was the designer of any other series of cuts, or even of a single cut, or painting, of the same subject, becomes increased tenfold. Mr. Douce, with the gross inconsistency that distinguishes the whole of his arguments on this subject, ascribes the alphabet of the Dance of Peasants to Holbein, and yet cautiously avoids mentioning him as the designer of the alphabet of the Dance of Death, though the reasons for this conclusion are precisely the same as those on which he rests the former assertion. Nay, so confused and contradictory are his opinions on this point, that in another part of his book he actually describes both alphabets as being the work of the same designer and the same engraver.

"Some of the writers on engraving," says Mr. Douce, "have manifested their usual inaccuracy on the subject of Holbein's Dance of Peasants. . . . . . . There is, however, *no doubt* that his beautiful pencil was employed on this subject in various ways, of which the following specimens are worthy of being recorded. In a set of initial letters frequently used in books printed at Basle and elsewhere," &c. After thus having unhesitatingly ascribed the Dance of Peasants to Holbein, Mr. Douce, in a subsequent page,—when giving a list of cuts which he ascribes to Hans Lutzelburger,—writes as follows: "8. An alphabet with a Dance of Death, the subjects of which, with a few exceptions, are the same as those in the other Dance ; the designs, however, occasionally vary," &c. On concluding his description of this alphabet, he thus notices the alphabet of the Dance of Peasants, having apparently forgot that he had previously ascribed the latter to Holbein. "9. Another alphabet *by the same artists*. It is a Dance of Peasants, intermixed with other subjects, some of which are not of the most delicate nature." *

It is, however, uncertain if Mr. Douce really did believe Holbein to be the designer of the alphabet of the Dance of Death, though from the preceding extracts it is plainly, though indirectly asserted, that he *was*. In his wish to claim the engraving of the Dance of Peasants for Lutzelburger, Mr. Douce does not seem to have been aware that from the words "by the same artists," coupled with his previous assertion, of Holbein being the designer of that alphabet, it followed as a direct consequence that he was also the designer of the alphabet of the Dance of Death. Putting this charitable construction on Mr. Douce's words, it follows that *his* assertion of Lutzelburger being the engraver of the Dance of Peasants is purely gratuitous. If Mr. Douce really believed

* Douce's Dance of Death, pp. 80, 100, and 101.

that Holbein was the designer of the alphabet of the Dance of Death, he ought in fairness to have expressly declared his opinion ; although such declaration would have caused his arguments, against Holbein being the designer of the cuts in the Lyons Dance of Death, to appear more paradoxical and absurd than they are when unconnected with such an opinion ; for what person, with the slightest pretensions to rationality, could assert that Holbein was the designer of the alphabet of the Dance of Death executed in 1530, the subjects, with few exceptions, the same as those in the Dance of Death published at Lyons in 1538, and yet in direct opposition to contemporary testimony, and the internal evidence of the subjects themselves, deny that he was the designer of the cuts in the latter work, on the sole authority of the nameless writer of a preface which only appeared in the first edition of the book, and which, there seems reason to suspect, was addressed to an imaginary personage ? Was Madame Jehanne de Touszele likely to feel herself highly complimented by having dedicated to her a work which contains undeniable evidences of the artist's having been no friend to popery ? In one cut a couple of fiends appear to be ridiculing his "Holiness" the pope ; and in another is a young gallant with a guitar, entertaining a nun in her bed-chamber. If a pious abbess of St. Peter's, Lyons, in 1538, should have considered that such cuts "tended to edification," she must have been an extremely liberal woman for her age. It is exceedingly amusing, in looking over the cuts of the Lyons Dance of Death, to contrast the drollery and satire of the designer with the endeavours of the textuary and versifier to give them a devout and spiritual turn.

As it is certain from the verses of Bourbon, in praise of Holbein as the painter or designer of a subject, or a series of subjects, representing "Death as if he were alive,"—ut mors vivere videatur,—that this celebrated artist *had designed* a Dance of Death, Mr. Douce, being unable to deny the evidence thus afforded, paradoxically proceeds to fit those verses to his own theory ; and after quoting them, at page 139, proceeds as follows: "It has already been demonstrated that these lines could not refer to the old painting of the Macaber Dance at the Dominican convent, whilst from the important dedication to the edition of the wood-cuts first published at Lyons in 1538, it is next to impossible that that work could then have been in Borbonius's contemplation. It appears from several places in his Nugæ that he was in England in 1535, at which time Holbein drew his portrait in such a manner as to excite his gratitude and admiration in another copy of verses . . . . . . He returned to Lyons in 1536, and it is known that he was there in 1538, when he probably wrote the complimentary lines in Holbein's Biblical designs a short time before their publication, either out of friendship to the painter, or at the instance of the Lyons publisher, with whom he was certainly connected.—Now, if Borbonius, during his residence at Lyons, had been assured that the designs in the wood-cuts of the Dance of Death were the production of Holbein, would not his before-mentioned lines on that subject have been likewise introduced into the Lyons edition of it, or at least into some subsequent editions, in none of which is any mention whatever made of Holbein, although the work was continued even after the death of that artist? The application, therefore, of Borbonius's lines must be sought for elsewhere ; but it is greatly to be regretted that he has not adverted to the place where the painting,* as he seems to call it, was made."

Mr. Douce next proceeds in his search after the " painting," and he is not long in finding what he wishes for. According to his statement, " *very soon after* the calamitous fire at Whitehall, 1697, which consumed nearly the whole of that palace, a person, calling himself T. Nieuhoff Piccard, probably belonging to the household of William III, and a man who appears to have been an amateur artist," made etchings after nineteen of the cuts in the Lyons Dance of Death. Impressions of those etchings, accompanied with manuscript dedications, appear to have been presented by this T. Nieuhoff Piccard to his friends or patrons, and among others to a Mynheer Heymans, and to " the high, noble, and well-born Lord William Benting, Lord of Rhoon, Pendraght," &c. The address to Mynheer Heymans contains the following important piece of information respecting a work of Holbein's, which appears most singularly to have escaped the notice of every other writer, whether English or foreign. " Sir,—The costly palace of Whitehall, erected by Cardinal Wolsey, and the residence of King Henry VIII, contains, among other performances of art, a Dance of Death, *painted by Holbein*, in its galleries, which, through an unfortunate conflagration, has been reduced to ashes."† In the dedication to the " high, noble, and well-born Lord William Benting," the information respecting this curious work of art,—all memory of which would have perished had it not been for the said T. Nieuhoff Piccard,—is rather more precise. " Sir, [not My Lord,] —In the course of my constant love and pursuit of works of art, it has been my good fortune to meet with that scarce little work of Hans Holbein, neatly engraved on wood, and which he himself had *painted as large as life*, in fresco, on the walls of Whitehall." Who Mynheer Heymans was will probably never be discovered, but he seems to have been a person of some consequence in his day, though unfortunately never mentioned in any history or memoirs of the period, for it appears that the court thought proper, in consideration of his singular deserts, to

---

* Mr. Douce here seems to lay some weight on the word *picta*, which, as has been previously observed, was applied equally to wood engravings and paintings.

† Douce, Dance of Death, p. 141.

cause a dwelling to be built for him at Whitehall. My Lord William Benting,*—though from his name and titles he might be mistaken for a member of the Bentinck family,—appears to have been actually born in the palace. It is, however, very unfortunate that his name does not occur in the peerage of that time ; and as neither Rhoon nor Pendraght are to be found in Flanders or Holland, it is not unlikely that these may be the names of two of his lordship's *castles in Spain*.

T. Nieuhoff Piccard's express testimony of Holbein having painted a Dance of Death in fresco, at Whitehall, is, in Mr. Douce's opinion, further corroborated by the following circumstances : 1. " In one of Vanderdort's manuscript catalogues of the pictures and rarities transported from St. James's to Whitehall, and placed there in the newly erected cabinet room of Charles I, and in which several works by Holbein are mentioned, there is the following article: 'A little piece, where Death with a green garland about his head, stretching both his arms to apprehend a Pilate in the habit of one of the spiritual Prince-Electors of Germany. Copied by Isaac Oliver from Holbein.' There cannot be a doubt that this refers to the subject of the Elector as painted by Holbein in the Dance of Death at Whitehall, proving at the same time the identity of the painting with the wood-cuts, whatever may be the inference. 2. Sandrart, after noticing a remarkable portrait of Henry VIII. at Whitehall, states ' that there yet remains at that palace *another work*, by Holbein, that constitutes him the Apelles of his time.' This is certainly *very like an allusion* to a Dance of Death. 3. It is *by no means improbable* that Matthew Prior may have alluded to Holbein's painting at Whitehall, as it is not likely that he would be acquainted with any other.

' Our term of life depends not on our deed,
Before our birth our funeral was decreed ;
Nor aw'd by foresight, nor misled by chance,
Imperious Death directs the ebon lance,
Peoples great Henry's tombs, and leads up Holbein's Dance.'
Prior, Ode to the Memory of George Villiers." +

Mr. Douce having previously *proved* that Holbein was *not* the designer of the cuts in the Lyons Dance of Death, thus, in a manner *equally*

---

* " The identification of William Benting," says Mr. Douce with exquisite bon-hommie, " must be left to the sagacity of others. He *could not have been* the Earl of Portland created in 1689, or he would have been addressed accordingly. He is, moreover, described as a youth born at Whitehall, and then residing there, and whose dwelling consisted of nearly the whole of the palace that remained after the fire."—Dance of Death, p. 244. It appears that these addresses of Piccard were written in a foreign language, though, whether Dutch, French, German, or Latin, Mr. Douce most unaccountably neglects to say : he merely mentions that his extracts are translated.

+ Douce's Dance of Death, pp. 144, 145.

satisfactory, accounts for the verses of Bourbon, by showing, on the *unexceptionable* evidence of "a person, calling himself T. Nieuhoff Piccard, *probably* belonging to the household of William III," that the great work of Holbein—by the fame of which he had made himself equal with the immortal gods—was painted as large as life, in fresco, on the walls of Whitehall. The ingenuity displayed in depriving Holbein of the honour of the Lyons cuts is no less exemplified in proving him to be the painter of a similar subject in Whitehall. The key-stone is worthy of the arch.

Though the *facts* and *arguments* put forth by Mr. Douce, in proof of Holbein having painted a Dance of Death on the walls of the old palace of Whitehall, and of this having been the identical Dance of Death alluded to by Bourbon, might be summarily dismissed as being of that kind which no objection could render more absurd, yet it seems necessary to direct the especial attention of the reader to one or two points ; and first to the assertion that "it is next to impossible that the Lyons Dance of Death of 1538 could then have been in Borbonius's contemplation." Now, in direct opposition to what is here said, it appears to me highly probable that *this* was the very work on account of which he addressed his epigram to Holbein ; and it is moreover evident that Bourbon expresses in Latin verse almost precisely the same ideas as those which had previously been expressed in French by the writer of the address to Madame Jehanne de Touszele, when speaking of the merits of the nameless artist who is there alluded to as the designer or engraver of the cuts.* As Holbein is not certainly known to be the painter or designer of any other Dance of Death which might merit the high praise conveyed in Bourbon's verses, to what other work of his will they apply? Even supposing, as I do, that the alphabet of the Dance of Death was designed by Holbein, I conceive it "next to impossible," to use the words of Mr. Douce, that Bourbon should have described Holbein as having attained immortality through the fame of those twenty-four small letters, a perfect set of which I believe is not to be found in any single volume.

---

* That the reader may judge for himself of the similarity of thought in the passages referred to, they are here given in juxta-position.

"Car ses histoires funebres, avec leurs descriptions severement rithmées, aux advisans donnent telle admiration, qu'ilz en *jugent les mortz y apparoistre tresvivement,* et les vifs tresmortement representer. Qui me faict penser, que la Mort craignant que ce excellent painctre ne la paignist tant vifve qu'elle ne fut plus crainte pour Mort, *et que pour celà luy mesme n'en devint immortel,* que a ceste cause," &c.—*Epistre des Faces de la Mort.*

> " Dum mortis Hansus pictor imaginem exprimit,
> Tanta arte mortem retulit, ut mors vivere
> Videatur ipsa : et ipse se immortalibus
> Parem Diis fecerit, operis hujus gloria."
> *Borbonius.*

That Bourbon *did* know who was the designer of the cuts of the Lyons Dance of Death there can scarcely be the shadow of a doubt; he was at Lyons in the year in which the work was published; he was connected with the printers; and another work, the Icones Historiarum Veteris Testamenti, also published by them in 1538, has at the commencement a copy of verses written by Bourbon, from which alone we learn that Holbein was the designer of the cuts,—the first four of which cuts, be it observed, being from the same blocks as the first four in the Dance of Death, published by the same printers, in the same year. What might be the motives of the printers for not inserting Bourbon's epigram in praise of Holbein in the subsequent editions of the Dance of Death, supposing him to be the designer of the cuts, I cannot tell, nor will I venture to *guess*. They certainly must have had some reason for concealing the designer's name, for the writer of the prefatory address to Madame Jehanne de Touszele takes care not to mention it even when speaking in so laudatory a style of the excellence of the designs. Among the other unaccountable things connected with this work, I may mention the fact of the French prefatory address to the abbess of St. Peter's appearing only in the first, and being omitted in every subsequent edition.

With respect to T. Nieuhoff Piccard, whose manuscript addresses to " Mynheer Heymans" and " Lord William Benting" are cited to *prove* that Bourbon's verses must relate to a painting of the Dance of Death by Holbein in the old palace of Whitehall, nothing whatever is known; and there is not the slightest reason to believe that a Lord William Benting, born in the old palace of Whitehall, " Lord of Rhoon, Pendraght," &c. ever existed. I am of opinion that the addresses of the person calling himself T. Nieuhoff Piccard are a clumsy attempt at imposition.* Though Mr. Douce had seen both those addresses, and also another of the same kind, he does not appear to have made any attempt to trace their former owners, nor does he mention the names of the parties in whose possession they were at the time that he saw them. He had seen the address to " Lord William Benting" previous to the publication of his

---

* Hegner, in his Life of Holbein, speaking of the Nieuhoff discovery, says: " Of this fable no notice would have been taken here had not Mr. Douce ascribed undeserved authority to it, and had not his superficial investigations found undeserved credit with English and other compilers." Hans Holbein der Jüngere, S. 338.

Mr. Douce, at page 240 of his Dance of Death, complains of Hegner's want of urbanity and politeness; and in return calls his account of Holbein's works *superficial*, and moreover says that " his arguments, if worthy of the name, are, generally speaking, of a most weak and flimsy texture." He also gives him a sharp rebuff by alluding to him as the " above *gentleman*," the last word, to give it point, being printed in Italics. Mr. Douce, when he was thus pelting Hegner, does not seem to have been aware that his own anti-Holbenian superstructure was a house of glass.

" Cedimus, inque vicem dedimus crura sagittis."

observations on the Dance of Death in 1794, when, if he had felt inclined, he might have ascertained from whom the then possessor had received it, and thus obtained a clue to guide him in his inquiries respecting the personal identity of the Loid of Rhoon and Pendraght. But this would not have suited his purpose; for he seems to have been conscious that any inquiry respecting such a person would only have tended to confirm the doubts respecting the paper addressed to him by Piccard. It is also uncertain at what time those pretended addresses were written, but there are impressions of the etchings which accompanied them with the date 1720; and I am inclined to think that if the paper and handwriting were closely examined, it would be found that those pretended presentation addresses were manufactured about the same, or perhaps at a later period. Whoever the person calling himself T. Nieuhoff Piccard may have been, or at whatever time the addresses to Mynheer Heymans and others may have been written, the only evidence of there having been a painting of the Dance by Holbein at Whitehall rests on his unsupported statement. Such a painting is not mentioned by any foreign traveller who had visited this country, nor is it noticed by any English writer prior to 1697; it is not alluded to in any tragedy, comedy, farce, or masque, in which we might expect that such a painting would have been incidentally mentioned had it ever existed. Evelyn, who must have frequently been in the old palace of Whitehall, says not a word of such a painting, though he mentions the Lyons Dance of Death under the title of Mortis Imago, and ascribes the cuts to Holbein;* and not the slightest notice of it is to be found in Vertue or Walpole.

The learned Conrad Gesner, who was born at Zurich in 1516, and died there in 1565, expressly ascribes the Lyons Dance of Death to Holbein;† and, notwithstanding the contradictory statement in the preface to the

---

* Evelyn is only referred to here on account of his *silence* with respect to the pretended painting at Whitehall. What he says of Holbein cannot be relied on, as will be seen from the following passage, which is a fair specimen of his general knowledge and accuracy. " We have seen some few things cut in wood by the incomparable Hans Holbein the Dane, but they are rare and exceedingly difficult to come by ; as his *Licentiousness of the Friars and Nuns ; Erasmus ; The Dance Macchabre ;* the *Mortis Imago,* which he painted in great in the Church of Basil, and afterwards graved with no less art."—Evelyn's Sculptura, p. 69. Edition 1769.

† " Imagines Mortis expressæ ab optimo pictore Johanne Holbein cum epigrammatibus Georgii Æmylii, excusæ Francofurti et Lugduni apud Frellonios, quorum editio plures habet picturas. Vidi etiam cum metris Gallicis et Germanicis, si bene memini." Mr. Douce cites this passage from Gesner's Pandectæ, " a supplemental volume of great rarity to his well-known Bibliotheca." The correct title of the volume in which it occurs is " Partitiones Theologicæ, Pandectarum Universalium Conradi Gesneri Liber Ultimus." Folio, printed by Christopher Froschover, Zurich (Tiguri) 1549. The notice of the Dance of Death is in folio 86, *a*.

first edition of this work, such appears to have been the general belief of all the artist's contemporaries. Van Mander, who was born in 1548, and who died in 1606, appears to have been the first person who gave any account of the life of Holbein. His work, entitled Het Schilder Boek, consisting of biographical notices of painters, chiefly Germans and Flemings, was first published in 1604; and, when speaking of Holbein, he mentions the Lyons Dance of Death among his other works. Sandrart, in common with every other writer on art of the period, also ascribes the Lyons work to Holbein, and he gives the following account of a conversation that he had with Rubens respecting those cuts : "I remember that in the year 1627, when the celebrated Rubens was proceeding to Utrecht to visit Honthorst, I accompanied him as far as Amsterdam; and during our passage in the boat I looked into Holbein's little book of the Dance of Death, the cuts of which Rubens highly praised, recommending me, as I was a young man, to copy them, observing, that he had copied them himself in his youth." Sandrart, who seems to have been one of the earliest writers who supposed that Durer, Cranach, and others engraved their own designs, without any just grounds describes Holbein as a wood engraver. Patin, in his edition of the "Stultitiæ Laus" of Erasmus, 1676, repeats the same story; and Papillon in his decisive manner clenches it by asserting that "most of the delicate wood-cuts and ornamental letters which are to be found in books printed at Basle, Zurich, and towns in Switzerland, at Lyons, London, &c. from 1520 to about 1540, were engraved by Holbein himself." Papillon also says that it is believed—on croit—that Holbein began to engrave in 1511, when he was about sixteen. "What is extraordinary in this painter," he further adds, "is, that he painted and engraved with the left hand, so that he consequently engraved the lines on the wood from right to left, instead of, as with us, engraving from left to right." * Jansen, and a host of other compilers, without inquiry, repeat the story of Holbein having been a wood engraver, and that the cuts of the Lyons Dance of Death were engraved by himself. That he was the designer of those cuts I am thoroughly convinced, though I consider it "next to impossible" that he should have been also the engraver.

Holbein's Bible Cuts, as they are usually called, were first published at Lyons, in 1538, the same year, and by the same printers, as the Dance of Death. The book is a small quarto, and the title is as follows: "Historiarum Veteris Testamenti Icones ad vivum expressæ. Una cum brevi, sed quoad fieri potuit, dilucida earundem et Latina et Gallica

---

* Traité de la Gravure en Bois, tom. i. p. 165. Van Mander asserts that Holbein painted with his left hand ; but Horace Walpole, however, in opposition to this, refers to a portrait of Holbein, formerly in the Arundelian collection, where he appears holding the pencil in his *right* hand.

expositione.   Lugduni sub scuto Coloniensi. M.D.XXXVIII."*   On the title-page is an emblematic cut, with the motto *Usus me genuit*, similar to that on the title-page in the first edition of the Dance of Death, but not precisely the same; and at the end is the imprint of the brothers Melchior and Gaspar Trechsel within an ornamental border, as in the latter work.   I am greatly inclined to think that the brothers were only the printers of the first editions of the Dance of Death and the Bible cuts, and that the real proprietors were John and Francis Frellon, whose names appear as the publishers in subsequent editions.

This opinion seems to be corroborated by the fact of there being an address from "*Franciscus Frellaeus*" to the Christian Reader in the Bible cuts of 1538 and 1539, which in subsequent editions is altered to "Franciscus *Frellonius*."   That the same person is designated by those names, I think there can be little doubt, as the addresses are literally the same.   From adopting the form "Frellaeus," however, in the editions of 1538 and 1539, it would seem that the writer was not wishful to discover his name.   When the work becomes popular he writes it Frellonius; and in the second edition of the Dance of Death, when the character of this work is also established, and there seems no longer reason to apprehend the censures of the church of Rome, we find the names of John and Francis Frellon on the title-page under the "shield of Cologne."   Whatever might be their motives, it seems certain that the first publishers of the Dance of Death were wishful to withhold their names; and it is likely that the designer of the cuts might have equally good reasons for concealment.   Had the Roman Catholic party considered the cuts of the Pope, the Nun, and two or three others as the covert satire of a *reformed* painter, the publishers and the designer would have been as likely to incur danger as to reap profit or fame.

The address of Franciscus Frellaeus is followed by a copy of Latin verses by Nicholas Bourbon, in which Holbein is mentioned as the designer; and immediately preceding the cuts is an address "aux lecteurs," in French verse, by Gilles Corrozet, who, perhaps, might be the poet that supplied the French expositions of those cuts, and the "descriptions severement rithmées" of the Dance of Death.   The following is an extract from Bourbon's prefatory verses, the whole of which it appears unnecessary to give.

---

* A copy of this edition is preserved in the Public Library at Basle, and there is another copy in the Royal Collection at Dresden. Another edition, in every respect similar to the first, was also printed by the brothers Trechsel in 1539. Hegner, in his Life of Holbein, does not seem to have known of this edition; speaking of that of 1538, he says, " It is probably the same as that to which Papillon gives the date 1539." There is a copy of the edition of 1539 in the British Museum.

"Nuper in Elysio cum fortè erraret Apelles
Una aderat Zeuxis, Parrhasiusque comes.
Hi duo multa satis fundebant verba ; sed ille
Interea mœrens et taciturnus erat.
Mirantur comites, farique hortantur et urgent :
Suspirans imo pectore, Coûs ait :
O famæ ignari, superis quæ nuper ab oris
(Vana utinam !) Stygias venit ad usque domos :
Scilicet, esse hodie quendam ex mortalibus unum
Ostendat qui me vosque fuisse nihil :
Qui nos declaret pictores nomine tantum,
Picturæque omneis ante fuisse rudes.
Holbius est homini nomen, qui nomina nostra
Obscura ex claris ac prope nulla facit.
Talis apud manes querimonia fertur : et illos
Sic equidem merito censeo posse queri,
Nam tabulam siquis videat, quam pinxerit Hansus
Holbius, ille artis gloria prima suæ,
Protinus exclamet, Potuit Deus edere monstrum
Quod video ? humanæ non potuere manus.
Icones hæ sacræ tanti sunt, optime lector,
Artificis, dignum quod venereris opus."

Besides those verses there is also a Greek distich by Bourbon, to which the following translation " pene ad verbum " is appended :

"Cernere vis, hospes, simulacra simillima vivis ?
Hoc opus Holbinæ nobile cerne manus."

When Mr Douce stated that it was " *extremely probable* that the anonymous painter or designer of the Dance might have been employed also by the Frellons to execute a set of subjects for the Bible previously to his death, and that Holbein was afterwards employed to complete the work," he seems to have forgot that such a testimony of Holbein being the designer was prefixed to the Bible cuts. In answer to Mr. Douce it may be asked, in his own style, if the Frellons knew that another artist was the designer of the cuts of the Dance of Death, and if he also had been originally employed to design the Bible cuts, how does it happen that they should allow Bourbon to give all the honour of the latter to Holbein, who, if the Dance of Death be not his, was certainly much inferior as a designer to the nameless artist whose unfinished work he was employed to complete ?

The total number of the Bible cuts in the first edition of the work is ninety, the first four of which are the same as the first four of the Dance of Death ; the other eighty-six are of a different form to the first four, as will be perceived from the specimens, which are of the same size as the originals. Those eighty-six cuts are generally much inferior in design to those of the Dance of Death, and the style in which they are engraved is very unequal, some of them being executed with considerable neatness and delicacy, and others in a much coarser manner. The following cut, Abraham about to sacrifice Isaac, Genesis XXII, is one of those which are the best engraved; but even these, so far as regards the expression of the features and the delicate marking of the hands, are generally much inferior to the cuts of the Dance of Death.

Though most of the Bible cuts are inferior both in design and execution to those of the Dance of Death, and though several of them are rudely drawn and badly engraved, yet many of them afford points of such perfect identity with those of the Dance of Death, that it seems impossible to come to any other conclusion than that either the cuts of both works have been designed by the same person, or that the designer of the one series has servilely copied from the designer of the other, and, what is most singular, in many trifling details which seem the least likely to be imitated, and which usually constitute individual peculiarities of style. For instance, the small shrubby tree in the preceding cut is precisely of the same species as that seen in the cut of the Old Woman in the Dance of Death; and the angel about to stay Abraham's hand bears a strong general resemblance to the angel in Adam and Eve driven out of Paradise.

The cut on the opposite page—the Fool, Psalm LIII—is copied from one of those executed in a coarser style than the preceding. The children in this cut are evidently of the same family as those of the Dance of Death.

In the first cut, the Creation, a crack is perceived running nearly down the middle from top to bottom, in the edition of the Dance of Death of 1545. It is also perceptible in all the subsequent Lyons editions of this work and of the Bible cuts. It is, however, less obvious in the Bible cuts of the edition 1549 than in some of the preceding, probably in consequence of the block having been cramped to remedy the defect. Mr. Douce speaks, at page 105, as if the crack were not discernible in the Bible cuts of 1549; it is, however, quite perceptible in every copy that has come under my notice. Some of the latter editions of this work contain four additional cuts, which are all coarsely executed. In the edition of 1547 they form the illustrations to Ezekiel XL; Ezekiel XLIII; Jonah I, II, and III; and Habakkuk. The Bible cuts were also printed with explanations in English. The title of a copy now before me is as follows: "The Images of the Old Testament, lately expressed, set forthe in Ynglishe and Frenche vuith a playn and brief exposition. Printed at Lyons by Johan Frellon, the yere of our Lord God, 1549," 4to. In the latter editions there are wood-cuts of the four Evangelists, each within an oval border, on the last leaf. They bear no tokens of Holbein's style.

Among the many instances of resemblance which are to be perceived on comparing the Dance of Death with the Bible cuts, the following may be enumerated as the most remarkable. The peculiar manner in which fire with smoke, and the waves of the sea, are represented in the Dance of Death can scarcely fail to strike the most heedless observer; for instance, the fire in the cut of Death seizing the child, and the waves in the cut of the Seaman. In the Bible cuts we perceive the same peculiarity; there is the same kind of fire in Moses directing the manner of burnt offerings, Leviticus I; in the burning of Nadab and Abihu, Leviticus X; and in every other one of those cuts where fire is seen. In the destruction of Pharaoh and his host, Exodus XIV, are the same kind of curling waves. Except in the Dance of Death and the Bible cuts, I

B B

have never seen an instance of fire or water represented in such a manner. If those cuts were designed by two different artists, it is certainly singular that in this respect they should display so perfect a coincidence of idea. The sheep in the cut of the Bishop in the Dance of Death are the same as those in the Bible cut of Moses seeing God in the burning bush, Exodus III; and the female figure in the cut of the Elector in the former work is perceived in the Bible cut of the captive Midianites, Numbers XXXI. The children introduced in both works are almost perfectly identical, as will be perceived on comparing the cut of Little Children mocking Elijah, chapter II, Kings II, with those of the Elector, and Death seizing the child, in the Dance of Death. The face of the Duchess in the latter work is the same as that of Esther in the Bible cut, Esther, chapter II; and in this cut ornaments on the tapestry, like fleurs-de-lis, behind the throne of Ahasuerus, are the same as those on the tapestry behind the King in the Dance of Death. The latter coincidence has been noticed by Mr. Douce, who, in direct opposition to the evidence of the German or Swiss costume of the living characters of the Dance of Death, considers it as contributing to demonstrate that both the series of those cuts are of Gallic origin.* It is needless to enumerate more instances of almost complete identity of figures and details in the cuts of the Dance of Death and those of the Bible illustrations; they are too frequent to have originated from a conventional mode of representing certain objects and persons; and they are most striking in minor details, where one artist would be least likely to imitate another, but where the same individual designer would be most likely to repeat himself. "As to the designs of these truly elegant prints," says Mr. Douce, speaking of the cuts of the Dance of Death, "no one who is at all skilled in the knowledge of Holbein's style and manner of grouping his figures would hesitate immediately to ascribe them to that artist."† As this opinion is corroborated by a comparison of the Dance of Death with the Bible cuts, and as the internal evidence of the cuts of the

* " A comparison of the 8th subject of the Simulachres," says Mr. Douce, " with that of the Bible for Esther I, II, where the canopy ornamented with fleurs-de-lis is the same in both, will contribute to strengthen the above conjecture, as will both the cuts to demonstrate their Gallic origin. It is most certain that the King sitting at table in the Simulachres is intended for Francis I, which if any one should doubt, let him look upon the miniature of that king, copied at p. 214, in Clarke's 'Repertorium Bibliographicum.'" The "above conjecture" referred to in this extract is that previously cited at page 367, where Mr. Douce conjectures that Holbein *might have been* employed to complete the Bible cuts which *might have been* left unfinished in consequence of the death of Mr. Douce's "great unknown" designer of the Dance of Death.—Dance of Death, p. 96. Mr. Douce, not being able to deny the similarity of many of the cuts, says it is highly probable that Holbein was merely employed to finish the Bible cuts, without ever considering that it is *primâ facie* much more probable that Holbein was the designer of the cuts in both works.

† Dance of Death, p. 82.

Dance of Death in favour of Holbein is confirmed by the testimony of his contemporaries, the reader can decide for himself how far Holbein's positive claims to the honour of this work ought to be affected by the passage in the anonymous address to Madame Jehanne de Touszele, which forms the groundwork of Mr. Douce's theory.

Having now examined the principal arguments which have been alleged to show that Holbein *was not* the designer of the Dance of Death, and having endeavoured to justify his claims to that honour by producing the evidences on which they rest, I shall now take leave of this subject, feeling thoroughly assured that HOLBEIN WAS THE DESIGNER OF THE CUTS OF THE FIRST EDITION OF THE LYONS DANCE OF DEATH; and trusting, though with no overweening confidence, that the preceding investigation will render it necessary for the next questioner of his title to produce stronger objections than the solitary ambiguous passage in the preface to the first edition of the work, and to support them with more forcible and consistent arguments than have been put forth by Mr. Douce. M. T. Nieuhoff Piccard, I am inclined to think, will never again be called as a witness in this cause; and before the passage in the preface can be allowed to have any weight, it must be shown that such a personage as Madame Jehanne de Touszele *was* prioress of the convent of St. Peter at Lyons at the time of the first publication of the work: and even should such a fact be established, the ambiguity of the passage—whether the pretendedly deceased artist were the engraver or designer, or both,—and the obvious desire to conceal his name, remain to be explained.

In 1538, the year in which the Dance of Death and the Bible cuts were first published at Lyons, Holbein was residing in England under the patronage of Henry VIII; though it is also certain that about the beginning of September in that year he returned to Basle and he remained there a few weeks.*

As the productions of this distinguished painter occupy so large a portion of this chapter, it perhaps may not be unnecessary to give here a few particulars of his life, chiefly derived from Hegner's work, previous to his coming to England. Hans Holbein, the Younger, as he is often called by German writers to distinguish him from his father, was the son of Hans Holbein, a painter of considerable reputation. The year and place of his birth have not been positively ascertained, but there seems reason to believe that he was born in 1498, at Augsburg,†

---

* " Venit nuper Basileam ex Anglia Ioannes Holbein, adeo felicem ejus regni statum prædicans, qui aliquot septimanis exactis rursum eo migraturus est." From a letter written by Rudolph Gualter to Henry Bullinger, of Zurich, about the middle of September 1538.— Quoted by Hegner, S. 246.

† Dr. Dibdin, in his Bibliographical Tour vol. iii. pp. 80, 81, Edit. 1829, mentions two paintings at Augsburg by the elder Holbein, one dated 1499 and the other 1501. The elder

of which city his father was a burgher, and from whence he appears
to have removed with his family to Basle, about the end of the
fifteenth or the beginning of the sixteenth century.   Young Holbein
was brought up to his father's profession, and at an early age displayed the germ of his future excellence.   There is a portrait in oil by
young Holbein of the date of 1513, which, according to Hegner, though
rather weak in colour and somewhat hard in outline, is yet clearly and
delicately painted.   From the excellence of his early productions, Patin,
in his Life of Holbein, prefixed to an edition of the Laus Stultitiæ of
Erasmus* thinks that he must have been born in 1495.   That he was
born in 1498 there can, however, be little doubt, for Hegner mentions
a portrait of him, at Basle, when in the forty-fifth year of his age,
with the date 1543.   Several anecdotes are told of Holbein as a jolly
fellow, and of his twice or thrice discharging his account at a tavern by
painting a Dance of Peasants.   Though there seems reason to believe
that Holbein was a free liver, and that he did paint such a subject in
a house at Basle, the stories of his thus settling for his liquor are highly
improbable.   He appears to have married young, for in a painting of
his wife and two children, executed before he left Basle for England
in 1526, the eldest child, a boy, appears to be between four and five
years old.†

The name of Holbein's wife is unknown; but it is said that, like
Durer's, she was of an unhappy temper, and that he enjoyed no peace
with her.   It is not, however, unlikely that his own unsettled disposition and straitened circumstances also contributed to render his home
uncomfortable.   Like most other artists of that period, he appears to
have frequently travelled; but his journeys do not seem to have
extended beyond Switzerland and Suabia, and they were for the most
part confined to the former country.   He seems to have travelled rather
in search of employment than to improve himself by studying the works

Holbein had a brother named Sigismund, who was also a painter, and who appears to have
established himself at Berne.   Papillon, in his usual manner, makes Sigismund Holbein a
wood engraver.   By his will, dated 1540, he appoints his nephew Hans the heir of all his
property in Berne.

    * Patin's edition of this work was published in octavo, at Basle, in 1676.   It contains
eighty-three copper-plate engravings, from pen-and-ink sketches, drawn by Holbein, in the
margin of a copy of an edition printed by Frobenius, in 1514, and still preserved (1860) in
the Public Library at Basle.   It is said that Erasmus, when looking over those sketches,
exclaimed, when he came to that intended for himself, " Oho, if Erasmus were now as he
appears here, he would certainly take a wife."   Above another of the sketches, representing
a man with one of his arms about a woman's neck, and at the same time drinking out of a
bottle, Erasmus is said to have written the name " *Holbein*." · In an edition of the Laus
Stultitiæ, edited by G. G. Becker, Basle, 1780, 8vo. those sketches are engraved (very
indifferently) on wood.

    † Hegner, Hans Holbein der Jüngere, S. 110.

of other masters. Perhaps of all the eminent painters of that period there is no one whose style is more original than Holbein's, nor one who owes less to the study of the works of his contemporaries or predecessors. Though there can be no doubt of his talents being highly appreciated by his fellow-townsmen, yet his profession during his residence at Basle appears to have afforded him but a scanty income. The number of works executed by him between 1517 and 1526 sufficiently testify that he was not deficient in industry, and the exercise of his art seems to have been sufficiently varied:—he painted portraits and historical subjects; decorated the interior walls of houses, according to the fashion of that period, with fanciful and historical compositions; and made designs for goldsmiths and wood-engravers. It is said that so early as 1520, the Earl of Arundel,* an English nobleman, having seen some of his works in passing through Basle, advised him to try his fortune in England. If such advice were given to Holbein at that period, it is certain that it was not adopted until several years after, for he did not visit this country till 1526.

Before he left Basle he had painted two or three portraits of Erasmus, and there is a large wood-cut of that distinguished scholar which is said not only to have been painted, but also engraved by Holbein. This cut is of folio size, and the figure of Erasmus is a whole length. His right arm rests upon a terminus, and from a richly ornamented arch is suspended a tablet, with the inscription, ER. ROT. Some old impressions have two verses printed underneath, which merely praise the likeness without alluding to the painter, while others have four which contain a compliment to the genius of Erasmus and to the art of Holbein.† The original block is still preserved in the Public Library at Basle; but there is not the slightest reason for believing that it was engraved by Holbein. In 1526 Holbein left Basle for England: Patin says, because he could no longer bear to live with his imperious wife. Though this might not be the chief cause, it is easy to conceive that a person of Holbein's character would feel but little regret at parting from such a helpmate. Van Mander says that he took with him a portrait which he had painted of Erasmus, with a letter of recommendation from the latter to Sir Thomas More, wherein it was observed that this portrait 'was

* It is conjectured by Walpole that this might be Henry Fitz-Alan, Earl of Arundel.

† The verses underneath the impressions which are supposed to be the earliest, are as follows :

"Corporis effigiem si quis non vidit Erasmi,
Hunc scite ad vivum picta tabella dabit."

The others :

"Pallas Apellæam nuper mirata tabellam,
Hanc, ait, æternum Bibliotheca colat.
Dædaleam monstrat musis Holbeinnius artem,
Et summi ingenii Magnus Erasmus opes."

THE SHEATH OF A DAGGER, INTENDED AS A DESIGN FOR A CHASER.*

much more like him than any of Albert Durer's.' Hegner, however, thinks that what Van Mander says about the contents of this letter is not

---

* It is impossible to exceed the beauty and skill that are manifested in this fine piece of art. The figures are, a king, queen, and a warrior; a young woman, a monk, and an infant; all of whom most unwillingly accompany Death in the Dance. The despair of the king, the dejection of the queen, accompanied by her little dog, the terror of the soldier who hears the

correct, as no such passage is to be found in the published correspondence of Erasmus with Sir Thomas More. Erasmus had already sent two portraits of himself to England ;* and as Sir Thomas More was personally acquainted with him, Hegner is of opinion that it would be unnecessary to mention that the portrait was a better likeness than any of those painted by Albert Durer. It is, however, by no means unlikely that Erasmus in speaking of a portrait of himself by Holbein—whether forwarded by the latter or not—might give his own opinion of it in comparison with one from the pencil of Durer.

It would appear that in 1525 Erasmus had already mentioned Holbein's desire of trying his fortune in England to Sir Thomas More, for in a letter written by Sir Thomas to Erasmus, dated from the court at Greenwich, 18th of December 1525, there is a passage to the following effect : "Your painter, dear Erasmus, is an excellent artist, but I am apprehensive that he will not find England so fruitful and fertile as he may expect. I will, however, do all that I can in order that he may not find it entirely barren." † From a letter, dated 29th of August 1526, written by Erasmus to his friend Petrus Aegidius at Antwerp, it seems reasonable to conclude that Holbein left Basle for England about the beginning of September. Though Holbein's name is not expressly mentioned in this letter, there cannot be a doubt of his being the artist who is thus introduced to Aegidius : "The bearer of this is he who painted my portrait. I will not annoy you with his praises, although he is indeed an excellent artist. Should he wish to see Quintin, and you not have leisure to go with him, you can let a servant show him the house. The arts perish here ; he proceeds to England to gain a few angels ; if you wish to write [to England] you can send your letters by him." ‡ In this extract we discover a trait of the usual prudence of Erasmus, who, in introducing his humbler friends to persons of power or influence, seems to have been particularly careful not to give annoyance

drum of Death, the struggling of the female, the reluctance of the monk, and the sorrow of the poor infant, are depicted with equal spirit and veracity. The original drawing is in the public library at Basle, and ascribed to Holbein.

* Erasmus, writing to Bilibald Pirkheimer, in 1524, says, " Rursus nuper misi in Angliam Erasmum bis pictum ab artifice satis eleganti." Hegner thinks that this artist was Holbein. In 1517 a portrait of Erasmus, with that of his friend Petrus Aegidius, was painted at Antwerp by Quintin Matsys. It was intended by Erasmus as a present to Sir Thomas More. This painting came subsequently into the possession of Dr. Mead, at whose sale it was purchased, as the production of Holbein, by Lord Radnor, for £110.

† " Pictor tuus, Erasme carissime, mirus est artifex, sed vereor ne non sensurus sit Angliam tam fœcundam ac fertilem quam sperarat. Quanquam ne reperiat omnino sterilem, quoad per me fieri potest, efficiam. Ex aula Grenwici. 18 Dec. 1525."

‡ " Qui has reddit, est is qui me pinxit. Ejus commendatione te non gravabo, quanquam est insignis artifex. Si cupiet visere Quintinum, nec tibi vacabit hominem adducere, poteris per famulum commonstrare domum. Hic frigent artes : petit Angliam ut corradat aliquot angelatos : per eum poteris quæ voles scribere."—Erasmi Epist.

from the warmth of his recommendations. How gently, yet significantly, does he hint to Aegidius that the poor painter who brings the letter is a person about whom he need give himself no trouble: if he has not *leisure* to introduce him personally to Quintin—that is, Quintin Matsys —he can send a servant to show him his house. The suggestion of the servant was a hint from Erasmus that he did not expect the master to go with Holbein himself.

Holbein on his arrival in England appears to have been well received by Sir Thomas More; and it is certain that he resided for some time with the learned and witty chancellor in his house at Chelsea. It is indeed said that he continued with him for three years, but Walpole thinks that this is very unlikely. Whether he may have resided during the whole of the intermediate time with Sir Thomas More or not, there seems reason to believe that Holbein entered the service of Henry VIII. in 1528. About the autumn of 1529,* he paid a short visit to Basle, probably to see his family, which he had left in but indifferent circumstances, and to obtain permission from the magistracy for a further extension of his leave of absence, for no burgher of the city of Basle was allowed to enter into the service of a foreign prince without their sanction. Patin, in his Life of Holbein, says that during his visit he spent most of his time with his old tavern companions, and that he treated the more respectable burghers, who wished to cultivate his friendship, with great disrespect. Hegner, however, considers all those accounts which represent Holbein as a man of intemperate habits and dissolute character, as unworthy of credit; in his opinion it seems impossible that he who was a favourite of Henry VIII, and so long an inmate of Sir Thomas More's house, should have been a dissolute person. M. Hegner throughout his work shows a praiseworthy regard for Holbein's moral character, but his presumption in this instance is not sufficient to counterbalance the unfavourable reports in the opposite scale.

About the latter end of 1532, or the beginning of 1533, Holbein again visited Basle; and his return appears to have been chiefly

---

* Erasmus, in a letter to Sir Thomas More, written from Freyburg in Brisgau, 5th September, 1529, alludes to a picture of More and his family which had been brought over by Holbein; and Margaret Roper, the eldest daughter of Sir Thomas More, writing to Erasmus in the following November, says, that she is pleased to hear of the painter's arrival with the family picture,—" utriusque mei parentis nostrumque omnium effigiem depictam." Hegner thinks that those portraits of Sir Thomas More and his family was only a drawing in pen-and-ink, which is now in the Public Library at Basle. The figures in this drawing are: Sir Thomas and his wife, his father, his son, and a young lady, three daughters, a servant, and Sir Thomas's jester. Over and under the figures are written the name and age of each. The drawing is free and light; and the faces and hands are very distinctly expressed.—Hans Holbein der Jüngere, S. 202—235—237. The drawing in the Public Library at Basle was probably a sketch of Holbein's large picture of the family of Sir Thomas More.

influenced by an order of the magistracy, which was to the following effect: "To M. Hans Holbein, painter, now in England. We Jacob Meier, burgomaster and councillor, herewith salute you our beloved Hans Holbein, fellow-burgher, and give you to understand that it is our desire that you return home forthwith. In order that you may live easier at home, and provide for your wife and child,* we are pleased to allow you the yearly sum of thirty guilders, until we can obtain for you something better. That you may make your arrangements accordingly, we acquaint you with this resolution. Given, Monday, 2nd September 1532."† It is uncertain how long Holbein remained at Basle on his second visit, but it was probably of short duration. Though he obeyed the summons of the magistracy to return, he seems to have had sufficient interest to obtain a further extension of his leave of absence. For the third and last time he revisited Basle in 1538 ; and from a licence, signed by the burgomaster Jacob Meier, dated 16th November in that year, it appears that he obtained permission to return to England and remain there for two years longer. In this licence fifty guilders per annum are promised to Holbein on his return to Basle, and till then the magistrates further agree to allow his wife forty guilders per annum to be paid quarterly, and the first quarter's payment to commence on the eve of St. Lucia next ensuing,—that is, on the 12th of December. As the mention of the allowance to Holbein's wife would seem to imply that she was not very well provided for by her husband, Hegner attempts to excuse his apparent neglect by suggesting "that the great sometimes forget to pay, and will not bear dunning ;" and in illustration of this he refers to the passage in Albert Durer's Journal which has been previously given at page 269.

Holbein's three visits to Basle have been here especially noticed in order that the reader might judge for himself as to the probability of his making the drawings for the Lyons Dance of Death on any of those occasions. As this work was published in 1538, and as Holbein on his last visit appears to have arrived at Basle about the beginning of September in that year, it is impossible that he should have made the drawings then; for if the forty-one cuts were executed by one person

---

* Holbein's wife and *child* only, not children, are mentioned in this licence. It is not known what became of Holbein's children, as there are no traces of his descendants to be found at Basle. Merian, a clergyman of Basle, in a letter to Mechel on this subject, in 1779, writes to this effect : "According to a pedigree of the Merian family, printed at Regensburg in 1727, Christina Syf, daughter of Rodolph Syf and Judith Weissin, and grand-daughter of Hans Holbein the unequalled painter, (born 1597,) was married on the 17th of November 1616 to Frederick Merian." Perhaps it is meant that Judith Weissin was Holbein's grand-daughter : there is evidently an error in the pedigree ; and if it be wrong in this respect, it is not entitled to much credit in another.

† Hegner, S. 242.

—as from the similarity and excellence of the style there seems every reason to believe—it would require at the least half a year to engrave them, supposing that the artist worked as expeditiously as a wood engraver of modern times. As it is highly probable that Holbein both made designs and painted on his former visits, in 1529, and in 1532 or 1533, I think it most likely that they were made on the latter occasion, —that is, supposing them to have been designed on one of those visits. It is, however, just as probable that the designs were made in England, and forwarded to a wood engraver at Basle.

Of the various paintings executed by Holbein during his residence in England it is not necessary to give any account here; those who wish for information on this point are referred to Walpole's Anecdotes of Painting.* Of his life in England there are few particulars. "In some household accounts of Henry VIII," says Mr. Douce, "there are payments to him in 1538, 1539, 1540, and 1541, on account of his salary, which appears to have been thirty pounds per annum. From this time little more is recorded of him till 1553, when he painted Queen Mary's portrait, and shortly afterwards died of the plague in 1554." Thomas Howard, Earl of Arundel, the great patron of artists, in the time of Charles I, was desirous of erecting a monument to the memory of Holbein, but gave up the intention as he was unable to discover the place of the artist's interment. As Holbein seems to have left no will, and as his death appears to have excited no notice, it is likely that he died poor, and in comparative obscurity. If his satirical drawings † of Christ's Passion, ridiculing the Pope and the popish clergy, were known to Mary, or any of her spiritual advisers, it could not be expected that he should find favour at her court.

Wood engraving in England during the time of Holbein's residence in this country appears to have been but little cultivated; but though there cannot be a doubt that the art was then practised here by native wood

* See Dallaway's edition, revised by R. N. Wornum. London, Bohn, 1849, 3 vols. 8vo. Vol. i. pp. 66 et seq.

† Those designs were engraved on sixteen small plates by Hollar, but without his name. The enemies of Christ are represented in the dress of monks and friars, and instead of weapons they bear croziers, large candlesticks, and other church ornaments; Judas appears as a capucin, Annas as a cardinal, and Caiaphas as a bishop. In the subject of Christ's Descent to Hades, the gates are hung with papal bulls and dispensations; above them are the Pope's arms, and the devil as keeper of the gate wears a triple crown. Underneath this engraving are the following verses, which are certainly not of the period of Holbein:

"Lo! the Pope's kitchin, where his soles are fried,
Called Purgatorie; see his pardons tied
On strings; his triple crown the Divell weares,
And o'er the door the Pope's own arms he beares."

In the subject of Christ before Caiaphas is the following inscription in German: "Wer wider die Römischen, der soll sterben,"—that is, "He who is against the Romans shall die."

engravers, yet I very much question if it were practised by any person in England as a distinct profession. It is not unlikely that many of the wood-cuts which appear in books printed in this country about that period were engraved by the printers themselves. It has indeed been supposed that most of the wood-cuts in English books printed at that period were engraved on the continent; but this opinion seems highly improbable—there could be no occasion to send abroad to have wood-cuts so rudely executed. Perhaps the difficulty, or rather the impossibility of finding a wood engraver in England capable of doing justice to his designs might be one reason why Holbein made so few for the booksellers of this country during his long residence here. The following portrait of Sir Thomas Wyatt, the poet, who died in 1541, was probably drawn on the block by Holbein. It is given on the reverse of the title of a small work in quarto, printed at London, 1542, and entitled "Næniæ in mortem Thomæ Viati equitis incomparabilis. Joanne Lelando antiquario autore." The verses, which are printed underneath the cut, seem decisive of the drawing having been made by Holbein. There is a drawing of Sir Thomas Wyatt by Holbein, in the Royal Collection, which is engraved in Chamberlain's work, entitled "Imitations of Original Drawings by Hans Holbein," folio, 1792. There is little similarity between the drawing and the cut, though on comparison it is evident that both are intended for the same person.

In effigiem Thomæ Viati.
Holbenus nitida pingendi maximus arte
Effigiem expressit graphicè : sed nullus Apelles
Exprimet ingenium felix animumque Viati.

It has been supposed that the original cut, of which the preceding is a fac-simile, was engraved by Holbein himself: if this were true, and the cut itself taken as a specimen of his abilities in this department of art, there could not be a doubt of his having been a very indifferent wood engraver, for though there be considerable expression of character in the drawing of the head, the cut is executed in a very inferior style of art.

The cuts in Cranmer's Catechism, a small octavo, printed in 1548,* have been ascribed to Holbein; but out of the whole number, twenty-nine, including the cut on the reverse of the title, there are only two which contain his mark. In the others the manner of pencilling is so unlike that of these two, and the drawing and composition bear so little resemblance to Holbein's usual style, that I do not believe them to have been of his designing. In the cut on the reverse of the title, the subject is Cranmer presenting the Bible to Edward VI.; the others, twenty-eight in number, but containing only twenty-six different subjects,—as two of them are repeated,—are illustrative of different passages of Scripture cited in the work. The following cut is one of

those designed by Holbein. It occurs at folio CL as an illustration of "the fyrst sermon. A declaration of the fyrst peticion" [of the Lord's Prayer]. Holbein's initials, H. H.—though the cross stroke of the first H is broken away—are perceived on the edge of what seems to be a book, to the left of the figure praying.

The other cut, designed by Holbein, and which contains his name at

---

* The following is the title of this scarce little volume. "Catechismus, that is to say, a shorte instruction into Christian religion for the singuler commoditie and profyte of childrē and yong people. Set forth by the mooste reverende father in God, Thomas Archbyshop of Canterbury, primate of all Englande and Metropolitane.—Gualterus Lynne excudebat, 1548." At the end of the book, under a cut of Christ with a child before him, is the colophon: "Imprynted at London, in S. Jhones Streete, by Nycolas Hyll, for Gwalter Lynne dwellyng on Somers kaye, by Byllynges gate." Mr. Douce, at page 96, mentions a cut with the name *Hans Holbein* at the bottom, as occurring in the title-page of "A lytle treatise after the manner of an Epystle wryten by the famous clerk Doctor Urbanus Regius," &c. also published by Walter Lynne, 1548.

full length,* occurs at folio CCI. The subject is Christ casting out Devils, in illustration of the seventh petition of the Lord's Prayer,—"Deliver us from evil." The following is a fac-simile.

For the purpose of showing the difference of style between those two cuts and the others contained in the same work, the three given on the following page have been selected. The first, illustrating the Creation, occurs at the folio erroneously numbered CXCV, properly CIX, No. 1 ; the second, illustrating the sermon of our redemption, at folio CXXI, No. 2 ; and the third, illustrating the third petition of the Lord's Prayer,—"Thy will be done,"—at folio CLXVIII, No. 3. The following are the introductory remarks to the explanation of what the archbishop calls the third petition : "Ye have herde how in the former petycions, we require of our Lorde God to gyve us al thinges that perteyne to his glorye and to the kyngdom of heaven, whereof he hath gyven us commaundemente in the three preceptes written in the first table. Nowe folowethe the thirde peticyon, wherein we praye God to graūte us that we may fulfyll the other seven commaūdementes also, the whiche intreat of matiers concerning this worldly kingdome and transitorye lyfe, that is to saye, to honoure our parentes and gouernours, to kyl no man, to committe none adulterye, to absteyne from thefte and lyinge, and to behave our selfes in all thinges obedientlye, honestlye, peaceably, and godly."

* Mr. Douce, in his observations prefixed to Hollar's etchings of the Dance of Death, published by Edwards in 1794, says, " A *set* of cuts with the latter mark [*Hans Holben*] occurs in Archbishop Cranmer's Catechism, printed by Walter Lyne, in 1548 ;" and in the same page he commits another mistake by describing the mark on the cut of the Duchess in the Lyons Dance of Death as **HB**, instead of **H**. It has been considered necessary to notice these errors, as it is probable that many persons who possess the work in which they occur, but who never may have seen a copy of the Lyons Dance of Death, nor of Cranmer's Catechism, may have been misled in those matters by implicitly relying on Mr. Douce's authority. A certain class of compilers are also extremely liable to transmit such mistakes, and, to borrow an expression of Hegner's, to give currency to them, as if they stood ready for use " in *stereotype*."

The feebleness of the drawing and the want of distinctness in these three cuts, are totally unlike the more vigorous delineation of

No. 1.

No. 2.

No. 3.

Holbein, as exemplified, though but imperfectly, in the two which are doubtlessly of his designing. None of them have the slightest pretensions to delicacy or excellence of engraving, though they may be considered as the best that had been executed in this country up to that time. Those which, in my opinion, were not designed by Holbein have the appearance of having been engraved on a *frushy* kind of wood, of comparatively coarse grain. It is not, however, unlikely that this appearance might result from the feebleness of the drawing, conjoined with want of skill on the part of the engraver.

The following cut will not perhaps form an inappropriate termination to the notice of the principal wood engravings which have been ascribed

to Holbein. It occurs as an illustration of the generation of Christ, Matthew, chapter I, in an edition of the New Testament, printed at Zurich, by Froschover, in 1554,* the year of Holbein's death. Though there be no name to this cut, yet from the great resemblance which it bears to Holbein's style, I have little doubt of the design being his.

The three following specimens of the cuts in Tindale's Translation of the New Testament, printed at Antwerp in 1534,† ought, in strict

---

* The title-page of this book—which has previously been referred to at page 357, in illustration of the word *picta*—is as follows: "Novi Testamenti Editio postrema per Des. Erasmum Roterodamum. Omnia picturis illustrata. Accesserunt Capitum argumenta Elegiaco carmine, Rudolpho Gualtero authore, conscripta. Tiguri, in Officina Froschoviana. Anno M.D.LIIII." 8vo.

† The volume is of octavo size, and the title is as follows: "The Newe Testament. Imprinted at Antwerp by Marten Emperour. Anno M.D.XXXIIII." The letters on the wood-cut of the printer's device, seen in the copies on paper, are M. K. The first edition of Tindale's Translation was printed in 1526. William Tindale, otherwise Hitchins, was born

chronological order, to have preceded those of the Dance of Death ; but as Holbein holds the same rank in this chapter as Durer in the

No. 1.   No. 2.

No. 3.

preceding, it seemed preferable to give first a connected account of the principal wood-cuts which are generally ascribed to him, and which

on the borders of Wales, but was of a Northumberland family, being descended from Adam de Tindale of Langley, near Haydon Bridge, in that county. He was strangled, and his body was afterwards burnt as that of a heretic by the popish party, at Vilvorde, near Brussels, in 1536.

there is the strongest reason to believe were actually of his designing. The celebrity of Tindale's translation, as the earliest English version of the New Testament which appeared in print, and the place which his name occupies in the earlier part of the history of the Reformation in England, will give an interest to those cuts to which they could have no pretensions as mere works of art. It is probable that they were executed at Antwerp, where the book was printed; and the drawing and engraving will afford some idea of the style of most of the small cuts which are to be found in works printed in Holland and Flanders about that period. The first of the preceding cuts represents St. Luke employed in painting a figure of the Virgin, and it occurs at the commencement of the Gospel of that Evangelist. The second, which occurs at the commencement of the General Epistle of James, represents that Saint in the character of a pilgrim. The third, Death on the Pale Horse, is an illustration of the sixth chapter of Revelations.

There is a beautiful copy, printed on vellum, of this edition of Tindale's Translation of the New Testament in the Library of the British Museum. It appears to have formerly belonged to Queen Anne Boleyn, and was probably a presentation copy from the translator. The title-page is beautifully illuminated; the whole of the ornamental border, which is seen in the copies on paper, is covered with gilding and colour, and the wood-cut of the printer's mark is covered with the blazoning of the royal arms. On the edges, which are gilt, there is inscribed, in red letters, ANNA REGINA ANGLIÆ. This beautiful volume formerly belonged to the Reverend C. M. Cracherode, by whom it was bequeathed to the Museum.

The first complete English translation of the Old and New Testaments was that of Miles Coverdale, which appeared in folio, 1535,* without the name or residence of the printer, but supposed to have been printed at

---

* The title of this edition is as follows : " BIBLIA. The Bible, that is, the holy Scripture of the Olde and Newe Testaments, faithfully translated out of Douche and Latyn in to Englishe. M.D.XXXV." This title is surrounded with an ornamental wood-cut border of ten compartments : 1. Adam and Eve. 2. The name of Jehovah in Hebrew characters in the centre at the top. 3. Christ with the banner of the cross trampling on the serpent, sin, and death. 4. Moses receiving the tables of the law. 5. Jewish High Priest,—Esdras. 6. Christ sending his disciples to preach the Gospel. 7. Paul preaching. 8. David playing on the harp. 9. In the centre at the bottom, King Henry VIII. on his throne giving a book— probably intended for the Bible—to certain abbots and bishops. 10. St. Paul with a sword. The day of the month mentioned in the colophon was probably the date of the last sheet being sent to press : " Prynted in the yeare of our Lorde M.D.XXXV, and fynished the fourth daye of October." Copies of this edition with the title-page are extremely rare. Some copies have a modern lithographed title prefixed, which is not exactly correct, though professedly a fac-simile : in one of the scrolls it has " telius meus " for " filius meus." In the corresponding scroll in a copy in the British Museum the words are in English : " This is my deare Son in whom I delyte, heare him,"—above the figure of Christ with the banner of the cross. I have not the least doubt of this title-page having been designed by Holbein.

C C

Zurich by Christopher Froschover. The dedication is addressed to Henry VIII, by "his Graces humble subjecte and daylie oratour, Myles Coverdale;" and in the copy in the British Museum the commencement is as follows: "Unto the most victorious Prynce and our most gracyous soveraigne Lorde, kynge Henry the eyght, kynge of Englonde and of Fraunce, lorde of Irlonde, &c. Defendour of the Fayth, and under God the chefe and supreme heade of the churche of Englonde. ¶The ryght and just administracyon of the laws that God gave unto Moses and unto Josua: the testimonye of faythfulnes that God gave of David: the plenteous abundance of wysdome that God gave unto Salomon: the lucky and prosperous age with the multiplicacyon of sede which God gave unto Abraham and Sara his wyfe, be gevē unto you most Gracyous Prynce, with your dearest just wyfe and most virtuous Pryncesse, Quene Anne. Amen." In most copies, however, "Quene Jane" is substituted for "Quene Anne," which proves that the original dedication had been cancelled after the disgrace and execution of Anne Boleyn, and that, though the colophon is dated 4th October 1535, the work had not been generally circulated until subsequent to 20th May 1536, the date of Henry's marriage with Jane Seymour.

This edition contains a number of wood-cuts, all rather coarsely engraved, though some of them are designed with such spirit as to be not unworthy of Holbein himself, as will be apparent from two or three of the following specimens. In the first, Cain killing Abel, the attitude of Abel, and the action of Cain, sufficiently indicate that the original designer understood the human figure well, and could draw it with great force in a position which it is most difficult to represent.

No. 1.

The figure of Abraham in No. 2 bears in some parts considerable resemblance to that of the same subject given as a specimen of Holbein's

Bible cuts at page 368; but there are several others in the work which are much more like his style; and which, perhaps, might be copied from

No. 2.

earlier cuts of his designing. The two preceding may be considered as specimens of the best designed cuts in the Old Testament; and the following, the return of the Two Spies, is given as one of the more ordinary.

No. 3.

The three next cuts are from the New Testament. The first forms the head-piece to the Gospel of St. Matthew; the second, which occurs on the title-page, and displays great power of drawing in the figure, is John the Baptist; and the third represents St. Paul writing, with his sword before him, and a weaver's loom to his left: the last incident,

c c 2

which is frequently introduced in old wood-cuts of this Saint, is
probably intended to designate his business as a tentmaker, and also to

No. 1.

No. 2.

No. 3.

indicate that, though zealously engaged in disseminating the doctrines of
Christ, he had not ceased to "work with his hands."

Many of the cuts in this work are copied in a subsequent edition, also in folio, printed in 1537 ; and some of the copies are so extremely like the originals—every line being retained—as to induce a suspicion that the impressions of the latter had been transferred to the blocks by means of what is technically termed "rubbing down."

About 1530 the art of chiaro-scuro engraving on wood, which appears to have been first introduced into Italy by Ugo da Carpi, was practised by Antonio Fantuzzi, called also Antonio da Trente. Most of this engraver's chiaro-scuros are from the designs of Parmegiano. It is said that Fantuzzi was employed by Parmegiano for the express purpose of executing chiaro-scuro engravings from his drawings, and that, when residing with his employer at Bologna, he took an opportunity of robbing him of all his blocks, impressions, and designs. Between 1530 and 1540 Joseph Nicholas Vincentini da Trente engraved several chiaro-scuros, most of which, like those executed by Fantuzzi, are from the designs of Parmegiano. From the number of chiaro-scuros engraved after drawings by this artist, I think it highly probable that the most of them were executed under his own superintendence and published for his own benefit. Baldazzar Peruzzi and Domenico Beccafumi, both painters of repute at that period, are said to have engraved in chiaro-scuro ; but the prints in this style usually ascribed to them are not numerous, and I consider it doubtful if they were actually of their own engraving.

From about 1530, the art of wood engraving, in the usual manner, began to make considerable progress in Italy, and many of the cuts executed in that country between 1540 and 1580 may vie with the best wood engravings of the same period executed in Germany. Instead of the plain and simple style, which is in general characteristic of Italian wood-cuts previous to 1530, the wood engravers of that country began to execute their subjects in a more delicate and elaborate manner. In the period under consideration, we find cross-hatching frequently introduced with great effect ; there is a greater variety of *tint* in the cuts ; the texture of different substances is indicated more correctly ; the foliage of trees is more natural ; and the fur and feathers of animals are discriminated with considerable ability.

The following cut will afford perhaps some idea of the best Italian wood-cuts of the period under consideration. It is a reduced copy of the frontispiece to Marcolini's Sorti,* folio, printed at Venice in 1540.

* The following is the title of this curious and scarce work : " Le Sorti di Francesco Marcolini da Forli, intitolate Giardino di Pensieri." Dedicated, " Allo Illustrissimo Signore Hercole Estense, Duca di Ferrara." At the conclusion is the colophon : " In Venetia per Francesco Marcolini da Forli, ne gli anni del Signore MDXXXX. Del mese di Ottobre." In a *proemio*, or preface, the author explains the manner of applying his

There is an impression of this cut on paper of a greenish tint in the Print Room of the British Museum, and from this circumstance it is placed, though improperly, in a volume, marked I. W. 4, and lettered " Italian chiaro-scuros."   Underneath this impression the late Mr. Ottley has written, " Not in Bartsch ; " and from his omitting to mention the work for which it was engraved, I am inclined to think that he himself

was not aware of its forming the frontispiece to Marcolini's Sorti. Papillon, speaking of the supposed engraver, Joseph Porta Garfagninus, whose name is seen on a tablet near the bottom towards the right, says, " J'ai de lui une fort belle Académie des Sciences," * but seems not to have known of the work to which it belonged.   This cut is merely a copy, reversed, of a study by Raffaele for his celebrated fresco, usually

'*piacevole inventione*," which is nothing more than a mode of resolving questions by cards, and was probably suggested by Fanti's Triompho di Fortuna, of which some account is given at page 315.

* Papillon, Traité de la Gravure en Bois, tom. i. p. 137.

called the School of Athens, in the Vatican. It is engraved in a work entitled "Vies et Oeuvres des Peintres les plus célèbres," 4to. Paris, 1813; and in the Table des Planches at the commencement of the volume in which it occurs, the subject is thus described: "Pl. ccccv. Étude pour le tableau de l'Ecole d'Athènes. Ces différens episodes ne se retrouvant pas dans le tableau qui a été exécuté des mains de Raphaël, ne doivent être considérées que comme des essais ou premières pensées. *Grav. M. Ravignano.*" From this description it appears that the same subject had been previously engraved on copper by Marco da Ravenna, who flourished about the year 1530. Though I have never seen an impression of Marco's engraving of this subject, and though it is not mentioned in Heineken's catalogue of the engraved works of Raffaele,* I have little doubt that Porta's wood-cut is copied from it.

Joseph Porta, frequently called Joseph Salviati by Italian authors, was a painter, and he took the surname of Salviati from that of his master, Francesco Salviati.† There are a few other wood-cuts which contain his name; but whether he was the designer, or the engraver only, is extremely uncertain.

Marcolini's work contains nearly a hundred wood-cuts besides the frontispiece, but, though several of them are designed with great spirit, no one is so well engraved.‡ The following is a fac-simile of one which occurs at page 35. The relentless-looking old woman is a personification of *Punitione*—Punishment—holding in her right hand a tremendous scourge for the chastisement of evil-doers. Though this cut be but coarsely engraved, the domestic Nemesis, who here appears to wield the retributive scourge, is designed with such spirit that if the figure were executed in marble it might almost pass for one of Michael

---

* This catalogue is printed in the second volume of Heineken's Nachrichten von Künstlern und Kunst-Sachen, 8vo. Leipzig, 1768-1769. This work, which appeared two years before his Idée Générale d'une Collection complette d'Estampes, contains much information on the early history of art, which is not to be found in the latter. All the fac-similes of old engravings in the Idée Générale originally appeared in the Nachrichten. Heineken, in the first volume of this work, p. 340, mentions Porta's cut, but says nothing of its being copied from a design by Raffaele.

† Heineken, in his Nachrichten, 1er. Theil, S. 340, says that Joseph Porta "was a pupil of *Cecchino* Salviati, who is not to be confounded with *Francesco* Salviati;" and yet in his Idée Générale, published subsequently, page 134, we find "Francesco del Salviati, autrement Rossi, de Florence, et son disciple Giuseppe Porta, appellé communément Giuseppe Salviati." Heineken, in his first work, committed the mistake of supposing that Francesco Salviati's *to*-name was the Christian name of another person. In Huber's Notice Générale des Graveurs et Peintres, Francis Salviati appears as "François Cecchini, dit Salviati."

‡ The first forty-six cuts are the best, generally, both in design and execution. The others, commencing at page 108, are illustrative of the sayings and doctrines of ancient philosophers and moralists, and one or two of the cuts are repeated. In this portion of the work, each page, except what is occupied by the cut, is filled with explanatory or illustrative verses arranged in triplets.

Angelo's. The drapery is admirably cast; the figure is good; and the action and expression are at once simple and severe.

The preceding cut, also a fac-simile, occurs at page 81 as an illustration of Matrimony. The young man, with his legs already tied, seems to be deliberating on the prudence of making a contract which may possibly add a yoke to his shoulders. The ring which he holds in his hand appears to have given rise to his cogitations.

The following small cuts of cards—" Il Re, Fante, Cavallo, e Sette di denari "—are copied from the instructions in the preface ;* and

the beautiful design of Truth rescued by Time—VERÏTAS FILIA TEMPORIS—occurs as a tail-piece on the last page of the work. This cut occurs nôt unfrequently in works published by Giolito, by whom I believe the Sorti was printed ; and two or three of the other cuts contained in the volume are to be found in a humorous work of Doni's, entitled " I Marmi," printed by Giolito in 1552.

The wood engravers of Venice about the middle of the sixteenth century appear to have excelled all other Italian wood engravers, and for the delicacy of their execution they rivalled those of Lyons, who at that period were chiefly distinguished for the neat and delicate manner of their engraving small subjects. In the pirated edition of the Lyons Dance of Death, published at Venice in 1545 by V. Vaugris, the cuts are more correctly copied and more delicately engraved than

---

* The first hundred and seven pages of the work are chiefly filled with similar figures of cards variously combined, with short references. How Marcolini's pleasant invention is to be applied to discover the secrets of Fate, I have not been able to comprehend.

those in the edition first published at Cologne by the heirs of Arnold Birkman in 1555. In fact, the wood engravings in books printed at Lyons and Venice from about 1540 to 1580 are in general more delicately engraved than those executed in Germany and the Low Countries during the same period. Among all the Venetian printers of that age, Gabriel Giolito is entitled to precedence from the number and comparative excellence of the wood-cuts contained in the numerous illustrated works which issued from his press. In several of the works printed by him every cut is surrounded by an ornamental border; and this border, not being engraved on the same block as the cut, but separately as a kind of frame, is frequently repeated : sixteen different borders, when the book is of octavo size and there is a cut on every page, would suffice for the whole work, however extensive it might

be. The practice of *ornamenting* cuts in this manner was very prevalent about the period under consideration, and at the present time some publishers seem inclined to revive it. I should, however, be sorry to see it again become prevalent, for though to some subjects, designed in a particular manner, an ornamental border may be appropriate, yet I consider the practice of thus *framing* a series of cuts as indicative of bad taste, and as likely to check the improvement of the art. Highly ornamented borders have, in a certain degree, the effect of reducing a series of cuts, however different their execution, to a standard of mediocrity ; for they frequently conceal the beauty of a well-engraved subject, and serve as a screen to a bad one. In Ludovico Dolce's Transformationi—a translation, or rather paraphrase of Ovid's Metamorphoses—first printed by Giolito in 1553, and again in 1557, the cuts, instead of having a border all round, have only ornaments at the two vertical sides. The preceding is a fac-simile of one of those cuts, divested of its ornaments, from the edition of 1557. The subject is the difficult labour of Alcmena,—a favourite with Italian artists. This is the cut previously alluded to at page 217.

A curious book, of which an edition, in quarto, was printed at Rome in 1561, seems deserving of notice here, not on account of any merit in the wood-cuts which it contains, but on account of the singularity of four of them, which are given as a specimen of a "Sonetto figurato," in the manner of the cuts in a little work entitled "A curious Hieroglyphick Bible," first printed in London, in duodecimo, about 1782. The Italian work in question was written by "Messer Giovam Battista Palatino, Cittadino Romano," and from the date of the Pope's grant to the author of the privilege of exclusively printing it for ten years, it seems likely that the first edition was published about 1540. The work is a treatise on penmanship; and the title-page of the edition of 1561—which is embellished with a portrait of the author—may be translated as follows : "The Book of M. Giovam Battista Palatino, citizen of Rome, in which is taught the manner of writing all kinds of characters, ancient and modern, of whatever nation, with Rules, Proportions, and Examples. Together with a short and useful Discourse on Cyphers. Newly revised and corrected by the Author. With the addition of fifteen beautiful cuts."*

In Astle's Origin and Progress of Writing, page 227, second edition, Palatino's work is thus noticed : "In 1561, Valerius Doricus printed at Rome a curious book on all kinds of writing, ancient and modern. This book contains specimens of a great variety of writing practised in different ages and countries ; some of these specimens are printed from types to imitate writing, and others from carved wood-blocks. This book also contains a treatise on the art of writing in cipher, and is a most curious specimen of early typography."

After his specimens of " Lettere Cifrate," Palatino devotes a couple of pages to " Cifre quadrate, et Sonetti figurati," two modes of riddle-writing which, it appears, are solely employed for amusement. The

---

* The following is a literal copy of the title : " Libro di M. Giovam Battista Palatino, Cittadino Romano, Nelqual s'insegna à Scriver ogni sorte lettera, Antica & Moderna, di qualunque natione, con le sue regole, & misure, & essempi : Et con un breve, et util Discorso de le Cifre : Riveduto novamente, & corretto dal propri' Autore. Con la giunta di quindici tavole bellissime." At the end of the work is the imprint : " In Roma per Valerio Dorico alla Chiavica de Santa Lucia. Ad Instantia de M. Giovan della Gatta. L'Anno M.D.LXI." 4to. Papillon says that the work first appeared in 1540, and was reprinted in 1545, 1547, 1548, 1550, 1553, and 1556. An edition was also published at Venice in 1588.

"Cifro quadrato" is nothing more than a monogram, formed of a cluster of interwoven capitals, but in which every one of the letters of the name is to be found. In the following specimen the name thus ingeniously disguised is LAVINIA.

The following is a slightly reduced copy of the first four lines of the "Sonetto figurato;" the other ten lines are expressed by figures in a similar manner. "As to figured sonnets," says the author, "no better

rule can be given, than merely to observe that the figures should clearly and distinctly correspond with the matter, and that there should be as few supplementary letters as possible. Of course, orthography and pure

Italian are not to be looked for in such exercises ; and it is no objection that the same figure be used for the beginning of one word, the middle of another, or the end of a third. It is the chief excellence of such compositions that there should be few letters to be supplied."

The " interpretatio " of the preceding figured text is as follows :

> " Dove son gli occhi, et la serena forma
> Del santo alegro et amoroso aspetto ?
> Dov' è la man eburna ov' e 'l bel petto
> Ch' appensarvi hor' in fonte mi transforma ?"

This figured sonnet is a curious specimen of hieroglyphic and " phonetic " writing combined. For those who do not understand Italian, it seems necessary to give the following explanation of the words, and point out their phonetic relation to the things. *Dove*, where, is composed of *D*, and *ove*, eggs, as seen at the commencement of the first line. *Son*, are, is represented by a man's head and a trumpet, making a sound, *son*. The preceding figures are examples of what is called "phonetic" writing, by modern expounders of Egyptian antiquities,—that is, the figures of *things* are not placed as representatives of the things themselves, but that their names when pronounced may form a word or part of a word, which has generally not the least relation to the thing by which it is *phonetically*, that is, vocally, expressed. *Occhi*, eyes, is an instance of hieroglyphic writing ; the figure and the idea to be represented agree. *La*, the, is represented by the musical note *la ; serena*, placid, by a Siren,—*Sirena*,—orthography, as the author says, is not to be expected in figured sonnets ; and *forma*, shape, by a shoemaker's last, which is called *forma* in Italian.

In the second line, *Santo*, holy, is represented by a Saint, *Santo ; allegro*, cheerfulness, by a pair of wings, *ale*, and *grue*, a crane, the superfluous *e* forming, with the T following, the conjunction *et*, and. The words *amoroso aspetto* are formed of *amo*, a hook, *rosa*, a rose, and *petto*, the breast, with a supplementary *s* between the rose and the breast.

In the third line we have *ove*, eggs, and the musical *la* again ; *man*, the hand, is expressed by its proper figure ; *eburna*, ivory-like, is composed of the letters EB and an urn, *urna ;* and in the latter part of the line the eggs, *ov'*, and the breast, *petto*, are repeated.

At the commencement of the fourth line, a couple of cloaks, *cappe*, stand for *ch' appe* in the compound word *ch' appe*nsarvi ; *hor'*, now, is represented by an hour-glass, *hora*, literally, an hour ; *fonte*, a fountain, is expressed by its proper figure ; and the words *mi transforma*, are phonetically expressed by a mitre, *mitra*, the supplementary letters NS, and the shoemaker's last, *forma*.

In the reign of Queen Elizabeth, a taste for inventing devices in this manner seems to have been fashionable among professed wits ; and the practice of expressing a name by a rebus was not unfrequent in an earlier age. It is probable that the old sign of the Bolt-in-Tun in Fleet Street derives its origin from Bolton, a prior of St. Bartholomew's in Smithfield, who gave a bird-*bolt* in the bung-hole of a *tun* as the rebus of his name. The peculiarities of the Italian figured sonnet are not unaptly illustrated in Camden's Remains, in the chapter entitled "*Rebus,** or Name-Devises :*" " Did not that amorous youth mystically expresse his love to *Rose Hill,* whom he courted, when in a border of his painted cloth he caused to be painted as rudely as he devised grossely, a rose, a hill, an eye, a loafe, and a well,—that is, if you will spell it,

Rose Hill I love well."†

Among the wood engravers of Lyons who flourished about the middle of the sixteenth century, the only one whose name has come down to modern times is Bernard Solomon ; and if he were actually the engraver of the numerous cuts which are ascribed to him, he must have been extremely industrious. I am not, however, aware of any cut which contains his mark ; and it is by no means certain whether he were really a wood engraver, or whether he only made the designs for wood engravers to execute. Papillon, who has been blindly followed by most persons who have either incidentally or expressly written on wood engraving, unhesitatingly claims him as a wood engraver ; but looking at the inequality in the execution of the cuts ascribed to him, and regarding the sameness of character in the designs, I am inclined to think that he was not an engraver, but that he merely made the drawings on the wood. Sir E. L. Bulwer has committed a mistake of this kind in his England and the English : " This country," says he in his second volume, page 205, edition 1833, " may boast of having, in Bewick of Newcastle, brought wood engraving to perfection ; his pupil, Harvey, continues the profession with reputation." The writer here evidently speaks of that which he knows very little about, for at the time that his book was published, Harvey, though originally a wood engraver, and a pupil of

---

* There is a curious allusion to a *Rebus* in Horace, Satyr. Lib. I. Sat. V., Vers. 88, which has escaped the notice of all his commentators :

" Quatuor hinc rapimur viginti et millia rhedis,
Mansuri oppidulo, quod versu dicere non est,
Signis perfacile est."

The place which he did not think proper to name was undoubtedly Asculum, whose situation exactly corresponds with the distance from *Trivicum,* where he rested the preceding night. From the manner in which Horace alludes to the *signa—as* and *culum—*of which the name is composed, it seems likely that a certain vulgar benison was not unknown at Rome in the age of Augustus.

† Remaines concerning Britaine, with additions by John Philpot, Somerset Herald, p. 164. Edit. 1636.

Bewick, had abandoned the profession for about eight years, and had devoted himself entirely to painting and drawing for copper-plate and wood engravers. Indeed I very much question if Sir Edward Lytton Bulwer ever saw a cut—except, perhaps, that of Dentatus,—which was actually engraved by Harvey. With about equal propriety, a writer, speaking of wood engraving in England twenty years ago, might have described the late John Thurston as "continuing the profession with reputation," merely because he was one of the principal designers of wood engravings at that period.

Bernard Solomon, whether a designer or engraver on wood, is justly entitled to be ranked among the "little masters" in this branch of art. All the cuts ascribed to him which have come under my notice are of small size, and most of them are executed in a delicate manner; they are, however, generally deficient in effect,* and may readily be distinguished by the tall slim figures which he introduces. He evidently had not understood the "capabilities" of his art, for in none of his productions do we find the well-contrasted "black-and-white," which, when well managed, materially contributes to the excellence of a well-engraved wood-cut. The production of a good *black* is, indeed, one of the great advantages, in point of conventional colour, which wood possesses over copper ; and the wood engraver who neglects this advantage, and labours perhaps for a whole day to cut with mechanical precision a number of delicate but unmeaning lines, which a copper-plate engraver would execute with facility in an hour, affords a tolerably convincing proof of his not thoroughly understanding the principles of his art. In Bernard's cuts, and in most of those executed at Lyons about the same period, we find much of this ineffective labour ; we perceive in them many evidences of the pains-taking workman, but few traits of the talented artist. From the time that a taste for those little and laboriously executed, but spiritless cuts, began to prevail, the decline of wood engraving may be dated. Instead of confining themselves within the legitimate boundaries of their own art, wood engravers seem to have been desirous of emulating the delicacy of copper-plate engraving, and, as might naturally be expected by any one who understands the distinctive peculiarities of the two arts, they failed. The book-buyers of the period having become sickened with the glut of tasteless

* Papillon, who speaks highly of the execution of the cuts ascribed to Bernard Solomon, admits that they want effect. "La gravure," says he, speaking of the cuts contained in 'Quadrins Historiques de la Bible,' "est fort belle, excepté qu'elle manque de clair obscur, parce que les tailles sont presque toutes de la même teinte, ce qui fait que les lointains ne fuyent pas assez. C'est le seul defaut des gravures de Bernard Salomon ; ce qui lui a été commun avec plus de quarante autres graveurs en bois de son temps."—Traité de la Gravure en Bois, tom. i. p. 209.

and ineffective trifles, wood engraving began to decline: large well-engraved wood-cuts executed between 1580 and 1600 are comparatively scarce.

Bernard Solomon, or, as he is frequently called, *Little* Solomon, from the smallness of his works, is said to have been born in 1512, and the most of the cuts which are ascribed to him appeared in works printed at Lyons between 1545 and 1580. Perhaps more books containing small wood-cuts were printed at Lyons between those years than in any other city or town in Europe during the corresponding period. It appears to have been the grand mart for Scripture cuts, emblems, and devices; but out of the many hundreds which appear to have been engraved there in the period referred to, it would be difficult to select twenty that can be considered really excellent both in execution and design. One of the principal publishers of Lyons at that time was Jean de Tournes; many of the works which issued from his press display great typographic excellence, and in almost all the cuts are engraved with great neatness. The following cut is a fac-simile of one which appears in the title-page of an edition of Petrarch's Sonnetti, Canzoni, e Trionfi, published by him in a small octodecimo volume, 1545.

The design of the cut displays something of the taste for emblem and device* which was then so prevalent, and which became so generally diffused by the frequent editions of Alciat's Emblems, the first of which was printed about 1531. The portraits of Petrarch and Laura, looking not unlike "Philip and Mary on a shilling," are

* Several editions of Alciat's Emblems and Claude Paradin's Devises Heroïques were published at Lyons in the sixteenth century. The first edition of the latter work was printed there by Jean de Tournes, in 1557, 8vo.

seen enclosed within a heart which Cupid has pierced to the very core with one of his arrows. The volume contains seven other small cuts, designed and engraved in a style which very much resembles that of the cuts ascribed to Bernard Solomon; and as there is no mark by which his productions are to be ascertained, I think they are as likely to be of his designing as three-fourths of those which are generally supposed to be of his engraving.

The work entitled "Quadrins Historiques de la Bible," with wood-cuts, ascribed to Bernard Solomon, and printed at Lyons by Jean de Tournes, was undoubtedly suggested by the "Historiarum Veteris Testamenti Icones"—Holbein's Bible-cuts—first published by the brothers Frellon in 1538. The first edition of the Quadrins Historiques was published in octavo about 1550, and was several times reprinted within the succeeding twenty years. The total number of cuts in the edition of 1560 is two hundred and twenty-nine, of which no less than one hundred and seventy are devoted to the illustration of Exodus and Genesis. At the top of each is printed the reference to the chapter to which it relates, and at the bottom is a "Quadrin poëtique, tiré de la Bible, pour graver en la table des affeccions l'amour des sacrees Histories." Those "Quadrins" appear to have been written by Claude Paradin. The composition of several of the cuts is good, and nearly all display great *neatness* of execution. The following is a fac-simile of the seventh, Adam and Eve driven out of Paradise. It is, however, necessary to observe that this

is by no means one of the best cuts either in point of design or execution.

A similar work, entitled "Figures du Nouveau Testament," with
cuts, evidently designed by the person who had made the drawings
for those in the "Quadrins Historiques de la Bible," was also published
by Jean de Tournes about 1553, and several editions were subsequently
printed. The cuts are rather less in size than those of the Quadrins,
and are, on the whole, rather better engraved. The total number is
a hundred and four, and under each are six explanatory verses,
composed by Charles Fonteine, who, in a short poetical address at
the commencement, dedicates the work "A Tres-illustre et Treshaute
Princesse, Madame Marguerite de France, Duchesse de Berri." The
following, Christ tempted by Satan, is a copy of the sixteenth cut,
but like that of the expulsion of Adam and Eve, it is not one of the
best in the work.

Old engravings and paintings illustrative of manners or of costume
are generally interesting ; and on this account a set of large wood-cuts
designed by Peter Coeck of Alost, in Flanders, is deserving of notice.
The subjects of those cuts are the manners and costumes of the Turks ;
and the drawings were made on the spot by Coeck himself, who visited
Turkey in 1533. It is said that he brought from the east an important
secret relative to the art of dyeing silk and wool for the fabrication
of tapestries, a branch of manufacture with which he appears to have
been connected, and for which he made a number of designs. He
was also an architect and an author ; and published several treatises
on sculpture, geometry, perspective, and architecture. The cuts illustrative of the manners and costume of the Turks were not published
until 1553, three years after his decease, as we learn from an inscription

on the last.* They are oblong, of folio size; and the seven of which the set consists are intended to be joined together, and thus to form one continuous subject. The figures, both on foot and horseback, are designed with great spirit, but they want relief, and the engraving is coarse. One of the customs which he has illustrated in the cut No. 3 is singular; and though this *orientalism* has been noticed by a Scottish judge—Maclaurin of Dreghorn—Peter Coeck appears to be the only traveller who has graphically represented "*quo modo Turci mingunt,*" i. e. *sedentes.* Succeeding artists have availed themselves liberally of those cuts. As the Turks in the sixteenth century were much more formidable as a nation than at present, and their manners and customs objects of greater curiosity, wood engravings illustrative of their costume and mode of living appear to have been in considerable demand at that period, for both in books and as single cuts they are comparatively numerous.

Though chiaro-scuro engraving on wood was, in all probability, first practised in Germany, yet the art does not appear to have been so much cultivated nor so highly prized in that country as in Italy. Between 1530 and 1550, when Antonio Fantuzzi, J. N. Vincentini, and other Italians, were engaged in executing numerous chiaro-scuros after the designs of such masters as Raffaele, Corregio, Parmegiano, Polidoro, Beccafumi, and F. Salviati, the art appears to have been comparatively abandoned by the wood engravers of Germany. The chiaro-scuros executed in the latter country cannot generally for a moment bear a comparison, either in point of design or execution, with those executed in Italy during the same period. I have, however, seen one German cut executed in this style, with the date 1543, which, for the number of the blocks from which it is printed, and the delicacy of the impression in certain parts, is, if genuine, one of the most remarkable of that period. As the paper, however, seems comparatively modern, I am induced to suspect that the date may be that of the painting or drawing, and that this picture-print—for, though executed by the same process, it would be improper to call it a chiaro-scuro—may have been the work of Ungher, a German wood engraver, who executed some chiaro-scuros at Berlin about seventy years ago. Whatever may be the date, however, or whoever may have been the artist, it is one of the best executed specimens of coloured block printing that I have ever seen.

* The following explanatory title occurs on the first cut: "Ces moeurs et fachons de faire de Turcz avecq' les Regions y appartenantes, ont este au vif contrefactez par Pierre Coeck d'Alost, luy estant en Turquie, l'an de Jesu Christ M.D. 33. Lequel assy de sa main propre a pourtraict ces figures duysantes à l'impression d'ycelles." From another of the cuts we thus learn the time of his death: "Marie Verhulst vefue du dict Pierre d'Alost, trespasse en l'anne MDL, a faict imprimer les dicts figures soubz Grace et Privilege de l'Imperialle Maiestie. En l'Ann MCCCCCLIII."

This curious picture-print, including the border, is ten inches and three quarters high by six inches and three quarters wide. The subject is a figure of Christ; in his left hand he holds an orb emblematic of his power, while the right is elevated as in the act of pronouncing a benediction. His robe is blue, with the folds indicated by a darker tint, and the border and lighter parts impressed with at least two lighter colours. Above this robe there is a large red mantle, fastened in front with what appears to be a jewel of three different colours, ruby, yellow, and blue ; the folds are of a darker colour ; and the lights are expressed by a kind of yellow, which has evidently been either impressed, or laid on the paper with a brush, before the red colour of the mantle, and which, from its glistening, seems to have been compounded with some metallic substance like fine gold-dust. The border of the print consists of a similar yellow, between plain black lines. The face is printed in flesh colour of three tints, and the head is surrounded with rays of glory, which appear like gilding. The engraving of the face, and of the hair of the head and beard, is extremely well executed, and much superior to anything that I have seen in wood-cuts containing Ungher's mark. The globe is blue, with the lights preserved, intersected by light red and yellow lines ; and the small cross at the top is also yellow, like the light on the red mantle. The hands and feet are expressed in their proper colours ; the ground on which the Redeemer stands is something between a lake and a fawn colour ; and the ground of the print, upwards from about an inch above the bottom, is of a lighter blue than the robe. To the right, near the bottom, are the date and mark, thus:

·J 5 · 4 3   The figure like a winged serpent resembles a mark which was frequently used by Lucas Cranach, except that the serpent or dragon of the latter appears less crooked, and usually has a ring in its mouth. The letter underneath also appears rather more like an I than an L. The drawing of the figure of Christ, however, is very much in the style of Lucas Cranach, and I am strongly inclined to think that the original painting or drawing was executed by him, whoever may have been the engraver. There must have been at least ten blocks required for this curious print, which, for clearness and distinctness in the colours, and for delicacy of impression, more especially in the face, may challenge a comparison not only with the finest chiaro-scuros of former times, but also with the best specimens of coloured block-printing of the present day.*

---

* This interesting specimen of the combined arts of wood engraving and printing formerly belonged to the late Mr. Robert Branston, wood engraver, who executed several of the chiaro-scuros, and imitations of coloured drawings, in Savage's work on Decorative Printing. It is now in the possession of his son, Mr. Frederick Branston, who is of the same profession as his father.

In 1557, Hubert Goltzius, a painter, but better known as an author than as an artist, published at Antwerp, in folio, a work containing portraits, executed in chiaro-scuro, of the Roman emperors, from Julius Cæsar to Ferdinand I.* Descamps, in his work entitled "La Vie des Peintres Flamands, Allemands et Hollandois," says that those portraits, which are all copied from medals, were "engraved on wood by a painter of Courtrai, named Joseph Gietleughen;"† and Papillon, who had examined the work more closely, but not closely enough, says that the outlines are etched, and that the two *rentrées*—the subsequent impressions which give to the whole the appearance of a chiaro-scuro drawing —are from blocks of wood engraved in *intaglio*. What Papillon says about the outlines being etched is true ; but a close inspection of those portraits will afford any person acquainted with the process ample proof of the "rentrées" being also printed from plates of metal in the same manner as from engraved wood-blocks.

Each of those portraits appears like an enlarged copy of a medal, and is the result of three separate impressions; the first, containing the outlines of the head, the ornaments, and the name, has been printed from an etched plate of copper or some other metal, by means of a copper-plate printing-press ; and the two other impressions, over the first, have also been from plates of metal, mounted on blocks of wood, and printed by means of the common typographic printing-press. The outlines of the head and of the letters forming the legend are black ; the field of the medal is a muddy kind of sepia ; and the head and the border, printed from the same surface and at the same time, are of a lighter shade. The lights to be preserved have been cut in *intaglio* in the plates for the two "rentrées" in the same manner as on blocks of wood for printing in chiaro-scuro. The marks of the pins by which the two plates for the "rentrées" have been fastened to blocks of wood, to raise them to a proper height, are very perceptible ; in the field of the medal they appear like circular points, generally in pairs ; while round the outer margin they are mostly of a square form. It is difficult to conceive what advantage Goltzius might expect to derive by printing the "rentrées" from metal plates ; for all that he has thus produced could have been more simply effected by means of wood-blocks, as practised up to that time by all other chiaro-scuro engravers. Though those portraits possess but little merit as chiaro-scuros, they are yet highly interesting in the history of art, as affording the first instances of

---

* The title-page of this work is printed in three colours,—black, sepia, and green. The black ornamental outlines are from an etched plate ; the sepia and green colours are printed from wood-blocks. An edition of this work, enlarged by Gevartius, with portraits in two colours, and entirely engraved on wood, was printed at Antwerp in 1645.

† Tom. i. p. 129. Paris, 1753.

etching being employed for the outlines of a chiaro-scuro, and of the substitution, in surface-printing, of a plate of metal for a wood-block. Goltzius's manner of etching the outlines of a chiaro-scuro print was frequently practised both by French and English artists about the middle of the last century; and about 1722, Edward Kirkall engraved the principal parts of his chiaro-scuros in mezzo-tint, and afterwards printed a tint from a metal plate mounted on wood. In the present day Mr. George Baxter has successfully applied the principle of engraving the ground and the outlines of his subjects in aqua-tint; and, as in the case of Hubert Goltzius and Kirkall, he sometimes uses a metal-plate instead of a wood-block in surface-printing. In the picture-prints executed by Mr. Baxter for the Pictorial Album, 1837, the tint of the paper on which each imitative painting appears to be mounted, is communicated from a smooth plate of copper, which receives the colour, and is printed in the same manner as a wood-block.

Among the German artists who made designs for wood engravers from the time of Durer to about 1590, Erhard Schön, Virgil Solis, Melchior Lorich, and Jost Amman may be considered as the principal. They are all frequently described as wood engravers from the circumstance of their marks being found on the cuts which they undoubtedly designed, but most certainly did not engrave. Erhard Schön chiefly resided at Nuremberg; and some of the earliest cuts of his designing are dated 1528. In 1538 he published at Nuremberg a small treatise, in oblong quarto, on the proportions of the human figure, for the use of students and young persons.* This work contains several wood-cuts, all coarsely engraved, illustrative of the writer's precepts; two or three of them—where the heads and bodies are represented by squares and rhomboidal figures—are extremely curious, though apparently not very well adapted to improve a learner in the art of design. Another of the cuts, where the proportions are illustrated by means of a figure inscribed within a circle, is very like one of the illustrations contained in Flaxman's Lectures on Sculpture. Some cuts of playing-cards, designed by Schön, are in greater request than any of his other works engraved on wood, which, for the most part, have but little to recommend them. He died about 1550.

Virgil Solis, a painter, copper-plate engraver, and designer on wood, was born at Nuremberg about 1514. The cuts which contain his mark are extremely numerous; and, from their being mostly of small size, he is ranked by Heineken with the "Little Masters." Several of his cuts

---

* The following is a copy of the title : " Underweisung der Proportzion und Stellung der Possen, liegent und stehent ; abgestochen wie man das vor augen sieht, in dem puchlein, durch Erhart Schon von Norrenberg ; für die Jungen gesellen und Jungen zu unterrichtung die zu der Kunst lieb tragen. In den druck gepracht, 1538."

display great fertility of invention; but though his figures are frequently spirited and the attitudes good, yet his drawing is generally careless and incorrect. As a considerable number of his cuts are of the same kind as those of Bernard Solomon, it seems as if there had been a competition at that time between the booksellers of Nuremberg and those of Lyons for supplying the European market with illustrations of two works of widely different character, to wit, the Bible, and Ovid's Metamorphoses,— Virgil Solis being retained for the German, and Bernard Solomon for the French publishers. He designed the cuts in a German edition of the Bible, printed in 1560; most of the portraits of the Kings of France in a work published at Nuremberg in 1566; a series of cuts for Esop's fables; and the illustrations of an edition of Reusner's Emblems. Several cuts with the mark of Virgil Solis are to be found in the first edition of Archbishop Parker's Bible, printed by Richard Jugge, folio, London, 1568. In the second edition, 1572, there are two ornamented initial letters, apparently of his designing, which seem to show that his sacred and profane subjects were liable to be confounded, and that cuts originally designed for an edition of Ovid might by some singular oversight be used in an edition of the Bible, although printed under the especial superintendence of a Right Reverend Archbishop. In the letter G, which forms the commencement of the first chapter of St. Paul's Epistle to the Hebrews, the subject represented by the artist is Leda caressed by Jupiter in the form of a swan; and in the letter T at the commencement of the first chapter of the Epistle General of St. John, the subject is Venus before Jove, with Cupid, Juno, Mars, Neptune, and other Heathen deities in attendance.*

A series of wood-cuts designed by Virgil Solis, illustrative of Ovid's Metamorphoses, was published at Frankfort, in oblong quarto, by George Corvinus, Sigismund Feyerabend, and the heirs of Wigand Gallus, in 1569. Each cut is surrounded by a heavy ornamental border; above each are four verses in Latin, and underneath four in German, composed by Johannes Posthius, descriptive of the subject. In the title-page,† which is both in Latin and in German, it is stated that they are *designed—gerissen*—by Virgil Solis for the use and benefit of painters, goldsmiths, and statuaries. It is thus evident that they were not engraved by him; and in corroboration of this opinion it may be observed that several

---

* This last letter contains the mark $\mathcal{A}$, which is to be found on some of the cuts in the editions of the Dance of Death printed at Cologne, 1555—1572.

† The title is as follows: "Johan. Posthii Germershemii Tetrasticha in Ovidii Metam. Lib. xv. Quibus accesserunt Vergilii Solis figuræ elegantissimæ, primum in lucem editæ.— Schöne Figuren, auss dem fürtrefflichen Poeten Ovidio, allen Malern, Goldtschmiden, und Bildthauern, zu nutz und gutem mit fleiss gerissen durch Vergilium Solis, und mit Teutschen Reimen kürtzlich erkläret, dergleichein vormals im Druck nie aussgangen, Durch Johan. Posthium von Germerssheim. M.D.LXIX."

of them, in addition to his mark, **W**, also contain another, **h**, which is doubtless that of the wood engraver. The latter mark occurs frequently in the cuts designed by Virgil Solis, in the first edition of Archbishop Parker's Bible.

Evelyn, in his Sculptura, has the following notice of this artist: "Virgilius Solis graved also in wood *The story of the Bible* and *The mechanic arts* in little; but for imitating those vile postures of Aretine had his eyes put out by the sentence of the magistrate." There is scarcely a page of this writer's works on art which does not contain similar inaccuracies, and yet he is frequently quoted and referred to as an authority. The "mechanic arts" to which Evelyn alludes were probably the series of cuts designed by Jost Amman, and first published in quarto, at Frankfort, in 1564; and the improbable story of Virgil Solis having had his eyes put out for copying Julio Romano's obscene designs, engraved by Marc Antonio, and illustrated with sonnets by the scurrilous ribald, Pietro Aretine, is utterly devoid of foundation. No such copies have ever been mentioned by any well-informed writer on art, and there is not the slightest evidence of Virgil Solis ever having been punished in any manner by the magistrates of his native city, Nuremberg, where he died in 1570.

Wood-cuts with the mark of Melchior Lorich are comparatively scarce. He was a native of Flensburg in Holstein, and was born in 1527. He obtained a knowledge of painting and copper-plate engraving at Leipsic, and afterwards travelled with his master through some of the northern countries of Europe. He afterwards visited Vienna, and subsequently entered into the service of the Palsgrave Otho, in whose suite he visited Holland, France, and Italy. In 1558 he went with the Imperial ambassador to Constantinople, where he remained three years. His principal works engraved on wood consist of a series of illustrations of the manners and customs of the Turks, published about 1570. There is a very clever cut, a Lady splendidly dressed, with his mark and the date 1551; it is printed on what is called a "broadside," and underneath is a copy of verses by Hans Sachs, the celebrated shoe-maker and *meistersänger* of Nuremberg,* entitled "*Eer und Lob einer schön wolgezierten Frawen*"—The Honour and Praise of a beautiful well-dressed woman. A large cut of the Deluge, in two sheets, is

---

* Hans Sachs, whose poetical works might vie in quantity with those of Lope Vega, was born at Nuremberg in 1494. Notwithstanding the immense number of verses which he composed, he did not trust to his profession of Meistersänger for the means of living, but continued to carry on his business as a shoemaker till his death, which happened in 1576. His verses were much admired by his contemporaries; and between 1570 and 1579, a collection of his works was published in five volumes folio. Several short pieces by him were originally printed as "broadsides," with an ornamental or illustrative cut at the top.

considered one of the best of his designing. Among the copper-plates engraved by Melchior Lorich, a portrait of Albert Durer, and two others, of the Grand Signior and his favourite Sultana, are among the most scarce. The time of his death is uncertain, but Bartsch thinks that he was still living in 1583, as there are wood-cuts with his mark of that date.

Jost Amman, one of the best designers on wood of the period in which he lived, was born at Zurich in 1539, but removed to Nuremberg about 1560.* His designs are more bold, and display more of the vigour of the older German masters, than those of his contemporary Virgil Solis. A series of cuts designed by him, illustrative of professions and trades, was published in 1564, quarto, with the title "Hans Sachse eigentliche Beschreibung aller Stände auf Erden—aller Künste und Handwerker," &c.—that is, Hans Sachs's correct Description of all Ranks, Arts, and Trades; and another edition in duodecimo, with the descriptions in Latin, appeared in the same year.† For the correctness of the date of those editions I am obliged to rely on Heineken, as I have never seen a copy of either; the earliest edition with Hans Sachs's descriptions that has come under my notice is dated 1574. In a duodecimo edition, 1568, and another of the same size, 1574, the descriptions, by Hartman Schopper, are in Latin verse.‡ This is perhaps the most curious and interesting series of cuts, exhibiting the various ranks and employments of men, that ever was published. Among the higher orders, constituting what the Germans call the "*Lehre und Wehr Stande*"—teachers and warriors—are the Pope, Emperor, King, Princes, Nobles, Priests, and Lawyers; while almost every branch of labour or of trade then known in Germany, from agriculture to pin-making, has its representative. There are also not a few which it would be difficult to reduce to any distinct class, as they are neither trades nor honest professions. Of those heteroclytes is the "Meretricum procurator—der Hurenweibel"—or, as Captain Dugald Dalgetty says, "the captain of the Queans."

The subject of the following cut, which is of the same size as the

* Papillon, who appears to have been extremely wishful to swell his catalogue of wood engravers, describes Jost Amman of Zurich and Jost Amman of Nuremberg as two different persons.

† Heineken, Idée Générale, p. 244.

‡ The following is the title of the edition of 1568;—that of 1574 is somewhat different. "ΠΑΝΟΠΛΙΑ omnium Illiberalium mechanicarum aut sedentariarum artium, continens quotquot unquam vel a veteribus, aut nostri etiam seculi celebritate excogitari potuerunt, breviter et dilucide confecta: carminum liber primus, tum mira varietate rerum vocabulorumque novo more excogitatorum copia perquam utilis, lectuque jucundus. Accesserunt etiam venustissimæ Imagines omnes omnium artificum negociantes ad vivum lectori representantes, antehac nec visæ nec unquam æditæ: per Hartman Schopperum, Novoforens. Noricum.—Frankofurti ad Moenum, cum privelegio Cæsario, M.D.LXVIII."

original, is a *Briefmaler*,—literally, a card-painter, the name by which
the German wood engravers were known before they adopted the
more appropriate one of *Formschneider*. It is evident, that, at the
time when the cut was engraved, the two professions were distinct :*
we here perceive the Briefmaler employed, not in engraving cuts, but
engaged in colouring certain figures by means of a *stencil*,—that is,
a card or thin plate of metal, out of which the intended figure is cut.
A brush charged with colour being drawn over the pierced card, as
is seen in the cut, the figure is communicated to the paper placed
underneath. The little shallow vessels perceived on the top of the

large box in front are the saucers which contain his colours. Near
the window, immediately to his right, is a pile of sheets which, from
the figure of a man on horseback seen impressed upon them, appear
to be already finished.

The subject of the following cut, from the same work, is a
Formschneider, or wood engraver proper. He is apparently at work
on a block which he has before him ; but the kind of tool which he
employs is not exactly like those used by English wood engravers

---

* The *Briefmalers*, though at that time evidently distinct from the *Formschneiders*, still
continued to *print* wood-cuts. On several large wood-cuts with the dates 1553 and 1554 we
find the words, " Gedrukt zu Nürnberg durch Hanns Glaser, *Brieffmaler*."

of the present day. It seems to resemble a small long-handled desk-knife; while the tool of the modern wood engraver has a handle which is rounded at the top in order to accommodate it to the palm of the hand. It is also never held vertically, as it appears in the hand of the *Formschneider*. It is, however, certain, from other wood-cuts, which will be subsequently noticed, that the wood engravers of that period were accustomed to use a tool with a handle rounded at the top, similar to the graver used in the present day.*—The verses descriptive of the annexed cut are translated from Hans Sachs.

I am a wood-engraver good,
And all designs on blocks of wood
I with my graver cut so neat,
That when they're printed on a sheet
Of paper white, you plainly view
The very forms the artist drew :
His drawing, whether coarse or fine,
Is truly copied line for line.

Jost Amman died in 1591, and from the time of his settling at Nuremberg to that of his decease he seems to have been chiefly employed in making designs on wood for the booksellers of Nuremberg and Frankfort. He also furnished designs for goldsmiths ; and

* See the mark C. S. at page 413.

it is said that he excelled as a painter on glass. The works which afford the best specimens of his talents as a designer on wood are those illustrative of the costume of the period, first published between 1580 and 1585 by S. Feyerabend at Frankfort. One of those works contains the costumes of men of all ranks, except the clergy, interspersed with the armorial bearings of the principal families in Germany ; another contains the costume of the different orders of the priesthood of the church of Rome ; and a third, entitled Gynæceum sive Theatrum Mulierum, is illustrative of the costume of women of all ranks in Europe. A work on hunting and fowling, edited by J. A. Lonicerus, and printed in 1582, contains about forty excellent cuts of his designing. A separate volume, consisting of cuts selected from the four preceding works, and of a number of other cuts chiefly illustrative of mythological subjects and of the costume of Turkey, was published by Feyerabend about 1590. In a subsequent edition of this work, printed in 1599, it is stated that the collection is published for the especial benefit of painters and amateurs.* Among the numerous other cuts designed by him, the following may be mentioned : illustrations for a Bible published at Frankfort 1565 ; a series of subjects from Roman History, entitled Icones Livianæ, 1572 ; and the cuts in an edition of Reynard the Fox. The works of Jost Amman have proved a mine for succeeding artists ; his figures were frequently copied by wood engravers in France, Italy and Flanders ; and even some modern English paintings contain evidences of the artist having borrowed something more than a hint from the figures of Jost Amman.

Jost Amman was undoubtedly one of the best professional designers on wood of his time ; and his style bears considerable resemblance to that of Hans Burgmair as exemplified in the Triumphs of Maximilian. Many of his figures are well drawn ; but even in the best of his subjects the attitudes are somewhat affected and generally too violent ; and this, with an overstrained expression, makes his characters appear more like actors in a theatre than like real personages. In the cuts of the horse in the "Kunstbüchlein" the action of the animal is frequently represented with great spirit : but in points of detail the

---

* This work is entitled "Kunstbüchlein," and consists entirely of cuts without any explanatory letter-press. The first cut consists of a group of heads, drawn and engraved with great spirit. On what appears something like a slab of stone or wood—most unmeaningly and awkwardly introduced—are Jost Amman's initials, I. A., towards the top, and lower down the mark, M̄F which is doubtless that of the engraver. This mark, with a figure of a graver underneath, occurs on several of the other cuts. The three following marks, with a graver underneath each, also occur : L. F. C. S. G. H. These facts are sufficient to prove that Jost Amman was not the engraver of the cuts which he designed. In the edition of 1599 the cuts are said to have been *drawn* by "the late most excellent and celebrated artist, Jost Amman of Nuremberg."

artist is as frequently incorrect. Some of his very best designs are to be found among his equestrian subjects. His men generally have a good "seat," and his ladies seem to manage their heavy long-tailed steeds with great ease and grace.

Several of the views of cities, in Sebastian Munster's Cosmography—first published in folio, at Basle, 1550—contain two marks, one of the designer, and the other of the person by whom the subject was engraved, the latter being frequently accompanied by a graver, thus: **H·H** ; or with two gravers of different kinds, thus : **·C·S·** This last mark, which also occurs in Jost Amman's Kunst- büchlein, is said to be that of Christopher Stimmer, a brother of Tobias Stimmer, a Swiss artist, who is generally described as a designer and engraver on wood. The cuts with the former mark have been ascribed to Hans Holbein, but they bear not the least resemblance to his style of design, and they have been assigned to him solely on account of the letters corresponding with the initials of his name. Professor Christ's Dictionary of Monograms, and Papillon's Treatise on Wood-engraving, afford numerous instances of marks being assigned to persons on no better grounds.

A writer, in discussing the question, "Were Albert Durer, Lucas Cranach, Hans Burgmair, and other old German artists, the engravers or only the designers of the cuts which bear their mark?" has been pleased to assert that the mark of the actual engraver is usually distinguished by the graver with which it is accompanied. This statement has been adopted and further disseminated by others ; and many persons who have not an opportunity of judging for themselves, and who receive with implicit credit whatever they find asserted in a Dictionary of Engravers, suppose that from the time of Albert Durer, or even earlier, the figure of a graver generally distinguishes the mark of the *formschneider* or engraver on wood. So far, however, from this being a general rule, I am not aware of any wood-cut which contains a graver in addition to a mark of an earlier date than those in Munster's Cosmography, and the practice which appears to have been first introduced about that time never became generally prevalent. When the graver is thus introduced there can be no doubt that it is intended to distinguish the mark of the engraver ; but as at least ninety-nine out of every hundred marks on cuts executed between 1550 and 1600 are unaccompanied with a graver, it is exceedingly doubtful in most cases whether the mark be that of the engraver or the designer.

The wood-cuts in Munster's Cosmography are generally poor in design and coarse in execution. One of the best is that representing an encounter of two armed men on horseback with the mark **⧆·**, which also occurs in some of the cuts in Gesner's History of Animals, printed at Zurich, 1551—1558. This cut, as well as several others, is repeated in another part of the book, in the manner of the Nuremberg Chronicle, where the same portrait or the same view is used to represent several different persons or places. The cuts are not precisely the same in every edition of Munster's work, which was several times reprinted between 1550 and 1570. Those which are substituted in the later editions are rather more neatly engraved.

The present cut is copied from one at page 49 of the first edition, where it is given as an illustration of a wonderful kind of tree said to be found in Scotland, and from the fruit of which it was believed that geese were produced. Munster's account of this wonderful tree and its fruit is as follows : " In Scotland are found trees, the fruit of which

appears like a ball of leaves. This fruit, falling at its proper time into the water below, becomes animated, and turns to a bird which they call the *tree goose*. This tree also grows in the island of Pomona [the largest of the Orkneys], not far distant from Scotland towards the north. As old cosmographers—especially Saxo Grammaticus—mention this tree, it is not to be considered as a fiction of modern authors. Aeneas Sylvius also notices this tree as follows : ' We have heard that there was a tree formerly in Scotland, which, growing by the margin of a stream, produced fruit of the shape of ducks ; that such fruit, when nearly ripe, fell, some into the water and some on land. Such as fell on land decayed, but such as fell into the water quickly became animated, swimming below, and then flying into the air with feathers and wings.

When in Scotland, having made diligent inquiry concerning this matter of King James, a square-built man, and very fat,* we found that miracles always kept receding ;—this wonderful tree is not found in Scotland, but in the Orcades.'"

The bird said to be the produce of this tree is the "Bernacle Goose, Clakis, or Tree Goose" of Bewick ; and the pretended *tree* from which it was supposed to be produced was undoubtedly a testaceous insect, a species of which, frequently found adhering to ships' bottoms, is described under the name of "*Lepas Anatifera*" by Linnæus, who thus commemorates in the trivial name the old opinion respecting its winged and feathered fruit. William Turner, a native of Morpeth in Northumberland, one of the earliest writers on British Ornithology, notices the story of the Bernacle Goose being produced from "something like a fungus proceeding from old wood lying in the sea." He says it is mentioned by Giraldus Cambrensis in his description of Ireland, and that the account of its being generated in this wonderful manner is generally believed by the people inhabiting the sea-coasts of England, Scotland, and Ireland. "But," says Turner, "as it seemed not safe to trust to popular report, and as, on account of the singularity of the thing, I could not give entire credit to Giraldus, I, when thinking of the subject of which I now write, asked a certain clergyman, named Octavianus, by birth an Irishman, whom I knew to be worthy of credit, if he thought the account of Giraldus was to be believed. He, swearing by the Gospel, declared that what Giraldus had written about the generation of this bird was most true; that he himself had seen and handled the young unformed birds, and that if I should remain in London a month or two, he would bring me some of the brood." † In Lobel and Pena's Stirpium Adversaria Nova, folio, London, 1570, there is a cut of the "Britannica Concha Anatifera," growing on a stalk from a rock, with figures of ducks or geese in the water below. In the text the popular belief of a kind of goose being produced from the shell of this insect is noticed, but the writer declines pronouncing any opinion till he shall have had an opportunity of visiting Scotland and judging for himself. Gerard, in his Herbal, London, 1597, has an article on the *Goose-tree;* and he says that its native soil is a small island, called the Pile of Fouldres, half a mile from the main land of Lancashire. Ferrer

---

* It is uncertain if James I. or James II. be meant. According to Sir Walter Scott,- Aeneas Sylvius, afterwards Pope Pius II, visited Scotland in 1448, when James II.—if Chalmers be correct, Caledonia, vol. i. p. 831,—was scarcely nineteen, and when his appearance was not likely to correspond with the learned prelate's description,—"hominem quadratum et multa pinguedine gravem."

† "Avium præcipuarum, quarum apud Plinium et Aristotelem mentio est, brevis et succincta historia. Per Dn. Gulielmum Turnerum, artium et medicinæ doctorem," 8vo. Coloniæ, M.D.XLIIII, fol. 9 *b.*

de Valcebro, a Spanish writer, in a work entitled "El Gobierno general hallado en las Aves," with coarse wood-cuts, quarto, printed about 1680, repeats, with sundry additions, the story of the Bernacle, or, as he calls it, the Barliata, being produced from a tree; and he seems rather displeased that his countrymen are not disposed to yield much faith to such singularities, merely because they do not occur in their own country.

There are two portraits of Erasmus in the first edition of Munster's Cosmography, one at page 130, and the other, with the mark ᕼᖇᐯᎠ, at page 407. The latter, as the author especially informs the reader, was engraved after a portrait by Holbein in the possession of Bonifacius Amerbach. The present is a reduced copy of a cut at page 361 of

Henry Petri's edition, 1554. On a stone, near the bottom, towards the left, is seen a mark *—probably that of the artist who made the drawing on the block—consisting of the same letters as the double mark just noticed as occurring in the portrait of Erasmus, H.R. M.D. A cut

---

* In Professor Christ's Dictionary of Monograms this mark is ascribed, though doubtfully, to "Manuel Deutsch." It is certainly not the mark of Nicholas Emanuel Deutsch of Bern, for he died several years before 1548, the date on several of the cuts with the mark H. R. M. D. in Munster's Cosmography, and which date evidently relates to the year in which the artist made the drawing. There can be no doubt that those four letters belong to a single name, for some of the cuts in which they occur also contain the mark of an engraver.

of the same subject, William Tell about to shoot at the apple on his son's head, was given in the first edition, but the design is somewhat different and the execution more coarse. The cut from which the preceding is copied may be ranked among the best in the work.

Though Sebastian Munster, in a letter, probably written in 1538, addressed to Joachim Vadianus, alludes to an improvement which he and his printer had made in the mode of printing maps, and to a project for casting complete words, yet the maps which appear in his Cosmography, with the outlines, rivers, and mountains engraved on wood, and the names inserted in type, are certainly not superior to the generality of other maps executed wholly on wood about the same period.* Joachim Vadianus, to whom Munster writes, and of whose assistance he wished to avail himself in a projected edition of Ptolemy, was an eminent scholar of that period, and had published an edition, in 1522, of Pomponius Mela, with a commentary and notes. The passage in Munster's letter, wherein maps are mentioned, is to the following effect: " I would have sent you an impression of one of the Swiss maps which I have had printed here, if Froschover had not informed me of his having sent you one from Zurich. If this mode of printing should succeed tolerably well, and when we shall have acquired a certain art of *casting whole words,* Henri Petri, Michael Isengrin, and I have thought of printing Ptolemy's Cosmography; not of so great a size as it has hitherto been frequently printed, but in the form in which your Annotations on Pomponius appear. In the maps we shall insert only the names of the principal cities, and give the others alphabetically in some blank space,—for instance, in the margin or any adjoining space beyond the limits of the map."† The art of casting whole words, alluded to in this passage, appears to have been something like an attempt at what has been called " logographic printing ; "‡ though it is not unlikely that

* A map of Russia, engraved wholly on wood, in a work entitled " Commentari della Moscovia e parimente della Russia," &c. translated from the Latin of Sigmund, Baron von Herberstein, printed at Venice, 4to. 1550, is much superior in point of appearance to the best in the work of Munster. This map, which is of folio size, appears to have been constructed by " Giacomo Gastaldo, Piamontese, Cosmographo in Venetia." The work also contains six wood-cuts, which afford some curious specimens of Russian and Tartar arms and costume.

† Philologicarum Epistolarum Centuria una, ex Bibliotheca M. H. Goldasti, p. 165. 8vo. Francofurti, 1610.

‡ According to this method, certain words, together with radices and terminations, of frequent occurrence, were cast entire, and not in separate letters, and placed in cases in such an order that the compositor could as " readily possess himself of the Type of a word as of the Type of a single letter." This method, for which a patent was obtained, is explained in a pamphlet entitled " An Introduction to Logography : or the Art of Arranging and Composing for Printing with Words entire, their Radices and Terminations, instead of single Letters. By Henry Johnson : London, printed Logographically, and sold by J. Walter, bookseller, Charing Cross, and J. Sewell, Cornhill, M.DCC.LXXXIII." Several works were

those "whole words" might be the names of countries and places intended to be inserted in a space cut out of the block on which the map was engraved. By thus inserting the names, either cast as complete words, or composed of separate letters, the tedious process of engraving a number of letters on wood was avoided, and the pressman enabled to print the maps at one impression. In some of the earlier maps where the names are printed from types, the letters were not inserted in spaces cut out of the block, but were printed from a separate form by means of a "re-iteration" or second impression.* In illustration of what Munster says about a certain art of casting whole words,—"*artem aliquam fundendarum integrarum dictionum*,"—the following extract is given from Dr. Dibdin's Bibliographical Tour, volume iii. page 102, second edition. "What think you of undoubted proofs of STEREOTYPE PRINTING in the middle of the sixteenth century? It is even so. What adds to the whimsical puzzle is, that these pieces of metal, of which the surface is composed of types, fixed and immovable, are some-times inserted in wooden blocks, and introduced as titles, mottoes, or descriptions of the subjects cut upon the blocks. Professor May [of Augsburg] begged my acceptance of a specimen or two of the types thus fixed upon plates of the same metal. They rarely exceeded the height of four or five lines of text, by about four or five inches in length. I carried away, with his permission, two proofs (not long ago pulled) of the same block containing this intermixture of stereotype and wood-block printing."

As the engraving of the letters in maps executed on wood—or indeed on any other material—is, when the names of many places are given, by far the most tedious and costly part of the process, the plan of inserting them in type by means of holes pierced in the block, as adopted

---

printed in this manner, and among others an edition of Anderson's History of Commerce, 4 vols. 4to. 1787—1789, by John Walter, at the Logographic Press, Printing-House-Square, Blackfriars. Logography has long been abandoned. The following account of this art is given in H. G. Bohn's Lecture on Printing, pp. 88, 89. "Something akin to stereo-typing is another mode of printing called Logography, invented by the late Mr. Walter, of the *Times*, in 1783, and for which he took out a patent. This means a system of printing from type cast in words instead of single letters, which it was thought would save time and corrections when applied to newspapers, but it was not found to answer. A joke of the time was a supposed order to the typefounder for some words of frequent occurrence, which ran thus:—'Please send me a hundred-weight, sorted, of murder, fire, dreadful robbery, atrocious outrage, fearful calamity, alarming explosion, melancholy accident; an assortment of honour-able member, whig, tory, hot, cold, wet, dry; half-a-hundred weight, made up in pounds, of butter, cheese, beef, mutton, tripe, mustard, soap, rain, &c.; and a few devils, angels, women, groans, hisses, &c.' This method of printing did not succeed: for if twenty-four letters will give six hundred sextillions of combinations, no printing office could keep a sufficient assortment of even popular words."

* See an edition of Ptolemy, printed at Venice by Jacobus Pentius de Leucho, in 1511, previously noticed at page 203.

in Munster's Cosmography, was certainly a great saving of labour; yet on comparing the maps in this work with those in Ptolemy's Cosmography, printed by Leonard Holl, at Ulm, 1482, and with others engraved in the early part of the sixteenth century, it is impossible not to perceive that the art of wood engraving, as applied to the execution of such works, had undergone no improvement : with the exception of the letters, the maps in Holl's Ptolemy—the earliest that were engraved on wood—are, in point of appearance, equal to those in the work of Munster, published about eighty years later. Considering that the earliest printed maps—those in an edition of Ptolemy, printed by Arnold Bukinck, at Rome, 1478*—are from copper-plates, it seems rather surprising that, until about 1570, no further attempt should have been made to apply the art of engraving on copper to this purpose. In the latter year a collection of maps, engraved on copper,† was published at Antwerp under the superintendence of Abraham Ortelius ; and so great was their excellence when compared with former maps executed on wood, that the business of map engraving was within a few years transferred almost exclusively to engravers on copper. In 1572 a map engraved on copper was printed in England, in the second edition of Archbishop Parker's Bible. It is of folio size, and the country represented is the Holy Land. Within an ornamented tablet is the following inscription : " Graven bi Humfray Cole, goldsmith, an English man born in yᵉ north, and pertayning to yᵉ mint in the Tower. 1572." In Walpole's Catalogue of Engravers the portraits engraved on copper of Queen Elizabeth, the Earl of Leicester, and Lord Burleigh, which appear in the first edition of Archbishop Parker's Bible, 1568,‡ are ascribed to Humphrey Cole, apparently on no better ground than that his name appears as the engraver of the map, which is given in the second. If Cole were really the engraver of those portraits, he was certainly entitled to a more favourable notice§ than he

---

* Some account of this work is given at page 200.

† At page 204 it is stated, on the authority of Breitkopf, that those maps were engraved by Ægidius Diest. Ortelius himself says in the preface that they were engraved by " Francis Hogenberg, Ferdinand and Ambrose Arsens, and others."

‡ The portrait of Queen Elizabeth appears on the title ; the Earl of Leicester's is prefixed to the Book of Joshua ; and Lord Burleigh's is given, with a large initial B, at the beginning of the first psalm. In the second edition, 1572, the portrait of Lord Burleigh is omitted, and the impressions of the other two are much inferior to those in the first edition in consequence of the plates being worn. Many of the cuts in the second edition are quite different from those in the first, and generally inferior to the cuts for which they are substituted.

§ " Humphrey Cole, as he says himself, was born in the North of England, and pertayned to the mint in the Tower, 1572. I suppose he was one of the engravers that pertayned to Archbishop Parker, for this edition was called Matthew Parker's Bible. I hope the flattery of the favourites was the incense of the engraver!" Catalogue of Engravers, p. 16. Edit. 1794.—Walpole does not appear to have paid the least attention to the engraver's merits—

receives from the fastidious compiler of the "Catalogue of Engravers who have been born or resided in England ;" for, considering *when* and *where* they were executed, the engraver is entitled to rank at least as high as George Vertue. In fact, the portrait of Leicester, considered merely as a specimen of engraving, without regard to the time and place of its execution, will bear a comparison with more than one of the portraits engraved by Vertue upwards of a hundred and fifty years later.

The advantages of copper-plate engraving for the purpose of executing maps, as exemplified in the work of Ortelius, appear to have been immediately appreciated in England, and this country is one of the first that can boast of a collection of provincial or county maps engraved on copper. A series of maps of all the counties of England and Wales, and of the adjacent islands, were engraved, under the superintendence of Christopher Saxton, between 1573 and 1579, and published at London, in a folio volume, in the latter year. Though the greater number of those maps were the work of Flemish engravers, eight, at least, were engraved by two Englishmen, Augustine Ryther and Nicholas Reynolds.*   They appear to have been all drawn by Christopher Saxton, who lived at Tingley, near Leeds. Walpole says, that "he was servant to Thomas Sekeford, Esq. Master of the Court of Wards," the gentleman at whose expense they were engraved. He also states that many of them were engraved by Saxton himself ; but this I consider to be extremely doubtful. In his account of early English copper-plate engravers, Walpole is frequently incorrect : he mentions Humphrey Lhuyd—an author who wrote a short description of Britain, printed at Cologne in 1572†—as the *engraver* of the map of England in the collection of Ortelius ; and he includes Dr. William Cuningham, a physician of Norwich, in his catalogue of engravers, without the slightest reason beyond the mere fact, that a book entitled "The Cosmographical

---

supposing, as he does, the portraits to have been executed by him :—he sneers at him because he had engraved certain portraits for a *Bible*, and because he was supposed to have been patronised by a *bishop*. A more liberal writer on art would have praised Parker, although he were an *archbishop*, for his patronage of a native engraver.

* "Augustinus Ryther, *Anglus*," occurs on the maps of Cumberland and Westmorland, Gloucester, and Yorkshire. Ryther afterwards kept a bookseller's shop in Leadenhall-street. He engraved some maps and charts, which were published about 1588. On the map of the county of Hertford, Reynolds's name occurs thus : "Nicholas Reynoldus, Londinensis, sculpsit." Several of those maps were engraved by Remigius Hogenberg, one of the engravers who are said to have been employed by Archbishop Parker in his palace at Lambeth.

† This little work, entitled "Commentarioli Britannicæ Descriptionis Fragmentum," was sent by the author to Ortelius, and the prefatory address is dated Denbigh, in North Wales, 30th August 1568. A translation of it, under the title of a "Breviary of Britain," was printed at London in 1573.—Lhuyd had only furnished Ortelius with materials for the construction of the map of England.

Glasse," written by the Doctor, and printed in 1559, contains several *wood-cuts*. He might, with equal justice, have placed Archbishop Parker in his catalogue, and asserted that some of the *plates* in the Bible were " engraved by his own hand."

In connexion with the preceding account of the earliest maps executed in England on copper, it perhaps may not be unnecessary to briefly notice here the introduction of copper-plate engraving into this country. According to Herbert, in his edition of Ames's Typographical Antiquities, the frontispiece of a small work entitled " Galenus de Temperamentis," printed at Cambridge, 1521, is the earliest specimen of copper-plate engraving that is to be found in any book printed in England. The art, however, supposing that the plate was really engraved and printed in this country, appears to have received no encouragement on its first introduction, for after this first essay it seems to have lain dormant for nearly twenty years. The next earliest specimens appear in the first edition of a work usually called " Raynalde's Birth of Mankind," printed at London in 1540.* This work, which is a treatise on the obstetric art, contains, when perfect, three plates, illustrative of the subject. Not having had an opportunity of seeing any one of these three plates nor the frontispiece to " Galenus de Temperamentis," I am obliged to trust to Herbert for the fact of their being engraved on copper. In the third volume of his edition of Ames, page 1411, there is a fac-simile of the frontispiece to the Cambridge book ; and in the Preliminary Disquisition on Early Engraving and Ornamental Printing, prefixed to Dr. Dibdin's edition of the Typographical Antiquities, will be found a fac-simile, engraved on wood, of one of the plates in Raynalde's Birth of Mankind. In an edition of the latter work, printed in 1565, the " byrthe figures" are not engraved on copper, but on wood.

A work printed in London by John Hereford, 1545, contains several unquestionable specimens of copper-plate engraving. It is of folio size, and the title is as follows : " Compendiosa totius Anatomiæ delineatio ære exarata, per Thomam Geminum." The ornamental title-page, with the arms of Henry VIII. towards the centre, is engraved on copper, and several anatomical subjects are executed in the same manner.

* The name of " Thomas Raynalde, Physition," is not to be found in the edition of 1540. The title of the work is, " The byrth of Mankynd, newly translated out of Latin into Englysshe. In the which is entreated of all suche thynges the which chaunce to women in theyr labor," &c. At folio vi. there is an address from Richard Jonas, " Unto the most gracious, and in all goodnesse most excellent vertuous Lady Quene Katheryne, wyfe and most derely belovyd spouse unto the moste myghty sapient Christen prynce, Kynge Henry the VIII."—This " most excellent vertuous lady" was *Catherine Howard*. The imprint at the end of the work is as follows : " Imprynted at London, by T. R. Anno Domini, M.CCCCC.XL." Raynalde's name first appears in the second edition, 1545. Between 1540 and 1600 there were at least eight editions of this work printed in London.

Gemini, who is believed to have been the engraver of those plates, was not a native of this country.* In a dedication to Henry VIII, he says that in his work he had followed Andrew Vesalius of Brussels; and he further mentions that in the year before he had received orders from the King to have the plates printed off [*excudendas*]. A second edition, dedicated to Edward VI, appeared in 1553; and a third, dedicated to Queen Elizabeth, in 1559.† In the last edition the Royal Arms on the title-page are effaced, and the portrait of Queen Elizabeth engraved in their stead. Traces of the former subject are, however, still visible, and the motto, "Dieu et mon Droit," has been allowed to remain. One of the engravings in this work affords a curious instance of the original plate of copper having been either mended or enlarged by joining another piece to it. Even in the first edition, the zigzag line where the two pieces are joined, and the forms of the little *cramps* which hold them together, are visible, and in the last they are distinctly apparent.

The earliest portrait engraved on copper, printed singly, in this country, and not as an illustration of a book, is that of Archbishop Parker engraved by Remigius Hogenberg. It is a small print four and a half inches high by three and a half wide. At the corners are the arms of Canterbury, impaled with those of Parker; the archbishop's arms separately; a plain shield, with a cross and the letters ƚ; and the arms of Archbishop Cranmer. The portrait is engraved in an oval, round the border of which is the following inscription: "Mūdus transit, et cupiscētia ejus. Anno Domini 1572, ætatis suæ Anno 69. Die mensis Augusti sexto." In an impression, now before me, from the original plate, the date and the archbishop's age are altered to 1573 and 70, but the marks of the ciphers erased are quite perceptible. The portrait of the archbishop is a half-length; he is seated at a table, on which are a bell, a small coffer, and what appears to be a stamp. A Bible is lying open before him, and on one of the pages is inscribed in very small letters the following passage from the VI. chapter of Micah, verse 8 : "Indicabo tibi, o homo, quid sit bonum, et quid Deus requirat a te, utique facere judicium, et diligere misericordiam, et solicitum ambulare cum Deo tuo." The engraver's name, "*R. Berg f.*," appears at the bottom of the print to the right: a cross line from the R to the B indicates the abbreviation of the surname, which, written at length, was

---

* At the end of the dedication to Henry VIII. he signs himself "Thomas Geminus, Lysiensis."

† In the edition of 1559 there is a large wood-cut—"Interiorum corporis humani partium viva delineatio"—with the mark R. S. and a graver underneath. In this cut the interior parts of the body are impressed on separate slips, which are pasted, by one edge, at the side of the figure. Those slips on being raised show the different parts as they occur on dissection.

Hogenberg. Caulfield, speaking of this engraving in his Calcographiana, page 4, 1814, says,—"The only impression supposed to be extant is in the library at Lambeth Palace; but within the last two years, Mr. Woodburn, of St. Martin's Lane, purchased a magnificent collection of portraits, among which was a very fine one of Parker."

The number of books, containing copper-plate engravings, published in England between 1559 and 1600, is extremely limited; and the following list will perhaps be found to contain one or two more than have been mentioned by preceding writers: 1. Pena and Lobel's Stirpium Adversaria Nova, folio, 1570,—ornamented title-page, with the arms of England at the top, and a small map towards the bottom :—the ornaments surrounding the map are very beautifully engraved. 2. Archbishop Parker's Bible, 1568—1572, with the portraits, previously noticed at page 419. 3. Saxton's Maps, with the portrait of Queen Elizabeth on the title, 1579. 4. Broughton's Concent of Scripture, 1591,—engraved title, and four other plates. 5. Translation of Ariosto by Sir John Harrington, 1591,—engraved title-page, containing portraits of the author and translator, and forty-six other plates. 6. R. Haydock's Translation of Lomazzo's Treatise on Painting and Architecture, Oxford, 1598,—engraved title-page, containing portraits of Lomazzo and Haydock, and several very indifferent plates, chiefly of architecture and figures in outline.

Walpole mentions a plate of the arms of Sir Christopher Hatton on the title-page of the second part of Wagenar's Mariner's Mirrour, printed in 1588, and the plates in a work entitled " A True Report of the Newfoundland of Virginia," all engraved by Theodore de Bry. The first of these works I have not been able to obtain a sight of ;* and the second cannot properly be included in a list of works containing copper-plates published in England previous to 1600 ;† for though it appeared in 1591, it was printed at Frankfort. In the reigns of James and Charles I, copper-plate engraving was warmly patronised in England, and several foreign engravers, as in the reign of Elizabeth, were induced to take up their abode in this country. In the first edition of Chambers' Cyclopedia, it is stated that the art of copper-plate engraving was brought

* In Herbert's edition of the Typographical Antiquities, vol. iii. p. 1681, both parts of this work are said to have engraved titles, and the arms of Sir C. Hatton are said to occur at the back of the title to the first part. The work contains twenty-two maps and charts, probably copied from the original Dutch edition of Wagenar, who was a native of Enchuysen. There is no printer's name in the English edition.

† Walpole erroneously states that "Broughton's book was not printed till 1600," and he says that "the *cuts* were probably engraved by an English artist named William Rogers." The mark *WR* is to be found on some of the plates of the edition of 1600, but it is to be observed that they are not the same as those in the edition of 1591. The *first* edition of the work was printed in 1588.

to this country from Antwerp by Speed the historian,—an error which
is pointed out by Walpole : the writer it seems had not been aware of

any earlier copper-plates printed in England than Speed's maps, which
were chiefly executed by Flemish engravers.

Dr. William Cuningham, whom Walpole describes as an engraver, was a physician practising at Norwich ; and his book, entitled The Cosmographical Glasse,* some of the *plates* of which are said to have been "engraved by the doctor's own hand," was printed at London by John Day in 1559. It contains no *plates*, properly speaking, for the engravings are all from wood-blocks. At the foot of the ornamental title-page, and in a large bird's-eye view of Norwich, is the mark I. B. F, which, from something like a tool for engraving, between the B. and F in the original, is most likely that of the engraver. The principal cut is a portrait of the author, a fac-simile of which is given in the opposite page.

It is much more likely that some of those cuts were engraved by the printer of the book, John Day, than by the author, Dr. Cuningham ; for the initials I. D. appear on a cut at the end of the book,—a skeleton extended on a tomb, with a tree growing out of it—and also on two or three of the large ornamental letters. John Day, in a book printed

* The following is the title of this work : " The Cosmographical Glasse, conteinyng the pleasant Principles of Cosmographie, Geographie, Hydrographie or Navigation. Compiled by William Cuningham, Doctor in Physicke. Excussum Londini in officina Joan. Daii, Anno 1559.

In this Glasse, if you will beholde
The starry skie and yearth so wide,
The seas also, with the windes so colde,
Yea, and thy selfe all these to guide :
What this Type mean first learne a right,
So shall the gayne thy travaill quight."

The " *Type* " mentioned in these verses relates to the various allegorical and other figures in the engraved title-page.

by him in 1567, says that the Saxon characters used in it were *cut* by himself. The cut on page 425 and the three following are specimens of some of the large ornamental letters which occur in the Cosmographical Glasse. The first, the letter D, inclosing the arms of Lord Robert Dudley, afterwards Earl of Leicester, to whom the work is dedicated. The second, the letter A, Silenus on an ass, accompanied by satyrs ; the mark, a C with a small ɪ within the curve, is perceived near the bottom, to the right.*

The third, the letter I, with a military commander taking the angles between three churches ; and the mark I. D. at the bottom to the left.

* This mark, which occurs in two other cuts of large letters in the Cosmographical Glasse, is also to be found on a large ornamented letter in Robert Record's Castle of Know-

The fourth, the letter T, a ship with a naked figure as pilot, preceded by Neptune on a dolphin. A mark, H, is perceived in the right-hand corner, at the bottom.

Of all the books printed in England in the reigns of Queen Mary and Queen Elizabeth, those from the press of John Day generally contain the best executed wood-cuts; and even though he might not be the engraver of the cuts which contain his initials, yet it cannot be doubted that he possessed a much better taste in such matters than any other English printer of his age. Some of the large ornamental letters in works printed by him are much superior to anything of the kind that had previously appeared in England. In the "Booke of Christian Prayers" printed by John Daye 1569, which goes by the name of "Queen Elizabeth's Prayer Book," there is a portrait of her Majesty, kneeling upon a superb cushion, with elevated hands, in prayer, of which the

ledge, folio, printed at London, by Reginald Wolfe, 1556. This work, like that of Cuningham, is a treatise on Geography. A mark, I. C., with a graver between the letters, occurs frequently in cuts which ornament the margins of a work entitled "A Book of Christian Prayers," &c. 4to. first printed by John Day in 1569. It is usually called "Queen Elizabeth's Prayer Book." In Herbert's edition of the Typographical Antiquities it is erroneously stated that such of the cuts as relate to the History of Christ are "after Albert Durer and his wife, *Agnes Frey*." They are *not* copied from any cuts designed by Albert Durer, and his wife most certainly neither drew nor engraved on wood. It is also incorrectly stated "that a Dance of Death, in the same work, is after Hans Holbein."—The cuts in this work are very unequal in point of execution. The best are those of the Senses—without any mark—Sight, Hearing, Taste, Smelling, and Touch. A mark not unlike that in the letter A, from Cuningham's Cosmographical Glass, occurs on several of the smaller cuts.

following is a fac-simile. The book is decorated with wood-cut borders of considerable spirit and beauty, representing, among other things, some of the subjects of Holbein's Dance of Death.

Our next cut is a copy, slightly reduced, of a large letter, C, at the commencement of the dedication of Fox's Acts and Monuments to Queen Elizabeth, in the edition printed by Day in 1576. The Queen, appearing more juvenile than she is usually represented, is seen seated on a throne, attended by three persons, supposed to be intended for one of her council, John Day, the printer, and John Fox, the author of the work. A cherub, with an immense cornucopia over his shoulder, holds a rose and a lily in one hand, and with the other supports the arms or England; while underneath a representation of the Pope is introduced, holding in his hands the broken keys.*

Though it be beyond the plan of the present work to trace the progress of the various kinds of large ornamental letters engraved on wood that have been from time to time introduced by the principal German, French, Italian, and English printers from the invention of typography, it may not be unnecessary to say a few words on this subject. In the earliest works of the German printers, as the type was a close imitation of the handwriting of the period, as used in Bibles and Missals, the large ornamental letters occasionally introduced are distinguished by their flourishes and grotesque work extending on the margin both above and below the body of the letter, as is frequently seen in illumined manuscripts of the period. Large initial letters of this kind are not

* This work contains a considerable number of wood-cuts, all undoubtedly designed and engraved in England. Two of the best are Henry VIII, attended by his council, giving his sanction to the publication of the Bible in English, with the mark I. F.; and a view of Windsor Castle, with the mark M. D. Both these cuts are in the second volume of the edition of 1576.

unfrequent in early French works ; but are comparatively scarce in books printed in England, where a letter, engraved on a square block, appearing, with the ornaments, white on a black ground, was adopted shortly after the introduction of printing by Caxton.* As the capitals of the Roman character used in Italy did not admit of the flourishes which accorded so well with the curves of Gothic or German capitals, the printers of that country, towards the end of the fifteenth century, began to introduce flowers, figures of men, birds, and quadrupeds, as back-grounds to their large initial letters. Between 1520 and 1530 this mode of ornamenting their large Roman letters was in great repute with the printers of Basle, Geneva, and Zurich, and to this taste we owe the small alphabet of the Dance of Death. Subsequently the Italian wood engravers, employed by the printers, carried this style of ornament a step further by introducing landscapes as well as figures to form a back-ground to the letter. The following specimen of letter thus ornamented is from a work printed by Giolito at Venice about 1550. The large capitals, in Cuningham's Cosmographical Glasse, were doubtless suggested by Italian letters in the same taste.

The borders which appear in the title-pages of Italian books of this period, and more especially in those printed at Venice, frequently display considerable excellence both in design and execution. They are generally much lighter and more varied in design than the borders in German books ; and cross-hatching, which is seldom seen in Italian wood-cuts executed previous to 1520, is so frequently introduced that it would seem that this mode of producing a certain effect—which might often have been accomplished by simpler means—was then considered as a proof of the engraver's talent. Some of the Italian printers' marks and devices, on the title-page, or at the end of a work, are drawn and engraved with great spirit. The following devices occur in a folio

* Dr. Dibdin, in his Preliminary Disquisition on Early Engraving and Ornamental Printing, in his edition of Ames and Herbert's Typographical Antiquities, has given several curious specimens of large ornamented capitals.

edition of Dante—known to bibliographers as the *cat edition*—published by the brothers Sessa, at Venice, in 1578. The smaller cut—with

ornamental work on each side, occupying nearly the width of a page, but omitted in the copy—is several times repeated; the larger—where Grimalkin "sits like an eastern monarch upon his throne"*—forms the tailpiece at the end of the volume.

In the latter part of the sixteenth and the beginning of the seventeenth century, an Italian artist named Andrea Andreani executed a

* Bibliographical Decameron, vol. i. p. 289.

considerable number of chiaro-scuros on wood. He was born at Mantua in 1540, and one of his earliest and largest works in this style is dated 1586. The subject is the History of Abraham, from the pavement of the cathedral of Siena ;* the first compartment consists of twelve pieces, printed in three colours, forming, when joined together, a large composition about five feet six inches wide by about two feet six inches high. The second compartment, Moses breaking the Tables of the Law, is not properly a chiaro-scuro, but a large wood-cut, consisting of several pieces, printed in ink in the usual manner. It is about six feet wide by about four feet high. Another large work of Andreani's is the Triumphs of Julius Cæsar, from the designs of Andrea Mantegna, dedicated to Vincentius Gonzaga, Duke of Mantua, and published in a folio volume in 1598. Andreani having obtained the blocks of several of the chiaro-scuros executed by Ugo da Carpi, Antonio da Trente, Nicholas da Vincenza, and others, reprinted them with the addition of his own mark; and from this circumstance he frequently obtains the credit of having engraved many pieces which were really executed by his predecessors and superiors in the art. The chiaro-scuros which he reprinted are generally superior to those pieces which were engraved by himself from original designs, and in the execution of which he had to depend on his own judgment and taste. He continued to engrave in this manner till he was upwards of seventy years old, for there are one or two subjects by him dated 1612. Bartsch says that he died in 1623, but observes that some writers place his death in 1626.

Henry Goltzius, a painter and engraver, born in 1558, near Venloo, in Flanders, executed several chiaro-scuros, chiefly from his own designs. The most of them are from three blocks ; and among the best executed are Hercules and Cacus, and four separate pieces representing the four elements. Like most of the other productions of this artist, whether paintings or copper-plate engravings, his chiaro-scuros are designed with great spirit, though the action of the figures is frequently extravagant. He imitated Michael Angelo, but not with success ; he too frequently mistakes violence of action for the expression of intellectual grandeur, and displays the "contortions of the pythoness without her inspiration." The cut in the opposite page is a reduced copy of the subject intended

---

* "The pavement of this cathedral is the work of a succession of artists from Duccio down to Meccarino, who have produced the effect of the richest mosaic, merely by inserting grey marble into white, and hatching both with black mastic. The grandest composition is the History of Abraham, a figure which is unfortunately multiplied in the same compartments ; but, when grasping the knife, the patriarch is truly sublime. These works lay exposed at least for a hundred years to the general tread, and have been rather improved than defaced by the attrition ; for one female figure which had never been trodden looks harsher than the rest. Those of the choir were opportunely covered two centuries ago."— Forsyth's Italy, p. 102, 2nd Edit.

to represent the element of water. In the original the impression is from four blocks; one with the outlines and shaded parts black, as in the copy here given; the other three communicating different tints of sepia. Henry Goltzius died in 1617. His mark, an H combined with a G, is seen at the bottom of the cut.

The cuts contained in a work on ancient and modern costume, printed at Venice in 1590,* are frequently described as having been drawn by Titian and engraved by his *brother*, Cesare Vecellio. That this person might have been a relation of Titian, whose family name was Vecelli, is not unlikely, but it is highly improbable that he was his brother; for

---

* The following is the title of this work, which is a large octavo: "De gli Habiti Antichi et Moderni di diverse Parti del Mondo Libri due, fatti da Caesare Vecellio, & con Discorsi da lui dichiriati. In Venetia, MD.XC." This work is thus mentioned in the notes to Rogers's Italy: " Among the Habiti Antichi, in that admirable book of wood-cuts ascribed to Titian, (A. D. 1590,) there is one entitled Sposa Venetiana à Castello. It was taken from an old painting in the Scuola di S. Giovanni Evangelista, and by the writer is believed to represent one of the brides here described."—Italy, p. 257, note. Edit. 1830.

Titian died in 1576, aged ninety-nine, and the dedication of the work to
Pietro Montalbano by Cesare Vecellio is dated October, 1589. In the
title it is stated that the costumes in question were "done"—*fatti*—by
Vecellio himself; but whether this word relates to the drawing or the
engraving, or to both, it would be exceedingly difficult to ascertain.
Those cuts have the appearance of having been drawn on the block
with pen-and-ink; and some of the best display so much "character"
that they look like portraits of individuals freely sketched by the hand
of a master. It was first stated in an edition of the work, printed in
1664, that the cuts were drawn by Titian and engraved by Cesare
Vecellio, his brother. The improbable assertion was merely a bookseller's trick to attract purchasers. It has also been frequently asserted,
that the cuts in Vesalius's Anatomy, printed at Basle in 1548, were drawn
by Titian. The Abbé Morelli has, however, shown that they were not
drawn by him, but by John Calcar, a Flemish painter, who had been
one of his pupils.

Papillon, who in his desire to dignify his art claims almost every
eminent painter as a wood engraver, pretends that Titian executed
several large cuts from his own designs. He says that Titian began
to engrave on wood when he was twenty-five years old [in 1502], and he
mentions a cut of the Virgin and the infant Christ, with other figures,—
probably intended to represent the marriage of St. Catherine,—as one of
the earliest specimens of his talents as a wood engraver. Papillon also
informs us that Titian engraved a large cut of the Triumph of Christ, or
of Faith, in 1508; and in another part of his work he describes several
others as engraved by Titian himself.

Several of the cuts after designs by Titian, but which were certainly
not of his engraving, are of large size, and executed in a free, coarse
manner, as if they were rather intended to paste against a wall than
to be inserted in a portfolio. One of the largest is the destruction of
Pharaoh and his host; it consists of several pieces, which, when united,
form a complete subject about four and a half feet wide by about three
feet high. A dog, which the painter has introduced in a peculiar
attitude,* gives to the whole the air of burlesque. The person by whom
it was engraved styles himself " depintore," a word perhaps intended to
imply that he was a brother of the guild, or society of painter-stainers,
stencillers, and wood engravers.† His name, with the date, is engraved
thus at the bottom of the cut, which is one of those which Papillon says

* A dog performing the same act occurs as a tail-piece in the first edition of Bewick's
Quadrupeds, 1790, page 310.
† I have seen a large head, which at first sight might be mistaken for an impression from
a wood-block, executed by means of a stencil after a design of Correggio. It was unquestionably old, and was about three feet high by two and a half wide.

were executed by Titian himself : "In Venetia p. dominico dalle greche depintore venetiano. M.DXLIX."

The following is a reduced copy of a cut designed by Titian, and said to have been intended by him to ridicule those painters who, not being able to succeed in colouring, recommended ancient sculptures, on account of the correctness of the forms, as most deserving of a painter's diligent

study. The subject is a caricature of the Laocoon; and the professed admirers of antiquity, who, above all, insisted on correct drawing, and thought slightly of colouring, are represented by the old ape wanting a tail, seen in the distance, attended by three of her young ones. The original cut is fifteen inches and seven-eighths wide by ten inches and a half high. It is coarsely engraved, and contains neither name nor date.* There are several chiaro-scuros after designs by Titian, engraved by Boldrini, Andreani, and others.

Wood engraving in Germany at the close of the sixteenth century appears to have greatly declined; the old race of artists who furnished designs for the wood engraver had become extinct, and their places were not supplied by others. The more expensive works were now illustrated with copper-plates; and the wood-cuts which appeared in the commoner kinds of books were in general very indifferent both in design and

---

* The following is Papillon's description of this cut : " Une Estampe que je possede, et que l'on regarde assez indifférement, est le Laocoon gravé en bois par le Titien, représenté sous la figure d'un singe et ses deux petits entourés de serpens. Il fit ce morceau pour railler les Peintres de son temps qui étudoient cette figure et les Statues antiques ; et il prétendit démontrer par cette Estampe qu'ils ressembloient aux singes, lesquels ne font qu'imiter ce qu'ils voyent, sans rien inventer d'eux mêmes."—Traité de la Gravure en Bois, tom. i. p. 160.

execution. As Germany was the country in which wood engraving was first encouraged and fostered, so was it also the country in which the art earliest declined and subsequently became most thoroughly neglected. In France and Italy, wood engraving had also by this time experienced a considerable decline, but not to such an extent as in Germany.

Between 1590 and 1610, when the art was rapidly declining in other countries, the wood-cuts which are to be met with in English books are generally better executed than at any preceding period. Engraved title-pages were then frequent, and several of them are executed with considerable skill. A large wood-cut, with the date 1607, in particular displays great merit both in design and engraving. The following is a reduced copy of an impression preserved in the Print Room of the British Museum.* The original, exclusive of the verses, and the ornaments at each side of them, is about fourteen inches high by about fourteen and a half wide.

The following are the six concluding lines of the sonnet underneath the cut: in the original they are printed in smaller type than the others, and in a double column. In the copy they are merely indicated to show the relative size of the type to that of the first eight lines.

> And (thus) to these to stand still open wide,
> He neither wrings with Wrongs nor racks his Rents ;
> But saves the charge of wanton Waste & Pride :
> For, Thrift's right Fuel of Magnificence :
> As Protean Fashions of new Prodigalitie
> Have quight worn out all ancient Hospitalitie.

The flowers at each side of the verses are, in the original, very coarsely executed. They are merely printers' ornaments, engraved

---

* There is also in the Print Room of the British Museum a curious wood-cut, of large size, engraved on several blocks, apparently of the time of James I. The title at the top, in Latin and English, is as follows : " HUMANÆ VITÆ IMAGO OLIM AB APELLE IN TABULA QUADAM DEPICTA. The image of the lyfe of man that was painted in a table by Apelles." The subject, however, is not so much a general representation of the life of man in its several stages, as an allegorical representation of the evils attendant on sensual indulgence. Several of the figures are designed with great spirit, and the explanations underneath the principal are engraved on the same block, in Latin and English. It seems likely that this cut was engraved for the purpose of being pasted or hung against a wall. It is about five feet four inches wide by about three feet high. Some of the figures are engraved with considerable spirit, but the groups want that well-contrasted light and shade which give such effect to the large cuts of Durer and Burgmair. It is likely that large cuts of this kind were intended to be pasted on the walls of rooms, to serve at once for instruction and ornament, like " King Charles's Golden Rules and the Royal Game of Goose " in later times.—*To this note Mr. Jackson adds in his annotated copy:* " The drawing appears to have been executed by an artist who was rather partial to cross-hatching, and the engraving by one who knew how to render every line before him with a degree of sharpness and delicacy by no means common at that period."

on separate pieces of wood, and not on the same block as the cut above them.

From one or two worm-holes, which have been in the block when it was printed in 1607, and which are apparent in the impression, it seems probable that this cut had been engraved some time previous to the date which appears at the bottom. As it is, however, very likely that the block was of pear-tree, which is extremely liable to the attacks

of the worm, it is possible that it might have been injured in this manner within a year or two of its being finished. The bold, *cleanly cut* lines of the original are very much like the work of Christopher Jegher, one of the best wood engravers of that period. He resided at Antwerp, but he is said to have been born in Germany in 1578. His best works are several large cuts which he engraved for Rubens from drawings made on the block by Rubens himself, who appears to have originally

published them on his own account. From the manner in which the
great painter's name is introduced at the bottom of each—" *P. P. Rub.
delin. & excud.*"—it would appear that they were both designed and
printed by him. Impressions of those cuts sometimes occur with a tint
printed over them, in sepia, from a second block, in the manner of
chiaro-scuros. We here give a reduced copy of one of the largest.[*]

As profit could not have been Rubens's motive for having these
cuts engraved, it is not unlikely that his object was to compare his
designs when executed in this manner with those of the older German
masters—Durer, Burgmair, and Cranach. The best, however, differ
considerably in the manner of their execution from the best old German
wood-cuts, for the lines are too uniform and display too much of art ;
in looking at those which consist chiefly of figures, attention is first
called to the *means* by which an effect is produced, rather than to the
effect itself in connexion with the entire subject. This objection applies
most forcibly to the cut which represents the Virgin crowned by the
Almighty and Jesus Christ. The design displays much of Rubens's
grandeur, with not less of his extravagance in the attitude of the
figures ; but he seems to have studied less the effect of the whole, than
to have endeavoured to express certain parts by a peculiar arrangement
of lines and hatchings. The subject does not produce that feeling,
which it is the great object of art to excite, in consequence of the
attention being diverted from the contemplation of the whole to the
means by which it is executed. In such impressions, however, as have

* The original cut is twenty-three inches and a half wide by eighteen inches high.

a tint of sepia printed over them from a second block, the hardness of the lines and heaviness in the hatchings are less apparent. The following is a reduced copy of another of those cuts, which, for the beautiful simplicity of the design, is perhaps the most pleasing of the whole. The execution of the original is, however, coarse, a defect which is not so apparent in the copy in consequence of the small scale on which it is engraved.

P.P.Rub delin.
& exrudit.   CVM PRIVILEGIIS.   C.Jeghenjculp.

Cornelius van Sichem,† a contemporary of Christopher Jegher, appears to have been one of the most industrious wood engravers of his time. He was a native of Holland, and is supposed to have resided at Amsterdam. One of his best cuts is a large head, engraved from a drawing by Henry Goltzius, with the date 1607. This and several other large cuts, which he probably engraved about the same time, are so much superior to the smaller cuts, with his mark, which appear in books, that I am inclined to think that most of the latter must have been engraved by his pupils; they are indeed so numerous that it seems almost impossible that he should have engraved them all himself. He seems at first to have worked for fame, and afterwards to have turned a manufacturer of wood-cuts for money. The cuts with his mark contained in a quarto book entitled "Bibels Tresoor," printed at Amsterdam

* The original is eighteen inches wide by thirteen inches and a half high, including the margin with the inscription "Cum privilegiis," which is engraved on the same block.
† Papillon, tom. i. p. 274—276, calls this engraver *C. S. Vichem ;* and charges Professor Christ with confounding three *Sichems* with three *Vichems.* The name at the bottom of the cut, in the following page, is most certainly intended for C. V. *Sichem.*

in 1646, by no means afford an idea of his ability as a wood-engraver ; many of them are wretched copies of old wood-cuts designed by Albert Durer and other old masters, discreditable alike to the engraver and to the originals. The following is a slightly reduced copy of a cut, engraved by Van Sichem, from a design by Henry Goltzius. The original, which was probably engraved about 1607, may be considered as an average specimen of the engraver's talents ; it is not so well executed as some

of his best large cuts, while it is much superior to the greater number of the small cuts which contain his mark. The subject is Judith with the head of Holofernes.

About 1625 a French wood engraver of the name of Businck executed several chiaro-scuros chiefly from designs by Lalleman and Bloemart ; and between 1630 and 1647, Bartolomeo Coriolano, who sometimes styles himself " Romanus Eques," practised the same art at Bologna with great reputation.* In an edition of Hubert Goltzius's Lives of the Roman Emperors, enlarged by Casper Gevartius, folio, printed at Antwerp in 1645, the portraits, in the manner of chiaro-scuros, from two blocks, are executed with great spirit. The name of the engraver is not mentioned, but from the mark I. C. I. on a tail-piece at the end of the work, I am inclined to think that he was the same person who engraved the cuts in a little book of devotion, first printed in Latin, French, Spanish, and Flemish, at Antwerp, about 1646.† The number of cuts in this little work is forty, and most of them contain the mark of the designer, 𝕭, as well as that of the engraver. From the drawing of these cuts it would seem that the designer was either a pupil of Rubens, or had closely copied his manner. In Professor Christ's Dictionary of Monograms the mark 𝕭 is ascribed to Andrea Salmincio, "an engraver and pupil of Valesius." Papillon, Traité de la Gravure en Bois, tom. i. p. 274, adopting Professor Christ's explanation of the mark, mentions "Andrea Salmincio" as the designer of those cuts ; but in page 461 of the same volume, he says, referring to his former statement, that he had since been informed by M. Eisen, a painter, and a native of Valenciennes, that they were designed by "a famous Flemish painter and engraver on wood, named Sallarte, a contemporary of Rubens, and who is supposed to have assisted the latter in some of his great works." Those cuts may perhaps be considered as the last series that were expressly designed by an artist of talent in the seventeenth century, for the purpose of being engraved on wood. The style in which they are executed is not worthy of the designs, though, considering the period, they are not without merit. The engraver appears to have been extremely partial to a kind of cross-hatching, in which the interstices are more like squares than acute-angled lozenges, thus giving to the figures and draperies a hard and unpliable appearance.

Though several English wood engravings of the reigns of James I. and Charles I. have evidently been executed by professed wood engravers, yet a great proportion of those contained in English books and pamphlets printed in this country during the seventeenth century appear to have been the work of persons who had not learnt and did not regularly practise the art. The cuts of those occasional wood engravers, who were

---

* The twelfth volume of Bartsch's Peintre-Graveur contains an ample list of Italian chiaro-scuros, together with the names of the painters and engravers.

† The only perfect copy which I have seen of this little work is in Spanish. The title is as follows : " La Perpetua Cruz, o Passion de Jesu Christo Nuestro Señor, desde el principio de su encarnacion hasta su muerte. Representada en quarenta estampas que se reparten de balde, y explicada con differentes razones y oraciones de devocion. En Amberes, en la emprenta de Cornelio Woons, 1650." The cuts were engraved at the instance of the Arch-bishop of Malines. Before the Spanish edition appeared, thirty thousand copies of the work in Flemish and Latin had already been circulated.

most likely printers, are as rude in design as they are coarse in execution, frequently displaying something like the fac-simile of a boy's drawing in his first attempts to sketch "the human *form* divine." Such cuts, evidently executed on the spur of the moment, are of frequent occurrence in tracts and pamphlets published during the time of the war between Charles I. and the Parliament. Evelyn, in the first edition of his Sculptura, published in 1662, thus mentions Switzer as a wood engraver of that period : "We have likewise Switzer for cutting in wood, the son of a father* who sufficiently discovered his dexterity in the *Herbals* set forth by Mr. Parkinson, Lobel, and divers other works." The cuts of plants in the work, usually called Lobel's Botany, were most certainly not engraved by the elder Switzer; they are much superior to the cuts of the same kind which are undoubtedly of his engraving, and the work in which they first appeared was printed in London in 1571. He engraved the cuts in Speed's History of Britain, folio, 1611 ; and, though the author calls him " the most exquisite and curious hand of that age," they abundantly testify that he was a very ordinary workman. They are executed in a meagre, spiritless manner ; the best are those which represent the portraitures of the ancient Britons. The cuts in Parkinson's Paradisus Terrestris, folio, 1629, were also undoubtedly engraved by him ; his name, " *A. Switzer*," with a graver underneath, occurs at the bottom of the very indifferent cut which forms the title-page. The portrait of the author is scarcely superior to the title-page ; and the cuts of plants are the most worthless that are to be found in any work of the kind. It is not unlikely that the cuts in Topsell's History of Four-footed Beasts, 1607, and in Moffet's Theatre of Insects, 1634, were also engraved by the elder Switzer. The taste for wood-cuts must have been low indeed when such an engraver was considered one of the best of his age. Of the younger Switzer's abilities I have had no means of judging, never having seen a single cut which was known to be of his engraving.

Between 1650 and 1700 wood engraving, as a means of multiplying

* In Walpole's Catalogue of Engravers there is the following notice of the elder Switzer : " In the Harleian Library was a set of wooden cuts, representing the broad seals of England from the conquest to James I. inclusive, neatly executed. Vertue says this was the sole impression he had seen, and believed that they were cut by Chr. Switzer, and that these plates were copied by Hollar for Sandford. Switzer also cut the coins and seals in Speed's History of Britain, 1614 [1611], from the originals in the Cottonian Collection. Speed calls. him *the most exquisite and curious hand of that age.* He probably engraved the botanic figures for Lobel's Observations, and the plates [cuts] for Parkinson's Paradisus Terrestris, 1629. Chr. Switzer's works have sometimes been confounded with his son's, who was of both his names."—Catalogue of Engravers, p. 18 note, Edit. 1794. It is doubtful if the elder Switzer's Christian name were Christopher. The initial in Parkinson's Paradisus Terrestris is an A. It is, however, possible that this letter may be intended for a Latin preposition, and not for the first letter of the engraver's Christian name.

the designs of eminent artists, either as illustrations of books or as
separate cuts, may be considered as having reached its lowest ebb.
A few tolerably well executed cuts of ornaments are occasionally to
be found in Italian, French, and Dutch books of this period ; but
though they sufficiently attest that the race *of workmen* was not wholly
extinct, they also afford ample proof that *artists* like those of former
times had ceased to furnish designs for the wood engraver. The art
of design was then, however, in a languishing condition throughout
Europe ; and even supposing that wood engraving had been as much
in fashion as copper-plate printing then was for the purpose of illustrating books, it would be vain to expect in wood-cuts that excellence
of composition and drawing which is not to be found in the works
of the best painters of the time. Wood engravings to please must
possess *some* merit in the design—must show some trait of feeling
for his subject on the part of the designer. Deficiency in this respect
can never be compensated by dexterity of execution : in anything
that approaches to fine art, mere workmanship, the result of laborious
application, can never atone for want of mind. The man who drew
a portrait of Queen Anne with a pen, and wrote the Psalms in the
lines of the face, and in the curls of the hair, in characters so small
that it required a glass to read them, does not rank with a Vandyke
or a Reynolds, nor even with a Lely or a Kneller. At the period of
the greatest decline of wood engraving, the want that was felt was not of
working engravers to execute cuts, but of talented artists to design them.

The principal French wood engravers about the end of the seventeenth century were : Peter Le Sueur,—born in 1636, died 1716 ;
his two sons, Peter and Vincent ; John Papillon the elder—who died
in 1710 ; and his son, of the same name, who was born in 1661, and
died in 1723. Though John Michael Papillon, son of John Papillon
the younger, and author of the Traité de la Gravure en Bois, speaks
highly of the talents of the aforesaid members of the families of Le
Sueur and Papillon as wood engravers, yet, from his account of their
productions, it would seem that they were chiefly employed in engraving
subjects which scarcely allowed of any display of excellence either
in design or execution. Their fine works were ornamental letters,
flowered vignettes, and tail-pieces for the booksellers ; while their
staple productions appear to have been blocks for card-makers and
paper-stainers, with patterns for embroiderers, lace-workers, and ribbon-
manufacturers. In the succeeding century, J. M. Papillon, grandson
of the first John Papillon, and Nicholas le Sueur, grandson of the
elder Peter Le Sueur, fully supported the character of their respective
families as wood engravers. Some account of their works will be given
in the proper place.

The tail-piece at the conclusion of this chapter will afford some idea of the primitive style of the wood-cuts previously mentioned as occurring in tracts and pamphlets printed in England during the civil war. It is a fac-simile of a cut which originally appeared on the title-page to the first known edition of Robin Hood's Garland, printed in 1670.* The original block is now in the possession of Mr. William Garret of Newcastle-on-Tyne, and was frequently used by the late Mr. George Angus of that town, as it had also been by his predecessors in the same business, to decorate the title-pages of the penny histories and garlands, which they supplied in such abundance for the winter-evenings' entertainment of the good folks of Northumberland and the " Bishoprick." Mr. Douce, in the second volume of his Illustrations of Shakspeare, also gives a fac-simile of this cut; and the following is his explanation of the subject.

" Mr. Ritson has taken notice of an old wooden cut ' preserved on the title-page of a penny history (*Adam Bell, &c.*), printed at Newcastle in 1772,' and which represents, in his opinion, a morris dance, consisting of the following personages : 1. A bishop. 2. Robin Hood. 3. The potter or beggar. 4. Little John. 5. Friar Tuck. 6. Maid Marian. He remarks that the whole is too rude to merit a copy, a position that is not meant to be controverted ; but it is necessary to introduce the cut in this place for the purpose of correcting an error into which the above ingenious writer has fallen. It is proper to mention that it originally appeared on the title-page to the first known edition of Robin Hood's Garland, printed in 1670, 18mo. Now, this cut is certainly not the representation of a morris dance, but merely of the principal characters belonging to the Garland. These are Robin Hood, Little John, *Queen Catherine*, the bishop, the *curtal frier*, (not Tuck,) and the beggar. Even though it were admitted that Maid Marian and Friar Tuck were intended to be given, it could not be maintained that either the bishop or the beggar made part of a morris."

To give more specimens of wood engraving when in its lowest state of declension has not been thought necessary ; for even at this period it would not be difficult to produce cuts which in point of mere execution are superior to many which appeared when the art was at its height. It is sufficient to have stated that, towards the end of the seventeenth century, wood engraving for the higher purposes of the art had sunk into utter neglect ; that the best productions of the

---

* The cuts in an edition of " The most Delightful History of Reynard the Fox," 4to. London, printed for Thomas Passinger, 1681, are scarcely superior to this cut in point of execution, though it must be confessed that the figures are generally in better " keeping."

regular wood engravers of the period mostly consist of unmeaning ornaments which neither excite feeling nor suggest a thought ; and that the wood-cuts which appear to have been engraved by persons not instructed in the business partake generally of the character of the following tail-piece. Having now brought down the history of the art of wood engraving to the end of the seventeenth century, its revival in the eighteenth, with some account of the works of Thomas Bewick and the principal English wood engravers of his time, will form the subject of the next chapter.

CHAPTER VII.

REVIVAL OF WOOD ENGRAVING.

ENGLISH WOOD-CUTS IN 1712—HOWEL'S MEDULLA HISTORIÆ ANGLICANÆ—MAITTAIRE'S CLASSICS 1713—E. KIRKALL—HIS CHIARO-SCUROS—CUTS IN CROXALL'S ÆSOP, 1722—J. B. JACKSON— CHIARO-SCUROS ENGRAVED BY HIM AT VENICE, 1738-1742—FRENCH WOOD ENGRAVERS, 1710- 1768; J. M. PAPILLON, N. LE SUEUR, AND P. S. FOURNIER—ENGLISH WOOD-CUTS, 1760-1772— CUTS IN SIR JOHN HAWKINS'S HISTORY OF MUSIC, 1776—THOMAS BEWICK—HIS FIRST WOOD- CUTS, IN HUTTON'S MENSURATION, 1768-1770—CUTS BY HIM IN A HIEROGLYPHIC BIBLE—IN FABLES, 1779-1784—HIS CUT OF THE CHILLINGHAM BULL—HIS QUADRUPEDS, BRITISH BIRDS, AND FABLES—JOHN BEWICK—CUTS BY HIM IN EMBLEMS OF MORTALITY, AND OTHER BOOKS— POEMS BY GOLDSMITH AND PARNELL—SOMERVILE'S CHASE—ROBERT JOHNSON, DESIGNER OF SEVERAL OF THE TAIL-PIECES IN BEWICK'S WORKS—CHARLTON NESBIT—LUKE CLENNELL— WILLIAM HARVEY—ROBERT BRANSTON—JOHN THOMPSON, AND OTHERS.

 LTHOUGH wood engraving had fallen into almost utter neglect by the end of the seventeenth century, and con- tinued in a languishing state for many years afterward, yet the art was never lost, as some persons have stated ; for both in England and in France a regular succession of wood engravers can be traced from 1700 to the time of Thomas Bewick. The cuts which appear in books printed in Germany, Holland, and Italy during the same period, though of very inferior execution, sufficiently prove that the art continued to be practised in those countries.

The first English book of this period which requires notice is an edition of Howel's Medulla Historiæ Anglicanæ, octavo, printed at London in 1712.* There are upwards of sixty wood-cuts in this work,

* Small wood-cuts appear to have been frequently used about this time in newspapers, for what the Americans call a "caption" to advertisements. "The great art in writing advertisements is the finding out a proper method to catch the reader's eye, without which many a good thing may pass over unobserved, or be lost among commissions of bankrupts. Asterisks and hands were formerly of great use for this purpose. Of late years the N.B. has

and the manner in which they are executed sufficiently indicates that the engraver must have either been self-taught or the pupil of a master who did not understand the art. The blocks have, for the most part, been engraved in the manner of copper-plates ; most of the lines, which a regular wood engraver would have left in relief, are cut in *intaglio*, and hence in the impression they appear white where they ought to be black. The bookseller, in an address to the reader, thus proceeds to show the advantages of those cuts, and to answer any objection that might be urged against them on account of their being engraved on wood. " The cuts added in this edition are intended more for use than show. The utility consists in these two particulars. 1. To make the better impression on the memory. 2. To show more readily when the notable passages in our history were transacted ; which, without the knowledge of the names of the persons, are not to be found out, by even the best indexes. As for example : In what reign was it that a rebellious rout, headed by a vile fellow, made great ravage, and appearing in the King's presence with insolence, their captain was stabbed upon the spot by the Lord-Mayor ? Here, without knowing the names of some of the parties, which a world of people are ignorant of, the story is not to be found by an index ; but by the help of the cut, which catches the eye, is soon discovered. We all have heard of the piety of one of our queens who sucked the poison out of her husband's wound, but very few remember which of them it was, which the cut presently shows. The same is to be said of all the rest, since we have chosen only such things as are NOTABILIA in the history to describe in our sculptures.— And if it be objected that the graving is in wood, and not in copper, which would be more beautiful ; we answer, that such would be much more expensive too. And we were willing to save the buyer's purse ; especially since even the best engraving would not better serve the purposes above-said."

Though no mark is to be found on any of those cuts, I am inclined to think that they were executed by Edward Kirkall, whose name appears as the engraver of the copper-plate frontispiece to the book. The accounts which we have of Kirkall are extremely unsatisfactory. Strutt says that he was born at Sheffield in 1695 ; and that, visiting London in search of improvement, he was for some time employed in graving arms, stamps, and ornaments for books. It is, however, likely that he was born previous to 1695 ; for the frontispiece to Howel's

been much in fashion, as also *little cuts and figures*, the invention of which we must ascribe to the author of spring trusses."—Tatler, No. 224, 14th September 1710. The practice is not yet obsolete. Cuts of this kind are still to be found in country newspapers prefixed to advertisements of quack medicines, horse-races, coach and steam-boat departures, sales of ships, and the services of *equi admissorii*.

Medulla is dated 1712, when, if Strutt be correct, Kirkall would be only seventeen. That he engraved on wood, as well as on copper, is unquestionable; and I am inclined to think that he either occasionally engraved small ornaments and head-pieces on type-metal for the use of printers, or that casts in this kind of metal were taken from some of his small cuts.*

The head-pieces and ornaments in Maittaire's Latin Classics, duodecimo, published by Tonson and Watts, 1713, were probably engraved on wood by Kirkall, as his initials, E. K., are to be found on one of the tail-pieces. Papillon speaks rather favourably of those small cuts, though he objects to the uniformity of the tint and the want of precision in the more delicate parts of the figures, such as the faces and hands. He notices the tail-piece with the mark E. K. as one of the best executed; and he suspects that these letters were intended for the name of an English painter—called *Ekwits*, to the best of his recollection,—who "taught the arts of painting and of engraving on wood to J. B. Jackson, so well known to the printers of Paris about 1730 from his having supplied them with so large a stock of indifferent cuts."†

The cuts in Croxall's edition of Æsop's Fables, first published by J. and R. Tonson and J. Watts, in 1722, were, in all probability, executed by the same person who engraved the head-pieces and other ornaments in Maittaire's Latin Classics, printed for the same publishers about nine years before; and there is reason to believe that this person, as has been previously observed, was E. Kirkall. Bewick, in the introduction prefixed to his "Fables of Æsop and others," first printed in 1818, says that the cuts in Croxall's edition were "on metal, in the manner of wood." He, however, gives no reason for this opinion, and I very much question its correctness. After a careful inspection I have not been able to discover any peculiar mark which should induce me to suppose that they had been engraved on metal; and without some such mark indicating that the engraved surface had been fastened to the block to raise it to the height of the type, I consider it impossible for any person to decide merely from the appearance of the impressions that those cuts were printed from a metallic surface. The difference, in point of impression, between a wood-cut and an engraving on type-metal in the same manner, or a cast in type-metal from a wood-cut, is not to be distinguished. A wood engraver of the present day, when casts

---

* Some of the cuts in an edition of Dryden's plays, 6 vols. 12mo. published by Tonson and Watts in 1717, have evidently been either engraved on some kind of soft metal or been casts from a wood-block. In the corner of such cuts, the marks of the pins, which have fastened the engraved metal-plate to a piece of wood below, are quite apparent.

† Papillon, Traité de la Gravure en Bois, tom. i. p. 323.

from wood-cuts are so frequently used instead of the original engraved block, decides that a certain impression has been from a cast, not in consequence of any peculiarity in its appearance denoting that it is printed from a metallic surface, but from certain marks—little flaws in the lines and minute "picks"—which he knows are characteristic of a "cast." When a cast, however, has been well taken, and afterwards carefully cleared out with the graver, it is frequently impossible to decide that the impression has been taken from it, unless the examiner have also before him an impression from the original block with which it may be compared ; and even then, a person not very well acquainted with the practice of wood engraving and the method of taking casts from engraved wood-blocks, will be extremely liable to decide erroneously.

Though it is by no means improbable that a person like Kirkall, who had been accustomed to engrave on copper, might attempt to engrave on type-metal in the same manner as on wood, and that he might thus execute a few small head-pieces and flowered ornaments, yet I consider it very unlikely that he should *continue to prefer metal* for the purpose of relief engraving after he had made a few experiments. The advantages of wood over type-metal are indeed so great, both as regards clearness of line and facility of execution, that it seems incredible that any person who had tried both materials should hesitate to give the preference to wood. If, however, the cuts in Croxall's Æsop were really engraved on metal in the manner of wood, they are, as a series, the most extraordinary specimens of relief engraving for the purpose of printing, that have ever been executed. When Bewick stated that those cuts were engraved on metal, I am inclined to think that he founded his opinion rather on popular report than on close and impartial examination of the cuts themselves ; and it is further to be observed that Thomas Bewick, with all his merits as a wood engraver, was not without his weaknesses as a man ; he was not unwilling that people should believe that the art of wood engraving was lost in this country, and that the honour of its re-discovery, as well as of its subsequent advancement, was due to him. Though he was no doubt sincere in the opinion which he gave, yet those who know him are well aware that he would not have felt any pleasure in calling the attention of his readers to a series of wood-cuts executed in England upwards of thirty years before he was born, and which are not much inferior— except as regards the animals—to the cuts of fables engraved by himself and his brother previous to 1780.* The cuts in Croxall's Æsop not only

---

* "The Fables of Mr. John Gay," with cuts by Thomas and John Bewick, was published in 1779. "Select Fables, a new edition improved," with cuts by the same, appeared in 1784 ; both in duodecimo, printed by T. Saint, Newcastle-on-Tyne. The cuts in the latter work are considerably better than those in the former. Several of the cuts

display great improvement in the engraver, supposing him to be the same person that executed the head-pieces and ornaments in Maittaire's Latin Classics printed in 1713, but are very much superior to any cuts contained in works of the same kind printed in France between 1700 and 1760.*

FROM A COPPER-PLATE BY S. LE CLERC.

FROM A WOOD-CUT IN CROXALL'S ÆSOP.

Many of the subjects in Croxall are merely reversed copies of engravings on copper by S. Le Clerc, illustrative of a French edition

which originally appeared in those two works are to be found in " Select Fables ; with cuts designed and engraved by Thomas and John Bewick, and others," octavo, printed for Emerson Charnely, Newcastle-on-Tyne, 1820.

* The cuts in two different editions of Æsop's Fables, published at Paris,—the one by Charles Le Clerc in 1731, and the other by J. Barbou in 1758,—are most wretchedly executed. The mark of Vincent Le Sueur appears on the frontispiece to Le Clerc's edition.

of Æsop's Fables published about 1694. The first of the preceding cuts is a fac-simile of one of Le Clerc's engravings; and the second is a copy of the same subject as it appears in Croxall. The fable to which they both relate is the Fox and the Goat.

The above cut is by no means one of the best in Croxall: it has not been selected as a specimen of the manner in which those cuts are executed, but as an instance of the closeness with which the English wood-cuts have been copied from the French copper-plates. In several of the cuts in Bewick's Fables of Æsop and others, the arrangement and composition appear to have been suggested by those in Croxall; but in every instance of this kind the modern artist has made the subject his own by the superior manner in which it is treated : he restores to the animals their proper forms, represents them *acting* their parts as described in the fable, and frequently introduces an incident or sketch of landscape which gives to the whole subject a natural character. The following copy of the Fox and Goat, in the Fables of Æsop and others, 1818–1823, will serve to show how little the modern artist has borrowed in such instances from the cuts in Croxall, and how much has been supplied by himself.

Between 1722 and 1724, Kirkall published by subscription twelve chiaro-scuros engraved by himself, chiefly after designs by old Italian masters. In those chiaro-scuros the outlines and the darker parts of the figures are printed from copper-plates, and the sepia-coloured tints afterwards impressed from wood-blocks; though they possess considerable merit, they are deficient in spirit, and will not bear a comparison with the chiaro-scuros executed by Ugo da Carpi and other early

Italian wood engravers. Most of them are too smooth, and want the bold outline and vigorous character which distinguish the old chiaro-scuros : what Kirkall gained in delicacy and precision by the introduction of mezzotint, he lost through the inefficient engraving of the wood-blocks. One of the largest of those chiaro-scuros is a copy of one of Ugo da Carpi's—Æneas carrying his father on his shoulders—after a design by Raffaele. In Walpole's Catalogue of Engravers, a notice of Kirkall's "new method of printing, composed of etching, mezzotinto, and wooden stamps," concludes with the following passage : "He performed several prints in this manner, and did great justice to the drawing and expression of the masters he imitated. This invention, for one may call it so, had much success, much applause, no imitators.—I suppose it is too laborious and too tedious. In an opulent country where there is great facility of getting money, it is seldom got by merit. Our artists are in too much hurry to gain it, or deserve it."

About 1724 Kirkall published seventeen views of shipping, from designs by W. Vandevelde, which he also called "prints in chiaro-scuro." They have, however, no just pretensions to the name as it is usually understood when applied to prints, for they are merely tinted engravings worked off in a greenish-blue ink. These so-called chiaro-scuros are decided failures.

Kirkall engraved, on copper, the plates in Rowe's translation of Lucan's Pharsalia, folio, published by Tonson, 1718 ; the plates for an edition of Inigo Jones's Stonehenge, 1725 ; and a frontispiece to the works of Mrs. Eliza Haywood, which is thus alluded to in the Dunciad :

> " See in the circle next Eliza placed,
> Two babes of love close clinging to her waist ;
> Fair as before her works she stands confest,
> In flowers and pearls by bounteous *Kirkall* drest."

A considerable number of rude and tasteless ornaments and head-pieces, with the mark F. H., engraved on wood, are to be found in English books printed between 1720 and 1740. Several of them have been cast in type-metal,* as is evident from the marks of the pins, in the impressions, by which they have been fastened to the blocks ; the same head-piece or ornament is also frequently found in books printed in the same year by different printers. Some of the best headings and tail-pieces of this period occur in a volume of "Miscellaneous Poems, original and translated, by several hands. Published

---

* It is not unlikely that the frequency of such casts has induced many persons to suppose that most of the cuts of this period were " *engraved* on metal in the manner of wood."

by Mr. Concanen," London, printed for J. Peele, octavo, 1724. The subjects are, Apollo with a lyre; Minerva with a spear and shield; two men sifting corn; Hercules destroying the hydra; and a man with a large lantern. They are much superior to any cuts of the same kind with the mark F. H.; and from the manner in which they are executed, I am inclined to think that they are the work of the person who engraved the cuts in Croxall's Æsop. The following is a fac-simile of one of the best of the cuts that I have ever seen with the mark F. H. It occurs as a tail-piece at the end of the preface to "Strephon's Revenge: A Satire on the Oxford Toasts," octavo, London, 1724.*

John Baptist Jackson, an English wood engraver, was, according to Papillon, a pupil of the person who engraved the small head-pieces and ornaments in Maittaire's Latin Classics, published by Tonson and Watts in 1713; and as the cuts in Croxall's Æsop were probably engraved by the same person, as has been previously observed, it is not unlikely that Jackson, as his apprentice, might have some share in their execution. Though these cuts were much superior to any that had appeared in England for about a hundred years previously, wood engraving seems to have received but little encouragement. Probably from want of employment in his own country, Jackson proceeded to Paris, where he remained several years, chiefly employed in engraving head-pieces and ornaments for the booksellers. Papillon, who seems to have borne no good-will towards Jackson, thus speaks of him in the first volume of his "Traité de la Gravure en Bois."

* Two cuts, with the same mark, are to be found in Thoresby's Vicaria Leodinensis, 8vo. London, 1724; one at the commencement of the preface, and the other at the end of the work.

" J. Jackson, an Englishman, who resided several years in Paris, might have perfected himself in wood engraving, which he had learnt of an English painter, as I have previously mentioned, if he had been willing to follow the advice which it was in my power to give him. Having called on me, as soon as he arrived in Paris, to ask for work, I for several months gave him a few things to execute in order to afford him the means of subsistence. He, however, repaid me with ingratitude ; he made a duplicate of a flowered ornament of my drawing, which he offered, before delivering to me the block, to the person for whom it was to be engraved. From the reproaches that I received, on the matter being discovered, I naturally declined to employ him any longer. He then went the round of the printing-offices in Paris, and was obliged to engrave his cuts without order, and to offer them for almost nothing ; and many of the printers, profiting by his distress, supplied themselves amply with his cuts. He had acquired a certain insipid taste which was not above the little mosaics on snuff-boxes ; and with ornaments of this kind, after the manner of several other inferior engravers, he surcharged his works. His mosaics, however delicately engraved, are always deficient in effect, and display the engraver's patience rather than his talent ; for the other parts of the cut, consisting of delicate lines without tints or a gradation of light and shade, want that force which is necessary to render the whole striking. Such wood engravings, however deficient in this respect, are yet admired by printers of vulgar taste, who foolishly pretend that they most resemble copper-plates, and that they print better than cuts of a picturesque character, and containing a variety of tints.

"Jackson, being obliged, through destitution, to leave Paris, where he could get nothing more to do, travelled in France ; and afterwards, being disgusted with his profession, he accompanied a painter to Rome, from whence he went to Venice, where, as I am informed, he married, and subsequently returned to England, his native country." *

Though Papillon speaks disparagingly of Jackson, the latter was at least as good an engraver as himself. Jackson appears to have visited Paris not later than 1726, for Papillon mentions a vignette and a large letter engraved by him in that year for a Latin and French dictionary, printed in 1727 by the brothers Barbou ; and it is likely that he remained there till about 1731. In an Italian translation of the Lives of the Twelve Cæsars, printed there in quarto 1738, there is a large ornamental title-page of his engraving ; and in the same year he engraved a chiaro-scuro of Christ taken down from the cross, from a

---

* Traité de la Gravure en Bois, tom. i. pp. 327, 328.

painting by Rembrandt,* in the possession of Joseph Smith, Esq. the British consul at Venice, a well-known collector of pictures and other works of art. Between 1738 and 1742, when residing at Venice, he also engraved twenty-seven large chiaro-scuros,—chiefly after pictures by Titian, G. Bassano, Tintoret, and P. Veronese,—which were published in a large folio volume in the latter year. They are very unequal in point of merit ; some of them appearing harsh and crude, and others flat and spiritless, when compared with similar productions of the old Italian wood engravers. One of the best is the Martyrdom of St. Peter Dominicanus, after Titian, with the date 1739 ; the manner in which the foliage of the trees is represented is particularly good. On his return to England he seems to have totally abandoned the practice of wood engraving in the ordinary manner for the purpose of illustrating or ornamenting books ; for I have not been able to discover any English wood-cut of the period that either contains his mark, or seems, from its comparative excellence, to have been of his engraving. Finding no demand in this country for wood-cuts, he appears to have tried to render his knowledge of engraving in chiaro-scuro available for the purpose of printing paper-hangings. In an " Essay on the Invention of Engraving and Printing in Chiaro Oscuro,"† published in his name in 1754, we learn that he was then engaged in a manufacture of this kind at Battersea. The account given in this essay of the origin and progress of chiaro-scuro engraving is frequently incorrect ; and from several of the statements which it contains, it would seem that the writer was very imperfectly acquainted with the works of his predecessors and con- temporaries in the same department of wood engraving. From the following passage, which is to be found in the fifth page, it is evident that the writer was either ignorant of what had been done in the six- teenth and seventeenth centuries, and even in his own age, or that he was wishful to enhance the merit of Mr. Jackson's process by concealing what had recently been done in the same manner by others. " After having said all this, it may seem highly improper to give to Mr. Jackson the merit of inventing this art ; but let me be permitted to say, that an art recovered is less little than an art invented. The works of the former artists remain indeed ; but the manner in which they were done is entirely lost : the inventing then the manner is really due to this latter undertaker, since no writings, or other remains, are to be found by

---

* This painting, which is wholly in chiaro-scuro, is now in the National Gallery, to which it was presented by the late Sir George Beaumont.

† The title at length is as follows : " An Essay on the Invention of Engraving and Printing in Chiaro Oscuro, as practised by Albert Durer, Hugo di Carpi, &c., and the Application of it to the making Paper Hangings of taste, duration, and elegance, by Mr. Jackson of Battersea. Illustrated with Prints in proper colours." 4to. London, 1754.

which the method of former artists can be discovered, or in what manner they executed their works ; nor, in truth, has the Italian method since the beginning of the sixteenth century been attempted by any one except Mr. Jackson." What is here called the " Italian method," that is, the method of executing chiaro-scuros entirely on wood, was practised in France at the end of the seventeenth century : and Nicholas Le Sueur had engraved several cuts in this manner about 1730, the very time when Jackson was living in Paris. The principles of the art had also been applied in France to the execution of paper-hangings upwards of fifty years before Jackson attempted to establish the same kind of manufacture in England. Not a word is said of the chiaro-scuros of Kirkall,* from whom it is likely that Jackson first acquired his knowledge of chiaro-scuro engraving : with the exception of the outlines and some other parts in these chiaro-scuros being executed in mezzotint, the printing of the rest from wood-blocks is precisely the same as in the Italian method.

The Essay contains eight prints illustrative of Mr. Jackson's method ; four are chiaro-scuros, and four are printed in " proper colours," as is expressed in the title, in imitation of drawings. They are very poorly executed, and are very much inferior to the chiaro-scuros engraved by Jackson when residing at Venice. The prints in " proper colours" are egregious failures. The following notices respecting Mr. Jackson are extracted from the Essay in question.

" Certainly Mr. Jackson, the person of whom we speak, has not spent less time and pains, applied less assiduity, or travelled to fewer distant countries in search of perfecting his art, than other men ; having passed twenty years in France and Italy to complete himself in drawing after the best masters in the best schools, and to see what antiquity had most worthy the attention of a student in his particular pursuits. After all this time spent in perfecting himself in his discoveries, like a true lover of his native country, he is returned with a design to communicate all the means which his endeavours can contribute to enrich the land where he drew his first breath, by adding to its commerce, and employing its inhabitants ; and yet, like a citizen of it, he would willingly enjoy some little share of those advantages before he leaves this world, which he must leave behind him to his countrymen when he shall be no more."

" During his residence at Venice, where he made himself perfect

---

* There can be no doubt that the mention of Kirkall's name is purposely avoided. The "attempts" of Count Caylus, who executed several chiaro-scuros by means of copper-plates and wood-blocks subsequent to Kirkall, are noticed ; but the name of Nicholas Le Sueur, who assisted the Count and engraved the wood-blocks, is never mentioned. It is also stated in the Essay, page 6, that some of the subjects begun by Count Caylus were finished by Mr. Jackson, and " approved by the lovers and promoters of that art in Paris."

in the art which he professes, he finished many works well known to the nobility and gentry who travelled to that city whilst he lived in it.— Mr. Frederick, Mr. Lethuillier, and Mr. Smith, the English consul at Venice, encouraged Mr. Jackson to undertake to engrave in chiaro-oscuro, blocks after the most capital pictures of Titian, Tintoret, Giacomo Bassano, and Paul Veronese, which are to be found in Venice, and to this end procured him a subscription. In this work may be seen what engraving on wood will effectuate, and how truly the spirit and genius of every one of those celebrated masters are preserved in the prints.

"During his executing this work he was honoured with the encouragement of the Right Honourable the Marquis of Hartington, Sir Roger Newdigate, Sir Bouchier Wrey, and other English gentlemen on their travels at Venice, who saw Mr. Jackson drawing on the blocks for the print after the famous picture of the Crucifixion painted by Tintoret in the albergo of St. Roche. Those prints may now be seen at his house at Battersea.—Not content with having brought his works in chiaro-oscuro to such perfection, he attempted to print landscapes in all their original colours ; not only to give to the world all the outline light and shade, which is to be found in the paintings of the best masters, but in a great degree their very manner and taste of colouring. With this intent he published six landscapes,* which are his first attempt in this nature, in imitation of painting in *aquarillo* or water-colours ; which work was taken notice of by the Earl of Holderness, then ambassador extraordinary to the republic of Venice ; and his excellency was pleased to permit the dedication of those prints to him, and to encourage this new attempt of printing pictures with a very particular and very favourable regard, and to express his approbation of the merit of the inventor."

John Michael Papillon, one of the best French wood engravers of his age, was born in 1698. His grandfather and his father, as has been previously observed, were both wood engravers. In 1706, when only eight years old, he secretly made his first essay in wood engraving ; and when only nine, his father, who had become aware of his amusing himself in this manner, gave him a large block to engrave, which he appears to have executed to his father's satisfaction, though he had previously received no instructions in the art.† The block was intended

---

* I have only seen one of these landscapes ; and from it I form no very high opinion of the others. It is scarcely superior in point of execution to the prints in " proper colours" contained in the Essay.

† Papillon, in the Supplement to his " Traité de la Gravure en Bois," page 6, gives a small cut—a copy of a figure in a copper-plate by Callot—engraved by himself when nine years old. If the cut be genuine, the engraver had improved but little as he grew older.

for printing paper-hangings, the manufacture of which was his father's principal business. Though until the time of his father's death, which happened in 1723, Papillon appears to have been chiefly employed in such works, and in hanging the papers which he had previously engraved, he yet executed several vignettes and ornaments for the booksellers, and sedulously endeavoured to improve himself in this higher department of his business.

Shortly after the death of his father he married; and, having given up the business of engraving paper-hangings, he laboured so hard to perfect himself in the art of designing and engraving vignettes and ornaments for books, that his head became affected; and he some-times displayed such absence of mind that his wife became alarmed, fancying that "he no longer loved her." On his assuring her that his behaviour was the result of his anxiety to improve himself in drawing and engraving on wood, and to write something about the art, she encouraged him in his purpose, and aided him with her advice, for, as she was the daughter of a clever man, M. Chaveau, a sculptor, and had herself made many pretty drawings on fans, she had some knowledge of design. Papillon's fits of absence, however, though they may have been proximately induced by close application and anxiety about his success in the line to which he intended to apply himself in future, appear to have originated in a tendency to insanity, which at a later period displayed itself in a more decided manner. In 1759, in consequence of a determination of blood to the head, as he says, through excessive joy at seeing his only daughter, who had lived from the age of four years with her uncle, combined with a recollection of his former sorrows, his mind became so much disordered that it was necessary to send him to an hospital, where, through repeated bleedings and other remedies, he seems to have speedily recovered. He mentions that in the same year, four other engravers were attacked by the same malady, and that only one of them regained his senses.*

Papillon's endeavours to improve himself were not unsuccessful; the cuts which he engraved about 1724, though mostly small, possess

---

* Traité de la Gravure en Bois, Supplement, tom. iii. p. 39. In the first volume, page 335, he alludes to the disorder as " un accident et une fatalité commune à plusieurs graveurs, aussi bien que moi." Has the practice of engraving on wood or on copper a tendency to induce insanity ? Three distinguished engravers, all from the same town, have in recent times lost their reason ; and several others, from various parts of the country, have been afflicted with the same distressing malady. These facts deserve the consideration of parents who design to send their sons as pupils to engravers. When there is the least reason to suspect a hereditary taint of insanity in the constitution of the youth, it perhaps would be safest to put him to some other business or profession where close attention to minute objects is less required.

considerable merit ; they are not only designed with much more feeling than the generality of those executed by other French engravers of the period, but are also much more effective, displaying a variety of tint and a contrast of light and shade which are not to be found in the works of his contemporaries. In 1726, in order to divert his anxiety and to bring his cuts into notice, he projected *Le petit Almanach de Paris,* which subsequently was generally known as "Le Papillon." The first that he published was for the year 1727 ; and the wood-cuts which it contained equally attracted the attention of the public and of connoisseurs. Monsieur Colombat, the editor of the Court Calendar, spoke highly of the cut for the month of January ; the cross-hatchings, he said, were executed in the first style of wood engraving, and he kindly predicted to Papillon that he would one day excel in his art. From this time he seems to have no longer had any doubt of his own abilities, but, on the contrary, to have entertained a very high opinion of them. He appears to have considered wood engraving as the highest of all the graphic arts, and himself as the greatest of all its professors, either ancient or modern.

From this, to him, memorable epoch,—the publication of "Le petit Almanach de Paris," with cuts by PAPILLON,—he appears to have been seldom without employment, for in the Supplement to the "Traité de la Gravure en Bois," he mentions that in 1768, the "Collection of the Works of the Papillons," presented by him to the Royal Library, contained upwards of *five thousand* pieces of his own engraving. This "Recueil des Papillons," which he seems to have considered as a family monument "ære perennius," is perpetually referred to in the course of his work. It consisted of four large folio volumes containing specimens of wood engravings executed by the different members of the Papillon family for three generations — his grandfather, his father, his uncle, his brother, and himself.

Papillon was employed not only by the booksellers of his own country, but also by those of Holland. A book, entitled "Historische School en Huis-Bybel," printed at Amsterdam in 1743, contains two hundred and seventeen cuts, all of which appear to have been either engraved by Papillon himself, or under his superintendence. His name appears on several of them, and they are all engraved in the same style. From a passage in the dedication, it seems likely that they had appeared in a similar work printed at the same place a few years previously. They are generally executed in a coarser manner than those contained in Papillon's own work, but the style of engraving and general effect are the same. The cut on the next page is a copy of the first, which is one of the best in the work. To the left is

Papillon's name, engraved, as was customary with him, in very small letters, with the date, 1734.

Papillon's History of Wood Engraving, published in 1766, in two octavo volumes, with a Supplement,* under the title of "Traité Historique et Pratique de la Gravure en Bois," is said to have been projected, and partly written, upwards of thirty years before it was given to the public. Shortly after his being admitted a member of the Society of Arts, in 1733, he read, at one of the meetings, a paper on the history and practice of wood engraving; and in 1735 the Society signified their approbation that a work written by him on the subject should be printed. It appears that the first volume of such a work was actually printed between 1736 and 1738, but never published. He does not explain why the work was not proceeded with at that time; and it would be useless to speculate on the possible causes of the interruption. He mentions that a copy of this volume was preserved in the Royal Library ; and he charges Fournier the younger, who between 1758 and 1761 published three tracts on the invention of wood engraving and printing, with having availed himself of a portion of the historical information contained in this volume. The public, however, according to his own statement, gained by the delay ; as he grew older he gained more knowledge of the history of the art, and "invented" several important improvements in his practice, all of which are embodied in his later work. In 1758 he also discovered the memoranda which he had made at Monsieur De Greder's, in 1719 or 1720, relative to the interesting twins,

---

* The Supplement, or " Tome troisième," as it is also called, though dated 1766, was not printed until 1768, as is evident from a " Discours Nuptial," at page 97, pronounced on 13th June 1768. Two of the cuts also contain the date 1768.

Alexander Alberic Cunio and his sister Isabella, who, about 1284, between the fourteenth and sixteenth years of their age, executed a series of wood engravings illustrative of the history of Alexander the Great.* However the reader may be delighted or amused by the romantic narrative of the Cunio, Papillon's reputation as the historian of his art would most likely have stood a *little* higher had he never discovered those memoranda. They have very much the character of ill-contrived forgeries ; and even supposing that he believed them, and printed them in good faith, his judgment must be sacrificed to save his honesty.

The first volume of Papillon's work contains the history of the art ; it is divided into two parts, the first treating of wood engraving for the purpose of printing in the usual manner from a single block, and the second treating of chiaro-scuro. He does not trace the progress of the art by pointing out the improvements introduced at different periods ; he enumerates all the principal cuts that he had seen, without reference to their execution as compared with those of an earlier date ; and, from his desire to enhance the importance of his art, he claims almost every eminent painter whose name or mark is to be found on a cut, as a wood engraver. He is in this respect so extremely credulous as to assert that Mary de Medici, Queen of Henry IV. of France, had occasionally amused herself with engraving on wood ; and in order to place the fact beyond doubt he refers to a cut representing the bust of a female, with the following inscription : " Maria Medici. F. M.D.LXXXVII." " The engraving," he observes, with his usual *bonhomie*, " is rather better than what might be reasonably expected from a person of such quality ; it contains many cross-hatchings, somewhat unequal indeed, and occasionally imperfect, but, notwithstanding, sufficiently well engraved to show that she had executed several wood-cuts before she had attempted this. I know more than one wood engraver—or at least calling himself such—who is incapable of doing the like." In 1587, the date of this cut, Mary de Medici was only fourteen years old ; and since its execution, according to Papillon, shows that she was then no novice in the art, she must have acquired her practical knowledge of wood engraving at rather an early age,—at least for a princess. Papillon never seems to have considered that F is the first letter of " Filia " as well as of " Fecit," nor to have suspected that the cut was simply a portrait of Mary de Medici, and not a specimen of her engraving.

From the following passage in the preface, he seems to have been

---

* Papillon's account of the Cunio, with an examination of its credibility, will be found in chapter i. pp. 26—39.

aware that his including the names of many eminent painters in his list of wood engravers would be objected to. " Some persons, who entertain a preconceived opinion that many painters whom I mention have not engraved on wood, may perhaps dispute the works which I ascribe to them. Of such persons I have to request that they will not condemn me before they have acquainted themselves with my researches and examined my proofs, and that they will judge of them without prejudice or partiality." The "researches" to which he alludes, appear to have consisted in searching out the names and marks of eminent painters in old wood-cuts, and his "proofs" are of the same kind as that which he alleges in support of his assertion that Mary de Medici had engraved on wood,—a fact which, as he remarks, "was unknown to Rubens." The historical portion of Papillon's work is indeed little more than a confused catalogue of all the wood-cuts which had come under his observation ; it abounds in errors, and almost every page affords an instance of his credulity.

In the second volume, which is occupied with details relative to the practice of the art, Papillon gives his instructions and enumerates his " inventions" in a style of complacent self-conceit. The most trifling remarks are accompanied by a reference to the " Recueil des Papillons ; " and the most obvious means of effecting certain objects,—such means as had been regularly adopted by wood engravers for upwards of two hundred years previously, and such as in succeeding times have suggested themselves to persons who never received any instructions in the art,—are spoken of as important discoveries, and credit taken for them accordingly. One of his fancied discoveries is that of lowering the surface of a block towards the edges in order that the engraved lines in those parts may be less subject to the action of the *plattin* in printing, and consequently lighter in the impression. The Lyons Dance of Death, 1538, affords several instances of blocks lowered in this manner, not only towards the edges, but also in the middle of the cut, whenever it was necessary that certain delicately engraved lines should be lightly printed, and thus have the appearance of gradually diminishing till their extremities should scarcely be distinguishable from the paper on which they are impressed. Numerous instances of this practice are frequent in wood-cuts executed from 1540 to the decline of the art in the seventeenth century. Lowering was also practised by the engraver of the cuts in Croxall's Æsop ; by Thomas Bewick, who acquired a knowledge of wood engraving without a master ; and by the self-taught artist who executed the cuts in Alexander's Expedition down the Hydaspes, a poem by Dr. Thomas Beddoes, printed in 1792, but never published.* As the

---

* This poem was privately printed and never published. It was written expressly in imitation of Dr. Darwin, some of whose friends had contended that his style was inimitable,

same practice has recently been claimed as an "invention," it would seem that some wood engravers are either apt to ascribe much importance to little things, or are singularly ignorant of what has been done by their predecessors. Such an "invention," though unquestionably useful, surely does not require any particular ingenuity for its discovery ; such "discoveries" every man makes for himself as soon as he feels the want of that which the so-called invention will supply. The man who pares the cork of a quart bottle in order to make it fit a smaller one is, with equal justice, entitled to the name of an inventor, provided he was not aware of the thing having been done before : such an "adaptation of means to the end" cannot, however, be considered as an effort of genius deserving of public commendation.

In Papillon's time it was not customary with French engravers on wood to have the subject perfectly drawn on the block, with all the lines and hatchings pencilled in, and the *effect* and the different tints indicated either in pencil or in Indian ink, as is the usual practice in the present day. The design was first drawn on paper ; from this, by means of tracing paper, the engraver made an outline copy on the block ; and, without pencilling in all the lines or washing in the tints, he proceeded to "translate" the original, to which he constantly referred in the progress of his work, in the same manner as a copper-plate engraver does to the drawing or painting before him. Papillon perceived the disadvantages which resulted from this mode of proceeding ; and though he still continued to make his first drawing on paper, he copied it more carefully and distinctly on the block than was usual with his contemporaries. He was thus enabled to proceed with greater certainty in his engraving ; what he had to effect was immediately before him, and it was no longer necessary to refer so frequently to the original. To the circumstance of the drawings being perfectly made on the block, Papillon ascribes in a great measure the excellence of the old wood engravings of the time of Durer and Holbein.

Papillon, although always inclined to magnify little things connected with wood engraving, and to take great credit to himself for trifling "inventions," was yet thoroughly acquainted with the practice of his art. The mode of thickening the lines in certain parts of a cut, after it has

but were deceived into a belief that this poem was written by him, until the real author avowed himself. In the Advertisement prefixed to it Dr. Beddoes speaks thus of the engraver of the cuts : "The engravings in the following pages will be praised or excused when it is known that they are the performance of an uneducated and uninstructed artist, if such an application be not a profanation of the term, in a remote village. All the assistance he received was from the example of Mr. Bewick's most masterly engravings on wood." The name of this self-taught artist was Edward Dyas, who was parish-clerk at Madeley, Shropshire, where the book was printed. The *compositor*, as is stated in the same Advertisement, was a young woman.—See *Bibliotheca Parriana*, p. 513.

been engraved, by scraping them down, was frequently practised by him, and he explains the manner of proceeding, and gives a cut of the tools required in the operation.* As Papillon, previous to the publication of his book, had contributed several papers on the subject of wood engraving to the famed Encyclopédie, he avails himself of the second volume of the Traité to propose several additions and corrections to those articles. The following definition proposed to be inserted in the Encyclopédie, after the article GRATUIT, will afford some idea of the manner in which he is accustomed to speak of his "inventions." The term which he explains is "GRATTURE ou GRATTAGE," literally, "SCRAPING," the practice just alluded to. "This is, according to the new manner of engraving on wood, the operation of skilfully and carefully scraping down parts in an engraved block which are not sufficiently dark, in order to give them, as may be required, greater strength, and to render the shades more effective. This admirable plan, utterly unknown before, was accidentally discovered in 1731 by M. Papillon, by whom the art of wood engraving is advanced to a state tending to perfection, and approaching more and more towards the beauty of engraving on copper." The tools used by Papillon to scrape down the lines of an engraved block, and thus render them thicker and, consequently, the impression darker, differ considerably in shape from those used for the same purpose by modern wood engravers in England. The tool now principally used is something like a copper-plate engraver's burnisher, and occasionally a fine and sharp file is employed.

In Papillon's time the French wood engravers appear to have held the graver in the manner of a pen, and in forming a line to have cut *towards them* as in forming a down-stroke in writing, and to have engraved on the longitudinal, and not the cross section of the wood. Modern English wood engravers, having the rounded handle of the graver supported against the hollow of the hand, and directing the blade by means of the fore-finger and thumb, cut the line *from them ;* and always engrave on the cross section of the wood. Papillon mentions box, pear-tree, apple-tree, and the wood of the service-tree, as the best for the purposes of engraving : box was generally used for the smaller and finer cuts intended for the illustration or ornament of books ; the larger cuts, in which delicacy was not required, were mostly engraved on pear-tree wood. Apple-tree wood was principally used by the wood engravers of Normandy. Next to box, Papillon prefers the wood of the service-tree. The box brought from Turkey, though of larger size, he considers inferior to that of Provence, Italy, or Spain.

---

* "Manière de Gratter les tailles déjà gravées pour les rendre plus fortes, afin de les faire ombrer davantage."—Supplément du Traité de la Gravure en Bois, p. 50.

Although Papillon's *modus operandi* differs considerably from that of English wood engravers of the present day, I am not aware of any supposed discovery in the modern practice of the art that was not known to him. The methods of lowering a block in certain parts before drawing the subject on it, and of thickening the lines, and thus getting more *colour*, by scraping the surface of the cut when engraved, were, as has been observed, known to him; he occasionally introduced cross-hatchings in his cuts;* and in one of his chapters he gives instructions how to insert a *plug* in a block, in order to replace a part which had either been spoiled in the course of engraving or subsequently damaged. One of the improvements which he suggested, but did not put in practice, was a plan for engraving the same subject on two, three, or four blocks, in order to obtain cross-hatchings and a variety of tints with less trouble than if the subject were entirely engraved on the same block. Such cuts were not to be printed as chiaro-scuros, but in the usual manner, with printer's ink. It is worthy of observation that Bewick in the latter part of his life had formed a similar opinion of the advantages of engraving a subject on two or more blocks, and thus obtaining with comparative ease such cross-lines and varied tints as could only be executed with great difficulty on a single block. He, however, proceeded further than Papillon, for he began to engrave a large cut which he intended to finish in this manner; and he was so satisfied that the experiment would be successful, that when the pressman handed to him a proof of the first block, he exclaimed, "I wish I was but twenty years younger!"

Papillon, in his account of the practice of the art, explains the manner of engraving and printing chiaro-scuros; and in illustration of the process he gives a cut executed in this style, together with separate impressions from each of the four blocks from which it is printed. There is also another cut of the same kind prefixed to the second part of the first volume, containing the history of engraving in chiaro-scuro. Scarcely anything connected with the practice of wood engraving appears to have escaped his notice. He mentions the effect of the breath in cold weather as rendering the block damp and the drawing less distinct; and he gives in one of his cuts the figure of a "mentonnière,"—that is to say, a piece of quilted linen, like the pad used by women to keep their bonnets cocked up,—which, being placed

---

* Several cuts in which cross-hatching is introduced occur in the "Traité de la Gravure en Bois;" and the author refers to several others in the "Recueil des Papillons" as displaying the same kind of work. He considers the execution of such hatchings as the test of excellence in wood engraving; "for," he observes, "when a person has learnt to execute them he may boast of having mastered one of the most difficult parts of the art, and may justly assume the name of a wood engraver."—Tom. ii. p. 90.

before the mouth and nostrils, and kept in its place by strings tied behind the head, screened the block from the direct action of the engraver's breath.

He frequently complains of the careless manner in which wood-cuts were printed;* but from the following passage we learn that the inferiority of the printed cuts when compared with the engraver's proofs did not always proceed from the negligence of the printer. " Some wood engravers have the art of fabricating proofs of their cuts much more excellent and delicate than they fairly ought to be ; and the following is the manner in which they contrive to obtain tolerably decent proofs from very indifferent engravings. They first take two or three impressions, and then, to obtain one to their liking, and with which they may deceive their employers, they only ink the block on those places which ought to be dark, leaving the distances and lighter parts without any ink, except what remained after taking the previous impressions. The proof which they now obtain appears extremely delicate in those parts which were not properly inked ; but when they come to be printed in a page with type, the impression is quite different from the proof which the engraver delivers with the blocks ; there is no variety of tint, all is hard, and the distance is sometimes darker than objects in the fore-ground. I run no great risk in saying that all the three *Le Sueurs* have been accustomed to practise this deception."†

All the cuts in Papillon's work, except the portrait prefixed to the first volume,‡ are his own engraving, and, for the most part, from his own designs. The most of the blocks were lent to the author by the different persons for whom he had engraved them long previous to the appearance of his work.§ They are introduced as ornaments at the beginning and end of the chapters ; but though they may enable the reader to judge of Papillon's abilities as a designer and engraver on wood, beyond this they do not in the least illustrate the progress of the art.

* He complains in another part of the work that many printers, both compositors and pressmen, by pretending to engrave on wood, had brought the art into disrepute. They not only spoiled the work of regular engravers, but *dared* to engrave wood-cuts themselves.

† Traité de la Gravure en Bois, tom. ii. p. 365.

‡ The portrait was engraved " *in venerationis testimonium*," and presented to Papillon by Nicholas Caron, a bookseller and wood engraver of Besançon. The following complimentary verses are engraved below the portrait :

" Tu vois ici les traits d'un Artiste fameux
Dont la savante main enfanta des merveilles ;
Par ses travaux et par ses veilles
Il resuscita l'Art qui le trace à tes yeux."

Papillon speaks favourably of Caron as a wood engraver ; he says that " he is much superior to Nioul, Jackson, Contat, Lefevre, and others his contemporaries, and would at least have equalled the Le Sueurs had he applied himself to drawing the figure."

§ From several of those blocks not less than sixty thousand impressions had been previously taken, and from one of them four hundred and fifty-six thousand had been printed.

The execution of some of the best is extremely neat ; and almost all of them display an effect—a contrast of black and white—which is not to be found in any other wood-cuts of the period. A few of the designs possess considerable merit, but in by far the greater number simplicity and truth are sacrificed to ornament and French taste. Whatever may be Papillon's faults as a historian of the art, he deserves great credit for the diligence with which he pursued it under unfavourable circumstances, and for his endeavours to bring it into notice at a time when it was greatly neglected. His labours in this respect were, however, attended with no immediate fruit. He died in 1776, and his immediate successors do not appear to have profited by his instructions. The woodcuts executed in France between 1776 and 1815 are generally much inferior to those of Papillon ; and the recent progress which wood engraving has made in that country seems rather to have been influenced by English example than by his precepts.

Nicholas Le Sueur—born 1691, died 1764,—was, next to Papillon, the best French wood engraver of his time. His chiaro-scuros, printed entirely from wood-blocks, are executed with great boldness and spirit, and partake more of the character of the earlier Italian chiaro-scuros than any other works of the same kind engraved by his contemporaries.* He chiefly excelled in the execution of chiaro-scuros and large cuts ; his small cuts are of very ordinary character; they are generally engraved in a hard and meagre style, want variety of tint, and are deficient in effect.

P. S. Fournier, the younger, a letter-founder of considerable reputation,—born at Paris 1712, died 1768,—occasionally engraved on wood. Papillon says that he was self-taught ; and that he certainly would have made greater progress in the art had he not devoted himself almost exclusively to the business of type-founding. Monsieur Fournier is, however, better known as a writer on the history of the art than as a practical wood engraver. Between 1758 and 1761 he published three tracts relating to the origin and progress of wood engraving, and the invention of typography.† From these works it is evident that, though

---

* In the chiaro-scuros from original drawings in the collection of Monsieur Crozat, with the figures etched by Count Caylus, the wood-blocks from which the sepia-coloured tints were printed were engraved by Nicholas Le Sueur.—About the same period Arthur Pond and George Knapton in England, and Count M. A. Zanetti in Italy, executed in the same manner several chiaro-scuros in imitation of drawings and sketches by eminent painters. The taste for chiaro-scuros seems to have been revived in France by the Regent-Duke of Orleans, who declared that Ugo da Carpi's chiaro-scuros afforded him more pleasure than any other kind of prints.

† The following are the titles of those tracts, which are rather scarce. They are all of small octavo size, and printed by J. Barbou. 1. Dissertation sur l'Origine et les Progrès de l'Art de Graver en Bois, pour éclaircir quelques traits de l'Histoire de l'Imprimerie, et prouver que Guttemberg n'en est pas l'Inventeur. Par Mr. Fournier le Jeune, Graveur et Fondeur de Caractères d'Imprimerie, 1758. 2. De l'Origine et des productions de

he takes no small credit to himself for his practical knowledge of wood engraving and printing, he was very imperfectly acquainted with his subject. They abound in errors which it is impossible that any person possessing the knowledge he boasts of should commit, unless he had very superficially examined the books and cuts on which he pronounces an opinion. He seems indeed to have thought that, from the circumstance of his being a wood engraver and letter-founder, his decisions on all doubtful matters in the early history of wood engraving and printing should be received with implicit faith. Looking at the comparatively small size of his works, no writer, not even Papillon himself, has committed so many mistakes; and his decisions are generally most peremptory when utterly groundless or evidently wrong. He asserts that Faust and Scheffer's Psalter, 1457–1459, is printed from moveable types of wood, and that the most of the earliest specimens of typography are printed from the same kind of types ; and in the fulness of his knowledge he also declares that the text of the Theurdank is printed not from types, but from engraved wood-blocks. Like Papillon, he seems to have possessed a marvellous sagacity in ferreting out old wood engravers. He says that Andrea Mantegna engraved on wood a grand triumph in 1486 ; that Sebastian Brandt engraved in 1490 the wood-cuts in the Ship of Fools,* after the designs of J. Locher ; and that Parmegiano

l'Imprimerie primitive en taille en Bois, 1759.   3. Remarques sur un Ouvrage intitulé, Lettre sur l'Origine de l'Imprimerie, &c. 1761.   This last was an answer to a letter written by M. Bär, almoner of the Swedish chapel in Paris, in which the two former tracts of Fournier were severely criticised.—Fournier was also the author of a work in two small volumes, entitled " Manuel Typographique, utile aux Gens de lettres, et à ceux qui exercent les differentes parties de l'Art de l'Imprimerie."

    * The cut here introduced is the first in the *Stultifera Navis*, or " Ship of Fools," and is copied from Pyason's edition of 1509. The following lines accompany it :

        " ——this is my mynde, this one pleasure have I,
        Of bokes to have great plenty and aparayle.
        I take no wysdome by them ; nor yet avayle
        Nor them perceyve not : And then I them despyse.
        Thus am I a foole and all that serve that guyse."

executed several wood-cuts after designs by Raffaele. He decides positively that Albert Durer, Lucas Cranach, Titian, and Holbein were wood engravers, and, like Papillon, he includes Mary de Medici in the list. Papillon appears to have had good reason to complain that Fournier had availed himself of his volume printed in 1738. His taste appears to have been scarcely superior to his knowledge and judgment : he mentions a large and coarsely engraved cut of the head of Christ as one of the best specimens of Albert Durer's engraving ; and he says that Papillon's cuts are for excellence of design and execution equal to those of the greatest masters !

From a passage in one of Fournier's tracts—Remarques Typographiques, 1761,—it is evident that wood engraving was then greatly neglected in Germany. It relates to the following observation of M. Bär's, almoner of the Swedish chapel at Paris, on the length of time necessary to engrave a number of wooden types sufficient to print such a work as Faust and Scheffer's Psalter : " M. Schœpflin declares that, by the general admission of all experienced persons, it would require upwards of six years to complete such a work in so perfect a manner." The following is Fournier's rejoinder : " To understand the value of this remark, it ought to be known that, so far from there being many experienced wood engravers to choose from, M. Schœpflin would most likely experience some difficulty in finding one to consult." The wood-cuts which occur in German books printed between 1700 and 1760 are certainly of the most wretched kind ; contemptible alike in design and execution. Some of the best which I have seen—and they are very bad—are to be found in a thin folio entitled " Orbis Literatus Germanico-Europaeus," printed at Frankfort in 1737. They are cuts of the seals of all the principal colleges and academical foundations in Germany. The art in Italy about the same period was almost equally neglected. An Italian wood engraver, named Lucchesini, executed several cuts between 1760 and 1770. Most of the head-pieces and ornaments in the Popes' Decretals, printed at Rome at this period, were engraved by him ; and he also engraved the cuts in a Spanish book entitled " Letania Lauretana de la Virgen Santissima," printed at Valencia in 1768. It is scarcely necessary to say that these cuts are of the humblest character.

Though wood engraving did not make any progress in England from 1722 to the time of Thomas Bewick, yet the art was certainly never lost in this country ; the old stock still continued to put forth a branch—*non deficit alter*—although not a golden one. Two wood-cuts tolerably well executed, and which show that the engraver was acquainted with the practice of " lowering," occur in a thin quarto, London, printed for H. Payne, 1760. The book and the cuts are thus noticed in Southey's Life

of Cowper, volume I. page 50.   The writer is speaking of the Nonsense
Club, of which Cowper was a member.

"At those meetings of

> Jest and youthful Jollity,
> Sport that wrinkled Care derides,
> And Laughter holding both his sides,

there can be little doubt that the two odes to Obscurity and Oblivion
originated, joint compositions of Lloyd and Colman, in ridicule of Gray
and Masòn.   They were published in a quarto pamphlet, with a vignette,
in the title-page, of an ancient poet safely seated and playing on his
harp ; and at the end a tail-piece representing a modern poet in huge
boots, flung from a mountain by his Pegasus into the sea, and losing
his tie-wig in the fall."   The following is a fac-simile of the cut
representing the poet's fall.   He seems to have been tolerably confident
of himself, for, though the winged steed has no bridle, he is provided
with a pair of formidable spurs.

The cuts in a collection of humorous pieces in verse, entitled
" The Oxford Sausage," 1764, are evidently by the same engraver,
and almost every one of them affords an instance of " lowering."
At the foot of one of them, at page 89, the name " Lister " is seen ;
the subject is a bacchanalian figure mounted on a winged horse,
which has undoubtedly been drawn from the same model as the
Pegasus in Colman and Lloyd's burlesque odes.   In an edition of the

Sausage, printed in 1772, the name of "T. Lister" occurs on the title-page as one of the publishers, and as residing at Oxford. Although those cuts are generally deficient in effect, their execution is scarcely inferior to many of those in the work of Papillon; the portrait indeed of "Mrs. Dorothy Spreadbury, Inventress of the Oxford Sausage," forming the frontispiece to the edition of 1772, is better executed than Monsieur Nicholas Caron's votive portrait of Papillon, "the restorer of the art of wood engraving."

In 1763, a person named S. Watts engraved two or three large wood-cuts in outline, slightly shaded, after drawings by Luca Cambiaso. Impressions of those cuts are most frequently printed in a yellowish kind of ink. About the same time Watts also engraved, in a bold and free style, several small circular portraits of painters. In Sir John Hawkins's History of Music, published in 1776, there are four wood-cuts; and at the bottom of the largest—Palestrini presenting his work on Music to the Pope—is the name of the engraver thus: *T. Hodgson. Sculp.* Dr. Dibdin, in noticing this cut, in his Preliminary Disquisition on Early Engraving and Ornamental Printing, prefixed to his edition of the Typographical Antiquities, says that it was "done by Hodgson, the master of the celebrated Bewick."* If by this it is meant that Bewick was the apprentice of Hodgson, or that he obtained from Hodgson his knowledge of wood engraving, the assertion is incorrect. It is, however, almost certain that Bewick, when in London in 1776, was employed by Hodgson, as will be shown in its proper place.

Having now given some account of wood engraving in its languishing state—occasionally showing symptoms of returning vigour, and then almost immediately sinking into its former state of depression—we at length arrive at an epoch from which its revival and progressive improvement may be safely dated. The person whose productions recalled public attention to the neglected art of wood engraving was

HOMAS EWICK.

---

* Dr. Dibdin adds : " Mr. Douce informs me that Sir John Hawkins told him of the artist's obtaining the prize for it from the Society for the Encouragement of Arts."

This distinguished wood engraver, whose works will be admired as long as truth and nature shall continue to charm, was born on the 10th or 11th of August, 1753, at Cherry-burn, in the county of Northumberland, but on the south side of the Tyne, about twelve miles westward of Newcastle.

THE HOUSE IN WHICH BEWICK WAS BORN.

His father rented a small land-sale colliery at Mickley-bank, in the neighbourhood of his dwelling, and it is said that when a boy the future wood engraver sometimes worked in the pit. At a proper age he was sent as a day-scholar to a school kept by the Rev. Christopher Gregson at Ovingham, on the opposite side of the Tyne. The Parsonage House, in which Mr. Gregson lived, is pleasantly situated on the edge of a sloping bank immediately above the river; and many reminiscences of the place are to be found in Bewick's cuts; the gate at the entrance is introduced, with trifling variations, in three or four different subjects; and a person acquainted with the neighbourhood will easily recognise in his tail-pieces several other little local sketches of a similar kind. In the time of the Rev. James Birkett, Mr. Gregson's successor, Ovingham school had the character of being one of the best private schools in the county; and several gentlemen, whose talents reflect credit on their teacher, received their education there. In the following cut, representing a view of Ovingham from the south-westward, the Parsonage House, with its garden sloping down to the Tyne, is perceived immediately to the right of the clump of large trees. The bank on which those trees grow is known as the *crow-tree bank.* The following lines, descriptive of a view from the Parsonage House, are from "The School Boy," a poem, by Thomas Maude, A.M., who received his early education at Ovingham under Mr. Birkett.

PARSONAGE AT OVINGHAM.

"But can I sing thy simpler pleasures flown,
   Loved OVINGHAM ! and leave the *chief* unknown,—
Thy *annual Fair*, of every joy the mart,
That drained my pocket, ay, and took my childish heart ?
Blest morn ! how lightly from my bed I sprung,
When in the blushing east thy beams were young ;
While every blithe co-tenant of the room
Rose at a call, with cheeks of liveliest bloom.
Then from each well-packed drawer our vests we drew,
Each gay-frilled shirt, and jacket smartly new.
Brief toilet ours ! yet, on a morn like this,
Five extra minutes were not deemed amiss.
Fling back the casement !—Sun, propitious shine !
How sweet your beams gild the clear-flowing Tyne,
That winds beneath our master's garden-brae,
With broad bright mazes o'er its pebbly way.
See Prudhoe ! lovely in the morning beam :— ⎞
Mark, mark, the ferry-boat, with twinkling gleam, ⎬
Wafting fair-going folks across the stream. ⎠
Look out ! a bed of sweetness breathes below,
Where many a rocket points its spire of snow ;
And from the *Crow-tree Bank* the cawing sound
Of sable troops incessant poured around !
Well may each little bosom throb with joy !
On such a morn, who would not be a boy ?"

Bewick's school acquirements probably did not extend beyond English reading, writing, and arithmetic ; for, though he knew a little

Latin, he does not appear to have ever received any instructions in that language. In a letter dated 18th April, 1803, addressed to Mr. Christopher Gregson,* London, a son of his old master, introducing an artist of the name of Murphy, who had painted his portrait, Bewick humorously alludes to his *beauty* when a boy, and to the state of his coat-sleeve, in consequence of his using it instead of a pocket-handker-chief. Bewick, it is to be observed, was very hard-featured, and much marked with the small-pox. After mentioning Mr. Murphy as " a man of worth, and a first-rate artist in the miniature line," he thus proceeds : " I do not imagine, at your time of life, my dear friend, that you will be solicitous about forming new acquaintances ; but it may not, perhaps, be putting you much out of the way to show any little civilities to Mr. Murphy during his stay in London. He has, on his own account, taken my portrait, and I dare say will be desirous to show you it the first opportunity : when you see it, you will no doubt conclude that T. B. is turning *bonnyer* and *bonnyer†* in his old days ; but indeed you cannot *help knowing this,* and also that there were *great indications* of its turning out so *long since.* But if you have forgot our earliest youth, perhaps your brother P.‡ may help you to remember what a *great beauty* I was at that time, when the grey coat-sleeve was *glazed* from the cuff towards the elbows." The words printed in Italics are those that are underlined by Bewick himself.

Bewick, having shown a taste for drawing, was placed by his father as an apprentice with Mr. Ralph Beilby, an engraver, living in Newcastle, to whom on the 1st of October 1767 he was bound for a term of seven years. Mr. Beilby was not a wood engraver ; and his business in the copper-plate line was of a kind which did not allow of much scope for the display of artistic talent. He engraved copper-plates for books, when any by chance were offered to him ; and he also executed brass-plates for doors, with the names of the owners handsomely filled up, after the manner of the old " *niellos,*" with black sealing-wax. He engraved crests and initials on steel and silver watch-seals ; also on tea-spoons, sugar-tongs, and other articles of plate ; and the engraving of numerals and ornaments, with the name of the maker, on clock-faces,—which were not then enamelled,—seems to have formed one of the chief branches of his very general business. §

* Mr. Christopher Gregson, who was an apothecary, lived in Blackfriars. He died about the year 1813. As long as he lived, Bewick maintained a friendly correspondence with him.
† *Prettier* and *prettier.*   ‡ Philip.
§ " While with BEILBY he was employed in engraving clock-faces, which, I have heard him say, made his hands as hard as a blacksmith's, and almost disgusted him with engraving."—Sketch of the Life and Works of the late Thomas Bewick, by George C. Atkinson. Printed in the Transactions of the Natural History Society, Newcastle, 1830.

Bewick's attention appears to have been first directed to wood engraving in consequence of his master having been employed by the late Dr. Charles Hutton, then a schoolmaster in Newcastle, to engrave on wood the diagrams for his Treatise on Mensuration. The printing of this work was commenced in 1768, and was completed in 1770. The engraving of the diagrams was committed to Bewick, who is said to have invented a graver with a fine groove at the point, which enabled him to cut the outlines by a single operation.

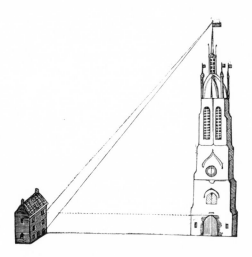

The above is a fac-simile of one of the earliest productions of Bewick in the art of wood engraving. The church is intended for that of St. Nicholas, Newcastle.

Subsequently, and while he was still an apprentice, Bewick undoubtedly endeavoured to improve himself in wood engraving; but his progress does not appear to have been great, and his master had certainly very little work of this kind for him to do. He appears to have engraved a few bill-heads on wood; and it is not unlikely that the cuts in a little book entitled "Youth's Instructive and Entertaining Story Teller," first published by T. Saint, Newcastle, 1774, were executed by him before the expiration of his apprenticeship.

Bewick, at one period during his apprenticeship, paid ninepence a week for his lodgings in Newcastle, and usually received a brown loaf every week from Cherry-burn. "During his servitude," says Mr. Atkinson, "he paid weekly visits to Cherry-burn, except when the river was so much swollen as to prevent his passage of it at Eltringham, when he vociferated his inquiries across the stream, and then returned to Newcastle." This account of his being accustomed to *shout* his enquiries

across the Tyne first appeared in a Memoir prefixed to the Select Fables,
published by E. Charnley, 1820. Mr. William Bedlington, an old friend
of Bewick, once asked him if it were true? "Babbles and nonsense!"
was the reply. "It never happened but once, and that was when the
river had suddenly swelled before I could reach the top of the *allers*,*
and yet folks are made to believe that I was in the habit of doing it."

On the expiration of his apprenticeship he returned to his father's
house at Cherry-burn, but still continued to work for Mr. Beilby. About
this time he seems to have formed the resolution of applying himself
exclusively in future to wood engraving, and with this view to have
executed several cuts as specimens of his ability. In 1775 he received
a premium of seven guineas from the Society of Arts for a cut of the
Huntsman and the Old Hound, which he probably engraved when
living at Cherry-burn after leaving Mr. Beilby.† The following is a

fac-simile of this cut, which was first printed in an edition of Gay's
Fables, published by T. Saint, Newcastle, 1779. Mr. Henry Bohn, the
publisher of the present edition, happening to be in possession of the
original cut, it is annexed on the opposite page.

In 1776, when on a visit to some of his relations in Cumberland,‡ he
availed himself of the opportunity of visiting the Lakes ; and in after-

---

* Alders—the name of a small plantation above Ovingham, which Bewick had to pass
through on his way to Eltringham ferry-boat.

† The Reverend William Turner, of Newcastle, in a letter printed in the Monthly
Magazine for June 1801, says that Bewick obtained this premium "*during his apprenticeship.*" This must be a mistake ; as his apprenticeship expired in October 1774, and he
obtained the premium in 1775. It is possible, however, that the engraving may have been
executed during that period.

‡ Bewick's mother, Jane Wilson, was a daughter of Thomas Wilson of Ainstable in
Cumberland, about five miles north-north-west of Kirk-Oswald

life he used frequently to speak in terms of admiration of the beauty of the scenery, and of the neat appearance of the white-washed, slate-covered cottages on the banks of some of the lakes. His tour was made on foot, with a stick in his hand and a wallet at his back ; and it has been supposed that in a tail-piece, to be found at page 177 of the first volume of his British Birds, first edition, 1797, he has introduced a sketch of himself in his travelling costume, drinking out of what he himself would have called the *flipe* of his hat. The figure has been copied in our ornamental letter T at page 471.

In the same year, 1776, he went to London, where he arrived on the 1st of October. He certainly did not remain more than a twelvemonth in London,* for in 1777 he returned to Newcastle, and entered into partnership with his former master, Mr. Ralph Beilby. Bewick—who does not appear to have been wishful to undeceive those who fancied that

he was the person who rediscovered the "long-lost art of engraving on wood"†—would never inform any of the good-natured friends, who fished for intelligence with the view of writing his life, of the works on which he was employed when in London. The faith of a believer in the story of Bewick's re-discovering "the long-lost art" would have received too great a shock had he been told by Bewick himself that

---

* Bewick, in London, in 1828, observed to one of his former pupils, that it was then fifty-one years since he left London, on his first visit, to return to Newcastle.

† Mr. Atkinson talks about wood engraving having taken a nap for a century or two "after the time of Durer and Holbein," and of Bewick being the restorer of the "long-lost art ;" and yet, with singular inconsistency, in another part of his Sketch, he refers to Papillon, whose work, containing a minute account of the art as then practised, was published about two years before Bewick began to engrave on wood.—The Reverend William Turner, who ought to have known better, also speaks of the "long-lost art," in his Memoir of Thomas Bewick.

on his arrival in London he found professors of the "long-lost art" regularly exercising their calling, and that with one of them he found employment.

There is every reason to believe that Bewick, when in London, was chiefly employed by T. Hodgson, most likely the person who engraved the four cuts in Sir John Hawkins's History of Music. It is at any rate certain that several cuts engraved by Bewick appeared in a little work entitled " A curious Hieroglyphick Bible," printed by and for T. Hodgson, in George's Court, St. John's Lane, Clerkenwell.* Proofs of three of the principal cuts are now lying before me. The subjects are : Adam and Eve, with the Deity seen in the clouds, forming the frontispiece ; the Resurrection ; and a cut representing a gentleman seated in an arm-chair, with four boys beside him : the border of this cut is of the same kind as that of the large cut of the Chillingham Bull engraved by Bewick in 1789. These proofs appear to have been presented by Bewick to an eminent painter, now dead, with whom either then, or at a subsequent period, he had become acquainted. Not one of Bewick's biographers mentions those cuts, nor seems to have been aware of their existence. The two memoirs of Bewick, written by his "friends" G. C. Atkinson and John F. M. Dovaston,† sufficiently demonstrate that neither of them had enjoyed his confidence in matters relative to his progress in the art of wood engraving.

Mr. Atkinson, in his Sketch of the Life and Works of Bewick, says that when in London he worked with a person of the name of Cole. Of this person, as a wood engraver, I have not been able to discover any trace. Bewick did not like London ; and he always advised his former pupils and north-country friends to leave the " province covered with houses " as soon as they could, and return to the country to there enjoy the beauties of Nature, fresh air, and

---

* I have not been able to discover the date of the first edition of this work. The third edition is dated 1785.

† " Some Account of the Life, Genius, and Personal Habits of the late Thomas Bewick, the celebrated Artist and Engraver on Wood. By his Friend John F. M. Dovaston, Esq. A.M.," was published in Loudon's Magazine of Natural History, 1829–1830. Mr. Dovaston seems to have caught a knowledge of Bewick's personal habits at a glance ; and a considerable number of his observations on other matters appear to have been the result of a peculiar quickness of apprehension. What he says about the church of Ovingham not being "parted into proud pews," when Bewick was a boy, is incorrect. It had, in fact, been pewed from an early period ; for, on the 2nd of September, 1763, Dr. Sharp, Archdeacon of Northumberland, on visiting the church, notices the pews as being "very bad and irregular ;" and on a board over the vestry-door is the following inscription : "This Church was new pewed, A. D. 1766." No boards from this church containing specimens of Bewick's early drawing were ever in the possession of the Duke of Northumberland. Mr. Dovaston is frequently imaginative, but seldom correct. His personal sketch of Bewick is a ridiculous caricature.

content. In the letter to his old schoolfellow, Mr. Christopher Gregson, previously quoted, he thus expresses his opinion of London life. "Ever since you paid your last visit to the north, I have often been thinking upon you, and wishing that you would *lap up*, and leave the metropolis, to enjoy the fruits of your hard-earned industry on the banks of the Tyne, where you are so much respected, both on your own account and on that of those who are gone. Indeed, I wonder how you can think of turmoiling yourself to the end of the chapter, and let the opportunity slip of contemplating at your ease the beauties of Nature, so bountifully spread out to enlighten, to captivate, and to cheer the heart of man. For my part, I am still of the same mind that I was in when in London, and that is, *I would rather be herding sheep on Mickley bank top than remain in London, although for doing so I was to be made the premier of England.*" Bewick was truly a *country* man; he felt that it was better "to hear the lark sing than the mouse cheep;" for, though no person was capable of closer application to his art when within doors, he loved to spend his hours of relaxation in the open air, studying the character of beasts and birds in their natural state; and diligently noting those little incidents and traits of country life which give so great an interest to many of his tail-pieces. When a young man, he was fond of angling; and, like Roger Ascham, he "dearly loved a main of cocks." When annoyed by street-walkers in London, he used to assume the air of a stupid countryman, and, in reply to their importunity, would ask, with an expression of stolid gravity, if they knew "Tommy Hummel o' Prudhoe, Willy Eltringham o' Hall-Yards, or Auld Laird Newton o' Mickley?"* He thus, without losing his temper, or showing any feeling of annoyance, soon got quit of those who wished to engage his attention, though sometimes not until he had received a hearty malediction for his stupidity.

In 1777, on his return to Newcastle, he entered into partnership with Mr. Beilby; and his younger brother, John Bewick, who was then about seventeen years old, became their apprentice. From this time Bewick, though he continued to assist his partner in the other branches of their business,† applied himself chiefly to engraving on

---

* Humble, Eltringham, and Newton were the names of three of his country acquaintances; Prudhoe, Hall-Yards, and Mickley are places near Ovingham.

† Bewick could engrave on copper, but did not excel in this branch of engraving. The following are the principal copper-plates which are known to be of his engraving. Plates in Consett's Tour through Sweden, Swedish Lapland, Finland, and Denmark, 4to. Stockton, 1789; The Whitley large Ox, 1789; and the remarkable Kyloe Ox, bred in the Mull, Argyleshire, 1790—A set of silver buttons, containing sporting devices, engraved by Bewick for the late H. U. Reay, Esq. of Killingworth, which passed into the possession of Mr. Reay's son-in-law, Matthew Bell, Esq. of Wolsingham.

wood. The cuts in an edition of Gay's Fables, 1779,* and in an
edition of Select Fables, 1784, both printed by T. Saint, Newcastle,
were engraved by Bewick, who was probably assisted by his brother.
Several of those cuts are well engraved, though by no means to be
compared to his later works, executed when he had acquired greater
knowledge of the art, and more confidence in his own powers. He
evidently improved as his talents were exercised; for the cuts in the
Select Fables, 1784, are generally much superior to those in Gay's
Fables, 1779 ; the animals are better drawn and engraved ; the
sketches of landscape in the back-grounds are more natural ; and the
engraving of the foliage of the trees and bushes is, not unfrequently,
scarce inferior to that of his later productions. Such an attention to
nature in this respect is not to be found in any wood-cuts of an
earlier date. The following impressions from two of the original cuts

in the Select Fables are fair specimens ; one is interesting, as being
Bewick's first idea of a favourite vignette in his British Land

* Mr. Atkinson says that " about the same time he executed the cuts [sixty-two
in number] for a small child's book, entitled ' A pretty Book of Pictures for little Masters
and Misses, or Tommy Trip's History of Beasts and Birds.' "—An edition of the Select
Fables, with very bad wood-cuts, was printed by Mr. Saint in 1776. The person by whom
they were engraved is unknown. Bewick always denied that any of them were of his
engraving.

Birds; the other as his first treatment of the lion and the four bulls, afterwards repeated in his Quadrupeds. In the best cuts of the time of Durer and Holbein the foliage is generally neglected; the artists of that period merely give general forms of trees, without ever attending to that which contributes so much to their beauty. The merit of introducing this great improvement in wood engraving, and of depicting quadrupeds and birds in their natural forms, and with their characteristic expression, is undoubtedly due to Bewick. Though he was not the discoverer of the art of wood engraving, he certainly was the first who applied it with success to the delineation of animals, and to the natural representation of landscape and woodland scenery. He found for himself a path which no previous wood engraver had trodden, and in which none of his successors have gone beyond him. For several of the cuts in the Select Fables, Bewick was paid only nine shillings each.

In 1789 he drew and engraved his large cut of the Chillingham Bull,* which many persons suppose to be his master-piece; but though it is certainly well engraved, and the character of the animal is well expressed, yet as a wood engraving it will not bear a comparison with several of the cuts in his History of British Birds. The grass and the foliage of the trees are most beautifully expressed; but there is a want of variety in the more distant trees, and the bark of that in the foreground to the left is too rough. This exaggeration of the roughness of the bark of trees is also to be perceived in many of his other cuts. The style in which the bull is engraved is admirably adapted to express the texture of the short white hair of the animal; the dewlap, however, is not well represented, it appears to be stiff instead of flaccid and pendulous; and the lines intended for the hairs on its margin are too *wiry*. On a stone in the fore-ground he has introduced a *bit* of cross-hatching, but not with good effect, for it causes the stone to look very much like an old scrubbing-brush. Bewick was not partial to cross-hatching, and it is seldom to be found in cuts of his engraving. He seems to have introduced it in this cut rather to show to those who knew anything of the matter that he could engrave such lines, than from an opinion that they were necessary, or in the slightest degree improved the cut. This is almost the only instance in which Bewick has introduced black lines crossing each other, and thus forming what is usually called " cross-hatchings." From the commencement of his career as a wood engraver, he adopted a much more simple method of obtaining colour. He very justly considered, that, as impressions of wood-cuts are printed from lines engraved in *relief*, the unengraved

* This cut was executed for Marmaduke Tunstall, Esq. of Wycliffe, near Greta Bridge, in Yorkshire.

I I

surface of the block already represented the darkest colour that could be produced ; and consequently, instead of labouring to produce colour in the same manner as the old wood engravers, he commenced upon colour or black, and proceeded from *dark to light* by means of lines cut in intaglio, and appearing white when in the impression, until his subject was completed. This great simplification of the old process was the result of his having to engrave his own drawings ; for in drawing his subject on the wood he avoided all combinations of lines which to the designer are easy, but to the engraver difficult. In almost every one of his cuts the effect is produced by the simplest means. The colour which the old wood engravers obtained by means of cross-hatchings, Bewick obtained with much greater facility by means of single lines, and masses of black slightly intersected or broken with white.

When only a few impressions of the Chillingham Bull had been taken, and before he had added his name, the block split. The press-men, it is said, got tipsy over their work, and left the block lying on the window-sill exposed to the rays of the sun, which caused it to warp and split.* About six impressions were taken on thin vellum before the accident occurred. Mr. Atkinson says that one of those impressions, which had formerly belonged to Mr. Beilby, Bewick's partner, was sold in London for twenty pounds ; A. Stothard, R.A., had one, as had also Mr. C. Nesbit.

Towards the latter end of 1785 Bewick began to engrave the cuts for his General History of Quadrupeds, which was first printed in 1790.† The descriptions were written by his partner, Mr. Beilby, and the cuts were all drawn and engraved by himself. The comparative excellence of those cuts, which, for the correct delineation of the animals and the natural character of the *incidents*, and the back-grounds, are greatly superior to anything of the kind that had previously appeared, insured a rapid sale for the work ; a second edition was published in 1791, and a third in 1792.‡

The great merit of those cuts consists not so much in their execution as in the spirited and natural manner in which they are drawn. Some of the animals, indeed, which he had not had an opportunity of seeing, and for which he had to depend on the previous engravings of others, are not correctly drawn. Among the most incorrect are the Bison, the

---

* The block remained in several pieces until 1817, when they were firmly united by means of cramps, and a number of impressions printed off. These impressions are without the border, which distinguishes the earlier ones. The border, which was engraved on separate pieces, enclosed the principal cut in the manner of a frame.

† A Prospectus containing specimens of the cuts was printed in 1787.

‡ The first edition consisted of fifteen hundred copies in demy octavo at 8s., and one hundred royal at 12s. The price of the demy copies of the *eighth* edition, published in 1825, was £1 1s. A proof of the estimation in which the work continued to be held.

Zebu, the Buffalo, the Many-horned Sheep, the Gnu, and the Giraffe or Cameleopard.* Even in some of our domestic quadrupeds he was not successful; the Horses are not well represented; and the very indifferent execution of the Common Bull and Cow, at page 19, edition 1790, is only redeemed by the interest of the back-grounds. In that of the Common Bull, the action of the bull seen chasing a man is most excellent ; and in that of the Cow, the woman, with a *skeel* on her head, and her petticoats tucked up behind, returning from milking, is evidently a sketch from nature. The Goats and the Dogs are the best of those cuts both in design and execution ; and perhaps the very best of all the cuts in the first edition is that of the Cur Fox at page 270. The tail of the animal, which is too long, and is also incorrectly marked with black near the white tip, was subsequently altered.

In the first edition the characteristic tail-pieces are comparatively few ; and several of those which are merely ornamental, displaying neither imagination nor feeling, are copies of cuts which are frequent in books printed at Leipsic between 1770 and 1780, and which were probably engraved by Ungher, a German wood engraver of that period. Examples of such tasteless trifles are to be found at pages 9, 12, 18, 65, 110, 140, 201, 223, and 401. Ornaments of the same character occur in Heineken's "Idée Générale d'une Collection complette d'Estampes," Leipsic and Vienna, 1771. Bewick was unquestionably better acquainted with the history and progress of wood engraving than those who talk about the "long-lost art" were aware of. The first of the two following cuts is a fac-simile of a tail-piece which occurs in

an edition of "Der Weiss Kunig,"† printed at Vienna, 1775, and which Bewick has copied at page 144 of the first edition of the

---

* The cut of the Giraffe in the edition of 1824 is not the original one engraved by Bewick. In the later cut, which was chiefly engraved by W. W. Temple, one of Bewick's pupils, the marks on the body of the animal appear like so many white-coloured lines crossing each other, and enclosing large irregular spots.

† Some account of this work is previously given at page 287.

Quadrupeds, 1790. The second, from one of the cuts illustrative of Ovid's Metamorphoses, 1569, designed by Virgil Solis,* is copied in a tail-piece in the first volume of Bewick's Birds, page 330, edition 1797.

The following may be mentioned as the best of the tail-pieces in the first edition of the Quadrupeds, and as those which most decidedly display Bewick's talent in depicting, without exaggeration, natural and humorous incidents. In this respect he has been excelled by no other artist either of past or present times. The Elephant, fore-shortened, at page 162; the Dog and Cat, 195; the Old Man crossing a ford, mounted on an old horse, which carries, in addition, two heavy sacks, 244; the Bear-ward, with his wife and companion, leading Bruin, and accompanied by his dancing-dogs,—a gallows seen in the distance, 256; a Fox, with Magpies flying after him, indicating his course to his pursuers, 265; Two unfeeling fellows enjoying the pleasure of hanging a dog,—a gibbet, seen in the distance, to denote that those who could thus quietly enjoy the dying struggles of a dog would not be unlikely to murder a man, 274; a Man eating his dinner with his dog sitting beside him, expecting his share, 285; Old Blind Man led by a dog, crossing a bridge of a single plank, and with the rail broken, in a storm of wind and rain, 320; a Mad Dog pursued by three men,—a feeble old woman directly in the dog's way, 324; a Man with a bundle at his back, crossing a stream on stilts, 337; a winter piece,—a Man travelling in the snow, 339; a grim-visaged Old Man, accompanied by a cur-dog, driving an old sow, 371; Two Boys and an Ass on a common, 375; a Man leaping, by means of a pole, a stream, across which he has previously thrown his stick and bag, 391; a Man carrying a bundle of faggots on the ice, 395; a Wolf falling into a trap, 430; and Two Blind Fiddlers and a Boy, the last in the book, at 456. In this cut Bewick has represented the two blind fiddlers earnestly scraping away, although there is no one to listen to their strains; the bare-legged *tatty*-headed boy who leads them, and the half-starved melancholy-looking dog at their heels, are in admirable keeping with the principal characters.

On the next page is a copy of the cut of the Two Boys and the Ass, previously mentioned as occurring at page 375. This cut, beyond any other of the tail-pieces in the first edition of the Quadrupeds, perhaps affords the best specimen of Bewick's peculiar talent of depicting such subjects; he faithfully represents Nature, and at the same time conveys a moral, which gives additional interest to the sketch. Though the ass remains immoveable, in spite of the application of

* This work is noticed at page 407.

a branch of furze to his hind quarters, the young graceless who is mounted evidently enjoys his seat. The pleasure of the twain con-

sists as much in having *caught* an ass as in the prospect of a ride To such characters the stubborn ass frequently affords more *amusement* than a willing goer; they like to flog and thump a thing well, though it be but a gate-post. The gallows in the distance—a favourite *in terrorem* object with Bewick—suggests their ultimate destiny; and the cut, in the first edition, derives additional *point* from its situation among the animals found in *New South Wales,*—the first shipment of convicts to Botany Bay having taken place about two years previous to the publication of the work. This cut, as well as many others in the book, affords an instance of lowering,—the light appearance of the distance is entirely effected by that process.

The subsequent editions of the Quadrupeds were enlarged by the addition of new matter and the insertion of several new cuts. Of these, with the exception of the Kyloe Ox,* the tail-pieces are by far the best. The following are the principal cuts of animals that have been added since the first publication of the work; the pages annexed refer to the edition of 1824, the last that was published in Bewick's life-time: the Arabian Horse, page 4,—the stallion, seen in the background, has suffered a dismemberment since its first appearance; † the Old English Road Horse, 9; the Improved Cart Horse, 14; the Kyloe Ox, 36; the Musk Bull, 49; the Black-faced, or Heath Ram, 56; Heath Ram of the Improved Breed, 57; The Cheviot Ram, 58; Tees-water Ram of the Old Breed, 60; Tees-water Ram, Improved Breed, 61; the American Elk, 125; Sow of the Improved Breed, 164; Sow

---

* The Kyloe Ox, which occurs at page 36 of the edition of 1824, the last that was published in Bewick's life-time, is one of the very best cuts of a quadruped that he ever engraved. The drawing is excellent, and the characteristic form and general appearance of the animal are represented in a manner that has never been excelled.

† The Lancashire *Bull,* of the first edition, by a similar process has been converted into the Lancashire *Ox.*

of the Chinese Breed, 166 ; Head of a Hippopotamus, (engraved by
W. W. Temple,) 185 ; Indian Bear, 293 ; Polar, or Great White Bear,
substituted for another cut of the same animal, 295 ; the Spotted
Hyena, substituted for another cut of the same animal, 301 ; the
Ban-dog, 338 ; the Irish Greyhound, 340 ; the Harrier, 347 ; Spotted
Bavy, substituted for another cut of the same animal, 379 ; the Grey
Squirrel, 387 ; the Long-tailed Squirrel, 396 ; the Jerboa, substituted
for another cut of the same animal, 397 ; the Musquash, or Musk
Beaver, 416 ; the Mouse, substituted for another cut of the same
animal, 424 ; the Short-eared Bat, 513 ; the Long-eared Bat, 515 ; the
Ternate Bat, 518 ; the Wombach, 523 ; and the Ornithorhynchus
Paradoxicus, 525. The cut of the animal called the Thick-nosed
Tapiir, at page 139 of the first edition, is transposed to page 381 of
the last edition, and there described under the name of the Capibara :
it is probably intended for the Coypu rat, a specimen of which is at
present in the Gardens of the Zoological Society, Regent's Park.
Bewick was a regular visitor of all the wild-beast shows that came
to Newcastle, and availed himself of every opportunity to obtain drawings from living animals.

The tail-pieces introduced in subsequent editions of the Quadrupeds
generally display more humour and not less talent in representing
natural objects than those contained in the first. In the annexed cut

of a sour-visaged old fellow going with corn to the mill, we have an
exemplification of cruelty not unworthy of Hogarth.* The over-laden,

* The originals of this and the three following cuts occur respectively at pages 13, 15, 69,
and 526 of the edition of 1824. The other principal tail-pieces in this edition are :
Greyhound-coursing, (originally engraved on a silver cup for a person at Northallerton,)
drawn by Bewick on the block, but engraved by W. W. Temple, page x, at the end of the
Index ; the Old Coachman and the Young Squire, 12 ; Tinker's Children in a pair of

half-starved old horse,—broken-kneed, greasy-heeled, and evidently troubled with the string-halt, as is indicated by the action of the *off* hind-leg,—hesitates to descend the brae, at the foot of which there is a stream, and the old brute on his back urges him forward by *working* him, as jockeys say, with the halter, and beating him with his stick. In the distance, Bewick, as is usual with him when he gives a sketch of cruelty or knavery, has introduced a gallows. The miserable appearance of the poor animal is not a little increased by the nakedness of his hind quarters ; his stump of a tail is so short that it will not even serve as a *catch* for the crupper or *tail-band.*

In the cut of the child, unconscious of its danger, pulling at the long tail of a young unbroken colt, the story is most admirably told. The nurse, who is seen engaged with her sweetheart by the side of the hedge, has left the child to wander at will, and thus expose itself to destruction ;

while the mother, who has accidentally perceived the danger of her darling, is seen hastening over the stile, regardless of the steps, in an agony of fear. The backward glance of the horse's eye, and the heel raised ready to strike, most forcibly suggest the danger to which the unthinking infant is exposed.

Though the subject of the following cut be simple, yet the *sentiment* which it displays is the genuine offspring of true genius. Near to a ruined cottage, while all around is covered with snow, a lean and hungry ewe is seen nibbling at an old broom, while her young and

panniers on the back of an Ass, 21 ; a Cow drinking, 28 ; Winter scene, 34 ; Two Men digging, (engraved by H. White, who also engraved the cut of the Musk Bull at page 49,) 37 ; Dog worrying a Sheep, 62 ; Old Soldier travelling in the rain, 117 ; Smelling, tail-piece to the Genet, a *strong bit,* 269 ; Drunken Man making his Dam, 378 ; and Seals on a large piece of floating ice, 510.

weakly lamb is sucking her milkless teats. Such a picture of animal want—conceived with so much feeling, and so well expressed,—has perhaps never been represented by any artist except Bewick.

The original of the following cut forms the tail-piece to the last page of the edition of 1824. An old man, wearing a parson's cast-off beaver and wig, is seen carrying his young wife and child across a stream. The complacent look of the cock-nosed wife shows that she enjoys the treat, while the old drudge patiently bears his burden, and with his right hand keeps a firm *grip* of the nether end of his better part. This cut is an excellent satire on those old men who marry young wives and become dotingly uxorious in the decline of life ; submitting to every indignity to please their youthful spouses and reconcile them to their state. It is a *new reading* of January and May,—he an old travelling beggar, and she a young slut with her heels peeping, or rather staring, through her stockings.

Mr. Solomon Hodgson, the printer of the first four editions of the Quadrupeds, had an interest in the work ; he died in 1800 ; and in consequence of a misunderstanding between his widow and Bewick, the latter had the subsequent editions printed at the office of Mr. Edward Walker. Mrs. Hodgson having asserted, in a letter printed in the Monthly Magazine for July 1805, that Bewick was neither the author nor the projector of the History of Quadrupeds, but "was employed merely as the engraver or wood-cutter," he, in justification of his own claims, gave the following account of the origin of the work.* "From my first reading, when a boy at school, a sixpenny History of Birds and Beasts, and a then wretched composition called the History of Three Hundred Animals, to the time I became acquainted with works on Natural History written for the perusal of men, I never was without the design of attempting something of this kind myself; but my principal object was (and still is) directed to the mental pleasure and improvement of youth; to engage their attention, to direct their steps aright, and to lead them on till they become enamoured of this innocent and delightful pursuit. Some time after my partnership with Mr. Beilby commenced, I communicated my wishes to him, who, after many conversations, came into my plan of publishing a History of Quadrupeds, and I then immediately began to draw the animals, to design the vignettes, and to cut them on wood, and this, to avoid interruption, frequently till very late in the night; my partner at the same time undertaking to compile and draw up the descriptions and history at his leisure hours and evenings at home. With the accounts of the foreign animals I did not much interfere; the sources whence I had drawn the little knowledge I possessed were open to my coadjutor, and he used them; but to those of the animals of our own country, as my partner before this time had paid little attention to natural history, I lent a helping hand. This help was given in daily conversations, and in occasional notes and memoranda, which were used in their proper places. As the cuts were engraved, we employed the late Mr. Thomas Angus, of this town, printer, to take off a certain number of impressions of each, many of which are still in my possession. At Mr. Angus's death the charge for this business was not made in his books, and at the request of his widow and ourselves, the late Mr. Solomon Hodgson fixed the price; and yet the widow and executrix of Mr. Hodgson asserts in your Magazine, that I was 'merely employed as the engraver or wood-cutter,' (I suppose) by her husband! Had this been the case, is it probable that Mr. Hodgson would have had the cuts printed in any other office than his own? The fact is the reverse of Mrs. Hodgson's statement; and although I have never, either 'insidiously' or otherwise, used any means to cause the reviewers, or others, to hold me up as the 'first and sole mover of the concern,' I am now dragged forth by her to declare that *I am the man.*

* This account is extracted from a letter written by Bewick, and printed in the Monthly Magazine for November 1805.

" But to return to my story :—while we were in the progress of our work, prudence suggested that it might be necessary to inquire how our labours were to be ushered to the world, and, as we were unacquainted with the printing and publishing of books, what mode was the most likely to insure success. Upon this subject Mr. Hodgson was consulted, and made fully acquainted with our plan. He entered into the undertaking with uncommon ardour, and urged us strenuously not to retain our first humble notions of 'making it like a school-book,' but pressed us to let it 'assume a more respectable form.' From this warmth of our friend we had no hesitation in offering him a share in the work, and a copartnership deed was entered into between us, for that purpose, on the 10th of April 1790. What Mr. Hodgson did in correcting the press, beyond what falls to the duty of every printer, I know not ; but I am certain that he was extremely desirous that it should have justice done it. In this *weaving of words* I did not interfere, as I believed it to be in hands much fitter than my own, only I took the liberty of blotting out whatever I knew not to be truth."

The favourable manner in which the History of Quadrupeds was received determined Bewick to commence without delay his History of British Birds. He began to draw and engrave the cuts in 1791, and in 1797 the first volume of the work, containing the Land Birds, was published.* The letter-press, as in the Quadrupeds, was written by his partner, Mr. Beilby, who certainly deserves great praise for the manner in which he has performed his task. The descriptions generally have the great merit of being simple, intelligible, and correct. There are no trifling details about system, no confused arguments about classification, which more frequently bewilder than inform the reader who is uninitiated in the piebald jargon of what is called "Systematic nomenclature." He describes the quadruped or bird in a manner which enables even the most unlearned to recognize it when he sees it ; and, like one who is rather wishful to inform his readers than to display his own acquaintance with the scientific vocabulary, he carefully avoids the use of all terms which are not generally understood. Mr. Beilby, though in a different manner and in a less degree, is fairly entitled to share with Bewick in the honour of having rendered popular in this country the study of the most interesting and useful branches of Zoology—Quadrupeds and Birds —by giving the descriptions in simple and intelligible language, and presenting to the eye the very form and character of the living animals. As a copper-plate engraver, Mr. Beilby has certainly no just pretensions

---

* Of this edition, 1,874 copies were printed,—one thousand demy octavo, at 10s. 6d. ; eight hundred and fifty thin and thick royal, at 13s., and 15s. ; and twenty-four imperial at £1 1s. The first edition of the second volume, 1804, consisted of the same number of copies as the first, but the prices were respectively 12s., 15s., 18s. and £1 4s.

to fame; but as a compiler, and as an able coadjutor of Bewick in simplifying the study of Natural History, and rendering its most interesting portions easy of attainment to the young, and to those unacquainted with the " science," he deserves higher praise than he has hitherto generally received. Roger Thornton's Monument, and the Plan of Newcastle, in the Reverend John Brand's History of that town, were engraved by Mr. Beilby. Mr. Brand's book-plate was also engraved by him. It is to be found in most of the books that formerly belonged to that celebrated antiquary, who is well known to all collectors from the extent of his purchases at stalls, and the number of curious old books which he thus occasionally obtained.—The Reverend William Turner, of Newcastle, in a letter printed in the Monthly Magazine for June 1801, vindicates the character of Mr. Beilby from what he considers the detractions of Dr. Gleig, in an article on Wood-cuts in the Supplement to the Encyclopedia Britannica. Mr. Beilby was a native of the city of Durham, and was brought up as a silversmith and seal-engraver under his father. He died at Newcastle on the 4th of January 1817, in the seventy-fourth year of his age.

The partnership between Beilby and Bewick having been dissolved in 1797, shortly after the publication of the first volume of the Birds, the descriptions in the second, which did not appear till 1804, were written by Bewick himself, but revised by the Reverend Henry Cotes, vicar of Bedlington. The publication of this volume formed the key-stone of Bewick's fame as a designer and engraver on wood; for though the cuts are not superior to those of the first, they are not excelled, nor indeed equalled, by any that he afterwards executed. The subsequent additions, whether as cuts of birds or tail-pieces, are not so excellent as numerous—in this respect the reverse of the additions to the Quad-rupeds. Though all the birds were designed, and nearly all of them engraved by Bewick himself, there are yet living witnesses who can testify that both in the drawing and the engraving of the tail-pieces he received very considerable assistance from his pupils, more especially from Robert Johnson as a draftsman, and Luke Clennell as a wood engraver.* Before saying anything further on this subject, it seems

* Pinkerton having stated in his Scottish Gallery, on the authority of Messrs. Morison, printers, of Perth, that Bewick, " observing the uncommon genius of his late apprentice, Robert Johnson, employed him to trace the figures on the wood in the History of Quad-rupeds," Bewick, in his letter, printed in the Monthly Magazine for November 1805, previously quoted, thus denies the assertion : " It is only necessary for me to declare, and this will be attested by my partner Mr. Beilby, who compiled the History of Quadrupeds, and was a proprietor of the work, that neither Robert Johnson, nor any person but myself, made the drawings, or traced or cut them on the wood."—Robert Johnson was employed by Messrs. Morison to copy for the Scottish Gallery several portraits at Taymouth Castle, the seat of the Earl of Breadalbane. Bewick in this letter carefully avoids pleading to that

necessary to give the following passage from Mr. Atkinson's Sketch of the Life and Works of Bewick. " With regard to the circumstance that the *British Birds*, with very few exceptions, were finished by his own hand, I have it in my power to pledge myself. I had been a good deal surprised one day by hearing a gentleman assert that very few of them were his own work, all the easy parts being executed by his pupils. I saw him the same day, and, talking of his art, inquired if he permitted the assistance of his apprentices in many cases ? He said, ' No ; it had seldom happened, and then they had injured the cuts very much.' I inquired if he could remember any of them in which he had received assistance ? He said, ' Aye : I can soon tell you them ;' and, after a few minutes' consideration, he made out, with his daughter's assistance, *the Whimbrel, Tufted Duck,* and *Lesser Tern :** he tried to recollect more, and turning to his daughter, said, ' Jane, honey, dost thou remember any more ?' She considered a little, and said, ' No : she did not ; but that certainly there were not half a dozen in all :' those we both pressed him to do over again. ' He intended it,' he said ; but, alas ! this intention was prevented. In some cases, I am informed, he made his pupils block out for him ; that is, furnished them with an outline, and let them cut away the edges of the block to that line ; but as, in this case, the assistance rendered is much the same as that afforded by a turner's apprentice when he rounds off the heavy mass of wood in readiness for a more experienced hand, but not a line of whose performance remains in the beautiful toy it becomes, it does not materially shake the authenticity of the work in question."

Though it is evident that Bewick meant here simply to assert that all the *figures* of the *birds*, except the few which he mentions, were entirely engraved by himself, yet his biographer always speaks as if *every one* of the cuts in the work—both birds and tail-pieces—were exclusively engraved by Bewick himself; and in consequence of this erroneous opinion he refers to seven cuts† as affording favourable

with which he was not charged ; he does not deny that several of the drawings of the tail-pieces in the History of British Birds were made by Robert Johnson. A pupil of Bewick's, now living, saw many of Johnson's drawings for these cuts, and sat beside Clennell when he was engraving them.

* These three cuts were engraved by one of Bewick's pupils, named Henry Hole. Neither Bewick's memory nor his daughter's had been accurate on this occasion ; but not one of the other cuts which they failed to recollect can be compared with those engraved by Bewick himself. In addition to those three, the following, not engraved by Bewick himself, had appeared at the time the above conversation took place—some time between 1825 and 1826 :—the Brent Goose, the Lesser Imber, and the Cormorant, engraved by L. Clennell ; the Velvet Duck, the Red-breasted Merganser, and the Crested Cormorant, by H. Hole ; the Rough-legged Falcon, the Pigmy Sand-piper, the Red Sand-piper, and the Eared Grebe, by W. W. Temple.

† " He never could, he said, please himself in his representations of water in a state of motion, and a horse galloping : his taste must have been fastidious indeed, if that beautiful

instances of Bewick's manner of representing water, although *not one* of them was engraved by him, but by Luke Clennell, from drawings by himself or by Robert Johnson. Mr. Atkinson, in his admiration of Bewick, and in his desire to exaggerate his fame, entirely overlooks the merits of those by whom he was assisted. Charlton Nesbit and Luke Clennell rendered him more assistance, though not in the cuts of birds, than such as that "afforded by a turner's apprentice when he rounds off the heavy mass of wood;" and Robert Johnson, who designed many of the best of the tail-pieces, drew the human figure more correctly than Bewick himself, and in landscape-drawing was at least his equal. These observations are not intended in the least to detract from Bewick's just and deservedly great reputation, but to correct the erroneous opinions which have been promulgated on this subject by persons who knew nothing of the very considerable assist- ance which he received from his pupils in the drawing and engraving of the tail-pieces in his history of British Birds.

Though three of the best specimens of Bewick's talents as a designer and engraver on wood—the Bittern, the Wood-cock, and the Common Duck*—are to be found in the second volume, containing the water-

birds, yet the land-birds in the first volume, from his being more familiar with their habits, and in consequence of their allowing more scope for the display of Bewick's excellence in the representation of

moonlight scene at sea, page 120, vol. ii. [edition 1816]; the river scene at page 126; the sea breaking among the rocks at page 168, or 177, or 200, or 216 ; or the rippling of the water as it leaves the feet of the old fisherman, at page 95, did not satisfy him." In scarcely one of the cuts engraved by Bewick himself is water in a state of motion well represented. He knew his own deficiency in this respect ; though Mr. Atkinson, not being able to distinguish the cuts engraved by Bewick himself from those engraved by his pupils, cannot perceive it.

* The cut here given is engraved by Bewick at a somewhat earlier date, for a once popular work entitled the History of Three Hundred Animals, since incorporated in Mrs. Loudon's " Entertaining Naturalist."

foliage, are, on the whole, superior both in design and execution to the others; their characteristic attitude and expression are represented with the greatest truth, while, from the propriety of the back-grounds, and the beauty of the trees and foliage, almost every cut forms a perfect little picture. Bewick's talent in pourtraying the form and character of birds is seen to great advantage in the hawks and the owls; but his excellence, both as a designer and engraver on wood, is yet more strikingly displayed in several of the other cuts contained in the same volume, and among these the following are perhaps the best. The numbers refer to the pages of the first edition of the Land Birds, 1797. The Field-fare, page 98; the Yellow Bunting, a most exquisite cut, and considered by Bewick as the best that he ever engraved, 143; the Goldfinch, 165; the Skylark, 178; the Woodlark, 183; the Lesser and the Winter Fauvette, 212, 213; the Willow Wren, 222; the Wren, 227; the White-rump, 229; the Cole Titmouse, 241; the Night-Jar, 262; the Domestic Cock, 276; the Turkey, 286; the Pintado, 293; the Red Grouse, 301; the Partridge, 305; the Quail, 308; and the Corncrake, 311.—Among the Birds in the second volume, first edition, 1804, the following may be instanced as the most excellent. The Water Crake, page 10; the Water Rail, 13; the Bittern, 47; the Woodcock, 60; the Common Snipe, 68; the Judcock, or Jack Snipe, 73; the Dunlin, 117; the Dun Diver, 257; the Grey Lag Goose, 292; and the Common Duck, 333.

Nothing of the same kind that wood engraving has produced since the time of Bewick can for a moment bear a comparison with these cuts. They are not to be equalled till a designer and engraver shall arise possessed of Bewick's knowledge of nature, and endowed with his happy talent of expressing it. Bewick has in this respect effected more by himself than has been produced by one of our best wood engravers when working from drawings made by a professional designer, but who knows nothing of birds, of their habits, or the places which they frequent; and has not the slightest feeling for natural incident or picturesque beauty.—No mere fac-simile engraver of a drawing ready made to his hand, should venture to speak slightingly of Bewick's talents until he has both *drawn and engraved* a cut which may justly challenge a comparison with the Kyloe Ox, the Yellow-hammer, the Partridge, the Wood-cock, or the Tame Duck.

Bewick's style of engraving, as displayed in the Birds, is exclusively his own. He adopts no conventional mode of representing texture or producing an effect, but skilfully avails himself of the most simple and effective means which his art affords of faithfully and efficiently representing his subject. He never wastes his time in laborious trifling to display his skill in execution;—he works with a higher aim, to represent nature ; and, consequently, he never bestows his pains except to express a meaning. The manner in which he has represented the feathers in many of his birds, is as admirable as it is perfectly original. His feeling for his subject, and his knowledge of his art, suggest the best means of effecting his end, and the manner in which he has employed them entitle him to rank as a wood engraver—without reference to his merits as a designer—among the very best that have practised the art.

Our copy of his cut of the Partridge, though not equal to the original, will perhaps to a certain extent serve to exemplify his practice. Every line that is to be perceived in this bird is the best that could have been devised to express the engraver's perfect idea of his subject. The soft downy plumage of the breast is represented by delicate black lines crossed horizontally by white ones, and in order that they may appear comparatively light in the impression, the block has

in this part been lowered. The texture of the skin of the legs, and the marks of the toes, are expressed with the greatest accuracy ; and the varied tints of the plumage of the rump, back, wings, and head, are indicated with no less fidelity.—Such a cut as this Bewick would execute in less time than a modern French wood engraver would require to cut the delicate cross-hatchings necessary, according to French taste, to denote the grey colour of a soldier's great coat.

The cut of the Wood-cock, of which that on the next page is a copy, is another instance of the able manner in which Bewick has availed himself of the capabilities of his art. He has here produced the most perfect likeness of the bird that ever was engraved, and at the same time given to his subject an effect, by the skilful management of light and shade, which it is impossible to obtain by means of copper-plate engraving. Bewick thoroughly understood the advantages of his art in this respect, and no wood engraver or designer, either ancient or modern, has employed them with greater success, without sacrificing nature to mere effect.

Among the very best of Bewick's cuts, as a specimen of wood engraving, is, as we have already said, the Common Duck. The round, full form of the bird, is represented with the greatest fidelity ; the plumage in all its downy, smooth, and glossy variety,—on the sides, the rump, the back, the wings, and the head,—is singularly true to nature ; while the legs and toes, and even the webs between the toes, are engraved in a manner which proves the great attention that Bewick, when necessary, paid to the minutest points of detail. The effect of the whole is excellent, and the back-ground, both in character and execution, is worthy of this master-piece of Bewick as a designer and engraver on wood.

The tail-pieces in the first editions of the Birds are, taken all together, the best that are to be found in any of Bewick's works ; but, though it is not unlikely that he suggested the subjects, there is reason to believe that many of them were drawn by Robert Johnson, and there cannot be a doubt that the greater number of those contained in the second volume were engraved by Luke Clennell. Before saying anything more about them, it seems necessary to give a list of those which were either not drawn or not engraved by Bewick himself ; it has been furnished by one of his early pupils who saw most of Johnson's drawings, and worked in the same room with Clennell when he was engraving those which are here ascribed to him. The pages show where those cuts are to be found in the edition of 1797 and in that of 1821.

This list might be considerably increased by inserting many other tail-pieces engraved by Clennell; but this does not appear necessary, as a sufficient number has been enumerated to show that both in the designing and in the engraving of those cuts Bewick received very considerable assistance from his pupils. In the additional tail-pieces to be found in subsequent editions the greater number are not engraved by Bewick himself. In the last edition, published in 1832, there are at least thirty engraved by his pupils subsequent to the time of Clennell.

The head-piece at the commencement of the introduction, volume I. page vii. drawn and engraved by Bewick himself, presents an excellent view of a farm-yard. Everything is true to nature ; the birds assembled near the woman seen winnowing corn are, though on a small scale, represented with the greatest fidelity ; even among the smallest the wagtail can be distinguished from the sparrow. The dog, feeling no interest in the business, is seen quietly resting on the dunghill ; but the chuckling of the hens, announcing that something like eating is going forward, has evidently excited the attention of the old sow, and brought her and her litter into the yard in the expectation of getting a share. The season, the latter end of autumn, is indicated by the flight of field-fares, and the comparatively naked appearance of the trees ; and we perceive that it is a clear, bright day from the strong shadow of the ladder projected against the wall, and on the thatched roof of the out-house. A heron, a crow, and a magpie are perceived nailed against the gable end of the barn ; and a couple of pigeons are seen flying above the house. The cut forms at once an interesting picture of country life, and a graphic summary of the contents of the work.

Among the tail-pieces drawn and engraved by Bewick himself, in the first edition of the Birds, the following appear most deserving of notice. In volume I. : A traveller drinking,—supposed to represent a sketch of his own costume when making a tour of the Lakes in 1776,—introduced twice, at the end of the contents, page xxx. and again at page 177. A man *watering*, in a different sense to the preceding, a very natural, though not a very delicate subject, at page 42. At page 62, an old miller, lying asleep behind some bushes ; he has evidently been tipsy and from the date on a stone to the left, we are led to suppose that he had been indulging too freely on the the King's birth-day, 4th June. The following is a copy of the cut.   Two cows standing in a pool, under

the shade of a *dyke-back*, on a warm day, page 74.   In this cut Bewick has introduced a sketch of a magpie chased by a hawk, but saved from the talons of its pursuer by the timely interference of a couple of crows. Winter scene, of which the following is a copy, at page 78.   Some boys

have made a large snow man, which excites the special wonderment of a horse ; and Bewick, to give the subject a moral application, has added *"Esto perpetua !"* at the bottom of the cut : the great work of the little men, however they may admire it, and wish for its endurance, will be dissolved on the first thaw.   At page 97 the appearance of mist and rain is well expressed ; and in the cut of a poacher tracking a hare, the snow is no less naturally represented.   At page 157, a man riding with a *howdy*—a midwife—behind him, part of the cut appears covered with a leaf.   Bewick once being asked the meaning of this, said that " it was done to indicate that the scene which was to follow required to be concealed."   At page 194 we perceive a full-fed old churl hanging his cat ; at page 226, a hen attacking a dog ; and at page 281, two cocks fighting,—all three excellent of their kind.

K K 2

Bewick's humour occasionally verges on positive grossness, and a *glaring* instance of his want of delicacy presents itself in the tail-piece at page 285. After the work was printed off Bewick became aware that the nakedness of a prominent part of his subject required to be covered, and one of his apprentices was employed to blacken it over with ink. In the next edition a plug was inserted in the block, and the representation of two bars of wood engraved upon it to hide the offensive part. The cut, however, even thus amended, is still extremely indelicate.*

The following is a copy of the head-piece at the commencement of the advertisement to the second volume. It represents an old man

saying grace with closed eyes, while his cat avails herself of the opportunity of making free with his porridge. The Reverend Henry Cotes, vicar of Bedlington, happening to call on Bewick when he was finishing this cut, expressed his disapprobation of the subject, as having a tendency to ridicule the practice of an act of devotion; but Bewick denied that he had any such intention, and would not consent to omit the cut. He drew a distinction between the act and the performer; and though he might approve of saying grace before meat, he could not help laughing at one of the over-righteous, who, while craving a blessing with hypocritical grimace, and with eyes closed to outward things, loses a present good. The head-piece to the contents presents an excellent sketch of an old man going to market on a windy and rainy day. The old horse on which he is mounted has become restive, and the rider has both broken his stick and lost his hat. The horse seems determined not to move till it suits his own pleasure; and it is evident that the old man dare not get down to recover his hat, for, should he do so, encumbered as

* The subject of this cut is thus explained in Brockett's Glossary of North Country Words : " Neddy, Netty, a certain place that will not bear a written explanation ; but which is *depicted to the very life* in a tail-piece in the first edition of Bewick's Land Birds, p. 285. In the second edition a bar is placed against the offending part of this *broad* display of native humour."

he is with a heavy basket over his left arm and an egg-pannier slung over his shoulder, he will not be able to remount. The following are the principal tail-pieces drawn and engraved by Bewick himself in the first edition of the second volume of the Birds, 1804. A shooter with a gun at his back crossing a stream on long stilts, page 5. An old wooden-legged beggar gnawing a bone near the entrance to a gentleman's house, and a dog beside him eagerly watching for the reversion, page 27. A dog with a kettle tied to his tail, pursued by boys,—a great hulking fellow, evidently a blacksmith, standing with folded arms enjoying the sport, page 56. A man crossing a frozen stream, with a branch of a tree between his legs, to support him should the ice happen to break, page 85. A monkey basting a goose that is seen roasting, page 263. An old woman with a pitcher, driving away some geese from a well, page 291. An old beggar-woman assailed by a gander, page 313.

One of the best of the tail-pieces subsequently inserted is that which occurs at the end of the description of the Moor-buzzard, volume I. in the editions of 1816 and 1821, and at page 31 in the edition of 1832. It represents two dyers carrying a tub between them by means of a cowl-staff; and the figures, Mr. Atkinson says, are portraits of two old men belonging to Ovingham,—"the one on the right being 'auld Tommy Dobson of the Bleach Green,' and the other 'Mat. Carr.'"* The action of the men is excellent, and their expression is in perfect accordance with the business in which they are engaged—to wit, carrying their tub full of *chemmerly*—chamber-lye—to the dye-house. The olfactory organs of both are evidently affected by the pungent odour of their load. It may be necessary to observe that the dyers of Ovingham had at that time a general reservoir in the village, to which most of the cottagers were contributors; but as each family had the privilege of supplying themselves from it with as much as they required for scouring and washing, it sometimes happened that the dyers found their trough empty, and were consequently obliged to solicit a supply from such persons as kept a private stock of their own. As they were both irritable old men, the phrase, "He's like a *raised* [enraged] dyer begging *chemmerly*," became proverbial in Ovingham to denote a person in a passion. This cut, as I am informed by one of Bewick's old pupils, was copied on the block and engraved by Luke Clennell from a water-colour drawing by Robert Johnson.

When the second volume of the History of British Birds was pub-

* "Mr. Atkinson must have· misunderstood Bewick, as the old man's name was George, not Matthew, Carr. He was grandfather to Edward Willis, one of Bewick's pupils, and to George Stephenson, the celebrated engineer. Matthew Carr was a tailor, who lived and died at Righton, in Durham."—Jno. Jackson.

lished, in 1804, Bewick had reached his fiftieth year; but though his powers as a wood engraver continued for long afterwards unimpaired, yet he subsequently produced nothing to extend his fame. The retouching of the blocks for the repeated editions of the Quadrupeds and the Birds, and the engraving of new cuts for the latter work, occupied a considerable part of his time. He also engraved, by himself and pupils, several cuts for different works, but they are generally such as add nothing to his reputation. Bewick never engraved with pleasure from another person's drawing; in large cuts, consisting chiefly of human figures, he did not excel. His excellence consisted in the representation of animals and in landscape. The Fables, which had been projected previous to 1795, also occasionally occupied his attention. This work, which first appeared in 1818, was by no means so favourably received as the Quadrupeds and the Birds; and several of Bewick's greatest admirers, who had been led to expect something better, openly expressed their disappointment. Dr. Dibdin, speaking of the Fables, says, "It would be a species of *scandalum magnatum* to depreciate any production connected with the name of Bewick; but I will fearlessly and honestly aver that his Æsop disappointed me; the more so, as his Birds and Beasts are volumes perfectly classical of their kind." The disappointment, however, that was felt with respect to this work resulted perhaps rather from people expecting too much than from any deficiency in the cuts as *illustrations of Fables*. There is a great difference between representing birds and beasts in their natural character, and representing them as actors in imaginary scenes. We do not regard the cock and the fox holding an imaginary conversation, however ably represented, with the interest with which we look upon each when faithfully depicted in its proper character. The tail-piece of the bitch seeing her drowned puppies, at page 364 of the Quadrupeds, edition 1824, is far more interesting than any cut illustrative of a fable in Æsop;—we at once feel its truth, and admire it, because it is natural. Birds and beasts represented as performing human characters can never interest so much as when naturally depicted in their own. Such cuts may display great fancy and much skill on the part of the artist, but they never can excite true feeling. The martyr Cock Robin, killed by that malicious archer the Sparrow, is not so interesting as plain Robin Redbreast picking up crumbs at a cottage-door in the snow :—

"One touch of nature makes the whole world kin."

Whatever may be the merits or defects of the cuts in those Fables, Bewick most certainly had very little to do with them; for by far the greater number were designed by Robert Johnson, and engraved by W. W. Temple and William Harvey, while yet in their apprenticeship. In the whole volume there are not more than three of the largest cuts engraved by Bewick himself.* The tail-pieces in this work will not bear a comparison with those in the Birds; the subjects are often both trite and tamely treated; the devil and the gallows—Bewick's two stock-pieces—occur rather too frequently, considering that the book is chiefly intended for the improvement of young minds; and in many instances nature has been sacrificed in order that the moral might be obvious.

THE CROW AND THE LAMB.

The letter-press was entirely selected and arranged by Bewick himself, and one or two of the fables were of his own writing. Though an excellent illustrator of Natural History, Bewick is but an indifferent fabulist.† Though the work is professedly intended for the instruction of the young, there are certainly a few tail-pieces introduced for the *entertainment* of the more advanced in years; and of this kind is the old beggar and his trull lying asleep, and a bull looking over a rail at them. The explanation of this subject would certainly have little tendency to improve young minds. Bewick, though very fond of introducing the devil in his cuts to frighten the wicked, does not appear to have been willing that a ranting preacher should in his discourses avail himself of the same character, though to effect the same purpose, as we learn from the following anecdote related by Mr. Atkinson. "Cant and hypocrisy he (Bewick) very much disliked. A ranter took up his abode near Cherry-burn, and used daily to horrify the country people with very familiar details of ultra-stygian proceedings. Bewick went to hear him, and after listening patiently for some time to

* The cuts engraved by Bewick himself are: a tail-piece (a Cow standing under some bushes) to "The Two Frogs," page 200. The fable of "The Deer and the Lion," page 315. "Waiting for Death," page 338. He also engraved the figure of the *Lion* in the fable of "The Lion and the four Bulls," page 89 (see cut at our page 480). The Man, Crow, and Sheep in the fable of the "Eagle and the Crow," of which we give the original cut. The Man and two Birds in the fable of "The Husbandman and the Stork."
† The fable of the Ship Dog is one of those written by Bewick.

a blasphemous recital of such horrors, at which the poor people were
gaping with affright, he got behind the holder-forth, and pinching his
elbow, addressed him when he turned round with great solemnity : ' Now
then thou seems to know a great deal about the devil, and has been
frightening us a long while about him : can thou tell me whether he
wears his own hair or a wig ? ' "—This is a bad joke ;—the query might
have been retorted with effect.   The engraver, it seems, might introduce
his Satanic majesty *ad libitum* in his cuts ; but when a ranting preacher
takes the same liberty in his discourses, he is called upon to give proof
of personal acquaintance.

Bewick's morality was rather rigid than cheerful ; and he was but too
prone to think uncharitably of others, whose conduct and motives, when
weighed in the scales of impartial justice, were perhaps as correct and as
pure as his own.   His good men are often represented as somewhat cold,
selfish individuals, with little sympathy for the more unfortunate of their
species, whose errors are as often the result of ignorance as of a positively
vicious character.   As a moralist, he was accustomed to look at the dark
rather than the bright side of human nature, and hence his tendency to
brand those with whom he might differ in opinion as fools and knaves.
One of the fables, written by himself, was objected to by the printer,
the late Mr. E. Walker, and at his request it was omitted.   We give
a copy of the cut intended for it.   The world is represented as having

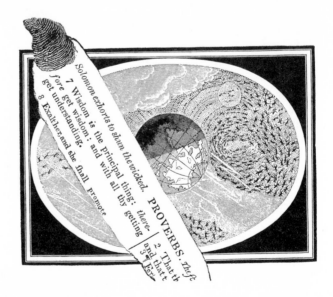

lost its balance, and legions of his favourite devils are seen hurled about
in a confused vortex.   The fable, it is said, was intended as a satire on

the ministerial politics of the time. A thumb-mark is seen at the upper end of what is intended to represent a piece of paper forming part of the page of a Bible pasted across the cut. A similar mark is to be found at page 175 of the Land Birds, first edition, 1797, and in the bill and receipt prefixed to the Fables, 1818–1823.

In a novel, entitled "Such is the World," there is the following erroneous account of Bewick's reason for affixing his thumb-mark to this bill.* "Having completed his task to the entire satisfaction of his own mind, Mr. Bewick bethought him of engraving a frontispiece. But having some suspicion that the said frontispiece might be pirated by some of those corsairs who infest the ocean of literature, he resolved to put a mark on it, whereby all men might distinguish it as readily as a fisherman distinguishes a haddock† from a cod-fish. Accordingly, he touched with his thumb the little black ball with which he was wont to ink his cuts, in order to take off proof impressions of his work: he then very deliberately pressed his thumb on the frontispiece which he was at that moment engraving, and cut the most beautiful image of the original, which he designated by the appropriate words 'John Bewick, his mark.'" Had the writer looked at the "frontispiece," as he calls it, he would have found "*Thomas*," and not "*John.*" The conclusion of this account is a fair sample of its general accuracy. In a preliminary observation the author, with equal correctness, informs his readers that the work in which this "frontispiece" appeared was "a superb edition of *Gay's* Fables."

Bewick's *mark* is, in fact, added to this bill merely as a jest; the mode which he took to authenticate the copies that were actually issued by himself, and not pilfered by any of the workmen employed about the printing-office,‡ was to print at his own work-shop, in red ink from a copper-plate, a representation of a piece of sea-weed lying above the wood-cut which had previously been printed off at a printing-office. This mode of printing a copper-plate over a wood-cut was a part of

---

* Mr. Atkinson says that this account determined Bewick to write a life of himself. It appears that he actually completed such a work, but that his family at present decline to publish it. [Mr. Jackson adds, " I engraved two portraits for it: one was a portrait of the Rev. Wm. Turner, of Newcastle, the other that of an engineer or millwright, at Morpeth, named Rastack, or Raistick.]

† " There is a tradition that the two black marks on the opposite sides of the haddock were occasioned by St. Peter's thumb and fore-finger when he took the piece of money out of the fish's mouth to give it as a tribute to Cæsar."

‡ Bewick's suspicions in this respect were not altogether groundless. Happening to go into a bookbinder's shop in Newcastle in 1818, he found a copy of his Fables, which had been sent there to bind before the work had been issued to the public. He claimed the book as his property, and carried it away ; but the name of the owner who had purchased it, knowing it to have been dishonestly obtained, was not publicly divulged.

one of the plans which he had devised to prevent the forgery of bank-notes.*

The first of the two following cuts, copied from his Fables, records the decease of Bewick's mother, who died on the 20th of February 1785, aged 58 ; and the second that of his father, who died on the 15th of November in the same year, aged 70. The last event also marks the day on which he began to engrave the first cut intended for the Quadrupeds. This cut was the Arabian Camel, or Dromedary, and he had made very little progress with it when a messenger arrived from Cherry-burn to inform him of his father's death.

Several years previous to his decease Bewick had devised an improvement, which consisted in printing a subject from two or more blocks,— not in the manner of chiaro-scuros, but in order to obtain a greater variety of *tint*, and a better effect than could be obtained, without great labour, in a cut printed in black ink from a single block. This improvement, which had been suggested by Papillon in 1768, Bewick proceeded to carry into effect. The subject which he made choice of to exemplify what he con_ sidered his original discovery, was an old horse waiting for death.† He accordingly made the drawing on a large block consisting of four different pieces, and forthwith proceeded to engrave it. He however did not live to complete his intention ; for even this block, which he meant merely for the first impression—the subject having to be completed by a second —remained unfinished at his decease.‡   He had, however, finished it all

* About 1799 Bewick frequently corresponded with Mr. Abraham Newland, cashier of the Bank of England, respecting a plan which he had devised to prevent the forgery of bank notes.   He was offered a situation in the Bank to superintend the engraving and printing of the notes, but he refused to leave Newcastle.   The notes of Ridley and Co.'s bank were for many years engraved and printed under the superintendence of Bewick, who, after Mr Beilby's retirement, still continued the business of copper-plate engraving and printing, and for this purpose always kept presses of his own.

† A small cut of the same subject, though with a different back-ground, occurs as a tail-piece in the Fables, 1818–1823.

‡ The last *bird* that Bewick engraved was the Cream-coloured Plover, at page 383, vol. i. of the Birds, in the edition of 1832.   Several years previous to his death he had projected a History of British Fishes, but very little progress was made in the work.   A few cuts of fishes were engraved, chiefly by his pupils; that of the John Dory, an impression of which is

with the exception of part of the horse's head, and when in this state he had four impressions taken about a week before his death. It was on this occasion that he exclaimed, when the pressman handed him the proof, " I wish I was but twenty years younger ! "

This cut, with the head said to have been finished by another person, was published by Bewick's son, Mr. Robert Elliott Bewick, in 1832. It is the largest cut that Bewick ever engraved,* but having been left by him in an unfinished state, it would be impossible to say what he might have effected had he lived to work out his ideas, and unfair to judge of it as if it were a finished performance. It is, however, but just to remark, that the miserable appearance of the poor, worn-out, neglected animal, is represented with great feeling and truth,—excepting the head, which is disproportionately large and heavy,—and that the landscape displays Bewick's usual fidelity in copying nature.

Bewick's life affords a useful lesson to all who wish to attain distinction in art, and at the same time to preserve their independence. He diligently cultivated his talents, and never trusted to booksellers or designers for employment. He did not work according to the directions of others, but struck out a path for himself ; and by diligently pursuing it according to the bent of his own feelings, he acquired both a competence with respect to worldly means and an ample reward of fame. The success of his works did not render him inattentive to business ; and he was never tempted by the prospect of increasing wealth to indulge in expensive pleasures, nor to live in a manner which his circumstances did not warrant. What he had honestly earned he frugally husbanded ; and, like a prudent man, made a provision for his old age. " The hand of the diligent," says Solomon, "maketh rich." This Bewick felt, and his life may be cited in the exemplification of the truth of the proverb. He acquired not indeed great wealth, but he attained a competence, and was grateful and contented. No favoured worshipper of Mammon, though possessed of millions obtained by " watching the turn of the market," could say more.

He was extremely regular and methodical in his habits of business : until within a few years of his death he used to come to his shop in Newcastle from his house in Gateshead at a certain hour in the morning, returning to his dinner at a certain time, and, as he used to say, *lapping*

---

said to have been sold for a considerable sum, is one of those not engraved by Bewick himself. As a work of art the value of an India paper impression. of the John Dory may be about twopence. This cut is an early performance of Mr. Jackson's, who also engraved, in 1823, about twenty of the additional tail-pieces in the last edition of the Birds, 1832.

* This cut is eleven inches and five-eighths wide by eight inches and three-fourths high. It is entitled, " Waiting for Death : Bewick's last work, left unfinished, and intended to have been completed by a series of impressions from separate blocks printed over each other."

up at night, as if he were a workman employed by the day, and subject to a loss by being absent a single hour. When any of his works were in the press, the first thing he did each morning, after calling at his own shop, was to proceed to the printer's to see what progress they were making, and to give directions to the pressmen about printing the cuts.* It is indeed owing to his attention in this respect that the cuts in all the editions of his works published during his life-time are so well printed. The edition of the Birds, published in 1832, displays numerous instances of the want of Bewick's own superintendence : either through the careless-ness or ignorance of the pressmen, many of the cuts are quite spoiled.

The following cut represents a view of Bewick's workshop in St. Nicholas' Churchyard, Newcastle. The upper room, the two windows of

which are seen in the roof, was that in which he worked in the latter years of his life. In this shop he engraved the cuts which will perpetuate his name ; and there for upwards of fifty years was he accustomed to sit, steadily and cheerfully pursuing the labour that he loved. He used always to work with his hat on ; and when any gentleman or nobleman

---

* When Bewick removed the printing of his works from Mr. Hodgson's office to that of Mr. E. Walker, a pressman, named Barlow, was brought from London for the purpose of printing the cuts in the second volume of the Birds in a proper manner. Bewick's favourite pressman at Mr. Hodgson's was John Simpson.

called upon him, he only removed it for a moment on his first entering. He used frequently to whistle when at work, and he was seldom without a large quid of tobacco in his mouth. The prominence occasioned by the quid, which he kept between his under lip and his teeth, and not in his cheek, is indicated in most of his portraits.

A stick, which had been his brother John's, was a great favourite with him, and he generally carried it in his walks, always carefully putting it in a certain place when he entered his workroom. He used to be very partial to a draught of water in the afternoon, immediately before leaving work. The water was brought fresh by one of the apprentices from the *pant* at the head of the Side, in an earthenware jug, and the glass which Bewick used to drink the water out of, was, as soon as done with, carefully locked up in his book-case. One of his apprentices once happening to break the jug, Bewick scolded him well for his carelessness, and made him pay twopence towards buying another.

Bewick was a man of athletic make, being nearly six feet high, and proportionably stout. He possessed great personal courage, and in his younger days was not slow to repay an insult with personal chastisement. On one occasion being assaulted by two pitmen on returning from a visit to Cherry-burn, he resolutely turned upon the aggressors, and, as he said, "*paid* them both well." Though hard-featured, and much marked with the small-pox, the expression of Bewick's countenance was manly and open, and his dark eyes sparkled with intelligence. There is a good bust of him by Bailey in the Library of the Literary and Philosophical Society of Newcastle, and the best engraved portrait is perhaps that of Burnet, after a painting by Ramsey.* The portrait on page 510, engraved on wood, is another attempt to perpetuate the likeness of one to whom the art owes so much.

In the summer of 1828 Bewick visited London ; but he was then evidently in a declining state of health, and he had lost much of his former energy of mind. Scarcely anything that he saw interested him, and he longed no less than in his younger years to return to the banks of

---

* The following is a list of the principal engraved portraits of Bewick : on copper, by J. A. Kidd, from a painting by Miss Kirkley, 1798. On copper, by Thomas Ranson, after a painting by William Nicholson, 1816. On copper, by I. Summerfield, from a miniature by Murphy—that alluded to in Bewick's letter to Mr. C. Gregson, previously quoted—1816. On copper, by John Burnet, from a painting by James Ramsey, 1817. Copies of all those portraits, engraved on wood, are given in Charnley's edition of Select Fables, 1820 ; and there is also prefixed to the work a portrait excellently engraved on wood by Charlton Nesbit, one of Bewick's earliest pupils, from a drawing made on the block by William Nicholson.—In the Memoir of Thomas Bewick, prefixed to the Natural History of Parrots, Naturalist's Library, vol. vi., it is incorrectly stated that Ranson, the engraver of one of the above portraits, was a pupil of Bewick's. He was a pupil of J. A. Kidd, copper-plate engraver, Newcastle.

the Tyne.   He had ceased to feel an interest in objects which formerly afforded him great pleasure ; for when his old friend, the late Mr. William Bulmer, drove him round the Regent's Park, he declined to alight for the purpose of visiting the collection of animals in the Gardens of the Zoological Society.

THOMAS BEWICK.

On his return to Newcastle he appeared for a short time to enjoy his usual health and spirits.   On the Saturday preceding his death he took the block of the Old Horse waiting for Death to the printer's, and had it proved ; on the following Monday he became unwell, and after a few days' illness he ceased to exist.   He died at his house on the Windmill-hills, Gateshead, on the 8th of November, 1828, aged seventy-five.   He was buried at Ovingham, and the following cut represents a view of the place of his interment, near the west end of the church. The tablets seen in the wall are those erected to the memory of himself and his brother John.

The following are the inscriptions on the tablets :

In Memory of
JOHN BEWICK,
Engraver,
Who died December, 5, 1795,
Aged 35 years.

His Ingenuity as an
Artist
was excelled only by
his Conduct as a
Man.

The
Burial Place
of
THOMAS BEWICK,
Engraver,
Newcastle.
Isabella, his Wife,
Died 1st February, 1826,
Aged 72 years.
THOMAS BEWICK,
Died 8th of November, 1828,
Aged 75 years.

In an excellent notice of the works of Bewick—apparently written by one of his townsmen (said to be Mr. T. Doubleday)—in Blackwood's Magazine for July, 1825, it is stated that the final tail-piece to Bewick's Fables, 1818–1823, is " A View of Ovingham Churchyard ;" and in the Reverend William Turner's Memoir of Thomas Bewick, in the sixth volume of the Naturalist's Library, the same statement is repeated. It is, however, erroneous ; as both the writers might have known had they thought it worth their while to pay a visit to Ovingham, and take a look at the church.   The following cut, in which is introduced an imaginary representation of Bewick's funeral, presents a correct view of the place. The following popular saying, which is well known in Northumberland, suggested the introduction of the rain-bow :

> " Happy is the bride that the sun shines on,
> And happy is the corpse that the rain rains on,—"

meaning that sunshine at a wedding is a sign of happiness in the marriage state to the bride, and that rain at a funeral is a sign of future happiness to the person whose remains are about to be interred.

The following eloquent tribute to the merits of Bewick is from an article on Wilson's Illustrations of Zoology in Blackwood's Magazine for June, 1828.

" Have we forgotten, in our hurried and imperfect enumeration of wise worthies,—have we forgotten

> ' The Genius that dwells on the banks of the Tyne,' *

the Matchless, Inimitable Bewick ?   No.   His books lie on our parlour, bed-room, dining-room, drawing-room, study table, and are never out of

---

* This line is adapted from Wordsworth, who, at the commencement of his verses entitled "The Two Thieves, or The Last Stage of Avarice," thus expresses his high opinion of the talents of Bewick :

> "O now that the genius of Bewick were mine,
> And the skill which he learned on the banks of the Tyne !
> Then the Muses might deal with me just as they chose,
> For I'd take my last leave both of verse and of prose."

Lyrical Ballads, vol. ii. p. 199. Edition 1805.

place or time. Happy old man! The delight of childhood, manhood, decaying age!—A moral in every tail-piece—a sermon in every vignette. Not as if from one fountain flows the stream of his inspired spirit, gurgling from the Crawley Spring so many thousand gallons of the element every minute, and feeding but one city, our own Edinburgh. But it rather oozes out from unnumbered springs. Here from one scarcely perceptible but in the vivid green of the lonesome sward, from which it trickles away into a little mountain rill—here leaping into sudden life, as from the rock—here bubbling from a silver pool, overshadowed by a birch-tree—here like a well asleep in a moss-grown cell, built by some thoughtful recluse in the old monastic day, with a few words from Scripture, or some rude engraving, religious as Scripture, OMNE BONUM DESUPER—OPERA DEI MIRIFICA."

John Bewick, a younger brother of Thomas, was born at Cherryburn in 1760, and in 1777 was apprenticed as a wood engraver to his brother and Mr. Beilby. He undoubtedly assisted his brother in the execution of the cuts for the two editions of Fables, printed by Mr. Saint in 1779 and 1784; but in those early productions it would be impossible, judging merely from the style of the engraving, to distinguish the work of the two brothers. Among the earliest cuts known to have been engraved by John Bewick, on the expiration of his apprenticeship, are those contained in a work entitled "Emblems of Mortality," printed in 1789 for T. Hodgson, the publisher of the Hieroglyphic Bible, mentioned at page 478. Those cuts, which are very indifferently executed, are copies, occasionally altered for the worse, of the cuts in Holbein's Dance of Death. Whether he engraved them in London, or not, I have been unable to ascertain; but it is certain that he was living in London in the following year, and that he resided there till 1795. When residing in the metropolis he drew and engraved the cuts for "The Progress of Man and Society," compiled by Dr. Trusler, and published in 1791; the cuts for "The Looking Glass of the Mind," 1796; and also those contained in a similar work entitled "Blossoms of Morality," published about the same time. Though several of those cuts display considerable talent, yet the best specimens of his abilities as a designer and engraver on wood are to be found in Poems by Goldsmith and Parnell, 1795, and in Somervile's Chase, 1796, both printed in quarto, to display the excellence of modern printing, type-founding, wood-engraving, and paper-making. Mr. Bulmer, who suggested those editions, being himself a Northumbrian, had been intimately acquainted with both Thomas and John Bewick. In the preface to the Poems by Goldsmith and Parnell, he is careful to commemorate the paper-maker, type-founder, and the engravers; but he omits to mention the name of Robert Johnson, who designed three of the principal

L L

cuts.* The merits of this highly-talented young man appear to have been singularly overlooked by those whose more especial duty it was to notice them. In the whole of Bewick's works he is not once mentioned. Mr. Bulmer also says, that all the cuts were engraved by Thomas and John Bewick; but though he unquestionably believed so himself, the statement is not strictly correct; for the four vignette head and tail-pieces to the Traveller and the Deserted Village were engraved by C. Nesbit. The vignettes on the title-pages, the large cut of the old woman gathering water-cresses, and the tail-piece at the end of the volume, were drawn and engraved by John Bewick; the remainder were engraved by Thomas.

The cuts in this book are generally executed in a free and effective style, but are not remarkable as specimens of wood engraving, unless we take into consideration the time when they were published. The best in point of execution are, The Hermit at his morning devotion, and The Angel, Hermit, and Guide, both engraved by Thomas Bewick; the manner in which the engraver has executed the foliage in these two cuts is extremely beautiful and natural. It is said that George III. thought so highly of the cuts in this book that he could not believe that they were engraved on wood; and that his bookseller, Mr. George Nicol, obtained for his Majesty a sight of the blocks in order that he might be convinced of the fact by his own inspection. This anecdote is sometimes produced as a proof of the great excellence of the cuts, though it might with greater truth be cited as a proof of his Majesty being totally unacquainted with the process of wood engraving, and of his not being able to distinguish a wood-cut from a copper-plate. If Bewick's reputation as a wood engraver rested on those cuts, it certainly would not stand very high. Much better things of the same kind have been executed since that time by persons who are generally considered as having small claims to distinction as wood engravers.

The cuts in the Chase were all, except one, designed by John Bewick; but in consequence of the declining state of his health he was not able to engrave them. Soon after he had finished the drawings on the block he left London for the north, in the hope of deriving benefit from his native air. His disorder, however, continued to increase; and, within a few weeks from the time of his return, he died at Ovingham, on the 5th of December, 1795, aged thirty-five.

The cuts in the Chase, which were all, except one, engraved by Thomas Bewick, are, on the whole, superior in point of execution to those in the Poems of Goldsmith and Parnell. Though boldly designed, some of them display great defects in composition, and among the most objectionable in this respect are the Huntsman and three Hounds, at

* The cut of the Hermit at his morning devotion was drawn by John Johnson, a cousin of Robert, and also one of Bewick's pupils.

page 5 ; the conclusion of the Chase, page 31; and George III. stag-hunting, page 93. Among the best, both as respects design and execution, are : Morning, vignette on title-page, remarkably spirited ; Hounds, page 25 ; a Stag drinking, page 27; Fox-hunting, page 63 ; and Otter-hunting, page 99. The final tail-piece, which has been spoiled in the engraving, was executed by one of Bewick's pupils.

John Bewick, as a designer and engraver on wood, is much inferior to his brother. Though several of his cuts possess considerable merit

with respect to design, by far the greater number are executed in a dry, harsh manner. His best cuts may be readily distinguished from his brother's by the greater contrast of black and white in the cuts engraved by John, and by the dry and withered appearance of the foliage of the trees. The above is a reduced copy of a cut entitled the "Sad Historian," drawn and engraved by John Bewick, in the Poems by Goldsmith and Parnell.

The most of John Bewick's cuts are much better conceived than engraved ; and this perhaps may in a great measure have arisen from

their having been chiefly executed for children's books, in which excellence of engraving was not required. His style of engraving is not good;
for though some of his cuts are extremely *effective* from the contrast of
light and shade, yet the lines in almost every one are coarse and harsh,
and "laid in," to use a technical expression, in a hard and tasteless
manner. Dry, stiff, parallel lines, scarcely ever deviating into a pleasing
curve, are the general characteristic of most of his small cuts. As he
reached the age of thirty-five without having produced any cut which
displays much ability in the execution, it is not likely that he would
have excelled as a wood engraver had his life been prolonged. The
following is a fac-simile of one of the best of his cuts in the Blossoms of
Morality, published about 1796. It exemplifies his manner of strongly
contrasting positive black with pure white; and the natural attitudes of
the women afford a tolerably fair specimen of his talents as a designer.

Robert Johnson, though not a wood engraver, has a claim to a brief
notice here on account of the excellence of several of the tail-pieces
designed by him in Bewick's Birds, and from his having made the
drawings for most of the wood-cuts in Bewick's Fables. He was born
in 1770, at Shotley, a village in Northumberland, about six miles to the
south-west of Ovingham; and in 1778 was placed by his father, who at
that time resided in Gateshead, as an apprentice to Beilby and Bewick
to be instructed in copper-plate engraving. The plates which are generally supposed to have been executed by him during his apprenticeship
possess very little merit, nor does he appear to have been desirous to
excel as an engraver. His great delight consisted in sketching from
nature and in painting in water-colours; and in this branch of art,
while yet an apprentice, he displayed talents of very high order.* He

* Johnson's water-colour drawings for most of the cuts in Bewick's Fables, are extremely
beautiful. They are the size of the cuts; and as a set are perhaps the finest small drawings
of the kind that were ever made. Their finish and accuracy of drawing are admirable—they

was frequently employed by his master in drawing and making designs, and at his leisure hours he took every opportunity of improving himself in his favourite art. The Earl of Bute happening to call at Beilby and Bewick's shop on one occasion when passing through Newcastle, a portfolio of Johnson's drawings, made at his leisure hours, was shown to his lordship, who was so much pleased with them that he selected as many as amounted to forty pounds. This sum Beilby and Bewick appropriated to themselves, on the ground that, as he was their apprentice, those drawings, as well as any others that he might make, were legally their property. Johnson's friends, however, thinking differently, instituted legal proceedings for the recovery of the money, and obtained a decision in their favour. One of the pleas set up by Beilby and Bewick was, that the drawings properly belonged to them, as they taught him the art, and that the making of such drawings was part of his business. This plea, however, failed; it was elicited on the examination of one of their own apprentices, Charlton Nesbit, that neither he nor any other of his fellow apprentices was taught the art of drawing in water-colours by their masters, and that it formed no part of their necessary instruction as engravers.

On the expiration of his apprenticeship Johnson gave up, in a great measure, the practice of copper-plate engraving, and applied himself almost exclusively to drawing. In 1796 he was engaged by Messrs. Morison, booksellers and publishers of Perth, to draw from the original paintings the portraits intended to be engraved in "the Scottish Gallery," a work edited by Pinkerton, and published about 1799. When at Taymouth Castle, the seat of the Earl of Breadalbane, copying some portraits painted by Jameson, the Scottish Vandyke, he caught a severe cold, which, being neglected, increased to a fever. In the violence of the disorder he became delirious, and, from the ignorance of those who attended him, the unfortunate young artist, far from home and without a friend to console him, was bound and treated like a madman. A physician having been called in, by his order blisters were applied, and a different course of treatment adopted. Johnson recovered his senses, but it was only for a brief period; being of a delicate constitution, he sank under the disorder. He died at Kenmore on the 29th October, 1796, in the twenty-sixth year of his age.*

look like miniature *Paul Potters.* It is known to only a few persons that they were drawn by Johnson during his apprenticeship. Most of them were copied on the block by William Harvey, and the rest chiefly by Bewick himself.

* John Johnson, a cousin of Robert, was also an apprentice of Beilby and Bewick. He was a wood engraver, and executed a few of the tail-pieces in the History of British Birds. Like Robert, he possessed a taste for drawing; and the cut of the Hermit at his morning devotion, engraved by T. Bewick, in Poems by Goldsmith and Parnell, was designed by him. He died at Newcastle about 1797, shortly after the expiration of his apprenticeship.

The following is a copy of a cut—from a design by Johnson himself—
which was drawn on the wood, and engraved by Charlton Nesbit, as a
tribute of his regard for the memory of his friend and fellow-pupil.

The next cut represents a view of a monument on the south side
of Ovingham church, erected to the memory of Robert Johnson by a few

friends who admired his talents, and respected him on account of his
amiable private character.

Charlton Nesbit, who is justly entitled to be ranked with the best wood engravers of his time, was born in 1775 at Swalwell, in the county of Durham, about five miles westward of Gateshead, and when about fourteen years of age was apprenticed to Beilby and Bewick to learn the art of wood engraving. During his apprenticeship he engraved a few of the tail-pieces in the first volume of the History of British Birds, and all the head and tail-pieces, except two, in the Poems by Goldsmith and Parnell, printed by Bulmer in 1795. Shortly after the expiration of his apprenticeship he began to engrave a large cut, containing a view of St. Nicholas Church, Newcastle-on-Tyne, from a drawing by his fellow-pupil, Robert Johnson. We here present a reduced copy of this cut, which is one of the largest ever engraved in England.* The original was engraved on a block consisting of twelve different pieces of box, firmly cramped together, and mounted on a plate of cast iron to prevent their warping. For this cut, which was first published about 1799, Mr. Nesbit received a medal from the Society for the Encouragement of Arts and Manufactures.

About 1799 Mr. Nesbit came to London, where he continued to reside till 1815. During his residence there he engraved a number of cuts for various works, chiefly from the designs of the late Mr. John Thurston, †

---

* The original cut, including the border, is fifteen inches wide by about twelve inches high.

† Mr. Thurston was a native of Scarborough, and originally a copper-plate engraver. He engraved, under the late Mr. James Heath, parts of the two celebrated plates of the death of Major Peirson and the Dead Soldier. He was one of the best designers on wood of his time. He drew very beautifully, but his designs are too frequently deficient in natural character and feeling. He died in 1821.

who at that time was the principal, and indeed almost the only artist of any talent in London, who made drawings on the block for wood engravers. Some of the best of his cuts executed during this period are to be found in a History of England printed for R. Scholey, and in a work entitled Religious Emblems, published by R. Ackermann and Co. in 1808. The cuts in the latter work were engraved by Nesbit, Clennell, Branston, and Hole, from drawings by Thurston; and they are unquestionably the best of their kind which up to that time had appeared in England. Clennell's are the most artist-like in their execution and effect, while Nesbit's are engraved with greater care. Branston, except in one cut,—Rescued from the Floods,—does not appear to such advantage in this work as his northern rivals. There is only one cut— Seed sown—engraved by Hole. The following may be mentioned as the best of Nesbit's cuts in this work :—The World Weighed, The Daughters of Jerusalem, Sinners hiding in the Grave, and Wounded in the Mental Eye. The best of Clennell's are :—Call to Vigilance, the World made Captive, and Fainting for the Living Waters. These are perhaps the three best cuts of their kind that Clennell ever engraved.

In 1815 Mr. Nesbit returned to his native place, where he continued to reside until 1830. While living in the country, though he did not abandon the art, yet the cuts executed by him during this period are comparatively few. In 1818, when residing in the North, he engraved a large cut of Rinaldo and Armida for Savage's Hints on Decorative, Printing : this cut and another, the Cave of Despair, in the same work and of the same size, engraved by the late Robert Branston, were expressly given to display the perfection to which modern wood engraving had been brought. The foliage, the trees, and the drapery in Nesbit's cut are admirably engraved; but the lines in the bodies of the figures are too much broken and "*chopped up.*" This, however, was not the fault of the engraver, but of the designer, Mr. J. Thurston. The lines, which now have a dotted appearance, were originally continuous and distinct; but Mr. Thurston objecting to them as being too dark, Nesbit went over his work again, and with immense labour reduced the strength of his lines, and gave them their present dotted appearance. As a specimen of the engraver's abilities, the first proof submitted to the designer was superior to the last.

In order to give a fictitious value to Mr. Savage's book, most of the cuts, as soon as a certain number of impressions were taken, were sawn across, but not through, in several places, and impressions of them when thus defaced were given in the work.* Nesbit's cut was, however,

---

* The practice of thus giving a fictitious value to works of limited circulation, and which are not likely to reach a second edition during the lifetime of their authors, is less frequent now than it was a few years ago. It is little more than a trick to enhance the price of the

carefully repaired, and the back part of Armida's head having been altered, the impressions from the block thus amended were actually given in the work itself as the *best*, instead of those which were taken before it was defaced. This re-integration of the block was the work of the late Mr. G. W. Bonner, Mr. Branston's nephew. The transverse pieces are so skilfully inserted, and engraved so much in the style of the adjacent parts, that it is difficult to discover where the defacing saw had passed.

In 1830 Mr. Nesbit returned to London, where he continued to reside until his death, which took place at Queen's Elms, the 11th of November 1838, aged 63. Some of the best of his cuts are contained in the second series of Northcote's Fables ; and the following, of his execution, may be ranked among the finest productions of the art of wood engraving in modern times :—The Robin and the Sparrow, page 1 ; The Hare and the Bramble, page 127 ; The Peach and the Potatoe, page 129 ; and The Cock, the Dog, and the Fox, page 238. Nesbit is unquestionably the best wood engraver that has proceeded from the great northern hive of the art—the workshop of Thomas Bewick.

Luke Clennell, one of the most distinguished of Bewick's pupils as a designer and painter, as well as an engraver on wood, was born at Ulgham, a village near Morpeth, in Northumberland, on the 8th of April, 1781. At an early age he was placed with a relation, a grocer in Morpeth, and continued with him, assisting in the shop as an apprentice, until he was sixteen. Some drawings which he made when at Morpeth having attracted attention, and he himself showing a decided predilection for the art, his friends were induced to place him as a wood engraver with Bewick, to whom he was bound apprentice for seven years on the 8th of April, 1797. He in a short time made great proficiency in wood engraving ; and as he drew with great correctness and power, Bewick employed him to copy, on the block, several of Robert Johnson's drawings, and to engrave them as tail-pieces for the second volume of the History of British Birds. Clennell for a few months after the expiration of his apprenticeship continued to work for Bewick, who chiefly employed him in engraving some of the cuts for a History of England, published by Wallis and Scholey, 46, Paternoster Row. Clennell, who was paid only two guineas apiece for each of those cuts, having learnt that Bewick received five, sent to the publisher a proof of one of them— Alfred in the Danish Camp—stating that it was of his own engraving. In the course of a few days Clennell received an answer from the publisher, inviting him to come to London, and offering him employment

book to subscribers, by giving them an assurance that no second edition can appear with the same embellishments. In three cases out of four where the plates and cuts of a work have been intentionally destroyed, there was little prospect of such work reaching a second edition during the writer's life.

until all the cuts intended for the work should be finished. He accepted the offer, and shortly afterwards set out for London, where he arrived about the end of autumn, 1804.*

Most of Clennell's cuts are distinguished by their free and *artist-like* execution and by their excellent effect ; but though generally spirited, they are sometimes rather coarsely engraved. He was accustomed to improve Thurston's designs by occasionally heightening the effect.+   To such alterations Thurston at first objected ; but perceiving that the cuts when engraved were thus very much improved, he afterwards allowed Clennell to increase the lights and deepen the shadows according to his own judgment. An admirable specimen of Clennell's engraving is to be found in an octavo edition of Falconer's Shipwreck, printed for Cadell and Davies, 1808. It occurs as a vignette to the second canto at p. 43, and the subject is a ship running before the wind in a gale. The motion of the waves, and the gloomy appearance of the sky, are represented with admirable truth and feeling. The dark shadow on the waters to the right gives wonderful effect to the white crest of the wave in front ; and the whole appearance of the cut is indicative of a gloomy and tempestuous day, and of an increasing storm. Perhaps no engraving of the same kind, either on copper or wood, conveys the idea of a storm at sea with greater fidelity.‡ The drawing was made on the block by Thurston ; but the spirit and *effect,*—the lights and shadows, the apparent seething of the waves, and the troubled appearance of the sky,—were introduced by Clennell. All the other cuts in this edition of the Shipwreck are of his engraving ; but though well executed, they do not require any especial notice. Two of them, which were previously designed for another work, are certainly not *illustrations* of Falconer's Shipwreck.

Clennell's largest cut is that which he engraved for the diploma of the Highland Society, from a design by Benjamin West, President of the

* Between the expiration of his apprenticeship and his departure for London he appears to have engraved several excellent cuts for a school-book entitled " The Hive of Ancient and Modern Literature," printed by S. Hodgson, Newcastle.—Clennell's fellow-pupils were Henry Hole and Edward Willis. Mr. Hole engraved the cuts in M'Creery's Press, 1803, and in Poems by Felicia Dorothea Browne, (afterwards Mrs. Hemans) 1808. Mr. Hole gave up wood engraving several years ago on succeeding to a large estate in Derbyshire. Mr. Willis, who was a cousin of Mr. George Stephenson, the celebrated engineer, died in London, the 10th of February, 1842, aged 58 ; but had for some time previously entirely abandoned the art.

+ He also invariably corrected the *outline* of Thurston's animals ; " Fainting for the Living Waters" in the Religious Emblems, and a little subject in an edition of Beattie's Minstrel, published at Alnwick, representing a shepherd and dog on the brow of a hill, were thus improved by Clennell.

‡ Mr. Jackson was in possession of the first proof of this pretty wood engraving, inscribed Twickenham, September 10, 1807, where Clennell was residing at the time.

Royal Academy; and for this he received fifty guineas. The original drawing was made on paper, and Clennell gave Thurston fifteen pounds for copying on the block the figures within the circle: the supporters, a Highland soldier and a fisherman, he copied himself. The block on which he first began to engrave this cut consisted of several pieces of box veneered upon beech; and after he had been employed upon it for about two months, it one afternoon suddenly split when he was at tea. Clennell, hearing it crack, immediately suspected the cause; and on finding it rent in such a manner that there was no chance of repairing it, he, in a passion that the labour already bestowed on it should be lost,

B. WEST. ESQ P R A PINX'   L. CLENNELL. SCULP.

DIPLOMA OF THE HIGHLAND SOCIETY.
Reduced to one-fourth of the original size.

threw all the tea-things into the fire. In the course of a few days however, he got a new block made, consisting of solid pieces of box firmly screwed and cramped together; and having paid Thurston fifteen pounds more for re-drawing the figures within the circle, and having again copied the supporters, he proceeded with renewed spirit to complete his work. For engraving this cut he received a hundred and fifty guineas—he paying Thurston himself for the drawing on the block; and the Society for the Encouragement of Arts and Manufactures presented him with their gold medal, May 30, 1809. This cut is characteristic of Clennell's style of engraving—the lines are in some places coarse, and in others the execution is careless ; the more important parts are, however, engraved with great spirit ; and the cut, as a whole, is bold and effective. Cross-hatchings are freely introduced, not so much, perhaps, because they were necessary, as to show that the engraver could execute such kind of work,—the vulgar error that cross-hatchings could not be executed on wood having been at that time extremely prevalent among persons who had little knowledge of the art, and who yet vented their absurd notions on the subject as if they were undeniable truths. The preceding is a reduced copy of this cut.* The original block, when only a very limited number of impressions had been printed off, was burnt in the fire at Mr. Bensley's printing-office. The subject was afterwards re-engraved on a block of the same size by John Thompson.

The illustrations to an edition of Rogers's Poems, 1812, engraved from pen-and-ink drawings by Thomas Stothard, R.A., may be fairly ranked among the best of the wood-cuts engraved by Clennell. They are executed with the feeling of an artist, and are admirable representations of the original drawings.† Stothard himself was much pleased with them ; but he thought that when wood engravers attempted to express more than a copy of a pen-and-ink drawing, and introduced a variety of tints in the manner of copper-plate engravings, they exceeded the legitimate boundaries of the art. A hundred wood-cuts by Bewick, Nesbit, Clennell, and Thompson might, however, be produced to show that this opinion was not well founded.

Clennell, who drew beautifully in water-colours, made many of the drawings for the Border Antiquities ; and the encouragement which he received as a designer and painter made him resolve to entirely abandon wood engraving. With this view he laboured diligently to improve himself in painting, and in a short time made such progress that his pictures attracted the attention of the Directors of the British Institution. In 1814, the Earl of Bridgewater employed him to paint a large picture of the entertainment given to the Allied Sovereigns in the Guildhall by the city of London. He experienced great difficulty in obtaining sketches of the numerous distinguished persons whose portraits it was necessary to give in the picture ; and he lost much time, and suffered considerable anxiety, in procuring those preliminary materials for his work. Having at length completed his sketches, he began the picture, and had made considerable progress in it when, in April 1817, he suddenly became insane, and the work was interrupted.‡ It has

---

* The original cut is about ten inches and a half high, measured from the line below the inscription, by about thirteen inches and a half wide, measured across the centre.

† Several additional cuts of the same kind, engraved with no less ability by J. Thompson, were inserted in a subsequent edition.

‡ This painting was afterwards finished by E. Bird, R.A., who also became insane.

been said that his malady arose from intense application, and from anxiety respecting the success of his work. This, however, can scarcely be correct; he had surmounted his greatest difficulties, and was proceeding regularly and steadily with the painting, when he suddenly became deprived of his reason. One of his fellow-pupils when he was with Bewick, who was intimate with him, and was accustomed to see him frequently, never observed any previous symptom of insanity in his behaviour, and never heard him express any particular anxiety about the work on which he was engaged.

Within a short time after Clennell had lost his reason, his wife also became insane;* and the malady being accompanied by a fever, she after a short illness expired, leaving three young children to deplore the death of one parent and the confirmed insanity of the other. These most distressing circumstances excited the sympathy of several noblemen and gentlemen; and a committee having been appointed to consider of the best means of raising a fund for the support of Clennell's family, it was determined to publish by subscription an engraving from one of his pictures. The subject made choice of was the Decisive Charge of the Life Guards at Waterloo, for which Clennell had received a reward from the British Institution. It was engraved by Mr. W. Bromley, and published in 1821. The sum thus raised was, after paying for the engraving, vested in trustees for the benefit of Clennell's children, and for the purpose of providing a small annuity for himself.

Clennell, after having been confined for three or four years in a lunatic asylum in London, so far recovered that it was no longer necessary to keep him in a state of restraint. He was accordingly sent down to the North, and lived for several years in a state of harmless insanity with a relation in the neighbourhood of Newcastle; amusing himself with making drawings, engraving little wood-cuts, and occasionally writing *poetry*. Upwards of sixty of those drawings are now lying before me, displaying at once so much of his former genius and of his present imbecility that it is not possible to regard them, knowing whose they are, without a deep feeling of commiseration for his fate. He used occasionally to call on Bewick, and he once asked for a block to engrave. Bewick, to humour him, gave him a piece of wood, and left him to choose his own subject; and Clennell, on his next visit, brought with him the cut finished: it was like the attempt of a boy when first beginning to engrave, but he thought it one of the most successful of his productions in the art. The following specimens of his cuts and of his poetry were respectively engraved and written in 1828.

---

* Clennell's wife was a daughter of the late C. Warren, one of the best copper-plate engravers of his time.

SONG.

Good morning to you, Mary,
  It glads me much to see thee once again ;
What joy, since thee I've heard !
  Heaven such beauty ever deign,
          Mary of the vineyard !

THE EVENING STAR.

Look ! what is it, with twinkling light,
That brings such joy, serenely bright,
That turns the dusk again to light ?—
    'Tis the Evening Star !
What is it with purest ray,
That brings such peace at close of day,
That lights the traveller on his way ?—
    'Tis the Evening Star !
What is it, of purest holy ray,
That brings to man the promised day,
And peace ?—
    'Tis the Evening Star !

COMPENDIUM POETICA.

A drop of heaven's treasure, on an angel's wing,
Such heaven alone can bring ;—
The painted hues upon the rose,
In heaven's shower reposing,
Is an earthly treasure of such measure.
The butterfly, in his spell,
Upon the rosy prism doth dwell,
And as he doth fly, in his tour
From flower to flower,
Is seen for a while
Every care to beguile,
And so doth wing his little way,
A little fairy of the day !

A FLOWERET.

Where lengthened ray
Gildeth the bark upon her way ;
Where vision is lost in space,
    To trace,
As resting on a stile,
In ascent of half a mile—
It is when the birds do sing,
In the evening of the spring.
The broad shadow from the tree,
    Falling upon the slope,
You may see,
O'er flowery mead,
Where doth a pathway lead
    To the topmost ope—
The yellow butter-cup
    And purple crow-foot,
The waving grass up,

Rounding upon the but—
The spreading daisy
In the clover maze,
The wild rose upon the hedge-row,
And the honey-suckle blow
    For village girl
To dress her chaplet—
Or some youth, mayhap, let—
Or bind the linky trinket
    For some earl—
Or trim up in plaits her hair
With much seeming care,
As fancy may think it—
Or with spittle moisten,
Or half wink it,
Or to music inclined,
Or to sleep in the soft wind.

St. Peter's, August 1828.

L. C.

About 1831, Clennell having become much worse, his friends were again compelled to place him under restraint. He was accordingly conveyed to a lunatic asylum near Newcastle, where he is still living. Until within this last year or two, he continued to amuse himself with drawing and writing poetry, and perhaps may do so still. It is to be hoped that, though his condition appear miserable to us, he is not miserable himself ; that though deprived of the light of reason, he may yet enjoy imaginary pleasures of which we can form no conception; and that his confinement occasions to him

       " Small feeling of privation, none of pain." [*]

William Harvey, another distinguished pupil of Bewick, and one whose earlier engravings are only surpassed by his more recent productions as a designer on wood, was born at Newcastle-on-Tyne, 13th of July 1796. Having from an early age shown great fondness for drawing, he was at the age of fourteen apprenticed to Thomas Bewick to learn the art of engraving on wood.[†] In conjunction with his fellow-pupil, W. W. Temple, he engraved most of the cuts in Bewick's Fables, 1818 ; and as he excelled in drawing as well as in engraving, he was generally entrusted by Bewick to make the drawings on the block after Robert

---

[*] Clennell died in the Lunatic Asylum, Feb. 9, 1840, in his fifty-ninth year.

[†] Isaac Nicholson, now established as a wood engraver at Newcastle, was the apprentice immediately preceding Harvey. W. W. Temple, who abandoned the business on the expiration of his apprenticeship for that of a draper and silk-mercer, came to Bewick shortly after Harvey ; and the younger apprentice was John Armstrong.

Johnson's designs. One of the best cuts engraved by Harvey during his apprenticeship was a vignette for the title-page of a small work entitled "Cheviot: a Poetical Fragment," printed at Newcastle in 1817. This cut, which was also drawn by himself, is extremely beautiful both in design and execution; the trees and the foliage are in particular excellently represented; and as a small picturesque subject it is one of the best he ever engraved.

Harvey was a great favourite of Bewick, who presented him with a copy of the History of British Birds as a new year's gift on the 1st of January 1815, and at the same time addressed to him the following admonitory letter. Mr. Harvey is a distinguished artist, a kind son, an affectionate husband, a loving father, and in every relation of life a most amiable man: he has not, however, been exposed to any plots or conspiracies, nor been persecuted by envy and malice, as his master anticipated; but, on the contrary, his talents and his amiable character have procured for him public reputation and private esteem.

"Gateshead, 1st January, 1815.

"DEAR WILLIAM,

"I sent you last night the History of British Birds, which I beg your acceptance of as a new year's gift, and also as a token of my respect. Don't trouble yourself about thanking me for them; but, instead of doing so, let those books put you in mind of the duties you have to perform through life. Look at them (as long as they last) on every new year's day, and at the same time resolve, with the help of the all-wise but unknowable God, to conduct yourself on every occasion as becomes a good man.—Be a good son, a good brother, (and when the time comes) a good husband, a good father, and a good member of society. Peace of mind will then follow you like a shadow; and when your mind grows rich in integrity, you will fear the frowns of no man, and only smile at the plots and conspiracies which it is probable will be laid against you by envy, hatred, and malice.

"To William Harvey, jun. Westgate. *Thomas Bewick.*"

In September, 1817, Mr. Harvey came to London; and shortly afterwards, with a view of obtaining a correct knowledge of the principles of drawing, he became a pupil of Mr. B. R. Haydon, and he certainly could not have had a better master. While improving himself under Mr. Haydon, he drew and engraved from a picture by that eminent artist his large cut of the Death of Dentatus, which was published in 1821.*

---

* This cut is about fifteen inches high by about eleven inches and one quarter wide. It was engraved on a block consisting of seven different pieces, the joinings of which are apparent in impressions that have not been subsequently *touched* with Indian ink.

As a large subject, this is unquestionably one of the most elaborately engraved wood-cuts that has ever appeared. It scarcely, however, can be considered a successful specimen of the art; for though the execution in many parts be superior to anything of the kind, either of earlier or more recent times, the cut, as a whole, is rather an attempt to rival copper-plate engraving than a perfect specimen of engraving on wood, displaying the peculiar advantages and excellences of the art within its own legitimate bounds. More has been attempted than can be efficiently represented by means of wood engraving. The figure of Dentatus is indeed one of the finest specimens of the art that has ever been executed, and the other figures in the fore-ground display no less talent; but the rocks are of too uniform a *tone*, and some of the more distant figures appear to *stick* to each other. These defects, however, result from the very nature of the art, not from inability in the engraver; for all that wood engraving admits of he has effected. It is unnecessary to say more of this cut here: some observations relating to the details, illustrated with specimens of the best engraved parts, will be found in the next chapter.

About 1824 Mr. Harvey entirely gave up the practice of engraving, and has since exclusively devoted himself to designing for copper-plate and wood engravers. His designs engraved on copper are, however, few when compared with the immense number engraved on wood. The copper-plate engravings consist principally of the illustrations in a collected edition of Miss Edgeworth's Works, 1832; in Southey's edition of Cowper's Works, first published in 1836, and since by Mr. Bohn in his Standard Library; and in the small edition of Dr. Lingard's History of England.

The beautiful vignettes and tail-pieces in Dr. Henderson's History of Ancient and Modern Wines, 1824, drawn and engraved by Mr. Harvey, may be considered the ground-work of his reputation as a designer, and by the kindness of Dr. Henderson we are enabled (in this second edition) to present impressions of seven of them. The cuts in the first and second series of Northcote's Fables, 1828, 1833;* in the Tower Menagerie,

---

* What may be considered the sketches for the principal cuts were supplied by Northcote himself. The following account of the manner in which he *composed* them is extracted from a Sketch of his Life, prefixed to the second series of his Fables, 1833 :—" It was by a curious process that Mr. Northcote really made the designs for these Fables the amusement of his old age, for his talent as a draftsman, excelling as he did in animals, was rarely required by this undertaking. His general practice was to collect great numbers of prints of animals, and to cut them out ; he then moved such as he selected about upon the surface of a piece of paper until he had illustrated the fable by placing them to his satisfaction, and had thus composed his subject ; then fixing the different figures with paste to the paper, a few pen or pencil touches rendered this singular composition complete enough to place in the hands of Mr. Harvey, by whom it was adapted or freely translated on the blocks for the

1828 ; in the Gardens and Menagerie of the Zoological Society, 1831 ; and in Latrobe's Solace of Song, 1837, were all drawn by him.

SPECIMENS OF MR. HARVEY'S WOOD-ENGRAVING.

FROM DR. HENDERSON'S HISTORY OF ANCIENT AND MODERN WINES.

engravers."—Mr. Harvey's work was something more than free translation. He *completed* that which Northcote merely suggested. The tail-pieces and letters are all of Mr. Harvey's own invention and drawing.

Among the smaller works illustrated with wood-cuts, and published about the same time as the preceding, the following may be mentioned as containing beautiful specimens of his talents as a designer on wood: —The Blind Beggar of Bethnal Green ; The Children in the Wood ; A Story without an End, translated from the German by Mrs. Austin ;

and especially his one hundred and twenty beautiful designs for the Paradise Lost, and other poems of Milton, and his designs for Thomson's Seasons, from which two works we select four examples with the view of exhibiting at the same time the talents of the distinguished engravers, viz., John Thompson and Charles Gray. For various other

M M 2

works he has also furnished, in all, between three and four thousand

designs. As a designer on wood, he is decidedly superior to the

majority of artists of the present day; and to his excellence in this respect, wood engraving is chiefly indebted for the very great encouragement which it has of late received in this country.

The two cuts on pages 533 and 534 are also from drawings by Mr. Harvey; and both are printed from casts. The first is one of the illustrations of the Children in the Wood, published by Jennings and

Chaplin, 1831; and the subject is the uncle bargaining with the two ruffians for the murder of the children. This cut is freely and effectively executed, without any display of useless labour.

The second is one of the illustrations of the Blind Beggar of Bethnal Green, published by Jennings and Chaplin, in 1832. The subject represents the beggar's daughter and her four suitors, namely,—the gentleman of good degree, the gallant young knight in disguise, the merchant of London, and her master's son. This cut, though well engraved, is scarcely equal to the preceding. It is, however, necessary to observe that these cuts are not given as specimens of the engravers' talents, but merely as two subjects designed by Mr. Harvey.

What has been called the "London School" of wood engraving produced nothing that would bear a comparison with the works of

Bewick and his pupils until the late Robert Branston began to engrave on wood. About 1796, the best of the London engravers was J. Lee. He engraved the cuts for the "Cheap Repository," a collection of religious and moral tracts, printed between 1794 and 1798, and sold by J. Marshall, London, and S. Hazard, Bath. Those cuts, though coarsely executed, as might be expected, considering the work for which they were intended, frequently display considerable merit in the design ; and in this respect several of them are scarcely inferior to the cuts drawn and engraved by John Bewick in Dr. Trusler's Progress of Man and Society. Mr. Lee died in March, 1804; and on his decease, his apprentice, Henry White, went to Newcastle, and served out the remainder of his time with Thomas Bewick. James Lee, a son of Mr. J. Lee, the elder, is also a wood engraver; he executed the portraits in Hansard's Typographia, 1825.

Rob. Branston.

Robert Branston, like Bewick, acquired his knowledge of wood engraving without the instructions of a master. He was born at Lynn, in Norfolk, in 1778, and died in London in 1827. He served his apprenticeship to his father, a general copper-plate engraver and heraldic painter, who seems to have carried on the same kind of miscellaneous business as Mr. Beilby, the master of Bewick. About 1802 Mr. Branston came to London, and finding that wood engraving was much encouraged, he determined to apply himself to that art. Some of his first productions were cuts for lottery bills ; but as he improved in the practice of engraving on wood, he began to engrave cuts for the illustration of books. His style of engraving is peculiarly his own, and perfectly distinct from that of Bewick. He engraved human figures and in-door scenes with great clearness and precision ; while Bewick's chief excellence consisted in the natural representation of quadrupeds, birds, landscapes, and *road-side* incidents. In the representation of trees and of natural scenery, Branston has almost uniformly failed. Some of the best of his earlier productions are to be found in the History of England, published by Scholey, 1804—1810 ; in Bloomfield's Wild Flowers, 1806 ; and in a quarto volume entitled " Epistles in Verse," and other poems by George Marshall, 1812.

The best specimen of Mr. Branston's talents as a wood engraver is a large cut of the Cave of Despair, in Savage's Hints on Decorative Printing. It was executed in rivalry with Nesbit, who engraved the cut of Rinaldo and Armida for the same work, and it would be difficult to decide which is the best. Both are good specimens of the styles of their respective schools ; and the subjects are well adapted to display the peculiar excellence of the engravers. Had they exchanged subjects, neither of the cuts would have been so well executed ; but in this case there can be little doubt that Nesbit would have engraved the figure and the rocks in the Cave of Despair better than Branston would have engraved the trees and the foliage in the cut of Rinaldo and Armida. The cut on the previous page is a reduced copy of a portion of that of Mr. Branston.

Mr. Branston, like many others, did not think highly of the cuts in Bewick's Fables ; and feeling persuaded that he could produce something better, he employed Mr. Thurston to make several designs, with the intention of publishing a similar work. After a few of them had been engraved, he gave up the thought of proceeding further with the work, from a doubt of its success. Bewick's work was already in the market ; and it was questionable if another of the same kind, appearing shortly after, would meet with a sale adequate to defray the expense. The three cuts in the opposite page were engraved by Mr. Branston for the proposed work. The two first are respectively illustrations of the fables of Industry and Sloth, and of the Two Crabs ; the third was intended as a tail-piece. The cut of Industry and Sloth is certainly superior to that of the same subject in Bewick's Fables ; but that of the Two Crabs, though more delicately engraved, is not equal to the cut of the same subject in Bewick.

Mr. Branston also thought that Bewick's Birds were estimated too highly ; and he engraved two or three cuts to show that he could do the

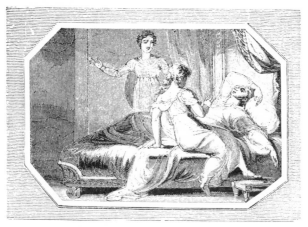

INDUSTRY AND SLOTH.—*Robert Branston.*

THE TWO CRABS.—*Robert Branston.*

TAIL-PIECE TO THE TWO CRABS.—*Robert Branston.*

same things as well, or better. In this respect, however, he certainly formed a wrong estimate of his abilities ; for, it is extremely doubtful if —even with the aid of the best designer he could find—he could have executed twenty cuts of birds which, for natural character, would bear a comparison with twenty of the worst engraved by Bewick himself. The great North-country man was an artist as well as a wood engraver ; and in this respect his principal pupils have also been distinguished. The cut on our present page is one of those engraved by Mr. Branston to show his superiority over Bewick. The bird represented is probably the Grey Phalarope, or Scallop-toed Sand-piper, and it is unquestionably executed with considerable ability ; but though Bewick's cut of the same bird be one of his worst, it is superior to that engraved by Mr. Branston in every essential point.

Between twenty and thirty years ago, a wood engraver named Austin executed several cuts, but did nothing to promote the art. William Hughes, a native of Liverpool, who died in February 1825, at the early age of thirty-two, produced a number of wood engravings of very considerable merit. He chiefly excelled in architectural subjects. One of his best productions is a dedication cut in the first volume of Johnson's Typographia, 1824, showing the interior of a chapel, surrounded by the arms of the members of the Roxburgh Club. Another artist of the same period, named Hugh Hughes, of whom scarcely anything is now known, executed a whole volume of singularly beautiful wood engravings, entitled " The Beauties of Cambria, consisting of Sixty Views in North and South Wales," London, 1823. The work was published by subscription at one guinea, or on India paper at two guineas, and was beautifully printed by the same John Johnson who printed William Hughes' cuts in the " Typographia," and who, a few years previously, had conducted the Lee Priory Press. The annexed four examples will give an idea of the high finish and perfection of this elegant series.

Hugh Hughes, del. et sc.

PISTILL CAIN.

Hugh Hughes, del. et sc.

MOEL FAMAU.

Hugh Hughes, del. et sc.

WREXHAM CHURCH.

Hugh Hughes, del. et sc.

PWLL CARADOC.

John Thompson,* one of the best English wood engravers of the present day, was a pupil of Mr. Branston. He not only excels, like his

SALMON.—*J. Thompson.*

GROUP OF FISH.—*J. Thompson.*

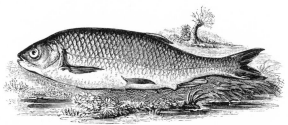

CHUB.—*J. Thompson.*

* Charles Thompson, the brother of John, is also a wood engraver. He resides at Paris, and his cuts are better known in France than in this country. Miss Eliza Thompson, a daughter of John Thompson, also engraves on wood.

master, in the engraving of human figures, but displays equal talent in the execution of all kinds of subjects. Among the very many excellent cuts which have been engraved in England within the last twenty years,

PIKE.—*R. Branston.*

those executed by John Thompson rank foremost. As he is rarely unequal to himself, it is rather difficult to point out any which are very

EEL.—*H. White.*

much superior to the others of his execution. The following, however, may be referred to as specimens of the general excellence of his cuts :— The title-page to Puckle's Club, 1817, and the cuts of Moroso, News-monger, Swearer, Wiseman, and Xantippe in the same work ; the Trout, the Tench, the Salmon, the Chub, and a group of small fish,* consisting

* The Salmon, Chub, and group of small fish are given on the preceding page from the actual cuts referred to.

of the Minnow, the Loach, the Bull-head, and the Stickle-back, in
Major's edition of Walton's Angler; * many of the cuts in Butler's
Hudibras, published by Baldwyn in 1819, and reprinted by Bohn, in
1859, of which we annex an example ; the portrait of Butler, prefixed

John Thompson.

to an edition of his Remains, published in 1827 ; and The Two Swine,
The Mole become a Connoisseur, Love and Friendship, and the portrait
of Northcote, in the second series of Northcote's Fables. One of his
latest cuts is the beautifully executed portrait of Milton and his
daughters, after a design by Mr. Harvey, already given at page 531.
The following cut—a reduced copy of one of the plates in the Rake's
Progress—by Mr. Thompson, engraved a few years ago for a projected
edition of Hogarth's Graphic Works, of which only about a dozen
cuts were completed, is one of the best specimens of the art that
has been executed in modern times. In the engraving of small

---

* Bewick was accustomed to speak highly of the cuts of fish in this beautiful work
(several of which are given on the previous pages) : the Salmon, engraved by J. Thompson,
and the Eel, by H. White, he especially admired. Among others scarcely less excellent
are the Pike, by R. Branston ; and the Carp, the Grayling, and the Ruffe, by H. White.
Major, in his second edition, went to great expense in substituting other engravings for most
of these, with the intention of surpassing all that, by the aid of artists, he had done before
—in which he to some extent succeeded. In this second edition, the Salmon is engraved
by John Jackson. All Mr. Major's wood-cuts, as well as many of Bewick's, having passed
into the hands of Henry G. Bohn (the present publisher), his edition of Walton's Angler
is extensively enriched by them.

cuts of this kind Mr. Thompson has never been surpassed; and it is
beyond the power of the art to effect more than what has here been
accomplished.

The English wood engravers, who next to Charlton Nesbit and
John Thompson seem best entitled to honourable mention, are:—
Samuel Williams ; * Thomas Williams ; Ebenezer Landells ; John Orrin
Smith ;* George Baxter ; Robert Branston ; Frederick W. Branston ;
Henry White, senior, and Henry White, junior ; Thomas Mosses ;*
Charles Gorway ; Samuel Slader ;* W. T. Green ; W. J. Linton ; John
Martin ; J. W. Whimper ; John Wright ; W. A. Folkard ; Charles
Gray ;* George Vasey ; John Byfield ;* John Jackson ;* Daniel Dodd,
and John Dodd, brothers.—William Henry Powis, who died in 1836,
aged 28, was one of the best wood engravers of his time. Several
beautiful cuts executed by him are to be found in Martin and Westall's
Pictorial Illustrations of the Bible, 1833, and in an edition of Scott's
Bible, 1834 ; both works now published by Mr. Bohn. The following
examples, principally taken from Martin and Westall's Illustrations,
will exemplify the talents of a few of the distinguished artists above
mentioned. It would swell the book beyond its limits to give more,
otherwise we might select from the same work, which contains one
hundred and forty engravings, by all the principal wood engravers of
the day.

---

* All the engravers to whose names an asterisk is added are now deceased.

JOHN MARTIN

JOHN JACKSON

The above cut was engraved by Mr. John Jackson in 1833. Abundant evidences of the versatility of his xylographic talent, are scattered throughout the present volume, of which, though not the author in a literary sense, he was at least the conductor and proprietor. Among the subjects pointed out by Mr. Chatto as engraved by Mr. Jackson, those on pages 473, 495, 496, 512, 605, 614, deserve to be mentioned.

JOHN MARTIN

F. W. BRANSTON

Mr. F. W. Branston, brother of Mr. Robert Branston, has long been known as one of our best engravers, as the annexed Specimen will shew.

JOHN MARTIN   E. LANDELLS

MR. EBENEZER LANDELLS, the engraver of this beautiful cut, has quite recently been lost to us. He was projector, and for a long time proprietor, of The Ladies' Illustrated Newspaper, and has engraved an immense number of subjects of all classes.

JOHN MARTIN   W. H. POWIS

The talented engraver of the present subject has already been named, with commendation, at page 544. We learn that the sum paid him for engraving it was fifteen guineas, being three guineas more than the average price. Mr. Wm. Bagg, now a successful draftsman of anatomical subjects, made this and all the other drawings on the blocks at the rate of five guineas each, and Mr. John Martin had ten guineas each for the designs. As the volume contains 144 subjects it must have cost the projectors, Messrs. Bull and Churton, upwards of four thousand guineas : it may now be bought for a dozen shillings.

JOHN MARTIN   THOS. WILLIAMS

MR. THOMAS WILLIAMS ranks high as an engraver on wood, and the illustrated works of the last twenty years teem with his performances. Some of the engravings in the Merrie Days of England, 1859, are by him.

JOHN MARTIN   W. T. GREEN

The only other Illustration which we shall take from Martin and Westall's Bible Prints is the above, engraved by Mr. W. T. Green, who continues to exercise his burin with great skill, and has recently engraved one of the plates in Merrie Days of England, and Favourite English Poems, and several of Maclise's designs for Tennyson's Princess.

To this is added, as a vignette finish to the chapter, an engraving recently executed by him for an illustrated edition of Milton's Paradise Lost, now published in Bohn's Library, and already mentioned at page 531.

One of the principal wood engravers in Germany, about the time that Bewick began to practise the art in England, was Unger. In 1779 he published a tract, containing five cuts of his own engraving, discussing the question whether Albert Durer actually engraved on wood : his decision is in the negative. In the same year, his son also published a dissertation, illustrated with wood-cuts, on the progress of wood engraving in Brandenburg, with an account of the principal books containing wood-cuts printed in that part of Prussia. They jointly executed some chiaro-scuros, and a number of trifling book-illustrations such as are to be found in Heineken's Idée Générale d'une Collection complette d'Estampes. These cuts are of a very inferior character. Gubitz, a German wood engraver, who flourished about thirty years ago, executed several cuts which are much superior to any I have seen by the Ungers. Several of those engraved by Gubitz, bear considerable resemblance to the cuts of Bewick. The principal French wood engravers in the eighteenth century, subsequent to Papillon, were Gritner and Beugnet ; but neither of them produced anything superior to the worst of the cuts to be found in the work of Papillon. With them wood engraving in France rather declined than advanced. Of late years the art has made great progress both in Germany and France ; and should the taste for wood-cuts continue to increase in those countries, their engravers may regain for the art that popularity which it enjoyed in former times, when Nuremberg and Lyons were the great marts for works illustrated with wood engravings.

W. HARVEY   W T. GREEN

CHAPTER VIII.

ARTISTS AND ENGRAVERS ON WOOD OF THE PRESENT DAY.

THE present chapter, which is additional to the former edition, had not been contemplated until the previous pages were printed off. But it was then suggested to the publisher, by one who was able and willing to co-operate in the object, that although the book was intended to be merely an improved reprint of what had been given before, a short chapter might advantageously be added respecting those Artists of the present day who were omitted by Jackson, or have risen to eminence since his time.

Applications in the form of a circular were accordingly issued, and have resulted in the Specimens now presented. They must speak for themselves, it not being within the province of the publisher to pronounce as to their respective merits. Besides which, the art of wood-engraving, owing to the enormous impulse given to it during the last twenty years, has attained such a pitch of excellence, that it would be somewhat difficult to determine who, if sufficiently stimulated, could produce the most perfect work. Artists in Wood, like Artists in Oil, have their specialties, and excel relatively in Landscape, Cattle, or Figure drawing; Architecture, Natural History, Diagrams, or Humour. But though each may acquire distinction in the department which choice or accident has assigned him, some can undertake all departments equally well. In saying this we refer to engraving rather than designing, for Harrison Weir would hardly undertake Architecture; Orlando Jewitt, Animals; or George Cruikshank, Mathematical Diagrams.

When, with the age of Bewick, wood-engraving began to reassume its importance for book illustration, both designing and engraving were generally performed by the same hand; but, in the present day, the professions are becoming too important to be joined, and those who, like William Harvey, Samuel Williams, and others, commenced by practising both, now, recognising the modern policy of a division of labour, confine themselves with few exceptions to one. Our business here, so far as designs are concerned, is almost limited to those draughtsmen who habitually draw on wood, for it is unnecessary to say that every drawing or painting may be transferred to wood by the practical operator.

The following Specimens are given in accidental order rather than with any notion of precedence or classification.

PERCIVAL SKELTON   JAMES COOPER

THE SIERRA MORENA.

The present and following specimens are engraved by JAMES COOPER.
The first one is from Mr. Murray's illustrated edition of Childe Harold,
published in 1859, which contains eighty engravings, all designed by
Mr. Percival Skelton ; the others from the Select Poems and Songs of
Robert Burns, published by Kent & Co. in 1858.   Mr. Cooper is favourably known to the artistic world by his engravings in Rhymes and
Roundelayes, a volume to which we shall presently refer again ; Poetry
and Pictures from Thomas Moore, Longmans, 1858 ; The Merrie Days
of England, 1859 ; Favourite English Poems, 1858 ; and Bloomfield's
Farmer's Boy, 1858—mostly after designs by Birket Foster, and all
produced under the superintendence of Mr. Joseph Cundall.

BIRKET FOSTER

JAMES COOPER

BANKS OF THE NITH.
BURNS' POEMS.

HARRISON WEIR

JAMES COOPER

THE TWA DOGS.
BURNS' POEMS

HARRISON WEIR   JAMES COOPER

TO AULD MARE MAGGIE.
BURNS' POEMS.

This and the preceding three specimens complete what we have to adduce of Mr. Cooper's engraving: the designers will be spoken of in subsequent pages.

HARRISON WEIR   J. GREENAWAY

THE POETRY OF NATURE.

MR. HARRISON WEIR is distinguished for his spirited drawings of animals and rural landscapes, as will be seen in the annexed examples, which are engraved by W. Wright (formerly with Vizetelly) and John Greenaway. He has contributed to most of the popular works of recent date, in which animals form a feature. Among them may be named : The Poetry of the Year ; Poems and Songs by Robert Burns ; Poetry and Pictures from Thomas Moore ; Favourite English Poems ; Barry Cornwall's Dramatic Scenes and Poems ; Fable Book for Children ; James Montgomery's Poems, 1860, and Wood's Natural History.

o o *

HARRISON WEIR   W. WRIGHT

BLOOMFIELD'S FARMER'S BOY.

HARRISON WEIR   GREENAWAY

CAMPBELL'S PLEASURES OF HOPE.

HARRISON WEIR   J. GREENAWAY

Both this and the specimen on the preceding page are from the illustrated edition of Campbell's Pleasures of Hope, of which all the plates are engraved by MR. JOHN GREENAWAY.

Mr. Greenaway has contributed to many other of the illustrated publications of the present day, and among them to the Poetry of Nature, edited by Mr. J. Cundall, with thirty-six cuts all designed by Harrison Weir. Low and Son, 1860. Bloomfield's Farmer's Boy, 1858 ; Favourite English Ballads, 1859.

BIRKET FOSTER

E. EVANS S^c

EDMUND EVANS

WILD FLOWERS.

Engraved by EDMUND EVANS from a design by Birket Foster for
Rhymes and Roundelayes, published by Mr. Bogue in 1857, and since
by Messrs. Routledge. Mr. Evans has likewise engraved the Landscapes
in Cowper's Task, after designs by the same artist, Herbert's Poetical
Works, and Graham's Sabbath, all published by Nisbet & Co.; the
Landscapes in Scott's Lay of the Last Minstrel, and Marmion, published
by Adam Black & Co.; many of the subjects in Poems and Songs by
Robert Burns, from which we have given several specimens, The
Merrie Days of England, &c.; and all the illustrations in Goldsmith's
Poetical Works, which are printed in Colours by himself.

BIRKET FOSTER   W. J. PALMER

LAYS OF THE HOLY LAND.

Engraved by W. J. PALMER, after a design by Birket Foster, for Lays of the Holy Land, published by Nisbet & Co. Mr. Palmer has also contributed to the Illustrated edition of Thomson's Seasons, The Merchant of Venice, Gray's Poems, published by Low and Son ; The Merrie Days of England, Kent & Co., and other pictorial works, chiefly after the designs of Birket Foster, and under the superintendence of Mr. Cundall.

Although several specimens have already been given of Birket Foster's powers of design, in speaking of the engravers, we give another, one of his earliest, that we may have occasion to say something of himself.

BIRKET FOSTER   H. VIZETELLY

EVANGELINE.

MR. BIRKET FOSTER was a pupil of Mr. Landells, who, discerning his artistic talent, employed him from an early age in the superior department of his profession. After he commenced on his own account, his first important illustrations were for Longfellow's Poetical Works, of which the above is a specimen. He has since partly or wholly illustrated, besides those works already mentioned under the name of the engraver, Adams's Allegories, published by Messrs. Rivington; The Book of Favourite Modern Ballads, Poets of the Nineteenth Century, Christmas with the Poets, Favourite English Poems, Home Affections, The Merrie Days of England, Barry Cornwall's Dramatic Scenes and Poems, Southey's Life of Nelson, Gosse's Rivers of the Bible, and many other of the best works of the period. In 1859 he was elected a member of the Old Water Colour Society, and has since then devoted himself almost exclusively, and with great success, to painting in Water Colours.

JOHN TENNIEL   DALZIEL

MR. JOHN TENNIEL is a successful illustrator of Historical subjects, and Ballad poetry, and has produced many fine examples of his pencil. His most recent work is a series of sixty-nine designs for the illustrated edition of Moore's Lalla Rookh, engraved by the Messrs. Dalziel, which the "Times" of Nov. 1, 1860, calls the "greatest illustrative achievement of any single hand," and of which we here present an example. He is now engaged in illustrating Shirley Brooks' story called The Silver Cord, in "Once a Week;" and in 1857 he contributed a number of spirited designs to the illustrated edition of Barry Cornwall's Poetical Works. Among Mr. Tenniel's earlier works are several in the Book of British Ballads, edited by Samuel Carter Hall, in 1843; and among his popular designs, sketched with a free pencil, are his large cuts in "Punch," and his small ones in Punch's Pocket Book.

DEATH OF SFORZA.

SFORZA.

Both these examples are from Barry Cornwall's dramatic sketch, entitled Ludovico Sforza, published in the illustrated edition of his Poems.

JOHN GILBERT.   DALZIEL BROTHERS.

ANTONY AND CLEOPATRA.

Engraved by MESSRS. DALZIEL, BROTHERS, after the designs of MR. JOHN GILBERT. These highly appreciated Artists appear together in a considerable number of the illustrated publications of the present day. Messrs. Dalziel are among the most extensive of our wood-engravers, and have taken part in all the illustrated works of importance which have been produced during the last twenty years. Among the recent ones are:—Staunton's Illustrated Shakspeare, from which the above specimen is taken, and Longfellow's Poems, Routledge, 1859; Barry Cornwall's Dramatic Scenes and Poems, with fifty-seven wood-engravings, published by Chapman and Hall in 1857, now republished by Henry G. Bohn; and Tennyson's Princess, after drawings by Maclise. These artists are at present engaged in engraving Millais' Designs in the "Cornhill Magazine."

THOMAS DALZIEL

DALZIEL, BROTHERS

THE FLORENTINE PARTY.

The present engraving, executed by the Brothers Dalziel, for Barry Cornwall's Poems, gives a pleasing example of Mr. Thomas Dalziel's drawing.

The next two are early designs by Mr. John Gilbert. The first is from the Percy Tales of the Kings of England, originally published in 1840, by Mr. Cundall, and since by Henry G. Bohn; the other from Maxwell's Life of the Duke of Wellington, in which there are upwards of one hundred similar vignettes, originally published in 1840, by Messrs. Baily, Brothers.

JOHN GILBERT   KIRCHNER

PRINCE ARTHUR AND HUBERT DE BOURG.
FROM PERCY TALES OF THE KINGS OF ENGLAND.

JOHN GILBERT

W. A. FOLKARD.

THE DEMON LOVER.

JOHN GILBERT.

We have here, engraved by MR. W. A. FOLKARD, another of the early designs of MR. JOHN GILBERT. It is one of the illustrations to the Book of English Ballads, edited by S. C. Hall, in 1843, which contains upwards of four hundred wood-engravings, and was the first work of any consequence that presented a combination of the best artists of the time. Indeed, it was the leader in what may be called the Illustrated Christmas Books of the present day. Since this period, Mr. Gilbert has probably produced more drawings on wood than any other artist, and has contributed to almost every illustrated book of any importance. He is a member of the Old Water Colour Society, and has sent many fine drawings to the Exhibition.

G. H. THOMAS   W. L. THOMAS

FROM HIAWATHA.

WILLIAM L. THOMAS deserves to rank among the foremost of our wood-engravers, as will be seen by the present specimen. He engraved most of the subjects to Hiawatha, all of which were drawn by his brother George H. THOMAS, and are now included in Bohn's Illustrated edition of Longfellow's Works; many of Mr. Maclise's masterly designs for Tennyson's Princess, and all the subjects for the Boys' Book of Ballads, from drawings by John Gilbert. They have also contributed, separately or together, to the Book of Favourite Modern Ballads, Poetry and Pictures from Thomas Moore, Burns' Poems, The Merrie Days of England, Favourite English Poems, and many other illustrated works.

GEORGE H. THOMAS   HORACE HARRAL

HIAWATHA.

Engraved by HORACE HARRAL (a pupil of the late John Orrin Smith), after a design by George Thomas, for the illustrated edition of Longfellow's Poems, formerly published in detached portions by Kent & Co., and now completely by H. G. Bohn. These artists have also contributed to the illustrated editions of Coleridge's Ancient Mariner, Burns' Poems, Campbell's Pleasures of Hope, the Merchant of Venice, and The Merrie Days of England; also to the

DALZIELS

Poetry and Pictures from Thomas Moore. Mr. George Thomas, who has long ranked as one of our best draughtsmen of figure subjects, has of late turned his attention almost exclusively to painting in oils, and is a successful exhibitor.

G. H. THOMAS   E. EVANS

JOHN ANDERSON MY JO.
BURNS' POEMS.

G. H. THOMAS   E. EVANS

These pleasing specimens conclude our examples of the drawing of Mr. George Henry Thomas. Of Mr. Evans the engraver we have already spoken.

D. MACLISE   W. THOMAS

FROM TENNYSON'S PRINCESS

The illustrated volume from which this is taken has twenty-six illustrations, engraved by W. Thomas, W. T. Green, E. Williams, and Dalziel, Brothers. Miss E. Williams is a daughter of the late talented Samuel Williams.

I. MACLISE, R.A.   LEONORA   J. THOMPSON

Here is another Design by MR. D. MACLISE, R.A., who in his own
peculiar manner has furnished drawings on wood for several finely
illustrated publications, among which may be enumerated Longman's
edition of the Poems and Songs of Thomas Moore, and especially
Tennyson's Princess, of which we have given an example on a previous
page. The present is the smallest of a series of designs engraved by
Mr. John Thompson, for that stirring Ballad, Bürger's Leonora.

PERCIVAL SKELTON   CHILDE HAROLD.   J. W. WHYMPER

MR. PERCIVAL SKELTON has been mentioned incidentally on a previous page, and we should have given in addition a fine example of his
pencil from the Book of Favourite Modern Ballads, but the plate is too
large. This present small specimen is to introduce the name of MR.
J. W. WHYMPER, who has been concerned in many of the illustrated
publications of the last thirty years, and especially those published by
the Christian Knowledge Society.

CLARKSON STANFIELD, R.A.   H. VIZETELLY

ANDERSON READING THE BIBLE TO JACK.

MR. HENRY VIZETELLY has been so indefatigable for the last twenty years in producing illustrated works in every department, that examples of his wood engraving are extensively distributed. He is besides a printer, well skilled in bringing up wood-cuts, which is a most delicate and artistic process. All the engravings in Miller's Boy's Country Year Book, and the Book of Wonderful Inventions, are engraved by him, or under his direction, as are also most of the charming series of designs made by CLARKSON STANFIELD, R.A. for Marryat's Poor Jack, of which the annexed is a specimen; many of the plates in Bohn's illustrated edition of Longfellow's Poems; and the entire series of Christmas with the Poets, fifty-three subjects, printed in tints by himself.

BIRKET FOSTER   H. VIZETELLY

CHRISTMAS IN THE OLDEN TIME.

We here present a specimen of a series of engravings executed by Mr. Vizetelly, for a work projected by the late Mr. Bogue, and yet unpublished.

SAMUEL WILLIAMS (recently deceased) deserves a conspicuous niche in the Walhalla of Artists for his forty-eight beautiful illustrations of Thomson's Seasons, all drawn and engraved by himself. The annexed

specimens selected from that volume (now about to be published by Mr. Bohn in his Illustrated Library) will give a fair example of his peculiar taste in the miniature treatment of rural subjects.

JOHN WOLF

G. PEARSON

EAGLES, STAGS AND WOLVES.

This and the following engraving were executed by MR. GEORGE PEARSON, a rising artist, after drawings made by JOHN WOLF, for the illustrations of T. W. Atkinson's Travels in the Region of the Upper and Lower Amoor (in Eastern Asia). Mr. Wolf, like Mr. Harrison Weir, has a preference for animal drawing, and excels in it.

JOHN WOLF   G. PEARSON

HARE HAWKING.

This well-executed cut of Hare Hawking is from Messrs. Freeman and Salvin's Work on Falconry, recently published by Messrs. Longman.

Mr. Pearson has lately been engaged in engraving Icthyological subjects for Hartwig's Sea and its Living Wonders, and some other works of Natural History, a department which he is cultivating by preference.

FALLS OF NIAGARA.   G. PEARSON

The Vignette by the same engraver is one of the Illustrations of Bohn's Pictorial Hand-book of Geography just published.

H. ANELAY   MEASOM

FROM SANDFORD AND MERTON.

Mr. H. Anelay is well known to the public as a draughtsman on wood, especially in the departments of portrait and figure drawing. The present example, taken from Bohn's Illustrated edition of Sandford and Merton, is engraved by Mr. Measom, whose practice is extensive and of long standing. Several of the figure subjects in Merrie Days of England, recently published by Kent and Co., and in Favourite English Poems, published by Low and Co. are by him.

JOHN ABSOLON   THOMAS BOLTON

MILES STANDISH.

Mr. J. Absolon has for many years been an illustrator of popular
story books and poems, most of which have been published or edited
by Mr. Cundall.   Among them may be named, Favourite English
Poems, published by Low and Co., in 1859; Rhymes and Roundelayes,
Routledge, 1858; Goldsmith's Poetical Works; and Lockhart's Spanish
Ballads, published by Murray.   The present specimen is from Bohn's
Illustrated edition of Longfellow's Poems, in which the Miles Standish
is chiefly illustrated by the designs of Mr. Absolon, and entirely engraved
by Mr. Thomas Bolton, an artist of considerable repute, whose name
appears in many of the books quoted in these pages, and among others,
in the Poems and Songs of Robert Burns.

Mr. Bolton has just invented a process by which the powers of
photography may be applied direct to the production of subjects from
nature or art on wood, and from which the engraving can be made without the intervention of drawing.   We annex his first specimen; others
are about to appear in the illustrated edition of Miss Winkworth's
Lyra Germanica.

FLAXMAN

THOMAS BOLTON

This specimen of MR. BOLTON's new process is taken from the well-known relief of Flaxman, *"Deliver us from evil."* It is one of the first successful photographs on wood, and was printed and engraved by MR. THOMAS BOLTON, from Mr. Leighton's negative.

R R *

R. DOYLE   JOHN SWAIN

MONTALVA'S FAIRY TALES.

MR. RICHARD DOYLE's manner of drawing is fairly exemplified in the present engraving, executed by him for Montalva's Fairy Tales of all Nations, published by Chapman & Hall in 1859. Mr. Doyle has illustrated a considerable number of books of a popular character, among which may be named: The Scouring of the White Horse; The Newcomes; The Continental Tour of Brown, Jones, and Robinson, of which we give an example on the next page; Manners and Customs of the English: and Pips' Diary.

RICHARD DOYLE   JOHN SWAIN

BROWN, JONES, AND ROBINSON IN VENICE.

Mr. Doyle's "Foreign Tour of Brown, Jones, and Robinson, what they saw and did in Belgium, Germany, Switzerland, and Italy," published in 1855, has acquired great popularity among the lovers of comic literature, and by the kindness of the publishers, Messrs. Bradbury and Evans, we are enabled to give a specimen.

JOHN LEECH   ORRIN SMITH

FROM UNCLE TOM'S CABIN.

Mr. JOHN LEECH is so well known to every reader of "Punch," that we need hardly do more here than merely mention his name as one of the best and most extensive of our graphic humorists.

Among the many books to which he has contributed are: The Comic History of England; Comic History of Rome; Comic Aspects of English Social Life; Tour in Ireland; Soapy Sponge's Sporting Tour; Young Troublesome; Mr. Jorrocks' Hunt; Punch's Almanack; and several editions of Uncle Tom's Cabin, from one of which (our own) the above specimen is taken, drawn, as we have reason to believe, in the course of two or three hours.

JOHN LEECH   JOHN SWAIN

PEASANTRY ON THEIR WAY TO AN IRISH FAIR.

TOUR IN IRELAND.

Another specimen of Mr. Leech's comic humour, taken from his Tour in Ireland, published at the Punch Office.

JOHN LEIGHTON   HENRY LEIGHTON

HASTEN AT LEISURE.

We here present a specimen of that curious work, "Moral Emblems of all Ages and Nations," published by Messrs. Longman & Co. The whole book has been drawn after the originals and superintended throughout by MR. JOHN LEIGHTON, who is well known under his pseudonyme of "Luke Limner." The engraving is by HENRY LEIGHTON.

THE BLOWING UP OF
L'ORIENT.

EDWARD DUNCAN   HORACE HARRAL

EDWARD DUNCAN, a member of the Old Water Colour Society, often draws on wood, especially Landscapes and Naval subjects. He has contributed to the Book of Favourite Modern Ballads, Favourite Englis Poems, Rhymes and Roundelayes, Poetry and Pictures from Thomas Moore, the Soldier's Dream, and Lays of the Holy Land.

E. DUNCAN   H. HARRAL

These two examples of his style are engraved by HORACE HARRAL for Bohn's Illustrated edition of Southey's Life of Nelson.

O. JEWITT

NORTH PORCH OF STA. MARIA MAGGIORE, BERGAMO.

The wood-engravings in the present and following pages are by
MR. ORLANDO JEWITT, who devotes himself almost exclusively to
Gothic Architecture and Ornament, in which he is pre-eminent. He
is one of the very few who continue to combine designing and drawing

with engraving. The first specimen here presented is from Street's
Brick and Marble Architecture of Italy in the Middle Ages, 8vo., published by Mr. Murray in 1855.

SHRINE IN BAYEUX CATHEDRAL.

Our second specimen, and two of those on the next page, are from
Mr. Pugin's splendid work, the "Glossary of Ecclesiastical Ornament,"
published by Henry G. Bohn in 1846.

HEARSE OF MARGARET, COUNTESS OF WARWICK.

CAPITAL OF THE PRESBYTERY, LINCOLN CATHEDRAL.

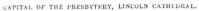

SPECIMENS OF ENGRAVING BY ORLANDO JEWITT.

●. JEWITT, del. et sc.

BRICK TRACERY, ST. STEPHEN'S CHURCH, TANGERMUNDE, PRUSSIA.
Unpublished.

Among the many works to which Mr. Jewitt has contributed, besides those already mentioned, are Bloxam's first principles of Gothic Architecture; the Glossary of Architecture published by Mr. Parker of Oxford; Rickman's Gothic Architecture, fifth edition; and the Baptismal Fonts, published by Mr. Van Voorst. He is now engaged in drawing and engraving Murray's Handbook of English Cathedrals.

THE NUT BROWN MAID.

T. CRESWICK   J. WILLIAMS

Mr. CRESWICK, R.A. the distinguished painter, has occasionally drawn on wood, but more as a favour than part of his *métier*. The present specimen, one of a series contributed to the Book of British Ballads, is so highly praised by Mr. Ruskin, and at the same time so elaborately criticised, that we think it in place to quote his words. After comparing him advantageously with Poussin, he proceeds to say, "Who with one thought or memory of nature in his heart could look at the two landscapes, and receive Poussin's with ordinary patience? Take Creswick in black and white, where he is unembarrassed by his fondness for pea-green, the illustrations, for instance, to the *Nut-Brown Maid*, in the Book of English Ballads. Look at the intricacy and fulness of the dark oak foliage, where it bends over the brook; see how you can go through it, and into it, and come out behind it, to the quiet bit of sky. Observe the grey aërial transparency of the stunted copse on the left, and the entangling of the boughs where the light near foliage detaches itself. Above all, note the forms of the masses of light. Not things like scales or shells, sharp at the edge, and flat in the middle, but irregular and rounded, stealing in and out accidentally from the shadow, and presenting in general outline, as the masses of all trees do, a resemblance to the specific forms of the leaves of which they are composed. Turn over the page, and look into the weaving of the foliage and sprays against the dark-night-sky, how near they are, yet how untraceable; see how the moonlight creeps up underneath them, trembling and shivering on the silver boughs above; note also, the descending bit of ivy, on the left, of which only a few leaves are made out, and the rest is confusion, or tells only in the moonlight like faint flakes of snow.

"But nature observes another principle in her foliage, more important even than its intricacy. She always secures an exceeding harmony and repose. She is so intricate that her minuteness of parts becomes to the eye, at a little, one united veil or cloud of leaves, to destroy the evenness of which is perhaps a greater fault than to destroy its transparency. Look at Creswick's oak again, in its dark parts. Intricate as it is, all is blended into a cloud-like harmony of shade, which becomes fainter and fainter as it retires, with the most delicate flatness and unity of tone. And it is by this kind of vaporescence, so to speak, by this flat misty unison of parts, that nature and her faithful followers are enabled to keep the eye in perfect repose in the midst of profusion, and to display beauty of form wherever they choose, to the greatest possible advantage, by throwing it across some quiet visionary passage of dimness and rest."

Mr. Creswick has recently contributed several vignettes to Tennyson's Poems. The following, engraved by MASON JACKSON, is from Bohn's Illustrated edition of Walton's Angler, to which Mr. Creswick has contributed several others.

CRESWICK   MASON JACKSON

JOHN MARTIN   W. J. LINTON

MR. W. J. LINTON has for many years had extensive practice both as a draughtsman and an engraver on wood, and still continues to combine both professions. The specimens on the present page shew his early work; the first is after a drawing by John Martin from the series of Bible Prints before quoted; the second, a vignette after McIAN, from the Book of British Ballads.

R. R. McIAN   W. J. LINTON

His later work is beautifully exemplified on the opposite page by the subject called Death's Door, after a drawing by that remarkable man WILLIAM BLAKE, of whom some account will be found at p. 632. It was published in the Art Union Volume of 1859, and is by the kindness of the Council of that Society inserted here.

To complete this page we annex two other of Mr. Linton's late works. They are taken from Milton's L'Allegro, published by Low & Co.

STONHOUSE   W. J. LINTON
"SHALLOW BROOKS AND RIVERS WIDE."

Many of the illustrated books of the last twenty years exhibit the talents of Mr. Linton. We may name, besides the Book of Ballads, The Pictorial Tour of the Thames, The Merrie Days of England, 1859, Burns' Poems and Songs, Favourite English Poems, 1859, Shakspere's Birthplace, and the Illustrated edition of Milton's Poetical Works formerly published by Kent & Co. and now in Bohn's Illustrated Library.

J. C. HORSLEY, A.R.A.   W. J. LINTON
"SUCH AS THE MELTING SOUL MAY PIERCE."

F. W. FAIRHOLT

MR. F. W. FAIRHOLT is distinguished for his knowledge of Costume and Mediæval art, which he has exemplified in a considerable number of shaded outlines, mostly drawn and engraved by himself. The wood-engraving at the head of this page is from the Archæological Album published in 1845, under the auspices of the British Archæological Association, to whose journal Mr. Fairholt has contributed largely. Ten of the subjects in the Book of British Ballads, illustrative of the Story of Sir Andrew Barton, are designed by him and give a favourable specimen of his drawing. They are cleverly engraved by T. Armstrong.

The Vignette is from the illustrated edition of Robin Hood, edited by Mr. J. M. Gutch in 1847. Mr. Fairholt has also edited and illustrated a volume on the Costume of England; a History of Tobacco, published by Messrs. Chapman & Hall; and the Translation of Labarte's Arts of the Middle Ages, published by Mr. Murray.

F. W. FAIRHOLT

MR. JOSEPH DINKEL is a very accurate draughtsman of subjects of Natural History, especially of Fossil remains; but though he has most practice in this department, he also undertakes Architectural and Engineering drawings. The present specimens are skilfully engraved by MR. JAMES LEE. Nearly all the drawings of the great work of

JOSEPH DINKEL   JAMES LEE

SHELL-LIMESTONE FROM THE MOUTH OF THE THAMES.
From Dr. Mantell's Geological Work, Medals of Creation.

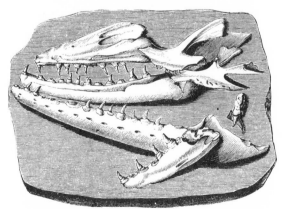

JOSEPH DINKEL   JAMES LEE

MOSASAURUS HOFMANNI.
From Dr. Mantell's Petrifactions and their Teachings.

Professor Agassiz, 'Poissons Fossiles,' published at Neuchatel, from 1833 to 1843, were executed by Mr. Dinkel; and he drew almost exclusively for the late Dr. Mantell. He is now much employed by Professor Owen; Thomas Bell, Esq. President of the Linnæan Society; and the Royal, Geological, and Palæontological Societies.

E. H. WEHNERT   HORACE HARRAL.

FROM COLERIDGE'S ANCIENT MARINER.

EDWARD H. WEHNERT, a member of the New Society of Painters in Water Colours, frequently draws upon wood. He illustrated Coleridge's Ancient Mariner, Grimm's Tales, Eve of St. Agnes, and contributed designs to Bohn's edition of Longfellow's Poems and to many other popular works of poetry and fiction. His style is essentially German. He has recently contributed thirty-four subjects to the Favourite English Poems and completed a number of drawings for Andersen's Tales, the electrotypes of which are produced by a new process by Mr. W. J. Linton.

GEORGE CRUIKSHANK is especially celebrated for the felicitous humour which he throws into every subject that comes under his pencil or burin. His works are legion and all highly prized, but his designs on wood are much less numerous than his etchings on copper. Mr. Ruskin, in his 'Modern Painters,' has lately expatiated as enthusiastically on the artistic merits of Mr. Cruikshank as he has done on those of Mr. Creswick, quoted by us in a previous page. He concludes by saying: "Taken all in all, the works of Cruikshank have the most sterling value of any belonging to this class produced in England." The present examples, taken from his 'Three Courses and a Dessert,' published in Bohn's Illustrated Library, will afford some idea of his peculiar talent. On the following page we give examples of his early work, being illustrations contributed to the 'Universal Songster,' a once popular work to which other artists including his late brother Robert

GEORGE CRUIKSHANK.

THE OLD COMMODORE.

Cruikshank also contributed. The engraver, rather a coarse hand, was
J. R. Marshall.

GEORGE CRUIKSHANK

GILES SCROGGINS AND MOLLY BROWN.

ALFRED CROWQUILL

THE MAN WHO WISHED TO BE TALLER.

ALFRED CROWQUILL

THE WOMAN WHO WISHED TO BE YOUNGER.

ALFRED CROWQUILL

DRINKING IS A VICE THAT LOWERS A MAN.

KENNY MEADOWS

Our last page of illustrations is devoted to humour. Three of the subjects are from the Pictorial Grammar, by ALFRED CROWQUILL (*i.e.* A. Forester), the fourth, a design by KENNY MEADOWS (from the Book of British Ballads), one of his early productions, but unsurpassed by anything he has since done.

These artists have in former years illustrated a number of books. Among Crowquill's may be named eight subjects to the Book of British Ballads. His latest work is ' The Adventures of Gooroo Simple and his Five Disciples.'

Among those by Kenny Meadows, we remember as his best an illustrated edition of Shakespeare, in three vols. royal 8vo. originally published by Mr. Tyas. London, 1843.

The Publisher here concludes his additional chapter; not for want of material, for he has more than enough to fill another volume, but for want of space. In endeavouring to give some indication of xylographic art-progress in England, he has made no attempt at completeness, and has said nothing whatever of foreign art, which has progressed quite as rapidly as our own. So much remains to be done in both domains, and so many fine examples are either lying before him, or placed at his disposal, which might advantageously have been adduced, that he contemplates following the present volume, at no very distant period, with one that shall supply what has now been necessarily omitted. Among the many skilful Artists whose names have not yet been mentioned are the following, arranged in three distinct alphabets. The first alphabet comprises those who are professionally painters in oil, but occasionally draw on wood; the second, those who make drawing on wood their leading profession, although many of them also paint in oil; the third, those who almost confine themselves to engraving the designs of others, although some of them are themselves good draughtsmen. One or more of the books to which they have contributed, are indicated.

Painters who occasionally Draw on Wood.

ANDREWS. G. H. *Figure subjects and Landscapes;* Ministering Children.—ANSDELL, Richard. *Animals;* Rhymes and Roundelayes.— ARMITAGE, Edward. *Figure subjects;* Winkworth's Lyra Germanica.— COPE, Charles West, R.A. *Figure subjects;* Book of Favourite Modern Ballads, Adams' Allegories, Excelsior Ballads, Burns' Poems, Poetry of Thomas Moore.—CORBOULD, E. H. *Figure subjects and Architecture;* Merrie Days of England, Book of Favourite Modern Ballads, Burns' Poems, Poetry of Thomas Moore, Barry Cornwall's Poems.—CROPSEY, Jasper. *Landscapes;* Poetry of Thomas Moore, Poe's Poems.—DODGSON, G. *Landscape;* Lays of the Holy Land.—FRITH, William Powell, R.A. *Figure subjects;* Book of British Ballads.—GOODALL, Edward. *Landscapes;* Rhymes and Roundelayes. — GRANT, W. J. *Figure subjects;* Favourite Modern Ballads, Bloomfield's Farmer's Boy.—HICKS, G. E. *Figure subjects;* Favourite Modern Ballads.—HORSLEY, John Calcott, A.R.A. *Figure subjects;* Poetry of Thomas Moore, Burns' Poems, Tennyson's Poems, Favourite English Poems, Favourite Modern Ballads. —HUNT, W. Holman. *Figure subjects;* Tennyson's Poems, Mrs. Gatty's Parables, Once a Week.—LE JEUNE, H. *Figure subjects;* Poetry of Thomas Moore, Lays of the Holy Land, Ministering Children.—MILLAIS, John Everett, A.R.A. *Figure subjects;* Tennyson's Poems, Lays of the Holy Land, Once a Week. Mr. Millais is now engaged in illustrating a volume of Parables to be engraved by the Dalziels.—MULREADY,

William, R.A. *Figure subjects;* Tennyson's Poems, Vicar of Wakefield, (engraved by Mr. John Thompson).—NASH, Joseph. *Figures and Architecture;* Merrie Days of England.—PICKERSGILL, F. Richard, R.A. *Figure subjects;* Poetry of Thomas Moore, Book of British Ballads, Lays of the Holy Land. — REDGRAVE, Richard, R.A. *Figure subjects;* Favourite English Poems, Book of British Ballads. — ROBERTS, David, R.A. *Architectural Landscapes;* Lockhart's Spanish Ballads.—SELOUS, H. C. *Figure subjects;* Poems and Pictures, Book of British Ballads.—SOLOMON, A. *Figure subjects;* Book of Favourite Modern Ballads.—WARREN, H. *Figure subjects and Architecture;* Book of British Ballads, Lockhart's Spanish Ballads, Poetry of Thomas Moore, Lays of the Holy Land.— WEBSTER, Thomas, R.A. *Infantine subjects;* Favourite English Poems, Book of British Ballads.—WYBURD, F. *Figure subjects;* Poetry and Pictures of Thomas Moore.

Professional Draughtsmen on Wood.

ARCHER, J. W. *Antiquarian and Architectural;* Vestiges of Old London.—ARCHER, J. R.S.A. *Figure subjects;* Burns' Poems.—BENNETT, Charles. *Humorous subjects;* Poets' Wit and Humour, Quarles' Emblems, 1860, Proverbs in Pictures.—BRANDLING, H. *Figure subjects and Architecture;* Merchant of Venice.—CLAYTON, J. R. *Figure subjects;* Barry Cornwall's Poems, Lays of the Holy Land—COLEMAN, Wm. *Landscape and Figure subjects;* Mary Howitt's Tales.—DARLEY, Felix. *Figure subjects;* Poe's Poetical Works, Poets of the West—DICKES, William. *Figures and Landscape;* most of the subjects in Masterman Ready. Mr. Dickes' attention is now turned to Colour-printing.—EDMONSTON, S. *Figure subjects;* Burns' Poems.—FRANKLIN, John. *Figure subjects;* Book of British Ballads, Mrs. S. C. Hall's Midsummer Eve, Seven Champions of Christendom, Poets of the West.—GOODALL, Walter. *Figure subjects;* Rhymes and Roundelayes, Ministering Children.— HULME, F. W. *Landscapes;* Rhymes and Roundelayes. — HUMPHREYS, Noel. *Ornamental Vignettes;* Rhymes and Roundelayes.—JONES, Owen. *Moresque Ornaments and Architecture;* Lockhart's Spanish Ballads. —KEENE, Charles. *Figure subjects;* Punch, Once a Week, Voyage of the Constance.—LAWLESS, M. J. *Figure subjects;* Once a Week, Punch.—MACQUOID, Thomas. *Ornamental Letters and Borders;* Rhymes and Roundelayes, Burns' Poems, Favourite English Poems, &c.— MORGAN, Matthew S. *Figures and Landscape;* Miles Standish.—PHIZ (Hablot K. Browne). *Humour;* Bleak House, Martin Chuzzlewit, The Pickwick Series, Wits and Beaux of Society, Lever's St. Patrick's Eve, &c. He has executed more etchings on steel than drawings on wood.—PROUT, J. S. *Landscapes and Architecture ;* Rhymes and Roundelayes.—READ, Samuel. *Landscapes and Architecture ;* Rhymes and Roundelayes, contributes to the London News.—ROGERS, Harry. *Ornamental Letters and Vignettes ;* Quarles' Emblems, Poe's Poetical Works.—SCOTT, T. D. *Figure subjects and Landscapes ;* able reducer and copyist of Pictures on Wood ; Book of British Ballads.—SHAW, Henry. *Architectural Ornaments, Letters, Furniture, &c.;* has designed extensively on wood, chiefly for his own works.—STEPHENSON, James. *Figure subjects ;* Clever Boys, Wide Wide World (Bohn's Edition), &c. A skilful engraver on steel.—STOCKS, Lumb, A.R.A. *Figure subjects :* Ministering Children, Ministry of Life, English Yeomen, &c. Mr. Stocks has considerable reputation as an engraver on steel.—SULMAN, T. Jun. *Ornamental Borders and Vignettes ;* Lalla Rookh.—TOPHAM, F. W. *Irish Character ;* Poetry of Thomas Moore, Mrs. S. C. Hall's Mid-summer Eve, Burns' Poems.—WATSON, J. D. *Figure subjects ;* Pilgrim's Progress, 110 designs, Eliza Cook's Poems. — ZWECKER, John B. *Animals ;* mostly engraved by the Dalziels ; Wood's Natural History, &c.

Engravers on Wood not before mentioned.

ARMSTRONG, Wm. Don Quixote, 1841, Illustrated News, Clever Boys 1860.—GORWAY, C. has successfully engraved many of John Gilbert's designs.—HAMMOND, J. Poems and Songs of Robert Burns.—JACKSON, Mason, son of the Projector of the present volume, in which some of the subjects are engraved by him ; also Walton's Angler (Bohn's Edition), Ministering Children.—LOUDON, J. engraves for the Illustrated Times. —SMYTH, F. G. *Figure subjects ;* Illustrated News.—SWAIN, Joseph. *Figure subjects ;* Lyra Germanica.—WIMPERIS, E. Merrie Days of England.—WOODS, H. N. *Ornamental Borders and Vignettes ;* Moore's Lalla Rookh.

CHAPTER IX.

THE PRACTICE OF WOOD ENGRAVING.

ERRONEOUS OPINIONS ABOUT CROSS-HATCHING—THE CHOICE AND PREPARATION OF THE WOOD —MODE OF INSERTING A PLUG—MAGNIFYING GLASSES AND ENGRAVER'S LAMP—DIFFERENT KINDS OF TOOLS—CUTTING TINTS—ENGRAVING IN OUTLINE—CUTS REPRESENTING COLOUR AND TEXTURE—MAPS ENGRAVED ON WOOD—THE ADVANTAGES OF LOWERING A BLOCK PREVIOUS TO ENGRAVING THE SUBJECT—CHIARO-SCURO ENGRAVING ON WOOD, AND PRINTING IN COLOURS FROM WOOD-BLOCKS—METALLIC RELIEF ENGRAVING, BY BLAKE, BEWICK, BRANSTON, AND LIZARS—MR. C. HANCOCK'S PATENT—MR. WOONE'S PATENT—CASTS FROM WOOD-CUTS—PRINTING WOOD-CUTS—CONCLUSION.

ERHAPS no art exercised in this country is less known to the public than that of wood engraving; and hence it arises that most persons who have incidentally or even expressly written on the subject have committed so many mistakes respecting the practice. It is from a want of practical knowledge that we have had so many absurd speculations respecting the manner in which the old wood engravers executed their cross-hatchings, and so many *notions* about vegetable putties and metallic relief engraving. Even in a Memoir of Bewick, printed in 1836, we find the following passage, which certainly would not have appeared had the writer paid any attention to the numerous wood-cuts, containing cross-hatchings of the most delicate kind, published in England between 1820 and 1834: —" The principal characteristic of the ancient masters is the crossing of the black lines, to produce or deepen the shade, commonly called *cross-hatching*. Whether this was done by employing different blocks, one after another, as in calico-printing and paper-staining, *it may be difficult to say;* but to produce them on the same block is so difficult and *unnatural*, that though Nesbit, one of Bewick's early pupils, attempted it on a few occasions, and the splendid print of Dentatus by Harvey shows that it is not impossible even on a large scale, yet the waste

O O

of time and labour is scarcely worth the effect produced." * Now, the difficulty of saying whether the old cross-hatchings were executed on a single block, or produced by impressions from two or more, proceeds entirely from the writer not being acquainted with the subject ; had he known that hundreds of old blocks containing cross-hatchings are still in existence, and had he been in the habit of seeing similar cross-hatchings executed almost daily by very indifferent wood engravers, the difficulty which he felt would have vanished. "Unnatural" is certainly an improper term for a *philosopher* to apply to a process of art, merely because he does not understand it : with equal reason he might have called every other process, both of copper-plate and wood engraving, "unnatural;" nay, in this sense there is no process in arts or manufactures to which the term "unnatural" might not in the same manner be applied.

In giving some account of the practice of wood engraving, it seems most proper to begin with the ground-work—the wood. As it is generally understood that box is best adapted for the purposes of engraving, and that it is generally used for cuts intended for the illus- tration of books, there seems no occasion to enter into a detail of all the kinds of wood that might be used for the more ordinary purposes of large coarse cuts for posting-bills, and others of a similar character. Mr. Savage, in his Hints on Decorative Printing, has copied the principal part of what Papillon has said on the subject of wood, intending that it should be received as information from a practical wood engraver ; but he has omitted to notice that much of what Papillon says about the choice of wood, can be of little service in guiding the modern English wood engraver, who executes his subject on the cross-section of the wood, while Papillon and his contemporaries were accustomed to engrave upon the side, or the *long-way* of the wood. "There is no difficulty," says Papillon, as translated by Mr. Savage, "in distinguishing that which is good, as we have only need of taking a splinter of the box we wish to try, and break it between the fingers ; if it break short, without bending, it will not be of any value ; whereas, if there be great difficulty in breaking it, it is well adapted to our purpose."

Now, it is quite evident from this direction—independent of the fact being otherwise known—that the thin splinter by which the quality of the wood was to be tested was to be cut the long way of the wood : a similar cutting taken from the cross-section would break short, however excellent the wood might be for the purpose of engraving. Papillon's direction is therefore calculated to mislead, unless accompanied with an explanation of the manner in which the splinter is to be taken ; and it

* Memoir of Thomas Bewick, by the Reverend William Turner, prefixed to volume sixth of the Naturalist's Library, page 18.

is also utterly useless as a test of box that is intended to be engraved on the cross-section, or end-way of the wood.

For the purposes of engraving no other kind of wood hitherto tried is equal to box. For fine and small cuts the smallest logs are to be preferred, as the smallest wood is almost invariably the best. American and Turkey box is the largest; but all large wood of this kind is generally of inferior quality, and most liable to split; it is also frequently of a red colour, which is a certain characteristic of its softness, and consequent unfitness for delicate engraving. From my own experience, English box is superior to all others; for though small, it is generally so clear and firm in the grain that it never crumbles under the graver; it resists evenly to the edge of the tool, and gives not a particle beyond what is actually cut out. The large red wood, on the contrary, besides being soft, is liable to crumble and to cut short; that is, small particles will sometimes *break* away from the sides of the line cut by the graver, and thus cause imperfections in the work. Box of large and comparatively quick growth, is also extremely liable to shrink unevenly between the rings, so that after the surface has been planed perfectly level, and engraved, it is frequently difficult to print the cut in a proper manner, in consequence of the inequality of the surface.

As even the largest logs of box are of comparatively small diameter, it is extremely difficult to obtain a perfect block of a single piece equal to the size of an octavo page. In order to obtain pieces as large as possible, some dealers are accustomed to saw the log in a slanting direction—in the manner of an oblique section of a cylinder—so that the surface of a piece cut off shall resemble an oval rather than a circle. Blocks sawn in this manner ought never to be used; for, in consequence of the obliquity of the grain, there is no preventing small particles tearing out when cutting a line.

Large red wood containing *white spots* or streaks is utterly unfit for the purposes of the engraver; for in cutting a line across, adjacent to these spots or streaks, sometimes the entire piece thus marked will be removed, and the cut consequently spoiled. A clear yellow colour, and as equal as possible over the whole surface, is generally the best criterion of box-wood. When a block is not of a clear yellow colour throughout, but only in the centre, gradually becoming lighter towards the edges, it ought not to be used for delicate work; the white, in addition to its not cutting so " sweetly," being of a softer nature, absorbs more ink than the yellow, and also retains it more tenaciously, so that impressions from a block of this kind sometimes display a perceptible inequality of colour ;—from the yellow parts allowing the ink to leave them freely, while the white parts partially retain it, the printed cut has the appearance of having received either too much ink in one place, or too little in another. Besides this, the ink remaining on the white parts becomes so adhesive, that, should the sheet be rather too damp (as will frequently happen when much paper is wetted at one time), it will sometimes stick to the paper; a small spot of white will hence appear in the impression, while a minute piece of paper will remain adhering to the block, to be mixed up with the ink on the balls, and transferred as a black speck to another part of the cut in a subsequent impression. But this is not all: should the piece of paper remain unnoticed for some time it will make a small indention in the block, and occasion a white or grey speck in the impressions printed after its removal. Soft red and white box, more especially the latter, being more porous than clear yellow, blocks of those kinds of wood are most liable to be injured by the liquids used to clean them after printing. Should the printer wash them with either lees or spirits of turpentine, these fluids will enter the wood more freely than if it were yellow, and cause it to expand in proportion to the quantity used, and sometimes to such an extent as to distort the drawing. If a block of any kind of box, whether red, white, or yellow, be wetted or exposed to dampth, it will expand considerably;* but with care it will return to its former dimensions, should it have been sufficiently seasoned before being printed. When, however, the expansion has been caused by lees or spirits of turpentine, the block will never again contract to its original size.†

As publishers frequently provide the drawings which are to be engraved, perhaps a knowledge of the different qualities of box is as necessary to them as to wood engravers themselves. In reply to this it may be said, why not require the engraver who is to execute the cuts to supply proper wood himself? Where only one engraver is employed to execute all the cuts for a work, the choice of the wood may indeed be very properly left to himself. But where several are employed, and each required to send his own wood to the designer, very few are particular what kind they send; for when the designer receives the different pieces he generally consigns them to a drawer until wanted, and when he has finished a design, he not unfrequently sends it to an engraver who did

---

* The following is an instance of the effect of dampth upon box-wood. I placed one evening a block, composed of several pieces of box glued to a thick piece of mahogany, against the wall of a rather damp room, and on examining it the next morning I found that the box had expanded so much that the edges projected beyond the mahogany upwards of the eighth of an inch.

† Some of the blocks engraved for the Penny Magazine, measuring originally eight inches and a half by six inches, have, after undergoing the process of stereotyping and the subsequent washing, increased not less than two inches in their perimeter or exterior lineal dimension, as has been proved by comparing the measurement of a block in its present state with a first proof taken on India paper, which paper, being dry when the impression was taken, has not suffered any contraction.

not supply the identical piece of wood on which it is drawn. Hence scarcely any engraver pays much attention to the kind of wood he sends; for where many are employed in the execution of a series of cuts for the same work, it is very unlikely that each will receive the drawings on the wood supplied by himself. Even when the designer is particular in making the drawings of the subjects which he thinks best suited to each engraver's talents on the wood which such engraver has supplied, it not unfrequently happens that the person who employs the engravers will not give the blocks to those for whom the artist intended them. Publishers have a much greater interest in this matter than they seem to suspect. If soft wood be supplied, the finer lines will soon be bruised down in printing, and the cut will appear like an old one before half the number of impressions required have been printed; if red-ringed, the surface is extremely liable to become uneven, and also to warp and split.

As box can seldom be obtained of more than five or six inches diameter, and as wood of this size is rarely sound throughout, blocks for cuts exceeding five inches square are usually formed of two or more pieces firmly united by means of iron pins and screws. Should the block, however, be wetted or exposed to dampth, the joints are certain to open, and sometimes to such an extent as to require a piece of wood to be inserted in the aperture.* Perhaps the best way to guard against a large block opening at the joining of the pieces would be to enclose it with an iron hoop or frame; such hoop or frame being fixed when nearly red-hot in the same manner as a tire is applied to a coach or cart wheel. If the iron fit perfectly tight when forced on to the block in the manner of a tire, it will be the more likely, by its contracting in cold and damp weather, to resist the expansive force of the wood at such times.

Besides the hardness and toughness of box, which allows of clear raised lines, capable of bearing the action of the press, being cut on its surface, this wood, from its not being subject to the attacks of the worm, has a great advantage over apple, pear-tree, beech,† and other kinds of wood, formerly used for the purposes of engraving. Its preservation in this respect is probably owing to its poisonous nature, for other kinds of wood of greater hardness and durability are frequently pierced through and through by worms. The chips of box, when chewed, are certainly unwholesome to human beings. A fellow-pupil, who had acquired a habit of chewing the small pieces which he cut out with his graver,

---

* Sometimes a piece of metal—such as part of a thin rule—is inserted in the chink by printers, when the part injured is dark and the work not fine. Such a temporary remedy is sure to increase the opening in a short time, and make the block worse.

† One of the original blocks of Weever's Funeral Monuments, 1631, preserved in the Print Room of the British Museum, is of beech.

became unwell, and was frequently attacked with sickness. On mentioning the subject to his medical adviser, he was ordered to refrain from chewing the pieces of box; he accordingly took the doctor's advice, gave up his bad habit, and in a short time recovered his usual health.*

Box when kept long in a dry place becomes unfit for the purpose of engraving. I have at this time in my possession a drawing which has been made on the block about ten years, but the wood has become so dry and brittle that it would now be impossible to engrave the subject in a proper manner.

When the wood does not cut clear, but crumbles as if it were too dry, the defect may sometimes be remedied by putting the block into a deep earthenware jug or pan, and placing such jug or pan in a cool place for ten or twelve hours. When the wood is too hard and dry to be softened in the above manner, I would recommend that the back of the block should be placed in water—in a plate or large dish—to the depth of the sixteenth part of an inch, for about an hour. If allowed to remain longer there is a risk of the block afterwards splitting.

Box, of whatever kind, when not well seasoned, is extremely liable to warp and bend; but a little care will frequently prevent many of the accidents to which drawings on unseasoned wood are exposed by neglect. For instance, when a block is received by the engraver from the designer or publisher, it ought, if not directly put in hand, to be placed on one of its edges, and not, as is customary with many, laid down flat, with the surface on which the drawing is made upwards. If a block of unseasoned wood be permitted to lie in this manner for a week or two, it is almost certain to turn up at the edges, the upper surface becoming concave, and the lower convex, as is shown in the annexed cut, representing the section of such a block.

The same thing will occur in the process of engraving, though to a small extent, should the engraver's hands be warm and moist; and also when working by lamp-light without a globe filled with water between the lamp and the block. Such slight warping in the course of engraving is, however, easily remedied by laying the block with its face—that is, the surface on which the drawing is made—downward on the desk or table at all times when the engraver is not actually employed on the

---

* A few years ago I allowed a rabbit to have the run of a small garden, where it soon eat up everything except a small bush of box. Happening to leave home for two days without making any provision for the rabbit, I found it in a dying state, and all the leaves nibbled off the box. The rabbit died in the course of a few hours, and on opening it the cause of its death was apparent—the stomach was full of the leaves of the box.—See Brand's Popular Antiquities, vol. ii. page 265 (Bohn's edit.), for an account of yew poisoning two cows.

subject. The block so placed, provided that it be not of very dry wood, in a short time recovers its former level. When a block of very dry wood becomes *dished*, or concave, on its upper surface, as shown in the preceding cut, there is little chance of its ever again becoming sufficiently flat to allow of its being well printed. When the deviation from a perfect level at the bottom is not so great as to attract the notice of the pressman previous to taking an impression, the block not unfrequently yields to the action of the platten, and splits. The fracture remains perhaps unobserved for a short time, and when it is at length noticed, the block is probably spoiled beyond remedy.

When box is very dry it is extremely difficult to cut a clear line upon it, as it crumbles, and small pieces fly out at the sides of the line traced by the graver. The small white spots so frequently seen in the delicate lines of the sky in wood-cuts are occasioned by particles flying out in this manner. If a block consist partly of yellow wood and partly of wood with red rings, the yellow will cut clear, while in the red it will be almost impossible to cut a perfect line. When the same piece of wood is yellow and red alternately it is extremely difficult to produce an even *tint* upon it. Wood of this kind ought always to be rejected, both from the difficulty of engraving upon it with clearness, and from the uncertainty of the surface continuing perfectly flat, as the red rings are more liable to shrink in drying than the other parts, and, from their thus not receiving a sufficient quantity of ink, to appear like so many rainbows in the impression.

The spaces between those rings are greater or less, accordingly as the seasons have been favourable or unfavourable to the growth of the tree. Besides the injurious effect which those red rings are apt to produce in an impression, wood of this kind is very unpleasant and uncertain to engrave on ; for as the yellow parts cut pleasant and clear, the engraver, unless particularly on his guard, is betrayed to trust to the whole piece as being of the same uniform tenacity, and before he is aware of its inequality in this respect, or can check the progress of his graver, its point has entered one of those soft red rings, and, to the injury of his work, has either caused a small piece to fly out, or carried the line further than he intended. Wood of this kind is unfit for anything except very common work, and ought never to be used for delicate engraving. There is no certain means of forming a judgment of box-wood until it be cut into slices or trencher-like pieces from the log ; for many logs which externally appear sound and of a good colour, prove very faulty and cracked in the centre when sawn up. Turkey box is in particular so defective in this respect that a large slice can seldom be procured without a crack. This, probably, is occasioned by the manner in which the tree is felled. Previous to their beginning to cut down a tree the Turkish wood-cutters fasten a rope to the top, by means of which they break the tree down when the bole is little more than half cut through. The consequence is that a *shiver* frequently extends through the most valuable portion of the log.

Many artists, who are not accustomed to make drawings on wood, erroneously suppose that the block requires some peculiar preparation. Nothing more is required than to rub the previously planed and smoothed surface with a little powdered Bath-brick, slightly mixed with water : as little water as possible is, however, to be used, as otherwise the block will absorb too much, and be afterwards extremely liable to split. When this thin coating is perfectly dry, it is to be removed by rubbing the block with the palm of the hand. No part of the light powder ought to remain, for, otherwise, the pencil coming in contact with it will make a coarse and comparatively thick line, which, besides being a blemish in the drawing, is very liable to be rubbed off. The object of using the powdered Bath-brick is to render the surface less slippery, and thus capable of affording a better *hold* to the point of the black-lead pencil.

When the principal parts of the drawing are first washed in upon the block in Indian ink, it is of great advantage to gently rub the surface of the block, when dry, with a little dry and finely powdered Bath-brick, before the drawing is completed with the black-lead pencil. By this means the hard edges of the Indian-ink wash will be softened, the different tints delicately blended, and the subsequent touches of the pencil be more distinctly seen. Some artists, previous to beginning to draw on the block, are in the habit of washing over the surface with a mixture of flake-white and gum-water.* This practice is, however, by no means a good one. The drawing indeed may appear very bright and showy when first made on such a white surface, but in the progress of engraving a thin film of the preparation will occasionally rise up before the graver and carry with it a portion of the unengraved work, which the engraver is left to restore according to his ability and recollection. This white ground also mixes with the ink in taking a first proof, and fills up the finer parts of the cut. If a white wash be used without gum, the drawing is very liable to be partially effaced in the progress of engraving, and the engraver left to finish his work as he can. The risk of this inconvenience ought to be especially avoided in making drawings on a block, as the wood engraver has not the opportunity of referring to another drawing or to an original painting in the manner of an engraver on copper.

---

* Instead of gum-water, French artists, who are accustomed to make drawings on wood, use water in which parchment shavings have been boiled.

The less that is done to change the original colour of the wood—
by white or any other preparation—so much the better for the engraver;
a piece of clear box is sufficiently light to allow of the most delicate
lines being distinctly drawn upon it.   When the surface of the block is
whitened, another inconvenience arises besides those already noticed.   It
is this : when the drawing is made upon a white ground, and the subject
partially engraved, the effect of the whole becomes very confused and
perplexing to the engraver in consequence of the parts already engraved
appearing nearly of the original colour of the wood, while the ground of
the parts not yet cut is white, as first drawn.   The engraver's eye cannot
correctly judge of the whole, and the inconvenience is increased by
his neither having an original drawing to refer to, nor a proof to guide
him : until the cut be completed he has no means of correctly ascertaining whether he has left too much *colour* or taken too much away.

The engraver on copper or on steel can have an impression of his
etching as soon as it is *bit* in, and can take impressions of the plate
at all times in the course of his progress ; the wood engraver, on the
contrary, enjoys no such advantages ; he is obliged to wait until all be
completed ere he can obtain an impression of his work.   If the wood
engraver has kept his subject generally too dark, there is not much
difficulty in reducing it ; but if he has engraved it too light, there is no
remedy.   If a small part be badly engraved, or the block has sustained
an injury, the defect may be repaired by inserting a small piece of wood
and re-engraving it : this mode of repairing a block is technically termed
"*plugging.*"*

When a block requires to be thus amended or repaired, it is first
to be determined how much is necessary to be taken out that the restora-
tion may accord with the adjacent parts ; for sometimes, in order to
render the insertion less perceptible, it may be requisite to take out
rather more than the part imactually perfect or injured.   This being
decided on, a hole is drilled in the block, as is represented in the next
page, of a size sufficient to admit "the *plug.*"   The hole ought not to be
drilled quite through the block, as the piece let in would, from the shaking
and battering of the press, be very likely to become loosened.   Should
it receive more pressure at the top than bottom, it would sink a little
below the engraved surface of the block, and thus appear lighter in the
impression than the surrounding parts ; while should it be slightly
forced up from below it, would appear darker,—in each case forming

---

* This mode of repairing a block was practised by the German wood engravers of the
time of Albert Durer.   The "plug" which they inserted was usually square, and not
circular as at present.   The French wood engravers of the time of Papillon continued to
employ square plugs.   There are two or three instances of cuts thus repaired, in the
Adventures of Sir Theurdank, Nuremberg and Augsburg, 1517-1519.

a positive blemish in the cut.* When the shape of the part to be restored is too large to be covered with one circular plug, it is better to

THE PLUG OUT.

add one plug to another till the whole be covered, than to insert one of a different shape, and thus fill the space at once. When a single plug is

used the section appears thus; the plug being driven in like a wedge, and having a vacant space around it at the bottom. If an oblong space of the form No. 1. is to be restored, it will be best effected by first inserting a plug at each end, as at No. 2, then adding two others, as at No. 3, and finally wedging them all fast by a central plug, as at No. 4, like the key-stone in an arch. When a plug is firmly fixed, the top is carefully cut down to the level of the block, and the part of the subject wanting re-drawn and engraved. When these operations are well performed no trace of the insertion can

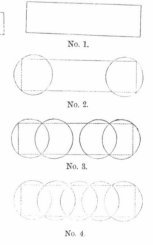

No. 1.

No. 2.

No. 3.

No. 4.

---

* In a tail-piece at page 52 of Bewick's Fables, edition 1823, a plug which has been inserted appears lighter than the adjacent parts, in consequence of its having sunk a little below the surface; and in the cut to the fable of the Hart and the Vine, in the same work, two large plugs, at the top, are darker than the other parts in consequence of their having risen a little above the surface.

be discovered, except by one who should know where to look for it.

When a cast is taken from a block which requires the insertion of a plug, the best mode is to have the part intended to be renewed cast blank. In this case a hole of sufficient size is to be drilled in the block, and afterwards filled up with plaster to the level of the surface. A cast being then taken, the part to be re-engraved remains blank, but of a piece with the rest of the metal, so that there is no possibility of its rising up above or sinking below the surface, as sometimes happens when a plug is inserted in a wood-block. When the part remaining blank in the cast is engraved in accordance with the work of the surrounding parts, it is almost impossible to discover any trace of the insertion. The following impression is from a cast of the block illustrating the "plug," with the part which appears white in the former

cut restored and re-engraved in this manner. A white circular line, near the handle of the pail, has been purposely cut to indicate the place of the plug.

Before beginning to engrave any subject, it is necessary to observe whether the drawing be entirely, or only in part, made with a pencil. If it be what is usually called a *wash* drawing, with little more than the outlines in pencil, it is not necessary to be so cautious in defending it from the action of the breath or the occasional touching of the hand ;

but if it be entirely in pencil, too much care cannot be taken to protect it from both.

Before proceeding to engrave a delicate pencil drawing the block ought to be covered with paper, with the exception of the part on which it is intended to begin. Soft paper ought not to be used for this purpose, as such is most likely to partially efface the drawing when the hand is pressed upon the block. Moderately stout post-paper with a glazed surface is the best; though some engravers, in order to preserve their eyes, which become affected by white paper, cover the block with blue paper, which is usually too soft, and thus expose the drawing to injury. The dingy, grey, and over-done appearance of several modern wood-cuts is doubtless owing, in a great measure, to the block when in course of engraving having been covered with soft paper, which has partially effaced the drawing. The drawing, which originally may have been clear and *touchy*, loses its brightness, and becomes indistinct from its frequent contact with the soft pliable paper; the spirited dark touches which give it effect are rubbed down to a sober grey, and all the other parts, from the same cause, are comparatively weak. The cut, being engraved according to the appearance of the drawing, is tame, flat, and spiritless.

Different engravers have different methods of fastening the paper to the block. Some fix it with gum, or with wafers at the sides; but this is not a good mode, for as often as it is necessary to take a view of the whole block, in order to judge of the progress of the work, the paper must be torn off, and afterwards replaced by means of new wafers or fresh gum, so that before the cut is finished the sides of the block are covered with bits of paper in the manner of a wall or shop-front covered with fragments of posting-bills. The most convenient mode of fastening the paper is to first wrap a piece of stiff and stout thread three or four times round the edges of the block, and then after making the end fast to remove it. The paper is then to be closely fitted to the block, and the edges being brought over the sides, the thread is to be re-placed above it. If the turns of the thread be too tight to pass over the last corner of the block, A, a piece of string, B, being passed within them and firmly pulled, in the manner here represented, will cause them to  stretch a little and pass over on to the edge without difficulty. When this plan is adopted the paper forms a kind of moveable cap, which can

---

* French wood engravers are accustomed to rub the sides of the block with bees'-wax, which on being chafed with the thumb-nail becomes slightly softened, and thus adheres to the paper.

be taken off at pleasure to view the progress of the work, and replaced without the least trouble.

I have long been of opinion that many young persons, when beginning to learn the art of wood engraving, have injured their sight by unnecessarily using a magnifying glass. At the very commencement of their pupilage boys will furnish themselves with a glass of this kind, as if it were as much a matter of course as a set of gravers; they sometimes see men use a glass, and as at this period they are prone to ape their elders in the profession, *they* must have one also; and as they generally choose such as magnify most, the result not unfrequently is that their sight is considerably impaired before they are capable of executing anything that really requires much nicety of vision.

I would recommend all persons to avoid the use of glasses of any kind, whether single magnifiers or spectacles, until impaired sight renders such aids necessary; and even then to commence with such as are of small magnifying power. The habit of viewing minute objects alternately with a magnifying glass and the naked eye—applying the glass every two or three minutes—is, I am satisfied, injurious to the sight. The magnifying glass used by wood engravers is similar to that used by watch-makers, and consists of a single lens, fitted into a short tube, which is rather wider at the end applied to the eye. As the glass seldom can be fixed so firmly to the eye as to entirely dispense with holding it, the engraver is thus frequently obliged to apply his left hand to keep it in its place; as he cannot hold the block with the same hand at the same time, or move it as may be required, so as to enable him to execute his work with freedom, the consequence is, that the engraving of a person who is in the habit of using a magnifying glass has frequently a cramped appearance. There are also other disadvantages attendant on the habitual use of a magnifying glass. A person using such a glass must necessarily hold his head aside, so that the eye on which the glass is fixed may be directly above the part on which he is at work. In order to attain this position, the eye itself is not unfrequently distorted; and when it is kept so for any length of time it becomes extremely painful. I never find my eyes so free from pain or aching as when looking at the work directly in front, without any twisting of the neck so as to bring one eye only immediately above the part in course of execution. I therefore conclude that the eyes are less likely to be injured when thus employed than when one is frequently distorted and pained in looking through a glass. I am here merely speaking from experience, and not professedly from any theoretic knowledge of optics; but as I have hitherto done without the aid of any magnifying power, I am not without reason convinced that glasses of all kinds ought to be dispensed with until impaired vision renders their use absolutely necessary. I am decidedly of opinion that to use glasses *to preserve* the sight, is to meet half way the evil which is thus sought to be averted. A person who has his sense of hearing perfect never thinks of using a trumpet or acoustic instrument in order to preserve it. All wood engravers, whether their eyes be naturally weak or not, ought to wear a shade, similar to that represented in the following figure, No. 1, as it both protects the eyes from too strong a light, and also serves to concentrate the view on the work which the engraver is at the time engaged in executing.

No. 1.   No. 2.

When speaking on this subject, it may not be out of place to mention a kind of shade or screen for the nose and mouth, similar to that in the preceding figure, No. 2. Such a shade or screen is called by Papillon a *mentonnière*,* and its object is to prevent the drawing on the block being injured by the breath in damp or frosty weather. Without such a precaution, a drawing made on the block with black-lead pencil would, in a great measure, be effaced by the breath of the engraver passing freely over it in such weather. Such a shade or screen is most conveniently made of a piece of thin pasteboard or stiff paper.

There are various modes of protecting the eyes when working by lamp-light, but I am aware of only one which both protects the eyes from the light and the face from the heat of the lamp. This consists in filling a large transparent glass-globe with clear water, and placing it in such a manner between the lamp and the workman that the light, after passing through the globe, may fall directly on the block, in the manner represented in the following cut. The height of the lamp can be regulated according to the engraver's convenience, in consequence of its being moveable on the upright piece of iron or other metal which forms its support. The dotted line shows the direction of the light when the lamp is elevated to the height here seen; by lowering the lamp a

---

* Papillon's description of a *mentonnière* is previously noticed at page 465.

little more, the dotted line would incline more to a horizontal direction, and enable the engraver to sit at a greater distance. By the use of those globes one lamp will suffice for three or four persons, and each person have a much clearer and cooler light than if he had a lamp without a globe solely to himself.*

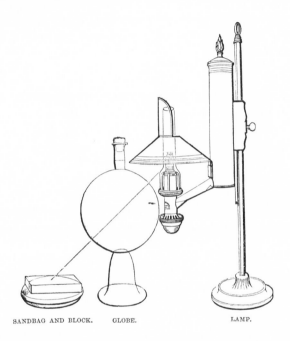

SANDBAG AND BLOCK.   GLOBE.   LAMP.

It has been said, and with some appearance of truth, that "the best engravers use the fewest tools;" but this, like many other sayings of a similar kind, does not generally hold good. He undoubtedly ought to be considered the best engraver who executes his work in the *best manner* with the fewest tools; while it is no less certain that he is a bad engraver who executes his work badly, whether he use many or few. No wood engraver who understands his art will incumber his desk or table with a number of useless tools, though, from a regard to his own time, he will take care that he has as many as are necessary. There are some who pride themselves upon executing a great variety of work with one

* Papillon preferred a kind of bull's-eye lens—*loupe*—of about three and a half inches diameter, flat on one side and convex on the other, to a globe filled with water—*un bocal*—for the purpose of bringing the light of the lamp to a focus. This bull's-eye he had enclosed in a kind of frame, which could be inclined to any angle, or turned in any direction by means of a ball-and-socket joint. He gives a cut of it at page 75, vol. ii. of his Traité de la Gravure en Bois.—I have tried the bull's-eye lens, but though the light was equally good as that from the globe, I found that the heat affected the head in a most unpleasant manner.

tool, and hence, firmly believing in the truth of the saying above quoted, fancy that they are first-rate engravers. Such would be better entitled to the name if they executed their work well. A person who makes his tools his *hobby-horse*, and who bestows upon their ornaments—ebony or ivory handles, silver hoops, &c.—that attention which ought rather to be devoted to his subject, rarely excels as an engraver. He who is vain of the beautiful appearance of his tools has not often just reason to be proud of his work.

There are only four kinds of cutting tools* necessary in wood engraving, namely :—gravers ; tint-tools ; gouges or scoopers ; and flat tools or chisels. Of each of these four kinds there are various sizes. The following cut shows the form of a graver that is principally used for outlining or separating one figure from another. A, is the back of the tool; B, the face ; C, the point ; and D, what is technically called the belly. The horizontal dotted line, 1, 2, shows the surface of the

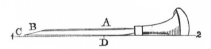

block, and the manner in which part of the handle is cut off after the blade is inserted.† This tool is very fine at the point, as the line which it cuts ought to be so thin as not to be distinctly perceptible when the cut is printed, as the intention is merely to form a termination or boundary to a series of lines running in another direction. Though it is necessary that the point should be very fine, yet the blade ought not to be too thin, for then, instead of cutting out a piece of the wood, the tool will merely make a delicate opening, which would be likely to close as soon as the block should be exposed to the action of the press. When the outline tool becomes too thin at the point the lower part should be rubbed on a hone, in order to reduce the extreme fineness.

About eight or nine gravers of different sizes, beginning from the outline tool, are generally sufficient. The blades differ little in shape, when first made, from those used by copper-plate engravers ; but in order to render them fit for the purpose of wood engraving, it is necessary to give the points their peculiar form by rubbing them on a Turkey stone. In this cut are shown the faces and part of the backs of nine gravers of different sizes ; the lower dotted line, A C, shows the extent to which the points of such

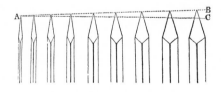

* A sharp-edged scraper, in shape something like a copper-plate engraver's burnisher, is used in the process of *lowering*.

† The handle, when received from the turner's, is perfectly circular at the rounded end ; but after the blade is inserted, a segment is cut off at the lower part, as seen in the above cut.

tools are sometimes ground down by the engraver in order to render them broader. When thus ground down the points are slightly rounded, and do not remain straight as if cut off by the dotted line A C. These tools are used for nearly all kinds of work, except for series of parallel lines, technically called "tints." The width of the line cut out, according to the thickness of the graver towards the point, is regulated by the pressure of the engraver's hand.

Tint-tools are chiefly used to cut parallel lines forming an even and uniform *tint*, such as is usually seen in the representation of a clear sky in wood-cuts. They are thinner at the back, but deeper in the side than gravers, and the angle of the face, at the point, is much more acute. About seven or eight, of different degrees of fineness, are generally sufficient. The following cut will afford an idea of the shape of the blades towards the point. The handle of the tint-tool is of the same form as that of a graver. The figure marked A presents a side view of the blade; the others marked B show the faces. Some engravers never use a tint-tool, but cut all their lines with a graver. There is, however, great uncertainty in cutting a series of parallel lines in this manner, as the least inclination of the hand to one side will cause the graver to increase the width of the white line *cut out*, and undercut the raised one *left*, more than if in the same circumstances a tint-tool were used. This

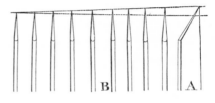

will be rendered more evident by a comparison of the points and faces of the two different tools: The tint-tool, being very little thicker at B than at the point A, will cause a very trifling difference in the width of a line in the event of a wrong inclination, when com-

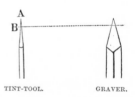

TINT-TOOL.   GRAVER.

pared with the inequality occasioned by the unsteady direction of a graver, whose angle at the point is much greater than that of a proper tint-tool. Tint-tools ought to be sufficiently strong at the back to prevent their bending in the middle of the blade when used, for with a weak tool of this kind the engraver cannot properly guide the point, and hence freedom of execution is lost. Tint-tools that are rather thick in the back are to be preferred to such as are thin, not only from their allowing of great steadiness in cutting, but from their leaving the raised lines thicker at the bottom, and conse-quently more capable of sustaining the action of the press. A tint-tool that is of the same thickness, both at the back and the lower part, cuts out

the lines in such manner that a section of them appears thus :
the black or raised lines from which the impression is
obtained being no thicker at their base than at the surface ;
while a section of the lines cut by a tool that is thicker at the back
than at the lower part appears thus.   It is evident that lines
of this kind, having a better support at the base, are much
less liable than the former to be broken in printing.
Gouges of different sizes, from A the smallest to B the largest, as here
represented, are used for scooping out the wood
towards the centre of the block ; while flat tools
or chisels, of various sizes, are chiefly employed
in cutting away the wood towards the edges.
Flat tools of the shape seen in figure C are
sometimes offered for sale by tool-makers, but
they ought never to be used ; for the projecting
corners are very apt to cut *under* a line, and thus
remove it entirely, causing great trouble to replace it by
inserting new pieces of wood.

GOUGES.

CHISELS.

    The face of both gravers and tint-tools ought to be
kept rather long than short ; though if the point be ground
too fine, it will be very liable to break. When the face
is long—or, strictly speaking, when the angle, formed by the plane
of the face and the lower line of the blade,
is comparatively acute—thus, a line is cut
with much greater clearness than when the
face is comparatively obtuse, and the small
shaving cut out turns gently over towards the hand. When, however, the face of the tool approaches to the shape seen in the
following cut, the reverse happens ; the small shaving is rather ploughed
out than cleanly cut out ; and the force necessary to push the tool
forward frequently causes small pieces to fly out at each side of the
hollowed line, more especially if the wood be dry.   The shaving
also, instead of turning aside over the face of
the tool, turns over before the point, thus,
and hinders the engraver from seeing that part
of the pencilled line which is directly under it.
A short-faced tool of itself prevents the engraver from distinctly seeing
the point. When the face of a tool has become obtuse, it ought to be
ground to a proper form, for instance, from the shape of the figure A
to that of B.

Gravers and tint-tools when first received from the maker are generally too hard,—a defect which is soon discovered by the point breaking off short as soon as it enters the wood. To remedy this, the blade of the tool ought to be placed with its flat side above a piece of iron—a poker will do very well—nearly red-hot. Directly it changes to a straw colour it is to be taken off the iron, and either dipped in sweet oil or allowed to cool gradually. If removed from the iron while it is still of a straw colour, it will have been softened no more than sufficient; but should it have acquired a purple tinge, it will have been softened too much; and instead of breaking at the point, as before, it will bend. A small grindstone is of great service in grinding down the faces of tools that have become obtuse. A Turkey stone, though the operation requires more time, is however a very good substitute, as, besides reducing the face, the tool receives a point at the same time. Though some engravers use only a Turkey stone for sharpening their tools, yet a hone in addition is of great advantage. A graver that has received a final polish on a hone cuts a clearer line than one which has only been sharpened on a Turkey stone; it also cuts more pleasantly, gliding smoothly through the wood, if it be of good quality, without stirring a particle on each side of the line.

The gravers and tint-tools used for engraving on a plane surface are straight at the point, as is here represented; but for engraving on a block rendered concave in certain parts by lowering, it is necessary that the point should have a slight inclination upwards, thus. The dotted lines show the direction of the point used for plane surface engraving. There is no difficulty in getting a tool to *descend* on one side of a part hollowed out or lowered; but unless the point be slightly inclined upwards, as is here shown, it is extremely difficult to make it *ascend* on the side opposite, without getting *too much hold*, and thus producing a wider white line than was intended.

As the proper manner of holding the graver is one of the first things that a young wood engraver is taught, it is necessary to say a few words on this subject. Engravers on copper and steel, who have much harder substances than wood to cut, hold the graver with the fore-finger extending on the blade beyond the thumb, thus, so that by its pressure the point may be pressed into the plate. As box-wood, however, is much softer than copper or steel, and as it is seldom of perfectly equal hardness

throughout, it is necessary to hold the graver in a different manner, and employ the thumb at once as a stay or rest for the blade, and as a check upon the force exerted by the palm of the hand, the motion being chiefly directed by the fore-finger, as is shown in the following cut.

The thumb, with the end resting against the side of the block, in the manner above represented, allows the blade to move back and forward with a slight degree of pressure against it, and in case of a slip it is ever ready to check the graver's progress. This mode of resting the thumb against the edge of the block is, however, only applicable when the cuts are so small as to allow of the graver, when thus guided and controlled, to reach every part of the subject. When the cut is too large to admit of this, the thumb then rests upon the surface of the block, thus :

still forming a stay to the blade of the graver, and a check to its slips, as before.

In order to acquire steadiness of hand, the best thing for a pupil to begin with is the cutting of tints,—that is, parallel lines; and the first attempts ought to be made on a small block such as is represented in No. 1, which will allow each entire line to be cut with the thumb resting against the edge. When lines of this length can be cut with tolerable precision, the pupil should proceed to blocks of the size of No. 2. He ought also

No. 1.

to cut waved tints, which are not so difficult; beginning, as in straight ones, with a small block, and gradually proceeding to blocks of greater

No. 2.

size. Should the wood not cut smoothly in the direction in which he has begun, he should reverse the block, and cut his lines in the opposite direction; for it not unfrequently happens that wood which cuts short and crumbles in one direction will cut clean and smooth the opposite way. It is here necessary to observe, that if a certain number of lines be cut in one direction, and another portion, by reversing the block, be cut the contrary way, the tint, although the same tool may have been used for all, will be of two different shades, notwithstanding the pains that may have been taken to keep the lines of an even thickness throughout. This difference in the appearance of the two portions of lines cut from opposite sides is entirely owing to the wood cutting more smoothly in one direction than another, although the difference in the resistance which it makes to the tool may not be perceptible by the hand of the engraver. It is of great importance that a pupil should be able to cut tints well before he proceeds to any other kind of work. The practice will give him steadiness of hand, and he will thus acquire a habit of carefully executing such lines, which subsequently will be of the greatest service. Wood engravers who have not been well schooled in this elementary part of their profession often cut their tints carelessly in the first instance, and, when they perceive the defect in a proof, return to their work, and, with great loss of time, keep thinning and dressing the lines, till they frequently make the tint appear worse than at first.

When uniform tints, both of straight and waved lines, can be cut with facility, the learner should proceed to cut tints in which the lines are of unequal distance apart.   To effect this, tools of different sizes are necessary ; for in tints of this kind the different distances between the black lines, are according to the width of the different tools used to cut them ; though in tints of a graduated tone of colour, the difference is sometimes entirely produced by increasing the pressure of the graver. In the annexed cut, No. 3, the black lines are of equal thickness, but the width of the white lines between them becomes gradually less from the top to the bottom. By comparing it with No. 4, the difference between a uniform tint, where the lines are of the same thickness and equally distant, and one where the distance between the lines is unequal, will be more readily understood.

No.3.

No. 4.

A straight-line tint, either uniform, or with the lines becoming gradually closer without appearing darker, is generally adopted to represent a clear blue sky.   In No. 3 the tint has been commenced with a comparatively broad-pointed tool ; and after cutting a few lines, less pressure, thus allowing the black lines to come a little closer together, has been used, till it became necessary to change the tool for one less broad in the face.   In this manner a succession of tools, each finer than the preceding, has been employed till the tint was completed. —To be able to produce a tint of delicately graduated *tone*, it is necessary that the engraver should be well acquainted with the use of his tools, and also have a correct eye.   The following is a specimen of a tint cut entirely with the same *graver*, the difference in the colour being

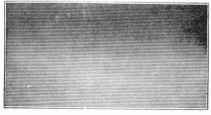

No. 5.

produced by increasing the pressure in the lighter parts.   Tints of this kind are obtained with greater facility and certainty by using a graver, and increasing the pressure, than by using several tint-tools. On comparing No. 3 with No. 5, it will be perceived that the black lines in the latter decrease in thickness as they approach the bottom of the cut, while in the former they are of a uniform thickness throughout. If a clear sky is to be represented, there is no other mode of making that part near the horizon appear to recede except by means of fine black lines becoming gradually closer as they descend, as seen in the tint No. 3. As the black lines in this tint are closer at the bottom than at the top, it might naturally be supposed that the colour would be proportionably stronger in that part. It is, however, known by experience that the unequal distance of the lines in such a tint does not cause any perceptible difference in the colour; as the upper lines, in consequence of their being more apart, print thicker, and thus counterbalance the effect of the greater closeness of the others.

The two following cuts are specimens of tints represented by means of waved lines: in No. 6 the lines are slightly undulated; in No. 7 they have more of the appearance of zig-zag.

No. 6.

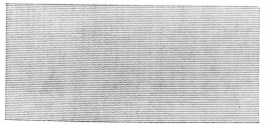

No. 7.

Waved lines are generally introduced to represent clouds, as they not only form a contrast with the straight lines of the sky, but from their form suggest the idea of motion. It is necessary to observe, that if the alternate undulations in such lines be too much curved, the tint, when printed, will appear as if intersected from top to bottom, like wicker-work with perpendicular stakes, in the manner shown in the following specimen, No. 8. This appearance is caused by the unequal

No. 8.

pressure of the tool in forming the small curves of which each line is composed, thus making the black or raised line rather thicker in some parts than in others, and the white interstices wide or narrow in the same proportion. The appearance of such a tint is precisely the same whether cut by hand or by a machine.* In executing waved tints it is therefore necessary to be particularly careful not to get the undulations too much curved.

As the choice of proper tints depends on taste, no specific rules can be laid down to guide a person in their selection. The proper use of lines of various kinds as applied to the execution of wood-cuts, is a most important consideration to the engraver, as upon their proper application all indications of form, texture, and conventional colour entirely depend. Lines are not to be introduced merely as such,—to display the mechanical skill of the engraver ; they ought to be the signs of an artistic meaning, and be judged of accordingly as they serve to express it with feeling and correctness. Some wood engravers are but too apt to pride themselves on the delicacy of their *lining*, without considering whether it be well adapted to express their subject ; and to fancy that excellence in the art consists chiefly in cutting with great labour a number of delicate unmeaning lines. To such an extent is this carried by some of this class that they spend more time in expressing the mere scratches of the designer's pencil in a shade than a Bewick or a Clennell would require to engrave a cut full of meaning and interest. Mere delicacy of lines will not, however, compensate for want of natural

* The sky in many of the large wood engravings executed in London is now cut by means of a machine invented by Mr. John Parkhouse. In many steel engravings the sky is ruled in by means of a machine by persons who do little else.

expression, nor laborious trifling for that vigorous execution which is the result of feeling. "Expression," says Flaxman, "engages the attention, and excites an interest which compensates for a multitude of defects —whilst the most admirable execution, without a just and lively expression, will be disregarded as laborious inanity, or contemned as an illusory endeavour to impose on the feelings and the understanding. ——Sentiment gives a sterling value, an irresistible charm, to the rudest imagery or the most unpractised scrawl. By this quality a firm alliance is formed with the affections in all works of art."[*] Perpetrators of laborious inanities find, however, their admirers; and an amateur of such delicacies is in raptures with a specimen of "exquisitely fine lining," and when told that such wood-*peckings* are, as works of art, much inferior to the productions of Bewick, he asks where his works are to be found; and after he has examined them he pronounces them "coarse and tasteless,—the rude efforts of a *country* engraver," and not to be compared with certain delicate, but spiritless, wood engravings of the present day.

With respect to the direction of lines, it ought at all times to be borne in mind by the wood engraver,—and more especially when the lines are not *laid in* by the designer,—that they should be disposed so as to denote the peculiar form of the object they are intended to represent. For instance, in the limb of a figure they ought not to run horizontally or vertically,—conveying the idea of either a flat surface or of a hard cylindrical form,—but with a gentle curvature suitable to the shape and the degree of rotundity required. A well chosen line makes a great difference in properly representing an object, when compared with one less appropriate, though more delicate. The proper disposition of lines will not only express the form required, but also produce more *colour* as they approach each other in approximating curves, as in the following example, and thus represent a variety of light and shade, without the necessity of introducing other lines crossing them, which ought always to be avoided in small subjects: if, however, the figures be large, it is necessary to break the hard appearance of a series of such single lines by crossing them with others more delicate.

In cutting curved lines, considerable difficulty is experienced by not commencing properly. For instance, if in executing a series of such lines as are shown in the preceding cut, the engraver commences at A, and works towards B, the tool will always be apt to cut through the black line already formed; whereas by commencing at B, and working towards A, the graver is always outside of the curve, and consequently

* Lectures on Sculpture, pp. 172—193.

never touches the lines previously cut.*　This difference ought always to be borne in mind when engraving a series of curved lines, as, by commencing properly, the work is executed with greater freedom and ease, while the inconvenience arising from slips is avoided.　When such lines are introduced to represent the rotundity of a limb, with a break of white in the middle expressive of its greatest prominence, as is shown in the following figure A, it is advisable that they should

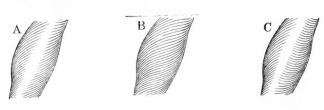

be first *laid in* as if intended to be continuous, as is seen in figure B, and the part which appears white in A *lowered* out before beginning to cut them, as by this means all risk of their disagreeing, as in C, will be avoided.

　　The rotundity of a column or similar object is represented by means of parallel lines, which are comparatively open in the middle where light is required, but which are engraved closer and thicker towards the sides to express shade. The effect of such lines will be rendered more evident by comparing the column in the annexed cut with the square base, which is represented by a series of equidistant lines, each of the same thickness as those in the middle of the column.

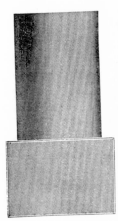

　　Many more examples of tints and simple lines might be given; but, as no real benefit would be derived from them, it is needless to increase the number, and make "much ado about nothing." Every new subject that the engraver commences presents something new for him to effect, and requires the exercise of his taste and judgment as to the best mode of executing it, so that the whole may have some claim to the character of a work of art.　If a thousand examples were given, they would not enable an engraver to

* As the drawing is the reverse of the impression, it is necessary to observe that the motion of the graver in this case is from right to left on the block,—that is, the point B forms the beginning, and not the termination, of the first line when the work is properly commenced.　The lines are represented in the cut as they would appear when drawn on a block to be engraved in the manner recommended.

execute a subject properly, unless he were endowed with that indefinable *feeling* which at once suggests the best means of attaining his end. Such feeling may indeed be excited, but can never be perfectly communicated by rules and examples. In this respect every artist, whether a humble wood engraver, or a sculptor or a painter of the highest class, must be self-instructed ; the feeling displayed in his works must be the result of his own perceptions and ideas of beauty and propriety. It is the difference in feeling, rather than any greater or less degree of excellence in the mechanical execution, that distinguishes the paintings of Raffaele from those of Le Brun, Flaxman's statues from those of Roubilliac, and the cuts in the Lyons Dance of Death from many of the laborious inanities of the present day.

Clear, unruffled water, and all bright and smooth metallic substances, are best represented by single lines ; for if cross-lines be introduced, except to indicate a strong shadow, it gives to them the appearance of roughness, which is not at all in accordance with the ideas which such substances naturally excite. Objects which appear to reflect brilliant flashes of light ought to be carefully dealt with, leaving *plenty of black* as a ground-work, for in wood engravings such lights can only be effectively represented by contrast with deep *colour*. Reflected lights are in general best represented by means of single lines running in the direction of the object, with a few touches of white judiciously taken out. In this respect Clennell particularly excelled as a wood engraver. Painting itself can scarcely represent reflected lights with greater effect than he has expressed them in several of his cuts. In Harvey's large cut of the Death of Dentatus, after Haydon's noble picture, the shield of Dentatus affords an instance of reflected light most admirably represented.

As my object is to point out to the uninitiated the method of cutting certain lines, rather than to engage in the fruitless task of showing how such lines are to be generally applied, I shall now proceed to offer a few observations on engraving in outline, a process with which the learner ought to be well acquainted before he attempts subjects consisting of complicated lines. The word *outline* in wood engraving has two meanings : it is used, first, to denote the distinct boundaries of all kinds of objects ; and secondly, to denote the delicate white line that is cut round any figure or object in order to form a boundary to the lines by which such figure or object is surrounded, and to thus allow of their easier liberation : it forms as it were a terminal furrow into which the lines surrounding the figure run. In speaking of this second outline in future, it will be distinguished as the *white outline ;* while the other, which properly defines the different figures and forms, will be called the true or proper outline, or simply the outline, without any distinctive additional term. As the white outline ought never to be distinctly visible in an impression, care ought to be taken, more especially where the adjacent tint is dark, not to cut it too deep or too wide. In the first of the two following cuts,

the white outline, intentionally cut rather wider than is necessary, is distinctly seen from its contrast with the dark parts immediately in contact with it. In the second cut of the same subject, with a different back-ground, it is less visible in consequence of the parts adjacent being

light. It is, however, still distinctly seen in the shadow of the feet; but it is shown here purposely to point out an error which is sometimes committed by cutting a white outline where, as in these parts, it is not required. The white outline is here quite unnecessary, as the two blacks ought not to be separated in such a manner; the proper intention of the white outline is not so much to define the form of the figure or object, but, as has been already explained, to make an incision in the wood as a boundary to *other lines* coming against it, and to allow of their being clearly liberated without injury to the proper outline of the object: when a line is cut to such a boundary, the small shaving forced out by the graver becomes immediately released, without the point of the tool coming in contact with the true outline. The old German wood engravers, who chiefly engraved large subjects on apple or pear tree, and on the *side* of the wood, were not in the habit of cutting a white outline round their figures before they began to engrave them, and hence in their cuts objects frequently appear *to stick* to each other. The practice is now, however, so general, that in many modern wood-cuts a white line is improperly seen surrounding every figure.

In proceeding to engrave figures, it is advisable to commence with such as consist of little more than outline, and have no shades expressed by cross-lines. The first step in executing such a subject is to cut a white line on each side of the pencilled lines which are to remain in relief of the height of the plane surface of the block, and to form the impression when it is printed. A cut when thus engraved, and previous to the parts which are white, when printed, being cut away, or, in technical language, *blocked out*, would present the following appearance.*

It is, however, necessary to observe that all the parts which require to be blocked away have been purposely retained in this cut in order to show more clearly the manner in which it is executed; for the engraver usually cuts away as he proceeds all the black masses seen within the subject. A wide margin of solid wood round the edges of the cut is,

* The subject of this cut is the beautiful monument to the memory of two children executed by Sir F. Chantrey, in Lichfield Cathedral.

however, generally allowed to remain until a proof be taken when the engraving is finished, as it affords a support to the paper, and prevents the exterior lines of the subject from appearing too hard. This margin, where room is allowed, is separated from the engraved parts by a moderately deep and wide furrow, and is covered with a piece of paper serving as a *frisket* in taking a proof impression by means of friction. In clearing away such of the black parts in the preceding cut as require to be removed, it is necessary to proceed with great care in order to avoid breaking down or cutting through the lines which are to be left in relief. When the cut is properly cleared out and blocked away, it is then finished, and when printed will appear thus :

Sculptures and bas-reliefs of any kind are generally best represented by simple outlines, with delicate parallel lines, running horizontally, to represent the ground. The following cut is from a design by Flaxman for the front of a gold snuff-box made by Rundell and Bridge for George IV. about 1827. The subject of this design was intended to com-

memorate the General Peace concluded in 1814 : to the left Agriculture is seen flourishing under the auspices of Peace ; while to the right a youthful figure is seen placing a wreath above the helmet of a warrior ; the trophy indicates his services, and opposite to him is seated a figure of Victory. The three other sides, and the top and bottom, were also embellished with figures and ornaments in relief designed by Flaxman. The whole of the dies were cut in steel by Henning and Son—so well known to admirers of art from their beautiful reduced copies and restorations of the sculptures of the Parthenon preserved in the British Museum—and from these dies the plates of gold composing the box were struck, so that the figures appear in slight relief. A blank space was left in the top of the box for an enamel portrait of the King, which was afterwards inserted, surrounded with diamonds, and the margin of the lid was also ornamented in the same manner. This box is perhaps the most beautiful of the kind ever executed in any country: it may justly challenge a comparison with the drinking cups by Benvenuto Cellini, the dagger hafts designed by Durer, or the salts by Hans Holbein. The process of engraving in this style is extremely simple, as it is only necessary to leave the lines drawn in pencil untouched, and to cut away the wood on each side of them. An amateur may without much trouble teach himself to execute cuts in this manner, or to engrave fac-similes of small pen-and-ink sketches such as the annexed.*

Having now explained the mode of procedure in outline engraving, it seems necessary, before proceeding to speak of more complicated subjects, to say a few words respecting drawings made on the block; for, however well the engraving may be executed, the cut which is a fac-simile of a bad drawing can never be a good one. An artist's knowledge of drawing is put to the test when he begins to make designs on wood; he cannot resort, as in painting, to the trick of colour to conceal the defects of his outlines. To be efficient in the engraving, his principal figures must be distinctly made out; a drawing on the wood admits of no *scumbling ;* black and white are the only means by which the subject can be represented; and if he be ignorant of the proper management of chiaro-scuro, and incorrect and feeble in his drawing, he will not be able

* This small cut is a fac-simile, the size of the original, of Sir David Wilkie's first sketch for his picture of the Rabbit on the Wall.

to produce a really good design for the wood engraver. Many persons can paint a tolerably good picture who are utterly incapable of making a passable drawing on wood. Their drawing will not stand the test of simple black and white ; they can indicate generalities "indifferently well" by means of positive colours, but they cannot delineate individual forms correctly with the black-lead pencil. It is from this cause that we have so very few persons who professedly make designs for wood engravers ; and hence the sameness of character that is to be found in so many modern wood-cuts. It is not unusual for many second and third rate painters, when applied to for a drawing for a wood-cut, to speak slightingly of the art, and to decline to furnish the design required. This generally results rather from a consciousness of their own inca-pacity than from any real contempt for the art. As greater painters than any now living have made designs for wood engravers in former times, a second or third rate painter of the present day surely could not be much degraded by doing the same. The true reason for the refusal, however, is generally to be found in such painter's incapacity.

The two next cuts, both drawn from the same sketch,* but by different persons, will show how much depends upon having a good,

No. 1.   No. 2.

artist-like drawing. The first is meagre ; the second, on the contrary, is remarkably spirited, and the additional lines which are introduced not only give effect to the figure, but also in printing form a support to the more delicate parts of the outline.

* The original sketch, from which the figure was copied, is by Morland.

Though a learner in proceeding from one subject to another more complicated will doubtless meet with difficulties which may occasionally damp his ardour, yet he will encounter none which will not yield to earnest perseverance. As it is not likely that any amateur practising the art merely for amusement would be inclined to test his patience by proceeding beyond outline engraving, the succeeding remarks are more especially addressed to those who may wish to apply themselves to wood engraving as a profession.

When beginning to engrave in outline, it is advisable that the subjects first attempted should be of the most simple kind,—similar, for instance, to the preceding figure marked No. 1. When facility in executing cuts in this style is obtained, the learner may proceed to engrave such as are slightly shaded, and have a back-ground indicated as in No. 2. He may next proceed to subjects containing a greater variety of lines, and requiring greater neatness of execution, but should by no means endeavour to get on too fast by attempting to do *much* before he can do a little *well*. Whatever kind of subject be chosen, particular attention ought to be paid to the causes of failure and success in the execution. By diligently noting what produces a good effect in certain subjects, he will, under similar circumstances, be prepared to apply the same means ; and by attending to the faults in his work he will be the more careful to avoid them in future. The group of figures here, selected from

Sir David Wilkie's picture of the Rent Day, will serve as an example of a cut executed by comparatively simple means ; the subject is also

such a one as a pupil may attempt after he has made some progress in engraving slightly shaded figures.   There are no complicated lines which are difficult to execute ; the hatchings are few, and of simple character ; and for the execution of the whole, as here represented, nothing is required but a *feeling* for the subject ; and a moderate degree of skill in the use of the graver, combined with patient application.

When the pupil is thus far advanced, he ought, in subjects of this kind, to avoid introducing more work, more especially in the features, than he can execute with comparative facility and precision ; for, by attempting to attain excellence before he has arrived at mediocrity, he will be very likely to fail, and instead of having reason to congratulate himself on his success, experience nothing but disappointment.   To make wood engraving an interesting, instead of an irksome study to young persons, I would recommend for their practice not only such subjects as are likely to engage their attention, but also such as they may be able to finish before they become weary of their task.   At this period every endeavour ought to be made to smooth the pupil's way by giving him such subjects to execute as will rather serve to stimulate his exertions than exhaust his patience.   Little characteristic figures, like the one here copied, from one of Hogarth's plates of the Four Parts of the

Day, seem most suitable for this purpose.   A subject of this kind does not contain so much work as to render a young person tired of it before

it be finished ; while at the same time it serves to exercise him in the practice of the art and to engage his attention.

When a pupil feels no interest in what he is employed on, he will seldom execute his work well ; and when he is kept too long in engraving subjects that merely try his patience, he is apt to lose all taste for the art, and become a mere mechanical cutter of lines, without caring for what they express.

Such a cut as the following—copied from an etching by Rembrandt —will form a useful exercise to the pupil, after he has attained facility in the execution of outline subjects, while at the same time it will serve to display the excellent effect in wood engravings of well contrasted light and shade. The hog—which is here the principal object—

immediately arrests the eye, while the figures in the back-ground, being introduced merely to aid the composition and form a medium between the dark colour of the animal and the white paper, consist of little more than outline, and are comparatively light. In engraving the hog, it is necessary to exercise a little judgment in representing the bristly hair, and in *touching* the details effectively.

When a learner has made some progress, he may attempt such a cut as that on the next page in order to exercise himself in the appropriate representation of animal texture. The subject is a dray-horse, formerly belonging to Messrs. Meux and Co., and the drawing was made on the block by James Ward, R.A., one of the most distinguished animal painters of the present time. Such a cut, though executed by simple

means, affords an excellent test of a learner's skill and discrimination :
the hide is smooth and glossy; the mane is thick and tangled; the
long flowing hair of the tail has to be represented in a proper manner;
and the markings of the joints require the exercise of both judgment

and skill. By attending to such distinctions at the commencement of
his career, he will find less difficulty in representing objects by appropriate texture when he shall have made greater progress, and will not
be entirely dependent on a designer to *lay in* for him every line. An
engraver who requires every line to be drawn, and who is only capable
of executing a fac-simile of a design made for him on the block, can
never excel.

As enough perhaps has been said in explanation of the manner of
cutting tints, and of figures chiefly represented by single lines, I shall
now give a cut—Jacob blessing the children of Joseph—in which single-
lined figures and tint are combined. It is necessary to observe that this
cut is not introduced as a good specimen of engraving, but as being
well adapted, from the simplicity of its execution, to illustrate what I
have to say. The figures are represented by single lines, which require
the exercise of no great degree of skill; and by the introduction of a
varied tint as a back-ground the cut appears like a complete subject, and
not like a sketch, or a detached group.

It is necessary to remark here, that when comparatively light objects,
such as the figures here seen, are to be relieved by a tint of any kind,
whether darker or lighter, such objects are now generally separated from
it by a black outline. The reason for leaving such an outline in parts
where the conjunction of the tint and the figures does not render it
absolutely *necessary* is this : as those parts in a cut which appear white

in the impression are to be cut away—as has already been explained,—
it frequently happens that when they are cut away *first*, and the tint
cut afterwards, the wood breaks away near the termination of the line
before the tool arrives at the blank or white. It is, therefore, extremely
difficult to preserve a distinct outline in this manner, and hence a black
conventional outline is introduced in those parts where properly there
ought to be none, except such as is formed by the tint *relieving* against
the white parts, as is seen in the back part of the head of Jacob in
the present cut, where there is no other outline than that which is
formed by the tint relieving against his white cap. Bewick used to
execute all his subjects in this manner; but he not unfrequently

carried this principle too far, not only running the lines of his tints
into the white on the *light* side of his figures,—that is, on the side
on which the light falls,—but also on both sides of a light object.

Before dismissing this part of the subject, it is necessary to observe
further, that when the white parts are cut away before the tint is
introduced, the conventional black outline is very liable to be cut
through by the tool slipping. This will be rendered more intelligible
by an inspection of the following cut,* where the house is seen finished,

* In this cut the *white* outline, mentioned at page 587, is distinctly seen at the top of the
buildings and above the trees.

and the part where a tint is intended to be subsequently engraved appears black. Any person in the least acquainted with the practice of wood engraving, will perceive, that should the tool happen to slip

when near the finished parts, in coming directly towards them, it will be very likely to cut the outline through, and to make a breach in proportion as such outline may be thin, and thus yield more readily to the force of the tool.

When the tint is cut *first*, instead of being left to be executed last, as it would be in the preceding cut, the mass of wood out of which the house is subsequently engraved serves as a kind of barrier to the tool in the event of its slipping, and allows of the tint being cut with less risk quite up to the white outline. By attending to such matters, and considering what part of a subject can be most safely executed first, a learner will both avoid the risk of cutting through his outline, and be enabled to execute his work with comparative facility. The following cut is an example of the tint being cut first. For the information of

those who are unacquainted with the process of wood engraving, it is necessary to remark that the parts which appear positively black are those which remain untouched by the graver.

The following subject, copied from one of Rembrandt's etchings, is chiefly represented by black lines crossing each other. Such lines, usually termed *cross-hatchings*, are executed with great facility in copper and steel, where they are cut *into* the metal; but in wood engraving, where they are left in *relief*, it requires considerable time and attention to execute them with delicacy and precision. In order to explain more clearly the difficulty of executing cross-hatchings, let it be conceived that this cut is a drawing made on a block, and that the engraver's object is to produce a fac-simile of it: now, as each black line is to be left in relief, it is evident that he cannot imitate the cross-hatchings seen

in the arms, the neck, and other parts, by cutting the lines continuously as in engraving on copper, which puts black *in* by means of an incision, while in wood engraving a similar line takes it *out.* As the wood engraver, then, can only obtain white by cutting out the parts that are to appear so in the impression, while the black is to be left in relief, the only manner in which he is enabled to represent *cross-hatchings*, or *black lines crossing each other*, is to cut out singly with his graver every one of the white interstices. Such an operation, as will be evident from an inspection of this cut, necessarily requires not only patience, but also considerable skill to perform it in a proper manner,—that is, to cut each white space cleanly out, and to preserve the lines of a regular thickness. From the supposed impossibility of executing such cross lines, it has been conjectured that many of the old wood-cuts containing such work were engraved in metallic relief: this opinion, however, is sufficiently refuted, by the fact of hundreds of blocks containing cross-hatchings being still in existence, and by the much more delicate and difficult work of the same kind displayed in modern wood engravings. Not only are cross-hatchings of the greatest delicacy now executed in England, but to such a degree of refinement is the process occasionally carried, that small black *touches*—such as may be perceived in the preceding cut in the folds of the sleeve above the elbow of the right arm—are left in the white interstices between the lines. Cross-hatchings, where the interstices are entirely white, are executed by means of a lozenge-pointed tool, and the piece of wood is removed at two *cuts*, each beginning at the opposite angles. Where a small black touch is left within the interstices, the operation becomes more difficult, and is performed by cutting round such minute touch of black with a finely pointed graver.

The various conjectures that have been propounded respecting the mode in which cross-hatchings have been effected in old wood-cuts require no argument to refute them, as they are directly contradicted both by undoubted historical facts, and by every day's experience. Vegetable putties, punches, and metallic relief are nothing but the trifling speculations of persons who are fonder of propounding theories to display their own ingenuity than willing to investigate facts in order to arrive at the truth. It has happened rather unfortunately, that most persons who have hitherto written upon the subject have known very little about the practice of wood engraving, and have not thought it worth their while to consult those who were able to give them information. There is, however, no fear now of a young wood engraver being deterred from attempting cross-hatchings on learning from certain heretofore authorities on the subject that such work could not be executed on wood. He now laughs at *vegetable putties, square-pointed punches* for indenting the block to produce cross-hatchings, and *metallic relief:* by means of his graver alone he produces a practical refutation of every baseless theory that has been propounded on the subject.

The right leg of Dentatus in Mr. Harvey's large wood engraving after Mr. Haydon's picture is perhaps the most beautiful specimen of cross-hatching that ever was executed on wood; and, in my opinion, it is the best engraved part of the whole subject. Through the kindness of Mr. Harvey, I have obtained a cast of this portion of the block, from which the present impression is printed. The lines showing the muscular rotundity and action of the limb are as admirably *laid in* as they are beautifully engraved. In the wider and stronger cross-hatchings of the drapery above, the small black touches previously mentioned are perceived in the lozenge-shaped interstices.

From an opinion that the excellence of an engraving consists chiefly in the difficulty of its execution, we now frequently find cross-hatchings in several modern wood-cuts, more especially in such as are manufactured for the French market, where a better effect would have been

produced by simpler means. Cross-hatchings, *properly introduced*, undoubtedly improve a subject; and some parts of large figures, such as the leg of Dentatus, cannot be well expressed without their aid, as a series of curved lines on a limb, when not crossed, generally cause it to appear stiff and rigid. By crossing them, however, by other lines properly *laid in*, the part assumes a most soft and natural appearance.

As the greatest advantage which wood engraving possesses over copper is the effective manner in which strongly contrasted light and shade can be represented, Rembrandt's etchings,—which, like his paintings, are distinguished by the skilful management of the chiaroscuro—form excellent studies for the engraver or designer on wood who should wish to become well acquainted with the capabilities of the art. A delicate wood-cut, executed in imitation of a smooth steel-engraving of "sober grey" tone, is sure to be tame and insipid; and whenever wood engravers attempt to give to their cuts the appearance of copper or steel-plates, and neglect the peculiar advantages of their own art, they

are sure to fail, notwithstanding the pains they may bestow. Their work, instead of being commended as a successful application of the peculiar means of the art, is in effect condemned by being regarded as " a clever *imitation* of a copper-plate."

The above cut of Christ and the Woman of Samaria, copied from an etching by Rembrandt, will perhaps more forcibly illustrate what has been said with respect to wood engraving being excellently adapted to effectively express strong contrasts of light and shade. The original etching—which has been faithfully copied—is a good example of

Rembrandt's consummate skill in the management of chiaro-scuro; everything that he has wished to forcibly express immediately arrests the eye, while in the whole design nothing appears abrupt. The extremes of light and shade concentre in the principal figure, that of Christ, and to this everything else in the composition is either subordinate or accessory. The middle tint under the arched passage forms a medium between the darkness of Christ's robe and the shade under the curve of the nearest arch, and the light in the front of his figure is gradually carried off to the left through the medium of the woman and the distant buildings, which gradually approach to the colour of the paper. Were a tint, however delicate, introduced in this subject to represent the sky, the effect would be destroyed; the parts which are now so effective would appear spotted and confused, and have a crude, unfinished appearance. By the injudicious introduction of a tinted sky many wood-cuts, which would otherwise be striking and effective, are quite spoiled.

It but too frequently happens when works are illustrated with wood-cuts, that subjects are chosen which the art cannot successfully represent. Whether the work to be illustrated be matter of fact or fiction, the designer, unless he be acquainted both with the capabilities and defects of the art, seldom thinks of more than making a drawing according to his own fancy, and never takes into consideration the means by which it has to be executed. To this inattention may be traced many failures in works illustrated with wood-cuts, and for which the engraver is censured, although he may have, with great care and skill, accomplished all that the art could effect. An artist who is desirous that his designs, when engraved on wood, should appear like impressions from *over-done* steel-plates, ought never to be employed to make drawings for wood engravers: he does not understand the peculiar advantages of the art, and his designs will only have a tendency to bring it into contempt, while those who execute them will be blamed for the defects which are the result of his want of knowledge.

Delicate wood engravings which are made to look well in a proof on India paper by rubbing the ink partially off the block in the lighter parts—in the manner described by Papillon at page 466—generally present a very different appearance when printed, either with or without types in the same page. Lines which are cut too thin are very liable to turn down in printing from their want of support; and hence cuts consisting chiefly of such lines are seldom so durable as those which display more black, and are executed in a more bold and effective style. A designer who understands the peculiarities of wood engraving will avoid introducing delicate lines in parts where they receive no support from others of greater strength or closeness near to them, but are exposed to the unmitigated force of the press. Cuts in proportion to the quantity of *colour* which they display are so much the better enabled to bear the action of the press ; the delicate lines which they contain, from their receiving support from the others, are not only less liable to break down, but, from their contrast with the darker parts of the subject, appear to greater advantage than in a cut which is of a uniformly grey tone. I am not, however, the advocate of *black*, and little else, in a wood-cut ; on the contrary, I am perfectly aware of the absurdity of introducing patches of black without either meaning or effect. What I wish to inculcate is, that a wood-cut to have a good effect must contain more of properly contrasted black and white than those who wish their cuts to appear like imitations of steel or copper-plate engravings are willing to allow. As wood engraving is not well adapted to represent subjects requiring great delicacy of lines and variety of tints, such will be generally avoided by a designer who understands the art ; while, on the contrary, he will avail himself of its advantages in representing well contrasted light and shade in a manner superior to either copper-plate or steel engraving. Of all modern engravers on wood, none understood the advantages of their art in this respect better than Bewick and Clennell : the cuts of their engraving are generally the most effective that have ever been executed.

Night-pieces, where the light is seen proceeding from a lantern, a lamp, or any other luminous object, can be well represented by means of wood engraving, although such subjects are very seldom attempted. An engraved wood-block, which contains a considerable proportion of positive black, prints much better than a copper-plate engraving of the same kind ; in the former the ink is distributed of an even thickness over the *surface*, and is evenly pressed upon the paper ; in the latter the ink forms a little pool in the *hollowed parts*, and, instead of being evenly taken up by the paper which is *pressed into* it, adheres only partially, thus giving in the corresponding parts a blurred appearance to the impression. For the effective representation of such scenes as Meg Merrilies watching by a feeble light the dying struggles of a smuggler, or Dirk Hatterick in the Cave, from Sir Walter Scott's Guy Mannering, wood engraving is peculiarly adapted,—that is, supposing the designer, in addition to possessing a knowledge of chiaro-scuro, to be also capable of drawing correctly, and of treating the subject with proper *feeling*. Some idea of the capability of the art in this respect may be formed from the following cut—the Flight into Egypt,—copied from an etching by Rembrandt. The mere work in this cut is of a very simple character ; there are no lines of difficult execution ; and the only parts that are lowered are those which represent the rays of light seen proceeding from the lantern.

As the wood engraver can always get his subject *lighter*, but cannot reproduce the black which he has cut away, he ought to be careful not to get his subject too light before he has taken a proof; and even in reducing the *colour* according to the touchings of the designer on the proof, he ought to proceed with great circumspection ; and where his own judgment informs him that to take out all the black marked for excision would be to spoil the cut, the safest mode would be to take out only a part, and not remove all at once ; for by strictly adhering to the

directions of an artist who knows very little of the real advantages of wood engraving, it will not unfrequently happen that the cut so amended will to himself, when printed, appear worse than it did in its first state. In the following cut too much has been done in this respect; it has been touched and retouched so often, in order to make it appear delicate, that the spirit of the original drawing has been entirely lost. In this instance the fault was not that of the artist, but of the engraver, who "would not let well alone;" but, in order to improve his work, as he fancied, kept *trimming* the parts which gave effect to the whole till he made it what it now appears. So far as relates to the execution of the lines, the subject need not have been better; but, from the engraver's

having taken away too much colour in places where it was necessary, the whole has the appearance of middle tint, the excellence of the original drawing is lost, and in its stead we have a dull, misty, spiritless wood engraving.

In every cut there ought to be a principal object to first arrest the attention; and if this cannot be effected from want of interest in such object considered singly, the designer ought to make the general subject pleasing to the eye by skilful composition or combination of forms, and the effective distribution of light and shade.

The preceding cut—a moonlight scene—when compared with the previous one, will show how much depends on an engraver having a proper *feeling* for his subject. So far as relates to the mere execution of the lines, this cut is decidedly inferior to the former; but, viewed as a production of art, and as a spirited representation of the original drawing, it is very much superior : in the former we see little more than mechanical dexterity ; while in the latter we perceive that the engraver has, from a greater knowledge of his art, produced a pleasing effect by comparatively simple means. The former cut displays more mechanical skill ; the latter more artistic feeling. The one contains much delicate work, but is deficient in spirit ; the other, which has been produced with little more than half the labour, is more effective because the subject has been better understood.

The following cut, representing a landscape, with the effect of the setting sun, displays great delicacy of execution ; but the labour here

is not thrown away, as in the sea-piece just mentioned: manual dexterity in the use of the graver is combined with the knowledge of an artist, and the result is a wood engraving at once delicate in execution and spirited in its general effect.

A volume might be filled with examples and comments on them, and I might, like Papillon, *instruct* the reader in the practice of the art, by informing him how many times the graver would have to enter the wood in order to produce a certain number of lines in relief ; but I have no inclination to do either the one or the other : my object is to make a few observations on some of the most important and least understood points in the practice of wood engraving, and to illustrate them with examples, rather than to enter into minute details, which would be uninteresting to the general reader, and useless to the learner who has made any progress in the art. The person who wishes to acquire a knowledge of wood engraving, with the view of practising it professionally, must generally be guided by his own judgment and feeling; for he who requires the aid of rules and examples in every possible case will never attain excellence. A learner ought not to put much trust in what is said about the beautiful wood-cuts—or *plates*, as some critics call them—which appear in modern publications. He ought to examine for himself, and not pin his faith to ephemeral commendations, which are often the customary acknowledgment for a presentation copy of the work. It is not unusual to find very ordinary wood-cuts praised as displaying the very perfection of the art, while others of much greater merit are entirely overlooked.

The person who wishes to excel as a wood engraver,—that is, to display in his cuts the knowledge and feeling of an artist, as well as the mechanical dexterity of a workman,—ought always to bear in mind that those who rank highest in modern times, not only as engravers, but also as designers on wood, have generally adopted the simplest means of effecting their purpose, and have never introduced unmeaning cross-hatchings, when working from their own drawings, merely to display their skill in execution. In representing a peasant supping his porridge, they have not spent a day on the figure, and two in delicately engraving the bowl. It may almost be said that Bewick never employed cross-hatchings; for, in the two or three instances in which he introduced such lines, it has been rather for the sake of experiment than to improve the appearance of the cut. Though one of the finest specimens of this kind of work ever executed on wood is to be found in Mr. Harvey's cut of Dentatus, yet, on other occasions, when he engraved his own designs, he seldom introduced cross-hatchings when he could accomplish the same object by simpler means. A wood engraving, viewed as a *work of art*, is *not* good in proportion as many of its parts have the appearance of fine lace. Bewick's birds and tailpieces are not, in my opinion, less excellent because they do not display so much *work* as a modern wood-cut which contains numerous cross-hatchings. Several of the best French designers on wood of the present day appear to have formed erroneous opinions on this subject; and hence we find in many of their designs much of the engraver's time spent in the execution of parts which are unimportant, while others, where expression or feeling ought to be shown, are treated in a careless manner. Many of their designs seem to have been made rather to test the patience of the engraver as a *workman* than to display his ability as an *artist*. The following cut, from a cast of a part of the Death of Dentatus, is introduced to show in how simple and effective a manner Mr. Harvey has represented the shield of the hero. An inferior artist would be very likely to represent such an object by means of complicated lines, which,

while they would be less effective, would require nearly a week to engrave.

Considering the number of wood engravings that are yearly executed in this country, it is rather surprising that there should hitherto have been so few persons capable of making a good drawing on wood. Till within the last few years, it might be said that there was probably not more than one *artist* in the kingdom possessing a knowledge of design who professionally devoted himself to making drawings on the block for wood engravers. Whenever a good original design is wanted, there are still but few persons to whom the English wood engraver can apply with the certainty of obtaining it; for though some of our most distinguished painters have occasionally furnished designs to be engraved on wood, it has mostly been as a matter of especial favour to an individual who had an interest in the work in which such designs were to appear. In this respect we are behind our French neighbours; the more common kind of French wood-cuts containing figures are much superior to our own of the same class; the drawing is much more correct, more attention is paid to costume, and in the details we perceive the indications of much greater knowledge of art than is generally to be found in the productions of our second-rate occasional designers on wood. It cannot be said that this deficiency results from want of encouragement; for a designer on wood, of even moderate abilities, is better paid for his drawings than a second-rate painter is for his pictures. The truth is, that a taste for correct drawing has hitherto not been sufficiently cultivated in England: our artists are painters before they can draw; and hence, comparatively few can make a good design on wood. They require the aid of positive colours to deceive the eye, and prevent it from resting upon the defects of their drawing. It is therefore of great importance that a wood engraver should have some knowledge of drawing himself, in order that he may be able to correct many of the defects that are to be found in the commoner kind of subjects sent to him to be engraved.

In the execution of subjects which require considerable time, but little more than the exercise of mechanical skill, it is frequently advisable to adopt the principle of *the division of labour*, and have the work performed, as it were, by instalments, allotting to each person that portion of the subject which he is likely to execute best. In this manner the annexed cut of Rouen Cathedral has been engraved by four different persons; and the result of their joint labours is such a work as not even the best engraver of the four could have executed by himself. Each having to do but a little, and that of the kind of work in which he excelled, has worked *con amore*, and finished his task before he became weary of it.

Though copper-plate engraving has a great advantage over wood when applied to the execution of maps, in consequence of the greater delicacy that can be given to the different shades and lines, indicating hills, rivers, and the boundaries of districts, and also from the number of names that can be introduced, and from the comparative facility of executing them; yet, as maps engraved on copper, however simple they may be, require to be printed separately, by means of a rolling-press

ROUEN CATHEDRAL.

the unavoidable expense frequently renders it impossible to give such maps, even when necessary, in books published at a low price. Under

R R 2

such circumstances, where little more than outlines, with the course of rivers, and comparatively few names, are required, wood engraving possesses an advantage over copper, as such maps can be executed at a very moderate expense, and printed with the letter-press of the work for which they are intended. As the names in maps engraved on wood are the most difficult parts of the subject, the method of drilling holes in the block and inserting the names in type—as was adopted in the

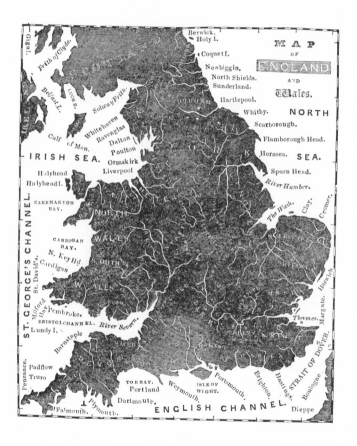

maps to Sebastian Munster's Cosmography, Basle, 1550,*—has recently been revived. The names in the outline maps contained in the Penny Cyclopædia are inserted in this manner. Had those maps not been engraved on wood, it would have been impossible that any could have been given in the work, as the low price at which it is published would

* Some account of the maps in Sebastian Munster's Cosmography is previously given at page 204, and page 417.

not have allowed of their being engraved on copper, and, consequently, printed by means of a rolling-press at an additional expense.

When, however, a map is of small dimensions, and several names in letters of comparatively large size are required to be given, this method of piercing the block can scarcely be applied without great risk of its breaking to pieces under the press, in consequence of its being weakened in parts by the holes drilled through it being so near together.* This inconvenience, however, may be remedied by engraving the names in *intaglio* where they are most numerous, and afterwards cutting a *tint* over them, so that when printed they may appear white on a dark ground. Other names beyond the boundary of the map can be inserted, where necessary, in type. The preceding skeleton map of England and Wales, showing the divisions of the counties and the course of the principal rivers, has been executed in this manner : all the names on the land, and the courses of the rivers, were first engraved on the smooth surface of the block in *intaglio*—in less than a third of the time which would have been required to engrave them in relief ; the tint was next cut ; and lastly, the block was pierced, and all the other names inserted in type, with the exception of the word " ENGLAND" in the title, which was engraved in the same manner as the names on the land.

As what has been previously said about the practice of the art relates entirely to engraving where the lines are of the same height, or in the same plane, and when the impression is supposed to be obtained by the pressure of a flat surface, I shall now proceed to explain the practice of lowering, by which operation the surface of the block is either scraped away from the centre towards the sides, or, as may be required, hollowed out in other places. The object of thus lowering a block is, that the lines in such places may be less exposed to pressure in printing, and thus appear lighter than if they were of the same height as the others. This method, though it has been claimed as a modern invention, is of considerable antiquity, having been practised in 1538, as has been previously observed at page 462. Instances of lowering are very frequent in cuts engraved by Bewick ; but until within the last five or six years the practice was not resorted to by south-country engravers. It is absolutely necessary that wood-cuts intended to be printed by a steam-press should be lowered in such parts as are to appear light ; for, as the pressure on the cut proceeds from the even surface of a metal cylinder covered with a blanket, there is no means of *helping* a cut, as is generally done when printed by a hand-press, by means of *overlays*. Overlaying consists in pasting pieces of

---

* When there is any danger of the block splitting from this cause, it is best to have a cast taken from it, as by this means the whole is obtained of one solid piece.

paper either on the front or at the back of the outer tympan, immediately over such parts of the block as require to be printed dark ; and the effect of this is to increase the action of the platten on those parts, and to diminish it on such as are not overlaid. When lowered blocks are printed at a common press, it is necessary that a blanket should be used in the tympans, in order that the paper may be pressed into the hollowed or lowered parts, and the lines thus *brought up*. The application of the steam-press to printing lowered wood-cuts may be

considered as an epoch in the history of wood engraving. Wood-cuts were first printed *by a steam-press* at Messrs. Clowes and Sons' establishment,* and since that time *lowering* has been more generally practised than at any former period.

* The first work containing lowered cuts printed by a steam-press was that on Cattle, published in numbers, under the superintendence of the Society for the Diffusion of Useful Knowledge, 1832.

By means of simply lowering the edges of a block, so that the surface shall be convex instead of plane, the lines are made to diminish in strength as they recede from the centre until they become gradually blended with the white paper on which the cut is printed. This is the most simple mode of lowering, and is now frequently adopted in such cuts as are termed *vignettes*,—that is, such as are not bounded by definite lines surrounding them in the manner of a border. In the preceding cut, representing a group from Sir David Wilkie's painting of the Village Festival, in the National Gallery, the light appearance of the lines towards the edges has been produced in this manner.

Mr. Landseer, in his Lectures on Engraving, observes that hard edges are incident to wood-cut vignettes. He was not aware of the means by which this objectionable appearance could be remedied. The following are his observations on this subject : " A principal beauty in most vignettes consists in the delicacy with which they appear to relieve from the white paper on which they are printed. The objects of which vignettes consist, themselves forming the boundary of the composition, their extremities should for the most part be tenderly blended—be almost melted, as it were, into the paper, or ground. Now, in printing with the letter-press, the pressure is rather the strongest at the extremities of the engraving, where we wish it to be weakest, and it is so from the unavoidable swelling of the damp paper on which the impressions are worked, and the softness of the blankets in the tympans of the press. Hence, hard, instead of soft edges, are incident to vignettes engraven on wood, which all the care of the printer, with all the modern accuracy of his machine, can rarely avoid."

Mr. Landseer's objection to vignettes engraved on wood applies only to such as are engraved on a plane surface, since by lowering the block towards the edges, lines gradually blending with the white paper can be obtained with the greatest facility. For the representation of such subjects,—supposing that their principal beauty consists in "the delicacy with which they appear to relieve from the white paper,"—wood engraving is as well adapted as engraving on copper or steel. Though it is certainly desirable that the lines in a vignette should gradually become blended with the colour of the paper, yet something more is required in an engraving of this kind, whether on wood or on metal. Much depends on its form harmonizing with the composition of the subject : a beautiful drawing reduced to an irregular shape, and having the edges merely softened, will not always constitute a good vignette. Of this we have but too many instances in modern copper-plate engravings, as well as wood-cuts. Of all modern artists J. M. W. Turner, R. A., and W. Harvey appear to excel in giving to their vignettes a form suitable to the composition.

Perhaps it may not be out of place to say a few words here on the original meaning of the word *vignette*, which is now generally used to signify either a wood-cut or a copper-plate engraving which is not inclosed by definite lines forming a border. The word is French, and is synonymous with the Latin *viticula*, which means a little vine, or a vine shoot, such as is here represented.

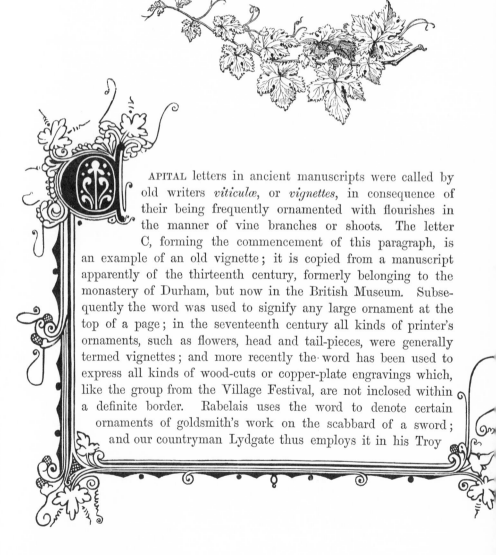

APITAL letters in ancient manuscripts were called by old writers *viticulæ*, or *vignettes*, in consequence of their being frequently ornamented with flourishes in the manner of vine branches or shoots. The letter C, forming the commencement of this paragraph, is an example of an old vignette; it is copied from a manuscript apparently of the thirteenth century, formerly belonging to the monastery of Durham, but now in the British Museum. Subsequently the word was used to signify any large ornament at the top of a page; in the seventeenth century all kinds of printer's ornaments, such as flowers, head and tail-pieces, were generally termed vignettes; and more recently the word has been used to express all kinds of wood-cuts or copper-plate engravings which, like the group from the Village Festival, are not inclosed within a definite border. Rabelais uses the word to denote certain ornaments of goldsmith's work on the scabbard of a sword; and our countryman Lydgate thus employs it in his Troy

Book to denote the sculptured foliage and tracery at the sides of a window :

> " And if I should rehearsen by and by
> The corve knots, by craft and masonry,
> The fresh embowing with virges right as lines,
> And the housing full of backewines,
> The rich coining, the lusty battlements,
> *Vinettes* running in casements."

The additional specimens of ornamental capitals on the preceding page are chiefly taken from Shaw's Alphabets, in which will be found a great variety of capitals of all ages.

Before introducing any examples of concave lowering in the middle of a cut, it seems necessary to give first a familiar illustration of the principle, in order that what is subsequently said upon this subject may be the more readily understood.—The crown-piece of George IV., which every reader can refer to, will afford the necessary illustrations. As the head of the King on the obverse, and the figures of St. George, the horse, and the dragon, on the reverse, are in *relief,*—that is, higher than the field,—it is evident, that if the coin were printed, each side separately, by means of pressure from an even surface, whether plane or cylindrical, covered with a yielding material, such as a blanket or woollen cloth, so as to press the paper against the field or lower parts, the impressions would appear as follows,—that is, with the parts in relief darkest, and the lower proportionably lighter from their being less exposed to pressure.

IMPRESSIONS FROM A SURFACE WITH THE FIGURES IN RELIEF.

If casts be taken of each side of the same coin, the parts which in the original are raised, or in *relief,* will then be concave, or in *intaglio ;* * and if such casts be printed in the manner of wood-cuts, the impressions will appear as in the opposite page,—that is, the field

* The *casts* are precisely the same as the *dies* from which the coin is struck.

being now highest will appear positively black, while the figures now in *intaglio*, or *lowered*, as I should say when speaking of a wood-cut, will appear lighter in proportion to the concavity of the different parts.

IMPRESSIONS FROM A SURFACE WITH THE FIGURES LOWERED, OR IN INTAGLIO.

Upon a knowledge of the principle here exemplified the practice of lowering in wood engraving entirely depends. When a block is properly lowered, there is no occasion for overlays; and when cuts are to be printed at a steam-press,—where such means to increase the pressure in some parts and diminish it in others cannot be employed without great loss of time,—it becomes absolutely necessary that the blocks should be lowered in the parts where it is intended that the lines should appear light.

In order that a cut should be printed properly without overlays, either at a common press with a blanket in the tympans, or at a steam-press where the cylinder is covered with woollen cloth, it is necessary that the parts intended to appear light should be lowered before the lines seen upon them are engraved; and the mode of proceeding in this case is as follows:—The designer being aware of the manner in which the cut is to be printed, and understanding the practice of lowering, first makes the drawing on the block in little more than outline,* and washes in with flake-white the parts which it is necessary to lower. The block is then sent to the engraver, who, with an instrument resembling a sharp-edged burnisher, or with a flat tool or chisel, scrapes or pares away the wood in the parts indicated. When the lowering is completed, the designer finishes the drawing, and the cut is engraved. It is necessary to observe, that unless the person who makes the drawing on the block perfectly understand the principle of lowering, and the purposes for which it is intended, he will never be able to design properly a subject intended to be printed by a steam-press.

---

* If the drawing were finished, the lines on the parts intended to be light would necessarily be effaced in lowering the block in such parts.

When an object is to be represented dark upon a light ground, or upon middle tint, the first operation in beginning to lower the block is to cut a delicate white outline round the dark object, and proceed with a flat tool or a scraper, as may be most convenient, to take a thin shaving or paring off those parts on which the background or middle tint is to be engraved. The extent to which the block must be lowered will depend on the degree of lightness intended to be given to such parts. In Bewick's time, when the pressmen used leather balls to ink the cuts and types, it was only necessary to take a very thin shaving off the block in order to produce the desired effect; as such balls, from the want of elasticity in the leather, which was comparatively hard and unyielding, would only touch lightly such parts as were below the level

of the other lines and the face of the types: had the block been lowered to any considerable depth, such parts would not have received any ink, and consequently would not have shown the lines engraved on them in the impression. In the present day, when composition rollers are used, it is necessary to lower the parts intended to appear light to a much greater depth than formerly;* as such rollers, in consequence of their greater elasticity, are pressed, in the process of inking, to a considerably greater depth between the lines of a cut than the old leather balls. The preceding cut—a Shepherd's Dog, drawn by W. Harvey,—is printed from

---

* In cuts printed by a steam-press it not unfrequently happens that lowering to the depth of the sixteenth part of an inch scarcely produces a perceptible difference in the strength of the impression. In cuts inked with leather balls, and printed at the common press, the lines in parts lowered to this depth would not be visible.

a block in which both the fore-ground and distance are lowered to give greater effect to the animal. If such a cut, printed in the same page with types, as it appears here, were inked with leather balls, a considerable portion of the lowered parts would not be visible. This cut illustrates the principle of printing from a surface—such as that of a coin—in which the head or figure is in relief.

In the next cut, an Egret, from a drawing by W. Harvey, the figure of the bird appears white on a dark ground,—the reverse of the cut of the Shepherd's Dog,—and is an example of lowering the block in the middle in the manner of a die with the figures in intaglio, or a cast from a coin in which the head or figures are in relief.

In a cut of this kind the general form of the principal object required to be light is first lowered out, and the drawing of the figure being next completed upon the hollowed part, the engraver proceeds to cut the lines, beginning with the back-ground and finishing the principal object last. In cutting the lines in the hollowed part, the engraver uses such a tool, slightly curving upwards towards the point, as has been previously described at page 579. In lowering the principal object in a cut of this kind, the greatest attention is necessary in order that the hollowed parts may be gradually concave, and also of a sufficient depth. In performing this operation, the engraver is solely guided by his own judgment; and unless he have some practical knowledge of the extent to which composition balls and rollers will penetrate in such hollowed parts, it is almost impossible that he should execute his work in a proper manner;—should he succeed, it will only be by chance, like a person shooting at a mark blindfolded. In such cases, though no special rules can be given, it is necessary to observe that the part lowered will, in proportion to its area, be exposed to receive nearly the same quantity of ink, and the same degree of pressure, as the lines on a level with the types. The *depth* to which such parts require to be lowered will consequently depend on their extent; and the degree of lightness intended to be given to the lines engraved on them. This, however, will be best illustrated by the annexed diagram. If, for instance, the part to be lowered extend from

A to B, it will be necessary to hollow the block to the depth indicated by the dotted line A c B. Should it extend from A to D, it will require to be lowered to the depth of the dotted line A e D in order to obtain the same degree of lightness in colour as in the lowered part A c B of less area,—that is, supposing the engraved lines in both cases to be of equal delicacy.

As overlaying such delicately engraved cuts as require the greatest attention in printing occupies much time, and lays the press idle during the process, the additional sum charged per sheet for works containing a number of such cuts has frequently operated to the disadvantage of

wood engraving, by causing its productions to be dispensed with in many books where they might have been introduced with great advantage, both as direct and incidental illustrations. It is, therefore, of great importance to adapt the art of wood engraving to the execution of cuts of all kinds, whether comparatively coarse or of the greatest delicacy, so that they may be properly printed at the least possible expense.

The preceding cut, with the two following, which have all been lowered, would, if printed at a steam-press, appear nearly as well as they do in the present work, where they have been printed by means of a common press with a blanket. But such a subject—a winter-piece, with an ass and her foal standing near an old outhouse,—cannot be properly represented without lowering the block; for no overlaying would cause the lines indicating the thatch on the houses and the stacks, as seen through the snow, to appear so soft as they now do.

In this cut of a Salmon Trout, with a view of Bywell Lock, on the river Tyne, both the fore-ground and the distance are lowered; the objects which appear comparatively dark in those parts are the least reduced, while those that appear lightest are such as are lowered to the greatest extent. The back of the fish, which appears dark in the impression, is in the block like a ridge, which is gradually lowered in a hollow curve towards the lower line. In such a cut as this, particular care ought to be taken not to lower too much those parts which come into immediate contact with a strong black outline, such as the back of the Salmon; for where the lowering in such parts is too abrupt, there is great risk of the lines engraved on them not being *brought up*, and thus causing the figure in relief to appear surrounded with a white line, as in the impressions from the crown-piece at page 618.

By means of lowering, the black pony, on which a boy is seen riding, in the following cut, is much more effectively represented, than if the whole subject were engraved on a plane surface. The grey horse, and the light jacket of the rider, the ground, the garden wall, and the

lightest of the trees, are all lowered in order to give greater effect to the pony.

A cut which is properly lowered may not only be printed by a steam-press without overlays, but will also afford a much greater number of

good impressions than one of the same kind engraved on a plane surface ; for the more delicate parts, being lower than those adjacent to them, are thus saved from too much pressure, without the necessity of increasing it in other places. The preceding cut will serve to show the advantages of lowering in this respect. It was originally engraved, from a drawing by William Harvey, for the Treatise on Cattle, published under the direction of the Society for the Diffusion of Useful Knowledge. Though twelve thousand impressions have already been printed from it by means of Messrs. Clowes and Sons' steam-press, it has not sustained the slightest injury in any part ; and the present impression is scarcely inferior to the first proof. With the exception of clearing out the ink in two or three places, it has required no preparation or retouching to give it its present appearance. Had such a work as the Treatise on Cattle been printed at a common press without the blocks having been lowered, the cost of printing would have been at least double the sum charged by Messrs. Clowes ; and the engraving, after so great a number of impressions had been taken, would have been considerably injured, if not quite spoiled.

In complicated subjects, consisting of many figures, and in which the light and shade are much diversified, it becomes necessary to combine the two principles of lowering, which have been separately illustrated by the Dog and the Egret, and to adapt them according to circumstances, forming some parts convex, and making others concave, respectively, as the objects engraved on them are to appear dark or light. In order to illustrate this process of combined lowering, I have chosen a subject from Rembrandt—the Descent from the Cross—in which several figures are introduced, and in which the lights and shades are so much varied—in some parts blended by a delicate middle tint, and in others strongly contrasted—as to afford the greatest possible scope for the illustration of what is termed *lowering* in a wood engraving.

The cut on the next page shows the appearance of an impression taken from the block before a single line had been engraved, except the *white* outline bounding the figures. All that is here seen has been effected by the flat tool and the scraper ; the lightest parts are those that are most concave, the darkest those that are most convex. The parts which have the appearance of a middle tint are such as are reduced to a medium between the strongest light and the darkest shade. The impression in its present state has very much the appearance of an unfinished mezzotint.

In order to render this example of complicated lowering more intelligible to those who have little knowledge of the subject, it seems necessary to give a detailed account of the process, even at the risk of repeating some previous explanations. In complicated as well as in simple subjects intended to be lowered, the design is first drawn in outline on the wood. In such a subject as that which is here given, the Descent from the Cross, it is necessary to cut a delicate *white* outline —such as is seen in the ladder—round all those parts where the true outline appears dark against light, previous to lowering out those light parts which come into immediate contact with such as are dark. When a white outline has been cut where required, a thin shaving is to be taken off those parts which are intended to be a shade lighter than the middle tints,—for instance, in the rays of light falling upon the cross, and in the lower part of the sky. After this, the light parts of the ground and the figures are to be lowered ; but, instead of taking a mere shaving off the latter, the depth to which they are to be hollowed out

will depend on the form and size of the parts, and the strength of the light intended to appear on them ; and where a series of delicate lines are to run into *pure white*, great care must be taken that the wood be sufficiently *bevelled* or rounded off to allow of their blending with the white, without their extremities forming a distinct line, more especially where rotundity is to be represented. In a block thus lowered, the parts intended to be lightest will be the most concave, and those intended to be darkest the most in relief; and, when printed, the impression will appear as in the following cut, in consequence of the lowered parts, in proportion to their depth, receiving both less ink and less pressure; while those that are to appear positively white are lowered to such an extent as to be neither touched by the ink, nor exposed to the action of the platten or cylinder.

When the block has been thus prepared, the subject is drawn upon it in detail, and the engraving of the lines proceeded with. The sky, and the lighter and more distant objects, should be engraved first: and

care ought to be taken not to get the lines too fine at the commencement, for, should this happen, there is no remedy for the defect. By keeping them comparatively strong, the darker objects can be executed in a corresponding degree of boldness; and should the proof be generally too dark, the necessary alterations can be easily made. The above cut of the Descent from the Cross is printed from the finished block; all the positive lines here seen having been engraved subsequent to the process of lowering.

It is necessary to observe that the process of engraving upon an uneven surface—such as that of the lowered block of the Descent from the Cross—is much more difficult than on a surface which is perfectly plane ; for the graver in traversing such parts as are lowered is apt to lose its hold, and to slip in descending, while in ascending it is liable to take too much hold, and to *tear* rather than to clearly cut out the wood in certain parts, thus rendering the raised lines rough at the sides, and sometimes breaking them quite through. In order to remedy in some degree such inconveniences, it is necessary to use a graver slightly curving upwards towards the point.

The process of lowering, as previously explained, is peculiarly adapted to give the appearance of proper texture to objects of Natural History, and in particular to birds, where it is often so desirable to impart a soft downy appearance to the plumage. Such softness can never be well represented by lines engraved on a perfectly level surface ; for, however thin and fine they may be, they will always appear too distinct, and want that softness which can only be obtained by lowering the block, and printing it with a blanket in the tympans at a common press. Those who in engraving birds on a plane surface are fond of imitating the delicacy of copper-plate or steel engravings, always fail in their attempts to represent that soft appearance so peculiar to the plumage of birds, whatever may be its colour. Bewick's Birds, in this respect, have never been equalled ; and the softness displayed in the plumage has been chiefly obtained by lowering, and thus preventing such parts receiving too much ink or too much pressure. The characteristic expression of the bird, and the variety of texture in the plumage, are not indeed entirely dependent on this process ; but the appearance of softness, and the general effect of the cut as a whole,—as exemplified in the Birds of Bewick,—are not otherwise to be obtained. Any wood engraver who doubts this, should attempt to copy, on an unlowered block, one of the best of Bewick's birds ; on comparing a printed impression of his work with the original, he will be likely to discover that he has thought too highly of his own practice, and too lightly of Bewick's.

Though chiaro-scuro drawings can be faithfully copied by means of wood engraving ; yet the art, as applied to the execution of such works, has met with but little encouragement in this country, and has consequently been little practised. From 1754—the date of J. B. Jackson's tract on the Invention of Engraving and Printing in Chiaro-scuro—to 1819, when the first part of Mr. Savage's Hints on Decorative Printing was published, the only chiaro-scuro wood engravings which appear to have been published in England were those executed about 1783, by an amateur of the name of John Skippe. The chiaro-scuros engraved by

Mr. Skippe do not appear to have been numerous; I have only seen three—St. John the Evangelist, St. Paul, and Hebe, all after drawings by Parmegiano. The latter is printed from four blocks, and each of the others from three. In point of execution, that of St. John is decidedly the best: it is much superior to any of the specimens given in J. B. Jackson's work, and will bear a comparison with some of the best chiaro-scuros of Nicholas Le Sueur.

Savage's Hints on Decorative Printing, in two parts, 1819—1823, contains several specimens, not only of chiaro-scuro wood engravings, but also of subjects printed in positive colours from several wood-blocks, in imitation of coloured drawings. Some of the chiaro-scuros, properly so called, are well executed, though they generally seem too soft and *woolly*. The following are those which seem most worthy of notice :— A female Bacchante, from a bas-relief in the British Museum ; Theseus, from the statue in the Elgin Collection of Marbles, in the British Museum ; Copy of a bust in marble in the British Museum ; Bridge and Landscape ; Passage-boats ; and a River Scene. For the representation of such subjects as the preceding, when drawn in sepia, wood engraving is peculiarly adapted.

The simplest manner of representing a chiaro-scuro drawing is by printing a tint, with the lights cut out, from a second block, over the impression of a cut engraved in the usual manner. Chiaro-scuros of this kind have the appearance of pen-and-ink drawings made on tinted paper, and heightened with touches of white. The illustrations to an edition of Puckle's Club were thus printed in 1820,—the year after they had appeared printed in the usual manner in a new edition of the work —but many of them are spoiled by the badly-chosen "fancy" colour of the tint.

From the time of the publication of the second part of Savage's Hints, and the tinted illustrations of Puckle's Club, no further attempts appear to have been made to improve or extend the practice of chiaro-scuro engraving and printing in colours till Mr. George Baxter turned his attention to the subject. His first attempts in chiaro-scuro engraving are to be found in a History of Sussex, printed by his father at Lewes, in 1835. Mr. Baxter tried various experiments, and at length succeeded so much to his satisfaction, that he took out a patent for printing in oil-colours. The manner in which he executes picture-prints in positive colours, after drawings or paintings in oil, is *nearly* the same as that in which Kirkall executed his chiaro-scuros. The ground, the outlines, and the more minute details, are first printed in neutral tint from a plate engraved in aquatint ; and over this impression the proper colours are printed from as many wood-blocks as there are different tints. The best specimens of Mr. Baxter's printing in oil-colours, from wood-blocks over an aquatint ground, are to be found in the Pictorial Album, published by Chapman and Hall, 1837 ; and among these the following appear to be most deserving of distinct enumeration :—Interior of the Lady Chapel, Warwick ; Lugano ; Verona ; and Jeannie Deans's Interview with the Queen. In some of the most elaborate subjects in this work, the colours have been communicated by not less than twenty blocks, each separately printed. So far as regards the landscapes, nothing of the same kind previously done will bear to be compared with them. But since this period, Mr. Baxter has brought his peculiar art to still greater perfection, and both large and small examples are to be met with abundantly. One of the most popular is his "Holy Trinity, after Raphael," a small plate of which no fewer than 700,000 copies have been sold. The subscribers to Bohn's Scientific Library will find a good specimen in the View of Chimborazo, prefixed to Humboldt's Views of Nature.

Another recent invention is that of "Knight's Patent Illuminated Prints and Maps." In every instance hitherto of surface-printing in colours, each colour, having a separate block, had to be worked off separately, which rendered such productions extremely expensive.* The new process has one great advantage over all its predecessors, in cheapness, and the facility with which it can multiply impressions. The general nature of the process will be best understood from a description of the mode of completing a coloured print.

In the first place, a subject is engraved upon wood in the usual manner, and the impression is coloured by a skilful artist. We will suppose four principal colours are introduced, red, blue, yellow, and brown. Separate and exact drawings of each colour are then made ; and four polished plates are prepared, each plate carrying one colour. These four plates are then firmly fixed in an ingeniously contrived frame, or table, moving upon the table of a common press, the motion being regulated by machinery, which ensures the most exact register, after it has once been obtained, and affords the greatest facility in obtaining it. The colours are then applied to their respective plates in precisely the same manner as ink to type, by means of rollers ; and four sheets of paper of the size intended for the print (or, for convenience, one large sheet to be afterwards cut up) are then placed on the frisket, which

---

* Sir William Congreve's mode of colour printing, however, patented many years ago, and now practised by Mr. Charles Whiting of Beaufort House, is one of the least expensive of all. It consists in printing several colours at one time, and may be thus described :—" A coloured design being made on a block, the various colours are cut into their respective sections, like a geographical puzzle, and placed in an ingeniously constructed machine, which inks them separately, and prints them together. By this mode speed is obtained in large operations, and the colours are prevented from running into each other. It is extensively applied to book-covers, decorative show-cards, the back of country notes, and labels, where the object is to prevent forgery."—*See Bohn's Lecture on Printing, page* 104.

is then turned down on the plates, and the pull applied. The table is then turned one quarter round, and the process is repeated, till each colour has, in succession, been printed upon the four sheets. Six or seven colours are sometimes produced by the same process, and from the same plates, by combination; and the union of two colours to produce a third is effected perfectly, in consequence of the rapidity of the process, which does not allow the colours to dry and become hard. The bright whites are, of course, formed by removing the surface in the requisite parts from all the plates, and suffering the ground to appear. Eight, or indeed any number of colours, can be introduced by using another press, or presses; in which case the frisket with the sheet or sheets fixed, is passed from one press to the other. The block of the drawing is always the last impressed.

From its extreme exactitude this invention seems peculiarly adapted for designs of patterns for shawls, ribbons, printed cottons, carpets, and such manufactures as have hitherto apparently been left to the fancy or the workman, or his employers, who in matters of art have frequently quite as little taste as the workman.

But probably the most favourable field for the display of the perfections of this invention, would be in subjects where only light and shade, or at most what are called neutral tints, are required, such as architectural drawings and sculptures, either statues or in relief. For such purposes the depth of tone obtainable, and the sharpness of the lights, seem peculiarly adapted.*

What is termed metallic relief engraving consists in executing subjects on plates of copper, or any other metal, in such a manner that the lines which form the impression shall be in relief, and thus allow of such plates being inked and printed in the same manner as a wood-cut. Since the revival of wood engraving in this country several attempts have been made to *etch* in metallic relief, and thus save the time necessarily required to cut out all the lines in a wood engraving. In etching upon copper, in order that the subject may be represented by lines *in relief*,—the reverse of the usual procedure in copper-plate engraving,—and that the plate may be printed in the same manner as a wood-cut, there are several methods of proceeding. In one, the subject is *drawn* upon the plate in Burgundy pitch, or any other substance which will resist the action of aquafortis, in the same manner

---

* The best specimen of this art will be found in Charles Knight's Old England's Worthies, a folio volume, containing twelve large plates of Architecture and Costume, printed in colours, and 240 portraits engraved on steel, folio (now published by H. G. Bohn), 15s. The practice of the art has not been continued, as it was only applicable to very large editions (ten thousand and upwards), and was more expensive than hand colouring where small editions were required. The machinery has been sold off and destroyed.

as copper-plate engravers in the ordinary process *stop out* the parts intended to be white. When the substance in which the drawing is made becomes *set*, or sufficiently hard, the plate is surrounded with a *wall*, as it is technically termed, and aquafortis being poured upon it, all the unprotected parts are corroded, and the drawing left in relief.

This was the method generally adopted by William Blake, an artist of great but eccentric genius, in the execution of his Songs of Innocence, the Book of Thel,* the Gates of Paradise, Urizen, and other works, published between 1789 and 1800. The following account of the origin of this new mode of engraving or etching in metallic relief, by corroding the parts intended to appear white in the impression, is extracted from the Life of William Blake, in Allan Cunningham's Lives of British Painters, Sculptors, and Architects :—

"He had made the sixty-five designs of his Songs of Innocence, and was meditating, he said, on the best means of multiplying their resemblance in form and in hue ; he felt sorely perplexed. At last he was made aware that the spirit of his favourite brother Robert was in the room, and to this celestial visitor he applied for counsel. The spirit advised him at once : 'Write,' he said, 'the poetry, and draw the designs upon the copper, with a certain liquid, (which he named, and which Blake ever kept a secret,) then cut the plain parts of the plate down with aquafortis, and this will give the whole, both poetry and figures, in the manner of stereotype.' The plan recommended by this gracious spirit was adopted, the plates were engraved, and the work printed off. The artist then added a peculiar beauty of his own : he tinted both the figures and the verse with a variety of colours, amongst which, while yellow prevails, the whole has a rich and lustrous beauty, to which I know little that can be compared. The size of these prints is four and a half inches high by three inches wide. The original genius of Blake was always confined, through poverty, to small dimensions. Sixty-five plates of copper were an object to him who had little money."

Blake subsequently executed, in the same manner, "the Gates of Paradise," consisting of sixteen small designs ; and "Urizen," consisting of twenty-seven designs. The size of the latter is four inches by six, and they are dated Lambeth, 1794. In 1800 he also engraved by a similar process, combined with the usual mode of etching *through* a prepared ground laid over the plate, two subjects to illustrate a song of his own writing, which was printed with them also from metallic relief. The title of this song is "Little Tom the Sailor," and the date is October 5, 1800. It appears to have been a charitable contribution

---

* The Book of Thel, which, with the titles, consists of seven quarto pages of verse and figures engraved in metallic relief, is dated 1789. A full list of the works of this remarkable artist will be found in Bohn's enlarged edition of Lowndes's Bibliographer's Manual.

of Blake's to the "Widow Spicer of Folkstone," the mother of little Tom ; and we learn from the imprint at the bottom that it was printed for, and sold by her for the benefit of her orphans.

Blake's metallic relief engravings were printed by himself by means of a rolling or copper-plate press, though the impression was obtained from the lines in relief in the same manner as from a wood-cut. The only difference in the printing consisted in the different manner in which the pressure was applied. As it is difficult, according to Blake's process, to corrode the large white parts to a depth sufficient to prevent their being touched by the dauber or ball in the process of inking, and thus presenting a soiled appearance in the impression, he was accustomed to wipe the ink out where it had touched in the hollows. As this occupied more time than the mere inking of the plate, his progress in printing was necessarily slow.

In another mode of engraving in relief on a plate of copper, the plate is first covered with an etching ground in the usual manner, and to this ground an outline of the subject is transferred by passing the plate with a pencil-drawing above it through a rolling-press. The engraver then proceeds to remove with his etching-point, or some other tool, as may be necessary, all such parts as are intended to be *white*. When this process, which may be termed *reverse etching*, is completed, the parts intended to be white are corroded by pouring aquafortis upon the plate in the usual manner, while the lines which represent the object remain in relief, in consequence of their being protected at the surface by the coating of etching ground.

Several persons have made experiments in this mode of metallic relief engraving. It was tried by Bewick, and also by the late Robert Branston ; but they did not succeed to their satisfaction, and none of their productions executed in this manner was ever submitted to the public. About twenty years ago, Mr. W. Lizars of Edinburgh appears to have turned his attention to the subject of metallic relief engraving, and to have succeeded better than either Bewick or Branston. One of the earliest-published specimens of his engraving in this style is the portrait of Dr. Peter Morris, forming the frontispiece to Peter's Letters to his Kinsfolk, printed at Edinburgh in 1819. This portrait has every appearance of being executed by the process of reverse etching,—that is, by first covering the plate with etching ground, and then removing the parts that are to be white, and leaving the lines that are to appear black in relief. The plate was printed by a common printing-press at the office of Ballantyne and Co. In the preface the "new invention" of Mr. Lizars is thus mentioned :—" The portrait of Dr. Morris is done in this new style ; and, had the time permitted, the others would have all been done so likewise. It is thrown off by the common printing-press, as the

reader will observe—but this is only one of the distinguishing excellences of this new and splendid invention of Mr. Lizars."

Within the last three or four years several plans for executing
engravings in metallic relief have been devised; and it has been pro-
phesied of each, that it would in a short time totally supersede wood
engraving. The projectors of those plans, however, seem to have taken
too narrow a view of the subject; and to have thought that the mere
novelty of their invention was sufficient to ensure it success. They
appear not to have considered, that it was necessary that their metallic
relief casts should not only be cheaper than wood-cuts, but that they
should be also as well executed.

Mr. Woone has taken out a patent for his invention, and the principle
upon which it is founded is that of taking a cast from a copper-plate,
whereby the lines engraved in *intaglio* are in the cast in *relief.* His
process of metallic relief engraving is as follows:—A smooth plate of
metal is covered with a coating of plaster of Paris, about equal in
thickness to the depth to which the lines are cut in engraving on copper
or steel. Upon this surface of plaster the engraver, with a fine point,
as in etching, cuts the lines of the subject *through* to the plate below.
When this plaster etching is completed, a cast is taken from it in type-
metal; and, after being *cleared out*, the subject in metallic relief can be
printed at a common press in the manner of a wood-cut. According to
this plan only *one* cast can be taken of each subject, as the plaster
is destroyed during the process, so that there is nothing left from which
a second mould can be made, as in the case of a wood-cut. The chief
advantage of this invention consists in the lines being of equal height
in the cast, in consequence of their being etched through the plaster
to the level surface of the plate beneath. As the coating of plaster is,
however, extremely thin, it is generally necessary to clear out with a
graver the interstices of the cast in order to prevent their being touched
by the inking roller.

A Mr. Schonberg has also made several experiments in metallic
relief engraving by means of etching on stone, and afterwards taking
a cast from his work. Though he has been for several years endeavouring to perfect his invention, he has not up to this time succeeded in
producing anything which it would be fair to criticise.

Many of the cuts of trees and shrubs in Loudon's Arboretum et
Fruticetum Britannicum are printed from casts in metallic relief, executed
by Mr. Robert Branston. The mode of procedure, according to Mr.
Branston's method, is extremely simple; the subject is first etched
on copper, and bit in by aquafortis in the usual manner; and from this
etching a cast is afterwards taken in type-metal. As the plate is not
corroded to an equal depth in every part, it is necessary to rub on a

stone the faces of the casts thus obtained in order to reduce the raised lines to the same level. There is also another inconvenience that attends casts in metallic relief taken from an etched copper-plate; for, as the aquafortis acts laterally as well as vertically, it is difficult to corrode the lines to a sufficient depth, without at the same time getting them too thick. It is hence necessary to clear out many of the hollow parts of such casts with a graver, in order to prevent their being touched by the balls or inking-roller, and thus giving to the impression a soiled appearance.

Casts in metallic relief from etchings always appear coarse; and, from the experiments hitherto made, it seems impossible to execute *fine* work in this manner. So far as relates to cheapness, such casts, however well they may be executed, being of a level surface, cannot be printed properly by a steam-press in the manner of lowered blocks, or casts from lowered blocks. For a work of extensive circulation, printed by means of a steam-press, a lowered block, or a cast from it, would be cheaper at five pounds, than a cast from an etching at four, even admitting that both were equally well executed.

The principal feature in Mr. C. Hancock's patent metallic relief engraving, which is quite original, is, that subjects resembling mezzotints can be inserted and printed with the text in the same manner as wood engravings. A mezzotint plate, if printed in the usual manner previous to being engraved upon, would appear black. On the other hand, if submitted to the same kind of printing as a wood-cut, it would scarcely discolour the paper. Upon this plate Mr. Hancock draws his subject with a broad steel point or burnisher, which polishes down the small prominences to a smooth surface in proportion to the pressure used in drawing. In proportion as the surface becomes smooth, so does it print dark, and have the appearance of a mezzotint. The reader will perceive that, according to this plan, Mr. Hancock can take a proof of his subject at any time, and procure either *dark* or *light* at pleasure, as the subject may appear to require it. The sparkling light can be touched in with the graver, in the same manner as on wood; so that such touches appear much sharper than in common mezzotint, where the lights are got by burnishing. As Mr. Hancock has not as yet brought anything before the public, it would be unfair to anticipate him, by introducing anything more in this place than a description of his process.

Wood engraving is necessarily confined, by the size of the wood, to the execution of subjects of comparatively small dimensions; and this limitation, together with the difficulty of printing even tints in positive colours, have combined to prevent it from being made extensively available in the production of works in chiaro-scuro, of large size, by the ordinary modes of surface-printing. Latterly, however, the demand which the progress of education has created for maps, school prints, elementary examples of fine art, and illustrations *on a large scale* for the illustrated newspapers, having called the attention of artists to the subject, many attempts have been made, and in some cases with success, to produce relief engravings on metal ; and also to combine that mode of engraving with analogous apparatus for the production of works in tints or colours, separate, combined, or mixed with line plates, in such degrees as particular cases might require. Several of these persons have been already named, and their processes described ; it only therefore remains to state, that Mr. Stephen Sly, in connexion with other artists, has for some years past been steadily engaged in making a series of experiments for giving a practical value, by various inventions, to the discoveries and experience of their predecessors in the art ; and with every prospect of success. Their method of procedure is : 1. To produce a finished drawing, in simple or crossed lines, with etching varnish on a plate prepared for the purpose ; 2. To bite away, with a compound acid, the spaces between the varnish lines ; and 3. To deepen and finish the work so produced, by the use of engraving tools, in the ordinary manner. The great difficulties in the way of these apparently simple operations have been, 1. To cast *sound* and durable plates of a large size, and of a texture sufficiently compact to produce sharp lines by the etching process, and at the same time soft enough to permit the surfaces to be lowered, and the cutting to be executed with facility ; 2. To remove the oxide formed by the combination of the acid with the metal from between the lines ; and 3. To carry the biting to a depth sufficiently great to permit the plate, with the addition of a small quantity of graver-work, to yield a clear impression.

Metallic relief engraving has not unfrequently been practised at Paris of late years. I have now lying before me an impression from a plate engraved in this manner by Messrs. Best, Andrew, and Leloir, of that city. The subject is a wild turkey, and it was engraved about three years ago for Mr. Audubon. Though it is the best specimen of metallic relief engraving that has come under my notice, I am yet of opinion that the subject could be better engraved on wood, and at a less cost. Ornaments and borders are sometimes engraved on solid brass by means of chisels and gravers in the same manner as a wood-cut. The head of Buchanan, and the border on the wrapper of Blackwood's Magazine, were engraved on brass in this manner, more than twenty years ago, by Messrs. Vizitelly, Branston, and Co. They were originally engraved on wood by Bewick The greater durability of ornaments engraved on brass, compensates for their additional cost. The *cheapest* mode, however, is to have such ornaments first engraved on wood, and casts afterwards taken from them in type metal. One great objection to *cutting* on metal with the graver is, that the metal *cuts the paper* in printing from it.

Duplicates of wood engravings may be readily obtained by means of casts from the original blocks ; and within the last twenty years, the practice of thus multiplying subjects originally engraved on wood, has become very prevalent both in this country and in France. Casts can be obtained from wood engravings by two different processes, and both are practised by two or three stereotype printers, to whom this business is usually entrusted. By the one mode, a mould is first made from the block in plaster of Paris, and from this mould or matrix a cast is afterwards taken in type metal. By the other mode—termed by the French *clichage* *—the mould or matrix is not formed of plaster ; but is

No. 1 (from Wood).   No. 2 (from Metal).

obtained by letting the block fall, with its engraved surface downwards, directly on a mass of metal,† just sufficiently fluid to receive the impression, and which becomes solid almost at the very instant it is touched by the block. From this mould or matrix a cast is afterwards taken in the same manner. In order to prevent the surface of the block becoming charred by the heat, it is previously rubbed over with a composition of common yellow soap and red ochre.

When it is particularly desirable to preserve the original block uninjured, the safest mode is that of forming a mould or matrix of plaster ; for by the process of *clichage* a delicately engraved block is extremely

---

* A cast from a form of types, as well as from an engraved wood-block, is by French printers termed a *cliché*.

† The metal of which this matrix is formed, is made several degrees harder than common type metal, by mixing with the latter a greater portion of regulus of antimony, otherwise the matrix and cast would adhere.

liable to receive damage.   As a cast, whether from a matrix of metal or of plaster, generally requires certain small specks of the metal to be removed, or some of the lines to be cleared out, this operation is frequently entrusted to a person employed in a printing-office where such cast is taken.   Such person, however, should never be allowed to do more than remove the specks ; for, should he attempt to re-enter or re-cut the lines or tints on metal, he will be very likely to spoil the work. It is extremely difficult, even to a dexterous engraver, to re-enter the lines that have been partially closed up in a tint, so that they shall appear the same as the others which have come off clear.   Should the printer's *picker* happen to re-enter them in a direction opposite to that in which they were originally cut on the block, the work is certain to be spoiled.   When a cast requires clearing out and retouching in this manner, the operation ought to be performed by a wood engraver, and, if possible, by the person who executed the original block.   When the subject is not very complicated, it is extremely difficult to distinguish which of two impressions is from a cast, and which is from the original block.   Those who profess to have great judgment in such matters are left to determine which of the preceding busts is printed from metal, and which from wood.

When a duplicate of a modern, or a fac-simile of an old wood-cut is required, the best mode of obtaining a correct copy, is to transfer the original, if not too large or too valuable, to a prepared block ; and the mode of effecting this is as follows :—The back of the impression to be transferred is first well moistened with a mixture composed of equal parts of concentrated potash and essence of lavender ; it is then placed above a block whose surface has been slightly moistened with water, and rubbed with a burnisher.   If the mixture be of proper strength, the ink of the old impression will become loosened, and be transferred to the wood.   Recent impression of a wood-cut, before the ink is set, may be transferred to a block without any preparation, merely by what is technically termed "rubbing down."   In order to transfer impressions from copper-plates, it is necessary to use the *oil* of lavender instead of the *essence :* if a very old impression, apply the preparation to its face.

Since the former edition of this work considerable improvements have been made in the mode of taking casts, of which the principal is *electrotyping*, by the galvanic precipitation of copper.   By this process all the finer lines of the engraving are so perfectly preserved, that impressions printed from the cast are quite undistinguishable from those printed from the original block.

Before closing this subject we think it right to introduce the notice of a new art, which, if it accomplishes all it professes, and as, judging by the annexed example, it seems capable of performing, will be a great acquisition. The art was first brought out as Collins's process, but is now called the *Electro-printing Block process*, and is managed under the inventor's direction by a company established at No. 27, New Bridge Street, Blackfriars. The object of the process is to reduce or extend, by means of transfer to an elastic material, maps or engravings of any size.

The specimen given in the present volume is reduced from a lithograph copy of an early block print, four times its size,* and then electrotyped

---

* Taken from Mr. S. Leigh Sotheby's *Principia Typographica*, 3 vols. folio—to whose kindness we are indebted for the reduced block.

into a surface block, so as to print in the ordinary manner of a wood-engraving. The reader will easily imagine that any plate transferred to an elastic surface distended equally, will, when collapsed, yield a reduced impression, and *vice versâ*. The only drawback to this process seems to be the want of depth in the electro-type where there are large unengraved spaces. Such plates will want good bringing-up and very careful printing.

The unequal manner in which wood-cuts are printed, is often injurious both to publishers and engravers; for, however well a subject may have been engraved, or whatever may have been the expense incurred, both the engraver's talents and the publisher's money will, in a great measure, have been thrown away unless the cut be properly printed. The want of cordial co-operation between printers and wood engravers is one of the chief causes of wood-cuts being so frequently printed in an improper manner. One printer's method of printing wood-cuts often differs so much from that of another, that it is generally necessary for an engraver who wishes to have justice done to his work, to ascertain the office at which a book is to be printed before he begins to execute any of the cuts. If they are intended to be printed at a steam-press, they require to be engraved in a manner suitable to that method of printing; and if it be further intended to take casts from them, and to print from such casts instead of the original blocks, it is necessary for the engraver to execute his work accordingly. Should they have to be printed at a common press *with a blanket*, it is necessary that they should be lowered in such parts as are most liable to be printed too heavy from the parchment of the tympan, when there is a blanket behind it, penetrating to a greater depth between the lines than when no blanket is used.* When it is intended to print cuts in what is called the *best* manner,—that is, at a common press without a blanket, and where the effect is brought up by means of overlaying,—the engraver has nothing to do but to execute his subject on a plane surface to the best of his ability, and to leave the task of bringing up the dark, and easing the light parts to the printer,—who, if he have not an artist's eye, can only by chance succeed in producing the effect intended by the draftsman and the engraver.

Should a series of wood-cuts be engraved with the view of their being printed at a steam-press, or at a common press with a blanket, and

* The principal difference, so far as relates to wood engravings, between printing by a steam-press with cylindrical rollers, and printing by a common press with a blanket, is, that the blanket or woollen cloth covering the cylinder of the steam-press comes into immediate contact with the paper, while in the common press the parchment of the tympan is interposed between the paper and the blanket. It is necessary that cuts intended to be printed by a steam-press should be lowered to a greater depth than cuts intended to be printed with a blanket at a common press, as the blanket on the cylinder penetrates to a greater depth between the lines.

should the publisher or proprietor of the work afterwards change his
intention, and decide on having them printed in the *best* manner,—
that is, by the common press without a blanket, and with overlays,—
such cuts, whatever pains might be taken, could not be properly and
efficiently printed ; for those parts which had been lowered in order to
obviate the *in*-pressure of the blanket, would either be totally invisible,
or would only appear imperfectly,—that is, with the lines indistinct and
broken, as if they had not been properly inked. The following cut, which
was lowered for machine-printing, or printing with a blanket, but has
been worked off at a common press without a blanket, when compared
with the same subject printed in the manner originally intended,—that
is, with a blanket,—will illustrate what has been previously said on the

subject. I by no means wish it to be understood, that any printer would
allow such a cut to appear quite so bad as it does in the present
impression ; he would do *something* to remedy the defects, but he could
not, without employing a blanket, cause it to have the appearance
originally intended by the designer and engraver. It is printed here
without any aid of overlaying, in order that the difference might be
the more apparent to those who are unacquainted with the subject. I
have, however, not unfrequently seen excellent cuts spoiled from inattention to bringing up the lowered parts, even when printed at the
office of printers who have acquired a high character for *fine* work, and
whose names on this account are announced in advertisements in
connexion with those of the author, designer, and publisher, as a

guarantee for the superior manner in which the cuts contained in the work will be printed.* The following cut, of the same subject as that given on the previous page, shows the appearance of the engraving when properly printed in the manner intended ; every line is here brought up by using a blanket, while from the block having been lowered, with a view to its being printed in this manner, there has been no occasion for overlays to increase the effect in the darker parts. The difference in the two impressions is entirely owing to the different manner of printing ; for the one is printed from the block, and the other from a cast.

Subjects engraved on lowered blocks, in the manner of the following cut, have always an unfinished appearance when printed without a

blanket, and the feebleness and confusion apparent in the lighter parts, instead of being remedied by overlaying the darker parts, are thus rendered more obvious. The connecting medium between the extremes of black and white being either entirely omitted or very imperfectly

---

* I have known a printer, who *once* had a high character for his *fine* work, charge and receive twelve guineas per sheet for a book containing a number of wood-cuts which required to be well printed, and I have known a similar work better printed from lowered blocks for less than half the sum per sheet. Publishers will at no distant time discover, that it is their interest rather to have their cuts first properly engraved than to pay a printer a large additional sum for the trouble of overlaying them, and thus giving them the appearance which they ought to have without such means and appliances, if the blocks were originally executed as they ought to be.

given, causes the impression to have that harsh and unfinished appearance which is frequently urged as one of the greatest objections to engraving on wood. It is indeed true, that many cuts have this objectionable appearance ; but it is also true that the fault does not originate in any deficiency in the art, but is either the result of want of knowledge on the part of the engraver, or is occasioned by improper printing. When wood engravers found that anything approaching to delicacy, in blending the extremes of black and white in their work, was extremely liable to be either lost or spoiled in the printing, it is not surprising that they should have paid comparatively little attention to the connecting tints. In many excellently engraved cuts, printed at the common press with overlays, the tint next in gradation to positive black is often perceived to be too dark, in consequence of the extra pressure on the adjacent parts ; while, on the other hand, the delicate lines intended to blend with the white, are either too heavy, or appear broken and confused. It is chiefly from this cause, that so much black and white, without the requisite connecting middle tints, is found in wood-cuts ; for the engraver, finding that such tints were frequently spoiled in the impression, omitted them whenever he could, in order to adapt his subject to the usual method of printing. When, in consequence of an improvement in the mode of printing wood-cuts, engravers can depend on finding all in the impression that can be executed on the block, it will no longer be an objection to the art that its productions have a hard and unfinished appearance, and that it is only capable of efficiently representing subjects displaying strong contrasts of black and white.

Should a wood-cut engraved on a plane surface, with the intention of its being printed in the *best* manner,—that is, at a common press with overlays, and *without* a blanket,—be printed at a steam-press, or at a common press *with* a blanket, it will present a very different appearance to the engraver's proof.* The following cut, which ought properly to have been printed in the *best* manner, is here printed improperly *with a blanket,* and the result is anything but satisfactory ; the parts which ought to have been delicately printed are, in consequence of the equality of the pressure on every part of the unlowered surface brought up too heavy, and from their appearing too dark, the effect intended by the designer and engraver is destroyed. The same cut, when printed at a common press with overlays, and without a blanket, as originally intended, would have the light parts relieved, and appear as it does on the following page.

---

* The cuts being arranged back to back, as at pages 641, 642, and thereby preventing the types appearing, as they do on the next page, is an advantage not to be overlooked.

The want of something like a uniform method of printing wood-cuts, and the high price charged by printers for what is called fine work, have operated most injuriously to the progress and extension of wood

engraving. The practice, however, of printing wood-cuts by a steam-press, or a press of any kind with a cylindrical roller instead of a platten, seems likely to introduce a general change in the practice of

the art. By the adoption of this cheap and expeditious method of printing, books containing the very best wood engravings can be afforded at a much cheaper rate than formerly. As cuts printed in this manner can receive no adventitious aid from overlays, the wood engraver is required to finish his work perfectly before it goes out of his hands, and not to trust to the taste of a pressman for its being properly printed. The great desideratum in wood engraving is to produce cuts which can be efficiently printed at the least possible expense ; and, as a means towards this end, it is necessary that cuts should require the least possible aid from the printer, and be executed in such manner that, without gross negligence, they will be certain to print well. The greatest advantage that wood engraving possesses over engraving on copper or steel is the cheap rate at which its productions can be printed at one impression, in the same sheet with the letter-press. To increase, therefore, by an incomplete method of engraving, the cost of printing wood-cuts, is to abandon the great vantage ground of the art.

The mode of printing by the common press without a blanket, and of *helping* a cut engraved on a plane surface by means of overlays, is not only much more expensive than printing from a lowered block by the steam-press, or a common press with a blanket and without over-laying, but is also much more injurious to the engraving. When a cut requires to be overlaid* in order that it may be properly printed, a piece of paper is first pasted on the tympan, and on this an impression is taken, which remains as a substratum for the subsequent overlays. A second impression is next taken, and in this the pressman cuts out the lighter parts, and notes such as are too indistinct and require *bringing up*. He then proceeds to paste scraps of paper over the corresponding parts in the first impression, on a sheet of thin paper, either in front or at the back of the parchment tympan, in order to increase in such parts the pressure of the platten ; and thus continues, sometimes for half a day, pasting scrap over scrap, until he obtains what he considers a perfect impression.

As the block is originally of the same height as the type, it is evident that the overlays must very much increase the pressure of the platten on such parts as they are immediately above. Such increase of pressure is not only injurious to the engraving, occasionally breaking down the lines ; but it also frequently squeezes the ink from the surface *into* the interstices, and causes the impression in such parts to appear blotted. While a block, with a flat surface, printed in this manner will scarcely afford five thousand good impressions without retouching, twenty thousand can be obtained from a lowered block printed by a steam-press, or by a common press with a blanket and without overlays ;

---

* What is called *underlaying* consists in pasting one piece of paper or more on the lower part of a block, in order to raise it, and increase the pressure. When a block is uneven at the bottom, in consequence of warping, underlaying is indispensable.

the darkest parts in a lowered block being no higher than the type, and not being overlaid, are subject to no unequal pressure to break down the lines, while the lighter parts being lowered are thus sufficiently protected. The intervention of the blanket in the latter case not only brings up the lighter parts, but is also less injurious to the engraving than the direct action of the wood or metal platten, with only the thin cloth and the parchment of the tympans intervening between it and the surface of the block.

When wood-cuts are printed with overlays, and the paper is knotty, the engraving is certain to be injured by the knots being indented in the wood in those parts where the pressure is greatest. When copies of a work containing wood-cuts are printed on India paper, the engraving is almost invariably injured, in consequence of the hard knots and pieces of bark with which such paper abounds, causing indentions in the wood. The consequence of printing off a certain number of copies of a work on such paper may be seen in the cut of the Vain Glow-worm, in the second edition of the first series of Northcote's Fables : it is covered with white spots, the result of indentions in the block caused by the knots and inequalities in bad India paper. Overlays frequently shift if not well attended to, and cause pressure where it was never intended.

In order that wood engravings should appear to the greatest advantage, it is necessary that they should be printed on proper paper. A person not practically acquainted with the subject may easily be deceived in selecting paper for a work containing wood engravings. There is a kind of paper, manufactured of coarse material, which, in consequence of its being pressed, has a smooth appearance, and to the view seems to be highly suitable for the purpose. As soon, however, as such paper is wetted previous to printing, its smoothness disappears, and its imperfections become apparent by the irregular swelling of the material of which it is composed. Paper intended for printing the best kind of wood-cuts ought to be even in texture, and this ought to be the result of good material well manufactured. Paper of this kind will not appear uneven when wetted, like that which has merely a *good face* put upon it by means of extreme pressure. The best mode of testing the quality of paper is to wet a sheet; however even and smooth it may appear when dry, its imperfections will be evident when wet, if it be manufactured of coarse material, and merely pressed smooth.

Paper of unequal thickness, however good the material may be, is quite unfit for the purpose of printing the best kind of wood engravings ; for, if a sheet be thicker at one end than the other, there will be a perceptible difference in the strength of the impressions of the cuts accordingly as they may be printed on the thick or the thin parts, those on the latter being light, while those on the former are comparatively heavy or dark. When it is known that an overlay of the thinnest tissue paper will make a perceptible difference in an impression, the necessity of having paper of even texture for the purpose of printing wood-cuts well is obvious. As there is less chance of inequality of texture in comparatively thin paper than in thick, the former kind is generally to be preferred, supposing it to be equally well manufactured.

Mr. Savage, at page 46 of his Hints on Decorative Printing, recommends that in a sheet which consists entirely of letter-press in one *form*, and of letter-press and wood-cuts in the other, the form without cuts should be worked first. His words are as follow :—" When there are wood-cuts in one form, and none in the other, then the form without the cuts ought to be worked first ; as working the cuts last prevents the indention of the types appearing on the engraving, which would otherwise take place to its prejudice."

My opinion on this subject is directly the reverse of Mr. Savage's, for, under similar circumstances, I should advise that the form containing the cuts should be printed first ; and for the following reason :—When any parts of a wood-cut require to be printed light—whether by lowering the block or by overlaying—the pressure in such parts must necessarily be less than on those adjacent. If then the form containing such cuts be printed first, the paper being perfectly flat, and without any indentions, all the lines will appear distinct and continuous, unless the pressman should grossly neglect his duty. If, on the contrary, the form containing such cuts be printed last, there is a risk of the lines in the lighter parts appearing broken and confused, in consequence of the inequality in the surface of the paper, caused by the indention of the types on the opposite side. Imperfections of this kind are to be seen in many works containing wood-cuts ; and they are in particular numerous in the Treatise on Cattle published under the superintendence of the Society for the Diffusion of Useful Knowledge. In many of the cuts in this work the lines representing the sky appear discontinuous and broken, and the imperfections are always according to the kind of type on the other side of the paper. When both forms contain wood-cuts, I should recommend that to be first which contains the best. Mr. Savage's reason, independent of the preceding objections, is scarcely a good one ; for admitting that the indention of the types of the second form does appear in the *clear* and *distinct* impressions from the cuts in the first, when the sheet is just taken from the press, are not such inequalities entirely removed when the sheet is *dried* and pressed ?

* The entire quantity of types, or of types and wood-cuts, which is locked up together, and printed on one side of a sheet at one impression, is called by printers a *form*.

In order to produce good impressions in printing wood-cuts, much more depends on the manner in which the subject is treated by the designer, and on the plate which the cut occupies in a page, than a person unacquainted with the nicety required in such matters would imagine. Wood-cuts which are delicately engraved, or which consist chiefly of outline, are the most difficult to print in a proper manner, in consequence of their want of dark masses to relieve the pressure in the more delicate parts, and thus cause them to appear lighter in the impression. There ought never to be a large portion of light delicate work in a wood-cut without a few dark parts near to it, which may serve as stays or props to relieve the pressure. In illustration of what is here said, I would refer to the cut of King Shahriyár unveiling Shahrazád, at page 15 of Mr. Lane's Translation of the Arabian Nights' Entertainments, where it will be seen, that certain dark parts are introduced as if at measured distances. It is entirely owing to the introduction of those dark parts that the press-man has been enabled to print the cut so well: they not only give by contrast the appearance of greater delicacy to the lightest parts; but they also serve to relieve them from that degree of pressure, which, if the cut consisted entirely of such delicate lines, would most certainly cause them to appear comparatively thick and heavy. Another instance of the advantage which a cut derives from its being placed in a certain situation in the page, is also afforded by the same work. The cut to which I allude is that of the Return of the Jinnee, at page 47, consisting chiefly of middle tint, with a pillar of smoke rising up from the ground, and gradually becoming lighter towards the top. Had this cut been intro-duced at the head of the page without any text above it, the light parts would not have appeared so delicate as they do now when the cut is printed in its present situation. The top of the cut, where the lines are required to be lightest, being near to the types, thus receives a support, and is by them relieved from that degree of pressure which would other-wise cause the lines to appear heavy. Towards the bottom of the cut, which also forms the bottom of the page, there are two or three dark figures which most opportunely afford that necessary degree of support which in the upper part is derived from the types.

The engraver by whom a cut has been executed is unquestionably the best person that the printer can apply to for any information as to the manner in which it ought to be printed, as he alone can be perfectly acquainted with the *state of the block*, and with any peculiarity in the engraving. If any light part should have been lowered to a very trifling extent, it is sometimes almost impossible that the printer should perceive such lowered part after the block has been covered with ink ; and hence, notwithstanding the proof which may have been sent by the engraver as a guide, such a cut is very likely to be worked off, to the great injury of the general effect of the subject, without the lowered part being properly brought up. In order to avoid such an occurrence, which is by no means unfrequent, it is advisable to send to the engraver a printed proof of his cut, in order that he may note those parts where the pressman has failed in obtaining a perfect impression. From the want of this precaution wood-cuts are but too often badly printed ; while at the same time the engraver is blamed for executing his work imperfectly, though in reality the defect is entirely occasioned by the cut not being properly printed.

The best mode of cleaning a block after the engraver has taken his first proof is to rub it well with a piece of woollen cloth. So long as anything remains to be done with the graver, the block, after taking a proof, ought never to be cleaned with any liquid, as by such means the ink on the surface would be dissolved, and the mixture getting between, the lines would thus cause the cut to appear uniformly black, and render it difficult for the engraver to finish his work in a proper manner from his inability to clearly distinguish the lines.* Turpentine or lye ought to be very sparingly used to clean a cut after the printing is finished, and never unless the interstices be choked up with ink which cannot otherwise be removed. When the surface of the block becomes foul, in consequence of the ink becoming hardened upon it, it is most advisable to clean it with a little soap and water, using as little water as possible, and afterwards to rub the block well with a piece of woollen cloth. When it is necessary to use turpentine in order to get the hardened ink out of the interstices, the surface of the block should immediately afterwards be slightly washed with a little soap and water, and afterwards rubbed with a piece of woollen cloth.† *Warm* water ought never to be used, as it is much more apt than cold to cause the block to warp and split. The practice of cleaning wood-cuts in the form by means of a *hard* brush, dipped in turpentine or lye, is extremely injurious to the finest parts, as by this means most delicate lines are not unfrequently broken. The use of anything damp to clean the cuts when the pressman finishes his day's-work, is to be avoided ; as a very small degree of damp is sufficient to cause the block to warp when left locked up over night in the form. Whenever it is practicable, the cuts ought to be taken out of the form at night, and placed on their edges till next morning ; as, by thus receiving a free circulation of air all round them, they will be much less liable to warp, than if allowed to remain in the form. As wood-cuts

---

* When a block, after being printed, requires retouching, it is generally necessary to cover it with fine whiting, which, by filling up the interstices, thus enables the engraver to distinguish the raised lines more clearly.

† When a block has been cleaned with turpentine, and not afterwards washed with soap and water, it will not receive the ink well when next used. The first fifty or sixty impressions subsequently taken, are almost certain to have a grey and scumbled appearance.

are often injured by being carelessly printed in a rough proof, it is advisable not to insert them in the form till all the literal corrections are made, and the text is ready for the press.

It is a fact, though I am unable to satisfactorily account for it, that an impression from a wood-block, taken by a common press, without overlaying, or any other kind of preparation, is generally lighter in the middle than towards the edges. Mr. Edward Cowper, who has contributed so much to the improvement of machine-printing, when engaged in making experiments with common presses constructed with the greatest care,* informs me, that he frequently noticed the same defect. Such inequality in the impression is not perceptible in cuts printed by a steam-press, where the pressure proceeds from a *cylinder* instead of a flat platten of metal or wood. Besides the advantage which the steam-press possesses over the common press in producing a uniformly regular impression, the ink in the former method is more equally distributed over every part of the form in consequence of the undeviating regularity of the action of the inking rollers. Though an equal distribution of the ink be of great advantage when all the cuts in a form require to be printed in the same manner,—that is, when all are of a similar *tone* of colour,— yet when some are dark, and others comparatively light, balls faced with composition are decidedly preferable to composition rollers, as by using the former the pressman can give to each cut its proper quantity of ink.

I very much doubt, if soft composition rollers, such as are now generally used, be so well adapted as composition balls for inking woodcuts engraved on a *plane* surface. The material of which the rollers are formed is so soft and elastic, that it does not only pass over the surface of the block, but penetrates to a certain depth between the lines, thus inking them at the sides, as well as on their surface. The consequence of this is, that when the pressure is too great, the paper is forced in between the lines, and receives, to the great detriment of the impression, a portion of the ink communicated by the soft and elastic roller to their sides. For inking cuts delicately engraved on *unlowered* blocks, I should recommend composition balls instead of composition rollers, whenever it is required that such cuts should be printed in the *best* manner.

The great advantage which modern wood engraving possesses over every other branch of graphic art, is the cheap rate at which its productions can be disseminated in conjunction with types, by means of the press. This is the stronghold of the art ; and whenever it has been abandoned in modern times to compete with copper-plate engraving, in point of delicacy or mere difficulty of execution, the result has been

---

* Some of those presses were so truly constructed, that if the table were wetted, and brought in contact with the platten, it could be raised from its bed by allowing the platten to ascend, in consequence of the two surfaces being so perfectly plane and level.

a failure. No large modern wood-cuts, published separately, and resting on their own merits as works of art, have repaid the engraver. The price at which they were published was too high to allow of their being purchased by the humbler classes, while the more wealthy collectors of fine prints have treated them with neglect. Such persons were not inclined to purchase comparatively expensive wood-cuts merely as curiosities, showing how closely the peculiarities of copper-plate engraving could be imitated on wood.

Though most of the large cuts designed by Albert Durer were either published separately without letter-press, or in parts with brief explanations annexed ; yet we cannot ascribe the favour with which they were unquestionably received, to the mere fact of their being executed *on wood.* They were adapted to the taste and feelings of the age, and were esteemed on account of the interest of the subjects and the excellence of the designs. Were a modern artist of comparatively equal talent to publish a series of subjects of excellence and originality, engraved on wood in the best manner, I have little doubt of their being favourably received ; their success, however, would not be owing to the circumstance of their being engraved on wood, but to their intrinsic merits as works of art.

On taking a retrospective glance at the history of wood engraving, it will be perceived that the art has not been regularly progressive. At one period we find its productions distinguished for excellence of design and freedom of execution, and at another we find mere mechanical labour substituted for the talent of the artist. As soon as this change commenced, wood engraving, as a means of multiplying works of art began to decline. It continued in a state of neglect for upwards of a century, and showed little symptoms of revival until the works of Bewick again brought it into notice.

The maxim that " a good thing is valuable in proportion as many can enjoy it," may be applied with peculiar propriety to wood engraving ; for the productions of no other kindred art have been more generally disseminated, nor with greater advantage to those for whom they were intended. In the child's first book wood-cuts are introduced, to enable the infant mind to connect words with things ; the youth gains his knowledge of the forms of foreign animals from wood-cuts ; and the mathematician avails himself of wood engraving to execute his diagrams. It has been employed, in the representation of religious subjects, as an aid to devotion ; to celebrate the triumphs of kings and warriors ; to illustrate the pages of the historian, the traveller, and the poet ; and by its means copies of the works of the greatest artists of former times, have been afforded at a price which enabled the very poorest classes to become purchasers. As at least one hundred thousand good impressions can be obtained from a wood-cut, if properly engraved and carefully printed ; and as the additional cost of printing wood-cuts with letter-press is inconsiderable when compared with the cost of printing steel or copper plates separately, the art will never want encouragement, nor again sink into neglect, so long as there are artists of talent to furnish designs, and good engravers to execute them.

INDEX.

Palmer, W. J. wood-engraver, 557.
Paper, proper for printing wood-cuts, 646;
India paper, injurious to wood-cuts, *ib.*
Paper-mark in an old book of wood-cuts,
107.
Paper money, early, 25 *n.*
Papillon, John, the elder, 443.
Papillon, John Michael, his story of the
Cunio, 26; his character, 35; notice of his
works, 457—467.
Parafe, or ruche, 14.
Parker, Archbishop, his portrait, engraved by
R. Hogenberg, 1572, 422.
Parkinson's Paradisus Terrestris, 442.
Parmegiano, chiaro-scuros after his designs,
403.
Pasti, Matteo, supposed to have designed the
cuts in Valturius de Re Militari, 1472, 186.
Patin's Life of Holbein. 372.
Patroner, the word explained, 330 *n.*
Paul of Prague, his definition of "libri-
pagus," 182.
Pearson, G. wood engraver, 573*, 574*.
Pepyr, Edmund, his mark, 18.
Peringskiold, 14.
Petit-Jehan de Saintré, Chronicle of, 41.
Petrarch's Sonnets, Lyons, 1545, cuts in,
400.
Petronius, 8, 15.
Pfintzing, Melchior, joint author of Sir Theur-
dank, 282.
Pfister, Albert, works printed by, at Bam-
berg in 1461 and 1462, 170, 181.
Phillery, properly Willem, de figursnider,
mistakes about a cut of his engraving, 310.
Phiz (H. K. Browne), draughtsman, 599*.
Piccard, T. Nieuhoff, an unknown discoverer
of a painting of the Dance of Death, by
Holbein, 360, 363.
Pickersgill, F. R. painter, 599*.
Pictura, a wood-cut sometimes called, 357.
Pilgrim, John Ulric, cuts ascribed to, 317.
Pinkerton, John, his statement that several
of the cuts in Bewick's Quadrupeds were
drawn on the block by R. Johnson, 491 *n.*
Pinx. et Scalp. not to be found on early wood-
cuts, 35.
Pirkheimer, Bilibald, letters written to him
by Albert Durer, 242; his letter to J.
Tscherte, announcing Durer's death, 273.
Pittacia, small labels, 8 *n.*
Playing cards, 40.
Plebanus, a curate or vicar, 61 *n.*
Pleydenwurff, William, with M. Wolgemuth,
superintends the cuts of the Nuremberg
Chronicle, 1491, 212.
Ploughman, Pierce, his Creed, 18.
Plug, mode of inserting in an engraved wood-
block, 549.
Poetry, specimen of Durer's, 260; specimens
of Clennell's, when insane, 526.
Poliphili Hypnerotomachia, 218, 220, 224.
Polo, Marco, 25.
Poor Preacher's Bible, 80—94, 175—179.
Portraits of Bewick, list of the principal, 509.
Powis, W. H. wood engraver, 544.
Prayer-book, Queen Elizabeth's, 1569, 427.
Prenters of Antwerp in 1442, 121.

Press made for Gutemberg previous to 1438,
127.
Press, rolling, for copper-plate printing, 4.
Press, steam, wood-cuts printed by, 644.
Preusch, his attempt to print maps by a typo-
metric process, 205.
Printing, Gutemberg occupied with the in-
vention of, in 1436, 127.
Printing in colours, a figure of Christ, with
the date 1543, 403; Savage's decorative
printing, 629; G. Baxter's improvements,
629; C. Knight's patent illuminated
prints and maps, 630.
Printing wood-cuts, best mode of, 640.
Priority of editions of the Speculum Salvationis, 100.
Procession, triumphal, of Maximilian, 288,
289.
Procopius, 13.
Proofs of wood engravings, mode of unfairly
taking, 466, 603.
Prout, J. S. draughtsman, 599*.
Psalter, printed by Faust and Scheffer in
1457, 164.
Ptolemy's Cosmography, with maps, engraved on wood, 1483, 199; an edition
printed by Dominico de Lapis, at Bologna,
201; at Venice, by J. Pentius de Leucho,
1511, 203.

Q.

Quadrin's Historiques de la Bible, 402.
Quadrupeds, History of, with cuts, by Bewick, 1791, 482—490.
Queen Elizabeth's Prayer-book, 427.
Quintilian, his notice of the manner of boys
learning to write by tracing the letters
through a stencil, 12.

R.

Raffaele, designs for the wood-cuts of the
Hypnerotomachia ascribed to him, 219;
a wood-cut after a drawing by, in Mar-
colini's Sorti, 389.
Rahmenschneiders, or border-cutters, 190,
319.
Raidel, his Dissertation on an edition of
Ptolemy, 201; dates, erroneous in books,
ib.
Raimbach, Abraham, his engraving of the
Rent-day, after Sir D. Wilkie, 213.
Randell, a printer's apprentice, wood-cuts by,
180.
Raynalde's Birth of Mankind, with three
copper-plate engravings, 1540, 421.
Read, S. draughtsman, 599*.
Rebus, or "name devises," 398.
Redgrave, R. painter, 599*.
Relief, metallic, engraving in, erroneous
statements about, 305; practised by Blake
and others, 632—636'
Rembrandt, cuts copied from etchings by,
595, 599, 602, 605.
Renaudot, l'Abbé, 24.
Rent-day, engraving of a group from, after
Sir D. Wilkie, 593.
Repairing wood-cuts, 569 *n.*

THE END